Bernardo de Gálvez

✳ ✳ ✳

Bernardo de Gálvez

Spanish Hero of the American Revolution

GONZALO M. QUINTERO SARAVIA

THE UNIVERSITY OF NORTH CAROLINA PRESS
Chapel Hill

This book was published with the assistance of
Joseph R. Godfrey, Ph.D.,
the National Society of the Sons of the American Revolution,
and Joseph W. Dooley; and with the assistance of the
Fundación Consejo España–Estados Unidos,
www.spainusa.org.

*Published with the assistance of the Anniversary Fund
of the University of North Carolina Press.*

© 2018 The University of North Carolina Press
All rights reserved
Designed by Rich Hendel
Set in Utopia by Tseng Information Systems, Inc.

Cover illustration: Friars Pablo Jesús and Jerónimo, *Pintura del Excelentisimo Señor Conde de Gálvez*, 1796. Museo Nacional de Historia, Castillo de Chapultepec, Mexico; reproduction authorized by the Instituto Nacional de Antropología e Historia, Mexico City. Technique: *sgrafitto*, a combination of painting and calligraphy. One of few examples of portraits of a Spanish viceroy on horseback; the position of the horse—*a la jineta*, with the two front legs in the air—was traditionally reserved for portraits of Spanish monarchs.

Library of Congress Cataloging-in-Publication Data
Names: Quintero Saravia, Gonzalo M., 1964– author.
Title: Bernardo de Gálvez : Spanish hero of the American Revolution /
Gonzalo M. Quintero Saravia.
Description: Chapel Hill : The University of North Carolina Press, [2018] |
Includes bibliographical references and index.
Identifiers: LCCN 2017050244 | ISBN 9781469640792 (cloth : alk. paper) | ISBN 9781469696126
(pbk : alk. paper) | ISBN 9781469640808 (epub) | ISBN 9798890853875 (pdf)
Subjects: LCSH: Gálvez, Bernardo de, 1746-1786. | Soldiers—Spain—Biography. |
Viceroys—New Spain—Biography. | Spain—Colonies—North America—History—
18th century. | United States—History—Revolution, 1775-1783—Participation,
Spanish. | Pensacola (Fla.)—History—Siege, 1781.
Classification: LCC DP199.9.G27 Q85 2018 | DDC 973.3/46 [B] —dc23
LC record available at https://lccn.loc.gov/2017050244

For product safety concerns under the European Union's General Product
Safety Regulation (EU GPSR), please contact gpsr@mare-nostrum.co.uk or
write to the University of North Carolina Press and Mare Nostrum Group B.V.,
Mauritskade 21D, 1091 GC Amsterdam, The Netherlands.

To

Elisa, Santiago, Salvador,

and my mother

Contents

Note on Terminology, Names, and
English Translations of Spanish Documents xi

Introduction 1

1. Early Years 9

2. New Spain: Fighting the Apache 21

3. Learning to Be an Officer and Tasting Defeat 62

4. Arrival in Louisiana and Preparations for War 79

5. Bernardo de Gálvez Takes the Initiative 137

6. His Finest Hour: Pensacola, "I Alone" 180

7. Objectives: Jamaica, Return to Europe, Cuba 245

8. Viceroy of New Spain 281

Afterword 340

Appendix 349

Acknowledgments 383

Notes 387

Bibliography 499

Index 585

Figures, Tables, Graphs, and Maps

FIGURES

Portrait of Bernardo de Gálvez	3
Engraving of José de Gálvez as Marquis of Sonora	10
View of Madrid from the south entrance to the city	11
Portrait of Matías de Gálvez, Bernardo's father, as viceroy of New Spain	12
Engraving of a private of the Royal Cantabre Regiment	16
Expulsion of the Jesuit order from the territories of the Spanish monarchy in 1767	25
Late eighteenth-century depiction of an Apache family	40
The Harvesters of Malaga before King Carlos III, by Joaquín Inza	64
View of the Bay of Algiers during the Spanish attack in 1775	74
Portrait of Alejandro O'Reilly as governor of Cadiz	77
King Carlos III wearing the Royal Order of Carlos III	81
Contemporary drawing of the flag of the Louisiana Fixed Infantry Regiment	92
Coat of arms of the province of Spanish Louisiana, 1786	109
Plan for the village of Galveztown in Louisiana	124
Two creole women	135
Map of the coast between New Orleans and Apalachicola Bay	148
Only surviving British flag of the several captured by Bernardo de Gálvez	158
Engraving published in London on March 8, 1780	162
Contemporary Spanish map of the landing at Mobile in 1780	167
Portrait of José de Ezpeleta	187
View of Havana's marketplace during the British occupation	191
Highly idealized view of Pensacola in the late 1770s	193
British brig	199
Map of the conquest of Pensacola in 1781	205
Portrait of Peter Chester, British governor of West Florida	208
Portrait of Francisco de Saavedra	215
Portrait of Admiral José Solano y Bote	217
Spanish map of the British forts and Spanish trenches at Pensacola, 1781	220

The explosion of the Queen's Redoubt in Pensacola	224
First accurate portrait of General George Washington, 1781	231
French map published in 1782	237
Engraving of Pensacola Bay, conquered by the Spaniards in 1781	239
Coat of arms granted by King Carlos III to Bernardo de Gálvez	243
Miniature depicting Bernardo de Gálvez on horseback	247
British lion confronting its four enemies	254
Portrait of Bernardo de Gálvez, 1782	258
John Jay	264
Cartoon by James Gillray, 1783	268
French engraving depicting several battles of the American War of Independence	271
Engraving of the "aerostatic fish" in flight	275
Testing Bernardo de Gálvez's invention	277
Mexico City's main square in 1769	282
Portrait of Miguel de Gálvez	297
Blueprint of the second floor of the Royal Palace of Chapultepec	324
Medals awarded by the Royal Academy of San Carlos in Mexico City	330
Detail of the design for the gardens of the Royal Palace of Chapultepec	344

TABLES

A. Louisiana's Colonial Population According to the May 1777 Census	111
B. Cost of the War with Britain, 1779–1783	143

GRAPHS

1. Annual Expenditures in the Defense of New Spain's Northern Frontier	37
2. Spanish Casualties at the Siege of Pensacola, 1781	226
3. Daily Average of Dossiers Processed by Bernardo de Gálvez as Viceroy of New Spain	333

MAPS

Treaty of Paris, Proposals	266
Treaty of Paris, 1783	267

Note on Terminology, Names, and English Translations of Spanish Documents

Since this book is based on research of documents and sources in several languages, it has been necessary to adapt the Spanish and French spellings of names and locations to the most-common ones used in modern English. The Spanish documents and archival terms have been translated as follows:

Apartado	section
bando	proclamation
carpeta	folder
carta	letter
carta reservada	confidential letter
cuaderno (*cuad.*)	notebook
despacho	dispatch
dictamen	ruling
expediente (*exp.*)	dossier (DF)
folio (f. or fol.); folios (ff.)	sheet/sheets
hoja	page
informe	report
instrucción	instruction
lámina (*lám.*)	plate
legajo (*leg.*)	bundle
memorial	memorial
minuta de carta	letter draft copy
minuta de oficio	official letter draft copy
oficio	official letter
ordenanza	ordinance
paquete (*paq.*)	parcel
pasquín	wall poster
real cédula	royal order
real decreto	royal decree

real orden	royal order
real ordenanza	royal ordinance
real resolución	royal decision
signatura	catalog number
tomo (*t.*)	volume

Bernardo de Gálvez

Introduction

Since early spring 1781, a Spanish army had been laying siege to Pensacola in British West Florida. By May, after having repelled a fierce British counterattack against the Spanish advanced positions, General Bernardo de Gálvez confided to his good friend Francisco de Saavedra his worries about the slow progress of His Catholic Majesty's arms against the British stronghold. Saavedra had been Gálvez's classmate in the Royal Military Academy of Avila and was in Pensacola as the personal representative of the powerful minister of the Indies, José de Gálvez, Bernardo's uncle.

More than two months after the arrival of the first Spanish forces at Pensacola Bay, the exhausting work of the engineers in excavating trenches and building artillery batteries and the exasperating routine of the exchange of artillery fire were beginning to undercut the morale of the troops. Gálvez was worried. The supplies brought from Havana were running out. Large-caliber cannonballs were so scarce that he was paying his soldiers two *reales* for each British cannonball retrieved so they could be refired against Pensacola. According to Saavedra, Gálvez "was determined to make a frontal assault on the enemy's Half-Moon Fort [Spanish name for the Queen's Redoubt], the conquest of which would soon force the surrender of the other two [positions], . . . and in this way he would shorten the siege, which was taking too long."[1]

Plans for what would have been a desperate, almost suicidal frontal assault had to be canceled since the Spanish forces arrived in front of the British fort when the sun was already up, and all surprise was lost. The following day, after the work on the Spanish battery closest to the Queen's Redoubt was finished, Gálvez ordered the Spanish cannons to open fire and reluctantly prepared himself and his troops for what everyone believed would be another routine day at the siege of Pensacola. But at half past nine on the morning of May 8, everything changed. A big explosion was heard. Gálvez rushed to the battery. Seeing the destruction at the Queen's Redoubt, he immediately ordered an attack. The Spanish troops quickly seized the fort. With

Pensacola now within firing range of the Spanish artillery, the British commander, General John Campbell, had no choice but to surrender. That same night, the articles of capitulation were signed, and Pensacola and all West Florida returned to the Spanish empire.[2]

On December 16, 2014, President Barack Obama signed a joint resolution of the U.S. Congress conferring honorary citizenship on Bernardo de Gálvez—the highest honor the U.S. government can bestow upon a foreign citizen and one that has been granted only eight times.[3] According to the resolution, Bernardo de Gálvez was "a hero of the Revolutionary War who risked his life for the freedom of the United States people." His "victories against the British were recognized by George Washington as a deciding factor in the outcome of the Revolutionary War." Thus, the "United States Continental Congress declared, on October 31, 1778, their gratitude and favorable sentiments to Bernardo de Gálvez for his conduct toward the United States" because he "played an integral role in the Revolutionary War and helped secure the independence of the United States." Despite these official recognitions and the fact that "several geographic locations, including Galveston Bay, Galveston, Texas, Galveston County, Texas, Galvez, Louisiana, and St. Bernard Parish, Louisiana, are named after Bernardo de Gálvez," his life and the role he played as the highest representative of the Spanish Empire in the American Revolutionary War remain grossly overlooked by mainstream history in the United States.[4]

The life story of Bernardo de Gálvez could be cast as an adventure novel. Even a cursory look at his life shows that, despite its brevity (he died at age forty), he enjoyed a military career full of action and daring. Although he was usually victorious in battle, he also knew defeat. His meteoric rise from simple lieutenant to lieutenant general is a tale of personal and family ambition, of courage, and sometimes of sheer luck. He was a colorful personality, impetuous and romantic, devoted to his wife, Felicitas, and passionate in his pursuits, whether playing the guitar or cheering the performance of a matador.

In the larger context, Gálvez's life can be viewed through the important role played by Spain during the American War of Independence, when Gálvez was supreme commander of the Spanish troops fighting the British in the present states of Mississippi, Alabama, and Florida and later of the joint Franco-Spanish forces in the Caribbean. A British map of North America published in 1783 shows that about three-quarters of what is today the United States was, at that time, part of the Spanish Empire, at least in theory—in theory because Spain had very little control over most of this huge territory,

The only contemporary portrait of Bernardo de Gálvez that could claim certain
accuracy since it was included in a book published in Mexico the year after his death.
(In Ventura Beleña, *Recopilación Sumaria de todos los autos acordados* . . . ;
Library of Congress, LCCN 28018536)

where the local indigenous populations were scarcely affected by Spain's sovereign claims over their lands.[5]

While sometimes the involvement of Spain in the Revolutionary War has been presented as a contribution to the independence of the United States, even as a gift, the reality is that Spain's decision to enter the war against Britain was based only on imperial policy considerations. Besides an opportunity for revenge for Spain's defeat in the Seven Years' War and the traditional confrontation between Britain and Spain in the Americas, the Spanish objectives in the war were to weaken the British Empire in general and to recover specific territories, especially Gibraltar. At the same time, the Spanish government considered the independence of the United States as a by-product of the war that could set a dangerous example for the Spanish possessions in the Americas. Confronted with the option of sharing North America with the British Empire or with a new and small republic with an extremely weak central government such as the one established by the Articles of Confederation, Spain chose the latter. In this context, it is not surprising that the Spanish government never considered the United States an ally. For Spain, the American Revolutionary War was just another imperial war between France and Spain against Britain.[6]

Well before war was officially declared, Gálvez was responsible for channeling most of the covert aid provided by the Spanish government to the American rebels. Although Spain was not a formal ally of the United States in its struggle for independence—strategic political considerations prevented this—its entry into the war tipped the balance definitively against Britain. The combined Franco-Spanish fleet was larger than the British navy, and Spain's attack on British-held Minorca and the siege of Gibraltar forced Britain to fight in several very distant places at the same time. Similarly, Gálvez's campaigns against British settlements on the Mississippi River and later against Mobile and Pensacola prevented British military and naval forces in North America from concentrating solely on the fight against George Washington's Continental army.

When the thirteen American colonies began the War of Independence, their theater would soon be part of a much greater struggle—that is, an Atlantic and eventually a global war. It was a war that would pit Britain against France, Spain, and the Dutch Republic on three continents. In the Americas, Britain had to fight the French on land and sea; the Dutch, meanwhile, would lose their Caribbean posts of Sint Eustatius, Saba, and Sint Maarten to the British, and Spain would fight the British not only on the Mississippi River and in Louisiana, Alabama, and Florida but also in Guatemala and New Providence (in today's Bahamas). In addition, jointly with the French,

Spain would aim at the conquest of Jamaica. In Europe, Spain conducted a long siege against Gibraltar, conquered the island of Minorca, and even laid plans with France for an invasion of the British Isles. In Asia, the siege of Pondicherry and the naval battle of Cuddalore set the French against the British, while the Dutch fought the latter in the Bay of Bengal.

Aside from being a rousing good tale, Bernardo de Gálvez's life offers a view of an individual deeply influenced by Enlightenment values. Gálvez's professional and social successes were possible only because of the political and social reforms that took place in the Spanish Empire during the second half of the eighteenth century. The rise of the Gálvez family, spurred mainly by the brilliant career of Bernardo's uncle José de Gálvez, minister of the Indies between 1776 and 1787, is an outstanding example of increasing social mobility in eighteenth-century Spain. José de Gálvez's patronage of his nephew was indispensable to Bernardo's success, as it allowed him to reach important positions at a young age and in so doing demonstrate his unusually strong military, administrative, and political talents.

Bernardo attended the Royal Military Academy of Avila, where young officers of the Spanish army were instructed in the principles of the new enlightened kind of modern warfare. There he joined the "mystery of Avila," a select group of determined, hardworking, and scientifically inclined young officers, whom their enemies called the *barbilampiños* or "beardless ones." Their baby faces were hated by the so-called *mozos viejos* or "old boys," who had no regard for newfangled things and insisted that promotions should be made on the basis of either seniority or courage in battle. The beardless ones favored a new model of warfare based on Frederick II of Prussia's scientific approach. They believed that merit, and merit alone, should be the criterion for advancement both in the army and in the state bureaucracy.

In the alliance between empire and science that emerged during the eighteenth century, military and naval officers were often at the forefront of the pursuit of useful knowledge for their countries. Their exploits created among other military and naval officers a sense that it was among their duties to be up to date and actively involved in the latest scientific and philosophic advances. In this context Bernardo de Gálvez pursued his own scientific interests. While in Madrid awaiting a new assignment in 1783–84, he devoted his free time to experimenting with military applications of the latest fashion among the educated class: hot-air balloons. But soon Gálvez had to abandon his technological pursuits since he would be busy upon his appointment as *capitán general* (governor) of Cuba.[7]

Well before that posting, though, Gálvez, on January 1, 1777, assumed his office as acting governor of Louisiana and colonel of Louisiana's Fixed Infantry Regiment. In Louisiana, Gálvez transformed the province's rebellious French population into a bastion of the Spanish Empire in North America. Obtaining the loyalty of this group of people was not easy because by "Louisiana's population," Spanish authorities mainly meant the French-origin creole elites. Both planters from the provinces and rich merchants from New Orleans found themselves in a strong position while negotiating with Spanish authority.[8] Gálvez offered trade concessions to the powerful merchants in New Orleans and to the rich planters of the province, and because of his charismatic personality he was able to captivate Louisiana's inhabitants within a year and a half of his arrival. When Spain declared war against Britain in June 1779, Gálvez not only could disregard all concerns about his rear guard but also could count on the strong support, even adoration, of the local population. Despite some tensions caused when the local elites tried to push too hard, the result would be that the Spanish authorities had no choice but to accommodate and adapt a substantial part of their model of empire to the interests of Louisiana's elite. Spain's accommodating stance had practical results when hundreds of men volunteered to fight against the English.

In administering Louisiana, Gálvez left no branch of the government unshaken. Under his governorship, new towns were founded and new crops introduced. Hundreds of settlers migrated from the Canary Islands and Malaga. Existing military units were reorganized and new ones created. Royal legislation against contraband was strictly enforced against British smugglers, while a much softer hand was applied against French ones. A policy of de facto religious toleration, unknown in the rest of the territories under Spanish rule, made it possible for non-Catholic citizens to prosper.

During his extremely short tenure (1785–86) as viceroy of New Spain, whose territory included today's southern United States, Mexico, and all of Central America to present-day Panama, Gálvez designed and implemented a vast array of reforms. For example, when dealing with the consequences of disastrous weather that caused the failure of most of the viceroyalty's crops and left the population on the verge of starvation, he put his Enlightenment ideals into practice by focusing on the welfare of poor peasants. He adopted the principle of "public happiness" (*felicidad pública*), a term that also included a unique sense of responsibility by the government toward the governed, especially those on the bottom rung of the social ladder.

One of Bernardo de Gálvez's most important and long-standing legacies as governor was his Indian policy. Building on his experience as captain of a small cavalry detachment fighting the Apache in the northern provinces of New Spain, he instituted a new Spanish policy toward indigenous groups living in the borderlands of the Spanish Empire in the Americas. Indeed, his *Noticia y reflexiones sobre la guerra que se tiene con los indios apaches en las provincias de Nueva España* (Account and reflections on the current war against the Apache Indians in the provinces of New Spain) still is one of the most important sources of knowledge about the eighteenth-century Apaches. Instead of succumbing to the warmongering attitudes prevalent in the region, he demanded from his countrymen that they "be impartial and acknowledge that if the Indians are not our friends, it is because they do not owe us any benefits, and if they take revenge on us, it is only in just compensation for the affronts we have caused them . . . , the lies we have told them, and the tyrannies they have suffered from us." He states clearly that the main cause of their war against the Spaniards was either "hatred or necessity"— that is, a hatred born of a desire for vengeance for the affronts they had suffered or a necessity rooted in "the extreme need in which they live." On their reputation for cruelty, he wondered "what their [the Apaches'] opinion is of us, most probably it would not be better, [and] for much better reason."[9]

Later, in his tenure as viceroy of New Spain, Gálvez completely reorganized New Spain's northern frontier with his *Instrucción formada en virtud de real orden de S.M.* (Instruction for governing the Interior Provinces of New Spain) of August 1786. In so doing he introduced a new model of relations between indigenous groups and European settlers. He abandoned the centuries-old model of sporadic confrontation, which had an endemic and almost permanent low-intensity warlike situation in which repeated attacks by indigenous groups elicited punitive military campaigns. Instead, Gálvez designed a new policy that aimed to attract indigenous groups by gift exchanges and commerce. The plan intended to make them dependent on the Spanish so that eventually they would be assimilated into Spanish-American society and would increase the state's presence throughout the region. By controlling both Spanish and indigenous populations, thereby preventing the multiple abuses inflicted on the latter, Gálvez's reorganization pacified the region for the duration of the Spanish presence in North America. But peace came with a price: since Spanish policies of assimilation were designed to bring indigenous communities into dependency, the Spanish took little or very limited account of indigenous peoples' interests.

Bernardo de Gálvez was one of those Spaniards who felt more at home in the Americas than in his native Iberian Peninsula. He spent most of his adult life in America, where he found his wife, where his three children were born, and where he decided that he would be buried. He was a friend of the American Revolution and a friend of an enlightened and progressive empire, friendships that in his mind, far from being contradictory, were mutually reinforcing.[10] Today, almost two and a half centuries after his death, I hope to cast a light on the last decades of the Spanish Empire in North America and on the role of Spain in the American Revolutionary War by bringing to life the world of Bernardo de Gálvez.

1. Early Years

Most people are born into a family. Bernardo de Gálvez was born into a clan. The origins of the Gálvez family in Macharaviaya, a small village near Malaga in southern Spain, can be traced to the sixteenth century, but the Gálvezes had been unable to acquire wealth or an outstanding social position in the village.[1] When Bernardo was born on July 23, 1746, the Gálvezes were mere "shepherds of Macharaviaya"[2]—that is, a long way from being members of that select group known as the "Spanish monarchy's watchmakers."[3] His father, Matías, was just another poor farmhand in a town with fewer than 300 inhabitants, where most of the men were "day laborers, since none can sustain himself on his own wealth."[4]

The family's limited social status and lack of relevant connections were confirmed by the choice of godparents for baby Bernardo. Without wealthy or noble patrons who could mentor their son, Bernardo's parents chose some close relatives from the near village of Benaque. At the time of his birth Bernardo seemed destined to continue on the family's undistinguished path. But his fortunes, like those of the rest of the Gálvez clan, were about to change. His uncle José, the driving force behind the family, had just set up shop in Madrid as an ambitious young lawyer. José de Gálvez's story is key to understanding the history of the entire Gálvez family.[5]

José was the smartest student in Macharaviaya's small parochial school, and when the bishop of Malaga paid a visit, José was asked to show off his abilities. So impressed was the bishop that he decided to enroll young José in the Malaga seminary. Discovering early that the church was not his calling, José switched to law and entered the old and prestigious University of Salamanca. After he graduated, in the mid-1740s, he moved to Madrid and married María Magdalena de Grimaldo, who died a year later.[6] In 1750 he married again, this time to a socially superior partner. Lucía Romet y Richelin was French and well connected to her embassy in Madrid. Through her, José entered the intimate circle of the French ambassador and in a short time became the embassy counsel. Under the patronage of the Marquis d'Ossun, José de Gálvez

Engraving of José de Gálvez as Marquis of Sonora. Bernardo de Gálvez's older uncle played a crucial role in his nephew's career. (Engraving by Jeronimo Antonio Gil, in Magro and Ventura Beleña, *Elucidationes ad quatuor libros Institutionum Imperatoris Justiniani*, vol. 1)

was introduced to the secretary of state the Marquis of Grimaldi, who appointed him as one of his clerks. In the early 1760s José won an appointment as the official lawyer to Crown Prince Carlos and the *alcalde de casa y corte*, a judge with jurisdiction over the capital. His real breakthrough came in 1764, when a candidate was urgently needed for the position of visitor-general of New Spain due to the sudden death of Francisco de Armona.

View of Madrid from the south entrance to the city. The painting by the Italian artist Antonio Joli dates from 1753, just three years before Bernardo de Gálvez arrived in Madrid at the age of ten. Prominent on the left is the royal palace, still under construction, built between 1738 and 1755. Unlike other empire's capitals, Madrid was not Spain's largest or richest city, and the kings used to live there only during the winter, spending the other seasons in different palaces (spring in Aranjuez, summer in El Escorial, and fall in La Granja). (Antonio Joli, *Vedutta di Madrid*, oil on canvas, 1753; private collection)

Little is known about Bernardo's early years. In 1748 his mother, María Josefa de Madrid, died giving birth to his brother, José.[7] Two years later his father married Ana de Zayas y Ramos. By 1756 the family was already living in Madrid, where his brother José died, leaving Bernardo the only son, as no children were born during his father's second marriage. Bernardo would be raised not only by his stepmother (his father would be absent in different military assignments) but also by his uncles from his father's side: the Gálvez clan.

Tragic as they would be in today's world, the impact of these losses in Bernardo's life should not be overestimated. During the Old Regime, both maternal and infant mortality were very high. In eighteenth-century Spain, infant mortality was between 240 and 400 per 1,000 births. That is, one in four children died during his or her first year, and only one in two lived to his or her fifth birthday.[8] If a child was motherless, as Bernardo was, life expectancy for that child was halved.[9] People at the time had to adapt to this reality by regarding death very differently than people do today. Death was intimately associated with everyday life, and profound religious convictions played an important part in helping individuals cope with grief and loss.[10] Thus, the loss of Bernardo's mother and brother was probably not as traumatic as it might be in the twenty-first century.

Portrait of Matías de Gálvez, Bernardo's father, as viceroy of New Spain, wearing his full regalia with the sash and insignia of the Royal Order of Carlos III. Above the right pocket of his general's full uniform is embroidered the key to the king's apartment, symbol of his condition of *gentilhombre de cámara del rey*. The parchment behind him lists some of his accomplishments, among them the foundation of the Royal Academy of Arts of Carlos III in Mexico City. (Ramón Torres, *Portrait of Viceroy Matías de Gálvez*, oil on canvas, 1783, in Museo de América, Madrid, inventory no. 1984/06/01)

According to Francisco de Miranda, Bernardo spent some years in the Canary Islands, where his father, Matías, an artillery captain, was posted from 1757 to 1778 as governor of the Castle of Paso Alto in the city of Santa Cruz.[11] Matías was also the king's lieutenant, a sort of deputy general commander of the island of Tenerife.[12] However, we have not found any documentary evidence or any mention by Bernardo de Gálvez himself that he lived in the Canary Islands with his father during this period. Matías de Gálvez's career would take off in 1778, two years after his brother José's appointment as minister of the Indies, when he was posted to Guatemala, first as inspector of the army and later as captain general and president of its *audiencia*. As for Bernardo, at the age of sixteen he entered the army.

JOINING THE ARMY

Becoming a soldier was the natural career path for a captain's son. The minimum age for signing up as a regimental cadet was sixteen,[13] and Spain's entry into the Seven Years' War the same year Bernardo reached that age provided a perfect opportunity. A "nice little war" could increase the prospects of a quick promotion. Indeed, by the middle of the eighteenth century, British naval officers raised a glass every Thursday for "a bloody war and a quick promotion!"[14] Similarly, in 1758 the Prussian colonel Wilhelm Sebastian von Belling used to pray in front of his regiment, "Thou seest, dear Heavenly Father, the sad plight of thy servant Belling. Grant him soon a nice little war that he may better his condition and continue to praise Thy name. Amen."[15]

Admission as a cadet depended on a vacancy in the regiment and the approval of its colonel, who required a personal recommendation. Even though Bernardo's father was a military officer, he had few friends in the top echelons of the army and in 1762, at the age of forty-five, was still a captain. So José de Gálvez through his connections at the French embassy in Madrid obtained for his nephew a commission as a lieutenant in the French army. At the time France was allied with Spain, and strange as it may seem, Bernardo de Gálvez was not the only Spanish military hero who started his career under the French flag. Admiral Blas de Lezo, who defeated the British at Cartagena de Indias in 1741, also began his career as a French midshipman in the battle of Vélez-Málaga on August 24, 1704.[16] Moreover, the French system had an important advantage over the Spanish one: the owners of French regiments were authorized to appoint officers to the rank of captain in exchange for an agreed-upon sum of money.[17] We have found no evidence of José de Gálvez paying any amount for his nephew's appointment as a French officer, but the fact remains that on June 12, 1762, Bernardo de Gálvez received his commission as lieutenant in the Royal Cantabre, one of the French regiments assigned to the joint Franco-Spanish force for the invasion of Portugal.[18]

THE SEVEN YEARS' WAR

In January 1762 Great Britain declared war on Spain. What would later be called the Seven Years' War had started several years earlier, in 1756.[19] About its origins, it is easy to agree with William Makepeace Thackeray, who in 1844 admitted that "it would require a greater philosopher and historian than I am to explain the causes of the famous Seven Years' War in which Europe was engaged."[20] What is relevant for the subject is that Spain needed little encouragement to fight the British. In fact, Spanish history can be divided into periods identified by the country's main enemy. During the eighteenth century that place of honor was occupied by Great Britain.

The rift with Britain started from afar and from the first was about control of Spain's overseas empire. The peace signed after the Spanish victory in the War of Jenkins' Ear, 1739–43 (known as "Guerra del Asiento" in Spain), was just the beginning of a long armistice full of problems and tensions.[21] The Spanish embassy in London complained, frequently but futilely, about attacks by British corsairs. At the same time, British settlements in Honduras and on the Mosquito Coast remained a thorn that the Spanish authorities could never accept. To these powerful political reasons a personal one was added: Carlos III wanted to avenge the humiliation he had suffered in 1742 as the king of Naples when a British squadron commanded by Admiral Thomas Mathews forced him to withdraw his troops from the northern part of the Italian peninsula.[22] As Portugal was Britain's ally, the Spanish contribution to the war effort would be its invasion of Portugal. The objective was not to conquer Portuguese territory but to end the use of its ports by the British Royal Navy. After the king of Portugal rejected a sugarcoated ultimatum, a joint Franco-Spanish force of 40,000 men crossed the border into his country. If there was ever such a thing as a nice little war, this was it. Armies marched back and forth, cities were laid to siege, and cannons were fired, but the troops saw little actual combat. The Royal Cantabre Regiment was no exception.

LIEUTENANT IN THE ROYAL CANTABRE REGIMENT

Between 8,000 and 15,000 French soldiers formed part of the joint army. The first figure comes from Spanish sources and the latter from French. Despite the discrepancy, both sides agreed that the French played a very secondary role in the campaign.

The Royal Cantabre Regiment was created in 1745 under the name Volontaires Cantabres.[23] Its officers and soldiers were meant to be Basques or "Cantabres" from a region that today encompasses Asturias, Navarre, the Basque country in Spain, and the French Basque country.[24] The regiment was initially formed with 1,500 infantry soldiers, about 300 hussars (cavalry), and a couple of pieces of artillery.[25] Its founder, Colonel Jeanne-Philippe de Béla, Chevalier de Béla, was a soldier of fortune who fought under the flags of France, Saxony, and Poland.[26] In 1749 he was dishonorably discharged after being accused of embezzlement. He retired from the military and devoted himself to writing local history.[27]

In 1747 the regiment changed its name to Royal Cantabre under the command of the Chevalier de Luppé.[28] It was reformed several times thereafter and then disbanded from 1749 to 1757.[29] In the latter year the regiment was formed again with 604 men in eight companies.[30] In 1760 the regiment's colonel was the Baron of Poudenx. Lieutenant Bernardo de Gálvez was assigned to its second battalion, under the command of Lieutenant Colonel the Chevalier of Beauteville.[31] On the last day of May 1762 the second battalion of the Royal Cantabre arrived in Bayonne, where it was joined by two more battalions from the Sarre regiment to form the sixth column of the French forces. Two weeks later the army crossed the Spanish border. Marching 220 miles in a month, or a little more than 7 miles per day, does not seem like much, but by the time the second battalion of the Royal Cantabre arrived in Valladolid on July 15, a third of its members were reportedly sick.[32] The battalion was in such bad shape that the Spanish commander, the Marquis of Sarriá, assigned it to garrison duty. Morale quickly deteriorated. On August 10, the commander of the French sixth column, Charles Juste de Beauvau-Craon, Prince of Beauvau, complained to the French supreme commander that "desertion, robbery, lack of discipline, and lack of decorum in the uniforms have reached their highest level: I will do everything I can to preserve the troops that I have the honor to command, but the bad examples have an advantage."[33] The Portuguese city of Almeida capitulated on August 25 without putting up a fight.

A new Spanish supreme commander, the Count of Aranda, arrived with a change of strategy. The objective would now be to take Abrantes, on the road to Lisbon. The meeting point was Penamacor, where the Spanish stayed until September 17 and the French a couple of days longer. The following months would see the Royal Cantabre Regiment moving back and forth across the

Engraving of a private of the Royal Cantabre Regiment, the French unit in which Bernardo de Gálvez served as a lieutenant in the war with Portugal during the Seven Years' War. The engraver struggled to represent the typical Basque *boina*, headgear traditional to that region of France and Spain that Bernardo, as a southerner, would find strange to wear. His experience during this short war, especially learning French, would be of enormous value for his military career. (Major d'après P. B. de la Rue, *Cantabres Volontaires*, engraving, Paris, F. Chereau, 1747, in *Nouveau recueil des troupes légères de France* . . . ; Bibliothèque nationale de France)

Spanish-Portuguese border.³⁴ On November 13 the Royal Cantabre Regiment was near Valencia de Alcántara when news arrived that an armistice had been signed. The nice little war was over. The Royal Cantabre spent the autumn in Cáceres and then at the end of November returned to France.

This was the part of the Seven Years' War in which Bernardo de Gálvez was involved. He was in no major engagements, and there is no evidence that he ever fired a shot. Bernardo left the Royal Cantabre as a lieutenant, discarding forever the original uniform with the *béarnaise* (Basque) beret, under which an Andalusian may not have felt very comfortable.³⁵ The regiment barely survived the end of the war: it was definitively abolished on November 25, 1762.³⁶ Most probably Bernardo then went to Madrid, where his uncle José was still working his way up through the royal civil service.

CONSEQUENCES OF THE SEVEN YEARS' WAR

Although the Seven Years' War was a conflict within the centuries-old confrontation between European powers in North America, it also represented a turning point in the history of that continent. This "crucible of war," as Fred Anderson has called it, had consequences of the utmost importance for everyone. France would disappear from the North American stage. For Britain, although completely victorious, the war would "set in motion the forces that created a hollow British empire."³⁷ Local populations would also be profoundly affected by the war and its outcome. For the thirteen colonies the Seven Years' War was not just the "backdrop to the American Revolution, but . . . both its indispensable precursor and its counterpart influence in the formation of the early republic."³⁸ For some of the French settlers in North America, especially for the Acadians, the end of the war would bring deportation and the beginning of an era of wandering across the Atlantic. The life of indigenous groups would also be deeply affected, inaugurating a period of increasing tensions with English settlers. As for Spain, the Iberian Peninsula theater was just one of many in which the war took place. Among others were America and the Philippines, both vitally important for Spain. The British captured both Havana and Manila, while Buenos Aires narrowly escaped the same fate.³⁹

The peace preliminaries were ratified by the kings of England, France, and Spain on November 12, 13, and 14, 1762; the Portuguese monarch did the same shortly thereafter. The peace treaty was signed in Paris on February 10, 1763. The Treaty of Paris ended French aspirations on the American continent, signaled the consolidation of Britain as a world power, and left behind a certain feeling of Spanish impotence. Most of the territories acquired by force during the war were returned to their previous owners, but there were also major changes. According to Guillermo Céspedes del Castillo, the peace treaty signed after the Seven Years' War brought an unnecessary humiliation to the defeated.[40] Furthermore, this would be a wake-up call for the Spanish court, which would soon seek its revenge. A new plan for imperial reforms was drafted at court in 1765, and its implementation started immediately afterward and culminated in 1776-79. These were intense years, during which the Spanish reformers engaged in unusual teamwork and placed in the highest positions of government ministers who came with the king from Naples (before becoming Carlos III of Spain, in 1759, he was Carlos VII of Naples).[41] In the telling of Céspedes del Castillo, this team of reformers was creative, optimistic, and bold, although tending toward a premature triumphalism.[42] All kinds of policy issues were addressed: population and industry; trade and the royal treasury; the army and the navy; society, uses, and customs; urbanism; and so on. Of all of the measures dictated during this reform period, those affecting America's defensive system had the most direct impact on the life and career of Bernardo de Gálvez.

Although Havana and Manila were returned to Spain, their temporary fall into British hands led to a revision of the system of defense of the American continent. Until the beginning of the eighteenth century, the main threat to Spain's overseas possessions was attacks by pirates and privateers. But from this time on, Spain had to deal with attempts by several European powers to establish themselves in Spanish territories on the American continent. If at first it was enough to strengthen certain ports with castles or fortresses and to make sure that convoys of the "fleet of the Indies" (*carrera de Indias*) were escorted by heavy warships, now it was necessary to design a whole new system of defense: one based in what Julio Albi has called the triad of navy, fortifications, and the army of America.[43]

This new army of America was made up of three distinct types of units: the *ejército de dotación*, the *ejército de refuerzo*, and the militia.[44] The *ejército de dotación* or *cuerpos fijos* (fixed corps) were military units permanently assigned to a place, hence their name. Almost all troops and most officers serving in them were Americans. They were the backbone of the whole defensive system. The *ejército de refuerzo* (reinforcement army) was formed by regiments or units based in the Iberian Peninsula and sent to America for a certain period of time through a system called the *noria* or waterwheel.[45] The militia comprised units of a territorial nature—that is, units were composed of troops recruited in the same place that they served and represented, at least in theory, all men between sixteen and forty-five who had an obligation to serve. The militiamen were locals who received weapons, uniforms, and a few training sessions, usually on Sunday mornings. They were instructed in little more than marching in close order and target practice. Both the officers and the troops in the militia were paid only when mobilized. Traditionally it has been thought that the militia's military relevance was negligible, although subsequent studies have questioned this idea.[46] In fact, militiamen should not be considered soldiers but civilians. As Allan J. Kuethe says about the militia's role in the defense of Havana in 1762, it was too much to ask for men without any systematic training and no knowledge of military discipline to behave as veteran soldiers.[47] Thus, the role usually assigned to militia units was to keep public order, and they were used for other duties only in case of emergency.

The new defensive system seemed to work reasonably well, but when Havana and Manila fell into British hands in 1762, the alarm sounded. How was it possible that two well-fortified cities, outfitted and equipped with theoretically sufficient troops, had succumbed to the enemy? Part of the answer was that the British had learned the lesson received when they had attacked Cartagena de Indias in 1741. The so-called miracle of Cartagena happened not only because of the courage of its defenders under the command of Viceroy Sebastián de Eslava and Admiral Blas de Lezo but also because the British troops were decimated by disease and local unsanitary conditions. In Havana, the British took advantage of their maritime supremacy in order to supply their troops, thus reducing the danger of diseases.[48] After the defeat, the Spanish governor of Cuba and other high-ranking officers were court-martialed.[49] The defeat could have been avenged, but to avoid a future humiliation it was clear that the *ejército de dotación* must be thoroughly reformed and the presence in America of the *ejército de refuerzo* augmented. In theory the task was easy, but its implementation was deemed very costly. Thus the Spanish government decided that the *ejército de dotación* would only reinforce essential cities, ports, castles, and strongholds, while the *ejército de refuerzo* and the militia would take up the responsibility of defending the rest of the American territory. To make the *ejército de dotación* and the militia into credible fighting forces, more than 700 men from several regiments from the Iberian Peninsula were sent to New Spain in 1764 under the command of General Juan de Villalba. Their mission was "the formation and training of Mexican recruits, who were to compose up to nine militia regiments of infantry, cavalry, and dragoons."[50] Villalba's work in New Spain went far beyond training the militia to a complete reform of the army. His plans were not finished during his posting and later would be continued by Bernardo de Gálvez during the 1780s.

The reform of the defensive system also touched the other two pillars of fortifications and the navy. Between 1763 and 1766 the number of military engineers in New Spain doubled.[51] In Cartagena de Indias, the work undertaken during the time of military engineer Antonio de Arévalo received an important boost when new funds were funneled into it.[52] In Havana, engineer Silvestre Abarca began drafting an ambitious project to prevent a recurrence of the 1762 failure.[53] Finally—and this list is not exhaustive—in Rio de la Plata, the engineers from Pedro de Cevallos's expedition to Colonia were entrusted with the construction and improvement of different strongholds in the estuary.[54]

As for the navy, it was ordered to speed up as much as possible the construction of new ships. The aim was to build thirty-six ships of the line (ships with sixty-four or more guns), eighteen frigates, ten *jabeques* (a small three-masted vessel of the Mediterranean), and seven galleys. Cartagena's naval yards received contracts for six more ships, and the yards in Guarnizo got a contract for another ship and four frigates. In addition to these new vessels, a faster communications system was created between Havana and Coruña, one of Spain's most important Atlantic ports.[55]

For Bernardo de Gálvez, the most important consequence of the Seven Years' War was that France disappeared from North America, transferring Louisiana to Spain, thus bringing Spanish and British possessions into direct contact.[56] Until that date, French colonies on both banks of the Mississippi River had served as a kind of buffer zone hindering the expansion of British colonies to the west. Now, however, Spain and England would share a long border along the Mississippi. In British hands, both East and West Florida constituted a spear dangerously pointed at Cuba and the Caribbean. An inevitable conflict was set up, a conflict in which Bernardo de Gálvez was to play a leading role.

2. New Spain

FIGHTING THE APACHE

In 1764, José de Gálvez, Bernardo's uncle, was appointed visitor-general for New Spain. The institution of the general visit was not new.[1] Juan de Solórzano, arguably the most important Spanish jurist of the seventeenth century, traced its origin back to Genesis 18: 20–21: "Then the Lord said, 'The outcry against Sodom and Gomorrah is so great and their sin so grievous that I will go down and see if what they have done is as bad as the outcry that has reached me. If not, I will know.'"[2] The legal framework for the general visit was established by the two main legal texts in force at the time, the *Nueva Recopilación* and the *Recopilación de Leyes de Indias*.[3]

The visit was, together with the *pesquisa* and *residencia*, among the institutions that the Spanish Crown used to oversee what today is known as the administration. The *pesquisa* investigated possible violations of the law by any person, not necessarily only royal officials. The *residencia* was an examination of the overall performance of a royal official at the end of his mandate. The *visita* sought full implementation by the administration of all relevant legislation regarding trade, finance, ecclesiastical matters, and justice.[4] There were two kinds of visit: particular and general. A particular visit focused only on a certain aspect of the administration. This practice was established in 1345. The general visit, created by King-Emperor Carlos V in 1515, looked at all branches of government.[5] At least that was the theory; in practice things were a bit more complex, depending on the powers attributed to a specific visitor. It could happen, for instance, that during a general visit the visitor-general would open a *pesquisa* if he found evidence of a crime or misconduct attributable to a royal civil servant.

On July 10, 1764, Francisco de Armona was appointed visitor-general for New Spain. Armona was one of the secretaries of the minister of war, the Marquis de Esquilache, who considered him "skillful, honest, and committed to the service of the king, who will not spare any hard work or diligence or fatigue in his service."[6] Although Armona tried to resist the appointment because of "the difficulty and complicated nature of the mission that Your Excellency deigns to assign me in New Spain," he finally accepted it and left for America in 1764.[7] But he died on September 26 that same year.[8] It is not known if José de Gálvez was next in line or volunteered for the position, but he was certainly aware that although the post was difficult, it also represented an unparalleled opportunity to distinguish himself in the eyes of his superiors. Since the objective of the general visit was not only to check on implementation of legislation in New Spain but also to gather information on ways to reform its administration, José de Gálvez was supplied with far-reaching powers. In fact, they were much greater than those granted to previous visitors-general. His instructions were laid out in four separate documents. Two of them were drafted by the Council of the Indies, one by the king himself, and one by the Marquis de Esquilache.[9] This last document was a secret instruction that had previously been issued to Armona before Armona's brother delivered it to Gálvez upon his arrival in Mexico City. It is of great importance since it reveals Esquilache's mistrust of New Spain's viceroy at the time, Joaquín de Montserrat, Marquis de Cruillas. In this instruction José de Gálvez was specifically ordered to find out "if it is true that he sells posts, hosts forbidden games at his home for the benefits he derives, grants pardons in exchange for money, delays the delivery of royal charters until the beneficiaries render him a service, [and] trades without paying duties through his nephew, D. Fernando Monserrat."[10]

JOSÉ DE GÁLVEZ'S ARRIVAL IN NEW SPAIN

José de Gálvez landed in Veracruz in July 1765. As soon as he set foot in the New World, he saw a significant discrepancy between the official reports the viceroy was sending back to Madrid and what was actually happening on the ground. For example, in the court it was believed that the tobacco monopoly was already in effect, but José de Gálvez realized "with the utmost despair, that in that port and in all the kingdom, tobacco was freely traded."[11] He also noted the sorry state of the defenses of Veracruz, even though more than 2 million pesos had already been spent on their improvement.[12] On August 21 he arrived in Mexico City, where he found that not everything was as bad as he had expected. For example, the *audiencia*, or supreme body for administration and justice in the viceroyalty, was doing a good job, even under the suspicious circumstance that most of its members were locals: "Despite the express prohibition by law, to give them [that is, the locals] credit, and in service of the truth, I must assure Your Excellency that I haven't experienced the qualms I anticipated because of the kinships and alliances they have with the city's most prominent families. When such cases [involving those families] come up, they simply excuse themselves from intervening in the procedures."[13]

José de Gálvez coped with the viceroy's reluctance to cooperate with him by deftly manipulating Cruillas's long-standing and open conflict with General Juan de Villalba, who, as was pointed out earlier, had been sent to New Spain to reorganize the army. Although allied with Villalba, Gálvez presented himself to the viceroy as a mediator between the two men.[14] His strategy was to buy time until the appointment of a new viceroy. At court loud rumors were already circulating that Cruillas would be replaced by the general Carlos Francisco de Croix, Marquis de Croix.[15] In fact, as early as November 1765 the marquis had been "advised to be in the knowledge" that the king was considering him for the position of New Spain's viceroy.[16] In any case, the situation must have been a tense one, and Gálvez's patience was tested. On one occasion his difficulties with Cruillas burst into the open. Early in 1766, when Gálvez sent a deputy to carry out some kind of fact-finding mission, the viceroy believed that the tone of Gálvez's report to him was not respectful enough and made no effort to hide his displeasure.[17]

Finally, on July 10, 1766, the Marquis de Croix landed at Veracruz.[18] On August 23, in Otumba, the Marquis de Cruillas solemnly transferred his command to the new viceroy.[19] From the beginning of his tenure in New Spain, Croix had a very good working relationship with José de Gálvez. The marquis was a French-born soldier who had been in the service of the Spanish Crown since the age of seventeen, and he enjoyed the king's utmost confidence. José de Gálvez's French connections would have been very useful in smoothing his relationship with the marquis. Certainly his command of the French language helped him a great deal, too. In a letter dated January 1767, the viceroy's nephew, Teodoro de Croix, described José de Gálvez as "an honest man, skilled, [who] gets along well with my uncle, because both are good men and loyal servants of their lord."[20] From the moment of their meeting until the end of Croix's mandate as viceroy in September 1771, José de Gálvez would act as the right hand of the Crown's highest representative in New Spain. He set out without delay to make changes that were impossible during Cruillas's tenure. He plunged into frantic activity covering nearly all areas of the administration: taxes, the tobacco monopoly as well as income produced by the postal system and other excises; institutions such as the judiciary and the treasury; and whole economic sectors, including salt and mercury mining—the latter of vital importance to Mexico, as mercury was essential for the smelting of silver.[21]

THE EXPULSION OF THE JESUITS

Among the official correspondences that arrived in Mexico on May 30, 1767, an envelope sent to the viceroy by the Count of Aranda stood out. On it was a very explicit warning: "Death sentence. Do not open this envelope until June 24 at nightfall."[22] The warning was not exaggerated. It contained detailed instructions for the expulsion of the Society of Jesus from New Spain.

King Carlos III had signed the order on February 27, 1767.[23] Whole libraries could be filled with the studies written about the motives, consequences, and meaning of the Jesuits' expulsion from the Spanish Empire. All of the studies agree only that it was a crucial event in the history of Spain. But here I will consider not the multiple causes or important consequences of the Jesuits' expulsion but the important role that José de Gálvez played in its implementation in New Spain.[24] According to Eva María St. Clair Segurado, in New Spain (772,000 square miles) alone, more than 500 priests had to be apprehended. Many of them worked in solitary devotion, spiritually ministering to the Indians in remote missions of which only the Jesuits knew the exact location and where few Spanish settlers lived.[25]

The general orders for the expulsion included an addition to the instruction that addressed the order's banishment from His Majesty's dominions in the Indies and the Philippines. This amendment, while stressing the importance of maintaining "the simultaneity of its implementation, with uniform procedures to ensure its success,"[26] left a wide margin for maneuvering by viceroys and governors, who were to proceed with "vigor, caution, and secrecy, not trusting this subject but to those strictly concerned with it."[27] Viceroy de Croix shared the news only with his two most trusted assistants: his nephew Teodoro and José de Gálvez.[28]

They worked tirelessly and in secret to prepare all of the details. On June 24, 1767, the command was given to the main public authorities. That same night all Jesuits in the capital were evicted from their residences. The next morning a proclamation was issued that concluded with a severe warning that perfectly sums up the philosophy of enlightened despotism: "For once and for all, the subjects of the great monarch who sits on the throne of Spain must know that they were born to keep silent and obey, and not to question or discuss important governmental matters."[29]

Anticipating difficulties, the viceroy ordered troops from various regions to collect in the capital city and in Puebla. The surprise played out in his favor, and Jesuits living in the capital were peacefully escorted to the port of Veracruz. It was not the same elsewhere in New Spain. According to Luisa Zahino Peñafort, six months after the implementation of the decree of expulsion, the situation in New Spain was very tense. Only a minority group

Contemporary engraving depicting the expulsion of the Jesuit order from the territories of the Spanish monarchy in 1767. The expulsion was done simultaneously throughout the Spanish Empire in a clockwork operation that tested the efficiency of the Spanish imperial bureaucracy to the limit. Under the command of Viceroy Carlos Francisco de Croix, José de Gálvez was put in charge of the complex operations that successfully apprehended more than 500 priests in the 772,000 square miles of the territory of the viceroyalty of New Spain. (*Expulsion et embarquement des Jésuites des états d'Espagne . . .* ; Bibliothèque nationale de France)

formed by the viceroy, composed of certain prelates and officials and some members of the secular clergy, supported the banishment.[30]

In December the viceroy warned the Crown in very clear terms that "if the increase of troops I asked for to rule this country and its large and varied population was necessary before the expulsion of the Jesuits, now that they are gone, it is needed even more. Although from the outside everything seems peaceful, there is a general ferment everywhere. Caution demands that we take necessary measures while we still can."[31]

The viceroy's fears would soon be realized in the rich mining areas of the country. According to José de Gálvez, "Even before [the expulsion], those people were already uneasy for other reasons, and they were getting used to independence."[32] The expulsion acted as a trigger for riots in San Luis de la Paz, Guanajuato, Pátzcuaro, and San Luis de Potosí, where the population hid Jesuit priests, raided the prisons, and attacked the authorities. The situation was so serious that to handle it the Marquis de Croix dispatched the one person in whom he had utmost confidence: José de Gálvez. Gálvez suppressed the revolt with extreme harshness. In addition to sentencing about eighty rebels to be hanged, he sent hundreds to forced labor, jail, or exile.[33] Once he had accomplished his mission, Gálvez returned to Mexico City, willing to embark on a new and ambitious project. He wrote, "[After I] restored and ensured calm in the provinces that are at the center of the realm, it was essential to look further and cast the attention of the government to those most remote areas. Sonora and Sinaloa had been agitated for some time now. [They were] almost completely destroyed by the barbaric hostilities of the fierce Apaches, and of the Seri, Pima, and Sububapas."[34]

But before he was able to think of any campaign against the Apache, José de Gálvez was sent to California. In April 1768, he left Mexico City toward the port of San Blas, near Puerto Vallarta on the Pacific coast. There he would be in charge not only of the preparations for the military expedition but also of ensuring the Pacific expansion of the Spanish Empire in North America, an expansion that in California, contrary to what happened at the time in other territories in the Spanish Empire, would not be accomplished mainly by military means but through religious ones. José de Gálvez's choice of the mission instead of the presidio as the colonizing institution in California would be based purely on economic considerations, since missions would be "less expensive and easier to establish than presidios." A consequence of his decision would be that while elsewhere in the Spanish Empire the colonization was focused on soldiers and settlers, in California it would develop around friars, priests, and indigenous populations.[35]

REASONS BEHIND THE CAMPAIGNS AGAINST THE "BARBARIC INDIANS"[36]
José de Gálvez's Personal Motives

The idea of carrying out a military expedition against the Seri and the Apache soon hatched in José de Gálvez's mind.[37] It was an initiative that had a great deal of support both in military circles and among the settlers and landowners on the northern border. To Gálvez the situation in the northern border region was unacceptable because it threatened the ambitious reform agenda that he had set for the entire viceroyalty. At the same time, an expedition could be the perfect opportunity to attract favorable attention from the court. As a *golilla*, a lawyer, perhaps he felt that he needed to acquire a certain amount of military experience to be eligible for important positions, since they were traditionally awarded to members of the military. A *golilla* was "a collar of lawn or linen, slightly rolled under at the edge and starched to stand out from the neckline, worn in Spain in the seventeenth century."[38] The term was applied also to "people trained in the humanities and law, usually *hidalgos*, who had studied and held administrative positions with the Catholic monarchy."[39] Historian John Lynch claims that José de Gálvez was "a *golilla* by definition"[40] to such an extent that when, in 1781, Francisco Javier de Santa Cruz y Espejo published his pamphlet *Portrait of a Golilla* attacking King Carlos III's government, he used José de Gálvez as his model.[41]

Whatever his personal motives and ambitions, José de Gálvez was not powerful enough to wage a war, as little as it might be, without the support of both Mexico City and Madrid. He won the authorities' concurrence because of a combination of factors that must be considered separately.

The Social Factor

A complex network of interests existed among people who saw the native population as a hindrance to the development of the northern border regions.[42] Some settlers, for example, were interested in exaggerating the Apache threat in order to obtain special grants or tax exemptions as compensation for the constant danger in which they claimed to live. Military officers posted in the region also tended to send alarming reports to earn supplemental pay for their hardships. In addition, royal officials could exaggerate their reports in support of their demands for more resources from the Royal Treasury. By waging a military campaign against the Indians, the viceregal authorities sought to win and maintain the support of these important social sectors.

The Military Factor

As seen earlier, General Juan de Villalba arrived in New Spain in 1764. With several officers and more than 700 soldiers, his troops were to become the backbone of a colonial army that in time would have as many as nine regiments.[43] Villalba recruited carefully and subjected his men to intense training, but to become real soldiers they needed combat experience. Although the number of forces assigned to José de Gálvez's campaign was not very large, it was sufficient to convey the message that the colonial army needed to be prepared at all times.

To civilian authorities, the presence of a standing army in New Spain was something new and problematic. Until the arrival of General Villalba, the viceroy had been the supreme and uncontested military authority of the viceroyalty. But with the creation of the position of deputy inspector general of troops, the viceroy's power was in reality diminished, which led to tensions between civilian and military authorities.[44] Although it cannot be claimed that the campaign was a ploy by civilian authorities to keep the newly formed army at a distance—even though idle troops near population centers were a predictable source of conflict—this was certainly an enabling factor.

The Political-Religious Factor

The Jesuits had borne much of the burden of establishing a Spanish presence in the territories along New Spain's northern border. The missionary work of Father Eusebio Francisco Kino in the Pimería Alta at the end of the seventeenth and the beginning of the eighteenth centuries provided a base for Spain's subsequent expansion into these lands. The role of the missionary as "agent both religious and royal," according to David Jacobo Calles Montaño, produced a close relationship between the presidios and the missions.[45] Both institutions "made possible the successful subjugation of indigenous people in the missions of the Northwest."[46] As José Marcos Medina Bustos notes, with the expulsion of the Jesuits from the missions of northwestern New Spain, a highly complex phase began, in which the norm was the presence in indigenous towns of hybrid forms of both spiritual and temporal governments, which varied according to the characteristics of the different areas.[47]

The withdrawal of the Jesuits did not lead to the imposition of a uniform model for transforming their missions. Although in most cases the missions were handed over to the Franciscans, sometimes they were simply secularized, creating a power vacuum that could trigger rebellion from the Seri and the Apache; it should not be forgotten that the memory was still fresh of the bloody revolts by the Seri and the Pimas in 1755 and 1760, respectively. The fear was justified. From January 1766 on, the Seri began to assemble on the mountain of Cerro Prieto, an almost impregnable bastion from which they launched attacks on nearby settlements. Their evident impunity was perceived as a threat to Spanish control of the region.

The Economic Factor

José de Gálvez was very skilled at proposing the military expedition. First, he pointed out the enormous wealth awaiting exploitation of those regions. As Domingo de Valcárcel, the auditor of the campaign, wrote, "If the stories are to be believed, in Sonora there are rich minerals, and even mountains of almost solid silver."[48] Elaborating on this theme, in April 1771, after the military campaign was over, a project was proposed in Mexico City with the title "Plan for a company to promote the benefits of the mines in Sonora and Sinaloa, and to restore the pearl fisheries in the Gulf of California."⁴⁹ Second, José de Gálvez stressed that the campaign would not be a burden to the Royal Treasury, since it would be financed totally by private sources. He worked tirelessly at the task of raising the necessary funds. In May 1767 he had already collected 189,628 pesos and was confident that he soon would have 300,000 pesos, the total sum needed.⁵⁰ The donors' list constituted a veritable who's who of individuals in Mexican society who had interests on the northern frontier.⁵¹ They included representatives of the chamber of commerce (*diputación del comercio*) of Jalapa; consulates and merchants from Mexico City, Puebla, and Veracruz; members of the ecclesiastical councils (*cabildos eclesiásticos*) of Durango and Oaxaca; and a goodly number of settlers in the region.⁵² Some of them were later generously rewarded for their financial support. For example, Manuel Varela of Puebla was appointed mayor for life (*regidor perpetuo*) of the village of Atlixco.⁵³ The merchant Pedro Antonio de Cossío of Veracruz was appointed by José de Gálvez as *superintendente de la real hacienda* (head of New Spain's treasury), although shortly afterward he was removed because of numerous wrongdoings.⁵⁴ Fernando Bustillo also received the job of *comisario de guías* (a collector of a specific kind of taxes) but for twelve years never rendered accounts of the taxes he was supposed to collect and at his death owed more than 7,000 pesos to the treasury.⁵⁵ Francisco Gil was rewarded in July 1770 with the post of *alcalde mayor* (judge) of Cuautla Amilpas.⁵⁶

OBJECTIVES OF THE CAMPAIGN

The political objective of the campaign was to pacify the northern frontier of New Spain, which was under the constant threat of raids by the several indigenous groups, particularly the Seri and the Apache. The strategic objective was to destroy the main Seri stronghold on Cerro Prieto, in the Ahome district of the present-day state of Sinaloa. From here the Seri "went out to deplete the land of both provinces [Sonora and Sinaloa], taking as many cattle as they could from the fertile countryside, and with mercy to no one, as all were victims of their atrocious cruelty."⁵⁷ The tactics were discussed during several meetings of royal officials during the first half of 1768. The size of the force grew from an initial 423 soldiers to more than 1,000. The duration of the campaign was predicted to be eight months. To speed the arrival of the troops and avoid a long march over hostile territory, the decision was made that they would travel by sea from San Blas to the base of operations in La Paz, in the present-day state of Baja California, from whence they would march into Sonora and Sinaloa.

A BRIEF DESCRIPTION OF THE CAMPAIGN

According to Mario Hernández Sánchez-Barba, the campaign must be divided into two very different periods: before and after the arrival of José de Gálvez.[58]

Before his arrival, troops were gathered in the villages of Pitic (today's Ciudad de Hermosillo, in the state of Sonora) and Guaymas (close to Ciudad de Hermosillo). Although their transport was to be by sea and to that purpose towboats had been built, bad weather, construction delays, red tape, and other incidents resulted in only the infantry going by ship. The cavalry, under the command of Colonel Domingo Elizondo, had to make its way overland. Making the best of the delay, Elizondo subjected his troops to a program of rigorous training. The military operations began in earnest in October 1768 with the reconnaissance of the territories surrounding Cerro Prieto. Weeks later, three separate columns departed from Guaymas and Pitic with orders to meet near Cerro Prieto. On October 23 they arrived near a place called Cajón de la Palma, where intelligence reports indicated the Seri were gathering. The attack was a complete failure. Spanish troops mistook some of their own Indian allies for the enemy and opened fire on them, alerting the Seri, who wasted no time in attacking them from the heights of Cerro Prieto. Elizondo had no choice but to return to camp. Another unsuccessful attack against Cerro Prieto took place in March of the following year. Despite its failure, too, the Seri were starting to feel pressured as they lost their much-needed mobility and the support of other groups. In any event, everything came to a standstill when new orders arrived from Madrid urging the hostilities to cease so that Elizondo could "try to attract the Seri through friendship."[59]

At this time José de Gálvez had been in California nearly a year. In May 1769, he arrived in the theater of operations against the Seri. Shortly afterward he issued an edict offering a royal pardon to all those who surrendered and laid down their arms.[60] A truce of forty days was decreed, after which "the day will arrive of their total ruin and exemplary punishment, which their many sacrilegious crimes deserve, because I will immediately treat them with all the rigors of war. No quarter will be granted. Their lives will not be spared. Although enough troops and weapons to suppress them are already in Sonora, I will increase their number with all the faithful vassals whom His Majesty has in the vast reaches of both provinces. I will personally go anywhere to let them experience the severity of justice, so they know (though belatedly) that they can neither hide nor avoid the blows of the supreme power of the kings of heaven and earth that threaten them."[61]

The offer of a royal pardon was essential, for the legality of the military campaign depended upon it. Only after the Seri had rejected his offer could José de Gálvez claim that he had carried out the royal order to use peaceful means to subdue their rebellion. Forty days passed, and to be on the safe side he issued an extension. Meanwhile, in the region of the Fuerte River, a small group of Indians rebelled but was easily put down. After the extension expired, José de Gálvez let loose the dogs of war. From then on it was no longer about pacification but punishment. The campaign grew in ferocity. Within a week he went from ordering his men "not to engage the enemy unless they were attacked" to instructing them to search for "victims who will be sacrificed on the altar of justice with the whole weight of my power, to serve as public warnings."[62] These were not empty threats. He did not hesitate to sentence three men and a woman to be hanged and shot, after which "the heads of all four [were to] be separated from their bodies, and put on pikes where they must remain until time consumes them."[63]

By the end of July 1769 everything was ready for what José de Gálvez believed would be the final offensive. The troops had been hardened in numerous encounters with the enemy; the military commander, Colonel Elizondo, was a professional soldier with ample experience; a new plan was adopted that was aligned with the tough terrain and even tougher fight; and the campaign had the total commitment of the highest authority on site, José de Gálvez, whom the viceroy had invested with his complete confidence. Precisely at this moment Gálvez was struck by what at the time was called "apoplexy and paralysis" but was probably malaria.[64] This was, at least, the official version of what happened. The truth, as always, was a bit more complex. The strange disease that afflicted José de Gálvez was the object of several interpretations at the time. Elizondo mentioned in passing "the constant indisposition of His Excellency ["Su Ilustrísma" in Spanish], which prevented him from tending to the government of the provinces and the campaign."[65] Eusebio Ventura Belcña wrote that from the end of June, Gálvez had had little sleep and began to suffer from fever caused by "the uneasiness he felt because of the delay in suppressing the rebellion."[66] Gabriel Antonio de Vildósola described him as having a "serious illness with a very high fever and some remnants of hypochondriac melancholy."[67] Last but not least, Juan Manuel de Viniegra, one of José de Gálvez's secretaries, insisted that his deep melancholy was caused by his frustration at seeing that "the rebels from Cerro Prieto were not surrendering, and the campaign was running out of funds."[68] The use of the term "melancholy" was ominous. Physicians at the time considered it a serious variety of mental illness.[69]

Hernández Sánchez-Barba suggests that José de Gálvez's insanity could have been feigned so that he would be relieved of the campaign without besmirching his honor, which would have been pledged to such a personal endeavor.[70] Héctor Cuauhtémoc Hernández Silva goes a step further and supposes that while Gálvez could have suffered a mental breakdown, it was probably only a part of a broader, obscure conspiracy woven by Gálvez and Viceroy de Croix to hide from Madrid the bleak reality of conditions on New Spain's northern frontier.[71]

Be that as it may, the fact is that from August 1769 the behavior of the visitor-general was increasingly erratic, and even deranged, to the point that by the end of that year the viceroy had no alternative but to order him back to Mexico City.[72] Without the presence of such a driving force, the days of the military campaign against the Seri of Cerro Prieto were numbered.

BERNARDO DE GÁLVEZ'S ASSIGNMENT TO LOPE DE CUÉLLAR'S CAMPAIGN

Bernardo de Gálvez did not arrive in New Spain until early 1769. Although several authors have placed him on American soil prior to that date, no documentation has been found to back up their assertions.[73]

What is certain is that Bernardo did not travel to New Spain with his uncle José. He was not among the members of the family, entourage, or servants who accompanied the visitor-general.[74] Moreover, there is evidence that Bernardo de Gálvez enlisted "as a volunteer in the expedition to Nueva Vizcaya against the Apaches under the command of Lope de Cuéllar," assuming his post in Chihuahua on April 11, 1769.[75] For a few months he was assigned to the company "to learn his trade" under the command of Lieutenant Diego Becerril, after which he was made captain in command of the Fourth Company.[76] Shortly afterward he was appointed as captain again to the New Spain Crown Regiment.

Bernardo had the full backing of his uncle and through him the support of the viceroy, the Marquis de Croix. Despite these well-placed mentors, his appointment was not without problems. For one thing, his posting to Lope de Cuéllar's forces was made "out of consideration for the visitor-general's merits"—that is, his uncle's merits but not Bernardo's.[77] This was normal in the eighteenth century. The word "nepotism" was not introduced into Spanish until 1843, when the Royal Academy's dictionary defined it as the "excessive preference that some give to their relatives for concessions or public employment." The key word here is "excessive," implying that if a preference were not excessive, it would not constitute nepotism.[78] Nepotism was widespread. For example, Francisco de Armona, the visitor-general before José de Gálvez, had his brother appointed governor of Lower California even before leaving for Mexico.[79] Lope de Cuéllar, the commander of the campaign against the Seri, had his brother assigned under him.[80] Even though the viceroy recommended Bernardo's appointment, the king did not confirm it but instead decreed that Bernardo would "have the grade [*grado*] and pay of an active [*vivo*] infantry lieutenant."[81] To understand this nuance it is important to explain the difference between grade (*grado*) and rank (*empleo*).

In the eighteenth century, military rank in the Spanish army "from sergeant major to general was granted with the King's approval."[82] Grade, in contrast, was "the honor superior to the rank of soldier, from corporal to colonel, [granted] as a reward for a commendatory deed or a distinguished action."[83] These technicalities meant that, although Bernardo was a lieutenant by rank, he was also a captain graduate, a rank he could not assume until a vacancy opened.[84] Army casualties suffered during the "nice little war" against the Apache would soon offer an opportunity for Bernardo's promotion; the death of Captain Juan de Solalinde left vacant the captaincy of a company in the Second Battalion of the New Spain Crown Regiment. Even though army regulations stipulated that merit was the main criterion, if not the only one, for promotion, in practice seniority also played a key role.[85] According to the promotion system, the colonel of a regiment had a list of the names of three men to promote, from which he could recommend one. But it was a recommendation only, since the king alone had the power to promote.

In this case, the colonel submitted his list of three names on June 21, 1769, putting in first place Lieutenant Joseph Cosido [José Cossío], Marquis de Torre Campo (with six years, nine months, and nineteen days of active service); in second place, Lieutenant Jayme Alsuvide of the grenadiers (with twenty years, seven months, and twenty-two days of service); and in third place, First Aide-de-Camp Francisco García (with nineteen years, seven months, and nine days). The colonel considered "the three candidates, all . . . worthy of promotion, especially the second, because of his longer service and war honors."[86] Despite the colonel's recommendation, the general inspector, the Marquis de la Torre, "in his report prefers the promotion of Joseph Cosido, listed in first place, because of his seniority, his performance, and for the extensive service of his father, the Marquis de Torre Campo, governor and general of the army of New Spain, as well for the service of his ancestors."[87] Both candidates were supported because of their years of service, but they had different kinds of seniority. While Lieutenants Alsuvide and García had been in service much longer than Cossío, the latter had served longer as a lieutenant. The fact that Cossío was a marquis had allowed him to enter the army directly with the grade and rank of lieutenant, while Alsuvide and García, without aristocratic pedigrees, had to serve first as cadets and then as second lieutenants.[88] But the final recommendation belonged to neither the colonel nor the inspector general but to New Spain's viceroy, and he had another candidate in mind for the captaincy. On July 27 the Marquis de Croix wrote, "Despite the recommendation in this proposal, he [that is, the viceroy] advises Your Majesty to award the captaincy vacant due to the death of Juan de Solalinde to Bernardo de Gálvez, nephew of the visitor-general, out of consideration of the distinguished service of this minister, and the good qualities and talent of Bernardo, who served with the greatest honor as lieutenant in the French auxiliary army during the last war with Portugal, and after returning from that kingdom immediately departed to enlist as a volunteer in Nueva Vizcaya's campaign against the Apache Indians under the command of Lope de Cuéllar, where he presently serves as captain of the First Company."[89]

In the cases of both Bernardo de Gálvez and the Marquis de Torre Campo, their merits were more familial than personal. More than twenty years of active duty by Alsuvide and nineteen years by García were not sufficient against such powerful family connections. Naively, it could be argued that faced with the difference between the colonel and the inspector-general, the viceroy chose the third candidate as a compromise. But this was not the first time Croix intervened in favor of the nephew of his closest adviser. In any case, the viceroy's recommendation was approved, and Bernardo de Gálvez was officially promoted to the full rank of captain.[90] In the New Spain Crown Regiment the news was most probably not much celebrated, and rightly so. Not only would one of its three lieutenants not get a captaincy, but also no sergeant major would get a lieutenancy, and so on. Since Bernardo de Gálvez would temporarily be assigned to the forces under Lope de Cuéllar, adding insult to injury was the fact that his captaincy in the New Spain Crown Regiment would remain reserved for him while his duties were most likely fulfilled for the time being by one of the three passed-over lieutenants. In any case, that would not be Bernardo's problem, since he actually never served in the regiment.

THE APACHE: A BRIEF INTRODUCTION

The eighteenth-century Apache Indians did not recognize themselves by this name. They used *diné*, *dné*, or *tin-ne-áh*, which in Athapaskan means "the people," the same word used by the Navajo to refer to themselves.[91] There are several theories about the origin of the term Apache.[92] The most accepted one is that it derives from the Zuñi word *ápachu*, or "enemy."[93] Others say it derives from the Chiricahua Apaches' facial war paint, which made them look like raccoons, *mapache* in Spanish; or from the Yuma word *e-pach*, meaning "man who fights"; or even from the Spanish word *apachurrar*, "smash."[94] Whichever is correct, the relevant issue is that the name "Apache" came from the outside, always bearing some kind of negative connotation and thus implying from the very beginning that knowledge about them was based more on stereotypes than on reality.[95]

While trying to understand the eighteenth-century Apache, we must contend with several difficulties. The first is that they had no writing and so were not able to record their impressions and opinions of European settlers. Outsiders, either contemporaneous witnesses or later researchers (whose testimonies always need to be analyzed with care), recorded their legends and stories.[96] The second difficulty relates to the dangers of the approach that tries to unveil a culture's unknown past from its present state.[97] The last difficulty is of a more general nature: at that time, history was written by the victors.[98]

The people known as the Apache had the Athapaskan language family and some cultural traits in common but little else. They never formed a political unit, and except in moments of extreme threat, they rarely acted in unison. Depending on the writer, the Apache are divided into various subgroups. But it is important to note that today's descriptions of them and even the names used to label them differ from those used in eighteenth-century Spanish sources.[99] Bernardo de Gálvez divided them into various subgroups depending on the moment he was considering the issue. While in 1771 he wrote about *gileños, mescaleros, natages, lipanes*, and *nizfandes*,[100] in 1786 he mentioned *lipanes, mezcaleros, jicarillas, navajos*, and *gileños*.[101] Today, modern scholars divide the Apache into three basic groups: eastern, including the Lipan, Jicarilla, and Kiowa Apache; central, comprising the Mescalero, Bedonkohe, and Chiricahua Apache, with the latter divided into several bands whose names vary according to the author; and western, including the Cibecue, Tonto (north and south), San Carlos, and White Mountain Apache.

While some subgroups, such as the Jicarilla and Lipan, were farmers and herders, most others were hunters and gatherers.[102] More because of these different lifestyles than because of the existence of an Apache territory per se, it is appropriate to talk about the zones in which the Apache presence was felt. This was exactly what contemporaries had in mind when they spoke of the "Apachería," which included, in the present-day United States, the eastern part of Arizona, a great part of New Mexico, Colorado's southeast portion, Oklahoma's western regions, and a big portion of Texas; and in Mexico, the northern parts of Sonora, Chihuahua, and Coahuila states.[103] In other words, it was a region almost as big as today's Spain or France, spanning 745 miles from east to west and 340 miles from north to south.[104] Of the Apache population at the time, some authors claimed that it comprised as many as 30,000 people.[105] But the number most widely accepted, at least at the beginning of the nineteenth century, is about 8,000.[106]

FIRST CONTACTS

Some authors mention the possibility that in 1528, Alvar Núñez Cabeza de Vaca encountered Apache Indians during his shipwrecks on the shores of the southern United States and northern Mexico or that Francisco de Coronado met up with them during his unsuccessful search for the seven cities of Cibola.[107] The group that attacked Gaspar Castaño de Sosa in 1590 could have been Apache, although the enemies were described only as Indian herdsmen. So we have to conclude that the first documented contact between the Spanish and the Apache took place in 1599, when the Apache supported the Pueblos against forces under the command of Juan de Oñate.[108] Aside from the interesting fact of the precise date, what is most important is that all of the early accounts describe the Apache as enemies.[109]

Within only a few years of these first contacts the Apache had already adapted to the newcomers, incorporating such elements from their culture as playing cards and mastering the horse.[110] Yet during the seventeenth century, confrontation was the norm.[111] The Apache raided Spanish settlements, and the Spaniards counterattacked in search of vengeance or even slaves, despite an express ban on the practice by the Crown.[112] The last decades of the century were the apogee of the Apache in the northern frontier of the viceroyalty of New Spain, since beginning in the eighteenth century, in a domino effect, they were pushed progressively farther from their lands by the Comanche, who in turn had been expelled from their own territories by the Sioux.[113] The war between the Comanche and the Apache lasted 120 years.[114] In the 1720s the Comanche finally succeeded in pushing the Apache southward against New Spain's expanding northern frontier.[115] More hostile confrontation was only a matter of time.

THE "APACHE PROBLEM" IN THE EIGHTEENTH CENTURY
The Organization of New Spain's Northern Frontier: The Regulations of 1729

Contemporaneous sources consider 1748 the "initial date of the era of unhappiness for Nueva Vizcaya, and in general for all of the Interior Provinces."[116] But problems had started well before that time.[117] Indian rebellions were not unknown in eighteenth-century New Spain. During the sixteenth century, the Chichimeca revolt was put down only after a war that

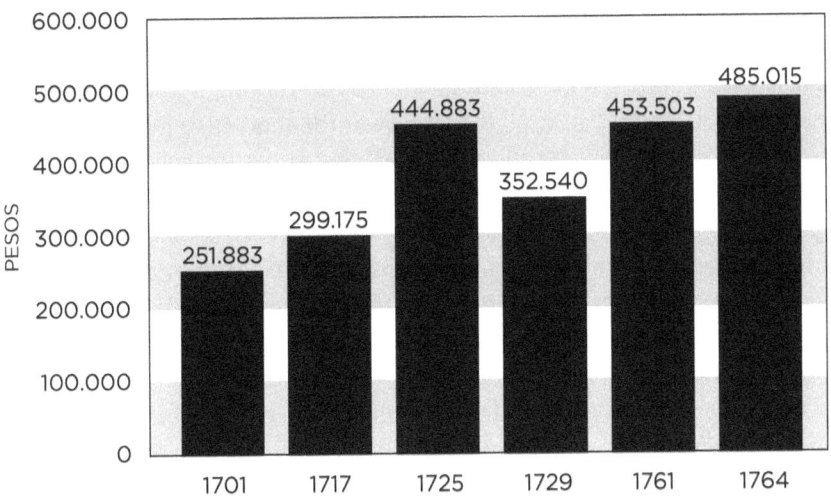

Graph 1. Annual Expenditures in the Defense of Spain's Northern Frontier
Data from Navarro Garcia, *José de Gálvez y la comandancia general*, 126 and 140–41.

lasted almost four decades. According to Philip Wayne Powell, this war was even costlier in terms of men, equipment, and money than the conquest of Mexico by Hernán Cortés.[118] The seventeenth-century Pueblo revolt took the Spaniards by surprise because of its unexpected beginning, sophisticated organization, and ferocity. It ended only after several fierce military campaigns between 1680 and 1693 and an agreement that would allow the Spanish back into Pueblos' land.[119] With these precedents it was logical that the Spanish authorities were watching for any trace of resistance. Continuous complaints from settlers and local authorities about the depredations suffered because of the Apache caused defense costs on the northern border of the viceroyalty to nearly double between 1701 and 1764.

Other factors conspired to complicate things even more. The territorial redistribution of North America through the 1763 Treaty of Paris increased pressure on the northern border of New Spain. Added to that was the second Seri rebellion the same year, the sighting of Russian ships on the Pacific coast, and one of the periodic Spanish obsessions to reduce public expenditures.[120] So it was a combination of old and new problems that triggered the Crown to consider that perhaps the time had come for an entirely new approach for organizing the frontier,[121] one based on the 1729 regulations, with origins in the costly suppression of the Pueblo rebellion between 1680 and 1693, which had emptied the Royal Treasury and severely weakened the presidio system.[122] In 1723 a visitor[123] had been sent to New Spain's northern frontier to identify problems and recommend solutions.[124] The visit con-

FIGHTING THE APACHE [37

cluded with a lengthy report that described the sorry state of the frontier's defenses, not to mention rampant corruption among the officials in the garrisons and the horrible conditions of day-to-day life in the presidios.[125] Based on this report, in 1729, the viceroy at the time, Juan de Acuña, promulgated "regulations for all of the presidios in the Interior Provinces of this government, with the number of officers and soldiers who are to be garrisoned there, the salaries that each one will receive, [and] ordinances for better governance and the military discipline of governors, officers, and soldiers, including clauses on the prices of the provisions and uniforms supplied to them."[126] This was the first attempt to reorganize the frontier. Two others followed, in 1771 and 1786.[127]

An important assumption shared by all of these reforms was that the real threat was not as serious as it appeared to be at first glance. Royal officials were increasingly suspicious that most of the alarms sounded by settlers on the frontier were nothing but self-interested exaggerations. Against this background, the 1729 regulations decreased the number of troops and presidios allocated to the defense of the frontier, which immediately produced significant savings for the Royal Treasury. Most of these measures targeted corruption and abuses among the officers and officials of the presidios and disregarded the effect they would have on defensive capabilities.[128] Salaries were also cut with the rationale that without corruption the price of merchandise in the presidios would fall, so soldiers and their families could live on less. But no policy has ever succeeded in completely eradicating corruption, and these measures served to undercut the power of the presidio officers and officials, whose interests were intimately intertwined with those of the elite groups of the populations they protected.[129] In the end, the main result of the 1729 regulations was that morale plummeted. Soon the royal authorities realized that the regulations solved very little, if anything. Attacks by the Apache and other groups continued to the point that some of the abandoned presidios had to be rebuilt. Even worse, the appetite for savings of central authorities in the capital did not abate with the new regulations, and to spend even less they considered renouncing any further expansion beyond the boundaries of the Spanish Empire. According to José de Carvajal, secretary of state at the time, efforts in America should be directed only toward consolidation within present limits. As for the protection of "the villages near savage Indians," he believed, "it would only be necessary to build a wall made of wooden sticks or just compacted soil, with little cannons placed on its angles."[130]

The complaints against the 1729 regulations were many. The most effective criticism emerged in 1748. That year José de Berrotarán sent an extensive report to the viceroy, the Count of Revillagigedo, in which he detailed the sorry state of the frontier, openly blaming the 1729 regulations.[131] Berrotarán's report was the origin of the idea to send to the north the first military campaign explicitly directed against the Apache.

However, neither costs nor complaints from villagers were the main reason for the Crown's decision to completely restructure the defense of the region. The new geographical framework after the Paris Treaty determined that New Spain's northern frontier was no longer the Spanish Empire's frontier but its heartland. The addition of Louisiana to His Catholic Majesty's territories in North America meant that the border was now much farther north, along the Mississippi River. This fact had a very important consequence for New Spain's northern regions. What was bearable in a region situated on the border of the empire could not be tolerated in its heartland. A new system was needed to ensure a reliable level of peace and tranquility.

It was in this context that the idea of creating a new viceroyalty was born. The idea was not original. During the eighteenth century, two new viceroyalties had already been created: Nueva Granada and Rio de la Plata.[132] A viceroyalty for northern New Spain was first suggested in an anonymous memorandum presented in 1760.[133] In the end, no new viceroyalty was established for northern New Spain, but a decade later the *comandancia general de las provincias internas* was created. It was the brainchild of José de Gálvez, who had long been working on this idea. In fact, only three months after he was made *secretario de estado de la secretaría del Despacho Universal de Indias* (minister of the Indies), he created the *comandancia general* and appointed a commandant responsible for "all branches of the governmental apparatus (administrative, judicial, military, financial, and ecclesiastical)" who, in theory at least, would be independent of New Spain's viceroy.[134]

Spaniards' Image versus Real Knowledge of the Apache

The eighteenth century witnessed a new European perception of the Indians. Far off were the days when their human condition was open to debate.[135] Now a more pragmatic, more enlightened approach was adopted. Viceregal officials weighed in on Indians' capacity to become active and productive vassals of His Majesty, while the church considered whether they had the capacity to understand fully the complexities of Roman Catholicism or whether it should be simplified for them.[136] At the time, almost all of the Indian population living within the Spanish imperial borders in America had already assumed the place allocated to them in society. Those in the borderlands needed to be incorporated, too. To achieve this, information about them was urgently needed. Therefore, it was no coincidence that dur-

Late eighteenth-century representation of an Apache family, one in a group of paintings depicting the different communities living in the viceroyalty of New Spain. This idyllic image, in which neither the dress nor the scenery bears any resemblance whatsoever to the reality of Apache life at the time, is direct heir to the idea of the "noble savage" popular during the Enlightenment. (*Castas, Indios apaches*, circa 1775, oil on copper, in Museo de América, Madrid, inventory no. 00065)

ing this period, reports, commentaries, descriptions, and narratives containing a wide variety of views of the Indians multiplied, ranging from those that directly reflected the recently created myth of the noble savage to those that insisted on their innate cruelty.[137] As for the Apache, in 1768 Nicolás de Lafora spoke in these terms: "They are extremely lazy; they sow little or nothing, so they are forced to steal to eat; as a mule, a horse, or a deer is the same for them, they prefer to go looking for the first thing they can find, taking from the Spaniards herds of horses, because with less fatigue than hunting they will assure food supplies more abundantly."[138]

By the end of the century, Colonel Antonio Cordero insisted that their nasty temper caused the Apache to be sly, suspicious, fickle, bold, proud, and jealous of their independence.[139] Others did not fully share these negative views. An important report in 1799 by the lieutenant of engineers José Cortés is a complete treatise on the Apache and opens with the direct accusation that those who speak about the northern frontier of the viceroyalty of New Spain do so with the same ignorance as if they were talking about Constantinople.[140] This report can be considered the first quasi-scientific study of the Apache and is in the Enlightenment tradition of Spanish scientific travelers who explored the world during the second half of the eighteenth century. But even so, Cortés's perspective never ceases to be that of an official searching for solutions to his country's problems. At the end of the day, as David J. Weber has concluded, "whether Spanish soldiers perceived Indians to be warlike or peaceful depended as much on Spaniards' designs on Indians as on Indians' behavior."[141] When a particular author sought to justify a military campaign against them, he focused on their cruelty, whereas if interested in signing alliances with Apache, he insisted on their reasonableness and the fact that their violence had been caused only by the affronts they had received.[142]

The Apache Threat: Real and Perceived

In the early 1760s, complaints multiplied about the cruelty of the Apache and the havoc they were creating. Reports reached the Crown from all directions that their bloody forays prevented the economic and demographic development of the northern frontier.[143] Despite this outcry, one must consider whether these complaints were justified. Sara Ortelli believes that from 1748 on, the issue of the proliferation of Apache attacks and the need to raise a war against them was the product of a real fear of an Indian uprising in Nueva Vizcaya, but it was also used as an argument in order to maintain the status quo in the region, a status quo tremendously favorable to the settlers and that was being challenged by the Crown, which was trying to increase its control over the territory and its population.[144]

This vision is certainly correct from the historian's global point of view, but it is also important not to underestimate the sufferings of the settlers. Max L. Moorhead estimates that between 1749 and 1769, about 800 people were killed by the Apache and more than 4 million pesos in property was stolen or destroyed.[145] Luis Navarro García increases the number of deaths to 1,973 between 1771 and 1776 in Nueva Vizcaya alone.[146] If these figures are accurate, it was to be expected that at the time the region suffered from an "authentic bellicose psychosis," as Mario Hernández Sánchez-Barba puts it—a psychosis that clouded all judgment and blamed all violence on the Apache.[147] Nevertheless, cooler heads were still to be found among some royal officials. In the 1770s, Luis Fernando de Oubel, head of the Royal Treasury in Chihuahua, reported that the decline of that mining area was due not to Apache attacks but to the decreasing productivity of the deposits.[148] In 1777 Viceroy Antonio Bucareli responded to an urgent request for more troops to "punish the Indians and keep the provinces in peace."[149] He believed that the depiction of the situation was "too sad" and that Indian attacks were just "stealing escapades" (*correrías rateras*).[150] The fact was that the settlers and the authorities had different interests. The former considered themselves victims abandoned to Apache cruelty by civil servants sitting comfortably in their offices in the capital. The latter judged the descriptions offered by the settlers as exaggerated and motivated by their particular interests and concluded that organizing a military campaign against the Apache would have only the one sure outcome of draining the Royal Treasury.

An "Apache Policy"

An "Apache policy" was formulated within the framework of two other distinct policies: the promotion of New Spain's northern frontier and the Crown's general policy toward the "barbaric Indians."

The declared aim of Spanish policy regarding the "barbaric Indians" in its possessions was to assimilate them into the existing social framework. In the period's words, the aim was to "render them to society, and in doing so to the knowledge of the true religion."[151] Thus, to "make them Christians, it was necessary first to make them men, and force and teach them to consider themselves and behave as such."[152] To accomplish this, peaceful methods were preferred, but the use of force was not ruled out if the first approach failed. A 1787 royal order for the *audiencia* of Guatemala stated that "many times the Church had resorted to the arms of the Catholic princes to force the infidels to hear the word of God."[153] This approach was designed with the Indians living within the borders of the empire in mind. Regarding those living in the borderlands, it was a little more difficult. A solution would come from the practices of local authorities on site, which, as is to be expected, varied a great deal, from peaceful means to war without mercy. The latter was the approach used most often in dealing with the Apache.

Before the arrival of the Europeans in North America, relationships among the various native groups were guided by rules known to everyone. For example, it was taken for granted that nomadic groups lived at the expense of sedentary groups. In this sense, the Apache considered their farmer or rancher neighbors their natural suppliers.[154] They saw the settlers as "a crop or renewable resource, taking what they needed in the way of stock and supplies, but always leaving enough behind for the people to rebuild."[155] When Spanish settlers arrived, the Apache placed them in the category formerly occupied by the Pueblo Indians. Thus a clash was inevitable, since the interests of each group pushed against the other. It got even messier when, as previously mentioned, the Sioux displaced the Comanche, and the latter did the same to the Apache. It is important to remember that the Apache did not form a nation or a political unit. As Jeffrey D. Carlisle points out, the Spaniards tended to lump all Apache into one group, even though each band operated independently. Thus, when one Apache band raided a Spanish outpost, the Spanish considered the peace broken. On the other hand, since the Apache considered each Spanish settlement a distinct "band," for them it was natural to make peace at one Spanish location while continuing to raid another.[156]

Even if a clash seemed unavoidable, the first institution the Spanish Crown used to integrate the Apache was not military but religious: that is, the mission. With the arrival of the Age of Enlightenment and the so-called Bourbon regalism, missions began to be considered with suspicion and their usefulness seriously questioned.[157] As their role diminished, missions were not replaced but were eclipsed in importance by the presidios. In time the presidios became not only military posts but also centers for trade and other economic activity as well as focal points for colonization. The presidial system has been the subject of many studies that stress its importance in "guaranteeing the very survival of Spanish civilization on the frontier" and planting the seeds of what would later become prosperous cities.[158] Presidios were at the origin of Tucson, Arizona, and El Paso and San Antonio, Texas. Because of this role, "forts in the eighteenth century now had no clear offensive or defensive function, but rather [served as points] of cultural contact, commercial penetration, and demographic occupation."[159] To us that seems a little extreme, but it is certainly true that "the expansion of the frontier, the characteristics of the indigenous population, and the shortage of Spanish population made the presidio an institution not only necessary but inevitable."[160] Either through the presidios or the missions, the Crown's official policy proclaimed Spain's intention to use peaceful means for conquest. The ordinances of Felipe II on the discovery, settlement, and pacification of the Indies, promulgated on July 13, 1573, were still in force. In them, article 20 stated, "The discoverers by sea or land do not over-indulge for any reason whatsoever in war or conquest in any way, or help the Indians against each other, or get involved in their quarrels, or hurt them, or do them any wrong, or take anything from them outside of trade or gifts."[161]

Whatever the law said, among the officers and soldiers on the ground there was a consensus that force was the only way possible to subdue the Apache, since they "have always been, are, and will always be enemies of

Spaniards and any rational being."[162] By the second third of the eighteenth century, this rationale was even embedded into the previously impervious minds of royal officials and became the Crown's official policy, as summarized in the 1772 regulations, which stated clearly that as "the purpose of war is to achieve peace," "a fiery and unremitting war (must be raised), and as soon as possible they should be attacked in their own villages and lands."[163]

BERNARDO DE GÁLVEZ'S BAPTISM BY FIRE: ARRIVAL IN NUEVA VIZCAYA

In March 1769 the viceroy, the Marquis de Croix, asked Madrid for confirmation of the appointment of Bernardo de Gálvez as volunteer captain in the campaign against the Apache in Nueva Vizcaya under the command of Lope de Cuéllar.[164] In June of that year the answer came reducing Bernardo's rank to active lieutenant.[165] If this seems important, what really mattered was that he was already campaigning to be where he could best distinguish himself.

Lope de Cuéllar's campaign was scheduled to start in May 1769. With a year's duration, it was to cover the region between the Pecos and Gil Rivers. As we have learned, when Bernardo arrived he was not immediately given any troops to command. Lope de Cuéllar was not happy to have had imposed on him "this young man who can be expected to be brave and well behaved, but because of his young age cannot offer the assurances and experience of the lieutenant of the dragoons, Diego de Becerril."[166] Because of this, Bernardo would have to spend several months under Becerril's command. Lope de Cuéllar's decision was justified from a military operations point of view, but it did not take into account another very important factor: politics. Standing in the way of the fulfillment of José de Gálvez's wishes could be as dangerous as facing Apache arrows.

At the end of June, Lope de Cuéllar left his headquarters and started chasing the Apache, who, true to their tactics, avoided combat while sending peace offers. Cuéllar ignored the offers and continued his pursuit toward the Paso del Rio Norte. Along the way he found two Apache settlements, killed about sixty Indians, and released some Spanish prisoners but had to retreat after a surprise attack in the Mimbres Mountains. Later he changed direction and headed toward Janos to protect the borders of Sonora and prevent the Gileño Apache from reinforcing the Seri and Pimas of Cerro Prieto. While he was thus occupied, a group of Apache warriors attacked the village of San Jerónimo near Chihuahua, and news arrived that another group had crossed the Rio Grande with the intention of simultaneously attacking Chihuahua, Durango, and Parras. Panic spread throughout the whole region. José de Fainí (or Fayní), Nueva Vizcaya's new governor, sent desperate messages to both the viceroy in Mexico City and to Lope de Cuéllar, somewhere in Sonora. Since he received no answer he could only raise a small group of volunteers in Durango. Fainí was furious, and since the viceroy was too far away and too highly placed for his anger to reach him, he turned it on Cuéllar.

Lieutenant Colonel José de Fainí had been made Nueva Vizcaya's governor in April 1768, but he did not arrive at his new post until the end of the year.[167] Even though there is no direct proof that he had obtained his appointment thanks to José de Gálvez, there is strong circumstantial evidence that such was the case. First, the appointment was made during the apogee of José de Gálvez's influence with New Spain's viceroy. Second, and much more important, Fainí was related to Gálvez. Fainí's maternal grandfather was José de Gálvez y Cabrera, so they shared not one but two surnames.[168] But their kinship did not prevent Fainí from criticizing José's nephew when he thought that he must. In a letter written to Julián de Arriaga, minister of the Indies at the time, he stated that the viceroy himself had appointed Bernardo and that while campaigning against the Apache Bernardo had disobeyed his orders, thus precipitating "the loss of the province."[169]

The situation in the region of Chihuahua deteriorated very quickly. The absence of troops at its garrison, who had left to become part of Lope de Cuéllar's forces, was exploited by the Apache to intensify their attacks. In June 1769 complaints from José de Fainí and the residents of Chihuahua were finally heard in Mexico City. Juan Velázquez, aide-de-camp in the regiment of dragoons of Spain, was immediately dispatched from the capital with orders to depose and arrest Lope de Cuéllar.[170] Luis Navarro García comments that this mysterious detention, undoubtedly related to the plot that was woven around the madness of Don José de Gálvez, ended months later with the return of Cuéllar to Mexico, and then to Spain, in the company of the visitor-general.[171]

The situation worsened to the point that just one month later, in mid-July 1769, José de Gálvez had no choice but to send some of his forces, which were then engaged in the campaign against the Seri of Cerro Prieto, immediately to Chihuahua "to reinforce the garrisons of the presidios on the frontier or other places where they can protect the country from the Apache's raids, and when this internal enemy has been vanquished, cavalry troops will proceed to search for those pirates in the Gila province, or wherever it is then resolved."[172]

Despite the arrival of these reinforcements and the dismissal of Lope de Cuéllar, the frontier continued to suffer under the Apache attacks during the second half of 1769 and the beginning of 1770.

ACCOMPANYING HIS UNCLE THROUGH THE "ELYSIAN FIELDS OF SONORA"[173]

Meanwhile, José de Gálvez's mental health was deteriorating rapidly. The order from the viceroy to send him to Mexico City caused Bernardo to leave immediately to join his uncle, with whom he was reunited sometime between the end of September and the beginning of November.[174] When Bernardo arrived in Pitic, near Hermosillo, the deliriums of his uncle included messages from Saint Francis of Assisi.[175] "From the mission's windows he shouted to all who passed that he was the generalissimo of those provinces with all the authority of the king and the pope," recorded one of José de Gálvez's secretaries, Juan Manuel de Viniegra, "and to others he made gifts and appointments well beyond his powers [as visitor-general]."[176]

José de Gálvez's entourage tried to conceal this behavior. Besides his nephew Bernardo, the immediate retinue of José de Gálvez was formed by his secretaries and assistants Viniegra, Miguel José de Azanza, and Juan Antonio Gómez de Argüello; Captain Lope de Cuéllar; the Franciscan monk Friar Mariano Antonio de Buena y Alcalde; the surgeon Guillermo de Cis; the naval officer and mathematician Antonio Faveau; the captain of the Fronteras presidio Gabriel Antonio de Vildósola; and his armed escort.[177] Juan de Pineda, governor of Sonora, refused even to talk about the visitor-general's behavior. When Juan Manuel de Viniegra tried to engage him, he answered simply, "Get yourself to bed, I'm deaf."[178] Bernardo de Gálvez has left no written testimony about his reaction to his uncle's mental illness, which is no surprise. At the time, medical science had just started to distinguish mental illness from demonic possession.[179]

At the end of October, José de Gálvez and his entourage arrived at Ures, where the visitor-general experienced a recovery. By December he was well enough to be allowed to write to the viceroy, telling him that he had been suffering from malign fevers.[180] He would soon relapse, however, with Bernardo witnessing his uncle's deliriums. Once he was even compelled to write at José's dictation a passport in which one of the servants was referred to as the new governor of the new kingdom of the Californias.[181] The situation became so complicated that several of José de Gálvez's secretaries (Viniegra, Azanza, and Gómez de Argüello), against the opinion of Pineda and Friar Buena y Alcalde, decided to write directly to the viceroy about the visitor-general's behavior. According to the not-always-reliable testimony of Viniegra, the letter bore the signatures of several witnesses, including Bernardo.[182]

This letter changed everything. Upon receiving this official communication, it was impossible for the viceroy to continue to pretend that nothing was wrong with the visitor-general. The matter ceased to be a private one and become a highly charged political one. José de Gálvez was one of the highest officials of New Spain. He was so committed to royal policies that he was identified with them, both by the people of New Spain and by himself. He had been the viceroy's most visible agent at the time of the expulsion of the Jesuits. He was, in a sense, too big to fail. As soon as the official communication arrived in Mexico City, the viceroy urgently dispatched the Bethlehemite friar Joaquín de la Santísima Trinidad to look after the visitor-general, with orders to inform him, and him alone, about José's health.[183] Meanwhile, beginning in March 1770, José de Gálvez arrived in Arispe, where his episodes of delirium continued. He signed a letter "by his own hand calling himself, Joseph the Gálvez, a fool to the world, miserable to himself, and I pray to God that he could be happy in the next."[184] During one of his seizures, "[he] called himself and believed himself to be the king of Prussia, King Charles XII of Sweden, the protector of the House of Bourbon, member of the Council of State, lieutenant of the admiral of Spain, immortal and stolid, Saint Joseph, the venerable bishop Palafox, and even the Eternal Father, and a multitude of personalities whose characters he imitated, to the point of presiding over the final judgment as if he were the divine word."[185]

When at the end of the month Friar Santísima Trinidad arrived in Chihuahua and met with Jose de Gálvez, he immediately informed him about his instructions and ordered the arrest of Viniegra, Azanza, and Gómez de Argüello, whose papers were confiscated. Their situation was very serious since they could be charged with a *lèse majesté* crime, second class. It sounds even worse when the lay word is used: treason. Spanish law at the time did not offer a definition of the *lèse majesté* second-class crime but only gave a few examples: "heresy, sedition, treason, currency counterfeiting, document forgery, highway robbery and banditry, murder (deliberate homicide), reoffending robbery (famous robber), sodomy, suicide, kidnapping and rape of unmarried women or nuns, etc."[186] The crimes were considered so heinous that death was not punishment enough. In the most severe cases, even the descendants of convicts could suffer consequences. Legal proceedings were simplified to "shorten the way for Justice to be rendered at the expense of the accused's defense."[187] In this simplified procedure, any person could denounce the accused, even those whose testimony in other cases would not be valid. All kinds of evidence were admitted, even if prohibited in other cases. All kinds of confession were valid, even if made during the sacrament of confession. All privileges could be removed from the accused.[188] Last but not least, torture was admitted during interrogations.[189]

Speed and secrecy in detaining all suspects were of the utmost importance to prevent them from hiding documents or, even worse, from making them public. Miguel José de Azanza, Juan Antonio Gómez de Argüello, and Antonio Faveau were arrested near Chihuahua and sent to Zacatecas. Juan Manuel de Viniegra, who had remained in the city of Leon because of illness, was arrested there. All of them were transferred to "the seminary of Tepotzotlán, where they remained under custody and incommunicado for several months, without being notified of the charges against them, or officially charged with any crime."[190]

On May 28, 1770, José de Gálvez reached Mexico City much recovered. A few days before, an impatient Bernardo de Gálvez had departed, in his own words, "with the intention of presenting myself before your Excellency prior to my uncle's arrival, but fate determined that my carriage overturned and I received a blow to the chest that prevented me from continuing my journey [to Mexico City]."[191] He asked the viceroy for permission to return to his post. The viceroy did not mince words in his reply: "Nothing could displease me more than you, sir, not complying with the orders to revere your uncle, and what you, sir, have done would be not only despicable but also worthy of the strongest reprimand."[192]

José de Gálvez's recovery did not diminish the pressure against witnesses of his temporary insanity.[193] Antonio Faveau was soon released. Since he had not signed any of the documents describing the visitor-general's condition, he was accused only of absence without leave. Miguel José de Azanza, Juan Antonio Gómez de Argüello, and Juan Manuel de Viniegra remained in custody. A visitor to their prison was Juan Antonio Valera, another one of José de Gálvez's secretaries who, to his good fortune, had remained in Mexico City. Valera admonished them to plead guilty to conspiracy to bear false witness against the visitor-general. When the accused refused to comply, they were sent to the port of Veracruz to await a ship to the Iberian Peninsula. While in Veracruz they received a visit from another envoy sent by José de Gálvez, Pedro Antonio de Cossío, who insisted on the plea and also, according to Viniegra, offered them important positions if they complied. The accused tried to obtain help from other members of José de Gálvez's entourage, but no one was willing to risk either his or the viceroy's wrath. Viniegra even tried to drag Bernardo into the fight. The following paragraph from the desperate letter from Viniegra, Azanza, and Gómez de Argüello to José de Gálvez is extremely revealing.

> It is also known that Your Excellency commissioned Bernardo de Gálvez, through the friar sent to Chihuahua from Mexico City, to deny to everyone, including the viceroy, your sorry state in Sonora; even

though he had informed the viceroy along with us about it. It is also known that during the conversation between the same friar and Bernardo de Gálvez in the hacienda in Zarza, when it was feared that your Excellency's nephew would not comply with your orders and could be an impediment to the abuse that was planned against us, it was decided that he would remain in Nueva Vizcaya. That same friar took the liberty of admonishing him not to have a *childish* [*muchachada*, underlined in the original] sense of honor by standing behind what he had written about Your Excellency's sickness. When Bernardo, following his honest way of thinking, did not comply with the friar's admonitions, he threatened him, telling him that his head was not secure on his shoulders and that he was a *treacherous rascal* [*pícaro traidor*, underlined in the original] like the rest of us. We cannot recall this event without feeling rage against what that infamous friar said, and surprise that Your Excellency's nephew would not answer him back and left without punishing the insolence against both himself and his friends. . . . Would Your Excellency say, as you did in Lagos and Guanajuato, that your nephew had been hallucinating? . . . Don Bernardo de Gálvez hallucinated, and it was induced by us! We all saw it with our own eyes for more than five months. He [Bernardo] is not capable of permitting such things to happen. Neither his age nor circumstances will allow it.[194]

There is no evidence that Viniegra's desperate appeal to Bernardo to testify in his favor succeeded. Most probably he, like the rest of the visitor-general's entourage, tried to keep as much distance as possible from the outcasts. In fact, nobody was interested in making public anything concerning the episode. Memory of it has survived only because of the Spanish administration's bureaucratic obsession with keeping every single piece of paper. It is an obsession that historians are particularly grateful for. There are two copies of Viniegra's papers, one in the National Library of Spain in Madrid and the other in the Bancroft Library at the University of California, Berkeley.[195] Eusebio Ventura Beleña's testimony is buried among the papers related to the Cerro Prieto military campaign in the Archivo General de Indias, Seville.[196] This archive also preserves an interesting folder under the title "Amusing episodes that happened to the visitor-general Don José de Gálvez before departing on the expedition to Sonora and California."[197] The folder is, not surprisingly, empty.

To close the case, just a few words about what eventually happened to the people involved in it. As has been stated, the main concern in the entire episode was to avoid scandal, so it is not unexpected that its long-term consequences were very few. Those who were involved but not charged never mentioned it again. Of the four initially detained, Antonio Faveau was quickly released on minor charges. A naval officer and a cartographer with wide experience in Asia's waters, he returned to his ship.[198] No trace has been found about the later fate of Juan Antonio Gómez de Argüello. But Miguel José de Azanza had an impressive career. From Mexico he went to Cuba, where he enrolled in the army, which he later left for the diplomatic service, with postings to Vienna and Saint Petersburg. He returned to the Iberian Peninsula to become *intendente*, a sort of governor, of Toro, Salamanca, and Valencia. In October 1796 he was made viceroy of New Spain.[199] Juan Manuel de Viniegra spent several years fighting José de Gálvez, calling him such names as "pompous ass"[200] and accusing him of being madder than Don Quixote.[201] He made such a nuisance of himself that the archbishop of Toledo, Francisco Antonio de Lorenzana, obtained a ruling from the minister of the Indies that Viniegra was to be "relieved of pursuing his lawsuit." It is not hard to find José de Gálvez's hand behind the archbishop's interest in Viniegra's case. Lorenzana's previous posting had been as archbishop of Mexico precisely during the Marquis de Croix's tenure as viceroy. Lorenzana's commitment to the expulsion of the Jesuits from New Spain can be compared only to that of Jose de Gálvez. In the end, Viniegra came to his senses and accepted the reality that José de Gálvez was too powerful for him, and in 1774 he accepted the post of treasurer with the Royal Treasury in Portobello, Panama.[202]

For Bernardo's military career, the episode had no negative consequences. He promptly returned from Mexico City to his post in Nueva Vizcaya. No reference to the affair has been found among his documents, although it certainly taught him valuable lessons for the future. He had learned to navigate the dangerous waters of politics. He had refrained from following his first impulse, which was to support his uncle's accusers, at least he so claimed.[203] He had learned always to place before anything else his family's interests, upon which his future depended. Cynical as it may sound, he had discovered that the world is a much more complicated place than he had envisioned. He had matured.

BERNARDO DE GÁLVEZ'S CAMPAIGN AGAINST THE APACHE

While Bernardo was accompanying his uncle, the situation in Nueva Vizcaya continued to deteriorate. In August 10, 1770, an Apache attack took place, during which more than 1,000 mules and horses were stolen.[204] Bernardo arrived in Chihuahua in July or August that year with an appointment as commander of the frontiers of Nueva Vizcaya and Sonora. With this promotion he was eager to prove his merits and immediately launched a military campaign against the Apache. The correspondence exchanged between the viceroy, the Marquis de Croix, and the minister of the Indies, Julián de Arriaga, includes "The account of the latest news of the second campaign against the barbarous Apache of Nueva Vizcaya," by Captain Don Bernardo de Gálvez.[205]

In Chihuahua, Nueva Vizcaya's governor, José de Fainí, immediately put 250 men with three months of provisions under Bernardo's command. Everything seemed to be ready, but the departure was postponed until after the bullfights in honor of Saint Phillip, patron saint of Chihuahua, had taken place. At first glance it seems strange, to say the least, that a military campaign against so powerful an enemy as the Apache would be delayed until after these celebrations. One possible explanation is that the Apache threat was not as urgent as it seemed. Another explanation could take into account the ritual character of bullfighting at the time. In periods of serious dislocation, societies tend to cling to certain traditions to establish much-needed normalcy. Whatever the reason, in 1770 in Chihuahua, the troops went to a bullfight before marching to war against the Apache.

First Sortie

At the head of 135 soldiers and 50 Opata Indian allies, Bernardo de Gálvez left Chihuahua to pursue the Apache who were ravaging the valleys of the Grande and Pecos Rivers. On October 21 they crossed the Rio Grande at a ford near the ruins of the abandoned presidio of the north. Decades later this ford was still known as the ford of Señor Gálvez.[206] On November 1 he was on the banks of the Pecos River. There, according to his own account, he addressed his men thus:

> Comrades! The day has arrived for the last effort, and to give the world proof of our resolve. Hunger, which is worse than any weather's harshness, is in sight. I do not know how many days or months will pass before we can encounter our enemies. Returning to Chihuahua, after spending so much time and money, is not an option for those of us who have a sense of shame. This kind of dishonor does not suit me. Alone I will go, if no one is found to accompany me. Either I will return to Chihuahua with a scalp, or I will pay with my life for the bread I have eaten from the king. Follow me, those who want to be part of my glorious endeavors, in the knowledge that there is nothing I can give to return their courtesy but my gratitude, and that they will forever live

in my memory and recognition. After pronouncing these words, the commander crossed the river while everyone cried out that they would follow him to the death, that they would eat the horses, and after that even rocks, and that they would never leave him.[207]

This statement deserves comment and analysis. First, in the last part of the transcribed paragraph, Bernardo de Gálvez referred to himself in the third person. It is a form of literary license with a long tradition in descriptions of military campaigns. Julius Caesar is reported to have been the first to exercise such license in his account of the Gallic wars. Second, in this text Bernardo de Gálvez states, "Alone I will go, if no one is found to accompany me." It is a phrase very similar to the one he would use several years later, which would become the origin of his famous motto.

A couple of days after crossing the Pecos River, the first combat with the Apache took place. Gálvez's troops attacked an Apache village where twenty-eight warriors were killed, thirty-six were captured, and more than 200 horses and pelts valued at more than 2,000 pesos were recovered.[208] Among the prisoners were two youngsters whom Bernardo ordered baptized with the names of his father and uncle; they would accompany him during all of his campaigns along the frontier.[209]

Bernardo's victory did not stop Apache raids in other parts of Nueva Vizcaya. By the end of December, another Apache attack wreaked havoc and ignited panic in the region. Governor José de Fainí ordered that, to protect the population, the campaign against the Apache was to be suspended and troops returned to the presidios. Fainí's decision was made against the express orders of the viceroy, the Marquis de Croix. The governor was on such bad terms with the viceroy that he was even sending his correspondence directly to Madrid without going through the viceroy, as required. Fainí finally had to comply when he received a direct order from the viceroy to move from Chihuahua to Durango. The governor's departure from Chihuahua left Bernardo de Gálvez with a free hand to continue the hostilities against the Apache.[210]

Second Sortie

On February 26, 1771, Bernardo left Chihuahua in command of a force of 110 soldiers and an indeterminate number of auxiliary Indians, probably Opata or Pimas. He spent three months searching for Apache without much success until, on April 21, near the Puerto River, a tributary of the Rio Grande in today's New Mexico, he ran into a group of 250 Apache. The results of the clash were very favorable for the Spaniards: a Spanish captive freed from the group; 1 Spanish and 22 auxiliary Indian casualties; and 58 Apache Indians killed. At the same time, Captain Leizaola, commander of the Janos presidio, patrolled the La Boca Mountains with 103 Opata Indians and several troops from both his presidio and that of San Buenaventura.[211]

A month later, the Apache attacked the presidios in Julimes and San Bartolomé y Parral, stealing more than 4,000 cows. In June they attacked some settlements near Chihuahua, and Bernardo de Gálvez went in pursuit but had to return empty-handed. By this time news of Bernardo's bellicose zeal had reached New Spain's capital. That same month, in a letter written to the court in Madrid, the viceroy praised him and recommended him for promotion to lieutenant colonel.[212]

Third Sortie

During August and September 1771, rumors circulated on the frontier about the Apache intentions to sue for peace.[213] To obtain some information, Gálvez sent a force of 300 soldiers to patrol around Chihuahua, but they returned without having made contact with the enemy. On the morning of October 11, while Bernardo was attending religious services in Chihuahua, the bells sounded the alarm. He rushed for his horse and leading only fourteen soldiers started a pursuit of the attackers. Soon he sighted them and without considering his numerical inferiority ordered an attack.[214] The result was disastrous. The Spaniards suffered ten casualties, and Bernardo was wounded thrice: an arrow in his left arm and two spears in his chest, one of them hurled so violently that it pierced his leather shield and wounded his horse.[215] Despite his wounds, Bernardo de Gálvez led a new sortie in December to punish an Apache attack against another settlement. This time 125 soldiers and 150 auxiliary Indians accompanied him, but he was forced to return to Chihuahua after receiving a strong blow to the chest.[216] This last wound would bother him to the end of his days.

RELIEVED OF COMMAND

On September 10, 1771, less than two weeks before ending his tenure, the viceroy appointed Hugo O'Conor commander inspector of the Interior Provinces.[217] The arrival of a new viceroy caused a delay since he, as a formality, had to confirm the appointment. The new viceroy, Antonio María de Bucareli y Ursúa, was delighted to oblige since O'Conor had been highly recommended by his cousin, Alejandro O'Reilly, one of the leading military figures in Spain during the second half of the eighteenth century. In a letter dated September 25 of the following year, O'Reilly thanked Bucareli for the appointment of O'Conor, who would certainly render good service since "none in his homeland is of more noble birth ... and [he] is a close relative of mine, whom I have had beside me since his tender years."[218]

Hugo O'Conor had arrived in Spain in 1750. At the age of fifteen he enrolled in the Hibernia Regiment, one of the Irish-born military units in the Spanish army. During the Seven Years' War he distinguished himself in the Portugal campaign, was promoted to captain, and was rewarded with membership in the Order of Calatrava.[219] In 1765 he arrived in New Spain as one of the officers selected to accompany Juan de Villalba in his military reform. Shortly afterward he was sent to Texas to investigate certain allegations of corruption. During this mission he also reformed several presidios so they could resist repeated attacks from Comanche and Apache. During this period he received his nickname "the Red Captain" because of the uncommon color of his hair.[220]

Bernardo de Gálvez's relief from command made perfect sense. In a letter to Alejandro O'Reilly dated October 1771, Viceroy Bucareli stated, "In the province of Nueva Vizcaya, on frontiers of Chihuahua, the war against the Indians continues. The troops posted there are presently under the command of the visitor-general's nephew, who I'm told has spirit but who because of his young age does not have the required experience, and since the visitor-general has asked for his nephew to accompany him on his return to Spain, I have resolved that he will be replaced by Don Hugo O'Conor, who departed in good spirits with the order to inform me about the real situation and to suggest what he would consider adequate."[221]

Besides his affection for his nephew and his need to be taken care of during his travel back to Madrid, José de Gálvez's wish to be accompanied by Bernardo could also have been dictated by the fear that Bernardo would be wasting his energy in a posting so far removed from the eyes of the court. A change of setting seemed to suit the ambitions of both members of the Gálvez clan.

Hugo O'Conor arrived in Chihuahua on November 17, 1771,[222] but he could not take his office right away because Bernardo de Gálvez was away fighting the Apache and would not return until December 10.[223] When they finally met, with Bernardo wounded and O'Conor sick, they spent four days in the transfer of command.[224] At the time Bernardo was a twenty-five-year-old captain and O'Conor a lieutenant colonel of thirty-six years. But despite the difference in rank and age, they were both the scions of families that had recently come to power in royal service. Bernardo's career was made possible by his uncle and O'Conor's by his cousin.

O'Conor was part of what has been called the Wild Geese, or Irish military in the service of France, Austria, and Spain.[225] Traditionally, these Irish soldiers fighting in other countries were studied only from the military history point of view, which saw them as romantic, almost legendary.[226] In recent years other important aspects of the Wild Geese phenomenon have received proper attention, such as the Irish priests in Catholic countries and the wider context of Irish emigration during the modern era, but as Óscar Recio Morales points out, not all Irish emigrants were soldiers, not all were men, and not all achieved the honors and social recognition they sought. In Spain they were victims of marginalization and caricature. Even the aristocrats among them had to go through a process of integration and, later, assimilation and were not exempt from difficulties or conflicts with other elite "natives" from Spain.[227]

Meeting O'Conor was the first contact Bernardo de Gálvez had with the Irish clan in the Spanish court. It would not be the last. Bernardo left Chihuahua at the end of December 1771 or the beginning of January 1772. His uncle José had requested and obtained from Viceroy Bucareli authorization for Bernardo to accompany him.[228] When Bernardo arrived in Mexico City on February 10, escorting a group of fourteen Apache from the Lipan, Gileño, and Nataje groups, who on his request were admitted to the San Gregorio School, he was informed that his uncle had already left for Veracruz.[229] In Mexico City he had to carry out certain formalities, such as the appointment of José de Echeveste as his representative before the royal court of auditors during the inspection of the account books of the Apache campaign.[230] When he reached Veracruz he was informed that he was late again. José de Gálvez had embarked for Havana just a few days earlier to accompany the former viceroy, the Marquis de Croix, on his return to the court. Bernardo took the first ship available for Havana on April 1, but on April 8 his uncle was already sailing toward Europe on board the *San Pedro de Alcántara*, while the former viceroy was on the *San Rafael*.[231] José de Gálvez arrived on May 20 and Bernardo probably a few weeks later.[232]

LESSONS LEARNED
Results and Assessments of the Campaigns

As expected, assessments of the campaigns against the Apache depended very much on the eye of the beholder. For José de Gálvez, not surprisingly, they were a major success. In June 1771 he wrote, "And as in these circumstances calm has been restored [to the frontier], what is left is only to continue to pursue the fierce Apache, who, being irreconcilable enemies of all nations that live in their neighborhood, continuously attack Nueva Vizcaya. To this end the infantry captain Don Bernardo de Gálvez is posted there to punish and contain them, and makes war against them with courage, sacrifice, and determination, due to his profession and inherited obligations. He has succeeded in destroying several Apache settlements, dispersing them far away from our borders, overcoming the roughness of such a big country, the speed of an errant nation, and the frequent calamities brought about by long days suffering hunger and thirst."[233]

The text is from a six-page pamphlet published in Mexico City under the explicit title *Noticia breve de la expedición Militar de Sonora y Cinaloa, su éxito feliz, y ventajoso estado en que por consecuencia de ella se han puesto ambas Provincias* (Brief account of the military expedition of Sonora and Sinaloa, its happy success, and the favorable state in which both provinces are because of it).[234] The work appeared anonymously, but there can be little doubt that José de Gálvez was directly behind it.[235] The second opportunity that José de Gálvez had to praise his own achievements was when he submitted his report to Viceroy Bucareli. On this occasion he does not mention his nephew even once. "About Nueva Vizcaya, I will not mention the measures and provisions taken by the Marquis de Croix to defend its frontiers and to help the important town of Chihuahua against the Apache's hostilities. Your Excellency knows well that it is essential to apply more forces to resist and chastise those barbarians, which were not available before because of the war in Sonora. To that end Your Excellency has appointed Lieutenant Colonel Hugo O'Conor as its commander, with the resolve to supply him with the resources he will need."[236]

José de Gálvez's legal training served him well. Why mention his nephew to a viceroy with whom he did not have an especially good relationship? It was enough to suggest subtly that if the campaign against the Apache had not been a complete success, it could be because not enough resources were allocated to it—a suggestion worded in such twisted terms that no one in either Madrid or Mexico City could resent it. José de Gálvez's report was supposed to be restricted, but, according to Clara Elena Suárez Argüello, at the time numerous manuscript copies were made that reached the hands of several important officials in Madrid responsible for conducting American affairs.[237]

For obvious reasons, New Spain's former viceroy, the Marquis de Croix, was also interested in presenting the Sonora campaign as a success. In March 1771, he brought it to a close, stating that its objectives had been achieved.[238] Three months later he sent in an account of the campaign and recommended Bernardo de Gálvez for promotion to lieutenant colonel.[239]

The assessment of the new viceroy, Antonio María de Bucareli, was very different. In a letter to Alejandro O'Reilly, dated October 1771, he stated that in Nueva Vizcaya "the war against the Indians was still on."[240] O'Reilly was of the same opinion. In a letter to Bucareli written in February 1772, he openly blamed both Lope de Cuéllar and Bernardo de Gálvez of having pushed and harassed the Apache Indians too much, which made any later peace negotiations with them impossible.[241] Hugo O'Conor, Bernardo de Gálvez's successor as military commander of the frontier, soon expressed his doubts about the usefulness of the military campaigns against the Apache. In a letter to the minister the of Indies, Viceroy Bucareli indicated that O'Conor had told him that the product of Bernardo de Gálvez's last sortie against the Apache was the capture of just one horse.[242] Years later O'Conor would write a full report, in which he stated, "I found all provinces under my command, especially Nueva Vizcaya, under the utmost unrest and complete terror because of frequent attacks by the Apaches; as soon as I gathered enough information I informed the government about the problems faced by the province, and its sorry condition since 1748, when non-stop war was declared against them. A war in which the Apaches always succeeded, with great loss of the king's wealth, the promulgation of illusory regulations, the reform of the province's government, and with not much honor to His Majesty's arms."[243]

Other contemporaries were of a different opinion but did not dare to express it until the tenure of Bucareli as viceroy was over. When Teodoro de Croix, nephew of the Marquis de Croix, was appointed commander general of the northern Interior Provinces, he succeeded in reversing the official peace policy toward the Apache. In defending his ideas he mentioned those of Bernardo de Gálvez as a positive precedent.[244]

Bernardo de Gálvez's Account and Reflections on the Apache War
I have left for the end of the contemporaneous assessments of the war against the Apache those made by Bernardo de Gálvez himself. In addition to the letters written during and immediately after the campaign, he also composed a very revealing document relating his experiences and lessons learned titled *Noticia y reflexiones sobre la guerra que se tiene con los indios apaches en las provincias de Nueva España* (Account and reflections on the current war against the Apache Indians in the provinces of New Spain).[245] Bernardo de Gálvez's *Noticia y reflexiones* is precisely what its title suggests: a description of the campaigns but also some thoughts about the causes and characteristics of the war against the Apache. Though its purpose was to find better ways to conduct military operations against this kind of enemy, Bernardo's approach went beyond simple military considerations. To defeat the Apache, he realized, he needed to understand them, and the document contains important information about eighteenth-century Spanish views of the Apache.[246]

Bernardo de Gálvez was fooled by neither the prevailing prejudices nor the "bellicose psychosis" rampant at the time in New Spain.[247] He was able to see the real causes of the war against the Apache. He asked of the Spaniards that they "be impartial and acknowledge that if the Indians are not our friends, it is because they do not owe us any benefits, and if they take revenge on us, it is only in just compensation for the affronts we have caused them."[248] Since revenge was answered with retaliation, thus generating new grounds for further revenge, a vicious circle of violence seemed impossible to break unless different measures were adopted.[249] Because of "the little faith we have kept with them, and the tyrannies they have suffered," the Apache went to war because of either "hate or necessity"—a hatred born of a desire for vengeance for the affronts inflicted on them, and a necessity rooted in "the extreme need in which they live, since as they do not sow, or farm the land, or breed cattle for their survival, they meet their needs by stealing from the Spaniards."[250]

In his description of the Apache he mentioned groups that, "despite all being Apaches and fierce, can be differentiated according to the land they inhabit."[251] These were Gileños, Mescaleros, Natages, Lipanes, and Nizfandes.[252] About what was called at the time their temperament and today their appearance, he said that the Apache were "healthy because of the harshness of the environment in which . . . [they are] raised and the simplicity of . . . [their] diet."[253] Bernardo de Gálvez approvingly reported that both men and women regarded fidelity as their supreme virtue, and their religion rewarded or punished them according to this criterion.[254] He mentioned the case of two warriors named Quitachin and Pitigacán who became his escorts and saved his life fighting against six of their own tribesmen, thus proving that "even in the most barbarous human heart there is place for gratitude."[255] The Apache were also very agile. Their character was grateful but also watchful and suspicious out of fear of the Spaniards.[256] About their alleged cruelty he wrote, "The Spaniards accuse the Indians of being cruel, but I do not know what their opinion is about us; maybe it would not be better, and with much more reason."[257] In fact, for the Apache, as well as for other indigenous groups such as the Comanche, Wichita, or Caddo, the "Spaniards operated as just another collection of bands like themselves in an equal, if not weaker, position to compete for socioeconomic resources in the region."[258] For Gálvez, if in the end it was found that they were truly vengeful, "we should forgive it of a nation that has not learned the philosophy that allows us to resist this natural feeling, that despite being pernicious it derives from a heroic cause, which is having a sensitive heart."[259]

As a soldier Bernardo de Gálvez paid particular attention to Apache combat tactics. The natives made extensive use of surprise, moving without a sound in small groups.[260] They were skilled in reconnaissance and camouflage, "crowning their heads with grass so when lying down they looked like small bushes."[261] They always watched their enemies closely to make sure that "they could deliver the blow with accuracy."[262] "No description is possible of the speed with which they attack, or the noise they make while fighting, how the terror spreads among our own, and the promptness with which it all ends," he noted.[263] In the words of Armstrong Starkey, "eighteenth-century Indian tactics resembled those of modern infantry more than did those of their European adversaries."[264] Their offensive weapons were just "the spear, sometimes the musket, a club, and arrows."[265] Their defensive ones were "a *chinal* or small shield and a leather protection, but otherwise they fight naked."[266]

To face them, Gálvez wrote, "the method that our soldiers use is very similar to that of the Indians"—similar but not the same, since the presidial soldiers "cannot walk long distances [as the Apache can], so they need to travel on horse."[267] The troops from the presidios had to carry very heavy equipment—each soldier with between 114 and 130 pounds in weight—which Bernardo described in detail.[268] Their main offensive weapon was the musket. Gálvez believed that Apache arrows were far deadlier.

The traditional view that the European soldier had armament far superior to that of the Native Americans is just another myth.[269] At the time of the first contact between Europeans and indigenous peoples, powder weapons and their noise inflicted psychological trauma.[270] But in the 1770s, that was already three centuries in the past. It is interesting to consider the respective accuracies and rates of fire of the musket and the bow and arrow. In terms of accuracy, arrows were far superior to the musket and, at least at short and medium ranges, equal to the rifle. Apache archers were famous for their accuracy; from a distance of 820 feet they were able to hit their targets with three of every four arrows.[271] By the end of the eighteenth century, several trials were conducted with professional soldiers. At a distance of 100 paces, or about 200 feet, soldiers were able to hit the target only 46 percent of the time.[272] This accuracy was achieved with muskets in perfect order and not with "bad quality muskets," which, as Bernardo de Gálvez complained, were supplied to the frontier troops.[273] Although accuracy was important, much more important was the rate of fire. Herein lay the supremacy of the bow and arrow. Bernardo de Gálvez considered that "the repetition of their shots is such that while a musket is being loaded an Indian can shoot twenty arrows, which can kill twenty men."[274]

It is important to take into account that the presidial troops were neither professional soldiers nor militia but something quite different.[275] But for Bernardo de Gálvez, "different" did not mean "inferior." European professional soldiers tended to believe that "the Americans lack spirit and generosity for the military,"[276] but Bernardo believed that "the creoles from the Interior Provinces are no less brave than the Indians whom they fight."[277] In fact, he considered them better suited to this kind of warfare. It was true that the *presidiales* were too informal with their officers, but Bernardo de Gálvez credited this to the fact that "those people had been raised in freedom and are used to independence." Thus their officers had to treat them differently than the European-born soldiers. "The presidial soldiers know by reason that they must obey, but they demand to be commanded through reason," Gálvez noted. "In this I am with them. I expect more from a man who respects himself than from another who had been a thousand times insulted and forever degraded."[278] Bernardo de Gálvez had very strong feelings about this issue. He emphatically asked, "What does the king care if his soldier is black or white, if the nobility of his heart denies the color of his face? . . . I have seen a flag more honored and better defended in the black hands of a mulatto than in other whiter but feebler hands."[279]

Since the *presidiales* were good soldiers, Bernardo de Gálvez had to blame their lack of success against the Apache on the fact that their command, tactics, training, and armament were not suited for the kind of warfare taking place on the northern frontier of New Spain's viceroyalty. In writing his "thoughts about how the frontier troops must be commanded to obtain their best obedience,"[280] he accused the officers of being interested only in getting rich.[281] According to Gálvez, officers should treat their men with "kindness and good manners," because when they do so, "their compliance and religious obedience is so great that they do not protest even when led to sacrifice."[282] He could have narrated numerous episodes to prove this point, but "modesty forbids me from mentioning them."[283] On the criteria for promoting officers, he insisted on the idea that merit alone should be taken into account and that "presidial soldiers should be preferred even if they do not belong to the cleanest races."[284]

Concerning tactics, he believed that even though the *presidiales* already used ones similar to those of the Apache, deep changes were needed.[285] More Indian auxiliaries were necessary, because "on foot they are as fast and dexterous as the Apaches, their arrows as deadly, and as cunning in their ways of exploring and surprising the enemy."[286] He successfully applied these ideas when he campaigned with seventy soldiers and 300 Indian auxiliaries, whereas the normal ratio between *presidiales* and Indians was two to one. The combat value of the Indian auxiliaries depended on their group.[287]

For Gálvez, the Concho were "good and loyal"; the Taraumares "although bad for war... are good for working"; the Tepeguane were "the best for campaigning, although unfriendly and distant with the Spaniards"; the Norteños and Cholorines were "lazy in general," but those "from Nueva Vizcaya are excellent for war"; the northern Suma [sic: Yuma] "are also brave but they are reported to be disloyal"; the Piros "though few in numbers are good"; the Tigua "though loyal... are not considered brave" (*guapo* in the Spanish original);[288] the Yaqui and Mayo were "first-rate mine workers but cowardly soldiers"; the Pimas were "good but rightly considered not trustworthy because of their rebellions"; the Opata were "the most courageous, noble, and loyal nation with the Spaniards... a loyalty that has earned them the consideration of the Tlascalteca from the Interior Provinces"; and last but not least, the Lanche were "very brave and useful in campaign... strongly built, daring in war, and very loyal." Despite their heterogeneity, all Indian auxiliary troops, according to Gálvez, should be "neither spoiled nor ill-treated, because too much kindness makes them insolent and too mush rashness exasperates them."[289] The best way to enforce discipline was to respect the authority of their own chiefs, letting them impose the punishments when they occurred. In this way "they do not feel as offended as when directly punished by the Spaniards."[290]

To conclude, Bernardo de Gálvez recommended the use of a new kind of troop who could "penetrate the mountains with less hindrance, leave fewer traces, and was less noisy during marches."[291] To that end, the first necessity was to reduce the *presidiales'* cumbersome equipment. "I will take off the saddles anything superfluous, no more big impedimenta, nor useless flaps."[292] The tactics were to be adapted to the peculiar nature of both the terrain and Apache combat.

Even though many at the time considered the war against the Apache "a sideshow to a sideshow," for Bernardo de Gálvez it was a turning point.[293] Fighting against the Apache, he experienced baptism by fire, received his first combat wounds, and acquired important experience that would be useful in his later career, not only when fighting the British in Louisiana and Florida but also when he returned to New Spain for what Kieran R. McCarty has called the education of a viceroy.[294]

3. Learning to Be an Officer and Tasting Defeat

The least-documented period of Bernardo de Gálvez's life and career is the five years between his return to Europe from New Spain and his departure for Louisiana. Although in previous works on Gálvez this gap has been the grounds for dismissing those years in just a few paragraphs, or for repeating errors and even sheer fabrications, this five-year period provides important clues to the formation of his character as a soldier.¹

SEVILLE INFANTRY REGIMENT

According to Bernardo de Gálvez's personal record written at the end of 1774, on October 9, 1772, he joined the Eleventh Infantry Regiment of Seville with the grade of captain.² This regiment, nicknamed "The Fighter," had been created in 1707.³ Despite its name, it was garrisoned in Cadiz in 1771 after serving several years in America—first in Louisiana, under the command of Alejandro O'Reilly, where it was part of the force sent to suppress the 1767–68 revolt against the Spanish governor, and later in Havana.⁴

In 1772 the regiment was under the command of Colonel Miguel Auler, who at age sixty-two had forty-six years of active service. His second was the Count of Argelejos, a lieutenant colonel who was fifty years old with thirty-nine years of service; and the first officer, then called "sergeant major" in the Spanish army, was Lieutenant Colonel Pascual de Ulloa, who two years later would be replaced by Lieutenant Colonel Miguel de Pedrosa. The rest of the staff consisted of eighteen captains, eighteen lieutenants, nineteen sergeant majors, seventeen first-class sergeants, and seventeen cadets. Not for the first time, nor for the last, Bernardo de Gálvez was among the youngest in his class. In 1774, at the age of twenty-eight, he was the second youngest of the eighteen captains, whose average age was forty-four. With twelve years, six months, and eighteen days of active service, he was far behind the average of twenty-eight years of active service of the other captains.⁵ His personnel record at the time assessed him thus: "courage: known; diligence: much; conduct: good; condition: single."[6] But too much credit should not be given to this assessment, which was made by his colonel in January 1775, as the personnel record of every single officer in the regiment contained exactly the same evaluation.[7] In any case, Bernardo de Gálvez spent only a few months assigned to the Seville Regiment. On March 18, 1773, he was granted leave from this unit. No documents have been found indicating Bernardo's whereabouts between March 1773 and April 1774.

ROYAL MILITARY ACADEMY OF AVILA

The Royal Military Academy of Avila de los Caballeros was created by royal decree on January 31, 1774.[8] Its purpose was "the education of officers of outstanding capability, good conduct, and brilliant aptitude in the art of war."[9] Although it is thought to have been the brainchild of the minister of war, the Count of Ricla, the real driving force behind its founding was Alejandro O'Reilly, who was appointed its first headmaster while keeping his post as inspector general of the army. Despite its name, it was closer to a staff college than a military academy, since its purpose was not to train all officers of the army but, in O'Reilly's words, to instruct only those "whose rapid training is most important to the service, because of their talent, conduct, and prospects of being promoted to corps commanders and generals."[10] The idea behind the academy was that "when they become governors of strongholds in Europe or America, they will not be at the mercy of the knowledge or impulses of their subordinates (who most of the time lack the necessary understanding, and when advice comes from several sources, there is always little unity and the requisite respect and obedience suffer); they will know how to make their posts combat ready; will ask from the king only what is needed; and will be ready for any eventuality; all of which will facilitate their success, and prevent any embarrassment caused by surprise or ignorance."[11]

Bernardo's appointment to serve "among those select officers who had demonstrated utmost determination and talent" was most probably helped by the fact that since 1774 his uncle Miguel de Gálvez had been the Supreme War Council's legal adviser, and Alejandro O'Reilly was one of the council's most important members.[12] Bernardo de Gálvez was at the military academy at its opening in April 1774, which explains his departure from the Seville Regiment.[13]

But the creation of the Royal Military Academy of Avila must be understood in a wider context than merely the improvement of the education of army officers. As Jesús Ignacio Martínez Paricio has remarked, the failure of the economic societies[14] to serve as a motor for change produced as their alternative what Antonio Elorza has called the "pedagogic utopia." The

The Harvesters of Malaga before King Carlos III, by Joaquín Inza, oil on canvas, 1776. The painting celebrates the founding, under the initiative of José and Miguel de Gálvez (Bernardo de Gálvez's uncles), of the Mutual Aid Society of Wine, Liquor, Raisins, Figs, Almonds and Oil Harvesters of Malaga (Montepío de Cosecheros de vino, aguardiente, pasa, higos, almendra y aceite de Málaga). The right side of the painting includes the portraits of both patrons, José (*standing, right*) and Miguel de Gálvez (*left*), wearing the traditional lawyer's black attire. This is the only surviving image of Miguel de Gálvez. (Sociedad Económica de Amigos del País de Málaga)

Economic Societies of Friends of the Country (Sociedades económicas de amigos del país) were institutions created by private citizens from the reformist elite but that had the decisive support of high-placed government officials, with the aim of increasing agricultural and industrial production, facilitating commerce, and fighting ignorance and poverty. Between 1770 and 1820, seventy Economic Societies were created on the Iberian Peninsula and fourteen more overseas.[15] But since the good intentions of the societies and its members were unable to lift the heavy stone of inertia, a new emphasis was put on the formation of leaders who, once they arrived in key posts, were to be responsible for implementing reform projects. A new ruling class had to be created. In this way, education was a major priority for men of the Enlightenment.[16]

The town of Avila was chosen for the academy, according to O'Reilly, because it "has few distractions, the weather is healthy, the country abundant in food, there are enough houses to lodge the officers, as well as a medium-sized barracks for an infantry regiment, which will be needed for drill practice."[17] The curriculum included both theory and practice. Every morning the students gathered "in a hall where a lecture is given in mathematics, with lessons in arithmetic and second-degree algebra; the elements of Euclid, with the notes of the famous Simpson,[18] professor of mathematics at the University of Glasgow; a concise practical geometry; and a treatise on fortification, with study of the plans of six acclaimed strongholds and castles. In artillery a short course is given that includes everything a high-ranking officer needs to know."[19]

The "library, although modest, contains the most brilliant military treatises written by the best authors."[20] To supplement this collection, several of the academy's professors and students were commissioned to translate additional works that were considered important. One of the students, Francisco de Saavedra, who would later become Bernardo's very close friend and have a life and career often intertwined with his, was in charge of translating the Count de Guibert's *Essai général de tactique* (General treatise on tactics), published in London just two years previously.[21] The need for good textbooks was also felt beyond the walls of Avila's military academy. During these years, both translations and original works flourished in Spain.[22] The Economic Society of the Basque Country commissioned an annotated edition of the works of Euclid; Benito Bails and Jerónimo de Capmany published their *Tratados de Mathematica* (treatises on mathematics); and Manuel de Aguirre published his *Indagación y reflexiones sobre la Geografía* (Studies and considerations on geography).[23] This last work is considered by Gregorio Valdelvira González to be the "most important treatment of geography from the Spanish Enlightenment."[24] At the academy all of this knowledge was complemented, in O'Reilly's words, "by the study of big maneuvers, the selection of the best places for encampments, the conduct of marches and convoys, the means for supplying the army, and other war operations."[25]

The practical part of the curriculum consisted of maneuvers with both infantry and cavalry troops. The Navarra Regiment garrisoned in Avila was assigned for that purpose, with "the idea that one or two more infantry regiments, a couple of cavalry squadrons, and six field cannons with their crew" would later arrive.[26] The academy students were to receive instruction "in big maneuvers, and the importance of speed while executing them; will see re-created the most famous orders of battle in the latest war and others before it; the way to fortify their [the students'] positions and encampments; to ensure supplies; the respective advantages of using the infantry and the cavalry; and other frequent and necessary operations in time of war."[27]

According to the testimony of Francisco de Saavedra, a normal day at the Royal Military Academy of Avila started early in the morning, when "we were taught theoretical and practical geometry with clarity and purpose. In the afternoon we gathered on the plain, called *la Dehesa*, where the Navarra Regiment maneuvered and performed as many exercises as we requested. At nightfall the students were divided into groups of eight to ten to read the best military authors and discuss the most important details of our art."[28]

One of the main challenges was finding a good faculty. The first professors were recruited from among young officers with some kind of scientific credentials. Shortly afterward the cartographer and engineer Jorge Sicre y Béjar, the engineer Miguel Ger, and Manuel de Aguirre would be teaching geography and José Ramón de Urrutia mathematics.[29] Among the few civilians on the faculty was Pierre Nicolás Chantreau, whose *Arte de hablar bien francés, ó gramática completa, dividida en tres partes* (Art of speaking French well, or a complete grammar, divided into three parts), published in 1781, became the eighteenth century's main textbook for learning French.[30] The lack of a solid teaching faculty was offset by what O'Reilly called "societies" or working groups in which students shared their progress, discussed their papers, and produced written conclusions, which were circulated among the rest of their classmates.[31] In this kind of autodidactic system, the key was having the very best students, and thus their selection was of the utmost importance.

The criterion was clear: merit, and merit alone. But critics soon questioned O'Reilly's interpretation and implementation of this criterion. The Count of Ricla, one of O'Reilly's fiercest political opponents, accused him of appointing only his supporters "with the sole aim of increasing his own power."[32] Either despite of or because of their method of selection, the students considered themselves members of an elite corps and destined to become the supreme commanders of the Spanish army. This esprit de corps reached such a height that outsiders began to speak of the "mystery of Avila."[33] The phrase had a double meaning, in that it referred both to the secretive manner in which these students conducted themselves and to the religious tradition of Avila as the hometown of Saint Teresa. Initiates in the "mystery" devoted themselves to their studies and shared their thoughts and ideas only with fellow members. The English traveler William Dalrymple, in a letter dated August 4, 1774, wrote that "the officers affected to be very mysterious; they told me, that they were enjoined, in the strictest manner, not to communicate what the king's intentions were for this assembly; and they were so very cautious, that they would not even show me the room intended for their study; but there was no reason for so much enigma, as they had little to conceal, and, of course, the veil was easily penetrated."[34]

Despite the Englishman's skepticism, the students' secrecy was partly justified, as they were aware that they formed the vanguard of what was intended to become a new model army, which, in Francisco de Saavedra's words, "would have to fight against ignorance linked with power."[35] This group of self-conscious, hardworking, and scientific young officers was called by their enemies the *barbilampiños*, or "beardless ones."[36] Their baby faces were hated by the so-called *mozos viejos*, or "old boys," who had no regard for newfangled things and protested that promotions should be made on the basis of either seniority or sheer battle courage.[37] The baby faces favored a new model of war, a Prussian model of clean war that aimed to limit bloody hand-to-hand combat through a more scientific approach. Not only age and ideas separated the two groups—their manners and appearances were also different. The old boys interpreted the neatness of the uniforms of the baby-faces as "a sign of effeminacy, since the veterans identified scruffiness with virility and courage."[38]

In addition to Saavedra, whose life and career would be closely linked to the Gálvez clan, Bernardo de Gálvez started a friendship with José de Ezpeleta, who was at the time posted with the Navarra Regiment garrisoned in Avila. Later they would be reunited in America.[39]

Alejandro O'Reilly paid his first visit to the Royal Military Academy at the end of July 1774, only three months after its opening. In his first report to King Carlos III, dated October 1, 1774, he noted, "I must convey deep satisfaction at being able to witness in Avila the great determination shown by those young officers in their studies; the honest competition that is flourishing among them; the frankness and camaraderie with which they treat each other; the help they give each other in their studies; and their commitment to this institution."[40]

At the end of October O'Reilly paid his second and last visit to the academy. In the course of eight days he was able to order the students to "re-enact the battle of Farsalia," using the troops of the Navarra Regiment.[41] Meanwhile, the academy was gaining in prestige as a first-rate educational institution. As Vicente de la Fuente has written, "In a very short time it attained a very good reputation thanks to the ingenuity of its officers."[42]

After the winter passed—which, in Avila's "healthy" weather, meant temperatures of between 28 and 44 degrees Fahrenheit, or much too cold for southerners such as Bernardo de Gálvez and Francisco de Saavedra—spring came with the news that troops were concentrating in Barcelona. Although the utmost secrecy surrounded their ultimate destination, "everyone believed that the expedition was to take revenge on the Moroccans."[43] As young and ambitious officers, all of the students at the Royal Military Academy wanted to join up. Francisco de Saavedra and Bernardo de Gálvez left almost immediately for Madrid to arrange a meeting with General O'Reilly. In his memoirs Saavedra recalled, "I started the journey on Easter Monday, that is, April 10th [1775], since Easter that year was on the 16th. I travelled in the company of Don Bernardo de Gálvez, captain of the Seville Regiment, toward whom I had great sympathy, despite having seldom talked to him. A feeling that, as usually happens, was mutual. We traveled by horse, and I had a very entertaining journey, because he related several episodes from his life, which were a real novelty. Anyway, we forged then a very close friendship, which in a certain way was to become the foundation of my destiny."[44] Saavedra's last remark was absolutely true, as would later be seen.

THE SPANISH MILITARY EXPEDITION AGAINST ALGIERS

Saavedra was right that the objective of the expedition being assembled in Barcelona was to "take revenge on the Moroccans."[45] In 1774 the Moroccans had broken the May 28, 1767, Peace and Commercial Treaty between Morocco and Spain by attacking Melilla and Vélez's Rock, two Spanish strongholds on the North African coast. A few days before the attack, Morocco's sultan, Sidi Muhámmad Ibn Abdallah, had sent a letter to King Carlos III stating that, in accordance with the wishes of his subjects and of Algiers, he would be attacking the Spanish strongholds, but this action should not be considered a breach of the maritime peace established by the peace treaty. This diplomatic subtlety was not appreciated in Madrid, though, which soon issued a declaration of war.[46] The Moroccan attacks took place between October 1774 and March of the following year, and they were both repelled by the garrisons of the Spanish strongholds. Despite the short and easy victory, the Spanish government concluded that the treacherous conduct of the sultan should not go unpunished. With this objective in mind, the idea of an expedition against Algiers was born.

This is the immediate background of the expedition put together in Barcelona, but the whole affair must be considered in the much larger context of Spain's African policy. That policy can be traced back as far as 1541, when the Holy Roman Emperor Carlos V personally led a force against Algiers. Since that time, according to José U. Martínez Carreras, the monarchy of Carlos III was the only one that showed particular attention to Africa. He was the only

Spanish king of the modern era who developed a real and coherent African policy, revealing his interest in and focusing on the relations and actions of Spain in that continent. It could be argued that the king laid the foundations for later Spanish Africanism.[47]

The main goal of Spanish Africanism in the second half of the eighteenth century was to protect eastern Spain's Mediterranean commerce from pirate attacks. To achieve this, King Carlos III favored the use of diplomacy.[48] In the words of the Count of Aranda, "We negotiate with them as if they were Frenchmen or Portuguese. . . . We are no longer in the time of the Crusades."[49] In this context, the military expedition against Algiers in 1775 needs explanation as an exception to the policy.

Why a military expedition? John Lynch points out that the war was important to Spaniards for reasons of pride, religion, and maritime security.[50] Also, legally the war between Morocco and Spain was still in force, although the sultan had written a letter, dated March 19, 1775, proposing a conference in Tangier to resolve their mutual differences. The Marquis of Grimaldi published the Spanish answer in the official journal *Gazeta de Madrid*, which stated clearly that the king of Morocco had been the aggressor, and "with such a precedent, His Majesty will not put down the sword without the compensations demanded by the decorum owed his sovereignty and the honor of Spanish arms."[51]

In today's terms, the "pride" mentioned by Lynch was international prestige, the need to carry out a foreign policy worthy of a world power.[52] While maritime security was an important factor behind the decision, the trigger was religion. According to Juan Antonio López Delgado,[53] who echoes traditional interpretations offered by the Count of Fernán-Núñez[54] and Antonio Ferrer del Río,[55] Carlos III decided in favor of a military intervention on the advice of his confessor, Friar Joaquín de Eleta, and the Franciscan friar Father Cano.[56] The latter had long experience in Africa, and for him this campaign was nothing short of a "crusade against the infidel."[57]

Moroccan and Algerian forces together had attacked Melilla and Vélez's Rock. Although Spanish wrath was directed against Morocco, its military action was against Algiers. But if the purpose was to punish the sultan of Morocco, why attack Algiers, which was not under his sovereignty but under the bey or dey[58] of Algiers? The reason was that Algiers had served as a pirate and corsair base for centuries, which made its port an important and rich commercial center.[59] As Fernand Braudel points out, piracy needs a market to sell its loot; it is inseparable from trade. Algiers could not have become an important corsair center without becoming at the same time a major commercial center.[60]

But what should Spain do with Algiers if it conquered the port? Two solutions were considered. Raze it completely, so it would never recover as a pirate center, or incorporate it into Spanish territories in North Africa. For the first option to succeed, a heavy naval bombardment would have been enough, as was already planned in 1751 and tried half-heartedly in 1783.[61] The second option was much more complicated. From Paris the Count of Aranda warned the Marquis of Grimaldi that the strongholds Spain already had in North Africa were more than enough, since they were "two huge nuisances and of no use whatsoever. . . . The way to force the Moroccans to a stable peace is to maintain fewer objects for them to attack—objects that we can sustain with such strength that when attacked, they will break their noses against them. This will make them lose any hope and will take away any temptation to revolt. The fact that we abandoned several strongholds there while reinforcing others will show them that what we keep will never be for their moustaches."[62]

The final decision to attack Algiers was taken in February 1775, but the urgency of sending the military expedition as soon as possible was set forth in two earlier military plans, which were more than twenty years old. The first had been drafted by the French in 1754 but never implemented for political reasons.[63] The second dated from the same year and had been sent to the Count of Aranda in 1757 by Francisco Ricaurd, a French engineer serving in the Spanish army.[64] The title of this second plan could not be more appropriate: "Memoir presented to force the Algerians to respect henceforth the sincerity of the treaties, and a plan for military operations."[65]

The supreme command of the expedition against Algiers was first offered to Lieutenant General Pedro de Ceballos, but his request for 40,000 men made the king reconsider his offer.[66] Instead, he appointed General Alejandro O'Reilly, who was willing to undertake the effort with half the number of men.[67] The naval forces were put under the command of Fleet Admiral Pedro González de Castejón.

Preparations began immediately. On March 24 orders were sent to consolidate troops and supplies in Barcelona and Cadiz. One of the main concerns was to get ready quickly and secretly so as to avoid giving any sign to the Algerians. Yet despite all precautions, the secret was soon out, even in remote Avila, where every student in the Royal Military Academy knew what was to happen.[68] On May 14 Admiral González de Castejón was already in Cartagena (in the Iberian Peninsula), and General O'Reilly arrived two days later. From Cadiz and Barcelona two separate convoys transported troops and equipment, and from the port of El Ferrol the escort ships departed. The expedition would finally total more than 20,000 troops (18,827 infantry, 954 cavalry, 736 artillery, and 16 engineer officers, plus 2,525 marines). Making up the Spanish naval forces were a total of 44 warships with between 331 and 348 transports of various sizes.[69] The Duke of Tuscany supplied two frigates under the command of the English naval officer John Acton, and the Knights of the Order of Malta contributed another frigate.

Bernardo de Gálvez arrived in Madrid during the night of April 11 and went directly to the home of his uncles Miguel and José in the "San Isidro el Real new street, near La Merced Street" (today Colegiata Street near Duque de Rivas Street).[70] With the help of his uncle Miguel, Bernardo had no difficulty rejoining the Seville Regiment, which had been assigned to the so-called Seville Brigade under the command of Brigadier General the Marquis of Villena, within the army group under Lieutenant General Luis de Urbina.[71] Bernardo was given the command of a light infantry company. At the time light infantrymen or skirmishers were chosen for "their agility and ease in handling weapons . . . to make reconnaissance and skirmishes."[72] "Left to their courage and resourcefulness," these soldiers "find the enemy's weakest points to infiltrate, draw the attention of their infantry, and taking advantage of the terrain they fire against their artillery with precision."[73] This kind of warfare was well suited for someone like Bernardo, with his combat experience against the Apaches.

The original plan was that the Spanish fleet would sail for Algiers by mid-June 1775, but bad weather delayed the departure several times. Finally, on June 30 the fleet arrived in the Bay of Algiers. From the bridge of the *Velasco* Alejandro O'Reilly could clearly see the Algerian troops deployed and waiting. Turning to the Count of Fernán-Núñez from the King's Immemorial Regiment (*Regimiento Inmemorial del Rey*), who would later publish his memoir about the expedition, O'Reilly said in French, "Ma foi, mon ami, le vin est versé, il faut le boire [My faith, my friend, the wine is shed, we must drink it]."[74] Even though it is well known that, as Helmut von Moltke the elder remarked, "no plan of operations extends with certainty beyond the first encounter with the enemy's main strength," the fact is that the entire Spanish plan was based on surprise, and when that fell through, instead of changing or adapting the plan, O'Reilly simply proceeded with it.[75] Perhaps he thought that a last-minute change would introduce chaos among his forces, but chaos was already present. The transport ships were scattered along the bay without any order whatsoever, so that the forces assigned to different waves of disembarkation were completely mixed up.[76] Harach Beach was chosen as the disembarkation point, but on the afternoon of July 2 bad weather made the first attempt to land the troops impossible. Meanwhile, new reconnaissance suggested that the place of disembarkation should be changed to Bad Woman's Beach, which was protected from dangerous eastern winds. New orders were circulated among the troops and ships, but while these were being implemented Alejandro O'Reilly changed his mind and returned to the original plan. Early on the morning of July 7 the troops were boarding the boats with such sluggishness that the whole operation was postponed until the next day, causing some units to spend more than twelve hours in their small boats. The next day the preparations started so early that most soldiers spent more than nine hours waiting for the rest of the force to assemble. They were barely able to eat some dry biscuits from their backpacks while in the boats, which were stinking with vomit.

The orders stated that upon arriving on the beach, a camp was to be built that could serve as a base for landing the rest of the infantry troops, especially the artillery.[77] The problem was that the first units to land were not those initially assigned to the mission but a hodgepodge in which the reserve battalions constituted the majority.[78] The original mission of these battalions was to reinforce the main infantry units rather than to fight directly with the enemy. Nevertheless, the officers succeeded in imposing some kind of order on their men, and the troops were formed into columns. Suddenly, and apparently without the issuance of any order, the troops started to change their formation into a line, so that marching inland was impossible, and the soldiers had to take cover from enemy fire behind a large dune close by. General O'Reilly watched everything from his command post on board the *Velasco* but did not order a change in the troops' formation.[79]

The Algerians' first attack was easily repelled by fire from His Majesty's ships, and a company of grenadiers from the *Guardias Españolas* succeeded in capturing an enemy standard. At this point O'Reilly ordered the troops to form a kind of hammer shape, the handle of which would reach the shore and serve as a conduit for reinforcements while the head would continue to engage the enemy. While these orders were carried out, a second enemy attack took place. Algerian cavalry were followed by unmounted camels carrying, according to one author, "flammable materials" to instigate panic among the Spaniards.[80] Again they were repelled by the combined fire of the infantry and the Tuscan frigates under the command of John Acton. Meanwhile, pressure was increasing in the flanks of the Spanish position, especially against the officers, who were the favorite target of Algerian sharpshooters. Amid the confusion some soldiers advanced against enemy positions, forcing the Algerians to retreat. While this was taking place, a second wave of Spanish troops landed with the same disorder as before, if not more. The original plan stipulated that as soon as troops set foot on shore, engineers would build a redoubt for their protection, but this effort did not start until three hours after the troops' arrival. The structure, after it was quickly finished, amounted to no more than some earth walls surrounded by a shallow trench. The order was given for all troops to take cover inside, and it was soon discovered that the redoubt was too small to hold them all. Even worse, only the outer lines were able to fire, thus eliminating the Spanish advantage in having larger numbers. In fact, the crowded Spanish redoubt offered a perfect target for the Algerian artillery, which, despite having only one twenty-four-pounder piece, opened fire again and again against the compact Spanish formation, causing heavy casualties and decimating, with shot after shot, Spanish morale. The Spanish were helpless against the Algerian cannon fire. Their biggest artillery pieces on land were only two twelve-pounders, whose effective range was 650 yards with solid shot and 430 yards with grapeshot, while the Algerian twenty-four-pounder could accurately hit up to 870 yards.[81]

Meanwhile, the Spanish light infantry was fighting outside the redoubt. It was especially difficult to repel the Algerian cavalry charge. Even though war theorists insist that a cavalry has little chance against infantry when charging directly against its solid formations, the truth was that the Spanish infantry formations were anything but solid.[82] The fact that the Spanish light troops successfully repelled the Algerian cavalry speaks volumes about their commitment and valor. Later, the light infantry was assigned to defend the Spanish advance posts outside of the perimeter of the redoubt.[83] Its last mission was to cover the general retreat or "re-embarkation," as it was officially called.

Captain Bernardo de Gálvez, one "of the best shooters of his regiment," was assigned to a company of skirmishers. In a letter later sent to Bernardo's uncle José, O'Reilly wrote that Bernardo "long remained with his men even after being wounded, and did not retreat from the field until specifically ordered to do so."[84] No details about his wound have been found, apart from the fact that it was to one of his legs.[85] Bernardo's actions would not go unnoticed.

Well after three in the afternoon, the first casualty report—or, as it was graphically called in the British army at the time, the Spanish "butcher's bill"—came out: more than 600 were dead and 1,800 wounded. The figure might not seem very high in relation to the total number of troops in the expedition, but it is completely disproportionate in comparison to the number of troops engaged in the action. Of the more than 20,000 Spanish troops, between 12,000 and 16,000 disembarked. When this figure is taken into account, the proportion of casualties rises to between 15 and 20 percent. This range was completely unacceptable at the time, especially since Spain had

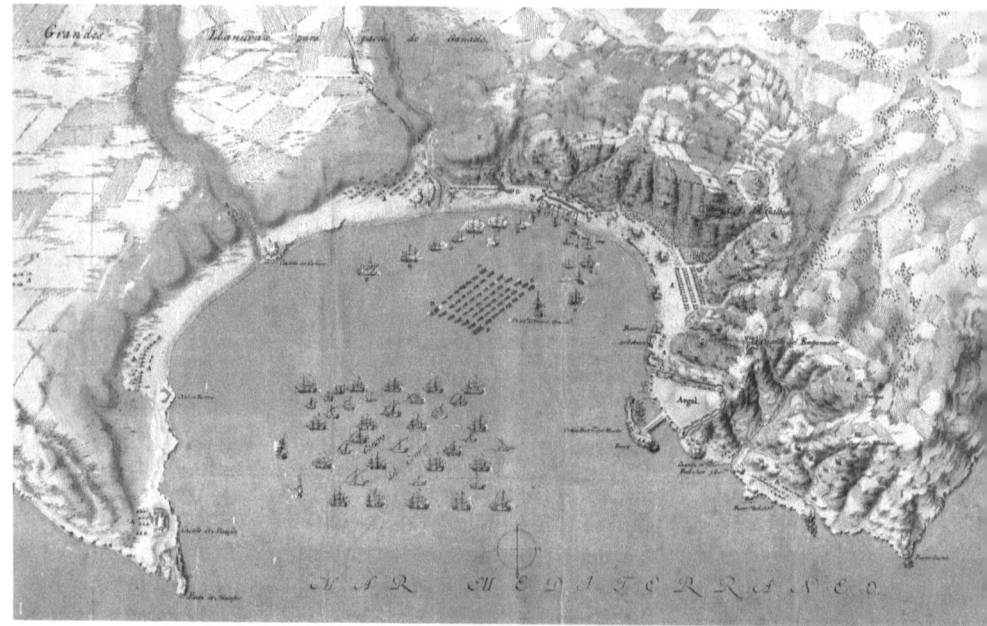

View of the Bay of Algiers during the Spanish attack in 1775 where Captain Bernardo de Gálvez commanded a unit of riflemen of the Seville Regiment and, according to the official report, "long remained with his men even after being wounded, and did not retreat from the field until specifically ordered to do so" (Alejandro O'Reilly to José de Gálvez, Puerto de Santa María, May 7, 1776, AGI, Santo Domingo, 2586, folder 11, ff. 927r–928v). (*Demostración de la baia de Argel* . . . ; Archivo General de Simancas, Secretaría de Guerra, Legajos, 02010, accompanying a letter from Francisco Sabatini to the count de Ricla, Madrid, 23 October 1775. España, Ministerio de Educación, Cultura y Deporte, Archivo General de Simancas, MPD, 10,004.)

such poor results in the action.[86] After nine hours of combat, the troops were still fighting on the beach more than five miles from the Algiers city walls.[87]

One hour later, General O'Reilly summoned all of his generals and colonels to a council of war. All were in favor of the re-embarkation. The supreme commander agreed and issued orders for it to start just before sunset. If the landing was a mess, the re-embarkation was even more so. Only the brilliant performance of the troops under the command of Victorio de Navia prevented a complete disaster. He was the last man to leave the beach.[88] But despite the bravery of Navia's men, some of the wounded were left behind and eventually executed on the spot. According to the *Chroniques de la régence d'Alger* (*Chronicles of the Algiers Regency*), the emir had promised "ten pieces of gold for every Christian head, but no reward for prisoners."[89] This same source claimed that the chaos of the re-embarkation was such that boats loaded with wounded men were rejected by their own ships and had no choice but to return ashore, where the men would face certain death.[90] If the three o'clock butcher bill was 2,400 casualties, the final tally was much higher, with between 3,000 and 5,000 wounded or dead.[91]

Once the troops were aboard their ships, O'Reilly ordered them to return to Spain. This decision led to additional criticism of the expedition's supreme commander. Accusations were leveled against him for not ordering the bombardment of the city. But in fact very little if anything could have been achieved by it. Furthermore, the few mortar ships included in the fleet were of no use, whereas exposing all of the ships to the long-range coastal cannons of Algiers would have only increased the already disproportionate butcher's bill.[92] Just a few days later, on July 14, 1775, the fleet arrived in Alicante on the eastern coast of Spain, and news of the defeat spread quickly. After the Bay of Algiers fiasco, fingers were pointed at two specific individuals identified as the authors of the defeat: General Alejandro O'Reilly and the Marquis of Grimaldi. About the latter, John Lynch sarcastically comments that he "was most successful when most inert."[93]

Aware of the danger of being considered responsible for such a defeat, O'Reilly soon began a propaganda campaign to hide or at least justify the failure. Even while sailing toward the Spanish coast he wrote a report to the king in which he attributed the bad results to the "excessive ardor of the troops . . . which led to an outcome not in accordance with the orders issued."[94] It lies somewhere between irony and sarcasm to attribute defeat to an excess of courage among one's own troops. The official report was published in the July 16, 1775, issue of the *Gazeta de Madrid*, followed by an addendum on July 25 that listed the official number of casualties as 27 officers and 501 men dead, and 191 officers and 2,088 soldiers wounded, a much smaller number than the real one. Outraged citizens lined the walls of Madrid with posters[95] bearing messages like these two:

> That everything went wrong,
> That the action was lost,
> That people died
> Because it was God's will,
> That, yes;
> But to try to persuade us
> That every wrong is a right,
> That those dead

Are not dead,
And that those who saw it lie,
That, no.⁹⁶

The *Gazeta* lied on Tuesday,
The supplement lied even more,
The two generals lie
For all eternity.⁹⁷

These popular but anonymous reactions to the official version of events have been considered a symptom of "something new entering the history of Spain," something that was later called public opinion.⁹⁸ But for the enlightened despotism of the second half of the eighteenth century, public opinion was not a factor to be taken into much account.

After one year, to let criticism die down, the Marquis of Grimaldi was sent to Rome as ambassador and Alejandro O'Reilly was appointed military governor of Andalusia. After his return from Algiers, Bernardo de Gálvez returned to his position with the Seville Regiment in Cadiz, where he spent some months recovering from his wounds. Here, in September 1775, he received a visit from his good friend Francisco de Saavedra, also wounded in Algiers. In his memoirs Saavedra recalled, "At that time he wrote a little song about the expedition and other funny little musical pieces. He was a man of huge talent and very fond of music."⁹⁹ At the end of January 1776 they met again: "In Seville I met my great friend don Bernardo de Gálvez, who was on his way to Madrid. He told me that the Minister of the Indies, Frey don Julián de Arriaga, had died, and the ministry divided into two: navy and Indies. The first was given to Don Pedro de Castejón, and the second to José de Gálvez, his uncle, to whom he offered to introduce me if we met in Madrid."¹⁰⁰

On January 30, 1776, the *Gazeta de Madrid* published the "infamous promotion of Algiers"—infamous not because those who fought in Algiers did not deserve recognition but because the list included almost everyone who had taken part, including those responsible for the defeat.¹⁰¹ The promotion list was meant to make the country forget about a defeat caused by a chain of errors, miscalculations, and lack of preparation by the Spanish army top brass. To that purpose, the promotions included four lieutenant generals, fifteen mayor generals, sixteen brigadier generals, seventeen colonels, forty-one lieutenant colonels, thirty-four captains, and seven lieutenants. Adding insult to injury, the promotion announcement stated that as "the king is satisfied by the good and long service of Count O'Reilly, he has agreed to bestow a five-thousand *reales* annual pension on each of his two elder

Portrait of Alejandro O'Reilly as governor of Cadiz. O'Reilly was part of what has been called the Wild Geese, or Irish military in the service of France, Austria, and Spain during the eighteenth century. He would rise to become a lieutenant general in the Spanish army, occupying very important positions, and would be instrumental in Bernardo de Gálvez's military career. O'Reilly selected Gálvez to attend the Royal Military Academy of Avila and appointed him colonel of the Louisiana Fixed Infantry Regiment and acting governor of the province. (Joaquín Güenen, *Retrato de Alejandro O'Reilly, conde de O'Reilly*, oil on canvas, 1786, in Museo de las Cortes de Cádiz)

sons."[102] Among the forty-one new lieutenant colonels was Bernardo de Gálvez. In an issue of the *Gazeta de Madrid* a few weeks later, it was specified that "His Majesty has also conferred the command of the grenadier companies of the Seville Regiment on the light infantry captains Don Bernardo Galvez, now ranked lieutenant colonel, and Don Nicolás de San Juan."[103] Hence, at the age of twenty-nine and with little more than thirteen and a half years of active service, Bernardo de Gálvez became a full lieutenant colonel. His career was on the right track, especially considering that in the 1770s the average age for a lieutenant colonel was fifty.[104]

BRIEF RETURN TO THE ROYAL MILITARY ACADEMY OF AVILA

In mid-1776 Bernardo de Gálvez returned to the Royal Military Academy of Avila, which was now under the direction of Francisco Estachería, former colonel of the Louisiana Fixed Infantry Regiment. On May 7, Alejandro O'Reilly, who, despite the debacle in Algiers, still had the king's confidence, wrote to the just-appointed minister of the Indies, José de Gálvez, to inform him of his intention to recommend Lieutenant Colonel Bernardo de Gálvez to fill the colonel position in the Louisiana Regiment. O'Reilly justified his recommendation thus: "It is time to fill the vacancy, and it goes to an officer of proven spirit and good conduct, who speaks the French language well, and who has knowledge of the character of that nation so that his manners and command will be agreeable to that colony, whose wealthier and most distinguished families serve in the said regiment."[105]

O'Reilly added that Bernardo's experience in New Spain would serve him well because, "since Louisiana is next to Mexico's presidios on the frontier, the practical knowledge that this officer has acquired of the Indians and the terrain will be useful in pacifying or employing them as appropriate to the service." On May 22, two weeks after this letter was written, Bernardo de Gálvez was officially appointed colonel of the Louisiana Fixed Infantry Regiment.[106]

4. Arrival in Louisiana and Preparations for War

On May 22, 1776, Bernardo de Gálvez was appointed colonel of the Louisiana Fixed Infantry Regiment, and several months later, on September 19, he was also designated acting governor of the province.[1] Before departing from Madrid he put his affairs in order: for example, he gave power of attorney to Diego Paniagua to carry on with the tedious and meticulous paperwork of his application to be admitted as knight of the Royal and Distinguished Spanish Order of Carlos III. Being a knight of the order meant much more than merely receiving a decoration for services rendered to the nation or the king; it would be an important contribution to both his military career and his social status. To be admitted it was necessary to prove, through an elaborate process, "the candidate's honest life and morality; his status as a legitimate son; his Catholicism; his racial and social purity [*limpieza de sangre y oficios*], as well as those of his parents, grandparents, and great-grandparents, both paternal and maternal; the nobility of blood, not of privilege [*nobleza de sangre, y no de privilegio*], of the candidate and his father and paternal grandfather, as well as his maternal grandfather."[2]

At first glance it would seem difficult for a son of shepherds to prove his "nobility of blood, not of privilege." According to María Elena Martínez, nobility of blood was "the most valued noble status in Spanish society because it implied being part of a privileged lineage since 'time immemorial,'" while nobility of privilege was the one granted "by kings to commoners who provided important military or public service or who were able to purchase patents of nobility. If the Crown allowed for its transmission from father to son the status would become *nobleza de sangre* (nobility of blood) on the third generation."[3] However, the Royal and Distinguished Spanish Order of Carlos III was created as an instrument of the enlightened social policies that promoted the advancement of members of what could be called the middle class. While it was true that during the admission process the candidate had to demonstrate his nobility of birth, this concept was interpreted in a lax way. All that was actually required was that among his ancestors the candidate had someone of "noble condition" (*hidalgo*). In this context, the most relevant consequence of becoming a member of the Royal Order of Carlos III would be that Bernardo de Gálvez, and by extension his family, had established their noble condition.[4]

Bernardo de Gálvez arrived in New Orleans at the end of 1776, and after a short transfer of power from his predecessor, Luis de Unzaga, on January 1, 1777, he assumed office as colonel and acting governor.[5] His long and detailed instructions were accompanied by extensive powers that gave him ample margin for maneuvering, which was necessary if he was to navigate the complex North American situation in 1777.[6]

By the end of 1776, the recently declared independent United States of America was facing what David Hackett Fisher has called "a cataract of disaster."[7] The arrival in New York in August 1776 of 30,000 English troops on board a powerful fleet had marked the beginning of a period of setbacks for the American patriots. According to Fisher, "Many on both sides thought that the rebellion was broken and that the American war was over."[8] After their quick conquest of New York, the British had a solid base of operations from which to launch two simultaneous offensives, one against Canada and the other to ensure control of the Hudson Valley.[9] Confronted with this thrust, the rebels could devise only a defensive strategy, the objective of which was to keep their army operational by avoiding any large-scale, direct confrontation that could destroy it.[10] The second half of 1776 was a succession of tactical retreats by the American forces under the command of George Washington, who at the time seemed to aspire only to preserve the remnants of his much-weakened Continental army. At this critical juncture, two important events occurred. The first was the publication in the *Pennsylvania Journal* of several articles by Thomas Paine, under the significant title "The American Crisis." In them Paine admitted how quickly panic can spread through a country, but he nevertheless concluded that "panics, in some cases, have their uses; they produce as much good as hurt. Their duration is always short; the mind soon grows through them, and acquires a firmer habit than before."[11] Paine's words spread like wildfire, lifting sagging spirits both in the Continental army and on the home front. The second event was the Continental Congress's decision, adopted on the same day that Washington's troops were fighting the British in Trenton, to abandon its policy of micromanaging the war and invest Washington with ample powers as the Continental army's commander in chief.[12]

Precisely at the moment that Bernardo de Gálvez was setting foot in

King Carlos III wearing the Royal Order of Carlos III, established in 1771 to reward his most distinguished vassals in Spain and the Indies for extraordinary services rendered to the king and the state. The creation of the Order of Carlos III must be considered within the wider context of the so-called Bourbon social reforms, and it was open to members of any profession, although it would be mostly awarded to members of the military and to civil servants. (Anton Rafael Mengs, *Portrait of Carlos III*, oil on canvas, 1774; © Madrid, Museo Nacional del Prado)

Louisiana, General Washington, fully aware of the desperate situation of the Continental army, and of the United States of America more broadly, decided to take advantage of the extended deployment of British troops in New Jersey to launch a surprise attack.[13] Crossing the partially frozen Delaware River to Trenton on Christmas Day, he succeeded in defeating—not once, but twice—an overly confident detachment of German mercenaries serving the British.[14]

The situation in North America was of particular worry to the Spanish on both sides of the Atlantic. Spanish concerns were manifested in a frantic search for reliable information about the real situation, as the first step toward establishing a policy coherent with its own interests.[15] In Paris the Spanish ambassador, the Count of Aranda, was convinced of the importance of early intervention against the British, to whom, in his words, "we should wish all lack of success."[16] Applying pressure on Madrid to take action, he reported not only on diplomatic overtures made by the French but also on his own contact with American diplomats at the court of Versailles. On December 28, 1776, the count met for the first time with Benjamin Franklin and Arthur Lee, and a second meeting followed on January 8. The arrival of his reports in Madrid several weeks later triggered a heated discussion in the Council of Ministers. On that occasion, José de Gálvez urged that for the moment both France and Spain should prepare themselves for a possible British attack. Even before Bernardo de Gálvez's departure for Louisiana, José de Gálvez had already taken steps to collect intelligence about the situation by dispatching orders to the governor of Cuba to send agents to Pensacola, Florida; Jamaica; and other British colonies.[17] From Havana, Luciano Herrero was sent to Florida, Antonio Raffelin to Jamaica, and Eduardo de Miguel to the soon-to-be-proclaimed United States of America. The latter was unlucky enough to be captured by an English frigate on his way to Philadelphia. Two more agents were sent to replace him, one to Philadelphia and the other to New York.[18]

In fact, the first contact between the rebels and Spain did not take place in Paris or Europe but in America. In May 1776 Charles Lee, who was to distinguish himself during the defense of Charleston in June, wrote on behalf of Virginia and the United Colonies to the Spanish governor of Louisiana asking for Spanish support for the American cause in the form of "muskets, uniforms, and medicines, especially quinine."[19] It is important to stress that about the same time, the Count of Aranda had already begun to fund the North American rebels through a financially complex undertaking with the French, using the services of the famous author Pierre-Augustin Caron de Beaumarchais.[20]

The tasks ahead of Bernardo de Gálvez as governor of Louisiana were multiple. But as important as they all were, both he and the royal authorities in Madrid had a clear priority: to follow the situation of the British colonies in North America closely and prepare Louisiana for an eventual war with Britain.

MONITORING TENSIONS IN NORTH AMERICA'S BRITISH COLONIES

Its geographical position made Louisiana the perfect location for monitoring the escalation of hostilities between Britain and its American colonies. As early as September 1775, Louisiana's governor at the time, Luis de Unzaga, received orders to gather as much information as possible.[21] But Unzaga was famous for procrastination, so he did not begin to comply until the following year.[22] As the conflict grew into full-scale war and the prospects for Spanish intervention increased, information gathering expanded from simple diplomatic interests to military intelligence. As John Keegan states, mere contact with military intelligence is extremely dangerous, because while one side or group believes it is using that intelligence, that group is always at a high risk of being used itself.[23] The so-called intelligence process can be divided into five parts: acquisition, transmission, analysis, counterintelligence, and covert action.[24] Bernardo de Gálvez would become involved in all of these stages, though not always with success.

Bernardo de Gálvez used all of the methods for acquiring information that, in 1838, the Baron of Jomini called indispensable to a good general, from reconnaissance to the questioning of prisoners and deserters, not to mention the use of spies.[25] Sometimes the amount of data available made him succumb to the "vacuum-cleaner syndrome"—sucking in everything without discrimination[26]—as happened, for example, while transmitting information supplied by a "Negro woman" on the Natchez blockade in May 1781.[27]

Once acquired, intelligence needs to be transmitted in a timely manner to the decision-making center. To fulfill this task in this context, an emergency mail system of fast ships was established linking the two sides of the Atlantic. The captains had an express order that "if at risk of being caught they should drop the documents into the sea."[28] Nonetheless, both the Spanish and English sides intercepted each other's communications. In December 1779, the Spaniards got hold of letters containing information about "great preparations for an attack against the *Dons* [underlined in the original] of New Orleans." A note in the document explains that "Dons" was the word used by the British to designate Spaniards "because of the treatment they use of Don Juan, Don Pedro."[29] A year and a half earlier, in May 1778, Bernardo de

Gálvez had ordered the capture of an Englishman because he wanted to see the papers he was supposedly carrying.[30] And in November 1779 Gálvez sent to Havana two letters intercepted from General John Campbell, which urged the settlers of Natchez to "join, in Manchac, Colonel Dickson and his company and the inhabitants of those districts, who would like to give proof of their fidelity and love of their King and Country against their perfidious and implacable enemies, the Spaniards."[31] In January 1780, on the other side of the Atlantic, José de Gálvez expressed to the governor of Cuba his displeasure about the British interception of a courier from Cuba, who carried Spain's plans to attack Pensacola.[32]

Despite José de Gálvez's obsessive control, New Orleans and Havana, for the obvious reason of location, became the two main centers for intelligence operations in America, particularly in taking charge of the analysis of the information gathered. In fact, the capital of Louisiana became a spy hub, where secrets were just another type of merchandise to exchange. In New Orleans, Little Page Robertson, an aid of the American adventurer James Willing, operated as a double agent, supplying important information to the British about the Spanish aid to the revolutionaries.[33]

Counterintelligence—that is, detecting enemy spies operating within the boundaries of Spanish North America—was of the utmost importance. To this end, Bernardo de Gálvez ordered in 1777 that a certain Nodbas Jamud be closely followed to ascertain if he was as close a friend of the American revolutionaries as he claimed to be.[34] In May of the following year Gálvez granted a passport to a British citizen while at the same time ordering his arrest and the seizure of all of his papers.

Within the realm of covert actions, Bernardo de Gálvez made extensive use of propaganda—as, for example, in April 1777, when with studied generosity he presented 150 barrels of flour to Pensacola to alleviate the food shortage that was ravaging the settlement.[35] He also used economic and commercial measures to put pressure on British settlements along the Mississippi River, seizing their ships or allowing covert commerce with the American rebels. These events will be discussed below.

Bernardo de Gálvez's use of spies was a complicated affair, since neither his character nor his previous experience prepared him to navigate such dangerous waters. In July 1777 he remitted to Madrid information gathered by a Spaniard about the defenses of Pensacola.[36] In August he received instructions to send a commissioner to the interior of the province of Louisiana;[37] he had already done so. Florida, too, hosted Spanish spies sent by Bernardo de Gálvez, who supplied him with maps and plans of the disposition of British troops in the region.[38]

The most successful mission carried out by Spanish spies was the journey of Jacinto Panis to Mobile and Pensacola. Under the cover of an official mission to present to Pensacola's English governor, Peter Chester, Spanish complaints about corsair activities on the Mississippi, Panis went to Pensacola and Mobile to gather as much intelligence as possible about their defenses, garrisons, and similar topics.[39] According to John Walton Caughey, "armed with a box of white sugar and a cask of wine" as a present for Governor Chester, Panis left New Orleans on February 22, 1778, reached Mobile on March 2, and proceeded a few days later to Pensacola.[40] There Peter Chester received him, and the two men immediately started discussing the Spanish complaints. Panis spent more than a month in Pensacola, and besides carrying out his secret instructions he was able to make a very good impression on the British governor. In a letter he sent to Gálvez, Chester states, "I am to return you many thanks for having sent an officer to me upon this occasion of Major Panis' rank & credit, who I have endeavored to receive with the distinction he is entitled to, not only from respect to your Excellency's introduction, but also from his own personal merit—and I wish he had given me an opportunity of rendering him any services."[41]

As soon as Panis returned to New Orleans, he submitted a thorough report to Bernardo de Gálvez, who immediately sent a copy of it to Madrid along with praise for Panis's work.[42] The importance of Panis's mission to Pensacola and Mobile cannot be overstated; the accuracy and precision of his report were to prove extremely useful in the coming military campaigns. But his contribution did not end there. A year later, Bernardo de Gálvez entrusted Panis with drafting military plans for the conquest of both British strongholds.[43] Again according to Caughey, author of the most comprehensive study of Bernardo de Gálvez's experiences in Louisiana, the best proof of the importance of Panis's mission was that when war broke out, his plans were followed almost to the letter.[44]

As good as the information supplied by Panis proved to be, Bernardo de Gálvez supplemented it with intelligence from other sources, such as information provided by Robert Holmes (or Roberto Holms), a wealthy planter of Pensacola, after he was arrested on Gálvez's orders, and the plans of Pensacola's defenses provided by several British deserters.[45]

But Bernardo de Gálvez's use of spies would not always be as successful as the Panis mission to Pensacola. In February 1777 he received orders to help Miguel Eduardo, who was posing as a merchant while channeling hypothetically secret Spanish aid to the American revolutionaries.[46] As soon as Eduardo arrived in New Orleans, rumors circulated that he was on an official mission.[47] Bernardo de Gálvez did his best to support his cover, and Eduardo continued to work in Louisiana.[48] Bernardo even wrote to his uncle about the convenience of keeping him in New Orleans.[49] But then Eduardo disappeared for two years without supplying any more information. When he suddenly returned in February 1779, he was immediately dismissed.[50] Another case of a disappearing spy was a certain Eligio de la Puente, who vanished after sending several reports with information of little or no importance.[51] As irrelevant or useless as the work of Miguel Eduardo or Eligio de la Puente might have been, both seemed to try their best. Such was not the case with Bartolomé Fernández Armesto.

Fernández Armesto's case constituted a big fiasco for Spanish intelligence. Bartolomé Fernández Armesto, if this was even his real name, offered to serve up Jamaica without having to fire a single shot. At the beginning of 1780 he presented himself in this way:

> The knowledge I have acquired during these [travels] and through commerce with foreigners, both American and European, apart from giving me the advantage of learning their languages, has made me elevate my spirit to higher designs, to rendering a very important service to the state which will . . . grant me the esteem of His Majesty (God bless him) and his wise ministers. . . . [I offer myself] to sow discord among the inhabitants of the islands of Jamaica and Tortola, raising a civil war that will keep busy and destroy the ground and naval forces that the British have in those parts, in such a way that will make them welcome the arrival of Spanish forces . . . on the understanding that I will be given funds only for my own sustenance for the duration of the operation and for spy ships to send information to our people.[52]

The possibility of conquering Jamaica in such a cheap and easy manner was difficult to resist. Shortly after receiving Fernández Armesto's offer, José de Gálvez instructed Santo Domingo's governor to start preparing for an invasion of Jamaica.[53] With his usual micromanagement he even determined the secret passwords to be used by those involved in the operation: "king" and "Spain."[54] Ten days later he ordered 5,000 pesos to be delivered to Fernández Armesto.[55] Months passed without any news about a slave rebellion in Jamaica. A year later the spy received another 400 pesos and a ship for sending his reports to Cuba. But by this time he was already under suspicion. From Havana, Juan Manuel de Cagigal wrote Bernardo de Gálvez several times warning him about Fernández Armesto.[56] José de Gálvez instructed Cuba's governor that "if he demands more [money] without delivering any results, his conduct will be examined and he is to be arrested in that place [Havana]."[57] By the end of 1781 it was clear that everything had been a hoax.

In May 1782 Bernardo de Gálvez met Fernández Armesto, and the spy could not have made a worse impression. According to Bernardo de Gálvez, "this individual, who I have been informed by Havana did not conduct himself or operate in accordance with the hopes and promises he had made, presented himself to me on his return from Jamaica. Indeed, his boisterous and unsound character has aroused my suspicions about his offers and information, as well as his [lack of] discretion and the expenses he has incurred. ... I have decided that it is best to keep him under surveillance so as not to waste the expense already paid or to lose any eventual fruit that his mission could render. When these are clear, there will be time enough to deal with him as we see fit."[58]

To understand how Fernández Armesto was able to fool so many important people for so long, he must be situated in the context of the Spanish obsession with Jamaica. Later I will return to Bernardo de Gálvez's employment of agents and spies during his campaign against Pensacola.[59] For the time being, it is relevant to add something on cost. As the Duke of Marlborough stated in 1712, intelligence is expensive.[60] Gálvez had to justify time and again the expenses he incurred in this area, such the 400,000 pesos he received in 1782 for "secret commissions."[61]

REORGANIZATION OF LOUISIANA'S MILITARY

Before considering Bernardo de Gálvez's reorganization of Louisiana's military forces, it is relevant to remember that one of his main priorities was to prepare the province for war against Britain, a task that involved not only reforming the military but also securing the loyalty of the local population to the Spanish Crown—a loyalty that was far from a given fact.

The territorial adjustments in North America following the 1763 Treaty of Paris (especially the transfer of Louisiana from France to Spain and of West Florida from Spain to Britain) confronted both Britain and Spain with the challenge of governing territories and populations that had been previously subjected to the sovereignty of another empire—an imperial adaptation that not only would involve the former and the new rulers of a particular territory but also would illustrate how the new authorities had to negotiate with the local populations. This negotiation required important transformations and even deep changes in the British and Spanish imperial models.[62]

Immediately after the Seven Years' War, France was forced to surrender its most septentrional North American possessions. Nonetheless, France was more than willing to transfer its southern ones to Spain. Louisiana was an extremely unproductive colony; in fact, when it was offered to Spain in compensation for its territorial losses after the war, the Spanish ministers long debated about the convenience of accepting it. It was a potentially poisonous gift. Besides the financial cost of supporting a new colony, there was also the danger of overstretching Spanish territory in North America, but the scenario of a British Louisiana determined that, in the end, the Spanish government took possession of Louisiana in order to use it as a buffer zone against the British colonies in North America.

The first years of the Spanish rule in Louisiana could not have been less auspicious. A combination of its first governor's ineptitude and the local population's resentment against new rulers triggered a revolt in 1768. After its suppression, the Spanish government embarked on an aggressive program of reforms in the province. This program needed to produce radical changes in a short period of time, since Spain knew that Louisiana was to play a major role in the next phase of the centuries-old British-Spanish confrontation in the Americas. This program also needed to take into account the peculiarities of Louisiana, where customs, institutions, and social and economic structures were, in some cases, very different from those of the American territories that had been ruled by Spain for more than two and a half centuries. In this dialogue at ground level between the new Spanish authorities and the population of Louisiana, each side would pursue its own interests, both taking advantage of their respective strengths. Far from simply being imposed on those governed, the state's authority in this dialogue had to be almost constantly negotiated, and in this negotiation the Spanish authorities had one clear priority: to win the support of the Louisianans in the upcoming war with Britain. The Spanish authorities had to identify the different interests of each social group and then decide which was more strategic to them in order to eventually accommodate its demands, if possible. In this complex process, Bernardo de Gálvez would demonstrate an exceptional capability for adaptation.[63]

When Gálvez arrived in Louisiana, the province was unable to defend itself against a British attack. To go on the offensive, much more had to be done.[64] Gilbert C. Din maintains that until 1776, the objective of the Spanish military presence in Louisiana was not to defend it but merely to assert the sovereignty of Spain on the western bank of the Mississippi River.[65] The main role of Spanish troops was to underscore Spanish claims to the country's newest American territory. Among what John Walton Caughey has called the "misunderstandings" between Louisiana's first governor, Antonio de Ulloa, and the local population, which were at the origin of the 1768 revolt, the absence of a visible military force was key.[66] This was an error that Ulloa's successor, General Alejandro O'Reilly, did not make when he arrived in New Orleans with 2,000 soldiers, three frigates, and five more warships.[67]

Such a display of power alone quickly put an end to the aspirations of the "driving forces and accomplices of the revolt."[68] O'Reilly laid the foundations for Louisiana's defenses, which Bernardo de Gálvez would find on his arrival. Most of the troops were posted in New Orleans, ending their previous costly dispersion.[69] O'Reilly also effectively raised the Fixed Infantry Battalion of Louisiana, which until then had existed only on paper. So while Luis de Unzaga's governorship was a relaxed period in which economic and social concerns were paramount and military considerations were left aside, the situation that Bernardo de Gálvez inherited was now completely different. As Bibiano Torres Ramírez points out, Spain's way of thinking about Louisiana changed when war broke out between Britain and its American colonies. It also coincided with the appointment of a minister of the Indies, José de Gálvez. Now the Spanish Crown needed more information. Spain was worried that the two warring sides would be able to sort out their differences and jointly attack Spanish Louisiana.[70]

The first measure taken by Bernardo de Gálvez was to continue repairs urged by José de Gálvez of the wooden palisades in New Orleans and at the San Juan Bayou fort. According to O'Reilly, these defenses were completely useless because the wooden structures rapidly decayed in the local climate.[71] But Bernardo de Gálvez had no choice but to obey his uncle's command.[72] He was learning his way around the Spanish colonial administration and knew by now that once the money had been allocated for a certain project, it was almost impossible to stop it from flowing. So instead of halting construction on the palisades, he demanded more funds to build several warships: "A couple of frigates would be of more use in the river than any other type of vessel. Since frigates can move by sail and oars, we will be superior to any warship that can enter through the river entrance. Because of its shallowness, they must be small and armed with twelve-pound cannons, which will allow them to choose their position and distance, from which they can inflict more damage on the enemy while receiving none themselves."[73]

The gunboats and the two frigates were enough to protect New Orleans, but they could not defend the mouth of the Mississippi or control the ships crossing through nearby waters. For this purpose, Bernardo de Gálvez asked for another warship to be sent from Havana.[74] A short time later, the frigate *Volante* was delivered with orders to remain under Bernardo de Gálvez's command until further notice.[75] In addition, in August 1777 Madrid ordered the governor of Cuba to dispatch to Louisiana a frigate and another small vessel.[76]

In 1776 gunpowder, empty gun carriages, and other items had arrived,[77] but cannons and handguns were still needed, although in truth there were not many men to arm. Nearly two decades later, in 1794, Francisco Sabatini estimated that "the number of troops I deem essential to guard the province in question [Louisiana] is four thousand veteran soldiers, most of them to be garrisoned in New Orleans," to which he thought that another 8,000 militiamen must be added.[78] Such troop numbers were considered essential in 1794, when the threat came from the newly established United States of America. But in 1777 the menace was Great Britain, a much more powerful adversary. So is reasonable to assume that the minimal number of troops needed for the defense of Spanish Louisiana at the end of the 1770s was much greater than Sabatini's estimate. In any case, the troops at Bernardo de Gálvez's disposal on his arrival in Louisiana were far fewer than Sabatini's recommendation. In order to secure a proper defense of the province, he would need both professional soldiers and militiamen enlisted in infantry, cavalry, and artillery units. Let us take a closer look at those troops.

THE FIXED INFANTRY REGIMENT OF LOUISIANA

When Bernardo de Gálvez disembarked in New Orleans as a colonel of the Fixed Infantry Regiment of Louisiana, the unit was a regiment on paper only since an infantry regiment needed at least two battalions.[79] The origin of the Louisiana's Fixed Infantry Battalion dated back to the time of Ulloa's governorship, when Madrid ordered its creation with twelve Spanish and twenty-four French officers under the command of a lieutenant colonel.[80] After suppressing the 1768 revolt, Alejandro O'Reilly decided to reinforce the battalion with troops from the Aragon, Guadalajara, and Milan Regiments. He was able to form eight companies with 8 officers, 19 sergeants, 7 drummers, 26 corporals, and 363 privates. Shortly afterward, they were joined by another 179 men from the Lisbon Regiment, who made the total force of the battalion more than 600 men (412 of the men were European Spaniards and the rest from other origins but mostly from Louisiana).[81] Under Governor Unzaga the battalion was neglected, along with many other official matters. Despite receiving a reinforcement of 100 privates in 1770, that same year the battalion had only 400 men, less than a third of the total number prescribed for a battalion by royal ordinances. According to the Reales Ordenanzas (Royal Military Regulations), infantry regiments must have at least two battalions. Each battalion consisted of nine companies (66 grenadiers and 80 regular infantrymen) and a staff of several officers, noncommissioned officers, and other servicemen. Taking this into account, the minimum number of men in an infantry regiment was 1,446.[82]

Gálvez's arrival, according to Juan José Andreu Ocariz, brought about a radical change.[83] He was colonel of a regiment, so he needed one—not just an emaciated battalion. Since a regiment is formed by at least two battalions, he had to fill all of the vacancies in the existing battalion before moving on to create a second one. The state of this first battalion was very sad. In a letter to his uncle José dated June 1778, Bernardo informed him that it was almost without personnel and most of its soldiers were near retirement age.[84] In May 1779 he confessed that the total force of the first battalion was only 14 officers and 439 men.[85] As he desperately needed more men, Madrid ordered that more soldiers be recruited in the Canary Islands and New Spain.

From the Canary Islands, 700 men were expected to arrive. Each of them, according to instructions sent to the recruitment parties by the king's lieutenant of Santa Cruz de Tenerife—Matías de Gálvez, Bernardo's father, who was a sort of second military commander of Tenerife Island[86]—was to be "robust, without any noticeable imperfection or injury, no indecorous vice, nor vile origin: mulatto, gipsy, executioner, butcher by trade, or convicted by justice."[87] The first contingent of recruits did not arrive in America until November 1778. In July of the following year, Bernardo de Gálvez informed Madrid that of the 1,582 immigrants arriving from the Canary Islands, only 153 men were incorporated into the regiment, as they were unmarried, whereas the remaining 329 married men along with 1,100 women and children were assumed to be settlers.[88]

Recruitment in New Spain was not much easier, due to the huge difference between Mexico and Louisiana in terms of both the soldiers' salaries and the cost of living.[89] This was the reason that by July 1779 only 109 recruits had arrived from New Spain.[90] Nevertheless, by that time Bernardo de Gálvez was able to consider the first battalion formally filled and raise the second one, despite being 218 men short.[91]

Another important feature of the Louisiana Regiment was its roster of officers. Most of the officers in the first battalion came from other Spanish military units, and only a few were from Louisiana, whereas in the second battalion the majority were locals. The local recruitment of officers was quite a different matter from the recruitment of privates. Whereas soldiers signed up for the Spanish army, the officers had to buy their commissions. In fact, Bernardo de Gálvez raised the price of commissions to 4,000 pesos for the privilege of becoming a captain, 2,000 for a lieutenant, and 1,000 for an ensign.[92] The idea behind this inflation, besides replenishing the always-meager Royal Treasury, was to ensure that the Louisiana Fixed Infantry Regiment was formed with the scions of New Orleans's elite families.

There were several reasons why Creoles not only in Louisiana but also all over Spanish America rushed to become officers in the Spanish army.

Contemporary drawing of the flag of the Louisiana Fixed Infantry Regiment, whose first colonel was Bernardo de Gálvez. Its design follows the traditional pattern for regimental flags in the Spanish army during the second half of the eighteenth century, with the red St. Andrew's cross topped with the regimental coat of arms, in this case the one awarded to Spanish Louisiana. (*Diseño de la bandera del Regimiento de Infantería fijo de la Luisiana*, Archivo General de Indias, Estado 41091, Mapas y Planos-banderas, 4; Ministerio de Educación, Cultura y Deporte, Archivo General de Indias)

According to Anthony McFarlane, they sought military commissions both for the prestige attached to the military and for the possibility of further promotions.[93] Other historians also mention the allure of the legal status conferred on members of the military at the time.[94] Among the privileges granted to officers was that they could be tried only before a military court—which meant, for example, that officers could not be imprisoned for debt. According to the 1768 Royal Army regulations, to become a cadet an applicant had to prove his noble status, have means enough to "decently provide for himself," or be the son of a captain.[95] In other words, if a family member obtained an officer's commission in the army, the rest of his family was also presumed to be of noble condition. Thus for creole families, having their sons wear the white and blue uniform of the Louisiana Fixed Infantry Regiment became an important source of pride as well as privilege.[96]

In addition to an infantry regiment, defense of New Orleans required mounted troops and artillery units. Although the cavalry Company of Louisiana, also known as New Orleans's Dragoons, was not created by Bernardo de Gálvez until 1780, it is included here to give a full picture of all of the units under his command as Louisiana's governor.[97] It was formed with a captain, a lieutenant, an under-lieutenant, two sergeants, a drummer, and twenty-five corporals and cavalrymen from dragoon regiments of Spain and Mexico.[98]

Although Bernardo de Gálvez tried to supply New Orleans's forts and defenses with proper regular artillery units, he did not have much success until the war with Britain began. Before then he could count only on a small artillery unit formed by two captains, one lieutenant, one under-lieutenant, a sergeant, and twelve artillerymen.[99]

To raise and strengthen regular army units such as the Louisiana Fixed Infantry Regiment, Bernardo de Gálvez needed the active involvement of authorities in Madrid. But with the militias he had much more freedom to act by himself. For this reason, the militias were a major focus of his efforts during his first months as governor. The first militias had been created during the government of Alejandro O'Reilly.[100] In 1770 O'Reilly considered a minimum of 700 militiamen necessary to protect Louisiana,[101] but on his arrival Bernardo de Gálvez found fewer than 175.[102] Since every man between fifteen and forty-five years of age was forced to serve in the militia, Bernardo de Gálvez needed to know exactly what Louisiana's population was to properly evaluate its recruitment potential.[103] For this purpose he turned to the May 1777 census, which identified 1,956 male settlers as able to bear arms.[104] With this figure in mind, he began an aggressive recruitment campaign both for the already existing unit as well as for new ones. The results were impressive. At the beginning of 1779, Louisiana had seventeen militia companies enrolled in several units, with a total of 1,478 men, including the New Orleans Infantry Militia Battalion, the New Orleans Artillery Militia Company, and the New Orleans Colored Militias.[105]

The New Orleans Infantry Militia Battalion had its origin in five infantry companies created in 1770 by Alejandro O'Reilly, each with a captain, a lieutenant, an ensign, a drummer, and sixty soldiers. In 1775 the unit was reinforced with another four companies to establish a battalion having one company of grenadiers and four of fusiliers for a total strength of about 600 men.[106] The New Orleans Artillery Militia Company was created in 1769, based on a previous French unit created in 1760. In 1777 the unit was reinstated, and in 1780 the former French captain Nicolás Favre D'Aunoy was appointed its commander.[107] The company had one captain, one lieutenant, one under-lieutenant, three sergeants, and sixty-five corporals and artillerymen.[108] The New Orleans Colored Militias were formed by a company of *pardos* (mulattoes) and another company of *morenos* (blacks, literally "of dark skin"), each with a captain, a lieutenant, an ensign, three sergeants, and eighty-seven corporals and privates.[109] If white Creoles found the incentives for enrolling in the military attractive, for free blacks and mulattoes in Louisiana they must have been almost irresistible. The legal status conferred by Spanish military law made their social position higher than that of poor white Creoles. Kimberly S. Hanger maintains that the colored militias "played a vital military role from the perspective both of the Spanish government and [of] the free population of color itself."[110]

Militias were raised not only in New Orleans. Other places in Louisiana had their own military units as well: Costa de Cabahanose (one company), Fourche de Chetimaches (one company), Valenzuela (one company), Costa de Iberville (one company), Galveztown (one company), Costa de Punta Cortada (two companies), Atakapas (one company), Pelouzas (one company), Nachitoches (one infantry company and one cavalry company), Onachita [*sic*: Ouachita] (one company), San Luis de Ilinueses (St. Louis, Missouri) (two companies), Santa Genoveva de Ilinoa (one company), Avaoyees [*sic*: Avoyelles] (half a company), and Costa Alemanes (two companies).[111]

The list of militias created by Bernardo de Gálvez ends with two more cavalry units. The Cavalry Company of Saint Louis, created in 1779 in San Luis de Ilinueses (present-day St. Louis, Missouri), had fifty-three members. The other unit was the New Orleans Militia Company of Distinguished Carabineros, created in 1779 with "the cream of the city's society."[112] Jack D. Holmes says about this militia unit that it was specifically designed to have "snob appeal." According to Holmes, the wealthy Creoles did not want to serve in military units with their shoemakers or barbers, so Bernardo de Gálvez decided to organize a company of cavalry formed of the most prominent men in New Orleans and environs with Gálvez himself as its captain so that they might enlist with greater goodwill.[113] In the beginning the men were armed only with cavalry sabers, but Gálvez later provided them with muskets and pistols at state expense. In addition, he requested a shipment of saddles, bridles, and other harnesses. The first group of forty-nine men paid for their uniforms and tack from their own pockets.[114]

THE FIGHT AGAINST CONTRABAND

According to John Walton Caughey, "Contraband trade with the English, especially the American English, had become a habit with the Louisianans, and a privilege which they cherished dearly."[115] The Spanish authorities had a completely different view of the matter, but the official policy was watered down because of lax implementation by royal civil servants on site, who either succumbed to the temptation of easy money or simply avoided confrontation by looking away.[116] To be fair, it was also true that even if Governor Ulloa had tried to control the contraband trade, he did not have the means to do so. Under Governor O'Reilly, the reinforced Spanish military presence in the colony was enough to reduce it significantly.[117] However, Governor Unzaga, Gálvez's predecessor, took a completely different tack. According to Charles Gayarré, one of Louisiana's first official historians, "Unzaga acted judiciously for the province and for Spain when he disregarded the Chinese-like regulations that he was commanded to enforce and winked at their violation."[118] It was a wink that, in the opinion of the anonymous author of the *Mémoire sur la Louisiane*, published in Paris in 1792, "left the impression [in the colony] of having served Louisiana's interests well *without neglecting his own* [italics in the original]."[119] The situation in 1775 was perfectly described by a French settler named La Frénière, who wrote that "we smuggle without problem, we sail by boat to ships to find everything we need."[120]

Under Bernardo de Gálvez, such impunity could no longer continue, but the issue was quite complex. In 1782 Martín Navarro, the head of the Royal Treasury in Louisiana, wrote a report titled "Political Considerations on the Present State of the Province of Louisiana" in which he described the situation at the time of Gálvez's arrival: "What a pain for a zealous governor like Don Bernardo de Gálvez, witnessing this heinous trade and not being able to take any measures without endangering either the sovereign authority [of Spain] or the happiness of the Province! What a conundrum without any solution but to keep the status quo! Sad consolation!"[121]

Among the various obligations stated in his orders as Louisiana's governor was to fight contraband by pardoning previous offences but warning clearly that this kind of activity would not be tolerated in the future.[122] In fact, contraband and commerce were but two sides of the same economic coin. The distance between them was not in the conscience of the economic agent or the lawmaker but simply in risk and cost analysis. In this context, any measures taken against smuggling would have to be accompanied by others promoting legal commerce.

So it was not a coincidence that the first step taken by Bernardo de Gálvez was to design a new general framework for commerce. It was to be a system in which, "as an exception to the just prohibition established in the laws of the Indies, which do not allow its subjects to directly or indirectly trade with foreigners," commercial exchanges between New Orleans and France and its American colonies were authorized on the condition that they were supervised by two French commissioners, were subject to a 5 percent tax, and took place in the presence of Spanish guardsmen on board ships, including the French ones.[123] Although it has been suggested that the measure was a limited trial for a later, more extensive liberalization of Spanish trade, in fact there is not enough evidence to support this attractive theory.[124] The new Louisiana trade regulation should more precisely be understood as a specific exception made in the particular context of the colony.[125] The trade regime for Louisiana later was expanded to allow direct commerce with New Spain through the port of Veracruz.[126] The benefits of this new trade regime for Louisiana were increased by its "generous" implementation by Bernardo de Gálvez. According to one of the two French commissioners, "the facilities granted by M. de Galvez to trade between Louisiana and the French islands, and also the liberal interpretation given by him to clauses of the treaty, have revived the industry and activity of merchants and planters, and opened a brilliant prospect to the colony."[127]

With the merchants as satisfied as they could be, it was time to move against the smugglers. Perfectly aware of Spanish political priorities for Louisiana, Bernardo de Gálvez decided not to fight all contraband trade, which would have been very costly, but to target that carried out by British citizens—which, to the injury of being conducted by subjects of Spain's sworn enemy, added the insult of depriving the Spanish Royal Treasury of much-needed taxes. In other words, the campaign against English smugglers in the Mississippi River should be understood as an economic measure as much as a strategic and political one.

Gálvez's generosity had convinced everyone that his tenure as governor would be as profitable for merchants and smugglers as Unzaga's had been. Nothing was further from the truth. He was simply waiting for an opportunity to strike, and it came, according to his own record, in April 1777, when a British ship seized a Spanish merchant ship with a consignment of tar for Havana.[128] The public uproar against the British was the opportunity Gálvez needed. Following his orders, Spanish troops boarded all English ships docked between La Balize and Manchac, in the estuary of the Mississippi, on the night of April 14, 1777. Of the fifteen ships, two managed to escape. Two others were the property of American rebels, but because of the difficulty of determining their proper ownership these too were seized. A few days later the thirteen ships and their cargoes were auctioned off for 53,000 pesos. Some 6,000 pesos had to be used to reimburse the American owners of the two ships, thanks to the intervention of Oliver Pollock, a key figure in the American Revolution in the South, who would work closely with Bernardo de Gálvez.[129]

Before April ended, Gálvez received a letter from Thomas Lloyd, commander of HMS *Atalanta*, in which he demanded to know "the reasons for this unexpected behavior, since it is my duty (having the honor of commanding one of His Majesty's warships) to be informed about the details of the matter."[130] Gálvez responded that it was a matter simply of Spanish trade along the Mississippi River.[131] According to contemporaneous testimonies cited by Caughey, on April 21, 1777, Captain Lloyd had stopped two merchant ships, one Spanish and the other French, opening fire against the first and boarding the second. Lloyd alleged that they were trading with American rebels.[132] After inspecting the French vessel for several hours, he let it continue its voyage. This incident was followed by a heated correspondence between Gálvez and Lloyd, which ended with a meeting between the two men. In his own words, the Spanish governor received Lloyd "with the fuse in my hand."[133]

Despite his defiant attitude, Gálvez was in a difficult position. For the British to threaten New Orleans, it was enough for them only to send another warship. To prevent this from happening he soothed the British governor of Pensacola by sending him 150 barrels of flour to help the local population, which was suffering from a food shortage during an epidemic.[134] The tense situation was eventually resolved with the help of British merchants in New Orleans, who, instead of siding with the British captain, recommended that Lloyd should leave things as they were, since they were convinced that Gálvez's seizure of the eleven British merchant ships had only been an impulsive reaction to the incident with the ship transporting tar to Havana. They even reminded Captain Lloyd that "British subjects here have been treated with the largest indulgence; every privilege we could have wished for has been fully granted, and from the well-known generosity and humanity of this gentleman [Gálvez] we have reason to expect that these advantages will last for a long time."[135] After this Captain Lloyd had no choice but to leave New Orleans under the pretext that he needed to pursue an American corsair ship sighted at the mouth of the Mississippi.

According to David Narrett, since Gálvez had no real military force to confront the British, he had to rely "on subterfuge and bluff, parrying British protests with rhetorical outrage, sharp aphorisms, and legalistic rejoinders."[136] He was so successful in this maneuver that British merchants in New Orleans trusted without reserve the Spanish justice in New Orleans, confident that in their courts they would receive a fair hearing. Ten years later their case would be dismissed. During the months following the seizure of the merchant ships, Gálvez seemed to continue his "indulgence" toward the British merchants. A few days after HMS *Atalanta* set sail, they expressed their satisfaction that trade had returned to normal.[137] In May they even mentioned the "contraband trade, a trade that hath for years past (on their paying a small share of the profits) been connived at, and even this Governor [Gálvez] who hath not been long appointed to the Government, had connived at it, until this period."[138] Their satisfaction was to be short-lived, though. That same month Gálvez published a whole battery of legislation opening up Louisiana's trade with Yucatán and Cuba, reducing the *almojarifazgo* (customs tariff) from 5 to 2 percent, and granting slave import licenses to French merchants.[139] In July 1778 the French commissioners in Louisiana informed Paris that "the British flag has not appeared in this river for more than three months, or, at least, it is only to be seen flying at the mast-head of a frigate destined to protect the Manchac settlement. The duties paid by our ships on their coming here are reduced every day, because the Spaniards are made more tractable by their need for our commerce. Finally all the trade of the Mississippi is now in our hands."[140]

The privileges granted to Louisiana's French merchants left their British counterparts with few alternatives. Some decided to continue their business with a little more caution. It was not always easy, as Robert Ross and John Campbell, a pair of Scottish merchant-smugglers, found out when they lost everything and their partner, Alexander Grayden, landed in a Cuban jail.[141] Others opted to join the winning side, including James Jones, who pledged allegiance to Spain while his brother remained a loyal British subject, at least until the die of the American Revolution was finally cast.[142] As Caughey writes, Gálvez's interpretation and implementation of the new Spanish commercial policy almost ended all English contraband trade with Louisiana even before Spain entered the war against Great Britain in 1779.[143]

INDIAN POLICY

As already seen, when Alejandro O'Reilly informed José de Gálvez of his intention to appoint José's nephew Bernardo as colonel of the Louisiana Fixed Infantry Regiment, he mentioned Bernardo's experience in Indian affairs: "Since Louisiana is next to Mexico's presidios on the frontier, the practical knowledge that this officer has acquired of the Indians and the terrain will be useful in pacifying or employing them as appropriate to the service."[144] Under the apparently simple phrase "in pacifying or employing them as appropriate to the service" was hidden a huge complexity. "Pacifying them" could be interpreted to mean the Spanish authorities' effective control of the Indians by incorporating them into the social structure designed for Spanish America. "Employing them as appropriate to the service" clearly states the Spanish priority at the time: preparing for war with the British, for which the Indians were considered essential. In designing means and policies directed toward these aims, Bernardo de Gálvez played a vital role, not only as governor of Louisiana but also later on when he was posted to the viceroyalty of New Spain. His previous experience with Indians on the northern frontier of New Spain and his family link to the supreme authority on all American affairs, the minister of the Indies, determined that his views were not only listened to carefully but also finally adopted as the Crown's official policy.[145] The result would be a whole new model of relations between Native American groups and Spanish authorities—a model that broke with traditional policies that had been in force for centuries all over Spanish America.

The presence of indigenous peoples in the borderlands of the empire always represented a challenge for Spanish authorities. For those who lived within the empire's confines, the general policy was integration into the American model of society, within which, according to Juan de Solórzano Pereira, arguably the most important political and legal theorist of Spanish American law, "the two republics of Spaniards and Indians are together today and form one body, both in the spiritual and the temporal realms."[146] The historian Abelardo Levaggi develops this idea further when he states that these two republics shared the same superior authorities and the same *derecho indiano* (Spanish law for the Spanish Americas), including the same political constitution, and under that common legal-political framework, each one had its own local authorities and laws.[147] According to Levaggi, the final objective was to create a *sociedad indiana* (Spanish-American society), where the native element would merge with the Spanish, both the spiritual as well as the temporal.[148] The differences between the French, British, and Spanish colonial models have been abundantly studied, and on the topic of Indian policy, the Spanish model could not be more different from the

French and British ones.¹⁴⁹ For John H. Elliott, in the Spanish borderlands a policy of inclusion was practiced, while in the British and to a great extent the French regions, the norm was exclusion.¹⁵⁰ The policy of exclusion or separate societies was structured on trade and regular gift-giving aimed at attracting indigenous communities with the design of blocking interference by other European colonial powers in their spheres of influence.¹⁵¹ The British and French models were severely tested in the Seven Years' War, during which both sides used any means necessary (appeals to honor, gifts, bribery, coercion, threats, and so on) to ensure indigenous peoples' loyalty in a war in which traditional European military tactics were not useful. Such irregular warfare was not completely new to the French and British armies, but during this conflict it would be taken to a completely new level. Combat took place in deep forests, where it was impossible to deploy the close-order lines of the infantry and where artillery fire was useless. Surprise attacks and guerrilla tactics made the Indians, who knew the territory intimately, better suited for this kind of war, and thus their services were in high demand.¹⁵² No wonder many groups took advantage of the opportunity to offer their services to the highest bidder.

As stated by Colin G. Calloway, the special conditions of Louisiana and the gathering storm between Spain and Britain demanded a specific Indian policy for the Spanish colony.¹⁵³ The policy needed to be oriented not toward the integration of the Indian communities, as in the Spanish-American model, but simply at controlling them or at least preventing their use by the enemy. The idea of adopting the French and British models did not originate with Bernardo de Gálvez. Much earlier, several Spanish officials had expressed their opinion that it would make sense. In Louisiana, Alejandro O'Reilly retained the French system implemented by former French subjects such as Athanase de Mézières.¹⁵⁴ The Spanish Indian policy in Louisiana had multiple objectives, of which Herbert Eugene Bolton mentions ten.¹⁵⁵ First and foremost among them was to attract the Indians to the Spanish side in the event of war. Gálvez was perfectly aware of this. In January 1777, he wrote to his uncle José:

> With the existing forces in this province, it is not possible to resist the slightest enemy attack without the Indians on our side. . . . All of the northern part of this province is covered by a multitude of Indian nations settled in British territory, living with the same unrestraint and freedom as all of the other Indians in New Spain, without any loyalty or friendship but to those who give them more; with this in mind, and in the event that war breaks with the British, it is necessary (even at

all costs) to attract the savages to our side. This, I think, will not be extremely difficult, for two reasons. First, because even today they have a certain attachment to the French, with whom they have lived many years; and second, after being properly pampered with our gifts, they will agree to everything we ask of them.[156]

In October of the following year he was less optimistic but insisted that the right course of action was to focus on trade and gifts:

> The experience I have acquired since my arrival in this colony about the way the British and French treat or have treated their Indians forces me to wish that in our own territories they would be treated the same way. I do not know if under the present conditions they could be kept on our side with gifts. . . . [But if this system could be applied] in our Interior Provinces [of New Spain], the Indians will forget how to make war against us, and if certain luxuries are introduced to them they could not, as happens in this province [Louisiana], be able to live without us, since they will have learned the comforts of a life previously unknown to them, which from that moment on they will regard as essential.[157]

Among these "certain luxuries," Bernardo de Gálvez intended several that Spanish law had expressly forbidden or restricted for Indians, such as guns, ammunition, and alcohol. In his January 1777 letter to his uncle, he warned that "maybe Your Excellency will be shocked by the inclusion of ammunition [among the list of merchandise to be presented as gifts], but you should not be when you consider that the English now and always have supplied them with more than they could ever use, since this is the main item of their trade and the one that the savages appreciate the most."[158]

The supply of guns was essential because the Indians were already receiving them from the British. According to Gálvez, the Indians of Louisiana were already "used to the fire guns and black powder presented to them, [and] they have forgotten the use and construction of their bows and arrows, not knowing other kinds of arms besides those that we [Europeans] give them, thus being subject to the event of being disarmed and dying of hunger from the very moment the European nations commonly decide to stop giving them the black powder they need."[159]

Bernardo de Gálvez knew firsthand the dangers of Indian arrows, and he preferred to fight Indians armed with guns rather than with their traditional weapons. Even though the law forbade Indians from possessing guns,[160] in Louisiana there was actually no choice, since they had already been supplied with guns by the French, and if the Spaniards did not give them guns they would simply turn to the British—which the Spanish could not afford.

The alcohol trade also was against traditional Spanish Indian policy, which permitted their traditional spirits, such as pulque in Mexico,[161] but forbade the consumption of European beverages such as wine[162] or *aguardiente* (any kind of liquor). In his letter to his uncle, Bernardo de Gálvez mentions the liquor trade as a usual practice among the Indians.

Besides trade, the other leg that supported European relations with the Indians was gifts, and the ability to provide both would be crucial in determining the Indian support for either side during the war.[163] The role played by gifts in traditional societies has been extensively studied by Marcel Mauss, who has shown that in theory they are voluntary, disinterested, and spontaneous but are in fact obligatory and given in expectation of receiving benefits.[164] As Bernardo de Gálvez stated to his uncle, the Spaniards had used gifts since the very beginning of their presence in America.[165] The sixteenth-century conquistador Bernardo de Vargas Machuca wrote a treatise on the best ways to subdue the native populations based on his experiences in what is today Colombia and Venezuela. In his *Indian Militia and Description of the Indies*, he advised would-be conquistadors to "present them with the trade items that they esteem, for all they desire is of such little value; there are no children who love toys more, with which they are so quickly contented."[166] Since those early days the practice of giving and receiving gifts had been regulated through rituals that determined what kind of merchandise should be presented in what way, on what occasions, and so forth. In May 1781, while besieging the English forts in Pensacola, Bernardo de Gálvez remembered that "one of my first concerns from the moment I arrived in the Province of Louisiana was to cultivate the friendship of the very numerous Indian nations around her."[167] In this same document he stressed the importance of that friendship not only for Louisiana but also for "all the king's other possessions in the vast empire of Mexico."[168] Gálvez believed that without "good harmony with the savages" it would be impossible to develop agriculture, and "the settlers will abandon their lands and those countries will perish little by little."[169] To ensure good harmony, Gálvez implemented a policy that followed the French and British models from the early days of Louisiana. But when this policy started to deliver its first results, he complained that "in those critical moments I lacked products and merchandise to give them, and the British, who had them in abundance, succeeded in luring a great part of the above-mentioned Indians, who had previously embraced the Spanish party."[170] This loss of support from the Indians would make things very difficult in his military campaigns and would lead to many casualties among his troops.

Among the most interesting of the different gifts that Europeans used to seal the loyalty of different indigenous groups were the Indian peace medals.[171] Giving medals to North American native populations was a practice that had started by the end of the seventeenth century. Among the discoveries in the excavations of a Native American settlement in Scipioville, in upstate New York,[172] where there was a Jesuit mission between 1756 and 1787, were several Mexican-made medals coined in honor of the beatification (1668) and canonization (1671) of Saint Rosa of Lima.[173] But in fact the first documented use of Indian peace medals was by the French. In the 1690s they began to present medals to the Indians honoring the 1693 birth of the dauphin, heir to the French throne.[174] These medals were later replaced by another medal specifically designed for the purpose of presentation to the natives.[175] The British soon joined in, coining their first medals in 1714 to commemorate the friendship between Great Britain and indigenous peoples.[176] The Indian peace medals so embodied the loyalty of a particular native group to their colonial power that when these loyalties changed, the medals had to change, too. The old ones were given away and new ones received. When this was not possible, the problem was solved simply by effacing the name of the former European friend or monarch and engraving a new one. Thus there are samples of a 1714 French Indian medal on which the name "LUDOVICUS XV, REX CHRISTIANISSIMUS" has been replaced by "GORGE [sic] III."[177]

By the middle of the eighteenth century the practice of presenting medals was so common that when Louisiana passed into Spanish hands, the new rulers had no choice but to continue it. In the autumn of 1769 the Spanish governor Alejandro O'Reilly had a meeting with representatives of several Indian groups, during which they asked that the new authorities continue to extend the same benefits and favors that they had received from the French. The meeting concluded with O'Reilly "bestowing medals hanging from a scarlet ribbon around the necks of several Indian chiefs."[178] The medals given by O'Reilly were ones known as *al mérito* (for merit), first coined in 1764.[179] Some samples of these medals are still found in museums and private collections in the southern United States, and they represent both the authority of the particular chief who received the medal[180] and his group's loyalty to Spain.[181] But the 1764 Spanish Indian peace medal had a flaw. In 1771, when Fernando de Leyba, representative of the Spanish Crown in Illinois, presented one of these medals to Cazenonpoint, chief of the Quapaw, he refused it and asked instead for the French medal, since it was bigger.[182] To avoid a repeat of such a snub, Bernardo de Gálvez asked for larger medals to be coined.[183] Almost immediately, on August 22, 1777, the royal court sent an order to the Royal Mint for the production of a new *al mérito* medal having a diameter of about two inches rather than the usual one and a half inches.[184] The practice of presenting Indian peace medals was so successful that several years after the Spanish began it, Bernardo de Gálvez had to instruct the authorities in Louisiana that there should be only "one medal chief per tribe."[185]

Indian peace medals were a way to make public a specific indigenous group's loyalty to Spain, but it was not the only way to do so. In a culture so profoundly legalistic as Spain was at the time, Spanish authorities wanted the Indians' commitment in writing, too. These documents had multiple names: peace, parliament, agreement, capitulation, articles of peace, and even treaty, although the latter term should not be interpreted in a strictly legal sense.[186] This method of expanding the boundaries of the Spanish Empire in America was to become so widespread that a historian has labeled it conquest by contract, as opposed to conquest by sword, which had been the norm during the previous two centuries. Historians differ about when this practice started.[187] While Charles Gibson states that in the whole early history of Spanish America he "could not recall anything that could properly be identified as an Indian treaty," Abelardo Levaggi maintains that despite no trace of documentation, the practice of signing agreements with Indians dates back to the Spanish Habsburg dynasty in the sixteenth and seventeenth centuries, adding that under the Bourbon kings in the eighteenth century the model already existed and was only consolidated and expanded.[188] Levaggi concludes that the custom of celebrating peace treaties extended to all borders in the Indies, and during the Hispanic period, it even survived—in certain cases—after the independence of the Latin American nations.[189] David J. Weber maintains that eighteenth-century treaties or agreements between Spaniards and Indians were of a different nature than those celebrated before that time, since they corresponded to a totally new model drawn from the systems that both the French and British had implemented with indigenous peoples in their territories.[190]

Under Bernardo de Gálvez, several of these agreements were signed. For example, after the conquest of Pensacola, the new Spanish governor appointed by Gálvez, Arturo O'Neill, resumed a practice dating back about twenty years by signing a treaty with the Talapuche. In it the tribal members stated "that they were born friends of the Spanish, that their friendship increases in proportion to their ages, that as good sons they arrive to the feet of their father and their protector, in the confidence that they [the Spaniards] would not cheat as the English did... and that they await the promises made by General Gálvez after taking Mobile and that after the conquest of Pensacola they should present themselves to the general to be presented with all kinds of gifts to establish a long-lasting and beneficial peace."[191]

Attracting the loyalty of the indigenous peoples through trade, gifts, or medals was just a part of the challenge. Just as important was ensuring peace among all of the native groups living in the area. This was the context for Bernardo de Gálvez's journey in September 1777 to Punta Cortada (Pointe Coupee), north of Baton Rouge on the west side of the Mississippi River, the aim of which was "to establish peace between two Indian nations."[192] Several months before, the Biloxi had asked for his blessing in declaring war on the Atakapa, who had killed one of their members.[193] The existence of the petition proves that his policy of attracting the Indians to the Spanish side was beginning to bear fruit, since it demonstrates that some groups recognized that the Spanish governor of Louisiana was a personage powerful or relevant enough to settle their disputes with other groups. In Punta Cortada, Gálvez met not only with representatives of the Biloxi and the Atakapa but also with envoys from sixteen other groups.[194] All of them received gifts from the hands of the governor, and he presided over a solemn ceremony in which their chiefs swore allegiance to Spain. Among the items listed as presented in this occasion was a bit of everything: 68 mattocks, 38 small axes, 68 rifles, 139 pounds of gunpowder, 19 dress coats, 16 hats, 2,888 sleigh bells, and 2 cane walking sticks.[195] Later they presented Gálvez with their British Indian peace medals, which he could not exchange for the new Spanish *al mérito* medals, as they would not be ready until the following year.[196] Unfortunately, no documentation has been found about the outcome of Gálvez's mediation between the Biloxi and the Atakapa groups.

When Gálvez was unable to travel, he demanded complete reports from his deputies about negotiations with the Indians, which, at the very least, had to include a list of the different groups along with their characteristics and disposition toward Spain. In December 1777 Francisco Cruzat sent him an exhaustive report from San Luis de Ilinueses (St. Louis), which included a list of the groups that usually went there to receive gifts, the names of their chiefs, the distance and directions to the places they lived, their main occupations, the benefits or injuries they had received in the past, and the names of their enemies.[197]

Step by step, Gálvez's efforts to woo the Indian groups in Louisiana were producing results. In December 1777 a Choctaw delegation asked him for Spanish flags to raise in their villages as proof of their loyalty. But Gálvez declined "for the moment" to "avoid complaints from the court of London if our flag were to be raised in their possessions."[198] Despite the negative answer, the Choctaw persevered in their efforts to show their commitment to Spain. In March of the following year they sent Gálvez another delegation to inform him of their attack on several British settlements as proof that they "want to be Spanish and English no more."[199] The Choctaw's action shows how much a coming war between Spain and Britain was taken for granted by all groups in the region.

We have seen how the Spaniards implemented a model of relations with Native Americans in Louisiana that was imported from the French and the British. But they departed from this model in one important aspect that, at least in theory, would help them in attracting the Indians' loyalty: an absolute and unrestricted prohibition of the practice of Indian slavery.[200] This was in theory because some of the Indian groups that the Spaniards were trying to draw to their camp were themselves involved in slave raiding and, thus, opposed to the end of slave trade. The principle against Indian slavery had deep roots in the so-called Spanish colonial model and dated back several centuries.[201] The last will and testament of Queen Isabel the Catholic, the Castilian monarch under whom Christopher Columbus sailed and discovered the Americas, stated clearly that the Indians should be "well and fairly treated."[202] Pope Paul III's decree or bull *Sublimis Deus*, issued in 1537, settled for good the dispute about the humanity of the Indians by categorically affirming that "all mankind is one."[203] King Felipe IV referred to them as his vassals, under his protection, thus rejecting that they could be considered as slaves.[204] The indigenous peoples had uncompromising defenders in Bartolomé de las Casas, Vasco de Quiroga, and Juan de Matienzo.[205] In the eyes of Spanish law the Indians were free, and any abuses inflicted on their freedom were to be harshly punished by Spanish authorities.[206] This general principle had few and limited exceptions: the Mindanaoans in the Philippines were enslaved because of their Muslim faith; the Caribe Indians because of their anthropophagy; certain groups in Chile and along the River Plate, Argentina, because of their serious rebellions against the Spanish authorities, although their enslavement was later revoked; and the peculiar and exceptional case of the Pijao Indians in today's Colombia, whose slavery lasted for a few months.[207]

In 1732, when Louisiana was still French, the region contained a significant population of Indian slaves. Of 841 slaves noted in the census that year, 161 were Indian and the rest were of African origin.[208] If these percentages were applied to figures in the 1777 census, the total number of Indian slaves would have been about 1,700.[209] But Charles R. Maduell Jr. mentions that there were only 100 slaves in all of the Lower Mississippi at the time, and Stephen Webre calculates the same figure for the previous decade.[210]

Despite all legal regulations, according to Kathleen DuVal, in Spanish Louisiana the prohibition against enslaving Indians was never seriously enforced, and those already in slavery were left in a kind of legal limbo.[211] They were not to be sold, and their servitude was to be terminated when their owners died.[212] This was the original policy implemented by Governor Alejandro O'Reilly, and by the end of the Spanish presence in Louisiana there were no Indian slaves left.[213] Besides protecting the Native Americans from the greed of the southern planters, the policy had the side effect of prompting a significant number of black slaves to demand their freedom in court, claiming that they were of Indian descent. Some of these cases would have to be adjudicated in U.S. courts after Louisiana passed into U.S. hands.[214] Among these cases, the story of Marguerite Scypion is worth mentioning as it would be the first of the so-called freedom suits that would pave the way for the notorious *Dred Scott* case. Marguerite Scypion, who in the legal proceedings is mentioned as "Marguerite, a free woman of color," was a black slave from St. Louis whose grandmother was a Natchez Indian. She argued that since Indian slavery was prohibited by Spanish law, her grandmother had been illegally held as slave. The first ruling in her favor was contested in 1826 by her current master, Jean Pierre Chouteau. Ten years later the original ruling was confirmed at the state level and two years after that by the Supreme Court, which asserted her freedom as well as that of her descendants. This marked the official end to Indian slavery in Missouri.[215]

A final important aspect of the Indian policy designed and implemented by Bernardo de Gálvez in Louisiana was its repercussion in other regions of North America. The royal authorities in Texas constantly complained about their difficult position, which demanded that they fight certain Indian activities that across the border in Louisiana were not only tolerated but encouraged. This tension between varying policies regarding Indian communities resulted in a significant number of Indian populations deciding to vote with their feet by migrating from Texas to Louisiana.[216]

His success in Louisiana made Bernardo de Gálvez an expert in Indian affairs. In October 1778 he was asked for advice by his uncle José. Bernardo expressed doubts about the success of an eventual military campaign against the Indians in the northern Frontier Province: "As many forces engage, they will never be enough to subdue the Apachería [Apache Nation], not in two or in three years."[217] Asked if 2,000 troops would be enough, he answered that it depended on the final objectives of the campaign. It was too many if the aim was to defend a village or a presidio but too few if they were to be sent to defend the entire frontier, because, it must not be forgotten, it spread across a territory "as great as the distance between Madrid and Constantinople." For this reason, Bernardo wondered if it would not be possible to implement with the Apache the same policy he had been developing in Louisiana, where gifts "could keep them happy for ten years with what we spend in one year on war. In our Interior Provinces the advantages would be even greater, because the Indians will forget how to wage war against us as the gifts will introduce a kind of luxury among them through trade. . . . I am fully aware that years will pass before we see the Indians of New Spain's frontier reach this point, and we will probably not see it during our own times, but the life of the kingdom is long."[218]

GOVERNMENT

The distinction between military and civilian governments in Louisiana would always be a bit artificial, for two reasons: first, because the top priority was always to prepare Louisiana for the war against the British; and second, because Bernardo de Gálvez was both supreme military commander and governor of the province. For example, granting land to Spanish settlers up the Mississippi River had to do with both increasing the province's population and reinforcing its defense against British intrusions west of the river. His heavy reliance on his colored troops would likewise have both civil and military objectives and implications. (The term "colored" as applied to military units, both regular army and militias, was widespread in the Spanish Empire.)[219]

Before we study Bernardo de Gálvez's actions as governor, it is necessary briefly to consider the economic and administrative conditions of Louisiana before his arrival. One of the reasons for France's generosity in handing over the colony to Spain was France's failure to make it profitable. Therefore it was natural for the new owners to explore every possibility for generating profits, or at least for limiting as far as possible the territory's cost to the Royal Treasury. But despite all of the efforts of Spanish authorities, Louisiana would always need *situados* (subsidies) from New Spain. This was not a situation particular to Louisiana, since other Spanish territories, including Cuba, Puerto Rico, Santo Domingo, and the Philippines, also had to rely on Mexican *situados* for their survival. Between 1766 and 1780, Louisiana received about 300,000 pesos, a figure that would rise to 315,000 pesos in the 1780s and 577,695 pesos in the last decade of the eighteenth century. To these amounts must be added 47,126 pesos for Pensacola and 151,031 pesos for St. Augustine in Florida. It was a significant amount of money but only a fifth of the cost of the much smaller island of Cuba.[220] However, the *situa-*

Coat of arms of the province of Spanish Louisiana granted by King Carlos III in 1786. (*Armas de la Provincia de la Luisiana,* Archivo General de Indias, Mapas y Planos-Escudos 129; Ministerio de Educación, Cultura y Deporte, Archivo General de Indias)

dos rarely arrived on time, and sometimes they were even sequestrated in Havana during transit, so that the Spanish governors of Louisiana frequently found themselves with no cash, even for paying the salaries of royal civil servants.[221] In this regard, Bernardo de Gálvez had the luck to find in New Orleans several devoted and loyal public servants whom he had the wisdom to promote to the most important positions in the colonial administration. Among them was Martín Navarro, who in 1777 was *contador* and *fiscal de la real hacienda* (deputy assistant of the Royal Treasury) and later would be a key figure in managing the complex logistics of the military campaigns against the British.[222] Navarro would also be invaluable in reorganizing the royal tobacco monopoly.[223] In 1780 Gálvez appointed him head of the Royal Treasury in Louisiana.

Another essential institution in the government of Louisiana was the cabildo, a kind of city council, which, besides performing certain administrative functions, served as the channel through which the local population, especially the local elite, expressed its interests and opinions.[224] Gálvez presided over its most important meetings, such as the one that took place every January 1, when most city officials were elected.[225] The relationship between Gálvez and the cabildo would not always be easy, since both were trying to assert their powers. But the fact that the relatively new Spanish subjects of New Orleans had this institution for interacting with the colony's supreme authority was essential to their involvement in the governments of the city and the province.[226]

POPULATION

When considering Louisiana's population it is important to remember that the data gathered during the eighteenth century refers only to free people and slaves. Indigenous peoples were not included in censuses made during either the French or Spanish periods. According to Antonio Acosta Rodríguez, in 1763 the whole region had scarcely 10,000 inhabitants, of which approximately 50 percent were slaves. About 25 percent of the total population, both free people and slaves, lived in New Orleans.[227] Six years later the census ordered by Governor Alejandro O'Reilly counted 13,000 inhabitants in the province.[228] This rapid increase in Louisiana's colonial population continued under Gálvez: between 1763 and 1777 Louisiana's free population increased 3.8 percent per year, and in the period from 1778 to 1783 it grew 4.5 percent each year.[229] According to Fernando Solano Acosta, the colonial population increase in Louisiana was so fast under Spanish domination that in less than twenty years it grew from 13,513 (O'Reilly's census) to 31,433 (1785 census).[230] Some parts of the province grew even more quickly. For example, in northern Louisiana the colonial population multiplied by a factor of ten during the Spanish period.[231] Such growth would be constant. At the end of the eighteenth century, a French traveler stated that the number of free inhabitants at the time was about 30,000—a figure that would be almost double if the slave population were taken into account. In May 1777 Gálvez sent Madrid the first of the censuses that were made under his tenure.[232]

A MULTIETHNIC AND MULTICULTURAL SOCIETY

Despite the efforts of all Spanish governors to populate Louisiana with Spaniards, at the end of Spain's sovereignty in the province Spaniards were a mere 15 percent of the total population.[233] The remaining 85 percent were free people of non-Spanish origin, slaves, and Native Americans. This meant

TABLE A. *Louisiana's Colonial Population According to the May 1777 Census*

Population		No. of Inhabitants	% of Total
Free	White	8,381	46.75
	Mulatto	273	1.52
	Black	263	1.47
	Subtotal	8,917	49.74
Slave	Mulatto	545	3.04
	Black	8,464	47.22
	Subtotal	9,009	50.26
Total		17,926	100.00
Population able to bear arms		1,956	10.91

Source: Certified copy of the census sent by Bernardo de Gálvez, New Orleans, May 12, 1777, Archivo General de Indias, Cuba, 2351.

that from the very beginning, Louisiana was a multicultural and multiethnic population, with a radically different social composition than that found in the rest of the American territories under the Spanish Crown. Even if, according to Jay Gitlin, empires were more able than nations to accommodate peoples from different cultures, the Spanish authorities had to design and implement a new type of policy to ensure their control.[234] From the beginning, Spanish authorities were aware of this fact and did not even try to apply the rules and regulations established for the rest of Spanish America. Among the instructions received by Bernardo de Gálvez from his uncle José was a clear statement that he was to welcome foreigners to settle in the province on the conditions that they were Catholic and swore allegiance to Spain.[235] While the second condition was followed to the letter, the first was not. It must be remembered that there were already some non-Catholic communities established in the Louisiana Territory, mainly composed of German-speaking settlers but also some with American and British refugees who had fled the war, as the case of Galveztown will show. In other cases the entry of new non-Catholic groups was also permitted. We will later return to these groups when considering the religious policy that Gálvez carried out.

Free Population

Although Louisiana's free population was less than half the total number of inhabitants recorded in the census, it was socially and economically the most important sector to keep peaceful—or, put more directly, it was the sector that could pose the most serious threat to Spanish domination in the province. For this reason, many of the measures taken by Spanish authorities directly targeted this social sector to ensure its loyalty to His Catholic Majesty.[236] Some of these measures were already considered in the discussion of the fight against the English contraband trade, which ensured the wealth of French-origin merchants of New Orleans. Others will be apparent in the later discussion on agriculture. Most if not all measures were based on an economic model that allowed the economic and social elite to survive and even flourish. Sometimes the interests of this elite were served by positive action (like granting special trade concessions) and at other times simply by under-zealously enforcing certain laws, rules, and regulations that came from across the Atlantic and, if strictly enforced, could harm the privileged class.

The free population was far from homogeneous. At the top of Louisiana's social pyramid were those who, with proof or a certain amount of creative genealogy, could trace their origins to noble lineages in France or Spain. Only these were the real Creoles. Under them was a plethora of groups and subgroups, for every one of which the Creoles had a specific name. The shopkeepers were *chacas*; those just arrived in New Orleans from rural areas were *chacalatas*; those with a drop of black blood in their veins were *achumas*; the French-Creole version of the famous *gachupines*, a term used in Mexico to designate the Spaniards just arrived from the Iberian Peninsula, were *catchoupines*; and *bambaras* and *bitacaux* were those working in unclean occupations, such as street sweepers and garbage collectors.[237]

The army played an important role in Gálvez's New Orleans, because the absence of a visible Spanish military force had been a key factor behind the 1768 revolt. This error would not be made again. From the time of Alejandro O'Reilly onward, Spain kept enough troops garrisoned in Louisiana to discourage this kind of temptation. But the role of the military as a control mechanism went further than mere deterrence, according to Gilbert C. Din. The army also served as a vehicle for social control because it incorporated many middle- and upper-class French Creoles serving as officers in the Fixed Infantry Regiment of Louisiana. For Din, "the loyalty of these troops to the Spanish Crown was never in question."[238]

Not all free men were white. Despite being a minority, free blacks had an important role in Louisiana's society and economy. According to Kimberly S. Hanger, white New Orleanians depended on free people of color to provide transportation, provisions, skilled labor, and all sorts of other services.[239] It is worth remembering that free blacks and mulattoes were enrolled in militia units, which were to play an important role during Gálvez's military campaigns against the British.

Slaves

More than half of Louisiana's colonial population was enslaved.[240] This demographic deeply affected its social, economic, and even political organization. The French model of slavery in Louisiana was quite different from the Spanish approach. It was based on the 1724 black legal code adapted from the *code noir* published in 1685 for the French West Indies.[241] The code was based on the legal proposition that black slaves were objects. It regulated every aspect of the "life of all colored people."[242] For example, article 7 of the 1685 code stated that on Sundays it was forbidden to have a "slave market or [sale] of any other kind of merchandise under the penalty of confiscation of all merchandise in those markets."[243] The cession of Louisiana from the French to the Spanish took place on the condition that its inhabitants' ways of life and laws would not be altered.[244] Accordingly, during the first years of Spanish rule, little happened to change the condition and regulation of slavery. Louisiana's first governor, Antonio de Ulloa, simply ignored the issue. The second governor, Alejandro O'Reilly, adopted a more cunning position: he declared in a proclamation of August 27, 1769, that as he did not have deep knowledge of the issue and his multiple occupations did not allow him time to study it himself, he was commissioning two experts, Messieurs Fleuriau and Ducros, to write a report proposing the best approach.[245] It is relevant that the 1724 French *code noir* had been translated into Spanish in 1767. Although Manuel Lucena Salmoral argues that the French code could have been in force in certain parts of Spanish America, since it was found among the documents used in a 1788 compilation of the laws on slavery, this point is not at all certain.[246] What is inarguable is that overall in Louisiana, the legal condition of slaves was subject to a degree of ambiguity, with important consequences both for the law and for its implementation.

The French *code noir* had an important influence on Spanish legislation at the end of the eighteenth century, moving the Spanish model of slavery closer to the French and British approaches. The three models had important differences. Frank Tannenbaum, in his classic study on slaves and citizens, mentions three traditions or historical forces that prevented Spanish law from considering a slave as a mere object: the influence of Roman law through the Code of Justinian; the role of the Catholic Church; and the long historical familiarity of Spaniards with Moors and blacks. He states that the law accepted the doctrine of the moral personality of the slave and made possible the gradual achievement of freedom implicit in such a doctrine.[247]

At the beginning of the seventeenth century, Juan de Hevia Bolaños, one of the most important Spanish legal thinkers at the time, clearly expressed that "rational men are not among the names of merchandise."[248] The draft of the never-enacted 1784 Spanish *code noir* for Santo Domingo included the statement that "the owners and holders of slaves ought not believe that they are a treasure or their own private property."[249] While this traditional view based on the legal framework has been questioned by scholars who argue that the study of the law can contribute little to the understanding of the experience of the slave in the Americas, Tamar Herzog asserts that it is time to take the law seriously and that the constant appeals to an alleged gap between "law" and "practice" should be definitively abandoned.[250]

The implication of considering slaves as chattel (objects) or as persons with limited—very limited—rights was of huge importance. As Spain's hold in Louisiana consolidated, the tension between these two models became more apparent, not as a question of principle but in everyday life, where Spanish authorities were forced progressively to incorporate the original French model into their own. One of the earliest points of friction was the means by which slaves could gain their freedom.[251] The Spanish legal institution of *coartación* meant that every slave had the right to buy his (or her) freedom through "payment of regular amounts of money to his owner up to the total of his value."[252] The authorities determined this value, and the owner had no choice but to accept it. The institution of *coartación* had its origin in customary law first incorporated into Spanish law in Cuba in 1768.[253] It was rigorously enforced by Spanish authorities in Louisiana, despite the problems it generated among the powerful planter elite. Thomas N. Ingersoll explains this apparent contradiction by observing that, as one of the main political aims of the Spanish authorities was to ensure the loyalty of the most important social and economic sectors, the possibility for slaves to buy their own freedom reduced their temptation to grab it through violence or escape. It also helped provide a much-needed labor force during the urban expansion under way in New Orleans. Finally, the promotion of saving among slaves helped curb, at least in part, the exit of cash in payments to foreigners for newly imported slaves.[254] Ingersoll concludes that the Spanish innovations were not intended to change the slave society of New Orleans but, on the contrary, to preserve it, yet the Spanish policy for developing the backward colony coincidentally provided more economic opportunities for slaves to earn money to free themselves and their relatives.[255] According to Jennifer M. Spear, the introduction of *coartación* was one of the most important policy changes that occurred under Spanish rule, and the slave population actively took advantage of this institution.[256]

One example sheds light on Bernardo de Gálvez's personal involvement in the matter: the case of Agnes Mathieu. On December 16, 1779, Governor Bernardo de Gálvez signed her freedom under the institution of the *coartación*. The governor's personal involvement in the case at a time when he was very busy fighting the British can be explained by the fact that the force behind the *coartación* dossier was Mateo Platilla, or Mathiey Platille, one of the fifty New Orleans militiamen who fought with Gálvez in Baton Rouge. The case had been at a standstill in court because Agnes's owner, Madame Arnaud, refused to accept the results of two appraisals establishing that she would be compensated 425 pesos for Agnes's release. Mateo Platilla had a personal interest in the outcome of the case: in his 1810 last will he revealed that Agnes was the mother of his children.[257]

As the Spanish model of slavery was progressively implemented in Louisiana toward the end of the Spanish domination over the province, the number and proportion of free blacks and mulattoes noticeably increased.[258] For the Crown, free men were far more profitable than slaves, since these new subjects of the king had to pay taxes, as the authorities reminded them from time to time.[259] So it was natural that the king ordered his officials "to take good care that free black men are well treated and their rights respected" or, when punishment was needed against fleeing slaves, to take particular care not to disturb peaceful free black men.[260]

Bernardo de Gálvez's policy on slavery was shaped by two considerations: the need to develop a labor force that could promote agriculture in the province and the need to ensure the loyalty of the local population in the expected war with the British. Both factors implied a need for more slaves. When planters demanded an easing of the requirements for importing slaves, after some hesitation he agreed.[261] First, he authorized their purchase on credit, and later, in November 1777, he published a decree authorizing their direct import from the Gulf of Guinea.[262] The effects of this decree, extended in 1782 to importing slaves from friendly or neutral countries, were extremely important since it reopened the slave trade in Louisiana after the French had outlawed the importation of new slaves since the Natchez War of 1729–30.[263] The consequence was that under Spanish rule, the number of slaves in Louisiana almost multiplied by four. According to Gwendolyn Midlo Hall, the numbers increased from 5,600 slaves in 1766 to 9,649 in 1777 to 20,673 in 1788. Such figures support Hall's assertion that Louisiana was "re-Africanized under Spanish rule."[264] Gálvez needed the planters' support, but that did not mean that he would yield to all of their demands. As has already been seen, the New Orleans institution of the cabildo ensured that the city's elite had a say in governmental affairs, and it was precisely in the cabildo that the tensions between the governor and the rich planters and merchants became most apparent.

In May 1777 a new tax was approved to raise funds for compensating the owners of runaway slaves. A new law also entrusted the cabildo with drafting new regulations on slave discipline. According to Gilbert C. Din and John E. Harkins, members of the cabildo took this opportunity to introduce tough new measures that in essence reintroduced aspects of the French *code noir* that were most favorable for them.[265] The problem was that the resuscitated articles about the punishment of *cimarrones* (runaway slaves) were in direct opposition to Spanish law. While the French punished all runaways in the same way, Spanish law distinguished between *bozales* (slaves who had been in America less than a year after their capture in Africa) and *ladinos* (all of the others) and stipulated a lenient punishment for the former and a harsher sentence for the latter. Spanish law also distinguished between simple escape (that is, with the purpose solely of escaping slavery) and aggravated escape (with the purpose of joining other runaways to form a band of robbers). These, too, had different punishments.[266] The specific punishments determined by Spanish and French law were also very different. The former stated, "To the black man or woman who has been absent from his or her master for four days, fifty lashes shall be given in the pillory, and he or she shall remain tied to the pillory till sunset. . . . If the black man or woman has been absent from his or her master for more than eight days, one hundred lashes shall be given, and heavy iron fetters [attached] for two months. . . . If absent for more than four months in the company of other *cimarrones*, six hundred lashes. . . . If absent for more than six months in the company of black rebels committing crimes, death by hanging."[267]

Article 38 of French Louisiana's code set even harsher punishments. "The runaway slave who escaped for a month, to be counted from the day his master notified the authorities, shall have his ears cut off and his shoulder branded with a *fleur de lys* using a hot iron; in the case of a second offense, his hamstring shall be cut and another *fleur de lys* branded on his other shoulder; in the case of a third offense, he shall be punished by death."[268]

The New Orleans cabildo spent several months working on a new *loi municipale* or slavery regulation that was supposed, in Gálvez's words, to accord with the laws of both the realm and the province. But when he was presented with the text, he refused to sign it and did not even send it to Madrid to be studied.[269] What had happened to cause the governor to so directly thwart the will of New Orleans's cabildo elite, when just a few months earlier he had been obliging them in every way? Barely a year before, he had strongly defended their interests against a court ruling in Havana, arguing that what was in force on that island did not apply in Louisiana, whose customs and laws could not be modified without the king's express consent.[270] Perhaps after a year in government, Gálvez felt more confident about his position and less dependent on the cabildo's goodwill. The cabildo, according to several historians, had forced the situation too much, misjudging its own influence and ultimately prompting Gálvez's urge to reassert his own powers.[271]

It is also important to mention that according to a 1750 royal decree, all English and Dutch fugitive black slaves were to be considered free on condition that they accepted the Catholic faith.[272] That this piece of legislation was in force during the American Revolutionary War is proven by the fact that Governor Gálvez sent a copy of it in September 1779 to Francisco Collell, Francisco Cruzat, Juan Delavillebeuvre, Carlos de Grand Pré, and Baltasar de Villiers.[273]

It is important to bear in mind that even though the suffering imposed by slavery was not substantially different under Spanish or French rule, according to Jennifer M. Spear both the Spanish rulers and the local Louisiana creole population believed that Spanish policies were more moderate. Spanish officials defended their laws as "just and fair," while local elites protested they were too lenient and inadequate for their circumstances.[274]

IMMIGRATION AND COLONIZATION

Increasing Louisiana's population was always a high priority for the Spanish authorities.[275] In his 1787 *Instrucción reservada* (Reserved instruction), King Carlos III stated clearly that "as for Louisiana, the design for it is to erect a barrier populated with men who will defend against advances and attacks from that area on New Mexico."[276] The population was to be developed in two ways: by "attracting foreign Catholic settlers" who must pledge allegiance to Spain and by organizing the migration of Spanish settlers into the province.[277]

Non-Spanish Immigration

During the period of French rule, two groups of non-French settlers had already arrived in Louisiana. The so-called Germans, or German-speaking groups who actually originated in Switzerland and Sweden, first arrived in about 1720, assisted by the Compagnie des Indes.[278] The area of their settlements on the banks of the Mississippi River southwest of New Orleans, near the lake that at the time was called Ouachas and today is known as Mechant, was known as the German Coast.[279] In 1765 they numbered 1,268 individuals.[280] As time went by they were progressively assimilated into the rest of

Louisiana's population, but during the last part of the eighteenth century they were still a separate community with a strong identity.

Another community of foreigners consisted of the Acadians, named after the Canadian region of Acadia, near the Gulf of St. Lawrence, where French Catholics had arrived at the beginning of the seventeenth century. Their settlement remained isolated from the rest of French Canada, since after the signature of the Treaty of Utrecht in 1713, Acadia, Newfoundland, and territories around the Hudson Bay passed to the British. They enjoyed a certain degree of prosperity because of their isolation, but in 1755 the British government decided to get rid of these potentially troublesome subjects during wartime and began to deport them, intensifying the effort between 1758 and 1762, to the point that the British policy toward this community has been considered a case of eighteenth-century ethnic cleansing.[281] During these years the first Acadians arriving in Louisiana were from Georgia, the two Carolinas, and Maryland, and they settled on the left bank of the Mississippi.[282] Shortly afterward more groups arrived from New York, Maryland, South Carolina (Charleston), and Haiti.[283] Between 1764 and 1767, a total of 1,486 Acadians arrived in Spanish Louisiana, and even as late as 1785 a group of 1,624 Acadian settlers arrived from France, where they had been returned after deportation but had never been able to adjust.[284] Gálvez also tried to attract Acadian migrants to the Upper Mississippi. In 1778 he instructed the authorities in St. Louis to "employ such means as prudence may dictate [to] increase the settlements committed to his charge, especially with French Canadian families living among the English." However, despite his orders and financial incentives, very few Acadians migrated to Upper Louisiana during his tenure as governor.[285]

Both Germans and Acadians were initially regarded with suspicion by Spanish authorities, since they had played an active role in the 1768 revolt against Governor Ulloa.[286] Since O'Reilly's time, though, every effort had been made to win their loyalty. According to Fernando Solano Acosta, this effort was successful: forgetting their former whims, the Germans and Acadians proved their firm support to the Spanish government, and many of them fought gallantly in Gálvez's units. Good workers and extremely prolific, their population rapidly increased.[287]

Louisiana, the Upper Mississippi, and later Florida also benefited from an important flow of refugees fleeing from the American Revolutionary War, part of whom remained in Spanish territories after the end of the conflict. Before Spain entered the war against the British, the Spanish authorities in America applied "a hospitality policy" allowing the entrance of refugees from British America, both Loyalist and rebel sympathizers. On March 3, 1778, the

Spanish governor of New Orleans published an order to all the inhabitants of the colony stating that although Spain was neutral in the present conflict, that would not mean that Spain would deny its hospitality to all those seeking it.[288] This policy would continue "until the fate of the war is decided."[289] Four months later, Governor Gálvez had to make clear that the hospitality policy applied to all Americans coming from British territories and specifically ordered the Spanish commanders of Punta Colorada and Manchac to grant asylum to all Englishmen demanding it.[290] The border region of the Upper Mississippi attracted war refugees but was not able to retain them; most continued their journey either to other parts of the Spanish territories in North America or to British colonies, mainly in the Caribbean.[291]

In the end, the Spanish authorities' failure in attracting European settlers would determine the opening of the region to Ohio Valley Indians, especially the Shawnee and the Delaware, who considered American independence the "greatest blow" to Ohio Valley Indians, short of their "total destruction."[292] In Florida, the flow of Loyalist refugees increased after the Spanish capture of Pensacola and West Florida. In the last years of the American Revolutionary War, the city of St. Augustine in Florida became a sort of hub for Loyalists fleeing from the United States. While most Loyalists stayed in St. Augustine for only a short period of time before leaving for other British American possessions or even England itself, a small number of them were allowed to settle in Mobile Bay, the Natchez region, and other areas of the Lower Mississippi valley.[293] Among the former was Elizabeth Lichtenstein Johnston, studied by Maya Jasanoff. Johnston arrived in St. Augustine during the last days of 1782 to find members of a busy Loyalist community immersed in plans to make West Florida their home.[294]

Spanish Immigration

The same treaty that gave Louisiana to Spain also determined that Spain lost Florida to Great Britain. It would have been natural for the Spanish population in Florida simply to move to Louisiana, but this did not happen. Spanish Floridians instead sailed to Cuba, mainly because the waters to Cuba were easier to navigate than the longer trip to Louisiana.[295]

Before the arrival of Gálvez in New Orleans, very few Spanish-origin people were in Louisiana. By the "scratch of a pen," all of Louisiana's inhabitants had been made loyal subjects of the Spanish monarchy in 1763, but they remained French in their language, culture, customs, and laws.[296] The idea of bringing Spanish settlers to Louisiana was first articulated by Francisco de Bouligny, who despite his French-sounding name was a Spaniard from Valencia. In August 1776 he wrote in his memoirs that he was sure that families from Valencia and Murcia in Spain would be happy to immigrate to Louisiana.[297] This proposal did not prosper, perhaps because of his bad relationship with Gálvez, but his idea was taken up by the governor with a slight but important change. Instead of bringing emigrants from Valencia, they were brought from Malaga and the Canary Islands.

Malaga seemed an obvious choice, since the Gálvez family was originally from the region and their connection to Malaga remained strong. They had transformed the poor and small village of Macharaviaya into a prosperous and beautiful place. But in choosing their fellow countrymen as emigrants, they were caught in a contradiction. If their aim was to develop their home village and region economically, why promote its depopulation? This can be explained only by Gálvez family nepotism, or the tendency always to favor their family, their clan, and their neighbors. It was a trait, or vice, that permeated actions taken by all members of the family.

In June 1778 the ship *San Josef* sailed from Malaga with sixteen families comprising eighty-two individuals. After an arduous trip they arrived in New Orleans on November 11.[298] They had to wait in the city for several months while their destination was decided. Francisco de Bouligny wanted them to settle in the region close to the Ouachita River, while Governor Gálvez considered that place unsuitable. After a time Gálvez's preferences prevailed, and they were sent to the village of Nueva Iberia (New Iberia), on the banks of Lake Tasse, today called Spanish Lake.[299]

Although most of these settlers were from Malaga, some were also from the neighboring region of Granada. All were expert farmers of flax and hemp. These two products were chosen to be economic motors for the region, since they were important for shipbuilding.[300] It must be remembered that at the time, Spain was implementing a very aggressive program of naval rearmament. Just for the rigging of a seventy-cannon warship, 138 tons of hemp were needed. In 1780 the Spanish Royal Navy was using 3,680 tons of hemp per year.[301]

The second and largest group of migrants came from the Canary Islands. Emigration from the Canaries to America is as old as the discovery of the continent and is deeply rooted in Canarian culture. As Francisco Morales Padrón states, "For the way he is raised, for custom, and for what he sees and what he hears, the men from the [Canary] Islands feel compelled to 'make the Americas.' The men from the Canary Islands since their early boyhood sigh for America as their own homeland."[302] If nepotism played an important role in selecting settlers from Malaga, it was also involved here. At this time, Matías de Gálvez, Bernardo's father, was governor of the Paso Alto

Castle in Santa Cruz de Tenerife, and since 1775 he had also been second in command of the island's military district.[303] On August 4, 1777, the minister of the Indies, José de Gálvez, ordered the deputy military commander of the island of Tenerife, his brother Matías, to start recruiting for the second battalion of Louisiana's Fixed Infantry Regiment, whose colonel was Bernardo de Gálvez. It all remained within the family.[304] Thus while people migrating from Malaga were settlers, at least in principle or origin, those from the Canary Islands were soldiers.[305]

The emigration from the Canary Islands was opposed by the Royal Economic Society of Friends of the Country as well as by large landowners who resented being deprived of their labor force.[306] Their opposition largely explains the delayed departure of the first contingent of recruits, which did not leave the Canary Islands until July 1778.[307] Between this date (when the *Santísimo Sacramento* sailed with 125 recruits, accompanied by 139 family members) and June 1779 (when the *Sagrado Corazón de Jesús* departed with 117 recruits and 306 family members), a total of 2,010 people from the Canary Islands arrived in Louisiana, 600 of them recruits for its infantry regiment.[308] Still waiting on the islands to migrate were 360 more people, 100 of them recruits, who were to complete the 700 soldiers required by royal ordinances to form the regiment's second battalion.[309] Their departure was so delayed that it had to take place after war broke out with Britain,[310] which made their travel very dangerous, to the point that of the three ships forming the convoy, one was diverted to Cuba and another to Caracas while the third was seized by a British warship and its passengers taken prisoner.[311]

The emigration from the Canary Islands was originally planned to be a military event, but, according to Antonio Acosta Rodríguez, once the Canarians arrived in the colony, and because of the problems faced by the Royal Treasury at the time, it was decided that the majority—at least those with families—would remain as settlers. This meant that there would be no need to pay them their intended military salaries and, at the same time, the colony would benefit by increasing its population and wealth.[312]

The results of the immigration of these two groups of Spaniards could not have been more different. While the farmers from Malaga prospered, the ex-recruits from the Canary Islands struggled to survive. On the basis of their different fates, a historian has deduced that Bernardo de Gálvez favored his fellow countrymen by providing them with more assistance and better land.[313] This is a possibility, but the outcome could also be explained by the fact that with their expertise as farmers, the settlers from Malaga could thrive better than the recruits from the Canary Islands, who had no expertise at all.

SETTLEMENT POLICY

If the king's strategy of a "barrier populated with men" was to succeed, it was necessary not only to attract men but also to settle them in specific places.[314] The settlement policy reached its peak during Bernardo de Gálvez's tenure as governor.[315] The task was not an easy one, as it required a complex administrative structure, detailed planning, and meticulous implementation. Bernardo de Gálvez created an administrative body in charge of everything related to the so-called new settlements, which was put under the command of a superintendent with whom he would have a difficult relationship: Francisco de Bouligny.[316] The planning involved a complex process of choosing locations, drawing plans, and preparing the necessities for construction. The implementation involved coordinating materials and a workforce as well as global supervision. An example of the level of detail involved in the planning was that it even took into account the need for so-called seed capital. In February 1778, the Spanish authorities determined that every settler would be provided, at the Spanish Crown's expense, with an ax, a hoe, a scythe or sickle, a shovel, two chickens, a rooster, and a two-and-a-half-month old piglet, besides a fixed amount of corn for each family member.[317]

The Spanish system of land tenure and registration also was important in attracting settlers. According to Richard C. Arena, this was a policy that had been developing for nearly three centuries in the Caribbean and continental possessions, juridically precise and conscientiously applied with realism and no false assumptions where Louisiana was concerned.[318] Following this model, large landowners initially lived with small farmers but eventually displaced them over time.

Some of the settlements that were either founded by or closely linked to the government of Bernardo de Gálvez should be mentioned (without attempting to be comprehensive) in order to properly assess his governorship.

Galveztown

Despite its name, this settlement was neither founded by nor named by Bernardo de Gálvez. In a letter to his uncle dated January 19, 1779, Gálvez explained that while on a journey to find the best locations for the new villages, he had discovered "a place of high lands near the confluence of the rivers Amite and Tuenville [today's Bayou Manchac], ignored until now by the locals and discovered by chance by British and American refugees [who were] in His Majesty's dominions because of past revolutions, where they founded a small village and gave it the name of Galbeztown [sic] (village of Gálvez), asking me not to change the name, because, as they had found refuge during the time of my command, they wished the above-mentioned name to be a token of their gratitude and a testimony to the time in which it was founded."[319]

Only six months after this letter, Galveztown already had forty-two wooden lodges, a nearly completed main square, and surroundings cleared of trees. The early settlers were joined by families from the Canary Islands and, in 1785, by Acadians. In 1779 its first pastor arrived, who helped build a church, which, not coincidentally, was put under the protection of Saint Bernardo.[320] A plan of the village, now in the Library of Congress, shows a main square surrounded by thirty-two blocks of houses.[321] The inscription states "*Carolo Regnante, Urbem aedificat amor, Galvez ad honorem, nomen dedit que suum*" (Under the reign of Carlos [III], city built [as a proof of] his love [for the king], in honor of Gálvez, who gave it her name). Despite this promising start, Galveztown soon suffered a series of setbacks. The first was due to its location, which made it a frequent victim of floods, which were followed by a series of epidemics. Gilbert C. Din called one of the most serious of these the "Galveztown tragedy."[322] It struck between March 1779 and March 1780, killing 161 inhabitants, many of them children.[323] These calamities, added to the fact that at the end of the war with Britain its location ceased to be of strategic importance, sealed Galveztown's fate. In 1804 the remaining settlers moved to Baton Rouge.[324] Today little trace of Galveztown remains. In an excavation in 2008 some ceramic fragments, porcelain, glass, buttons, nails, and clay pipes were found.[325]

It is important not to mistake this Galveztown with Galveston in Texas. The latter was named after Bernardo de Gálvez as well but not until the 1780s. When Bernardo de Gálvez was governor of Cuba, he commissioned José de Evia to draw maps of the reconquered Florida and the coast of New Spain. When the expedition arrived in the area south of what is today the city of Houston, Evia found an island and named it Galvezton, today's Galveston.[326]

Nueva Iberia (New Iberia)

A great deal of the tension between Bernardo de Gálvez and the superintendent of new settlements, Francisco de Bouligny, centered on Nueva Iberia.[327] One of Gálvez's duties was to travel throughout Louisiana. In November 1778, before departing on one such journey, he ordered Bouligny to draw up a plan of a new settlement that was not to be located in the region of the Ouachita River.[328] Probably to reduce the influence of settlers from Malaga, Bouligny obtained Gálvez's permission to populate it also with families of Irish, German, and French origin and later with farmers from the Opelousas and Atakapas regions. The expedition left New Orleans in the beginning of 1779 under Bouligny's command and in March of that year built the first

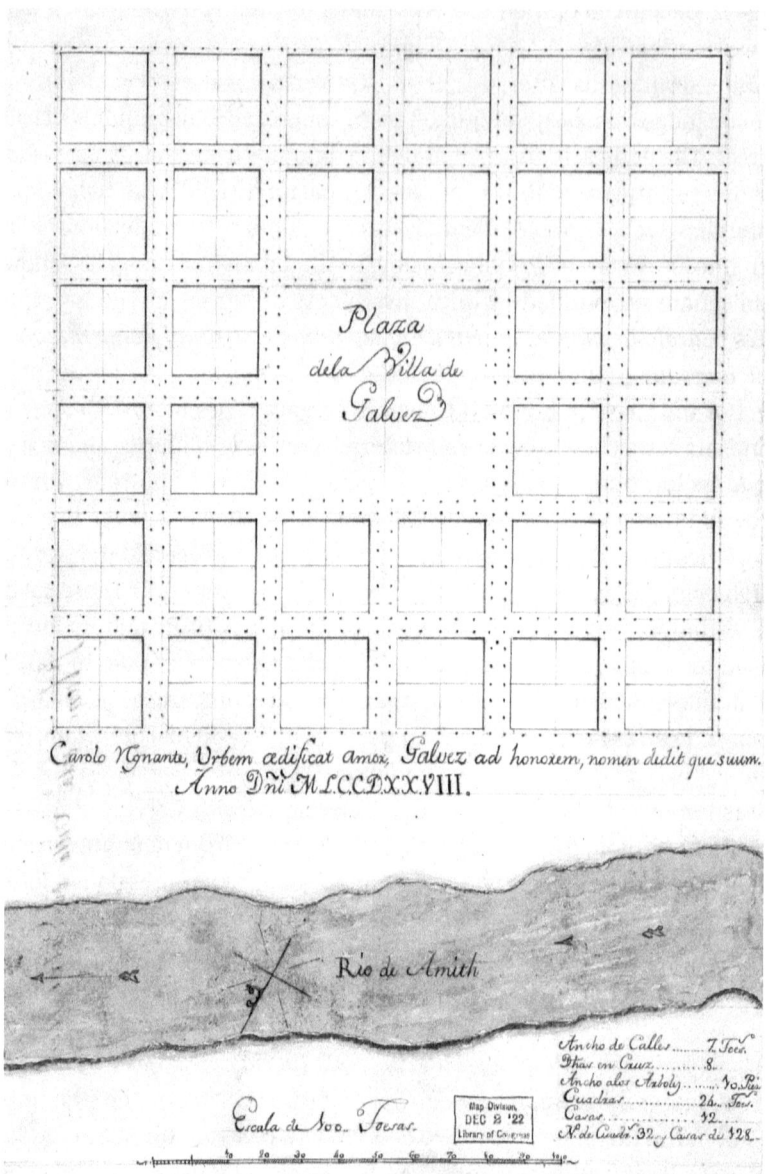

Plan for the village of Galveztown in Louisiana, not to be confused with Galveston, Texas. Despite its name, this settlement was neither founded by nor named by Bernardo de Gálvez but was named in his honor by the local population, mainly refugees from the American Revolutionary War, who wanted to guarantee his patronage for their village. A series of calamities and the loss of its strategic position after the war determined that the surviving settlers moved to Baton Rouge in 1804, abandoning a deserted Villa de Gálvez. (*Villa de Gálvez, Louisiana*, mss. map, 1778; Library of Congress, LC, G4014, G224 1778, P5 Vault)

houses in the Bayou Teche region. A month later severe floods forced Nueva Iberia to relocate to higher ground. In the face of these problems, its growth was slow, and the 1785 census registered only 125 inhabitants, 70 of them from Malaga.[329]

Valenzuela

This village of settlers from the Canary Islands was founded in 1782 some seventy-five miles west of New Orleans in a location that would be favorable for its rapid growth.[330] Its name was chosen to honor the third wife of Bernardo's uncle José, Concepción Valenzuela de Fuentes. In 1797 the village had grown to nearly 2,000 inhabitants.[331] The commission for its construction was awarded to Gilberto Antonio Saint-Maxent, a rich New Orleans merchant with whom Bernardo de Gálvez had a very close relationship.

Barataria

Very little is known about this settlement, which was located about twelve miles south of New Orleans and abandoned after the war with the British because it cost too much to maintain.[332] The name chosen for this village needs some explanation, since it possibly reflects something of Gálvez's character. Barataria Island was the fictitious governorship offered to Sancho Panza, the loyal squire of Don Quixote. Cervantes's description of Barataria is heavily influenced by Thomas More's utopian ideas, which were widespread in seventeenth-century Spain.[333] By choosing this name, Gálvez could have been showing off some of his culture. But aside from that, it is evident that the political ideas contained in Don Quixote's speech to Sancho on how to best govern his land were deeply appealing to Gálvez: "Take notice, Sancho, if you choose virtue for your medium, and pique yourself upon performing worthy actions, you will have no cause to envy noblemen and princes; for, blood is hereditary, but virtue is acquired; consequently, this last has an intrinsic value which the other does not possess."[334]

This idea of the supremacy of merit and virtue above all other considerations was doubly important for Bernardo de Gálvez. On the one hand, his family members were making their way up the social ladder, from impoverished shepherds in the miserable village of Macharaviaya in Malaga to the highest posts in the Spanish royal service. On the other hand, he may have felt the need to dispel accusations that his position as governor was due only to the fact that he was the nephew of the all-powerful minister of the Indies. He wished, almost needed, to reassert his own credentials by stressing, in Cervantes's words, that "everyone is the son of his own works."[335]

San Bernardo

In 1778 Gálvez commissioned Francisco Sosier to erect the settlement of San Bernardo or St. Bernardo.[336] By the beginning of the next year, thirty houses had been constructed.[337] San Bernardo's original name was La Concepción, and it was also referred to as Nueva Gálvez (New Gálvez) to differentiate it from Galveztown. It was later called Tierra de Bueyes (Land of Oxen) or by its French name, Terre-aux-Boeufs, because of its wealth in livestock. Its location east of New Orleans allowed for the easy transport of its products while at the same time isolated its inhabitants from the city's growth. This isolation was instrumental in preserving its Canary Islands traditions and culture. Even today, the town's inhabitants are still called *isleños* (islanders).[338]

Las Felicianas

Again, this was a settlement whose name reflected Gálvez's decisions and character. After his victories over the British, he decided to establish a couple of villages north of New Orleans to be populated mainly with Acadians. Nothing was more natural to him than proclaiming his love for his wife by naming these villages Las Felicianas, in honor of his wife, Felicitas, Feliciana in Spanish.[339]

Bayagoulas and Atakapas

Both settlements were founded in 1779. Juan Bautista Degruis erected Bayagoulas. The cost of building its twenty-four houses was 14,400 *reales*. Atakapas was populated mainly by families from Malaga but also received some Acadians.[340]

AGRICULTURE

Improving Louisiana's agriculture was an obvious way to make the province more profitable. But to achieve this, new crops and an appropriate and available labor force were needed. Several useful plants were introduced, with mixed results. The plan to introduce flax and hemp, for which expert farmers were brought from the Iberian Peninsula, was soon discarded.[341] Sugar cane was not easy to get started, and it was not until 1795 that the first harvests were obtained.[342] Indigo was one of Louisiana's main crops until the mid-eighteenth century, when a plague destroyed most of the plants and the crop was abandoned.[343] The cultivation of tobacco developed very slowly. During Luis de Unzaga's government, the first shipments of tobacco were sent to Mexico. Shortly before Gálvez's arrival, Mexican authorities were demanding more shipments of the crop, and his orders specifically stated that he must foster its cultivation.[344] Among the advice offered by Antonio Lavedan, army surgeon and physician to the royal family, was the assertion that tobacco had powerful virtues, such as "giving rest to a worked and tired body" when inhaled and "evacuating by nose and mouth the superficialities of the brain and surrounding lower parts" when sniffed.[345] Tobacco had even more beneficial effects on the Royal Treasury. The tobacco monopoly was a perfect business for the Royal Treasury to manage, and from 1636 on it determined the price, supervised its harvest, and had a monopoly over its manufacture, distribution, and sale.[346] So tight was the system that, according to Agustín González Enciso, the monopoly gave birth to contraband. The rigidity of the prices determined by the administration favored illegal trade. Smuggling tobacco flourished, thanks to customer demand, and the smugglers grew very rich.[347] The quota for Louisiana to produce, established by Madrid, was between 500,000 and 600,000 French livres or Spanish libras (in today's weight, approximately the same number of pounds), a fifth of Mexico's total demand or a seventh of that of the entire Iberian Peninsula.[348]

In June 1777, Bernardo de Gálvez called a meeting with the local tobacco planters to inform them about the Spanish Crown's formal commitment to buy all their production at a price that was satisfactory to them.[349] Several days later, he published a proclamation announcing the official tobacco prices and the process for its trade.[350] The prospects could not have been better. Louisiana was considered to "enjoy a better climate than Maryland and Virginia, [and] on account of its extent and fertility, could furnish the universe with tobacco."[351] The tobacco produced in Louisiana was of the Virginia type, one of the only two kinds imported to the Iberian Peninsula, so its market was assured.[352] Yet despite this auspicious start, its production did not meet the quota. In 1779 only 138,808 livres were shipped to Veracruz, far less than the half million expected. When the war against Britain demanded Gálvez's full attention, he turned over all tobacco issues to Martín Navarro. This loyal Royal Treasury civil servant worked with his usual expertise and zeal, and in six years Louisiana was able to not only meet but double the quota demanded by Madrid. In 1785, shipments to Mexico reached 1.15 million livres.[353]

The other side of the equation was the necessary workforce, and this was achieved by increasing the import of slaves and encouraging the emigration of Spaniards, Frenchmen, Germans, and refugees from the American War for Independence, both British and American.

RELIGIOUS POLICY

The religious policy of Spanish authorities in Louisiana not only was aimed at the spiritual life of the population but also had an important dimension of social control. Spanish Louisiana benefited from a policy of religious tolerance unknown in the rest of the territories under His Catholic Majesty, whether in America, Europe, Asia, or Africa. Religious tolerance did not mean religious freedom—that would be too much to ask of the eighteenth-century Spanish Enlightenment. No one in Louisiana was forced to convert to Catholicism, but neither were they allowed publicly to practice any non-Catholic religion.[354]

In French Louisiana, the task of caring for the souls of its inhabitants had been entrusted to the Order of the Capuchin Friars. During the initial period of Spanish domination, the lack of secular clergy meant that the congregation of French Capuchins under Friar Dagobert continued its work.[355] In 1772 six Capuchin friars and another from the Order of Saint Francis arrived from the Iberian Peninsula. Their head, Capuchin friar Cirilo de Barcelona, was armed with a ferocious zeal that he never abandoned, and he denounced the decadent moral state of the French Capuchin community and the disastrous condition of the parishioners.[356] Not knowing anything about the particularities of what Carl A. Brasseaux has called French Louisiana's moral climate, the Spanish friars suffered a significant culture shock upon their arrival in New Orleans.[357] The confrontation between Friar Dagobert and Friar Cirilo de Barcelona was a product of this shock but far from the only one. Gálvez's predecessor spent years writing letters and answering reports to and from authorities, both civil and religious, in an attempt to tone down their disputes.[358] Gálvez was luckier, since Friar Dagobert died a year before his arrival and the Spanish friar had his zeal rewarded with the Crown's approval of his efforts, so his combative spirit was calmed.[359] Calmed, that is, but not extinguished. Friar Cirilo continued to be a nuisance, to the point that Gálvez unsuccessfully tried to have him replaced.[360]

Friar Cirilo was not the only member of his order whose extreme zeal would create difficulties for civil authorities in Louisiana. Friar Luis de Quintanilla, who had also arrived in 1772, was sent to the border region of Natchitoches, in western Louisiana. According to Elizabeth Shown Mills, Quintanilla was a zealous crusader who felt the state existed to enforce church dogmas and who initiated a "cleanup campaign" that involved not only religious matters but also other aspects of social life: race relations, women's rights, public welfare and private morals, birth rate, and taxation.[361]

In 1777 Friar Quintanilla went to New Orleans, where he obtained Gálvez's support for his "cleanup campaign."[362] Invested with official backing, Quintanilla returned to his community and continued to interfere in all aspects of the day-to-day life of the Natchitoches settlers. To their relief he was finally removed in 1783.

Gálvez tried to make the bishop of Havana, under whom Louisiana was situated, pay closer attention to the province. He reported that that since no bishop had ever set foot in Louisiana, the sacrament of confirmation had not been conferred on individuals.[363] The bishop's pastoral visit never materialized, but at least he authorized five missionaries to administer sacraments.[364]

It is also important to mention that the Inquisition was never present in Louisiana.[365] Until the arrival in New Orleans of the Capuchin friar Antonio Sedella in 1781, matters of this sort were handled by an auxiliary vicar, who had to refer the most important cases to Inquisition courts in Havana.[366]

The convent of Ursuline nuns in New Orleans was an institution that, since its founding in 1727, was devoted to the education of girls. It also served as an orphanage; as a place where the wives of Creoles were left, for security reasons, when their husbands had to leave the city; and as a refuge for women abused by their husbands.[367] Initially the Spanish authorities considered moving the convent to Cuba, but Governor Unzaga succeeded in obtaining assurances for the nuns' maintenance from the Royal Treasury. However, according to José Antonio Armillas Vicente, it was Bernardo de Gálvez who became the champion of the continuity of the Ursuline nuns, obtaining from Madrid authorization for an increase in their numbers, thanks to an intervention by the Count of Aranda, Spanish ambassador to France, and a contribution of money from Gálvez's own pocket.[368] The decision to maintain the Ursuline convent in New Orleans was received with joy by the population, and a solemn Te Deum mass was celebrated in December 1777.[369] Following Emily Clark, Gálvez's support for the Ursuline convent should be viewed in the larger context of the power struggle between Spanish rulers and the French-origin local creole elite.[370] By defending the Ursulines, Gálvez was not only validating the nuns' "social" work but also ingratiating himself with the interests and traditions of the New Orleans elite.

Gálvez would remember the convent in his last will and testament, leaving it 10,000 pesos a year produced by the rent of several houses he owned in New Orleans.[371] From that moment on, the "twelve orphans of His Excellency the Count of Gálvez" no longer had financial problems, and the convent became a model institution.[372] In fact, when in 1793 the recently appointed bishop of Louisiana and the Floridas, Luis Ignacio Peñalver y Cárdenas, arrived in New Orleans, the convent was one of the few religious institutions earning his praise. On that same date, of all the funds in the convent's coffers, three-fourths were from the Gálvez donation.[373]

In conclusion, according to James Pitot, despite the efforts of civil authorities and the zeal of Spanish friars, religion was the area that was least influenced by the Spanish administration, which had no choice but to allow it to remain in the "relaxed status" it had enjoyed during the previous French period.[374]

BECOMING A CREOLE

In his book *Misión en Managua*, Pedro de Arístegui writes about the true, mysterious, and "unexplained" fact that makes every Spaniard who arrives in America—and that surely happened from the first day Columbus set foot on the island of Guanahani until today—become an American. He lives and walks as such and is unable to find any significant difference between what he had left behind in his old land and what he finds here.[375]

Bernardo de Gálvez was no exception: he, too, became an American. His youth, open character, and, not least important, rank as colonel and governor opened for him all doors to Louisiana's upper class. According to the contemporaneous testimony of Captain José Javier Delfau de Pontalba, a native of New Orleans who later moved to France, served in its army, and in 1801 sent Napoleon a memoir about Louisiana, "Count de Galvez appeared, and with him confidence, affability, gentleness, frankness, justice, and kindness. Soon the whole colony was devoted to him."[376]

When Bernardo de Gálvez arrived in New Orleans, he had just turned thirty. He had already spent time in America campaigning against the "barbaric Indians," but this was his first opportunity to live in a fairly important city. In New Orleans he attended the "brilliant assemblies where politeness, amiability, and gaiety reign supreme."[377] Among the doors opened for him, none was more imposing than that of the Saint-Maxent family.[378] Gilbert Antoine de Saint-Maxent (who under the Spanish rule hispanicized his name to Gilberto Antonio) was one of Louisiana's richest businessmen. Of noble origin, born in 1727 in the French city of Longy,[379] he immigrated to Louisiana, where he married the daughter of a wealthy merchant. In 1762 he and some partners established a company to trade with the Indians. It quickly prospered to the extent that he became one of the founders of the city of St. Louis, Missouri. When Louisiana was ceded to Spain, he was among the first to swear loyalty to the new government. He succeeded in winning the confidence of Governor Ulloa, as shown in the latter's agreement to stand as godfather for Saint-Maxent's daughter Marie-Anne Joseph. Saint-Maxent and his associates obtained several trade concessions, among them a special royal permit to import slaves. During the 1768 revolt, Saint-Maxent was the one who alerted Ulloa of the impending danger, and the governor sent him on an official mission to the German Coast, where he was almost killed by rioters.[380] When Alejandro O'Reilly arrived in New Orleans at the head of the army, Saint-Maxent was among his most ardent supporters and even served as witness for the prosecution of the main instigators of the revolt.[381] As a reward for his pro-Spanish zeal, he was appointed captain of the New Orleans militia and granted further royal permits for the Indian trade. During the governorship of Luis de Unzaga, Saint-Maxent continued to prosper, benefiting from the governor's blind eye to the contraband trade. According to Ramón Ezquerra, the relationship between Unzaga and Saint-Maxent "became so intimate that the elderly governor (Unzaga was 55 at the time) ended up marrying María Isabel Saint-Maxent, Gilbert's daughter."[382] The official ceremony took place in Venezuela on November 22, 1779, when Unzaga was no longer Louisiana's governor. It could well have been the sanctification of a previous secret marriage. If so, it would not be the only such case in the family.

With these credentials, it was natural for Gilberto Antonio Saint-Maxent to quickly become part of the new governor's inner circle. As the conflict between Gálvez and Francisco de Bouligny developed, Saint-Maxent was an unconditional ally of the former, which was probably the reason he was appointed contractor for the new settlement of Valenzuela, for which he received the handsome sum of 21,000 *reales* for materials.[383] He also had his privileges renewed to conduct the Indian trade.[384] Last but certainly not least, when war broke out with Great Britain, all of Saint-Maxent's men immediately volunteered and distinguished themselves on several occasions.

It seems that the relationship between Gálvez and Saint-Maxent turned rapidly into a mutually beneficial one, to the point that both became a little sloppy in business dealings. Bernardo de Gálvez forgot the multiple prohibitions established by Spanish law against governors conducting business or owning houses, farms, ranches, orchards, or land in the territory under their jurisdiction.[385] Years later, in his last will and testament, Gálvez confessed that "my possessions were acquired in Louisiana, and on expeditions I made in those lands, and through some commerce I made there before my marriage."[386] On his side, Saint-Maxent was sued by the Crown for tax evasion, which led to his arrest and the seizure of all of his property.[387] The final ruling by the Council of the Indies, issued on January 24, 1799, was that he and his associates had to pay 37,000 pesos to the Royal Treasury.[388]

This privileged relationship became much more intimate when Gilberto Antonio Saint-Maxent's second daughter was introduced to the young governor. Marie-Felicité, or Felicitas, was born in New Orleans on December 27, 1755. In 1772 she married Jean Baptiste Honore d'Estrehen, scion of another extremely prominent New Orleans' lineage, with whom she had a daughter, Adelaide, born shortly after her father died. Eyewitness accounts of the young widow concur about her beauty and her kind character, which made her beloved by everyone.[389] Even the famous Prussian geographer Alexander von Humboldt, usually impervious to feminine charms, was favorably impressed when he met her in 1803. Felicitas, who later hispanicized her name to Feliciana, was portrayed as the perfect example of what Berndt Ostendorf has called the "myth of Creole womanhood."[390] This myth has been hammered into today's collective imagination by the character of Scarlett O'Hara in *Gone with the Wind*,[391] and as George Orwell suggested that "myths which are believed tend to become true,"[392] it is worthy of a brief analysis. Its origin can be traced back to the description made by a contemporary, Guy Soniat du Fossat, for whom "the women, besides having the qualities above enumerated, are agreeable in figure, and seldom deformed.[393] They make good mothers, and are devoted to their husbands and their children: and in their marital relations seldom are they unfaithful."[394] The myth can also be found in A. Lussan's play *La famille creole*, first staged in New Orleans in 1837. William Darby's 1817 description of creole women's charms is also relevant:

> The women of Louisiana are, with few exceptions, well formed, with a dark piercing eye. Their movements bespeak warmth of imagination, and a high flow of animal spirits, whilst their features indicate good nature and intelligence. Tender, affectionate, and chaste, but few instances of connubial infidelity arise from the softer sex. With too often example to excuse, and neglect to stimulate, the most sacred of human contracts is fulfilled on their part with a fidelity that does honor to their sex. . . . As wives, sisters, or mothers, the Creole women hold a rank far above their apparent meanness of education. Frugal in the expenses of life, they seldom lead their families into distress, by gratifying their pleasures or pride. . . . Very seldom the victims of inordinate desires in any respect, their dress is regulated by neatness, decency, and frugality.[395]

Among the fathers of the myth of the southern belle—since these descriptions were all made by men—is Hains Boussuge, whose article on women appeared in 1837 in the first issue of the *Louisiana Creole: Gazette des salons, des arts et des modes*:

> The word woman is the secret of the art. . . . It is a mistake to represent poetry in the form of an angel. . . . The Creole woman is a Houri less the Quran, a Sultana for her beauty but without the Seraglio; a daughter of Smyrna or of Georgia who does not answer you, Allah is great and Mohamad its prophet! When you give her good morning; it is an angel with wings of fire . . . but who speaks French.[396]

Felicitas's charms were certainly encouraged by her father, since they served the family's interests well, at a time when marriage was a family alliance at the service of plans for social advancement more than a matter of sentiment.[397] Although this may be true in the case of Feliciana and Bernardo, sentiment also played a very important role. In terms of mid-eighteenth-century social conventions, their courtship was extremely short.[398] On November 2, 1777, they were married, and the circumstances of the marriage were not usual either. The official version is contained in the marriage certificate signed by Friar Cirilo de Barcelona: "Being seriously ill, he [Bernardo de Gálvez] informed me about his engagement with Doña Feliciana Maxent, widow of Don Juan Bautista Honorato Dethrean [Jean Baptiste Honore d'Estrehen], and that in the predicament in which he was, he wanted to marry the above-mentioned lady, so if God would take his life, he would die with the consolation of having honored his word. In consideration of these Christian reasons, and having been assured of his bachelorhood, I proceeded to take the mutual consent of the above mentioned Don Bernardo de Gálvez and Doña Feliciana Maxent."[399]

Marriage in extremis or in articulo mortis was a legal figure established in both Spanish and canon law.[400] If death threatened, marriage could be celebrated without all of the formalities required for a normal marriage. But in the case of Bernardo de Gálvez, the problem was double. On the one hand, at this time he was acting governor of Louisiana, and law 44, title 2, book 5 of the *Recopilación de Leyes de los Reynos de las Indias* (Legal code for Spanish America) expressly forbade governors and other royal officials to marry within their jurisdictions without a special royal permit in advance under "the penalty of being deprived of their office, and of being ineligible for any other in the Indies."[401] In addition, as colonel of the Louisiana Fixed Infantry Regiment, he also needed in advance a special royal license to marry.[402] The October 30, 1760, royal decree determined that "any officer who marries without royal license shall be disposed of his rank, stripped of his privileges, and his wife shall not be eligible for a widow's pension or *tocas*."[403]

Hence the marriage was secret, according to the documentation included in the file of their son, Miguel de Gálvez y Saint-Maxent, for admission to the aristocratic Order of Calatrava, which was processed in the late 1780s. In the marriage certificate, the bishop of Havana wrote, "[The usual] rite was omitted in the ceremony of their marriage, due to the necessary discretion with which it was executed, because of the lack of royal permission for it, and because [Bernardo de Gálvez] was at the time in command of Louisiana's provinces, where lady Doña María Felicia [*sic*] Maxent was born."[404]

According to Bernardo de Gálvez's own deposition in this document, the royal permission arrived a little later and the secret marriage could be unveiled. Naturally, no record has been found about how he managed to correct a situation that could seriously jeopardize his career. But it is not difficult to imagine the discreet intervention of his uncle José, the all-powerful minister of the Indies. His help most probably came after a reprimand for marrying a widow from Louisiana instead of one of the daughters of the Spanish aristocracy, as José himself had done two years earlier in marrying Concepción Valenzuela de Fuentes,[405] daughter of the fourth Count of Puebla de los Valles. Perhaps it was no coincidence that about this time Bernardo de Gálvez christened a village and a ship with the name of his uncle's wife. In any case, four years later, on November 26, 1781, in the bishop's palace in Havana, the "nuptial blessings" took place, and "His Excellency has esteemed it proper to make public his secret marriage, on behalf of the holy sacrament itself, and of its offspring, so no one ever could doubt their legitimate condition."[406]

Keeping such a secret in New Orleans could not have been easy, but it certainly became impossible in August of the following year.[407] That month, almost exactly nine months after the marriage, Matilde Bernarda Felipa Isabel Juana Felicitas y Fernanda de Gálvez y Saint-Maxent was born. So either Bernardo de Gálvez's illness was not serious enough to prevent him from consummating the marriage, or his marriage to Feliciana performed the miracle of his speedy recovery. Matilde's godparents, Lorenzo Montalvo Ruiz de Alarcón, first Count of Macuriges, and his wife, Teresa Ambulodi y Arriola, were chosen from among the titled Cuban aristocracy.[408] The proud father later christened a ship with the name of his daughter.[409]

Not only did Bernardo de Gálvez become a Creole, but New Orleans society also experienced a significant degree of hispanicization. Despite José Antonio Armillas Vicente's assertion that Spanish "Creolization" was impossible, on the contrary, it is easy to find extensive Spanish influence on Louisiana society at that time.[410] In addition to the Spanish imprint on New Orleans's urban landscape—most of which came because of the city's destruction by two major fires in 1788 and 1794, after Gálvez's governorship—it was precisely under Gálvez that Louisiana's tradition of French literature was born. In 1777 Julien Poydras, a rich planter, published two poems dedicated to Gálvez. In the first, *Le dieu et les nayades du fleuve St. Louis*, the god of the Mississippi and his naiads congratulate Gálvez for his recovery from serious illness. In the second, *Épître á Don Bernard de Galvez*, the excessive celebratory tone made Edward Larocque Tinker suspect that the author was paving the way for certain favors from the governor.[411] Not only was Gálvez popular, but Spanish customs and culture were also becoming increas-

A photograph by Edwin L. Wisherd of two creole women standing in the doorway to their uptown home, originally published in the April 1930 issue of *National Geographic*. Both are wearing their mantillas (Spanish shawls) and one is holding her fan in a typical Spanish pose, 150 years after their great-great-great-grandmothers, according to Bernardo de Gálvez, "willingly adopted the use of [Spanish] *sayas* [dresses] and mantillas, voluntarily leaving aside the French-style dresses" (Bernardo de Gálvez to José de Gálvez, dispatch no. 320, New Orleans, October 16, 1779, AGI, Santo Domingo, 2586). (Edwin L. Wisherd/National Geographic Creative)

ingly so. According to Alice Moore Dunbar-Nelson, at the outbreak of the American Revolutionary War, the natives of Louisiana began to tolerate, and even to like, their (up to that moment, hated) Spanish rulers.[412] Sybil Kein even claims that the typical creole dish of jambalaya is a version of Spanish paella.[413] Dress, as Sophie White studied for slaves' constructions of masculinity and ethnicity in French colonial New Orleans, was a valuable channel for social and economic agency, and the use of the Spanish mantilla or shawl by New Orleans's women is another example of hispanicization.[414] In Bernardo de Gálvez's words, from an October 1779 report to his uncle, "Believing that dress is one of the things that most define nations, I have the satisfaction of informing Your Excellency that all of the ladies in this town have willingly adopted the use of [Spanish] *sayas* [dresses] and mantillas, voluntarily leaving aside the French-style dresses they previously wore. . . . There is not a single white person who has not embraced the Spanish fashion with gusto."[415]

From Madrid, His Majesty congratulated Bernardo de Gálvez and ordered him that "on his behalf, please do inform these ladies of his royal gratitude and approval of such behavior."[416]

5. Bernardo de Gálvez Takes the Initiative

Despite an old Spanish foreign policy axiom that counseled "war with the whole world and peace with England," in fact for most of the modern age—and especially after the arrival of the house of Bourbon on the throne of Spain—this advice was seldom heeded.[1] Spain's alliance with France, built upon the three Family Compacts (Pactos de Familia), so-called because both countries had Bourbon kings, made confrontation with the British almost the norm for the foreign policy of the Spanish monarchy, at least until 1777, when José Moñino y Redondo, Count of Floridablanca, was appointed secretary of state. He introduced a new vision of international relations based more on diplomacy and trade than on sheer military power. From this moment on, the main objective would be "to keep the peace at all costs in order to develop our trade and industry."[2]

Ironically, precisely at this juncture a gathering storm of circumstances was setting Spain up to make war on Britain. Two years earlier, at the outbreak of the conflict between England and its colonies in North America, Carlos III had asked for the opinion of his ministers, who, according to Sylvia L. Hilton, gave him all sorts of advice.[3] Several historians argue that Spain was not able to correctly assess the new situation, in which its own national interests demanded a change of alliance—namely, that it leave the French to support British efforts to suppress the revolt in its North American colonies.[4] José Luis Villacañas Berlanga maintains that Spain was not strong enough either to separate from France or to confront Britain.[5] In this context, the Count of Floridablanca adopted a policy whose main objective was to prolong the war as long as possible in order to wear down both opponents, which would not only strengthen Spanish power against them but hopefully resolve once and for all Spain's grievances vis-à-vis the British concerning Gibraltar, Minorca, the coast of Campeche (Mexico), and Honduras.[6] The first two complaints dated back to the Treaty of Utrecht (1713), the third to the Treaty of Paris (1763), and the last to the late seventeenth century.

So it is within this framework that Spanish participation in the American War of Independence must be understood.[7] It is also relevant to take into account the fact that around 1775, Spanish foreign policy was under serious scrutiny and finally underwent a major change.[8] From a foreign policy based on defense, a new policy was built on the idea of security. And whereas defense was understood mostly in military terms, the new policy encompassed other, no less important considerations, such as economic and strategic concerns.[9]

SPANISH POLICY TOWARD THE WAR BETWEEN BRITAIN AND ITS NORTH AMERICAN COLONIES

Floridablanca's policy has been called Fabianism, in reference not to the nineteenth-century socialist political theorist but to the Roman consul Quintus Fabius Maximus, who used delaying tactics during the Second Punic War to earn himself the name Cunctator, or "delayer" in Latin.[10] This strategy was summed up by the count himself, who declared that he would "prepare for the war, as it is inevitable, but do everything to prevent it."[11] In his report to His Majesty King Carlos III, which was also sent to his successor, King Carlos IV, he justified himself thus: "Your Majesty knows well of all of the efforts, steps, reports, and work I made to follow your orders, to prevent that outbreak, and after it happened, what I did again to achieve reconciliation and restore peace under the mediation of Your Majesty, which both powers accepted. All of the time spent in these negotiations served to increase Your Majesty's preparations and arms, make Your Majesty respected, and assume a better position in case Your Majesty's peaceful wishes were not fulfilled and a declaration of war became necessary, as in fact happened."[12]

The offer of Spanish mediation between Britain and the rebellious North American colonies was ambiguously received by the former, partially welcomed by the latter, and strongly opposed by the French, who believed they would profit more from a military victory than from a diplomatic settlement.[13] The revolutionaries conditioned their support on Spain's recognition of their independence, a request that was impossible to grant.[14] The U.S. Congress, on the other hand, was not at all inclined to consider the proposed terms of Spanish mediation in the war between Britain and its American colonies. Floridablanca's suggested armistice, proffered in 1778–79, would have allowed Britain to maintain possession of American territories that its military forces currently held while peace talks went forward, so there was no guarantee that U.S. independence could be secured by such an arrangement. In fact, Floridablanca was generally contemptuous of the United States—a point that should not be minimized in early Spanish-U.S. diplomatic relations.

On July 19, 1778, the U.S. Congress Committee of Commerce wrote to Bernardo de Gálvez: "By authentic advices lately received from Europe, we learn that His Catholick Majesty has offered his mediation in order to adjust the disp[ute] now subsisting between France, England, and these United States, which we hope may have a salutary effect, and thereby put an end to a cruel and inhuman War hitherto carried on by Great Britain against the Inhabitants of these United States, by burning their Towns and Villages on the Sea Coasts, massacreing the innocent Inhabitants, Men, Women, and Children without distinction by the scalping Knife, Tomohawk and Bayonet."[15]

During the four years between the start of the Revolutionary War and Spain's declaration of war on Britain, Spain would officially proclaim its neutrality while doing everything it could to help the rebels' cause.[16] Spain's support aimed at weakening the British more than at strengthening the Americans, since it was clear to everyone that such an action could set a dangerous precedent for Spanish possessions in the Americas. The alliance was sort of another version of the old axiom that "the enemy of my enemy is my friend," which so many times in history has produced odd couples. On this occasion, it led to a joining of interests between an absolute monarch and the American revolutionaries, who would soon proclaim that all men are created equal.

SPAIN'S SUPPORT FOR THE AMERICAN REBELS

In March 1778 Bernardo de Gálvez announced that Spanish neutrality "would not compromise its hospitality" to the Americans.[17] This hospitality allowed him to carry out all sorts of covert actions in their support. A few months later, he confirmed that this policy would continue "until the fate of the war is decided."[18] Captain James Willing tested Spanish hospitality during the first months of 1778 when he and his company of marines attacked several British settlements along the Mississippi River.[19] Willing's raid probably had more to do with pillaging than with military operations, but in any case Bernardo de Gálvez, following the advice of Oliver Pollock, authorized Willing to sell most of his loot in New Orleans.[20] In fact, as Pollock wrote in the spring of 1777, the American revolutionaries were confident that Gálvez was ready to open Spanish ports to American vessels and to allow New Orleans to become a venue for the sale of British prizes by U.S. privateers and cruisers.[21] In this letter, Pollock confided to Robert Morris that "the more mischief the better sport."[22]

The presence of Willing's men in the capital of Louisiana was protested by John Ferguson, commander of HMS *Sylph*, in a confrontation that never went further than an exchange of letters with Governor Gálvez.[23] In a letter dated May 15, 1778, Gálvez wrote Ferguson to express his surprise at the British protest, since, following the practice in Europe, both the British and the Americans were welcome in Louisiana.[24] At the time Gálvez's claim was absolutely true. In an order dated July 14 that year, he reminded the commanders of Spanish outposts in Manchac and Punta Colorada on the Mississippi that they should grant asylum to all applicants of British origin.[25] Gálvez's support to Willing was always determined by what he perceived as Spanish interests, so, as David Narrett has remarked, Willing found himself both helped and constrained by Spanish authority. In May 1778, Willing was denied permission to carry out an expedition against Iberville and Manchac that Gálvez deemed counterproductive to his strategy of keeping up appearances with the British.[26]

As time went by, Spanish support for the Americans was increasingly difficult to cover up. The British continued to protest it while the rebels not only acknowledged it but also showed their gratitude. A year before Willing's raid, the U.S. Congress Secret Committee sent Gálvez a letter stating, "We are informed by means of Mr Oliver Pollock of the favorable disposition you have been pleased to manifest toward the Subjects, Interest and cause of the United, Free and Independent states of America upon every occasion that has presented since your Excellency's accession to the Government of New Orleans & Louisiana."[27]

The Committee of Commerce also expressed its gratitude to Gálvez for facilitating the delivery of supplies to U.S. troops through New Orleans.[28] This is the context for the resolution presented by the Board of War and approved by the Continental Congress in October 1778 that "Governor Galvez be requested to accept the thanks of Congress for his spirited and disinterested conduct toward these States, and be assured that Congress will take every opportunity of evincing the favorable and friendly sentiments they entertain of Governor Galvez, and all the faithful subjects of his Catholic Majesty inhabiting the country under his government."[29]

As important as was the aid channeled through Louisiana with Gálvez's support, it must be remembered that this was only part of the Spanish contribution, in both cash and supplies, to the American Revolution. There has been some debate over the scale of the aid.[30] Of all the Spanish contemporaneous testimonies, the two most important are those of Diego María de Gardoqui and the Count of Aranda. In 1794 Gardoqui, who would become the first ambassador of Spain to the United States and whose firm Gardoqui & Sons played a crucial role in channeling Spanish aid to the American revolutionaries, stated that between 1776 and 1778, Spain contributed a total of "7,944,906 *reales* and 16 *maravedíes de vellón*" in cash and supplies.[31] In settling the account so as to submit a claim to the new United States, the Count of Aranda, Spain's ambassador to France at the time, offered the figure of five and a half million *reales de vellón* for the same period.[32] To these figures must be added the contributions made after the official declaration of war. Taking all calculations into account, the total Spanish economic aid to the American revolutionaries would be closer to 13 million *reales de vellón* (around 2 billion in today's U.S. dollars)—to be exact, 12,906,560 *reales de vellón*, including 4,961,960 *reales de vellón* in loans and 7,944,600 in nonrepayable grants.[33] According to American sources, the total was even slightly higher, but this discrepancy can be attributed to the difficulty of converting Spanish *reales de vellón* to the French *livres tournoises*.[34] French financial aid to the Americans was about 46 million *livres tournoises* (34 million *livres tournoises* in loans and 12 million in nonrepayable grants), equivalent to nearly 167 million *reales de vellón*.[35]

Thus, according to these figures, total Spanish financial aid to the American Revolution was less than 10 percent of French financial aid. But other nonfinancial contributions by Spain must also be taken into account. Among the latter, the opening of Spanish Caribbean ports to U.S. trade was essential for the new nation to sustain a military effort.[36] From the start, this opening was conceived as temporary and limited to the duration of the war.[37] Later this condition created serious problems in bilateral relations between the two countries, since American merchants rapidly became accustomed to the benefits of Spanish ports and were reluctant to renounce them when peace arrived. This access was also important for the small U.S. navy, which benefited from safe docking places where crews could rest and ships could be repaired and provisioned—the latter sometimes even at the expense of the Spanish Royal Treasury.[38]

Another important factor in the story of Spanish support of the American rebels was the role played by the Spanish commercial firm Gardoqui & Sons from Bilbao. Since the 1760s the company had been part of the cod industry in Boston and Salem. Reyes Calderón Cuadrado states that "the Gardoqui firm performed, with the knowledge of Spain, the role of American agent in selling their American cod products in Spain and France, buying on their behalf military supplies that the Gardoqui ships brought to America, along with other merchandise paid secretly by the Spanish Royal Treasury."[39]

Gardoqui & Sons was also one of the routes that Governor Gálvez used to channel his aid to the American revolutionaries. Most of the supplies were shipped from the Iberian Peninsula to Havana and then on to New Orleans. In January 1777 the courier ship from Havana arrived in the port of New Orleans with uniforms, medicines, and 300 muskets, in theory destined for the Louisiana Fixed Infantry Regiment. British spies in the city sent notice about the shipment to the British governor of Pensacola, who officially complained to the Spanish authorities about its real final destination. Not willing to have a problem with the British at that time, Governor Gálvez staged a public auction of the textiles and medicines, while the muskets and ammunition were conveniently misplaced in the Royal Treasury's warehouse. From there they eventually landed in the hands of Oliver Pollock, who successfully smuggled them to American-controlled territory.[40] Not only supplies but also cash issued forth from Louisiana through Pollock, who was able to procure a Spanish loan to Virginia for the George Rogers Clark campaign into the Illinois country in June 1778. This particular loan resulted in problems for Pollock since the U.S. Congress declined responsibility for them and Pollock became liable for the loan.[41] Between 1776 and 1777, more than 1.5 million *reales de vellón* were transferred to the American cause from the Royal Treasury in both New Orleans and Havana.[42]

THE COST OF THE WAR WITH BRITAIN

Such was the Spanish aid supplied to the American revolutionaries, but it was only part of Spain's total financial output on the war. To complete the picture, the total cost of the war itself must be considered. This is more easily said than done because there is no separate record of the amounts effectively spent by Spain on its war with Britain. Thus I have taken an indirect approach, comparing the amounts spent in the defense of Spanish possessions before and after the war to the amounts spent during the war. The difference between these amounts can provide a rough idea of the cost of the war itself. An important portion of expenses before the war should also be considered as part of the real cost of the war, as these expenses included preparations for what was to follow, but available data does not provide enough detail to allow us to make such estimations.

With all these caveats in mind, I calculate that the total cost for Spain of its war with Britain is in the neighborhood of 431 million *reales de vellón*.[43] It was a significant sum, especially considering that at the time the total annual revenues of the Spanish Royal Treasury were almost exactly the same amount.

In 1779 the Junta de Medios or Treasury Council actively started the usual mechanisms for raising money to cover the cost of the war. Some were specifically designed for the Spanish possessions in America, such as donations from landowners and corporations of merchants and artisans, lotteries in the main cities, the sale of aristocratic titles and posts in the colonial administration to American-born Spaniards, authorization to viceroys to raise money in ways they deemed appropriate, and an increase in the sales tax on alcohol.[44] Soon it was clear that, with a war with two operational theaters as

TABLE B. *Cost of the War with Britain, 1779-1783*

Year	Amount	Average Defense Expenditures during Peacetime	Difference in Expenditures during the War over Average during Peacetime
1775	323,031,000		
1776	351,082,000		
1777	325,280,000		
1778	337,515,000		
1779	336,489,000		63,600
1780	462,678,000		126,252,600
1781	410,506,000		74,080,600
1782	502,240,000		165,814,600
1783	401,496,000		65,070,600
1784	345,219,000	336,425,400	
Total expenditures during the war over the average during peacetime			431,282,000

Sources: Merino, *Las cuentas de la Administración central española*; Tedde de Lorca, "La Real Hacienda de Carlos III," 221-24.
Notes: All the figures in *reales de vellón*. The figures of the average defense expenditures during peacetime are the result of adding the defense expenditures of the years 1775, 1776, 1777, 1778, and 1784 and dividing the result by 5 (the number of years). Spain declared war on Britain on June 22, 1779, so this year has been considered as a war year despite the fact that the defense expenditure during it was little increased, probably because 1779's war expenses were registered in the accounts of the 1780s. The peace was signed in January 1783, but following the previous reasoning we have considered it as a war year.

far apart as America and the Mediterranean to pay for, these usual resources would not be enough and new ones would need to be found. In the meetings of the Treasury Council on June 29, 1779, and July 22, 1781, it was agreed that the Royal Treasury must issue *vales reales*, a kind of government bond. These *vales reales* were the first banknotes in the history of Spain[45] and for Earl J. Hamilton represent a crucial instrument in Spain's road to capitalism.[46] Even though it was not the first time that the Royal Treasury resorted to debt, this time it was decided that to make the *vales reales* more attractive to investors they would yield 4 percent interest rather than the traditional 3 percent and that the notes must be accepted at their face value in certain transactions, including the payment of taxes.[47] During the war with Britain there were three issues of public debt certificates: in August 1780 for 149 million *reales de vellón*, in March 1781 for 79 million, and in May 1782 for almost 222 million, for a total of 450 million *reales de vellón*.⁴⁸ Taking away the banker's fee (10 percent in the first issue and 6 percent in the other two), a total of 417 million *reales de vellón* was raised for the Royal Treasury—a figure close to the 431 million *reales de vellón* that I estimated was the cost of the war (about 66 billion in today's U.S. dollars).⁴⁹

ENTERING THE WAR AGAINST BRITAIN

On June 21, 1779, Spain officially declared war on Britain. No one was surprised. It was the direct consequence of the Treaty of Aranjuez signed by Spain and France on April 12, 1779. In article 7, Spain detailed each one of its objectives in the war: "The Catholic king has the intention to acquire by war and the future peace treaty the following advantages: 1st, the restitution of Gibraltar; 2nd, the possession of the river and the fort on Mobile; 3rd, the restitution of Pensacola with all the coast of Florida near the Bahama Channel, expelling from it all foreign domination; 4th, the expulsion of the British from the Bay of Honduras and the fulfillment by them of the prohibition stated in the 1763 Treaty of Paris to establish neither there nor in any other Spanish territory any kind of settlement; 5th, the revocation of the privilege granted to the British of cutting logwood [*palo de tinte*] on the coast of Campeche; and 6th, the restitution of the island of Minorca."⁵⁰ It is a long and ambitious list that contains two direct orders for Governor Gálvez: to conquer the river and fort of Mobile and to take not only Pensacola but both Floridas, East and West. The New Bahama Channel was a stretch of sea off the Atlantic coast of Florida whose control was essential to Spain. The sea routes leading from Mexico and the Spanish Caribbean to European Spain went directly through it, and thus securing it was of strategic importance since the presence there of an enemy power could strangle communications between Spanish possessions on both sides of the northern Atlantic. Two months after the signing of the San Ildefonso Treaty, the minister of the Indies, José de Gálvez, issued specific orders to the governor of Cuba. In a letter dated August 29, 1779, he wrote, "The King has determined that the main objective of his arms in America during the war with the English will be to expel them from the Mexican Basin and from the banks of the Mississippi, where their settlements are harmful to our trade and to the security of our richest possessions.... His Majesty desires that, without any delay, an expedition be arranged with all the land and naval forces that can be assembled to attack Mobile and Pensacola, which are the keys of the Mexican Basin, detaching, before or after, divisions that cover and clean the Englishmen from the banks of the Mississippi, which must be considered as protection of the vast empire of New Spain."⁵¹

In the *note verbale*—which in the jargon of diplomacy meant an official written communication—signed by the Duke of Almodovar, the ambassador of Spain to the British court, and delivered on June 16, the ambassador concluded that the king of Spain "has no choice but to use all means granted to him by the Almighty to obtain justice, which has not been possible by other means. His Majesty, being confident in the justice of his cause, hopes that the consequences of this resolution will not be taken against him either by God or men; and that other nations will consider it proper, especially in comparison to that of the British ministry."[52] The ambassador's note was answered the very next day by a speech of King George III to Parliament, in which he "strongly trusts that this chamber will support him with the zeal and ardor so many times before proven in his decision to use all the might and all the resources of the nation to resist and repel the hostile designs of the court of Spain."[53]

It is relevant to mention that Spain entered the war against Britain with France as an ally, but not the United States of America. This important distinction is clearly explained by Diego José Navarro in a notice sent to several Spanish officials in America on June 27, 1779: "There is no positive order or political basis for the United States to be seen or considered under any other concept but that of neutrality, since, not acting as subjects of Great Britain, they do not deserve our hostility; and not openly being friends of the Spanish nation, they should not benefit from our war efforts. Thus you will observe with them, their ships, and [their] vassals the orders issued last November 6, limiting aid to them to what is demanded by the right of hospitality."[54]

This statement had profound implications. For example, even though both Spain and the United States shared a common enemy, it would not be possible to plan or execute joint military operations. This particular issue arose when Diego José Navarro received an American suggestion to plan, or at least to discuss, this kind of initiative. Knowing the general policy, Navarro gave a formal and cold answer to the American rebels, telling them that since the matter exceeded his own powers, he had to consult with his capital.[55] Three months later he received a letter from Madrid informing him that he had done the right thing by responding that he "had no orders to participate in such actions and that the naval and land forces in Cuba were busy with other objectives of the utmost importance."[56] In November 1781 the minister of the Indies wrote to his nephew that after the conquest of British Jamaica, which was being planned at the time, no more help should be given to the United States in its war against Britain.[57]

The official entry of Spain in the war not only tipped the balance of the conflict, making the Franco-Spanish naval forces superior in number to the

British ones, but also profoundly changed the general strategy of the war.[58] Britain would be forced to abandon a purely American perspective and adopt a more global view.[59] And the British were not the only ones who had to change their strategy; the French also had to modify theirs since the Spanish government succeeded in imposing its own priorities regarding the use of the combined forces, making the French hostage to Spain's war aims: "the regaining of Minorca, Gibraltar, West Florida and the coast of Honduras."[60]

TAKING THE INITIATIVE

On May 18, 1779, more than a month before the official declaration of war, Spanish officials in America were informed about its imminent launch.[61] On July 17 the news that Spain and Great Britain were at war arrived in Havana and a little later in New Orleans.[62] However, Bernardo de Gálvez did not wait for this official confirmation to begin his long-formulated plan for attack.[63] Despite the fact that during previous years the military forces available in Louisiana had increased in number, they were not enough to guarantee the province's defense.[64] In a council of war held on July 13, 1779, Gálvez admitted that Louisiana faced a British force "formed of more than 800 veterans, and with the knowledge that mine barely total 500 men, with 330 of them raw recruits recently arrived from Mexico and the Canary Islands."[65] The unanimous opinion of all officers present was that "if no reinforcements arrived from Havana it was possible only to fortify the city [New Orleans] and to be reduced to the defensive in case war breaks out." But Gálvez, who in his own words "would rather be accused of being a daredevil than of any other thing," informed his men that he was resolved to "go and find our enemies in their own fortresses and posts, because if not taken one by one, I knew full well they are going to come find me."

Bernardo de Gálvez was right, for he had spent considerable time and resources building a network of spies, which had informed him of British intentions to capture New Orleans as quickly as possible. On June 17, 1779, Lord George Germain, the British minister for the colonies, had sent a letter to Frederick Haldimand informing him of the declaration of war and ordering him to attack New Orleans and other Spanish ports along the Mississippi in coordination with an expedition under the command of General John Campbell, which was to be arriving with ships and troops at the Natchez River.[66] In Gálvez's own words,

> not taking into account the opinion of the council of war, and trusting to the support of the local population, I made my preparations without public knowledge, and I decided to march on August 22. . . . [But on

August 18] a violent hurricane arrived and in less than three hours sank all of the ships ... among them the small warships and gunboats I had ordered to be built for the defense of the river. Many houses in the city and most of those around it were also destroyed, supplies lost, trees torn, men dismayed, their women and children wandering through the deserted fields abandoned to the elements, the land flooded, and everything drowned in the river, along with my resources, supplies, and hopes.

Any other governor would have used the hurricane as an excuse for staying in New Orleans while trying to recover. Instead, Gálvez argued that if before the hurricane the British could hardly believe that the Spaniards were going to attack, now, "because of the destruction caused by the hurricane (destruction that has not affected their [the British] settlements), they will certainly believe that we are almost defeated." Thus it was the perfect opportunity for a surprise attack. The key was to secure the support of the local population while at the same time not revealing his true intention. So,

> with the arrival of the news of the war also came news that His Majesty had appointed me full governor,[67] which I hid so as not to be forced to reveal the arrival of the mail-ship. I assembled the inhabitants and gave them as emotional a speech as I was able, about the sad condition of the colony, and the unhappy coincidence that at this exact time orders had arrived from Havana to protect the province, since Spain, having recognized the independence of the Americans, expected that the British would begin hostilities against us without motive, as they had against the French; that peace remained in force and that Spain wished to preserve it as long as England did not break it. I used this pretext to hide the real objective of my movements, which I had to make in front of everyone.

Bernardo de Gálvez was taking a huge risk. By falsely claiming that Spain had recognized the independence of the United States of America and that peace was still in force with Britain, he could lose all of the prestige and popularity he had gained up to that moment. Once he reached the emotional peak of his speech, he concluded in this way: "I also told the inhabitants that I had another piece of news to share with them; and pulling out my appointment as full governor, I shared this new honor that His Majesty had bestowed upon me—an honor that could not be fulfilled until the cabildo had sworn to defend the province; that to spill the last drop of my blood in sacrifice to my sovereign I did not need to take any oath, but since I could

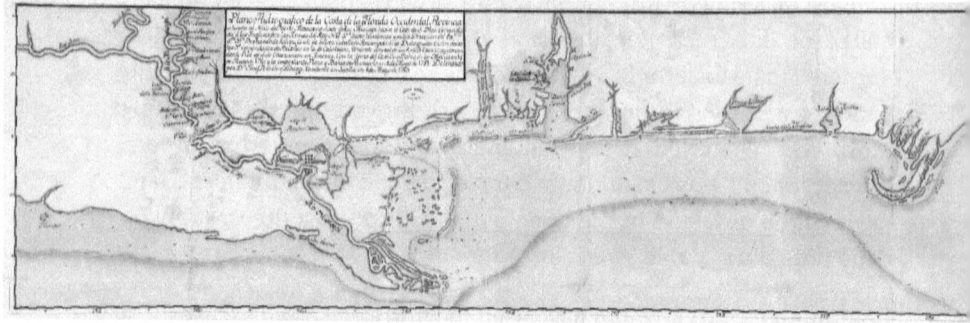

Manuscript map of the coast between New Orleans and Apalachicola Bay, drawn in 1783, showing the theater of operations of Bernardo de Gálvez's first campaigns against the British. (José Portillo y Labaggi, *Plano hidrográfico de la Costa de la Florida Occidental* . . . ; España, Ministerio de Educación, Cultura y Deporte, Archivo General de Simancas, MPD, 22,017)

not ensure the defense of the colony because of the few troops I had under my command, they should not expect me to take such an oath unless they promised to help me keep it."

It was a brilliant speech and also a clever political maneuver, reminiscent of the cunning of Julius Caesar when he addressed the mutinous men of his Tenth Legion as *quirites* rather than as soldiers.[68] In this moment Gálvez cashed in the capital of his popularity acquired during his tenure as acting governor. The people of New Orleans cheered him, and he was carried on their shoulders to the cabildo, whose "doors were broken rather than waiting until the keys were found, and I had the satisfaction of being received with the utmost expressions of joy." Once there, he received solemn promises that the city "would sacrifice its lives in the king's service and that they would gladly do the same with all their possessions if they had not already lost them." Immediately afterward they all tried to salvage anything that had survived the havoc left by the hurricane. Four small ships were removed from the bottom of the river, quickly repaired, and supplied with provisions, ammunition, and ten cannons. On August 26 Bernardo de Gálvez solemnly gave command of the city to Lieutenant Colonel Pedro Piernas, leaving him with only militias to defend it. The next day, four days behind the original schedule, "we set off, as they say, heading for adventure."

ATTACKS ON BRITISH SETTLEMENTS ALONG THE MISSISSIPPI

The force accompanying Gálvez "heading for adventure" was a small one: 170 veterans, 330 raw recruits, 20 carabineers, 60 militiamen, 80 free blacks and mulattoes, and Oliver Pollock, "an agent from the [U.S.] Congress, who made with me the whole campaign," along with 2 officers and 7 American volunteers. In Gálvez's words, he had "men of all conditions, nations, and colors, without an engineer or artillery officer."

The Attack on Fort Manchac

The first objective was Fort Manchac, also known as Fort Bute, on the left bank of the Mississippi south of Baton Rouge. This position had been completed in haste a month earlier and was manned by a very small garrison, as British commanders considered it quite difficult to hold.[69] For the British it was of limited strategic value anyway, but for Gálvez it was very important. On the one hand, it was on the way to Baton Rouge, whose conquest would deny the British a vital supply line; and on the other, Gálvez desperately needed a quick and easy victory. He was fully aware of the diverse composition and lack of experience of his "army," so it was essential to give them cohesion, experience, and high morale. For this there was nothing better than a victory, as small as it might be. On his way to Manchac he passed through the German Coast and the Acadian settlements, where he recruited another 600 men of all conditions and colors, as well as 160 Indians, so that his force now totaled 1,427 men. They marched the 100 miles from New Orleans to Manchac in eleven days. The slow pace, only 9 miles a day, was far less than the 15 miles stipulated by Frederick the Great[70] and the 18 miles specified in Spanish army regulations at the time.[71] To be fair to Gálvez's men, these figures were calculated for professional armies with well-trained veteran soldiers marching on even ground, neither of which was the case. Gálvez's troops were inexperienced and untrained, and they marched through "thick forests and impassable roads, without tents, baggage, and other essential equipment"—to which must also be added that the heat was suffocating and the marshes infested with mosquitoes carrying malaria, which would claim one-third of them.

Gálvez did everything possible to conceal his real objective. Before departing New Orleans he dispatched a letter to General John Campbell dealing with normal bureaucratic matters.[72] For their part, the British received news about a Spanish force on the move, but they were unable to gather details until it was too late.[73] On September 6 the Spaniards arrived in Manchac, where Gálvez announced that Spain was at war with Britain. The British garrison was caught totally by surprise, and to prevent the news from spreading Gálvez sent a small detachment north to cut off the road to Baton Rouge. In the early hours of the next day Gálvez gave the order to attack. Most probably the fort would have surrendered if offered the chance, but Gálvez needed to conquer it by assault as a morale-building symbol. The first man to enter the British position was the militia captain Gilberto Antonio Saint-Maxent, Gálvez's father-in-law. There were no casualties on either side, and one captain, one lieutenant, one under-lieutenant, and twenty-four privates—in other words, almost the entire British garrison— were made prisoners of war (six privates managed to escape during the first stages of the fight). As Charles Gayarré writes, "This certainly was no great exploit,"[74] but as John Walton Caughey accurately points out, it was a good initiation for the militia, and the victory improved their morale.[75] These were precisely Gálvez's aims. After taking possession of the fort and making the usual inventories, they remained in Manchac for a week to give the many sick men time to recover.

The Attack on Baton Rouge

The success against Manchac was made possible by the element of surprise. In Baton Rouge this was not an option. Despite having been raised in less than six weeks, the defenses of the fort at Baton Rouge were much more impressive than those at Manchac. They included a moat eighteen feet wide and almost nine feet deep, with "earth walls surrounded with *chevaux de frise*, protected by thirteen cannons and defended by 900 men, 400 of them veterans and the rest consisting of locals and armed black men." In theory the Spanish forces were 1,427 men strong, but with one-third of them sick or recovering and only 170 veterans, their only superiority, besides their commander, was from the artillery. Despite having three cannons fewer than the British, the Spanish cannons were of a larger caliber and thus of a longer range, giving an advantage that Bernardo de Gálvez was to use.

Perhaps the safest way to get hold of Baton Rouge would have been to starve the garrison, but Gálvez did not have the two months needed for this kind of siege. British reinforcements could arrive at any time, and so, "taking into account that my small army was mostly made up of civilians and that any setback would put all of the colony in mourning, I decided to excavate the trenches and position the batteries." Gálvez found "two suitable emplacements, and I chose the less convenient one, hoping to fool the enemies by drawing their attention to a different place from the one we were really going to use." With this idea of misleading the garrison, on September 20 he sent a detachment of white and colored militiamen and Indians to the edge of the forest that was closest to the fort. "By night, and protected by the trees, some men chopping wood, others excavating, and the rest firing toward the fort as if they were covering the workers, the result was that the enemies tired themselves in vain firing to that place with their cannons, both with cannonball and shrapnel, without hurting anyone, while on the other side [of the fort], making no noise and without being disturbed, the trenches were dug and the batteries placed behind an orchard which hid them."

Late in the evening the British realized their mistake, but it was too late, since the Spanish artillery was already under cover. Continuing with Gálvez's account:

> The following morning, at five and three quarters (because a thick fog did not allow it earlier), we started firing at them, directed by... Julián Álvarez, with so much accuracy that despite continuous fire from the enemy, after three and a half hours the fort was so dismantled that they sounded the bugle and two officers came with terms for their surrender, which I did not accept, demanding that the garrison must remain prisoners of war and that their surrender must include that of Fort Panmure in Natchez, which garrison was composed of eighty grenadiers and their officers. They agreed to all my demands, and after the twenty-four hours I had given them to consider my offer, which we saw they employed in burying their dead (which number they do not want to tell me on a whim), they came out with military honors to a distance of five hundred paces, where the 375 men (since I allowed the inhabitants and the black men to return to their homes) yielded their weapons and handed in their flags, becoming prisoners of war.

Even if the British officers did not, "on a whim," tell Gálvez the number of their casualties, they had to inform their superiors in London. Issue number 12070 of the *London Gazette* published a list of 36 dead and 10 wounded.[76] On the number of prisoners of war, the British and Spanish figures differed. According to the *London Gazette*, in all the operations carried out by Gálvez along the Mississippi, 485 prisoners were taken, 378 of them in Baton Rouge (15 officers, 6 surgeons, 17 noncommissioned officers, 5 others, and 335 privates; see appendix table 1).

For his part, Bernardo de Gálvez mentions 577 prisoners (21 officers, 3 surgeons, 3 others, and 550 soldiers),[77] not taking into account "the sailors of the eight ships captured, or the locals and black men fighting in Manchac, Baton Rouge, and other places, who, according to the Laws of War, should have been made prisoners, too, and who numbered about another five hundred; but their freedom was granted as a bequest from our sovereign's warm heart, and because it would have been impossible to guard them if the Second Battalion of the España Regiment had not arrived from Havana."

The troops from Cuba arrived too late to take part in the action against the fort, but they were used to guard the prisoners and especially to reinforce

New Orleans from the possibility of a British attack.[78] Despite Madrid's orders to send reinforcements to Gálvez, they arrived late because they lacked transports, since several merchant ships docked in Havana's port had been authorized to return to Europe "against the king's express orders."[79] This fact earned Juan Bautista Bonet, naval commander of Havana, a strong reprimand from his superiors.[80]

Spanish and British accounts do agree on one thing: the good treatment received by the British prisoners of war. King Carlos III conveyed to Gálvez his satisfaction with "the extraordinary humanity with which the vanquished were treated." In a letter to his superior officer in Pensacola, the British commander of Baton Rouge, General John Campbell, wrote that "I must do justice to His Excellency Don Bernardo de Gálvez by stating that officers and soldiers, prisoners of war in this place, are treated with the utmost generosity and kindness; not only the Spanish officers but also their soldiers are keen to be polite and kind to all prisoners."[81] Shortly afterward the prisoners were escorted to New Orleans, where officers in particular were granted a large amount of freedom under parole. Some of them returned to Pensacola or even to England on the condition they not bear arms against Spain until properly exchanged.[82]

Immediately after the surrender of Baton Rouge, Gálvez sent a detachment of fifty men, under the command of Captain Juan Delavillebeuvre, to Fort Panmure in Natchez, almost 125 miles up the Mississippi. Panmure was of strategic importance because it controlled a great part of the river's left bank. Its defenses were much more impressive than those of Manchac or Baton Rouge, so having included its surrender in the capitulation of Baton Rouge had been a master stroke on Gálvez's part.[83] Delavillebeuvre's mission was a delicate one, not from a military point of view but from a political one. Once more the services rendered by the American revolutionary Oliver Pollock were essential. He wrote a letter to the Natchez district's inhabitants congratulating them on now being under the protection of the armies of His Catholic Majesty and praising Gálvez's conduct.[84] Once at the gates of Fort Panmure, also known as Fort Rosalie, Delavillebeuvre delivered to Captain Anthony Forster, the garrison's commander, a document from Forster's superiors ordering him to surrender his position. On October 5 Captain Forster, two lieutenants, three sergeants, two drummers, and fifty-four privates, accompanied by thirteen women and children, exited the fort. Delavillebeuvre and his men entered and remained there as its garrison.[85] The Spanish military presence in Natchez was essential, as most of the settlers in the area were hostile to Spain. In fact, as Robert V. Haynes has hinted, the "only positive effect of the Spanish occupation" was to unite the inhabitants, who until that moment had been divided into pro-American and pro-British factions, against the Spanish.[86] This fact would be very important for the events that later unfolded in Natchez.

Before returning to New Orleans, Bernardo de Gálvez had to consolidate his conquests. He appointed Carlos Grand Pré district commander as a reward for capturing the British posts in Thompson's Creek and Amite River and Pedro José Favrot commander of the fort's garrison. On September 25 he issued a proclamation announcing that in six days all inhabitants had to take an oath of loyalty to the Spanish Crown or abandon the colony. To those who chose to depart, assurances were given that they could take with them all of their possessions and slaves, that they would not suffer any offense from the Spanish troops, and that none of their papers, public or private, would be confiscated or examined.[87] Despite this generous offer, according to Rose Meyers, the inhabitants of the Baton Rouge district, being mostly Anglo-Saxon and Protestant, still feared the Spanish government, and several incidents, such as the escape of a British officer who broke his parole, prompted Gálvez to issue an order to Pedro José Favrot to make clear to the population the serious consequences they would face if they sheltered or helped an enemy.[88]

Other Military Operations on the Mississippi

While the troops under the direct command of Bernardo de Gálvez were conquering British forts along the Mississippi, naval combat took place between the American corvette *Morris*, under the command of William Pickles, and the British ship *West Florida*, under (depending on the source) George Burdon or John Willet Payne, in the lake today called Pontchartrain near New Orleans.[89] After a brief exchange of fire, the Americans boarded the enemy ship and captured its crew. Gálvez remarked, "It is incredible that this ship [the *Morris*] was able to make this capture because of the differences of ships, artillery, etc. It is true that its crew was larger, and it boarded the enemy; if not it would have had a very difficult time. The royalists lost their captain and three other men were killed and five wounded." The importance of this naval action lies in the fact that HMS *West Florida* then joined the Spanish flotilla as a private corsair under the new name of *Galvezton* (it was also called the *Galveztown* or simply the *Gálvez*). The *Galvezton* would play an essential role in Bernardo de Gálvez's campaigns.

Finally, there were two minor actions to mention: the capture of several small British vessels near Galveztown, which were returning from Pensacola, and Vicente Rillieux's seizure of a British transport on its way to Manchac, with fifty-six soldiers from the Waldeck Regiment.[90]

Epilogue to the Expedition: The British Attack against San Luis de Ilinueses

After recovering from their initial surprise, the British responded by trying to regain control of the Mississippi with an attack against San Luis de Ilinueses, today's St. Louis, Missouri. In May 1780 they attacked the Spanish garrison under the command of Captain Fernando de Leyva. Leyva's 29 soldiers and 281 armed civilians were confronted by more than 300 British soldiers and 900 Indian warriors. The February 16, 1781, issue of the Spanish official newspaper, the *Gazeta de Madrid*, published an account of the defense emphasizing Captain Leyva's gallant defense and the cruelties committed by the enemy while retreating from San Luis de Ilinueses.[91]

John Walton Caughey mentions the British astonishment at a defeat by such inferior numbers.[92] Perhaps the key was the cohesion and discipline showed by the Spaniards, who made good use of their small artillery, while the attackers simply ran toward the enemy with no order. The combat tactics of the Indians were very effective on open ground and in guerrilla warfare but not very successful against well-planned defenses and well-trained troops. In this particular case, the British and their Indian allies quickly spent their strength in front of the St. Louis palisades and then turned their frustration against anything and anyone they found in their way. The report made by Martín Navarro to the court in Madrid is loaded with instances of the cruelties perpetrated by "these hungry wolves."[93]

Results

In his already extensively quoted "Excerpt of what happened in the expedition made by the brigadier Don Bernardo de Gálvez, governor of the province of Louisiana, against the settlements and forts the British had along the banks of the Mississippi River, which he succeeded in taking and completely evicting," Bernardo de Gálvez presented some of his achievements. "This was the end of our expedition, and His Majesty's troops had to return back for lack of anything else to conquer. The result was the acquisition of more than one thousand miles of the best lands along the Mississippi, with the best settlements, and mostly populated by nations who occupy themselves in the fur trade."[94] Gálvez showed his pride when he wrote, "His Majesty's troops had to return back for lack of anything else to conquer"—and it was warranted, although some contemporaries interpreted it as arrogance. His pride was often used against him by his enemies. As John Stuart Mill remarked, "the Spaniards pursued all their great men with it, embittered their lives, and generally succeeded in putting an early stop to their successes."[95] The Spanish general and war theorist the Marquis of Santa Cruz de Marcenado, in his *Military Reflections* first published in 1730, advised that "a commander achieves no greater happiness than to defeat his enemies in battle, and therefore never is his restraint more needed than after victory, since he then sets in motion against himself all the powers of envy."[96]

From the strategic point of view, Bernardo de Gálvez's conquests along the left bank of the Mississippi took a territory regarded by the Crown as vital to "the protection of the vast empire of New Spain" and also succeeded in dispersing British forces that otherwise could have united against him or the American rebels.[97] Furthermore, the campaign along the Mississippi helped to relieve pressure from the British against Georgia and South Carolina and made it impossible for the two British armies operating in the north and the south to reunite.[98] It additionally ensured that Spanish aid to the American Revolution would safely reach General Washington's Continental army via the Mississippi.[99] And last but certainly not least, it ended the menace of a British attack against New Orleans, as the British themselves recognized.[100] Several messengers intercepted in Natchez carried official dispatches on the subject.[101] In November 1779 a certain Mr. Gordon wrote to Thompson & Campbell Company in Jamaica about this situation: "Immediately after learning about the war with Spain we all thought that we must attack New Orleans; and preparations for that expedition started immediately, but to our great disappointment, precisely when everything was ready for departure, news arrived that Don Galwas [Gálvez] had forced our troops to surrender."[102]

Besides such strategic achievements, Gálvez's campaign on the Mississippi provided him with an important opportunity to develop his military leadership capabilities, such as his strategic vision. By starting with attacks on British settlements and forts along the Mississippi instead of on Spain's main objectives, Mobile and Pensacola, Gálvez was able to take the enemy by surprise and then proceed eastward after having secured his rear guard. While it is true that expelling the British from the banks of the Mississippi was among the orders sent by José de Gálvez to the governor of Cuba, it is important to remember that those orders, dated August 29, 1779, were received after Bernardo de Gálvez had already departed for Manchac with his small and diverse army.[103]

Another characteristic of Gálvez's military capability was his tactical intuition. By winning "three forts, one by assault, another by capitulation, and another by cession," he demonstrated his ability to use different methods in different situations.[104]

Gálvez also would always take good care of his men, or, as the 1768 Spanish army regulations stated, he would show "clear concern for his subordinates." As a colonel he was charged with paying special attention to "the well-being of his soldiers," and the evidence is that he always did that.[105] In a letter dated September 20, 1779, Martín Navarro, Louisiana's royal treasurer, wrote to José de Gálvez that Bernardo was "in total command of the troops, and to this end he employs the better policy, which must be a model for all generals, since he not only treats his troops with the cordiality that is natural for him and that wins his soldiers' hearts, but he also transforms himself into an Indian, a Creole, a soldier, to flatter each in his own way, without losing the decorum he owes to his own person."[106]

This quality also translated into preserving their lives as much as possible. Keeping morale high in an army formed mainly by militiamen and volunteers with little military training or experience demanded that casualties be kept to a minimum. In the letter his uncle sent him conveying His Majesty's congratulations on his victories, José expressly mentioned that "what has been of greatest interest to his [the king's] generous heart is the careful economy with which you have managed to handle the precious blood of his vassals, [and] the order, discipline, and harmony that reigned during the whole expedition."[107]

In addition, Gálvez led by example. In Navarro's letter to José de Gálvez, he wrote that "he, the first to sleep out in the open, because of the haste of the march and the lack of tents, was imitated by everyone; if the lack of bread makes him eat rice, everyone does the same as if they were feasting, and finally, he does what everyone does, but no one can do everything he does."[108]

One final, important result of Gálvez's victories along the Mississippi was to ensure Louisiana's full support for Spain, expressed in the devotion of the province's population to Spain's representative. When the victorious troops returned to New Orleans, the whole city gave them a hero's welcome, including a solemn Te Deum mass in the San Luis Cathedral.[109] Bernardo concluded his official report to Madrid with a request to his uncle "to convey to His Majesty that this same province, which in other times had been dubiously devoted to the Spanish nation, has now been able to give the clearest, most genuine, and most truthful evidence that their love and loyalty for their monarch is not surpassed by those of his own nationals."[110]

Julien Poydras, Louisiana's earliest poet, followed his early praises of Gálvez with a long poem published in 1779 under the title *La Prise du morne du Bâton Rouge par Monseigneur de Galvez*.[111] In it the Mississippi River, awakened by the sound of cannon fire, sends one of its nymphs to inquire about the origin of the noise. When she returns she describes all that she has seen and heard:

I've seen that hero, who caused your alarm,
He looks like a God, covered in his arms,
His superb Panache thorough at the discretion of the wind,
And his disheveled hair served him as ornament.
A noble and proud aspect announces his courage,
The heroic virtue shines over his face.[112]

Along with the mythological references, Poydras stresses throughout the poem the care Gálvez takes of his troops, his eagerness to be the first to confront any danger, and the devotion his men feel for him. He concludes:

As in our climates, this generous conqueror,
Of a People he loves he will bring happiness;
The God interrupting, allows his joy to burst,
I see him, he says, it's Heaven who sends him.
May he live embraced by prosperity,
May he enjoy the pleasure of being adored.
May his great virtues be celebrated by all,
May his beautiful actions get him trophies.[113]

Poydras's wishes for Gálvez were soon granted. Bernardo de Gálvez sent his brother-in-law, militia lieutenant Maximiliano Saint-Maxent, to Madrid to report his victories, knowing that the military custom was that the officer carrying good news was traditionally rewarded. But Lieutenant Saint-Maxent did not arrive at his destination; his ship was captured by the British, and he barely had time to throw his official dispatches overboard. He was soon exchanged and freed and promoted to the rank of captain, not in the militia but in the Spanish regular army's Louisiana Fixed Infantry Regiment.[114] In the end Captain José Valière served as messenger. He arrived in the port of El Ferrol on December 21, 1779, carrying several captured British flags.[115]

Maximiliano Saint-Maxent was only one recipient of the king's generosity. Bernardo de Gálvez was deeply satisfied with the performance of his men, particularly the militiamen, who, in his words, were "the ones who had done the most." He also claimed that "no less praise was due to the company of free blacks and mulattoes, who were always at the vanguard, both in simulated attacks and frontal assaults, always firing at the enemy, behaving with as much courage, humanity, and selflessness as the white [troops]." In addition, "the Indians have shown for the first time a beautiful example of a humanity superior to that which has been many times shown by some of the civilized nations from Europe."[116] Shortly after his return to New Orleans,

The only surviving British flag of the several captured by Bernardo de Gálvez during the American Revolutionary War. The flag, today preserved in the Spanish Army Museum in Toledo, was kept for centuries in the church of Macharaviaya, the Gálvez family village of origin. During the French invasion of Spain in 1808, the population of Macharaviaya rallied against the French invaders waving this flag while shouting "Gálvez!" Unfortunately, no record has been found about the reaction of the French soldiers after being attacked by a group of Andalusian peasants formed under a British flag. (*British Flag captured by Bernardo de Gálvez during his campaigns in America*, 1781; © Museo del Ejército, inventory no. 40390)

Gálvez sent Madrid a long list of the "officers and several others who, from their conduct during the expedition, it is considered should be promoted." The list included sixty-three people: forty-two military personnel (twenty-two regular soldiers, thirteen from the white militia, and seven from the colored militia), five civil servants from the Royal Treasury, and eight others who served in the expedition, to whom he would add two more officers, four cadets, and two sergeants.[117] Among the officers of the colored militia, thirty "silver double-sized *al mérito* medals" were distributed.[118]

All of the people included in Gálvez's list received the promotions he asked for, with one exception.[119] Gálvez proposed that Acting Lieutenant Colonel Esteban Miró be made full lieutenant colonel in the Louisiana Fixed Infantry Regiment. Instead, he was made full colonel since Gálvez was to be promoted to *mariscal de campo* (one-star general) and hence could no longer be in direct command of the Louisiana Fixed Infantry Regiment.[120]

Besides satisfying Bernardo de Gálvez's ambition, his promotion reaffirmed his position as the supreme commander of all military operations in the North American theater. In a letter to the governor of Cuba dated August 29, 1779, right around the time the expedition had set out, José de Gálvez had written,

> The king wishes that this expedition should be under the command of Brigadier Don Bernardo de Gálvez, governor in full of Louisiana, who being the author of the plan, has acquired a practical knowledge of those lands. He keeps intelligences [that is, spies] among the enemies, is well informed about the operations that the United States troops will conduct in Georgia, has earned the friendship of the Chactas [Choctaws] and other Indian nations, who will turn to the British if someone not known to them is put in command, and lately his successful actions and perhaps a combination of happy coincidences have rendered him much credit among the members of the [U.S.] Congress and spread respect for his name among the English settlements near Louisiana. Knowing the vital importance in war of reputation among the enemies, His Majesty has determined on the appointment of the above-mentioned governor [as military supreme commander], choosing him instead of other officers with more years of experience, who no doubt would be better for any other enterprise.[121]

The long list of reasons for appointing Bernardo de Gálvez clearly exposes José de Gálvez's nepotism in choosing his nephew, since there would have been no need to justify it if a more experienced officer had been selected for the job. Aware that Bernardo de Gálvez's promotion to brigadier general might be contested by other Spanish leaders, José de Gálvez reinforced his nephew's standing by severely reprimanding Cuba's governor, Diego José Navarro, for not supporting him enough. In a letter dated January 1780, he starts by lecturing the governor about the art of war: "In war action is at the origin of all success, and when precious time is wasted in consultations and changes of plans, it is impossible that the king's armies can obtain the glorious advantages that we should have [obtained] from our own situation and that of our enemies." He continues by informing the governor that the king "considers lost the auspicious momentum for implementing the planned enterprises, and is left with disgust that his royal orders were not put into practice with the speed and rigor they should inspire." He ends in the same recriminatory tone: "It is true that if, when the expedition in the Mississippi ended, when the British fleet was fleeing from the French, and when the Count d'Estaing threatened Georgia with more than twenty-six ships of the line, the Spanish forces had appeared in front of Pensacola, it is very likely that this important port would be now among our dominions. The king does not doubt that you did everything on your side, but it was necessary to push aside the difficulties, even risking something, so as not to spoil an opportunity that would hardly present itself again."[122]

In the United States the news of the Spanish victory was spread by Juan de Miralles. Miralles was the "secret" envoy of the Spanish court to the United States, since Spain and the United States would not establish official diplomatic relations until 1785. Between 1778 and 1780 he resided in Philadelphia, where he was responsible for channeling most of the aid that the United States received from Spain.[123] He developed a close relation with some of the Founding Fathers and died in April 28, 1780, in Morristown, New Jersey, while visiting George Washington's headquarters. His funeral, with military honors, was presided over by Washington.[124] In February 23, 1780, the following article, inspired by Miralles, appeared in the *Pennsylvania Journal and Weekly Advertiser*: "Account of the Operation and Advantages Acquired by His Catholic Majesty's Arms, under the Command of Brigadier General Don Bernardo De Galvez, Governor of the Province of Luciana, Against the English Situated on the River Mississippi; the possession taken of all their establishments, of three forts at Manchac and Natchez defended by 550 privates and a number of inhabitants and blacks who took up arms and were made prisoners of war under the dominion of the king of Spain, and about fifteen hundred miles of the very best fertile and prime grounds. This account has been sent to this town by the Governor of Havannah, under the date of November 23d, 1779."[125]

Just a few days later, Miralles informed José de Gálvez that the news about the Spanish conquest on the Mississippi was not well received. Some members of the Continental Congress as well as other important people were displeased, because with these lands in Spanish hands they would not be able to incorporate them into the new country. Miralles argued that this claim was absurd, since they did not possess the smallest part of this territory, and if they were incapable of keeping their conquests of 1778 under their control, how they could dream of conquering lands where the British had strong fortified positions and numerous armies? He informed José de Gálvez that members of Congress were well aware of these considerations, but they fooled themselves into thinking that in the future they could annex these lands to ones they already had along the Ohio River. They were also conscious that the Spanish conquests deprived them of any solid basis for freely navigating along the Mississippi, which was their real interest.[126] Proof of the importance of this issue for the Continental Congress was its order that all available information be sent to John Jay, the U.S. representative in Madrid.[127] George Washington wrote to Juan de Miralles: "I am happy in the opportunity of congratulating you on the important successes it announces to the arms [sic] of His Catholic Majesty, which I hope are a prelude to others more decisive. These events will not only advance the immediate interest of his Majesty, and promote the common cause, but they will probably have a beneficial influence on the affairs of the Southern states at the present juncture."[128]

In Spain, news of the victories on the Mississippi was published in the December 31, 1779, issue of the *Gazeta de Madrid* and a supplement that appeared two weeks later.[129] Although this could be considered the start of a propaganda campaign directed by José de Gálvez on behalf of his nephew, in fact the *Gazeta* was the official newspaper of the Spanish court, where all news was published, both national and international. In any case, thanks to this kind of publicity, Bernardo de Gálvez was beginning to be known for something other than being the nephew of the minister of the Indies.

In Britain, the reports of Gálvez's victories along the Mississippi were first received with surprise, which soon transformed into defiance against the Spanish aggression, as a print published in London in March 8, 1780, testifies.

MOBILE

Gálvez spent the months following his return to New Orleans making plans and preparations for a campaign against "Mobile and Pensacola, which are the keys to the Mexican Basin."[130] Quite a few people in the higher echelons of the Spanish administration, both civilian and military, believed that Bernardo de Gálvez was not the right person for this important job. They attributed his success on the Mississippi to sheer luck and insisted that the strength of the defenses of Mobile and Pensacola demanded a commander with more experience. Among the naysayers was the governor of Cuba, Diego José Navarro, who without ever directly confronting the all-powerful minister of the Indies did as much as he could to delay Bernardo de Gálvez's preparations. Besides ensuring the late arrival of the Second Battalion of the España Regiment in Baton Rouge, Navarro continued to procrastinate.

Plans and Preparations

Bernardo de Gálvez worked long and deliberately on his plans for attacking Mobile. As seen earlier, during the first months of 1778 he had sent Cap-

Engraving published in London on March 8, 1780. Britain, preparing for battle with her shield and spear, talks to America: "Daughter return to your duty, and let me punish those empty Boasters; those base Villains, who keep you from your allegiance and disturb our quiet." America, brandishing a knife and a tomahawk, responds, "Mother if you would punish these villains who forced me from my allegiance, and disturb our quiet, you must find them at home, those gentlemen are my allies, we are now amid and seek your life." On her right side, Don Carlos, a sixteenth-century dressed Spaniard, is ready to fight while saying, "Signiora Britania. I'll take care your daughter shall be true to me. I'll make her wear a Spanish Padlock." On America's left, Monsieur Louis, this time with a proper eighteenth-century tenure, warns with a heavy French accent, "Sacra Dieu, I will have your daughter vether you will let me or no, and vat you tink besides. By Gar I will make you my servant, to vair upon us, you shall roast your own bull for our wedding dinner." (*Britania and Her Daughter—A Song*, 1780, in Prints and Photographs Division, Library of Congress, control no. 2004673374)

tain Jacinto Panis to Mobile and Pensacola on a spy mission,[131] and after Panis's return he commissioned the captain to prepare a plan for their conquest.[132] Panis's plans, with only minor changes, became the basis for Gálvez's campaign.[133] For example, Panis's plans included a fleet and at least 7,000 men,[134] but Gálvez estimated four ships of the line and 4,000 men would be enough.[135] But even with these reduced numbers Gálvez needed reinforcements from Cuba, and if Navarro had not been enthusiastic about supporting him in the past, he was definitely not supportive this time. According to John Walton Caughey, "First, [Navarro] delayed any action until news arrived of the outcome of the Manchac expedition. Second, he offered a substitute plan for the seizure of West Florida, which would emphasize a naval onslaught on Pensacola. The plan, designed by the colonel of the engineer corps Luis Huet, considered that Pensacola would capitulate after a naval bombardment without troops having to be landed, and that Mobile and the other posts would automatically share the same fate."[136]

Bernardo de Gálvez considered Navarro's proposal totally wrong. First, according to information gathered by Panis, the cannons in Pensacola's fort were of a longer range than those on board the Spanish ships, so the latter would not be able to approach the fort without being blown to pieces.[137] Second, also from Panis's intelligence, the state of Mobile's defenses was less impressive and in fact easier to breach than Navarro thought.[138] Third, Mobile was on the supply route to Pensacola.[139] And fourth, Gálvez certainly remembered that a similar idea had led to the 1775 disaster in Algiers.

Navarro answered these objections with a new plan, also by Luis Huet, in which he abandoned the idea of a naval bombardment in favor of an amphibious assault against Mobile, from which they would then attack Pensacola.[140] Navarro accompanied his plan with a letter explaining that it was impossible to send Gálvez the men he requested, both because of the great number of prisoners on the island, which required troops to be properly guarded, and because, in his opinion, only half of that number was needed for the implementation of Gálvez's plan.[141] If Navarro had been sincere in his offer of 3,500 men, Gálvez would have been more than happy. But this, too, was nothing more than another delaying tactic. In a last effort to have his demands met, Gálvez sent Esteban Miró, lieutenant colonel of the Louisiana Fixed Infantry Regiment, to Havana. When Miró arrived at the end of January 1780, he confronted a wall of silence, which he tried to break through by haggling about the number of troops to be sent to Gálvez. First he asked for the 3,500 Navarro had seemingly conceded to, then requested 1,500, and then almost begged for 1,300.[142] In the end he had to settle for 567 men from the Navarra Regiment. According to a later official account of the expedition against Mobile, "From late October to early January Don Bernardo de Gálvez waited in New Orleans for the arrival of important reinforcements from Havana to start the expedition against Pensacola. ~~Guessing~~ [crossed out in the original] Persuaded by news arriving from the island that the reinforcements were on their way, he decided to depart with his people to meet them, and if unable to find them, to attack the castle of Mobile with only his own troops, and ~~reuniting there with the armaments from Havana~~ [crossed out in the original] while waiting there for reinforcements from Havana, and after accomplishing the mission there, to attack Pensacola."[143]

Gálvez's description was not totally accurate, because Esteban Miró did not arrive in Havana until the end of January, so it was not possible for him to know earlier that same month that reinforcements were coming from Cuba. The reality he could not put in writing was much simpler: that he was tired of delays and excuses from Spanish authorities on the island and so decided to confront them with the fait accompli of his attack on Mobile and force them to react.

Heading to Mobile

On January 2 Bernardo de Gálvez gave the final orders to the garrison staying behind in New Orleans. On January 11 he reviewed his troops and ships. Despite certain discrepancies in his three accounts of the expedition, the number of troops under his command when he left New Orleans was about 1,300 men (see appendix table 2).[144] The ships under his command were far from the powerful armada that Jacinto Panis had envisioned. It was a mere flotilla, with only three warships and several transports (see appendix table 3).

After a delay of several days due to bad weather, on January 14, 1780, Bernardo de Gálvez's flotilla sailed from New Orleans down the Mississippi River. The voyage was very slow, in part because of the need to avoid being spotted by a British warship and in part because of the difficult navigational conditions of the Mississippi delta. An almost contemporaneous Spanish description notes that the huge deposits of mud carried by the river made it flow "through a great number of mouths, which continuously change because of the frequent spills from the river, which with time has formed a vast artificial terrain, whose coast is so flat and low that it cannot be seen from a distance."[145] Four days later the fleet had to stop to send some boats to sound the water's depth. When they returned, Gálvez consulted with the seamen and decided to take a course near a sandbank to the east, which forced them to "lighten the boats of more than twelve feet of draft."[146] It took two weeks to reach the mouth of the Mississippi. On February 6 they tried for open sea but had to return because of "the very dark horizons ... and a very windy night with showers, thunder, and lightning, and hail, and a tornado that struck at ten thirty, which almost sank us." The following day the wind was still very bad, and they had "to hoist the storm trysails." The morning of February 8 was the worst. The *Galvezton* sailed at sunrise, accompanied by only three other ships, one of them in very bad condition. The following day they sighted Mobile and discovered a British armed merchant frigate, which they pursued with such bad luck that the *Galvezton*, the *Volante*, and four other ships ran aground. "Despite efforts all day long, the *Volante* remained stuck," Gálvez noted in his diary. "The *Galvezton* remained aground from midday to one in the morning, when, after a huge amount of work, it was freed, but with extensive damage and leaking more than nine inches of water per hour; of the other four ships, two were able to free themselves and the other two remained aground with their crews and troops embarked, asking for help."

The men on these last two ships had to spend two days on board before they could be rescued. On February 12 the weather improved and Gálvez "took the decision to unship, on the beach at the point of Mobile, the troops on board the sloops that had arrived unharmed, to make them rest a little, and at the same time I gave orders to do the same with the rest of the ships as soon as they appeared." Slowly several ships were able to disembark their troops, with the exception of the *Volante* and the hospital ship *Rosario*, which had to be abandoned. On February 18 the prospect was bleak. The troops were on a deserted beach, "(among which were about eight hundred castaways, who had saved only themselves, having lost their food provisions, most of their ammunition, cannons, and other artillery supplies) without any other hope but that which our bare arms could provide us."

This description is from Gálvez's journal, but in the official account published later in the Spanish newspaper *Mercurio Histórico Político* it was thought fit to add that "among these frightening calamities [the troops] always maintained the same desire to fight against the enemy."[147] This addition about the troops' high morale certainly tried to hide, as several historians have pointed out, a moment of hesitation on Gálvez's part.[148] If at this precise moment a British attack had occurred, his troops, despite their alleged high spirits, would have had no choice but to surrender. Aware that his troops' morale could vanish if they remained at ease, he ordered them to start making ladders for climbing the walls of Mobile and to disembark the cannons to erect a battery for protecting the entrance to its bay. As soon as they were finished, they started to re-embark for the mainland (Mobile).

While they were thus occupied, a sloop was sighted. It was the vanguard of the flotilla coming from Havana with ammunition and food supplies for the expedition. Two days later, seven more ships arrived (see appendix table 4).

Despite this support, Bernardo de Gálvez's situation was desperate, much more so than he was then or later willing to admit. The later testimony of one of his officers was more revealing of the real situation. Gerónimo (also spelled Jerónimo) Girón Moctezuma was a colonel of the Príncipe Regiment, Gálvez's second in command during the expedition against Mobile, and, as descendant of the Aztec emperor Moctezuma, third Marquis of the Amarillas. In his application for his promotion to lieutenant general he described how "the troops found themselves ashore without arms or ammunition, naked and with nothing to eat in a land surrounded by enemies. There they remained for twelve days without tents or food other than the rice arrived from Havana. But far from being disheartened with these misfortunes, when the reinforcements arrived they were found to be making ladders, which they were to carry on their shoulders the long distance that still separated them from the enemies' stronghold, where they were certain to find everything they needed in the enemies' stores."[149]

At this point the British garrison in Mobile already knew of the presence of Spanish troops nearby, and, according to Gálvez's account, they were "in high spirits with the news given to them by two of my deserters that we had lost seven hundred men."

Landing and Siege

On February 27 all of the troops and supplies were on shore. The following day military engineers inspected the placement of the encampment and the batteries as they prepared for the siege of Fort Charlotte at Mobile. The fort had originally been built in 1723 by the French, who had named it Fort Condé. It was a brick structure with stone foundations, and its seven-pointed star design was laid out according to the military construction theories of Sébastien Le Prestre de Vauban.[150] At the end of the Seven Years' War, it was handed to the British, who renamed it Fort Charlotte in honor of King George III's wife.[151]

When the Spanish arrived in 1780, Fort Charlotte no longer presented its best face. Ten years earlier, its commander, Elias Durnford, had informed his superiors that it was in a "sorry state" and its repairs would cost several thousand pounds. In 1774 it was further weakened when 16,000 bricks were taken from it to reinforce the nearby and much more important stronghold of Pensacola.[152] Nevertheless, Durnford managed to make some repairs, which, at least in theory, allowed Fort Charlotte to continue to protect Mobile.[153] With

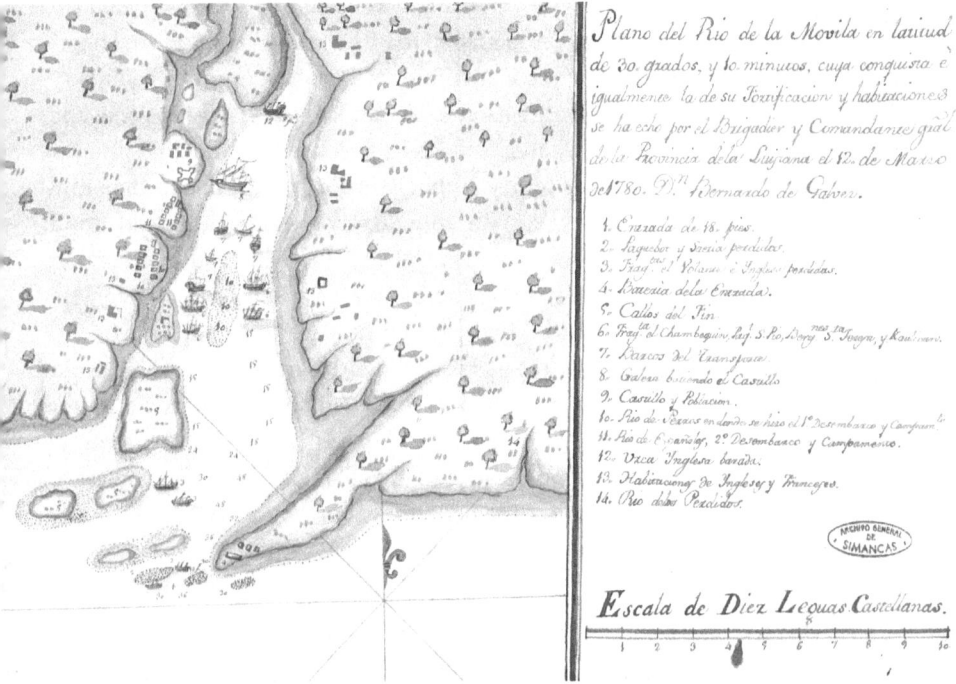

Contemporary Spanish map of the landing at Mobile of the forces under the command of Bernardo de Gálvez in February 1780. (*Plano del río de la Movila* .... España, Ministerio de Educación, Cultura y Deporte, Archivo General de Simancas, MPD, 15,006)

a garrison suiting its size and forty-nine cannons of various calibers, it still was an impressive structure.[154]

The Spanish military engineers informed Gálvez that the best site for starting the construction needed for the siege would be on the other side of the Dog River, south of Mobile. On February 29 the firsts shot were fired from the fort but with no losses on the Spanish side. On March 1 Gálvez made a reconnaissance of the enemy positions and sent Lieutenant Colonel Francisco de Bouligny to Fort Charlotte with a letter written in French, the eighteenth-century lingua franca, addressed to its commander, Elias Durnford. In it he informed Durnford of his "disposition to grant him a normal capitulation in accordance with the present circumstances," reminding him of the superior numbers on the Spanish side and, in case he refused his terms, threatening him "with all of the extremities of war, since a useless and out of place resistance irritates the patience of my troops, already annoyed by some mishaps."[155] The choice of Bouligny as emissary may have seemed strange because of his past confrontation with Gálvez, but his reputation throughout

Louisiana made him invaluable.[156] Bouligny was warmly received by Durnford "as an old acquaintance" and invited to lunch, which ended with cheerful toasts in honor of their respective monarchs and common friends.[157] During the meeting Durnford was able to confirm the hardships that the Spanish troops had suffered, about which he quickly informed his superior officer in Pensacola, General John Campbell. According to Durnford, before saying good-bye to his "guest," he summoned all of his men and read aloud to them the letter he had received from Gálvez, after which "they all joined in three cheers and then went to our necessary work like good men."[158] He then wrote out his answer to Gálvez, which he gave to Bouligny, who returned to the Spanish camp at four o'clock. Durnford stated that he could not accept Gálvez's offer because if he did he would be considered a traitor to his king and country, but then he ended on a much less resolute note. "My love for both [king and country] and my own honor direct my heart to refuse to surrender in this Fort until I am under conviction that resistance is in vain. The generosity of your Excellency's [Gálvez's] mind is well known to my brother officers and soldiers and should it be my misfortune to be added to their number a heart full of generosity and valor will ever consider brave men fighting for their country as objects of esteem and not revenge."[159]

Because of the absolutely inferior numbers of the defenders—between 120 and 300 British troops to 1,300 Spanish attackers[160]—Durnford's only hope was to receive reinforcements from Pensacola. At the very same time he was answering Gálvez's surrender proposal, he wrote to General John Campbell thanking him for the comfort offered by his announcement of an urgent relief expedition and informing him that "I need not say I will defend Fort to the last extremity."[161] Immediately after receiving Durnford's letter, Gálvez ordered work on the siege of Fort Charlotte to speed up.

On March 5 an interesting episode took place between the besieged and the besiegers. Durnford sent to the Spanish encampment, under a truce flag, a sergeant whose wife and children had been made prisoners. The sergeant carried a letter and, as a gift, a dozen bottles of wine, a dozen chickens, freshly baked bread, and a lamb. In his answer Bernardo de Gálvez wrote, "I am deeply honored by the courtesy you have done by sending me a snack. Please be aware that for my part I have the pleasure of sending you two cases of wine, one from Bordeaux and the other from Spain, a case of lemons and oranges, one full of biscuits, marzipan, and cakes, and another of cigars from Havana."[162] Behind this apparently random list of gifts there was a carefully thought-out message. Sending both Spanish and French wine stressed the alliance between these two countries against Britain. The fresh fruits and the biscuits, marzipan, and cakes were to be proof of how well supplied the

Spanish forces were. The Cuban cigars were testimony not only of the luxuries that were available to the besiegers but also of the fact that the Spanish navy was in control of all the trade and supply routes around the Caribbean. He ended his letter by assuring Durnford that the prisoners under his custody were always treated with as much care and courtesy as possible and that this would remain so until the fate of the war was decided.

Under the eighteenth-century norm of politeness between Gálvez and Durnford hid various intrigues. By sending the besiegers this sort of "snack," the besieged were in fact telling them that they had enough supplies to last for a long time. Bernardo de Gálvez's generosity similarly sent the message that despite all of the hardships endured by his troops, they too were well supplied. By sending a sergeant to meet with his imprisoned family in the Spanish camp, Durnford was also gathering information about how the Spaniards were treating those in their custody, perhaps in preparation for his and his men's near future.

In his letter to the fort's commander Gálvez protested the burning of several houses, which the British had set alight so as to prevent the enemy from using them as cover. Gálvez lamented the suffering this measure had caused the local population, adding, "Fortresses are generally erected to protect towns, while you start by destroying the town to protect a fortress, which is incapable of defending it."[163] He was well aware that Mobile had been in British hands for only two decades and that the majority of its population was of French origin, so his strong protest was a very intelligent way of increasing his support among them.[164] He reinforced this message by offering his promise that if the British committed to not destroying any more houses, he would not use them as cover for his artillery.[165]

The next day the exchange of letters continued. Durnford tried to take advantage of Gálvez's proposal, assuring him that only a few houses had been destroyed under his command and that he resented that Gálvez could believe that "I would tarnish my reputation by inflicting such harm on my fellow countrymen, whom I justly esteem and whom I would like to protect while it is in my power to do so." He added that he gladly accepted Gálvez's generous promise "not to advance, erect batteries, or occupy to my disadvantage that part of the town."[166] Gálvez immediately answered that he had written only that he would promise, not that he had already promised. His intention, as pointed out by John Walton Caughey, was to reach a mutual agreement, not to offer an unconditional pledge.[167] In any case, Gálvez concluded his letter, if the British commander considered in good faith that he had made such a promise, he would uphold it.[168]

This courteous exchange of letters between the two commanders did not slow down the work in the Spanish encampment, where engineers were quickly opening trenches and placing the batteries. On March 7 a British communication was intercepted, which said that the besieged were soon expecting the arrival of a relief expedition from Pensacola. To verify this, Gálvez sent a couple of platoons in reconnaissance. When they returned four days later, they confirmed that they had sighted a group of British troops near a place called Tenza (also spelled Tenza or Tensaw).[169] The first reports estimated its strength at between 400 and 600 men, but later reports counted more than 1,100.[170] This was the relief expedition that the garrison of Mobile had been promised, under the command of General John Campbell himself. Although Pensacola's British commander had been informed as early as February 12 of a strong Spanish military presence in the Mobile vicinity, he took a long time before departing to their aid.[171] The news of the proximity of the British detachment from Pensacola made the Spaniards redouble their efforts to conquer Fort Charlotte as soon as possible. As Gálvez later admitted to his uncle, "Your Excellency can imagine our situation on the eve of running out of food, with very little ammunition (most of it was lost in the shipwreck); 1,100 men in sight, who the above-mentioned general [John Campbell] had ordered to remove the flints from their muskets so to attack us with the bayonets; 300 in the castle [Fort Charlotte], who with the 1,100 under General Campbell totaled 1,400, a number similar to ours; the local population on their side; and the protection given by the fort. All of these discouraging omens did not take the confidence and hope of victory from our officers and men; on the contrary, making virtue of necessity, they worked even harder than before."[172]

Finally, at sunrise on March 12, the Spanish battery was in place. At ten o'clock it opened fire, and the enemy fired back. According to Gálvez, the shots hit their targets with great accuracy and "non-stop [fire] from both sides (since when one cannon was hit they quickly replaced it) lasted till sunset, when the enemy hoisted the white flag." Gálvez agreed to a ceasefire until next morning at seven, on the British "word of honor that they would not use that time to receive the help they were expecting, nor open the gates to the sailors and local population who had participated in the defense of the fort." At sunrise Durnford sent some emissaries with peace propositions, which Gálvez judged so inadmissible that he sent back an ultimatum: Durnford had four hours to surrender the fort. Gálvez reminded him that the breach in the walls was already practicable, even with a little difficulty. This point was of utmost importance, since according to rules of war at the time, the besieged could surrender up until the moment a breach in their walls appeared, at which point the fort, town, or city would be at the mercy of the besiegers, who could storm the place without giving quarter.[173] After a short negotiation, the two commanders in chief signed the articles of capitulation.[174] The surrender entered into force the following day. The Spaniards spent the night awake, as the proximity of 1,100 men under the command of General John Campbell could very well turn their victory into defeat. Gálvez ordered his troops to "be on guard all night, and patrol everywhere to prevent being surprised." At ten o'clock on March 14, the garrison of Fort Charlotte exited in surrender through the breach in the walls. The exit of a defeated garrison through the breach and not through the main gates of the fort was the custom at the time to prove that it was large enough for the enemy to enter through and thereby storm the fort, and therefore all resistance was useless.[175] This was one of the important rituals of surrender since it marked the formal change of the soldiers' condition from members of an active duty fighting force to prisoners of war.[176]

Bernardo de Gálvez granted the garrison the privilege of honorable defeat. The British marched out according to the traditional military ritual still in use at the time: "beating their drums, fuses lit, and flags unfurled," although the time was long past when the fuses of the muskets were lit.[177] This honor allowed Durnford to inform his superiors that no man from his garrison had tarnished the glory of the British army.[178] The British soldiers were taken prisoners of war, and the Spaniards hurried to assume positions inside Fort Charlotte in case of an attack by Campbell's forces. He did not attempt it and instead spent only a day near Mobile before retreating to Pensacola.

Impact of the Spanish Victory

Bernardo de Gálvez had reason to be satisfied. He had snatched victory from the nearly closed jaws of defeat. According to John Walton Caughey, "The assault was admirably planned; his men's spirits were kept up despite discouragements; the trench and battery were placed most effectively, and with a minimum of hazard to his men, the artillery fire battered the fort into submission promptly but without much loss of life on either side."[179]

As was his custom, in victory Bernardo de Gálvez showed magnanimity toward the defeated and extreme generosity toward all of his men. Immediately after taking possession of Fort Charlotte, "I thanked them on behalf of the king for their resolution in facing all of the hardships we endured, and for the zeal, courage, and determination that they displayed to achieve success, and I also offered them, also on the king's behalf, as a reward for their efforts, a third of the value of all that was captured inside the fort."[180]

After the inventory was made and a third of the goods distributed to his men as promised, Gálvez sent Manuel González, second lieutenant of the

Second Battalion of the España Regiment, "to submit to His Majesty's own hands the official report on the conquest of the fort of Mobile."[181] González fulfilled this commission on June 15 in Aranjuez and was rewarded with a promotion to captain.[182] Gálvez asked for pensions and promotions as a reward for those who had distinguished themselves during the campaign, which were all granted.[183] Among his men his second in command, Gerónimo Girón y Moctezuma, colonel of the Príncipe Regiment, stood out. Fully aware of his personal debt to him, Gálvez made a point of publicizing it widely, rather than try to hide it, as many leaders, both military and civilian, would do for fear that a brilliant subordinate could steal the show. In the *Gazeta de Madrid* of June 20, 1780, these words of the supreme commander of the expedition against Pensacola appeared:

> This Governor . . . wished to mention the particular merit incurred by the colonel of the Príncipe Regiment, D[on] Gerónimo Girón, second in command of the expedition. He [Gálvez] says that to reward this officer as deserved for services rendered during the voyage and shipwreck, he ordered him to take command of the attack on Mobile, while he reserved for himself that on Pensacola. At the same time, he [Gálvez] issued another order to his troops to recognize Girón as the supreme commander of that enterprise. He [Gálvez] adds, that as a result, Girón was in command from the beginning to the end; and although his modesty did not allow him to make such an order public, or to make a move without consulting him, he had the satisfaction of approving everything Girón suggested and witnessing the steady hand, sound judgment, and skill with which he was able to direct the action.[184]

After this kind of praise it was no surprise that in the same year, Gerónimo Girón y Moctezuma was promoted to brigadier general.[185] To have the whole picture, it must also be taken into account that Girón was the scion of one of the most noble and important families of Malaga, and their gratitude could be an important asset for the Gálvez clan.[186]

The conquest of Mobile had an important impact on both sides of the Atlantic. In New Orleans the news was received with a large public outpouring of joy.[187] In the United States, despite the somewhat strange silence in the correspondence of General George Washington, several important personalities took note of it. John Adams, at the time about to leave Paris, informed the president of the Continental Congress of its importance. In his opinion, "the conquest of Mobile, made by the Spaniards, the news of which has lately arrived here, appears so much the more important, as it leads infallibly to that of Pensacola, by which the Spaniards may cut off one of the principal avenues of Jamaica, and may, in time, intercept the commerce and the provisions of this Island."[188]

Adams also remarked to the French minister of foreign affairs, Count of Vergennes, that "the advantages which Spain has gained in West Florida, and particularly of late at Mobile, and the probability that they will succeed in acquiring both the Floridas, show that the English are on the losing hand in this quarter."[189] Bernardo de Gálvez himself sent a letter to the president of the Congress, which was read aloud in its June 6 session.[190] According to Representative William C. Houston, the news of the conquest represented that "the bitter Cup of ill Tidings is dashed with a little mixture of a different Quality."[191] The Congress also ordered that all information related to this matter be forwarded to John Jay, U.S. representative in Madrid.[192]

In England the government was silent on Mobile. But if the official press made no mention of it, the private one certainly did. The March 29, 1780, issue of the *Caledonian Mercury* published an "extract of a letter from a Gentleman at Pensacola, dated December 10, to his friend in Jamaica" that contained the information about "Don Galvez Governor, for his Catholic Majesty of Louisiana, had received a reinforcement from Havana, and is embarking troops for some expedition, supposed to be this place, or Mobile."[193] On August 16 the same paper published the false news that "it is reported [from Madrid], that Don Bernard de Galvez, after the taking of Fort Mobile, had marched against Pensacola, which place he took by storm, and put all the garrison to the sword, not, however, without great loss on our side, 1,000 of our men left on the field of battle, and 1,500 wounded."[194] During July and August that year, many newspapers wrote about the latest events in Mobile.[195] Two of them criticized as "very pompous" the account of the campaign that Bernardo de Gálvez published in his journal.[196]

In France, during the second half of July, news of the campaign was announced by the *Journal Politique, ou Gazette des Gazettes*, which also published Bernardo de Gálvez's letter to his uncle and an abridged version of his journal.[197] Also spreading the news were, among others, the *Journal Historique et Littéraire* and the *Courrier d'Avignon*, which in its July 4, 1780, issue wrote with just a bit of chauvinism that "this brave general, of only thirty-three years, is the nephew of Don Gálvez, Minister of the Indies; and his talents as well as his bravery have deservedly earned him the rank of brigadier general. He served as a volunteer in the French army during the last war with Portugal, and there early on he showed an active genius and a courage that revealed great military talent."[198]

The news arrived in Spain on June 15, 1780. The minister of the Indies was hugely pleased with his nephew. In a letter to him dated just one week later, he poured out praises and pride.[199] The next day he wrote him again announcing that, as proof of the king's approval, he had ordered that Bernardo's journal, his letter from June 22, and the entire articles of capitulation be published in the official court newspaper.[200] But despite the public jubilation, in private the most senior members of the Spanish court regretted that the blow to the British pride had not been stronger and deeper. As Bernardo de Gálvez confided in a letter to his uncle dated March 20, "We cannot consider without pain, that if the expedition from Havana had joined us in time, the British would have suffered as much as in Saratoga."[201] José de Gálvez was more than disappointed; he was furious, and in his correspondence with the governor of Cuba he let his rage run free. In a letter signed in Aranjuez on April 20, 1780, he expressed his disapproval of the conduct of the Spanish Royal Navy in Cuba and specifically criticized Juan Bautista Bonet, commander of the Navy Department, who, he wrote,

> delayed with baseless excuses, and against the explicit and communicated royal orders, the expedition decreed to conquer the strongholds of Pensacola and Mobile, which probably are the two most threatening English possessions. . . . For this serious damage . . . the king disapproves of the behavior of the head of the Royal Navy in Cuba. He [Bonet] is not the one to determine the greater or lesser importance of military operations that the king has ordered him to implement. . . . The ships of the Royal Navy, which cost the state so much, are first and foremost intended to attack and pursue our enemies, to contribute to the glory and security of the nation, and to make its flag respected at sea, and not to remain idle in the ports, as happened with the fleet of that [Navy] Department, against the wishes of His Majesty, and to the astonishment and disapproval of America and Europe.[202]

Four days later José de Gálvez was still boiling. In another letter to Cuba's governor he added,

> I make this consideration on the king's orders to convince you of how necessary it is to fulfill with the utmost punctuality his royal decrees, even if at first glance it may seem convenient to make some modification in them because of circumstances that may have developed between the time of their issue and their arrival; because such circumstances, as much as human knowledge can foresee things, were already considered by His Majesty before issuing his orders. This kind of behavior will open the door to leaving implementation of His Maj-

esty's orders to the whims of governors and other royal officials in the Indies.[203]

As harsh as these words may have sounded to the ears of senior army and navy chiefs in Havana, probably what enraged them was that a civilian like José de Gálvez should give them a lecture on military history, reminding them that "the experience of all centuries has shown that in war, the one who is more active and pays less attention to the attendant dangers, is the one who usually carries victory on his side."[204]

Another Opportunity Wasted

Bernardo de Gálvez spent the days following the British surrender in reconstructing Fort Charlotte, which he renamed Fort Carlota in honor of King Carlos III.[205] From Mobile he planned to go directly to Pensacola. According to John Walton Caughey, "An immediate attack would take advantage of the disorder incident to Campbell's fruitless journey to the Tensaw. Furthermore, it was advisable to invest [attack] Pensacola before reinforcements arrived, and the news of the fall of Mobile was certain to suggest such strengthening."[206] To make this possible he needed the reinforcements promised from Havana, but these were nowhere to be seen. In theory they had been ready since the beginning of December 1779. Indeed, on January 5, 1780, Diego José Navarro informed José de Gálvez that "the expedition is ready to sail from this port . . . under the command of the governor of the province of Louisiana, Brigadier Don Bernardo de Gálvez" (see appendix table 5).[207]

Bernardo de Gálvez was perfectly aware of the lack of enthusiasm about his expedition among the top brass in Havana. Precisely for this reason, as discussed earlier, on January 1780 he sent one of his most trusted men, Esteban Miró, to Havana to try to expedite the shipment of troops.[208] Miró arrived in Havana on January 24 and immediately made contact with Gálvez's old friend from the Royal Military Academy of Avila, José de Ezpeleta, colonel of the Navarra Regiment.[209] Miró tried his best with the military commanders in Havana but did not get far with them. He constantly heard positive words and promises, but very little was ever delivered. According to Miró's journal, in a conversation with Juan Bautista Bonet, head of the Navy Department of Cuba, the latter even confessed, "What is all this fuss about Mobile and Pensacola? This [Cuba] is far more valuable than fifty Mobiles and Pensacolas. It is true that there is the king's order to sail; but I do not know if sometime it would not be best to disobey the king's orders if you realize that if His Majesty were here he would do the same."[210]

This remark is totally in line with what, according to Ricardo Palma, many conquistadors had in mind when they received orders contrary to their wishes, interests, or opinions: "God is in heaven, the king is far away, and I am the one in command here."[211] Bonet's remark most probably reached José de Gálvez's ears in Aranjuez, where the court was spending the spring. In his letter to Diego José Navarro on April 24, 1780, he seems to respond directly to Bonet's idea.[212] For Ezpeleta it was crystal-clear that "the general of the navy [that is, the admiral] did not want the expedition to take place and he would find all possible means to delay it, trusting that news about the enemy's fleet would put it on hold."[213] It is certainly easy, perhaps too easy, to ridicule Bonet by portraying him as a timid old man opposed to the vigorous courage of young Bernardo de Gálvez, but it is worthwhile to pause to consider the reasons for his opposition. From a strategic point of view, no one doubted that one Cuba was worth more than fifty Mobiles and Pensacolas; thus, sending Bernardo de Gálvez the reinforcements he asked for would mean that the defense of the island would be seriously weakened. And as a seaman with more than fifty-two years' active service, it was perfectly natural for Bonet to be suspicious of Gálvez's aggressiveness.[214] But whatever opinion he had of the whole plan, Bonet could do nothing other than delay it, and he finally had to give way to pressure, especially from the court, and inform Cuba's governor that the fleet was ready to sail (see appendix table 6).

On February 15 the troops began to embark, but by February 21 Bonet had still not given the order to sail, arguing that the weather was unfavorable.[215] José de Ezpeleta was desperate. In a letter to his father dated that same day, he complained that "the expedition remains docked, despite the good weather and [the fact] that all the troops have been on board since February 15. On February 10, two hundred men sailed first, and the rest were to follow, which has not happened because of delays by the navy or the ill will of its commander. The truth is that the troops suffer, [and] the governor is concerned and does not dare to do anything more than to inform the court. See *Vuestra Merced* how far are we from the solution [to our problems]."[216]

Despite Ezpeleta's despair, Bonet was right. In the night between February 22 and 23 a violent storm forced the troops who had been on board eleven days to disembark. Now it was Esteban Miró's turn to express his frustration in his journal. He wrote that so many orders and counterorders had come that "the French people, the Americans, and the British prisoners are openly mocking our navy, which is a shame."[217]

After more than a week's delay, finally, on March 7, 1780, the fleet sailed from the port of Havana. Fifteen warships and twenty transports carried 2,148 officers and soldiers to "follow the army under the command of Brigadier and Governor of the Province of Louisiana Don Bernardo de Gálvez." Unfortunately, they were too late to participate in the conquest of Fort Charlotte and Mobile (see appendix table 7).

On March 15, 1780, a day after the surrender of the British garrison at Fort Charlotte, the fleet was still more than 240 miles from Mobile and would need a full two weeks before arriving on March 30. Once they were there, Gálvez ordered that the army headquarters be formed for the conquest of Pensacola.[218] In it, under his command, José de Ezpeleta would serve as his second and commander of the brigade of veteran troops; Gerónimo Girón y Moctezuma as major general; Francisco de Navas as lieutenant colonel of engineers and quartermaster; and Esteban Miró as his first aide-de-camp.

They immediately started to plan the best way to reach their objective. The naval commander Miguel de Goicoechea informed them that, according to the attack plan designed by Bonet, the troops must approach from land following the course of the Perdidos River.[219] Gálvez thought this plan impossible since the terrain was impenetrable.[220] Instead, he considered it far better for the navy to force entry into Pensacola Bay and, once inside, disembark troops for the assault against the fort. He suggested his plan to the navy—suggested and not ordered, since, although he was supreme commander of all army troops, the navy still reported directly to Bonet, who despite this responsibility had decided to remain in Havana. Bernardo de Gálvez had very complete information about the forces he would face at Pensacola: 1,302 veteran soldiers, 600 hunters and locals, 300 sailors, and 300 armed black men, totaling about 2,500 men. The enemy's naval forces consisted only of a thirty-six-cannon frigate and another smaller ship, so he decided that a Spanish Royal Navy man-of-war and several frigates were enough against them. The naval captain Gabriel de Aristizábal, commander of the man-of-war *San Ramón*, disagreed, arguing that his orders clearly stated that he must rendezvous with the rest of the fleet. The naval commander Goicoechea supported him by pointing out that, since Admiral Bonet was not far away, the decision should be his.[221]

On April 6 Gálvez asked the naval officers their opinion of the viability of his plan to attack Pensacola by sea.[222] But they declined to commit themselves, arguing that they would do as Admiral Bonet ordered. Tired of so many excuses, on April 11 Gálvez ordered his troops to embark and sail toward Pensacola on the few ships that had come from New Orleans and were under his command. That same day news arrived, to be confirmed two days later, that two British ships had entered Pensacola Bay.[223] Before departing Gálvez appointed Enrique Grimarest, captain of the Navarra Regiment, as acting military governor of the castle of Mobile and civilian chief of its district.[224]

On April 24 they were close to Mobile Point (near today's Fort Morgan), and the following day naval captain Gabriel de Aristizábal arrived with Admiral Bonet's answer, which stated only that because of fleet supply problems, the ships could be less than three weeks at sail.[225] The possibility of attacking Pensacola from sea was thus dead. Gálvez turned to Aristizábal to ask whether he considered it possible to attack using only the ships that at that moment were under his direct command. Aristizábal answered that it was not possible but that "he himself, with his officers and sailors, were willing to sacrifice themselves side by side with the army in the king's service, whether in land operations, on board their ships, or by going ashore to follow the flags."[226]

On May 4 Bernardo de Gálvez convened a council of war.[227] He addressed his officers in the following terms:

> You gentlemen have long witnessed my impatience and I your ardent desire to be of service to the king, without that desired moment arriving. The support we expected from His Excellency the commander of the navy has not materialized, and our hopes to make the expedition by sea have vanished. The time has passed for me to make a decision, as set forth in His Excellency's letter. It is a choice that I have described a thousand times and has always been misunderstood. We have no option but to abandon the enterprise or to do it by land. According to reports by naval officers, engineers, and artillery men, the enormous difficulty of dragging cannons and transporting supplies and ammunitions would force the troops to march with only the arms and supplies they could carry themselves, in an attempt to surprise Pensacola in a direct assault. I am perfectly aware of the problems and dangers of this kind of action, which would risk the honor of His Majesty's armies and our own reputations. But when there is no other choice but attack or retreat, I ask from you gentlemen your opinion as to what is best for the royal service.[228]

There was really no choice. All those present reluctantly agreed that the expedition should be called off. Gálvez immediately sent word of the resolution of the council of war to Admiral Bonet, in a letter in which he "more than suggested that the entire responsibility for this decision was Bonet's."[229] The following day the frigate *Príncipe de Asturias* arrived with new supplies, which were not enough to change the decision as made. With these problems among the leading officers, it was natural that the troops' morale would be affected. The men from New Orleans "started to cry out for their return home to help their families and tend to the harvest."[230] Confronted with this reality, Bernardo de Gálvez gave the order to return. Before leaving he appointed José de Ezpeleta commander of Mobile, while Enrique Grimarest would remain as head of Fort Charlotte's garrison.[231]

Bernardo de Gálvez returned to New Orleans victorious but with a sour feeling that the conquest of Pensacola had slipped from his hands. In a long report to his uncle from November 1780, he openly complained about Admiral Bonet, who, "under the pretext that the conquest of Pensacola was not now in the king's interests . . . only demanded for me to fortify and satisfy myself with Mobile; adding that the greatest service I could render to the king was that, and nothing would make me a better servant than to sacrifice the glory and promotions that could be awarded to me for the conquest of Pensacola. . . . It seems to me that the admiral was doing nothing but finding ways to deprive me of ships by using them for other pursuits and leaving us abandoned."[232]

Before departing for New Orleans, Bernardo de Gálvez ordered Ezpeleta to keep secret the dissolution of the expedition against Pensacola. It was useless, everybody knew. On May 13, the British commander of Pensacola, General John Campbell, informed his superiors that the town had not yet been attacked.[233] Three days later he asked for reinforcements to take the initiative and attack the Spaniards.[234]

6. His Finest Hour
PENSACOLA, "I ALONE"

In Mobile, Bernardo de Gálvez left 800 men under the command of José de Ezpeleta, who had to manage the hostility of the local population. At the end of March, Ezpeleta forced the locals to take an oath of allegiance to Spain. Those of French origin, and therefore mostly Catholic, had to swear "to God and under the sign of the cross . . . to behave as good and loyal subjects of His Catholic Majesty."[1] The British, who were non-Catholic, had to "promise on the Gospels and the sacred scriptures not to betray, or to cause, or to allow, any hostility, direct or indirect, against the Spanish nation, the fort, or the conquered country, or against the [Spanish] state during the entire time that we are under her [that is, Spain's] dominion."[2] In the end these precautions were unnecessary, since the threat materialized not from the local population but from the Native Americans. Gálvez's Indian policy has been described in previous chapters. Now it is time to consider its implementation during his military campaigns against the British.

While still in Mobile, Bernardo de Gálvez sent the following message to the British general John Campbell: "I propose to Your Excellency to separate the Indians from our national disputes, since the weapons in their hands are twice as deplorable for humanity. Your Excellency knows that I, for my part, do not employ them in any capacity, and that such allies degrade more than they help. I hope that Your Excellency, being aware that this is true and that your benevolence will result in benefit to the English settlers, will give me a favorable answer."[3]

Gálvez's recognition of the failure of his policy to attract the Indians in Florida to the Spanish side can be seen in his proposal for Indian neutrality. The widespread colonial assumption had been that all whites had a common interest in keeping the Indians outside the war, but at the time that notion had already been abandoned.[4] In the region surrounding Mobile were three important Indian groups: the Choctaw (in Spanish sources, referred to as Chactas), the Creek (Cric), and the Chickasaw (Chicasa or Chichaca). Two more groups lived nearby: the Cherokee (Cheroquis) and the Shawnee (Chavamones).

The Choctaw were the most numerous. Their loyalty to their French allies was legendary. In 1778 one of the chiefs told Charles Stuart, deputy British superintendent for Indian Affairs in the Southern District, that during French times, "the best of them would run for any white man by day, or by night, whether hot or cold, wet or dry, any distance for a small flap [breechcloth]."[5] As already seen, Bernardo de Gálvez succeeded in attracting to Spain's side some of the Choctaw within Louisiana's borders, but because most of them lived in territory under British control, they fell under British "protection."[6] The British high command even noted with a degree of surprise how some Choctaw warriors were harassing Spanish settlers in Mobile.[7]

Although fewer in number than the Choctaw, the Chickasaw "warriors were the most bellicose of all."[8] They had an ancient alliance with the British that the latter would try to enforce during the war.[9] Charles Stuart said that they were "a proud and politick people known to be brave and of a more free and independent spirit [than the Choctaw] ... [and they] very seldom come to this province to beg as the Choctaws do but pride themselves on hunting for their own maintenance."[10]

"Creek" was the name given by British settlers to a very heterogeneous group of Native Americans who lived mainly in the present states of South Carolina, Georgia, and Florida.[11] While British contemporaneous sources distinguished only between Lower and Upper Creeks, Spanish sources mentioned Alibamones, Talapuches, Abecas or Apizcas, and Caouitsas or Covetas.[12] Their importance for military campaigns was that they had "a strength of about 3,500 warriors, 2,000 from the upper tribes and the rest from the lower ones."[13] Of the other groups in the area, the Cherokee added 2,500 warriors[14] and the Shawnee hardly any, as their population was small.[15]

The historical debate about the contribution of Native American groups to the War of Independence exceeds the scope of this study. However, it is worth noting that far from being in agreement, historians have offered multiple views on the topic. Colin G. Calloway mentions a "national mythology" in which Native Americans have been assigned a minimal and negative role in the story of the Revolution since they chose the wrong side and lost.[16] This traditional view of the Native Americans taking sides with the British would make sense from a general political perspective since one of the grievances of the thirteen colonies was that the government in London had unilaterally imposed on them a limit to their westward expansion. The 1763 proclamation line restricted white settlements to the east of the Appalachian Mountains and reserved the land to the west to Indian communities.[17] Bernard W. Sheehan considers the Indian contribution to the American War of Independence to be marginal, more symbolic than substantial.[18] More recently, Elisabeth Whitman Schmidt states that today there is increasing awareness of the role played by African and Native Americans in the U.S. War of Independence.[19] But Bryan Rindfleisch points out that even if there is a growing awareness of the participation of these groups in the Revolution, significantly less research has been conducted on Native American involvement during the war compared to that of African Americans, which, in his opinion, makes possible the persistence of a national myth that Native Americans were mostly allies of the British.[20] Armstrong Starkey believes that the Indians' individual alliances depended on factors specific to each group and that therefore it is impossible to offer any universal judgment about their role.[21] Also relevant is what James H. O'Donnell III has written about the Indians' motives in allowing themselves to become involved in the war: they had already been dragged into every previous confrontation between Britain and France in North America, so by the time the Revolution started it was clear "to most of them that it was no longer a matter of playing off one suitor against another or of choosing the ally with the most gifts, but of preserving their lands and thereby, their autonomy."[22] Additionally, it is important to remember that, according to Calloway, "in Indian country the American Revolution often translated into an American civil war. While British regulars and Continental troops fought campaigns in the East, in the backcountry—which usually meant the Indians' backyards—whites killed Indians, Indians killed whites, Indians killed Indians, and whites killed whites in guerrilla warfare that was localized, vicious, and tolerated no neutrals."[23]

One of the conclusions of such debate is that the focus should be shifted from the traditional question about the role of Native American groups in the War of Independence toward an analysis of the reasons and backgrounds behind each and every group's participation, or not, in the war. Previous relations between Native American tribes and the British Americans was one important factor, as was the role played by specific individuals, on all sides (American revolutionary, British, Native American, French and Spanish), in influencing the final outcome—people like Samuel Kirkland (the persuasive Christian missionary who attracted the Oneida to the revolutionary side); William Johnson and Guy Johnson (British commissioners of Indian Affairs in the Northern District who secured the alliance of the Iroquois) and John Stuart (their counterpart in the Southern District who mobilized the Cherokee); Thayendanegea or Joseph Brant (charismatic leader of the Mohawk); and Athanase de Mézières (French-born commander of the Spanish post at

Natchitoches).²⁴ To further complicate the picture, tensions among Native American groups had an important impact on the outcome, as was the case among the Cherokee where a new generation of warriors headed by Dragging Canoe rejected the policies of their elders.²⁵

In addition, it must be stressed that all of the actors in the war gave serious consideration to Native American involvement. On the ground the British made extensive use of Indian groups bound to them by pacts or agreements—"on the ground" because in London, and more specifically in Parliament, and even more so among the opposition to Lord North's Tory government, the idea of "using" Native Americans against a people who were still considered fellow subjects was regarded as outrageous.²⁶ In British America, after an initial, very brief discussion of the wisdom of keeping the Indians out of the conflict, officers rarely showed similar moral or political misgivings about the Indians' role and assumed that they would make the same contribution as in previous conflicts.²⁷ For this reason, officers rushed to assure their superiors of the Indians' "love and attachment to the King, and [that they were] always ready to act in His Service."²⁸

In British West Florida, the policy for using Native Americans in warfare was, at best, erratic. According to Joseph Barton Starr, during the first fourteen years of British domination, Indian policy went in a complete circle, from being the direct responsibility of John Stuart, superintendent for Indian Affairs, to being under the control of colonial authorities, to returning to Stuart's portfolio in 1777.²⁹ According to Mark F. Boyd and José Navarro Latorre, John Stuart had immense influence among the Indians to the point that they consider that because of his efforts most of the Indians remained British partisans during the Revolution.³⁰ The British were very pragmatic about the issue. In 1784, the Upper Creek leader Alexander McGillivray, who would be commissioned as a colonel by the British, clearly stated that the "Indians will attach themselves to and serve them best who supply their necessities."³¹ In West Florida, English traders were able to satisfy most of the Native American groups' demands, so when the war with Spain broke out, most of the Indians sided with the British.³² In deciding the best way to involve the Indians to British advantage, John Stuart did not interpret his instructions as an order to have them attack settlers in the province. Instead, he felt it his duty that "no time be lost in employing the Indians of the different nations to give all the assistance in their power to such of His Majesty's faithful subjects as may already have taken or shall hereafter take arms, [and] to resist the lawless oppression of the rebels and their attempts to overturn the constitution and oppose His Majesty's authority."³³

Stuart's idea was that the Indians would be auxiliaries of the British regular army. However, the last British word on the subject was not his but General John Campbell's (the very last word, of course, would be from the Chickasaw, the Creek, and the Choctaw). While Stuart had a deep understanding of Indian culture and a certain respect for them, Campbell described them as of "a mercenary race ... the slaves of the highest bidder without gratitude or affection; However, ... I'm afraid that Europans themselves have taught them these Principles."[34] Despite this opinion, Campbell made extensive use of Indians during his campaigns, and he recognized in May 1780 that one of the reasons the Spaniards had abandoned their idea of attacking Pensacola at that time was "their fear of the savages."[35] This opinion was shared by Alexander Cameron, who two months later wrote, "[I] will venture to say that the possession of this place [Pensacola] is owing entirely to the great number of Indians who repaired here to assist, and who waited near a month for the Spaniards; then getting impatient wished to go and look for them."[36] Campbell's prejudices prevented him from making good use of Indian warriors, since he oscillated between recognizing his need for them and complaining about their cost. Therefore whenever rumors of the presence of Spanish troops in the region reached the British camp, he would rush to call for them, but after the emergency passed he would send them home again. According to Greg O'Brien, in April 1780 Campbell had 1,235 Creek, 236 Choctaw, and 31 Chickasaw, but most of them abandoned Pensacola shortly after when it was clear that a Spanish attack was not imminent. In February 1781, 744 Choctaw were present at Pensacola, but Campbell, convinced that the Spanish attack would not come in the near future, sent home 300 of them.[37] Because of this behavior, when they were really needed the Indians were so dispersed over the region that Campbell was unable to assemble a sufficient number of them to make a difference.[38] John Walton Caughey assesses the role that the Indians played in the defense of Pensacola as merely delaying its fall into Spanish hands.[39]

The U.S. theory and practice concerning the involvement of Native Americans in the war was also contradictory. The Continental Congress laid out the theory in June 1775, when it instructed the Committee on Indian Affairs "to prepare proper talks to the several tribes of Indians for engaging the continuance of their friendship to us, and neutrality in our present unhappy dispute with Great Britain."[40] The practice, however, was different, since even before the Battle of Lexington several Indians were among the famed minutemen.[41] A year later, George Washington questioned official theory when he wrote to the president of the Continental Congress, "In my opinion, it will be impossible to keep them in a state of neutrality. They must, and, no doubt, soon will take an active part either for or against us; and

I submit it to the consideration of Congress, whether it would not be best immediately to engage them on our side, and to use our utmost endeavors to prevent their minds being poisoned by ministerial emissaries."[42]

Washington expressed the widespread opinion that the policy of so-called Indian neutrality only benefited the British, who used the Indians extensively against American settlers and their families. This assumption even appeared in the Declaration of Independence. Among the many American grievances against the British monarch was that "he has excited domestic insurrections amongst us, and has endeavoured to bring on the inhabitants of our frontiers, the merciless Indian Savages, whose known rule of warfare, is an undistinguished destruction, of all ages, sexes and conditions."[43] A change in U.S. policy was evident when, in June 1776, the Continental Congress passed several resolutions authorizing the use of Indians in the war against the British army. But by then it was probably a bit late, since the British were already securing the support and loyalty of most Indian groups.[44]

As for Spain, it courted Indian groups settled in Louisiana by adopting the French and British model of trade and gift giving in exchange for their loyalty. Despite several communications to the court from Bernardo de Gálvez extolling the good results of this new policy, the truth is that its success was limited to only a few groups, most prominently the Choctaw.[45] As Colin G. Calloway has assessed, international competition as well as village politics worked against Spanish efforts to implement multitribal alliances.[46] Gálvez's realization of this limited success was in fact behind his "generous" offer to General Campbell "to separate the Indians from our national disputes."[47] Although George C. Osborn has called his proposal a "humanitarian" and "idealistic appeal," at almost the same time that Gálvez was writing to Campbell he had no problem giving orders to store gifts in Mobile "to procure the friendship of the Choctaws and the rest of the Indian nations, who demand them from the Spaniards, or could do so in the future."[48]

As the war continued, it was increasingly difficult for the Spaniards to continue to trade with and supply gifts to the Indians. On April 24, 1780, the acting governor of the fort of Mobile, Enrique Grimarest, informed Gálvez of the serious problems he was facing because he did not have gifts for the Choctaw and other tribes who demanded them.[49] The situation grew worse under Mobile's new governor, José de Ezpeleta. In early June Ezpeleta assured Gálvez that it was not his intention to use the Indians against the British, but just one week later he had already changed his mind because of the growing number of attacks by tribes loyal to the enemy.[50] As expected, General Campbell declined Gálvez's "humanitarian" and "idealistic" offer.

In his letter of April 20 he said it was "insulting and injurious to reason and common sense," adding that he could not agree because he himself would become the object of his king and country's contempt for not using all the means that God and his sovereign had put into his hands.[51] Meanwhile, in Mobile the pro-British Indians soon started to harass the Spaniards. Their first attacks took place as early as April and May 1780. José de Ezpeleta was desperate to attract the Indians to the Spanish side, but he lacked the necessary trade merchandise and gifts. He repeatedly asked for replenishments, but the stores in New Orleans were empty.[52] Aware of Ezpeleta's predicament, Gálvez could only recommend to his friend that he do all he could without insulting or despising the Indians. Ezpeleta and Gálvez were old and close friends, and this relationship allowed Ezpeleta to take liberties when writing to his superior.

On May 10, 1780, José de Ezpeleta wrote to Bernardo de Gálvez "concerning supplies for the Indians: I will not mention them again; if they arrive soon we will be able to get by; and since I come from a serious household, I do not know how to gyp them, as Señor Gálvez does, so I will need gifts to keep them happy." We have translated *gitanear*, the Spanish word used by Ezpeleta, as "gyp" since the word means literally "to do as the Gypsies do."[53] The Gypsies had a profound impact on the culture of southern Spain (seen most notably in flamenco), but they were also associated with robbery and a profound lack of honesty in their dealings with those outside of their own community. Ezpeleta knew that the Spanish governor of Louisiana had no problem at all in doing whatever necessary to win the favor of the Indians. As Alexander Cameron, British agent to the Choctaw and Chickasaw, wrote in 1780, "Gálvez will even humble himself so low as to kiss their warriors from ear to ear and pay them every respect that is due to great chiefs. He sent for them to visit him even in [New] Orleans."[54] But in the correspondence between Gálvez and Ezpeleta, there is no evidence that Gálvez took offense. On the contrary, he deeply sympathized with his friend's predicament, although there was nothing he could do to help him out.[55]

Without merchandise or gifts, it was only a question of time before the Indians surrounding Mobile turned against the Spaniards. On September 19, 1780, the first serious Indian attack took place when several Choctaw warriors raided a cavalry patrol. For Ezpeleta the episode announced the start of a "destructive war, in which they will burn and devastate the entire country."[56] Ezpeleta's response was to raise a general war against them, since he preferred to "have ten enemies in the open than four hidden."[57] This remark reveals Ezpeleta's inability to adapt to the rules and conditions of warfare

Late nineteenth-century copy of an early portrait of José de Ezpeleta. Gálvez and Ezpeleta met at the Royal Military Academy of Avila, where Gálvez was studying and Ezpeleta was captain in the Navarre Regiment. Through the years, they developed a very close friendship that not only survived but was strengthened when Gálvez became Ezpeleta's superior during the campaigns against the British. Ezpeleta's distinguished career included appointments as governor of Cuba, viceroy of New Granada (present day Colombia, Venezuela, Ecuador, and Panama), and viceroy of Navarre. He died at the age of eighty-four holding the rank of lieutenant general, the highest rank in the Spanish army at the time. (E. Carceller, *Portrait of José Ezpeleta Galdiano*, oil on canvas, 1879, in Ministerio de Defensa, Ejército de Tierra, Academia de Artillería)

both with and against Native Americans. In this kind of asymmetric warfare, of which the American Revolution offers one of the earliest examples, a certain flexibility is demanded that makes it very different from traditional warfare.[58] In late November of the same year, some 500 Six Towns Choctaw warriors arrived in Mobile to offer their services to Spain, but Ezpeleta's distant attitude caused them to leave and finally fight for the British.[59]

THE BRITISH ATTACK AGAINST MOBILE: "BUNKER HILL IN MINIATURE"

Abandoning for a short while the chronological progress of Bernardo de Gálvez's campaign against Pensacola, it is relevant to focus on the situation of the Spanish garrison in the recently conquered Mobile. Bernardo de Gálvez was deeply worried about the predicament of his compatriot Ezpeleta. In a letter dated November 20, 1780, he wrote to him, "Oh, Ezpeleta, my friend! How many worries, tragedies, and disasters you cost me. Nothing is more important to me than your situation. Do not ever think that I am capable of leaving you alone. With a little more patience and some resolve everything will be solved. I've written you a thousand letters since my arrival here [in Havana], but since I wasn't able to put anything new in them, I have torn them all to pieces. A thousand times I decided to send you letters, and a thousand times I determined that the first news you would have from us would be a report to you of the departure of your reinforcements."[60]

On Dauphin Island, a site called the Aldea de la Mobila ("Mobile Village" or "Spanish Fort") sat between Mobile Bay and the Perdidos River.[61] It was essential to guard this location so as to keep communications open between the two banks of the river. Aware of its strategic importance, Ezpeleta positioned 190 men and two cannons there.[62] He was right to do so, for on January 3, 1781, it was approached by a force of about 100 soldiers from the Third Waldeck Regiment (German troops under British command) and the Sixtieth Infantry Regiment, along with some provincials, several dragoons, an artillery detachment with two cannons, and between 400 and 500 Indians.[63] They were meant to launch a coordinated attack with the British warships *Mentor* and *Hound* so as to quickly overpower the Spanish garrison.[64] Then, with Mobile Village in British hands, the surrender of Mobile would be merely a question of time. At sunrise on January 7, the commander of the British forces, Colonel von Hanxleden, gave the order to attack. The Spanish guards were completely surprised, to the point of mistaking them for Spanish militias and allowing them to reach their trenches. Once there, the attackers divided themselves into two columns. The first column, under the command of Colonel von Hanxleden himself, tried to follow the trench.

But the Spanish soldiers, already realizing that it was an enemy attack—the fourth in the last few weeks—repelled the British soldiers with fixed bayonets, killing even the colonel.[65] The death of their commander made the attackers lose momentum, and they retreated in disarray. The second column, with soldiers from the Sixtieth Infantry Regiment and men from the Pennsylvania and Maryland Provincial Militia, under the command of militia captain Philip B. Key, succeeded in taking some of the Spanish positions, but as soon as these troops realized that they were on their own, a Spanish counterattack was enough to rout them back.[66] All this time the Indians were waiting for attack orders from Colonel von Hanxleden, but when these never came they retreated without taking part in the fight.

The British ships, for their part, "did not fully achieve their objectives but were more successful than the land troops," since they were able to prevent Spanish reinforcements from the Aldea de la Mobile to Mobile.[67] Mentioning in his report that HMS *Mentor* and HMS *Hound* were able to enter Mobile Bay without any problem, Ezpeleta added that "from this fact Your Excellency will infer that entry through this river is not as difficult as some would have us believe, and that the sand bar has not changed its location, as Don Josef Rada supposed."[68]

When the fighting ended, each side reported its butcher's bill. According to the incomplete official British report, their side incurred fifteen dead [one colonel, two lieutenants, and twelve men] and twenty-three wounded [one captain, two lieutenants, three sergeants, one fife, and sixteen men].[69] The Spanish tally of enemy casualties was fifteen dead and three wounded prisoners and of their own casualties fourteen dead and twenty-nine wounded.[70]

Beside these figures, the personal account of Loyalist Benjamin Baynton included in a letter to his brother is illuminating: "The particulars of this action you will I suppose see in the publick papers; but, this I will venture to assert, no action since the rebellion, (for the number) was more severe while it lasted, or where more honor has been reflected on the astonishing intrepidity of the British Troops. They pushed on upwards of two hundred yards through an incessant fire of grape & musket shot, from at least twice their number, entrenched up to their teeth. One continual sheet of fire presented itself for ten minutes. You may judge of the gallantry of the Officers, when you read in the papers that out of ten, six were killed and wounded. It was Bunkers hill in miniature."[71]

Of course, reports of the fighting in Mobile Village were not published in the newspapers, and its comparison to the Battle of Bunker Hill is a bit exaggerated. But it is worth remembering that, as the old military saying goes, for the soldier who dies in a small skirmish, that is his Waterloo. José de Ezpeleta ended his official report with a comment that clearly shows his northern character—short of words, but full of pride: "I believe that from what happened they [the British] are chastened, since although everything was in their favor, they have lost four officers, who for their courage deserved better luck, and I have no doubt they would have had it if they had not meet troops who knew how to confront them, and who did not know how to run."[72]

BERNARDO DE GÁLVEZ IN HAVANA

As he became exasperated with the delays, Bernardo de Gálvez left New Orleans for Havana, where he arrived on August 2, 1780. The following day, a fleet under the command of Admiral José Solano y Bote arrived from Cadiz in southern Spain. Gálvez's hope for a quick departure for Pensacola soon melted away when the sorry condition of the disembarking troops became apparent. Just one example: the King's Immemorial Regiment was 1,209 men strong when it left Cadiz, but on its arrival in Havana only 744 men were fit for service.[73] The troops would need weeks, if not months, to recover from the travel, which at the time was always unhealthy. Most of the men were sick with various diseases. Therefore Bernardo de Gálvez was immediately dragged into an exhausting series of war councils to plan every detail of the expedition.[74] The tensions that Gálvez had experienced earlier with Admiral Bonet were soon duplicated with his replacement, Victorio de Navia.[75] But at least the arrival of José Solano, chief of the fleet just arrived from Cadiz, made Gálvez's relationship with the navy easier. Solano played a key role in speeding up preparations for the departure of the expedition against Pensacola. Finally, on October 16, 1780, 3,822 soldiers and 169 officers, on board a fleet commanded by José Solano, set sail from the port of Havana for Pensacola (see appendix table 8).

Bernardo de Gálvez's joy lasted only a couple of days. On October 18, a nearly weeklong hurricane sank several ships, damaged most of the rest, and scattered them off course. Despite repeated efforts it was impossible to regroup, as the hurricane had thrown ships to such far-flung locations as Havana, Campeche (on the coast of Mexico), Mobile, and New Orleans (see appendix table 9).

CONTEMPORANEOUS ACCOUNTS OF THE EXPEDITION AGAINST PENSACOLA

Since Bernardo de Gálvez begins his account of the expedition against Pensacola with a description of the destruction caused by the hurricane, this seems an appropriate place to summarize other narratives from the time dealing with the same subject.

View of Havana's marketplace during the British occupation. The tension between the local population and the invaders can be clearly seen in the defiant attitude of the British soldiers in the foreground, one of them staring at the nearby group of priests while blowing smoke from his pipe. (Durnford, Canot, and Morris, *A view of the market place in the city of Havana* . . . ; Library of Congress Prints and Photographs Division, control no. 2009633664)

Two German accounts—the journals from two members of the Waldeck Regiment posted to Pensacola—have survived. The diary of Carl Philipp Steuernagel, logistics officer of the company under the command of Captain Teutzel, covers May 20, 1776, to his return to Germany after the end of the war. The other journal was by the chaplain, Ph. Waldeck.[76]

On the British side are three official reports sent by General John Campbell[77] to his superiors on April 9, May 7, and May 12, 1781, and testimonies by Sergeant James A. Mathews and officer Robert Adolphus Farmar.[78] It is worth mentioning that a copy of Farmar's "Journal of the Siege of Pensacola, from the time the Enemy's fleet first appeared to the 10th of May, the day we surrendered to the arms of Spain" was among the papers of Francisco de Miranda.[79]

Among documentation related to the expedition against Pensacola in the French National Archives is the correspondence of the Chevalier de Monteil, head of the French fleet, which gives a neutral perspective on the tensions between Gálvez and the naval commanders; a letter from Mr. de Champmeslin about the capture of Pensacola; copies of several letters to and from Gálvez and Solano; a copy of the articles of capitulation; and a French account of the capture of Pensacola, with details about the French contribution.[80]

Several Spanish participants in the siege of Pensacola have left their official or personal accounts: José Solano, Francisco de Miranda, Francisco de Saavedra, and Bernardo de Gálvez. José Solano kept a diary, the original of which is in the Spanish National Archives at Simancas. It offers details about the naval operations.[81] Francisco de Miranda, infantry captain in the Aragon Regiment and aide-de-camp to Juan Manuel de Cagigal, second in command of the expedition, who would go down in history as the father of the independence of Venezuela, kept two diaries during the expedition.[82] The first starts on February 28 and ends on April 18;[83] the second covers the period from April 9 to May 10.[84] Both documents along with others related to the expedition are in the Francisco Miranda Archives in Caracas, Venezuela.[85] Miranda's always lively pen supplies a lot of detail about the military operations as well as a firsthand account of Gálvez's problems with the naval commanders. Francisco de Saavedra, one of Bernardo de Gálvez's closest friends who played a key role behind the scenes, recorded his experiences in the Pensacola campaign twice. His journal covers the period between January 1 and May 26, 1781, and he also addresses the campaign in his memoirs, which he entitled *Los Decenios*.[86] José de Ezpeleta, Mobile's governor and also Gálvez's close friend, left important documentation and his own account of the expedition among his papers.[87]

Bernardo de Gálvez also kept a journal. Actually, despite the singular word, it actually exists in four versions: two in manuscript form and two in printed form. The first manuscript[88] covers all of the expeditions and includes the articles of capitulation as well as a list of casualties. Some details were later omitted to play down Bernardo's conflict with the naval commanders. The second manuscript covers only twelve days, March 9 to March 20.[89] This version seems to have been written in haste and contains some personal thoughts left out of the first manuscript and the two printed versions. Both manuscripts are in the General Archive of the Indies in Seville, Spain. The third version, which was the first to appear in print, was published in the August 10, 1781, issue of the *Gazeta de Madrid*, the official Spanish newspaper. The fourth version, which was the second to appear in print, is an offprint from the first printed edition and contains identical text. It has no date or place of publication, a fact that has created quite an energetic debate among historians and bibliophiles.[90] The printed copies used in this

A highly idealized view of Pensacola in the late 1770s, showing a prosperous port and a booming city. The reality was much more modest, as attested to by contemporary British travelers, settlers, and both officers and soldiers posted to its garrison. (*A view of Pensacola, in West Florida* . . . ; Library of Congress Prints and Photographs Division, control no. 2004672419)

work are those found in the National Library in Madrid and the library of Madrid's Royal Palace.[91]

In addition, fifteen maps and plans of the siege of Pensacola, drawn at the time or a short time later by Spanish, British (or British-employed), and French engineers and mapmakers, are preserved in several archives.[92] Two of these stand out: one by Francisco Miranda, because it was drawn during the operation itself, and another by Luis Huet, because of its detail about the military operations.

PREPARATIONS FOR THE SECOND ATTEMPT AGAINST PENSACOLA: BERNARDO DE GÁLVEZ'S "SECRET PLAN"

After the hurricane had destroyed his ships, Bernardo de Gálvez returned to Havana on November 17, 1780, where most of the top military hierarchy was waiting to witness the downfall of the ambitious young general. For them the situation was clear enough. The expedition had ended in failure, and if the king decided on a new adventure, it would be under a new commander in chief.[93] Gálvez rebutted their views by simply ignoring them and concentrating on preparations for a second attempt against Pensacola, this time with an important change in strategy.

In pressing for reorganizing the ongoing expedition against Pensacola, he started by talking up the great dangers facing Spanish possessions in North America, not only in recently conquered Mobile but also in Louisiana itself, which demanded immediate reinforcement. It was in this context that Miró's frustrated attempt to send supplies and troops to Mobile had taken place. Now, in Gálvez's words, it was time to "go against Pensacola, but if that is not possible, to keep in greater safety that which has already been conquered."[94] Such was what F. de Borja Medina Rojas[95] calls Gálvez's "secret plan." In furthering this idea, Gálvez asked Diego José Navarro for troops to be sent to Louisiana and Mobile that could be later used in the attack on Pensacola.[96] Bernardo de Gálvez shared the details of his plan only with his most trusted friends, José de Ezpeleta and Francisco Saavedra.[97] Saavedra had just arrived from European Spain, having been commissioned by José de Gálvez himself to be his eyes, ears, and mouth in Havana.[98] According to his journal, Bernardo de Gálvez confided in him that his intention was to get the military leaders in Havana to agree to reinforcements for Louisiana and Mobile and then, instead of taking the troops to those places, to lead them directly to Pensacola. On the evening of February 4 Saavedra had a private conversation with Gálvez.

> We talked at length about the expeditions against Pensacola, and he entrusted me with his plan, which seemed to me very well thought out, as I always believed that the forces at his disposal would not be enough. All of the troops sent from Havana plus those of Louisiana and Mobile totaled barely three thousand men, while the British had two veteran infantry regiments there, [with] the support of many Indian nations, and these could easily be reinforced from Jamaica. He knew better than I that his numbers were not enough, but he dared not ask for more troops so as not to delay their departure. It was agreed that I would try to get him more men and supplies as well as more warships after he departed, especially if the news arrived that the British were going to send reinforcements to Pensacola.[99]

Among the many councils of war held during this period, one that took place in Havana on November 30, 1780, needs to be considered in some detail.[100] Bernardo de Gálvez convened the meeting with the specific intention of having every participant set forth in writing his position on the expedition against Pensacola. Most of them agreed that under the present conditions it was impossible, mainly because of the lack of supplies. But then an important thing happened. Two newly arrived members of the navy, José Solano and Juan Tomaso, did not agree with the Havana leaders and stated simply that the expedition was the top priority. Juan Manuel de Cagigal, commander of the army who had just arrived from Cadiz, apparently sided with Gálvez more directly in asserting that "this second expedition" should be sped up, and "the general commissioned to command it will determine his own needs." Cagigal's carefully chosen words had extremely important implications. If it was a "second expedition," it would require new orders from Madrid, not only on the military operation itself but also on the specific appointment of a general to command it, a general that very well could not be Bernardo de Gálvez.

One by one Bernardo de Gálvez addressed the problems facing the expedition. He started by saying that the expedition against Pensacola should be "restored." In using this word he set aside Cagigal's argument and proceeded to ask for only 3,000 troops. He explained the figure thus: "If someone asks me why now I accept three thousand, I would answer that before I asked for more, because the number of troops on the island was higher, so I wanted to have victory more secured." About supplies, he said that if the troops already in Havana were being fed, it was pointless to argue "whether we have them [that is, supplies] or not; if we have them it is the same to eat them here or in another place." Regarding troops, he questioned official statements about their condition and numbers, saying that he judged there were more than enough for garrison duties. Of the possibility of a British attack on Cuba, he dismissed the idea, since they were not able to assemble enough forces to attempt it. And on the damages caused by the hurricane, he said, "It is true that lately fortune has been not favorable to us, but look at our enemies and you will see how they have also suffered from the ravages with which heaven has punished us. . . . With them [the British] the hurricane was more furious, and the damages caused were not limited to their fleets but also a part of the island of Jamaica has been devastated and destroyed. The eyes of God were kinder to us; it is true we have suffered from a heavy storm, but I consider this blow more a setback than a ruin."

He concluded his speech in the council of war by challenging those present to show as much resolve as the British in Charleston, when their fleet was similarly hit by a storm, and to speed up all preparations, because "perhaps peace will surprise us, and if this happens, all other ranks in society will rejoice; but we soldiers, whom the king paid during peace, will have been useless in time of war. With what panache can we still carry a rusty sword that was not unsheathed when it had to be?"

Despite these strong words, nothing was settled in this council of war or those that took place in the following two months. But at the end of January Gálvez's luck changed with the arrival of his good friend Francisco de Saavedra, who was indispensable for clearing the path for the expedition. Saavedra was the one who solved the problem of the lack of provisions by forcing bakers in Havana to supply their wares promptly to the military stores. He was the one who made the military leaders in Havana feel the pressure emanating from the Spanish royal court by insisting that His Majesty's wishes and orders needed to be carried out and obeyed. It was he, too, who succeeded in appeasing them. With courtesy, patience, and common sense, he ascertained clearly that "each chief argued in favor of the endeavor that would bring him the most personal glory."[101] He met separately with each of them. He judged it necessary to "win Admiral Bonet with kindness and skill, who at heart is of good character but stubborn in matters of military etiquette and indecisive when faced with a predicament."[102] Saavedra's portrait of Bonet was confirmed by the Chevalier de Monteil, commander of the French naval squadron.[103] With Governor Diego José Navarro, "well intentioned but weak because of his many years," Saavedra displayed every courtesy, as when Navarro asked him what place he would occupy in the council of war, and he answered merely that he "never argued about etiquette, and I would be deeply honored to sit anywhere, even in the last seat, in a gathering of persons so highly decorated."[104] He massaged Victorio de Navia's ego by paying him a visit immediately after returning from an audience with the governor.[105] Saavedra also had to exercise patience with his friend, with whom he shared long evenings at home, talking about his plans and problems.

Saavedra would prove so successful that by the end of February all problems had been solved and everything was ready to go. On February 28, 1781, "the expedition for the relief of Mobile and the conquest of Pensacola" set sail from Havana, with five warships, twenty-seven transports, and more than 1,500 soldiers (see appendix table 10).

"I ALONE"

The Island of Santa Rosa

In theory the troops were for the reinforcement of Mobile and New Orleans, but Bernardo de Gálvez did not even pretend to follow that course and instead headed directly for Santa Rosa Island, which lies at the entrance to Pensacola Bay in the south.[106] This time the voyage was uneventful, and on March 9 they sighted the island, where it was believed the British had erected a fort to defend the entrance to the bay. The same night a detachment disembarked to attack the enemy position from behind, but when the troops arrived they found only a couple of cannons and a mortar with a crew of seven artillerymen, who were soon made prisoners.[107] General Campbell had planned to build a battery there to support another one on the Red Cliffs, but, he said, the project was canceled for lack of tools, as they could not work in two places at one time.[108] Bernardo de Gálvez ordered a battery to be placed there to protect the rest of his troops as they disembarked. While his men were fulfilling this order, on March 17 news arrived that reinforcements from Mobile under the command of José de Ezpeleta, "with nine hundred men, two cannons, two artillery officers, an engineer, and mounted dragoons,"[109] were waiting for transports to cross the river. After securing his position on Santa Rosa Island, the next step for Gálvez was to take troops to the mainland to start the siege of Pensacola. But to do this Gálvez needed protection from the navy's warships.

Crossing the Bar to Pensacola

The main challenge of entering Pensacola Bay was the shallow water over a sandbank that connected Santa Rosa to the mainland. It was an especially worrying situation for the *San Ramón*, a ship of the line with a deeper draft than the rest of the fleet. On March 11 its commander, naval captain José Calvo, gave the order to enter the bay. According to his account, "following more my sense of duty in the king's service and my own honor than the advice of reason, I resolved to force entry with all ships of the escort and the convoy.... But with the entire convoy sailing close to the Barrancas Coloradas [Red Cliffs], my ship ran hopelessly aground, with the keel crushed in on the bottom. This event left me with the deep disappointment of never being able to enter the port."[110]

According to the colorful testimony of Francisco de Miranda, when Bernardo de Gálvez suggested to the naval officers that the *San Ramón* remain in the convoy's rear guard and be the last ship to force entry, "it was Troy." Naval captain Calvo interpreted his suggestion as an affront to the honor of the fleet's flagship. The commanders of the frigates, fearing that they did not have the support of the *San Ramón*'s firepower, "presented all kind of excuses (although the day before they had been competing among themselves to be the first to force entry), and it did not stop there; they so strongly supported Calvo, that it seemed they were going to abandon the expedition and leave the troops on an island that has nothing but sand. Since this happened, the days pass and letters go back and forth, but nothing is done."[111]

The letters mentioned by Miranda solved very little; in fact, their content escalated to personal insults.[112] Gálvez convened a council of war at which naval officers supported Calvo's position that it was impossible to enter the bay "without an exact map of it, with indications about its depth and configuration." This was not exactly accurate, as a handmade map with this information was already available, which, according to the Spanish army's official cartographic services, "seems to have been made in preparation for General Gálvez's operations against the British."[113] Gálvez was furious. "How can the possible loss of a frigate, in which surely not many people would perish, compare with the total destruction of all of the troops and some of the sailors?" Calvo responded, "Your Excellency, do not ignore the art of war, or the rules of military caution, which teach us to avoid extreme danger, haste, and delay.... To what purpose will we needlessly send, as sheep to the slaughter, the king's vassals under our command? ... I assure Your Excellency, that I do not want glory at such a cost."

The same day, Calvo sent Gálvez another letter containing a thinly veiled threat of insubordination. He said he would ask Havana for instructions, "since I am not in a position to take on by myself such great responsibility." Gálvez answered Calvo that he "should not mess in judgments that are beyond his authority." The following day, Calvo, perhaps aware that he had overstepped, offered to send some transports to carry the troops arriving from Mobile. Gálvez thanked him but added, "I take advantage of this occasion to ask you, Sir, if concerning this issue of entering the port, an operation among those necessary for the conquest of Pensacola, you consider yourself not under my command, since some of the language you used in previous communications has made me suspect that you, Sir, think with too much independence." Calvo responded, "My communications written to Your Excellency are far from showing any independence from Your Excellency's orders about the conquest of Pensacola, but my orders force me to behave in these proceedings according to my own judgment."

Each version of Gálvez's journal of the expedition devotes scarcely two paragraphs to this incident. But in his handwritten account of the disembarkation on Santa Rosa Island he deals with the episode more extensively.[114] No wonder this document never made it into the official account of the expedition. The other important source of what happened at this crucial juncture is Francisco Miranda:

> At two o'clock on the 18th [of March], a boat approached the ship of the line [the *San Ramón*] with the engineer officer Gilabert on board. From it, on behalf of the general [Gálvez], he presented a cannonball picked up in the encampment, one of those the British were shooting from the entrance to the bay, and bade those with honor and courage to fol-

A British brig sloop-of-war similar to HMS *West Florida*, which, after its capture at the battle of Lake Pontchartrain (September 10, 1779) by the Continental navy schooner USS *Morris*, was purchased by Bernardo de Gálvez as governor of Louisiana and renamed the *Galvezton*. (Francis Holman, *An English brig with captured American vessels*, oil on canvas, 1778, in National Maritime Museum, Greenwich, object ID BHC1061)

low him, since he was going on board the *Galvezton* to show them that they had nothing to fear. The message was delivered in a loud voice and thus heard by all the crew. The answer of the commander [Calvo] was that the general was rude and reckless, and a traitor to king and country, and that with the insult he had just made to him and all the navy, he would be laid at the king's feet. That he was the coward, and if he again sent that kind of message, he should do it through a common man rather than an officer, so he could hang him from the mast. The commander had all of his officers assembled so they could hear his answer.[115]

Later, Calvo justified his words in a letter to the minister of the navy: "This barbarous insult filled me with the greatest fury I have ever felt; I told him [Gálvez], almost losing my temper, everything that my just anger said to me."[116] Immediately after this challenge, Bernardo de Gálvez went into action. He boarded the *Galvezton*, a brig from New Orleans that was under his direct command as Louisiana's governor, where he ordered the sailors to hoist "the banner of the chief of squadron, making the ship the proper salute.... He freely entered the port followed by the ship under Don Juan de Riaño and the gunships, while the rest of the army, despite the noise made by the enemy's batteries, continued happily to cheer the king's name; he succeeded in entering and anchoring his three vessels without any harm."[117]

Although according to naval regulations at the time an army general had the same rank as a naval chief of squadron, hoisting his banner in the navy's way was a studied provocation on Gálvez's part.[118] In doing so he elevated the rank of the small flotilla from New Orleans to a naval squadron and, at the same time, succeeded in inspiring all of his men, soldiers and sailors alike.[119] Seizing the moment in a manner one author has called an indulgence in melodrama,[120] Bernardo de Gálvez addressed his men in the following terms, which deserve to be quoted at length:

> I, my sons, went alone to sacrifice myself, so as not to expose a single soldier, not a man of my army, and so the navy could see that there is no danger such as they say, and that I do not want to sacrifice such a respectable corps, despite all of the troubles they have caused me, and the deceptions they have practiced from the beginning.... In this predicament... I was forced to take this course of action to set an example, sending Don José Calvo a message through the engineer Don Francisco Gilabert, who carried the enemy's cannonball, of the same caliber that they were firing, to tell him that those were the ones I was going to confront bare chested while forcing entry into the port, with those with the honor and courage to follow me; and although I hoped to see them following us, I found that they did not, since he [Calvo] ordered his ships not to move; answering me with all kinds of insults, calling me reckless, and saying that if the enemy's cannonballs did not behead me, the king himself would chop off my head.
>
> At that time, in front of everyone, he received a thousand congratulations, and embracing his officers, he [Gálvez] showed his affection with hugs and kisses for the commander of the artillery, thanking him for the precision and good timing of his cover fire....[121]
>
> Everyone shouted three times, "God save the king!" and Gálvez ordered that each and every soldier of the army should receive a *real* from his own pocket.[122]

Gálvez's speech raised his men's morale, and more than two centuries later it still resounds. But we must overlook the emotion and consider its content. First, its context was that of a joint army-navy operation. This kind of operation is never easy, not only because of technical complexities but also because of the cultural differences between the two branches of the military. While soldiers tend to consider the navy merely a means of transportation and themselves those who in the end will do the real fighting, seamen complain that the army's demands rarely take into account the technical difficulties or the safety of the ships. In Spanish royal regulations at the time, both the army and the navy were to simply ignore each other.[123] This mutual silence was simply the lawmaker's way of acknowledging that a general criterion or solution was impossible, leaving problems to be solved on the spot.

There was also the question of the extent to which Gálvez's authority, as commander in chief of the expedition against Pensacola, extended over the navy. Despite John Walton Caughey's assertion that he had been appointed supreme commander of both naval and land forces, the appointment was made on February 12, 1781, and therefore could not have reached Havana before the expedition departed for Pensacola.[124] Two further details confirm this claim. The first is that Francisco Saavedra wrote in his journal on May 26 that several days earlier, a mail ship had arrived in Havana containing dispatches appointing Bernardo de Gálvez supreme commander.[125] The second detail is that Gálvez himself did not assume this office until May 29.[126]

Therefore the chain of command at the mouth of Pensacola Bay in 1781 was far from clear. In theory, as a brigadier general, Bernardo de Gálvez outranked José Solano, a navy captain (*capitán de navío*)—not to be confused with the Spanish admiral with the same name—the equivalent of an army colonel.[127] Solano's orders issued in Havana stated that he must implement Gálvez's orders, but he must do so "according to his well-known intelligence," without ever contravening the Royal Navy's regulations.[128] According to those regulations, a commander's first duty was to "preserve his ship," and the order from Gálvez to enter the bay could endanger it.[129] On top of this, as Caughey wisely remarks, "the loss of the *Volante* and the grounding of several other vessels at Mobile had not won Gálvez the reputation of being an expert authority on entering ports."[130]

Gálvez's speech at the mouth of Pensacola Bay in 1781 is the origin of his famous motto: *Yo solo* (I alone). It is a perfectly simple and suitable phrase that has been used extensively in references to Bernardo de Gálvez in history (and pseudo-history) books, historical fiction, press, theater, and even a king's speech.[131] But the truth is he never uttered these exact words. In his challenge he encouraged "those with honor and courage to follow me" and on his return said, "I, my sons, went alone to sacrifice myself, so as not to expose a single soldier, not a man of my army."[132] To change from "I went alone" to "I alone," the king's intervention was needed, and years later the king would add the motto "I alone" to Bernardo de Gálvez's coat of arms.[133] Bernardo de Gálvez was perfectly aware that despite his motto, "my desires would never have come true if the officers of the ship [the *Galvezton*] had lacked the courage, intelligence, and determination required in the situation. That it is to you, Monsieur Rousseau, as first in command, and to Monsieur Duparc, as second, that I owe success in that enterprise, I wish with the copy of the royal decree and this letter of gratitude to publicly acknowledge, until (as His Majesty promises) another reward more suitable and authentic arrives."[134]

A last comment about Gálvez's speech: his reward of a *real* from his own pocket to every soldier in the expedition was, certainly, proof of his generosity, but it was also a wise move to "buy" his troops' loyalty at a crucial moment when he could have been overstepping his military authority. This interpretation is reinforced by the fact that mention of the reward appears only in his journal of the Santa Rosa events and not in the official copy of the diary sent to his uncle or in the later published versions.[135]

Bernardo de Gálvez succeeded in forcing entry into Pensacola Bay "without any casualties, despite twenty-eight cannon shots fired from the fort."[136] But this would have meant nothing had the rest of the fleet and the convoy not followed him inside. According to Francisco de Miranda, "This unexpected example encouraged the frigate commanders to volunteer to enter the bay, but the fleet commander, unmoved by their repeated pleas both in person and in writing, would have none of it, and he furthermore gave the order to all of the warships and those in the convoy not to move from their positions without his express and specific orders, even if only to shorten their anchors. At eight o'clock Colonel Longoria came on board, sent by General [Gálvez] to make amends and offer himself as guarantor; with these assurances and redoubled pleas, the fleet commander agreed and gave the order to the warships and convoy to enter the port the following day."[137]

At two o'clock on March 19, 1781, all ships, with the exception of the *San Ramón*, entered Pensacola Bay. According to Calvo, "because of this insult, and to show him [Gálvez] what the navy could do to live up to its honor, on the 19th, the feast of Saint Joseph, I ordered the convoy to enter, which it did with great fortune, without death, or injury, or serious head wounds."[138] With these words Calvo put himself in a very difficult position, rendering invalid all of his previous arguments about caution and so on. Despite more than 140 rounds fired from the British battery on top of the Red Cliffs, the Spanish ships entered the bay undamaged.[139] Aware of the importance of sealing the entrance to the bay, British general John Campbell had ordered that a small fort be built there with a garrison formed from about fifty soldiers from the Waldeck Regiment and the crews of His Majesty's ships. Since the latter were in the majority, the site was named the Royal Navy's Redoubt. Five large-caliber cannons were positioned there, supported by six smaller ones. Hugely satisfied with this arrangement, Campbell informed his superiors of the surprise awaiting his enemy when faced with its fire.[140] But in fact, as Spanish engineers later found, the Royal Navy's Redoubt was positioned too far and too high from the water for its cannons to be able to aim properly at ships entering the bay.[141] Muzzle-loading cannons were unable to fire aiming downward, so the Spanish fleet and convoy simply entered the mouth of the bay underneath British fire, and not into it, as General Campbell had expected. Immediately afterward, José Calvo informed General Gálvez that he would return with the *San Ramón* to Havana, since his work was done.[142] Calvo later tried to justify his action by arguing that he was short of provisions and his ship's services were no longer needed.[143] But when news of the *San Ramón*'s return reached the Spanish authorities in Havana, Francisco de Saavedra commented that it was received with much surprise, "since its captain, Don José Calvo, was a seasoned officer, and we did not know for what reason he would leave the expedition before its completion."[144]

The departure of Fleet Commander Calvo did not end Bernardo de Gálvez's problems with the navy. On March 22, an incident took place that almost ended in direct confrontation. Francisco Miranda provided another engaging description:

> That same day several officers . . . dined with the general, and he talked about the conduct of Señor Castejón [minister of the navy], attributing to him the delay in the conquest of Pensacola, saying that he was a traitor to king and country, because of the influence and tears of his wife, General Campbell's niece; and that he had proof of it, with his delays in Havana and that fact that his officers had shown such *colloneria* [literally, "lack of guts," that is, cowardice] in their entrance into the port, and that he had no doubt that the whole navy was on the same page as its supreme commander. The naval officers, tired and ashamed of these derogatory remarks about their corps and commanders, retorted by asking him to withdraw them; but Gálvez in fury took his sword and hat and asked if they wished to insult him. At that moment Commander Alderete [fleet commander after the departure of Calvo] entered and the scene ended, but another even worse one began, with the general asking him if he recognized him as the supreme commander of all land and naval forces, since he had not properly saluted when he passed alongside the *Galvezton*. . . . Alderete answered that

since he had no orders to that effect, and royal regulations did not demand it, he would never do it. Gálvez in anger told him that he did not need the navy, and that they all could return to Havana as soon as they wished, where they could send regards to his wife, and turning on heel he left.[145]

Gálvez's rage, even if justified, could have jeopardized the whole expedition. True enough, the troops were disembarking on the mainland, and therefore the navy was no longer needed for their transport. But the navy was still essential to protecting the troops from any British attempt to reinforce or resupply Pensacola. Much to his good fortune, the new fleet commander, naval commander Miguel de Alderete, was a very different man from his predecessor. Instead of throwing fat on the fire, Alderete opted to keep his cool and wait until the following day, when, according to Miranda, "he received a letter from Gálvez offering to dine with him on board his frigate, to make amends with the navy, and to remain in good spirits for the sake of future operations, and [saying] that he would order all army officers never again to mention past matters."[146] Alderete accepted Gálvez's peace offer but not without informing José Calvo about the incident, including the testimony of those present.[147] Calvo did not waste time in complaining to the minister of the navy in Madrid: "If Your Excellency, on behalf of the whole navy, does not inform the king about these insults, you will contribute to his [Gálvez's] efforts, supported by HIS UNCLE [capitalized in the original], to discredit this useful and glorious corps . . . and will fall into disrepute in the king's eyes."[148] Calvo's thinly veiled threat to his superior in Madrid did not serve him well. He was desperate and oscillated between aggressiveness and humble pleas to "trust the almighty God and His Majesty's kindness . . . which will prove that had I a servile and low character and had given in to the general Don Bernardo de Gálvez's whims, as many others have, I would be free of such persecution."[149]

Little is known about José Calvo's later life—only that in trying perhaps to find consolation for his stranded career in the navy he devoted himself to poetry, which one critic has described as "modest."[150] Several surviving manuscripts of his verse give evidence of his struggle, and two titles in particular show how deeply he was wounded: "Poem on military caution, taken from and based on events told in the Holy Scriptures, which show the true reasons why generals, battles, and empires are lost" and "The ungodliness of this century, fought in different meters, in defense of virtue and religion."[151]

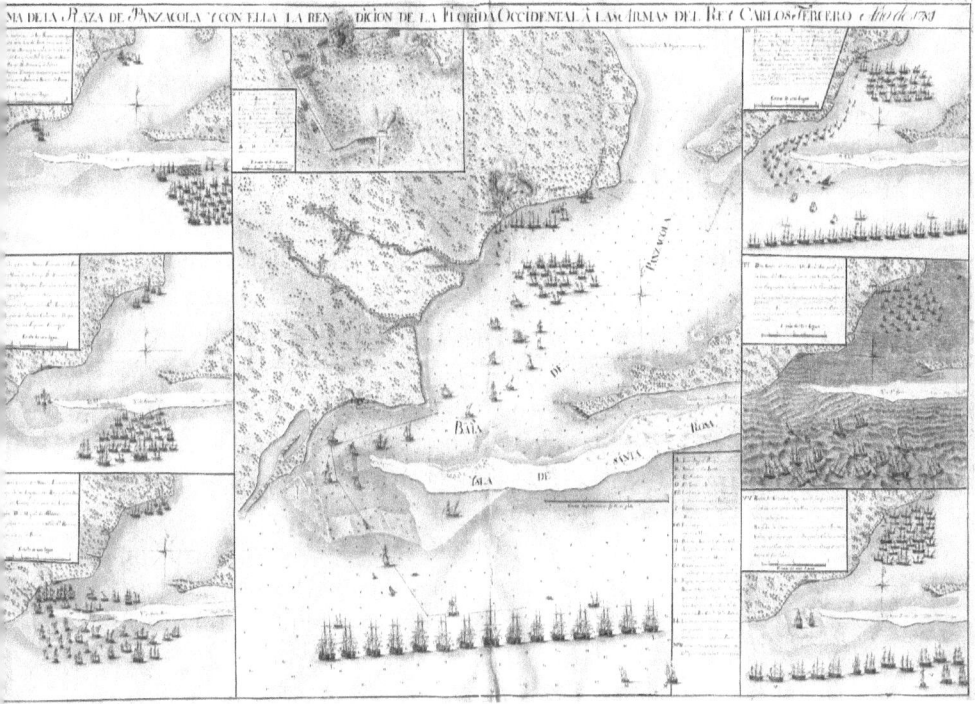

Map of the conquest of Pensacola in 1781. The anonymous and undated map focuses on the maritime operations, and the description of the siege closely follows the official reports by the Spanish naval officers. Of the eight partial maps, seven are of naval operations. The entrance to the bay by the ships under the command of Bernardo de Gálvez is described in the most neutral terms possible, with no reference to the problems between Gálvez and the navy commander. The end of the siege, with the explosion of the Queen's Redoubt, is portrayed almost as a fortuitous event (which it was, but in order to happen the Spanish trenches had to be excavated close enough to the British positions), and with no mention of Gálvez's involvement. According to the text inside the cartouche of this small map, the order to assault Pensacola was given by an unnamed army officer. In fact, Gálvez's name is mentioned only twice, while those of five naval officers are registered. The map's beautiful drawings of ships and troops compensate for its obvious pro-navy bias and the unknown author and date.
(*Toma de la plaza de Panzacola y rendición de la Florida Occidental a las armas de Carlos III*; España, Ministerio de Defensa, Archivo del Museo Naval, inventory no. AMN 6-A-20)

The Start of the Siege of Pensacola

Even with all of his troops safely on the mainland, Gálvez's position was still shaky. Breaking Pensacola's defenses with only 1,500 men was impossible. Military theorists at the time thought that successfully laying siege to a fortress with three or four redoubts required 6,000 to 8,000 men.[152] Besides these fortifications, Pensacola also had a seasoned garrison. When General John Campbell arrived as its commander, he had brought with him from New York an artillery detachment from the Waldeck Regiment and two provincial units, the Pennsylvania and Maryland Provincial militias.

The Waldeck Regiment was composed of German troops who fought on the British side during the Revolutionary War. Since they were mostly from the land of Hesse, they were called Hessians. The Waldeck Regiment was initially formed with 1,255 men, and by the end of the war, 720 of them had died in America. As seen earlier, some members of this regiment were defeated by the Spanish in Baton Rouge and Mobile.[153]

The Pennsylvania Loyalists were originally recruited in Philadelphia in October 1777. Their first commander was Lieutenant Colonel William Allen. In December 1770 the unit was temporarily merged into a unit called the United Corps of Pennsylvania and Maryland Loyalists, under the command of General John Campbell.[154] The Maryland Loyalists were recruited at the same time and in the same place as the Pennsylvania Loyalists. Their first commander was Lieutenant Colonel James Chalmers until December 1770, when they joined with the Pennsylvania Loyalists.[155]

In addition to these troops brought to Pensacola by General Campbell, some were already posted there: a battalion of the Sixteenth Infantry Regiment; another of the Sixtieth Infantry Regiment; three companies raised by Pensacola's governor, Peter Chester; a group of provincials; local militia raised by the superintendent of Indian Affairs, John Stuart; and a number of Indian warriors.[156] The Sixteenth Infantry Regiment was created in 1688. In 1767 it was sent from Ireland to Florida and garrisoned at Pensacola from 1768 until 1776, when it left for New York. Members of the regiment were made prisoner at Baton Rouge and later exchanged and returned to active duty. In 1781 a detachment was posted to Pensacola.[157]

The Sixtieth Infantry Regiment's original name was the Sixty-Second, also known as the Royal American Regiment of Foot. It was created in 1756, and its main part served not on the American continent but in the West Indies. But in 1780 four companies of its Fourth Battalion were sent to Mobile, where they were taken prisoner and later exchanged. In 1781 its Third Battalion was posted to Pensacola.[158] When the Spaniards arrived, the entire

British garrison of Pensacola amounted to between nearly 1,800 and almost 1,900 men (see appendix table 11).

This is the total figure, but to evaluate the British forces properly one must consider their condition and morale. In February 1779, John Campbell sent his superiors a sad picture of the troops under his command.[159] He said that the Sixteenth Regiment was half "composed of men worn out in the service" and half of inexperienced German recruits. Campbell wanted to dissolve this unit and transfer its few useful men to the Sixteenth, but he was unable to do so because the reinforcements he asked for never arrived.[160] The men of the Sixteenth Regiment had awful memories of Pensacola, where they had been garrisoned between 1763 and 1764, so they left their comfortable posting in Jamaica reluctantly.[161] The Sixteenth was formed of professional soldiers recruited in North America. According to Pensacola's civilian governor, Peter Chester, their training was poor.[162] In fact, Campbell's opinion of them was even worse: "Germans, condemned criminals, and other species of gaol birds." He thought their loyalty could not be trusted, except perhaps for certain veterans in the Sixteenth.[163]

About the Waldeck Regiment, Campbell wrote that he had "no objection to an account of military subordination . . . but I must say that I think them totally unfit for active service, their appointments, their dress, their discipline, nay their very make and form of body disable them from acting with that rapidity and spirit wherewith it might probably be necessary to repel an invading enemy, and indeed must at all times render them improper troops for the woods and wilds of America."[164] Campbell concluded that they could be useful for garrison duty but little else.

About the Pennsylvania and Maryland Loyalists, Campbell shared the contempt for provincials that was common among British officers fighting in North America. For him they were "composed of the greater part of Irish vagabonds (deserters from the rebels) who from natural fickleness and instability of their disposition, which has been confirmed by their late roaming way of life, would desert without any other temptation."[165] The merging of the Pennsylvania Loyalists and Maryland Loyalists was strongly contested by officers in the latter unit, to the point that Sir Henry Clinton, supreme commander of the British forces in North America, eventually had to order the two separate corps reinstated.[166]

Pensacola's defenses were formed by three structures: Fort George, the Queen's Redoubt, and the Prince of Wales Redoubt. Fort George was the most important structure. Initially built in 1772, it had a central square protected by brick and earthen walls, a tower at each corner, a surrounding

Undated portrait of Peter Chester, British governor of West Florida. The British leadership at Pensacola was divided between its civilian governor, Chester, and its military commander, General John Campbell. This fact and the lack of collaboration between both of them weakened the British efforts to defend Pensacola from the Spanish attack. (*Portrait of Peter Chester, governor of British West Florida*, University Archives and West Florida History Center, UWF Libraries, Pensacola)

moat with no water, and eleven cannons, five of them of large caliber.[167] The Queen and Prince of Wales Redoubts sat to the north of Fort George and were intended to protect it.[168] In addition to these three military structures, there were also the Royal Navy's Redoubt, erected on the Red Cliffs, and the planned but never fully constructed battery on Santa Rosa Island.

The British defensive system for Pensacola also included naval forces from both the Royal Navy and private sources, whose mission was to prevent the enemy from entering the bay. When Gálvez arrived, two British navy ships, the *Mentor* and the *Port Royal*, were protecting the bay. Until the end of February a third ship, the *Hound*, had also been present, but it then left for Jamaica. Up until the moment the Spaniards entered the bay, the navy played an important role in the defense of Pensacola, as can be seen in the *Mentor*'s log. The *Mentor* was a small ship built in Maryland by the American rebels and then captured by the British in 1779 and commissioned as a private corsair under the name of *Who's Afraid*. It was later bought by the Royal Navy, which renamed it the *Mentor*. Under the command of Captain Robert Deans, the *Mentor* had a short but lucrative corsair career, capturing six Spanish vessels in the waters near Florida and participating in the unsuccessful British attack on Mobile.[169] Despite their small number, the British ships could have easily prevented the Spanish ships from entering Pensacola Bay, but the fire from the Spanish battery on the island of Santa Rosa pinned them down. Once the Spanish fleet entered the bay, the British ships were no longer of use, and their crews were ordered to reinforce Pensacola's defenses. The *Mentor* was burned by its crew to prevent its capture by the enemy.[170]

While his troops were busy disembarking, Bernardo de Gálvez wrote the first of a series of letters to General John Campbell, in which he warned that "as the British had cautioned the defenders in Havana not to destroy the king's or private buildings or ships, I warn you of the same, under the penalty of treatment with the utmost severity."[171] General Campbell answered, "The threats of the enemy are nothing more than a ploy or scheme to be used to his own advantage. Be assured that in the defense of Pensacola (since I am the one being attacked), I will do nothing contrary to the laws and customs of war."[172] To clarify the way in which these laws and customs were applicable to Pensacola, Campbell wrote another letter to Gálvez the following day, in which he promised not to use official buildings for military purposes but only to shelter the civilian population. He concluded by informing Gálvez that if this was not respected, "you alone will be responsible in the eyes of God and of men for any calamities and misfortunes deriving from the situation. . . . But from the experience we have of your past behavior and noble sentiments, we do not think that horrors will happen."[173]

The same day two more letters arrived for Gálvez, both from Peter Chester, the civilian governor of Pensacola. In the first letter Chester offered to release all Spanish prisoners held in the town on the condition that they swear not to take up arms against Britain until properly exchanged. In the second he offered guarantees of protection for the women and children of Pensacola.[174] The importance of these letters is not in their content but in their mere existence, since instead of speaking with one voice the British in Pensacola spoke with two, which were not very well coordinated. Bad relations between military and civilian authorities in Pensacola had a long history, which can be traced back to the beginning of British domination over West Florida. As pointed out by Joseph Barton Starr, during the first twelve years of the British presence, "disputes between the governor and the military commander were common, and the province was often in a state of turmoil and confusion. The role of the military was in a constant state of change as troops arrived and were withdrawn with little apparent forethought as to the effect on the colony."[175]

On top of this serious problem, according to N. Orwin Rush, unlike Gálvez, General Campbell was far from enthusiastic about serving his king in this section of the empire.[176] As early as March 10, 1779, Campbell was writing to his superior "earnestly to solicit and entreat that Your Excellency will be pleased to release me from the command of West Florida as soon as you can conveniently, and beg as a particular favor, I may not be kept any length of time with a command I have so great an aversion to; give me leave to assure you, Sir, that I shall be very unhappy and discontented as long as I remain in this province. . . . I must own there is nothing I wish for so much as a relief from my present command, finding myself unable to undergo the fatigue and trouble of it. . . . You cannot therefore bestow a greater favor upon me, than to recall me from Western Florida."[177]

During his command in Pensacola, Campbell continued to complain and more importantly to convey a defeatist attitude. On May 18, 1780, after asserting that nothing would be spared in the defense of Pensacola, he asked "for permission to join the army, rather than remain here, with such troops as compose my pitiful command, without the least chance of serving with credit to myself or with honor and advantage to my Royal master, pestered with innumerable difficulties, and a multiplicity of perplexing business— you may therefore conceive my feelings in my present condition, which I humbly submit to your serious consideration."[178]

In September of the same year, he warned that he hoped "to be able to perform what can reasonably be expected from me in the circumstances in which I am situated."[179] The same attitude permeated his first report to Sir Henry Clinton.[180] In his second report to General Clinton, dated May 7, 1781, he wrote,

> To conclude my Lord our fate appears inevitable. We are attacked by an armament that shows the importance of the conquest in the estimation of Spain. We have notwithstanding your Lordship's repeated instruction to attend to the safety of Pensacola, been neglected by Jamaica—and the prospect, nay even the hope of relief is now vanished. I shall however preserve this place to His Majesty, while I shall think resistance justifiable, and of any profitable advantage to the King's interest. I apprehend, My Lord, my next will be the unpleasing and disagreeable task of reporting the triumph of Spain, and their acquisition of a province under their dominion. I only comfort myself with the hope that my endeavors, and those of the garrison under my command, for the defense [of Pensacola], will be acceptable to His Majesty.[181]

In the third and final report, written after his surrender of the town, he was even more direct in saying, "It has been my great misfortune to have been employed in this ill-fated corner of His Majesty's Dominion; but I trust, that the calamities that have befallen West Florida will not be imputed to me, my endeavors to put it in the best state of defense possible have been unremitting."[182] In further damage to morale in Pensacola, Campbell's pessimism was accompanied by several demonstrations of his contempt for the local population. During a meeting of the Pensacola city council in February 1780, he warned that if council members continued to do nothing against the approaching enemy, they would justifiably be despised by those with courage and that the misfortunes that would certainly befall them, if they persisted in their ways, would be lamented by neither friends nor foes.[183]

The situation in Pensacola could not have been more different from the one in the Spanish territories. In December 1779, Campbell himself, in a report to Lord George Germain, praised Gálvez's ability to attract to his side the people of Louisiana. "The Spanish ways [of government] was some time ago hateful to their French subjects, but since that time cajoling and lenient methods of managing them have been adopted, in which their present governor in particular has been very successful."[184] This impression was confirmed by a member of Pensacola's city council, who wrote in 1777, "In the event of war between our crown and theirs [Spain], it is generally believed that it would take thousands [of troops] whereas hundreds only would have been necessary before his arrival to make a conquest of the island [New Orleans]."[185]

To the three letters he received from Pensacola on March 21, Bernardo de Gálvez answered that, since he was "a little indisposed," he would write the following day.[186] His ailment did not prevent him from receiving Lieutenant Colonel Alexander Dickson, commander of Baton Rouge, who was in Pensacola under parole and thus unable to take arms against Spain.[187] For Dickson's benefit Gálvez ordered his troops to assemble "with the purpose of allowing Lieutenant Colonel Dickson to inform General Campbell about the sort of troops under my command and their total numbers."[188] Once again, under this show of eighteenth-century courtesy was a cold calculation, since the troops Gálvez presented to his guest were not all under his command, and he had already received news of the imminent arrival of important reinforcements from Mobile and New Orleans. The meeting with Dickson came to an abrupt end when the Spaniards saw the British burning houses to prevent the enemy from taking cover behind them. Bernardo de Gálvez wrote a furious letter to Campbell: "This act proves that you are not sincere; that humanity is just a phrase, that although you repeat it on paper, your heart does not know its meaning. . . . I will hear no more proposals from you other than those offering your surrender, and I assure Your Excellency, that, since it will not be my fault, I will see Pensacola burn with as much detachment as I will also see die over its ashes those who have burned it."[189]

This is the account Bernardo de Gálvez included in the versions of his journal he wanted read by others. But in the version he kept to himself, the one I have called the second manuscript, under the entry for March 20, he wrote that the enemy burned a house located directly in front of their own encampment.[190] If this was the same house burned by the British as was previously mentioned, the fire took place on the night of March 20 and not March 21. So Bernardo de Gálvez postponed his anger until he could display it in front of Lieutenant Colonel Dickson. General Campbell's answer to Gálvez was of no importance to him. Although the British commander justified his men's actions by the need to deprive the enemy of cover,[191] Gálvez was already focused on the preparations and the orders he must give to start the siege of Pensacola.

Reinforcements from Mobile and New Orleans

At nine-thirty on the morning of March 22, Bernardo de Gálvez had a little over 900 more men, who had arrived from Mobile under the command of his trusted friend José de Ezpeleta (see appendix table 12). At four o'clock the following day, a flotilla entered the bay carrying 1,378 more reinforcements, this time from New Orleans, and a couple of days later, 237 more troops arrived by land, also from Louisiana's capital (see appendix table 13).

With these additions Gálvez now commanded a little more than 4,000 men, but still not enough to lay a proper siege, which demanded between 6,000 and 8,000 troops.[192] It could be reckless even to imagine that with so few forces he could successfully lay siege to a fortress such as Pensacola. But Gálvez still had an ace up his sleeve: his friend and José de Gálvez's personal envoy, Francisco de Saavedra. Saavedra was still in Havana, charged with "helping him with anything necessary for the achievement of his objective."[193] While Saavedra was busy in Havana, Gálvez started the real preparations for the siege.

On March 24 all of the troops, except for a detachment of 200 men left to guard Santa Rosa Island, began working on the trenches needed to attack Fort George from the back.[194] But first it was necessary to build a position close to the Queen's Redoubt. The task was technically not difficult but was made so by constant harassment from the Indians, who were backed by some soldiers. Between March 25 and April 19 the Spanish troops were attacked ten times. During the attack that took place on April 12, according to Gálvez, "the enemy was coming from three different sides, with two small cannons. For this reason, he [Gálvez] advanced to see the place where they were going to cut off their retreat; when he reached the advanced batteries, he received a musket shot to a finger of his left hand, which also made a furrow in his gut. Because of this he had to return to his tent for the surgeons to dress the wounds, commanding General Ezpeleta to relieve him, and in his name give all of the orders needed until he could quickly return to the field."[195]

The attackers succeeded only in delaying the work on the siege for a whole day at the cost of one dead and nine wounded. Gálvez's injuries were minor, but on April 14, during a big storm, he suffered what the medicine at the time called the *pasmo* (literally, the shock or freeze),[196] most probably an episode of malaria, which was endemic in Florida until the twentieth century.[197]

Reinforcements from Havana

The morning of April 19 was spent measuring the distance from the Spanish positions to the Queen's Redoubt.[198] At two o'clock Bernardo de Gálvez received news that several sails were sighted near the entrance to the bay. Two hours later it was confirmed that they looked like Spanish ships. At eight o'clock in the evening, Gálvez received confirmation that "the fleet's commanders, Don Jose Solano and the chevalier de Monteil, were close to Santa Rosa Island with fifteen men-of-war, three frigates, and other vessels, and

1,600 men on board, under the command of Brigadier General Don Manuel de Cagigal, to reinforce our army."[199] From his diary it seems that once more, when he most needed it, luck came to his rescue. But while luck always plays an important part in any military operation, in fact, as the aphorism attributed to Field Marshal Helmut Graf von Moltke states, "luck in the long run is given only to the efficient."[200] Bernardo de Gálvez had wisely left his destiny in the hands of his most efficient friend, Francisco de Saavedra.

Saavedra's task in Havana was enormous. He was responsible for coordinating Spanish and French forces in preparation for what would become the next objective: the conquest of British Jamaica.[201] To accomplish this he started by gaining the trust of the initially reluctant French fleet commander, the Chevalier de Monteil, by making sure that his demands, which until then had been mostly ignored, were promptly satisfied.[202]

The main threat to the French-Spanish plans was that a British fleet could close off passage from Cuba to the North American continent. When news arrived on March 19, 1781, that some British ships had been sighted south of Cuba, the order went out to all available ships to find them. After several days with no enemy in sight, the French fleet commander informed his Spanish allies that he would disembark his sick men and depart for Haiti, where his presence was needed to defend the colony in the event a British fleet was sighted in those waters.[203] Orders received from Madrid by the Spanish naval commanders were far from clear; as Saavedra pointed out, "The king's orders stated that neither the fleet nor the squadron should leave Havana before receiving news that the French fleet was already approaching; but they also said that the fleet must be in Spanish ports all of April or at least until the British fleet had left their ports."[204]

The situation seemed to be at a standstill, but Saavedra came up with a solution that "solved all difficulties."[205] He proposed that the departure of the fleet be postponed until July, that two of the four men-of-war be added to the squadron leaving for Haiti, and that the remaining two men-of-war, as well as all of the troops on board, be added "to the army remaining in Havana for the relief of the expedition against Pensacola if *the need arose* [italics mine] . . . and that after news of the surrender of Pensacola arrives, that the thousand men remaining in Havana be sent to Haiti, since they will no longer be needed here." His suggestion was approved, and as it was accepted that a force would remain in Havana to assist in the conquest of Pensacola, all that was required was that the "need" arise before April 8. In Saavedra's own words, "At sunset [on April 7, 1781], the governor received an urgent message from La Filipina [in today's province of Holguin, Cuba] with information that a fisherman had just arrived there, claiming that on the

Portrait of Francisco de Saavedra. Born in the same year but from very different family backgrounds, Bernardo de Gálvez and Francisco de Saavedra met while studying at the Royal Military Academy of Avila. As personal envoy of José de Gálvez to the Spanish and French forces fighting the British in America, he was instrumental in the Spanish victory at Pensacola and beyond. Although this portrait was painted when Saavedra was almost seventy years old, his eyes still transmit the deep intelligence that made him indispensable to José de Gálvez and a bonhomie that cemented his lifelong friendship with Bernardo de Gálvez. Saavedra's memoirs and diaries are a source of the utmost importance in relation to his friend's career and personality. (*Portrait of Francisco de Saavedra y Sangronis*, 1814–1819, in Museo Nacional del Prado, inventory no. PO3433)

evening of March 30 he had seen eight British warships and a frigate sailing toward Cape San Antonio, and that they were firing shots as if making signals. A council of war was immediately called, at which all present agreed that the only possible destination was Pensacola. . . . It was decided that without wasting any time our squadron would sail with troops on board to help in that endeavor."[206]

In other words, less than twenty-four hours before the scheduled departure of the squadron from Guarico, Haiti, news arrived in Havana of a British fleet heading for Pensacola. It was very convenient for Bernardo de Gálvez, and highly suspicious, too—first, because receiving this information just one day before the squadron's departure was all too perfect, as it meant that all supplies and troops were already on board; and second, and even better suited for Gálvez's purposes, because the testimony of a simple fisherman, whose name was not recorded, was enough to change the plans of an entire squadron of His Catholic Majesty. It makes much more sense to believe that Saavedra and his allies had everything ready in advance and that the alarming news brought by the fisherman, if there ever really was a fisherman, was exactly the pretext they needed for sending the reinforcements that Gálvez desperately awaited. Of course, no documentation has been found to confirm this hypothesis. If there ever was any, Saavedra would have made it disappear, with his well-proven zeal.

At sunrise on April 9, 1781, the squadron left for Pensacola with more than 1,600 soldiers on board, along with 1,505 naval officers and sailors. The latter would be especially important, as most of them volunteered to disembark and fight on foot against the British (see appendix tables 14 and 15).

On their arrival in Pensacola on April 19, Bernardo had at his disposal more than 5,500 soldiers, 1,505 officers and sailors of the Spanish navy, and 725 French troops,[207] who volunteered "so they could share in the glory of this conquest."[208] The total number of men of the now Franco-Spanish force was 7,485,[209] but from the ramparts of Pensacola's forts they seemed like many more. The British military commander, General John Campbell, informed his superiors that the force just arrived had between 3,000 and 4,000 regular (professional, not militia or sailors) soldiers, while the real number of Spanish and French professional soldiers was only half that.[210] Even more distorted was the estimate of Carl Philipp Steuernagel, logistics officer of the Waldeck Regiment, who calculated that the total Spanish force was 22,000 soldiers.[211] But Gálvez's luck did not end with the arrival of these reinforcements. Commanding the squadron of the Spanish Royal Navy was José Solano, who would cause all of Gálvez's problems with the navy to evaporate. Bernardo de Gálvez was extremely relieved, since, as he confessed to

Portrait of Admiral José Solano y Bote, whose arrival as head of the Spanish navy fleet assigned to the expeditionary force in Pensacola contributed to a better coordination of naval and ground forces under the command of Bernardo de Gálvez. (*Portrait of José Solano y Bote, Marquis del Socorro*, Ministerio de Defensa, Archivo del Museo Naval)

Saavedra, when he first heard the news of sails approaching, he thought that "his expedition was doomed."[212] The reinforcements allowed Gálvez to speed up the work on the siege, which had been prepared for but not properly begun, since only a few trenches had been dug so far. At least that was the opinion of Sergeant James A. Mathews, who wrote in his diary that until that moment neither side had pushed very hard.[213]

THE SIEGE

With the new arrivals, Bernardo de Gálvez reorganized the men under his command (Spanish soldiers and French and Spanish naval officers and sailors) into four brigades, three divisions, and headquarters (see appendix tables 16 and 17).

Military Units

From this point on, Gálvez's troops were reinforced with soldiers from regiments with a long tradition and many battle honors. These forces consisted of several distinct units, some Spanish and some French. Among the Spanish were the Aragon Regiment, known as "The Formidable"; the Catalonia Volunteers Light Infantry Regiment (Regimiento de Infantería Ligera Voluntarios de Cataluña); the Spain Regiment, known as "The Martyr"; the Flanders Valon Infantry Regiment (Regimiento de Infantería Valona de Flandes); the Guadalajara Regiment, known as "The Tiger"; the Havana Fixed Infantry Regiment, or "The Noble" (Regimiento de Infantería Fijo de La Habana); the Hibernia Regiment, known as the "Hibernian Column"; the Mallorca Regiment, or "The Invincible"; the Navarra Regiment, or "The Triumphant"; the Prince's Regiment, or "The Bold"; the King's Regiment, or "The Brake"; the Soria Regiment, or "The Bloody"; the America's Dragoons; the Havana Fusiliers Company (Compañía de Fusileros de La Habana); the Battalion of Havana Free Blacks (Batallón de morenos libres de La Habana); and the New Orleans Colored Militia (Milicias de color de New Orleans).[214]

Depending on the source, the number of French troops that fought in Pensacola varies. In his order of April 23, 1781, Gálvez mentions 509 French soldiers, but probably additional men fought who were attached to other Spanish units.[215] The Spanish fleet commander, José Solano, mentions 700 men,[216] but probably the most accurate estimate of the total French troops is 800, a figure mentioned both by Gálvez and by the French fleet commander, the Chevalier de Monteil,[217] which included both soldiers and seamen.[218] Gálvez grouped the French fighters in his second division under the command of navy captain Boderut with Captain d'Amariton as his second.[219] The French army units came from regiments posted in the French Caribbean territories (the d'Agenois Regiment, the Cambresis Regiment, and the Poitou Regiment); in addition, some French seamen volunteered to fight.[220] Some sources mention the presence in Pensacola of two other French regiments, the Gatinais and the Orleans, but no confirmation has been found among the official documentation of the expedition.[221]

The Plan of Attack

The Spanish plan for the conquest of Pensacola was to attack Fort George from the rear, which meant that the Queen's and Prince's Redoubts had to be taken first. To do so it was necessary to dig trenches and place the batteries slowly, under cover but close enough so their fire could reach the British. Despite some work already under way, the truth is that the most important and difficult endeavors would not start until the arrival of the reinforcements from Havana. Although Bernardo de Gálvez was optimistic publicly, the task was far from easy. The Chevalier de Monteil wrote to his superiors in Paris that "the fortress seems to me harder to conquer than previously believed."[222] The work was hard, but it was really just a question of implementing the scientific approach to war that the French theoretician Sébastien Le Prestre de Vauban had championed. His books were preeminent and authoritative for generations of professional soldiers in all European armies.[223]

Siege Works and British Counterattacks

In the early hours of April 22, the top brass of the Spanish forces "went to inspect the attack position against the Half-Moon Fort [or the Queen's Redoubt in British sources], [but] were spotted and fired on, so they had to retreat," not before suffering some casualties.[224] Soon after, Lieutenant Hugh Mackey Gordon, one of General Campbell's aides-de-camp, went to the redoubt and found, according to Robert Farmar's account, "the plan of the enemy's works and the manner they mean to attack us. The advanced redoubt [Queen's Redoubt] is their chief object[;] finding this we imagine the engineer was killed by one of the cannon shot as the tree that he was standing [next to] was struck and near it a great quantity of blood."[225]

That the British had the Spanish plans was of no great importance, since they did not tell them anything they did not already know. The logical way to attack Fort George from the rear was through the Queen's Redoubt, which was why it was built in the first place. Moreover, the Spanish engineers had already been working in that location for several weeks in plain view of the British.

On April 24, according to Saavedra and Miranda, a frigate tested its cannons against Fort George and proved that it could be reached from the sea.[226] Since fire from the Spanish ships could destroy the town, the civilian governor of Pensacola wrote to Gálvez to discuss the town's neutrality.[227] That same day, after a skirmish with no major consequences, a salute was fired from the British position in honor of General Lord Charles Cornwallis's victory at Guilford.[228] If Campbell's intention was to raise his men's morale, he may have achieved it, but his gesture made no impression at all on the Spanish camp, since no one knew of Cornwallis's success. The only effect of the British feu de joie was to prove that they had enough ammunition for that kind of demonstration—a fact already known to the besiegers.[229]

Two days later, the British made a sortie to stop or delay the Spanish ad-

Plano de la Villa de Pansacola en la WE florida del fuerte Jorge y de las fortificacio
nes adjacentes ultimamente construidas para la defensa y seguridad de dicha
Plaza por la Nacion Británica, y atacada por las fuersas Españolas al mando
del Mariscal de Campo d. Bernardo de Galvez: rendida en 8 de Mayo de 1781

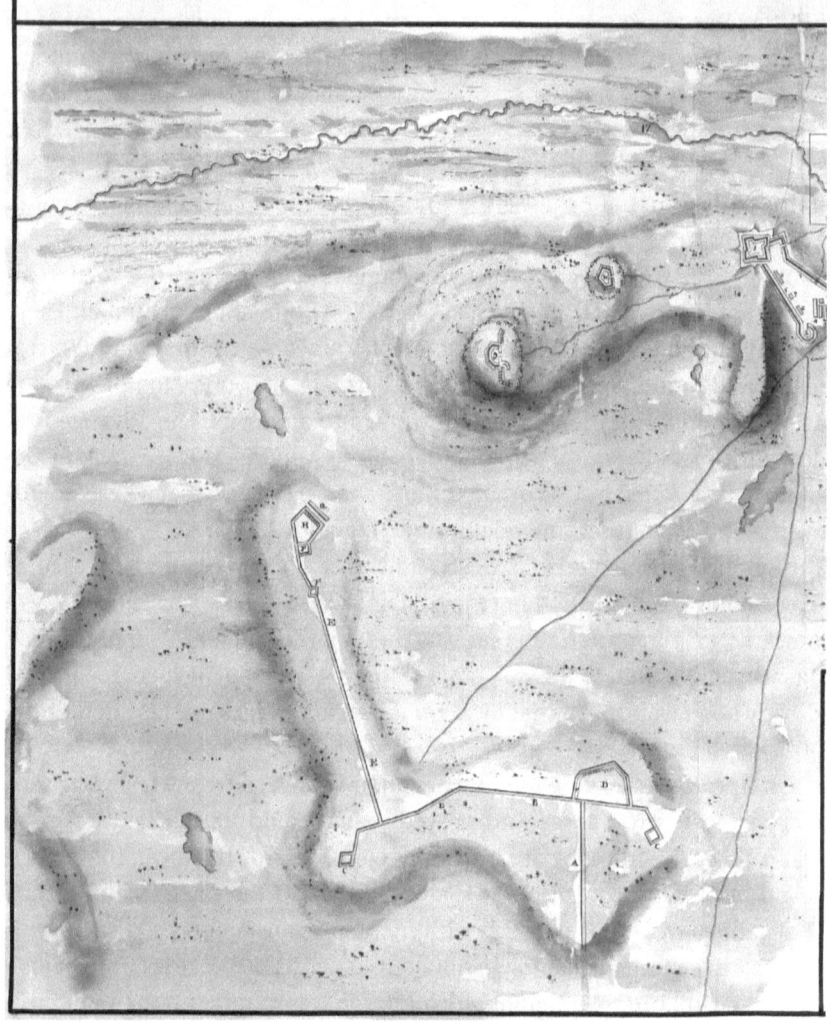

Spanish manuscript map of the British forts and Spanish trenches at Pensacola, 1781.
(Luis Huet, *Plano de la villa de Pansacola* [sic] *en WE Florida del Fuerte Jorge y de
las fortificaciones adyacentes últimamente construidas para la defensa y seguridad
de dicha plaza por la nación Británica, y atacada por las fuerzas españolas al*

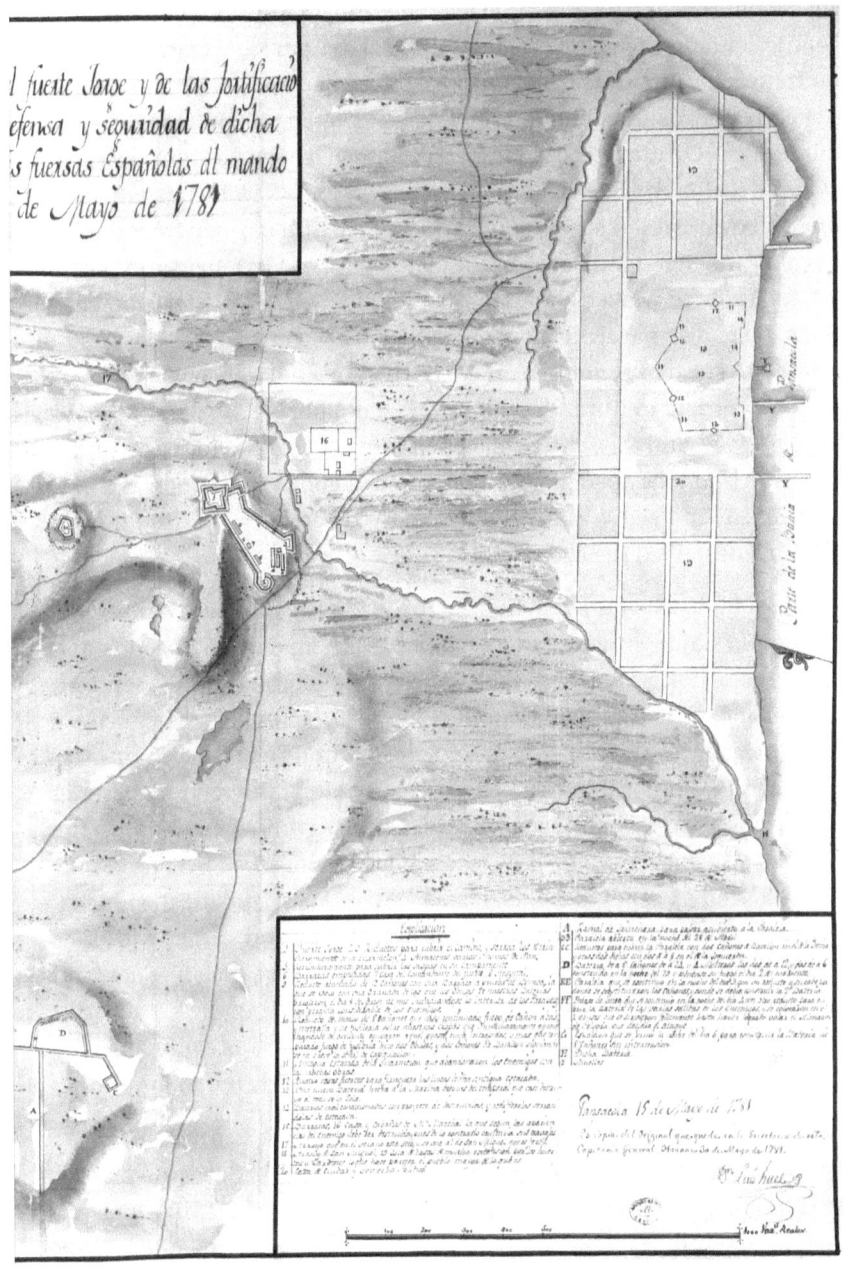

mando del mariscal de campo dn. Bernardo de Gálvez: rendida en 8 de Mayo de 1781, Pensacola 19 mayo 1781. Villa de Pensacola, con fuerte Jorge y otros; Archivo General de Indias, Mapas y Planos-Florida Luisiana 247, Ministerio de Educación, Cultura y Deporte, Archivo General de Indias)

vance, but they were easily repelled. The British also started to dig several counterbatteries, which were neutralized. The Spanish advance continued until their position was overexposed, so José de Ezpeleta ordered the construction of two more redoubts joined by a covered trench more than a half-mile long.[230] On May 2 work started on a new advanced position closer to the Queen's Redoubt. The British tried to delay the work with constant artillery fire, and two days later they launched an attack with 120 men from the Pennsylvania and Maryland Loyalists under Major John McDonald and 890 more troops from the Waldeck Regiment under Lieutenant Colonel Albrecht von Horn. A Spanish naval officer spotted the advance with his spyglass and "informed Don Pablo Figuerola, officer in charge of the trench, who dismissed it."[231] According to Miranda, the British hid among a small group of trees until midday, and then the English batteries opened fire to "cover and protect the assault they had planned against our redoubts." As soon as the artillery fire ended, "eighty of them ran with fixed bayonets against our troops." Miranda described the account:

> The soldier, who buried in his trench did not expect such a danger and had put down his weapons; the officer, who unaware was eating and therefore not as vigilant as the moment required; and the raw sentinel, who only looked straight in front of his post . . . were taken by surprise and ran away, such that disorder spread among all of the troops stationed in that location. The enemies got hold of the redoubt without any opposition whatsoever, and chasing all of those running with the point of their bayonets, they freely injured and killed everyone they could find. . . . They also took our second redoubt, spiking the four artillery pieces we had there, burning everything, and as they withdrew taking with them the Spanish officer's silver cutlery, their buckles, and the money from the dead and the wounded, who numbered between forty and fifty. . . . On their side only one sergeant was wounded, who died later, and they all withdrew to the forest amid cries of joy, throwing their hats in the air.[232]

As soon as he was informed of this turn of events, Bernardo de Gálvez sent four companies of light infantry to assist, under José de Ezpeleta. He arrived after all of the action had ended. According to the official report, the casualties numbered eighteen dead, sixteen wounded, and three officers taken prisoner. The following day was spent rebuilding the Spanish position in front of the Queen's Redoubt. That night a heavy storm forced all work to stop, and the ships sailed farther from shore so they would not be grounded. The weather was so bad that Gálvez granted his troops a much-needed rest to "dry their uniforms and enjoy a ration of liquor."[233] That same afternoon he revealed to his friend Francisco de Saavedra "the great predicament in which he found himself, and the ambitious plan he had in mind. From Havana very few cannonballs had come; not many of the twenty-four caliber, the most needed ones, remained; and he had enough only for two days of firing. All of those shot by the enemy were collected, and the soldiers were paid two *reales* for each one they brought, but even this did not suffice. . . . In this situation he was determined to make a frontal assault on the enemy's Half-Moon Fort [the Queen's Redoubt], the conquest of which would soon force the surrender of the other two [positions], which were controlled from it, and in this way he would shorten the siege, which was taking too long, and with its delay was jeopardizing his other plans."[234]

If Bernardo de Gálvez was in a "great predicament," the situation of the British was much worse. In General Campbell's second report dated May 7, 1781, he informed his superiors that "I apprehend, My Lord, my next [duty] will be the unpleasing and disagreeable task of reporting the triumph of Spain, and their acquisition of a province under their dominion."[235] In accordance with Gálvez's "ambitious plan," in the early hours of that day, 900 men of the First Brigade, under the command of General Gerónimo Girón, had started to approach the British position to attempt an attack. So as to take the enemy by surprise they made a detour, which took more time than expected, and did not arrive at their attack position until the sun was already up. Having lost all chance of surprise, Gálvez was counseled by Ezpeleta that he had no choice but to call off the attack. The following day, only an Indian attack on the Spanish took place, which resulted in three dead, one wounded, and a soldier taken prisoner.

At daybreak on May 8, construction finished on the battery closest to the Queen's Redoubt, and the exchange of fire began anew. Everything pointed to another long and uneventful day, with the siege continuing at its exasperatingly slow pace. But at half past nine in the morning, everything suddenly changed. Again in Miranda's words:

> From the encampment we heard a big explosion, which greatly alarmed us, for we did not know what it was. Immediately the general and his second went to the trench from whence the noise had come. From there we could see a big column of smoke reaching to the clouds, and later we were informed that an explosion had occurred inside the fort [the Queen's Redoubt], and that the entire battery was on fire, due to a bomb from our batteries.
>
> The general and the rest of the chief commanders immediately went

French engraving representing the moment the Queen's Redoubt exploded in Pensacola. This image, probably based on a previous design made in Mexico in 1785 by Jerónimo Antonio Gil, has become the most popular image of the siege of Pensacola. (Berteaux and Ponce, *Prise de Pensacola*; Library of Congress, control no. LC-USZ62-39588)

to the trench with some troops, leaving General Cagigal in charge of headquarters, and confirming what had happened and the destruction caused, ordered the advance of Girón's troops from the left, and under the cover of the burning battery, took possession of that position.

The speed and boldness with which it was done made the enemy retreat to the near fort or Prince of Wales Redoubt . . . leaving it ours to occupy without major opposition.[236]

VICTORY

Six hours later, the white flag was hoisted in Fort George. After negotiations lasting until eleven o'clock, the articles of capitulation were signed.[237] Their content was very similar to the agreement between Baton Rouge and Mobile. Honors were granted to the British garrison; the soldiers would become prisoners of war and later would be shipped to Cuba; the officers would keep their swords and would be sent to a British port under the condition that they would not take arms against Spain without first having been properly exchanged. Spain was to take possession of the fort, the town, and all of the territory, along with its contents, except for the personal belongings of those in the garrison. The population of Pensacola would be protected from any harassment. On May 10, 1781, the official surrender ceremony took place. "At three o'clock the six grenadier companies and those of French light infantry lined up before Fort George, the general [Campbell] exited with his troops, and after surrendering the Waldeck Regiment's flags and a flag from the artillery, with the usual ceremonies they surrendered their arms."[238]

The following day, a small Spanish detachment was sent to the Royal Navy's Redoubt in the Red Cliffs to take possession of it and imprison 139 men. British total casualties in Pensacola were 90 dead, 46 wounded, and 1,113 men taken prisoner. Some 54 men had deserted during the siege, and 300 more escaped to Georgia while the surrender of Pensacola was being negotiated. Among those who surrendered were 101 women and 123 children who, despite not being officially prisoners, had fates linked to those of their spouses, partners, or fathers.[239]

The prisoners were kept to the east of the town until June 4, when most of them embarked for Havana, where, after a stay of ten days, they set sail for New York. Their voyage was eventful. The small ship *San José y San Joaquín*, with the Pennsylvania and Maryland Loyalists on board, was captured by two American corsairs, the *Holker* and the *Fair American*, who forced the Spanish vessel to head for Philadelphia. Complaints from the Spanish captain and Captain Joseph Swift, commander of the Loyalists, were to no avail. Smith feared for his and his men's lives, since they were all American-born and thus could be regarded as traitors and executed. Francisco Rendón, Spain's representative to the U.S. Continental Congress, had to intervene and explain that under the terms of Pensacola's surrender, the Loyalists should be treated like any other British soldiers and respected.[240] Luckily for Captain Swift's men, before the two American corsair ships could enter the Delaware River, they were in turn captured by two other corsairs under the British flag, one of them with the infamous name of *General Arnold*. They escorted the *San José y San Joaquín* to New York, finally arriving on July 23, 1781, just one week after the other troops had arrived from Havana.[241]

Besides the casualties mentioned above, the British also lost matériel in Pensacola: 4 mortars, 143 cannons of different calibers, 6 howitzers and 40 *pedreros* (bombards), and plenty of ammunition and gunpowder, as well as 2,142 muskets, 30,712 cartridges, and other military supplies.[242]

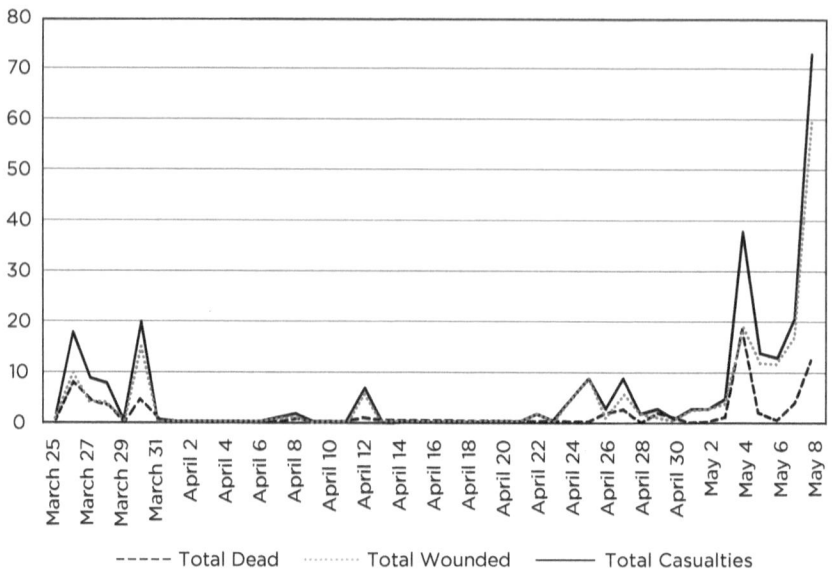

Graph 2. Spanish Casualties at the Siege of Pensacola, 1781
Sources: José de Ezpeleta, List of dead and wounded of the army under general Gálvez from its disembark in the Island of Santa Rosa to the surrender of Pensacola (*Relación de los muertos y heridos que ha tenido el ejército a las órdenes del mariscal de campo el sr. D. Bernardo de Gálvez, desde su desembarco en la isla de Sta. Rosa hasta el día 8 de mayo, en que se rindió la Plaza de Panzacola*), Pensacola, 12 May 1781, in *Diario de las operaciones . . .* , BPR, BN; "Diario de las operaciones . . ." (first manuscript), AGS, SGU, 6913, Ex3.

The total casualties on the Spanish side (74 dead and 198 wounded, 272 in total) were exactly double those of the British (90 dead and 46 wounded, 136 in total). A two-to-one ratio of casualties, with those suffered by the attacker much greater than those of the besieged, was considered normal for a siege, but—and a big "but" it is—one must take into account the fact that all of the Spanish casualties happened prior to the explosion inside the Queen's Redoubt, whereas almost all of the British casualties were a result of it. This means that until the moment of the explosion, the Spaniards were suffering a disproportionate number of casualties. It was true that Bernardo de Gálvez was in "a great predicament." It is important to note the precise time that the Spanish casualties happened. Fortunately, at the end of his diary of the siege, Bernardo de Gálvez includes a list of casualties by date.[243] They are represented in graph 2.

According to the graph, it is clear that most of the Spanish casualties occurred at the end of the siege, before the explosion at the Queen's Redoubt. In fact, up until April 24, the day on which the serious work of the siege started, 70 men had died, only 26 percent of eventual total casualties. In other words, it was not until the arrival of the reinforcements from Havana that Bernardo de Gálvez fully pushed for the siege works to be completed. Therefore he was waiting for these reinforcements, knowing that without them it would be impossible to take Pensacola by siege.

Another interesting aspect that can be deduced from the list of casualties by date is the contribution of Indian warriors to the defense of Pensacola. Through April 25, 96 percent of Spanish casualties were caused by Indians. In other words, of the eighty-four casualties during this period, both dead and wounded, eighty-one of them were the result of Indian attacks, of which sixty-nine were in attacks carried out only by Indians and twelve in joint British-Indian attacks. From that date on, no more Indians attacks took place, which confirms that the British used them to harass the enemy or for surprise attacks but not when war was waged according to traditional European rules of war. The figures do not confirm that the Indians were more bloodthirsty or cruel than the professional troops, since the ratio between Spanish dead and Spanish wounded is almost the same in combat against the Indians as against British soldiers. In the former, 33 percent were killed and 66 percent wounded, while in the latter 25.4 were killed and 74.6 percent wounded. A 7.6 percent difference in killed and an 8.6 percent difference in wounded does not seem extremely significant.[244]

Having concluded an inventory of goods captured from the British, Bernardo de Gálvez ordered the re-embarkment of his troops for Havana, so as "not to waste an instant."[245]

REPORTING THE VICTORY

Gálvez took some time sending his official reports on his victory at Pensacola. He wrote to Havana on May 15 and to Madrid on May 26. The delay can be explained by the need to finish the inventories and also to make clear copies of his diary and other accounts.[246]

In his letter to Diego José Navarro, governor of Cuba, he writes, "I assure Your Excellency, for your own satisfaction, that even if I did not lose hope of accomplishing the mission with the few forces I had, I had plenty of doubts about its final success, and that it was Your Excellency and other members of the council who made it possible through the speedy and timely assistance you sent me under the command of Señores Solano and Cagigal. Both generals did not waste any time in providing me with the reinforcements they brought, and to their actions I own a great deal of the happiness God has bestowed upon me."[247]

In addition to being generous, Bernardo de Gálvez was also intelligent. By allowing Navarro to share in his success, he hoped to win an ally for future military operations. By confessing his own doubts, he wanted to overcome his reputation of being too reckless and impulsive. He continued by praising the contribution of the navy and ended with a subtle gesture of personal revenge against the naval captain, José Calvo, in describing "the satisfaction we feel at the sight of fifteen anchored men-of-war . . . [and] with which we have publicly testified that Spanish ships can approach the worst reefs without being lost, when at the head of the squadrons are men of resolve, courage, love for their king, and true desire to serve him, as each day Señor Solano proves himself to be."[248]

Gálvez trusted this important document to his friend Francisco de Saavedra, who arrived in Havana on board the French cutter *Serpent* on May 26. Two days later, the governor dispatched a mail ship to Cadiz, "following royal orders that when the news is important it should be sent by three separate channels, and in this case by four."[249]

Gálvez's letter to his uncle on May 26, 1781, is especially revealing, since it shows that he had become a much more detached and professional soldier.[250] It starts with a paragraph that states simply that "on the ninth of this month, twelve days after the trenches were opened and sixty-one after the disembarkation on Santa Rosa Island, the forts and town of Pensacola surrendered to His Majesty's armies." He then added an overview of the supplies and goods captured. The second paragraph is devoted to the amount of money the British spent on Pensacola's defenses—72,000 pounds sterling just since the previous April—and includes an estimate that the total value of the town and forts was more than 1.5 million pesos.[251] The third paragraph announces that he would be soon sending his uncle all of the documentation related to the expedition—diaries, inventories, maps, and the like—and details about the casualties and prisoners taken. The last two-fifths of the letter are filled with mention of all those who had distinguished themselves in the victory, starting with an acknowledgment of how much he owed to military authorities in Havana, who sent him the timely reinforcements. After Solano he praised the French fleet commander, the Chevalier de Monteil, along with his officers, who also volunteered for land operations "with so much determination, it was as if the place was theirs, proving that all that you need to fight well is courage, honor, and good faith." He added that "our Spaniards, with their usual spirit and resolve, had done as they always do." He did not forget to stress the important contribution of other military chiefs and officers, including Juan Manuel de Cagigal, Gerónimo Girón, José de Ezpeleta, and naval captain Felipe Lopez Carrizosa, who commanded the seamen volunteering to fight on land. He ended the letter by announcing that he would soon send a list of all those who, in his opinion, deserved to be rewarded with His Majesty's generosity.

Bernardo de Gálvez sent this letter to his uncle on the ships *Caymán* and *Pío*, which left Pensacola at the end of May. But the news arrived at the Spanish court through a mail ship sent from Philadelphia, which arrived at Cadiz at the end of June.[252]

REACTIONS IN AMERICA AND EUROPE

In Cuba, as soon as Saavedra informed him about the important victory, Governor Navarro ordered that a solemn mass and Te Deum be held in the city's cathedral. The cannons were fired and the population celebrated joyfully, most probably because with this victory they considered themselves avenged from the recent British occupation of Havana.[253]

Shortly after the capitulation of Pensacola, Bernardo de Gálvez returned to New Orleans. No eyewitness account of his welcome has been found, but it is not difficult to imagine that it would have been something memorable. If his popularity was already enormous, upon his return the myth of the young hero was established in the history of the city, with his governorship considered a golden age of Spanish rule in Louisiana. As an example of the fervor of the people of New Orleans, on November 12, 1781, they humbly requested of King Carlos III, "as proof of their unshaken loyalty to their monarch, that he grant the title of count to the one who has restored these continents, the friend of the allied nations, which he kept united in harmony." The king explicitly mentioned this request later when he rewarded Gálvez. The same New Orleans gentry considered Bernardo de Gálvez "one of the great men of the century: *vidit, pugnavit, et vincit.*"[254]

In another petition dated March 18, 1782, this time to Esteban Miró, the inhabitants of Louisiana expressed their gratitude for "the many and repeated blessings that through this gentleman [Bernardo de Gálvez] the king has bestowed upon the province; the righteous administration of justice he has performed during his government, satisfying both the plaintiff and the defendant, which is extremely difficult to do; his friendly, affable, and popular manner, with which he honors everyone welcomed into his office; in one word, the ensemble of beautiful qualities that adorn him, [which are] the source of the respect and veneration that all inhabitants feel for him, with a kind of enthusiasm that may seem boundless to all of those who have not had the privilege of serving under his command."[255]

The confirmed news about the Spanish conquest of Pensacola reached the North American East Coast at the same time as the news of the incident involving the two American corsair ships, the *Holker* and the *Fair American*, and the Spanish vessel, the *San José y San Joaquín*, which had the Pennsylvania and Maryland Loyalists on board.[256] The latter incident tainted and tarnished the former, despite Samuel Huntington's statement to Bernardo de Gálvez that he "must sincerely congratulate Your Excellency, upon the Success of the Army of His Catholic Majesty, under your command, in the Reduction of Pensacola. You may rest assured, Sir, that we deem this a Common cause, and wish you future success, for we wish to maintain the most sincere and perpetual Friendship with your Nation."[257]

George Washington remained distant. First he simply responded to Francisco Rendón's letter that he would be very glad when the news was confirmed, and later he complained in his usual gentlemanly, indirect way about the conditions granted to British troops in the articles of capitulation:[258] "I am obliged by the extract of Don Galvez's letter to the Count de Grasse explaining at large the necessity he was under of granting the terms of Capitulation to the Garrison of Pensacola which the Commandant required— I have no doubt, from Don Galvez's well known attachment to the cause of America but he would have refused the Articles which have been deemed exceptionable, had there not been very powerful reasons to have induced his acceptance of them."[259]

According to the articles of capitulation, British soldiers and American Loyalists were precluded from action against Spain or its allies, and since Spain had no formal alliance with the United States, some of the men returning from Pensacola, around a thousand of them, were sent to reinforce British positions in New York. Several notable U.S. political leaders were astonished that Gálvez consented to conditions that were markedly unfavorable to the United States. Samuel Huntington, president of Congress, voiced his surprise in a letter of July 2, 1781, to Washington: "I cannot ... perswade myself that Governor Gálvez who commanded the Expedition, and who manifested the most friendly Sentiments, and attachment for us, would admit of terms so apparently detrimental to these States."[260] Huntington's surprise indicates a certain naïveté about Spanish war aims, which were geared toward gaining the Gulf Coast's northern rim and the Lower Mississippi as an exclusive imperial preserve. Spanish military collaboration with the United States proved to be more limited than Washington and others hoped. For example, General Benjamin Lincoln and his staff in South Carolina were greatly disappointed when Spanish authorities put off their pleas for assistance during the British siege of Charleston, which fell to English forces on May 12, 1780. This fact may explain why Washington faintly applauded the Spanish conquest of Mobile—an event that became known to him about the time that news of Charleston's surrender arrived. At the time

First accurate portrait of General George Washington, 1781. (V. Green, engrav., *General Washington, after a portrait by Trumbull, J. Esqr. of Connecticut, 1780*, in Prints and Photographs Division, Library of Congress, control no. 2004666688)

of the Spanish victory at Pensacola, Washington was as politic as possible about this turn of affairs because he still hoped for effective Spanish-U.S. cooperation in the war. It is also important to take into account, as David Narrett has pointed out, that the generous terms of the capitulation were dictated by Gálvez's priorities at the time: he wanted to avoid a prolonged fight that could delay his preparations for a joint Spanish and French assault against Jamaica.[261]

However, the real problem went beyond this particular case. With the conquest of Pensacola, Spain had acquired West Florida from the British, thereby blocking U.S. access to the Caribbean. The American rebels were fighting the British for their freedom and their land, not for their enemy's territories, which would be going to another colonial power. As much as a British defeat would always be welcomed, in this particular instance the Spanish conquest of Pensacola meant that the war in this theater was over and the British could concentrate their resources against the Americans. One of the main strategic contributions of Spain to the American cause had been precisely to open this second front against the British. Now that the Spanish victory had closed it, the Americans feared the worst. It was not surprising, then, that the annexation of West Florida by Spain was not enthusiastically welcomed by either the military or the politicians. It was in U.S. interests for Spanish troops to keep the British fighting, not to defeat them in such a way that they could redeploy their forces against the Americans. The situation was perfectly summed up by Edmund Jennings in a letter to John Adams from Brussels on March 4, 1782, who commented "on the confirmed news of the taking of Minorca. It is a greater blow on the English than they will be ready to acknowledge because it is of little consequence in the present war. But it must be of importance, if ever they attempt to recover the mediterranean Trade. I find by the capitulation that the Troops are not to act against Spain or her allies and as America does not come under the latter description they may be sent there as the Pensacola prisoners were—this confers no obligation on France or Us [capitalized in the original]." Other American politicians were even more critical of Gálvez. Richard Potts, a Maryland delegate, wrote that "the Success of the Spaniards [at Pensacola] will be more prejudicial to our Operations, than their failure would have been."[262]

The American press—that is, the press in America, since both Loyalists and rebels had their own newspapers—had followed Gálvez's campaign in Pensacola closely. If the House of Commons in London had believed that Pensacola would never fall into Spanish hands, Loyalists in America had shared the same feeling. On September 21, 1780, a short article had appeared in the *Royal American Gazette* offering a transcription of a letter received from Pensacola, dated August 25, which said, "Don Galvez has but a weak garrison at New Orleans; that country might be taken with a small body of troops. We have heard that he is afraid of an attack from the northward; it seems we have now possession of the Illinois Country, which alarms the Don."[263] A few months later, news started to spread about the arrival of Spanish forces in Pensacola.[264] The *Pennsylvania Journal* reported the first rumors of the surrender of Pensacola on May 23, 1781.[265] Shortly afterward, a number of newspapers confirmed the news and started to include as many information as was then available about the British defeat.[266] Although some of the Loyalist newspapers remained in denial for a time, they finally had to announce the Spanish victory.[267] It is relevant that the first news received on the Loyalist side was in a letter "from the Creek Nation," which stated that "I am just returned from Pensacola, and from that quarter have the disagreeable intelligence to give you of its fall, which happened on the 10th [of May]."[268] From July 18 onward, more detailed accounts started to appear in the press, and the articles of capitulation were published several times.[269] Finally, the *New-Hampshire Gazette State Journal, and General Advertiser*, although changing Gálvez's name, reported that "Don Juan de Galvez by his activity and indefatigable perseverance, taking with him a good part of this reinforcement, went, without losing a moment, to Pensacola. The English attempted in vain to throw seccours [sic] into the place; Don Galvez carried it; and we hope this intrepid commander will go on to make a rapid progress in Florida, & that he will add Augstin [sic] to the number of his conquests."[270]

Before the news of Pensacola's surrender reached London, a very interesting debate took place in the House of Commons on May 21, 1781.[271] The session started with the submission of a bill having a long and unappealing name that needed to be passed so the government could make several payments.[272] Among the payments were 20,500 pounds for "erecting a very useful and necessary fort in [West] Florida," which, according to Sir Charles Cocks,[273] quoting from a report by Pensacola's military governor, "was a very important and strong defense. The enemy had contrived two expeditions against [West] Florida, and had gone to an expence of blood and treasure more than it [the fort] was worth." Edmund Burke then took the floor and, according to the official transcription, "spoke for some time in a humorous stile" criticizing the government. After a few more speeches, Lord George Germain announced that since the issue was related more to his duties than to those of Sir Charles Cocks, he would answer all questions.[274]

> With regard to what gentlemen said relative to Pensacola; that place was certainly of very great importance to this country, as indeed the

Spaniards thought, having fitted out no less than two expeditions with the hopes of taking it, but they had happily been repulsed each time; and when they should attack it, such was the state of its strength, and such the safety airing from the new works lately erected there, that he flattered himself the Spaniards would not find it so easy a capture as they might imagine. His lordship had lately met with a very able and ingenious engineer by accident, who had put the works into a state of thorough repair, and had built two new forts, one of them at the mouth of the river to guard the entrance, so that he had no great apprehension with regard to the safety of Pensacola.[275]

Lord George Germain could not have been more wrong. When he pronounced these words, Pensacola had already surrendered twelve days earlier, and the troops whose security he was so certain of were Spanish prisoners of war.

Official news about the defeat in Pensacola would take some time to appear. The letter written on July 2 by Peter Chester in Charleston, South Carolina, to Lord George Germain and the articles of capitulation were not printed in the *London Gazette* until August 7.[276] They were followed, two days later, by a letter from General John Campbell accompanied by lists of members of the garrison and the casualties from the conflict.[277] Despite the official silence, the public was well fed by rumors. In its July 31 edition, the French *Courrier d'Avignon* reported that "rumors are spreading in London about the Spaniards having conquered Pensacola; even though the official newspapers do not mention it, the news has acquired an alarming consistency."[278] The French newspaper article ended by pointing out that if the rumors were confirmed, it would not be long before Don Gálvez attacked Jamaica. The official Spanish newspaper, the *Gazeta de Madrid*, mentioned in mid-May that rumors were circulating in England at the end of April and informed its readers that "it has been assured that it has been confirmed, no doubt by the frigate *Rawleygh* [*Raleigh*], which arrived in Portsmouth from New York on the 24th."[279] The rumors mentioned by the Spanish press were false this time, but that did not prevent it from continuing to report London's reaction to news about Pensacola—as on June 29, when the *Gazeta de Madrid* announced the arrival of the Spanish reinforcements but assured its readers that the place was "well fortified, well supplied, and with a reinforced garrison no doubt will resist the strongest enemy attacks."[280] Again on August 24, the *Gazeta de Madrid* reported on the British reaction to the loss of the town, which, according to British politicians, "was extremely useful to us [Spain], as the facilities allowed English merchants to carry out a very lucrative contraband trade with South America, which profited in part from the products of the mines of Mexico and even Peru."[281]

The British private press gave a great deal of attention to the Spanish campaigns along the Mississippi River and against Mobile and Pensacola.[282] The May 7 *Northampton Mercury* and the May 29 *Leeds Intelligencer* denied rumors that Pensacola had been taken, while the May issue of the *London Magazine* included a description of West Florida that mentioned the previous year's loss of Mobile.[283] During June and July the press mentioned the arrival of troops from "Don Galvez," the beginning of the siege, and the arrival of Spanish reinforcements from Havana.[284] Other papers even printed news about a Spanish defeat, adding that "it is said that Galvez died two days after the action [in January 1781]."[285] Among the first British newspapers to print articles about Spanish military victories was the *Derby Mercury*, whose July 26 issue mentioned General Gálvez as "the nephew of the Spanish minister of the Indies and the conqueror of Baton Rouge and Mobile."[286] After August 1 the fall of Pensacola was recorded in numerous newspapers.[287] Several sources mentioned the garrison's honorable surrender, and between August and December 1781 more than a dozen articles appeared that expressed worry about the fate of the British prisoners of war and their return home.[288] General John Campbell's and Governor Peter Chester's correspondence was widely quoted, and despite efforts to find consolation in the great number of Spanish casualties or the fact that the capture of Pensacola, even if important to Spain, was of little consequence for the war, most English newspapers started questioning how such a defeat had been possible.[289] Several publications studied the articles of capitulation and stressed that their soldiers were now free to return to the fight against the American rebels since, as the *Norfolk Chronicle* and the *Reading Mercury* stated, the Spaniards were not in alliance with the United States.[290]

To conclude this analysis of the British press, it is relevant to mention a significant detail that proves how different war in the eighteenth century was from today. Since the nineteenth century, war has involved the entire *nation*—a concept that had yet to be born a century earlier—and to serve that purpose propaganda for hating the enemy must be developed. During the Enlightenment, in contrast, war was a business executed by professionals, with a kind of detachment that is difficult to conceive of today. This detachment made it possible to respect and even admire the enemy. It was in this context that articles appeared in the July issue of the *London Magazine or Gentleman's Monthly Intelligencer*, which discussed the recently translated *Memoirs of Francisco de Quevedo*, which was part of a book titled *Letters from an English Traveler in Spain in 1778, on the Origin and Progress in that Kingdom; With Occasional Reflections on Manners and Customs; And Illustrations of the Romance of Don Quixote, Adorned with Portraits of the Most Eminent Poets.*[291]

The official news arrived in Versailles in dispatches from the Chevalier de Monteil to the French minister of the navy. In them the chevalier assured his superior that the conquest of Pensacola would never have been possible without the support of the French naval squadron.[292] But he also portrayed Bernardo de Gálvez as a courageous "general, who despite his wounds continued to pursue the siege with the utmost determination," and as "a patriot encouraged by a true zeal [for his country]" who had "overcome all of the obstacles of the [difficult] terrain and all others raised by the multitude of savages loyal to the English."[293]

The French press followed the military operations in America closely.[294] The June 1 issues of both the *Courrier d'Avignon* and the *Gazette de Leyde* informed readers of the failure of the British attack on Mobile.[295] The June 22 issues of both newspapers announced the news that had arrived on board the American ship *Príncipe Negro* of the departure for Pensacola of the relief expedition under the command of "Don Solano."[296] The *Courrier d'Avignon* also published detailed reports about the events in Pensacola.[297] Among them, the one appearing on July 3 stands out: "The news received from General Don Bernard Galvez dated April 6 before Pensacola announced that this general had changed his encampment several times while approaching his target, and that he had constantly been attacked by groups of hardened warriors, who make use of their fire weapons with the particular skill of people who hunt for a living, but that they had always been driven back, although not before causing thirty dead and the same number of wounded."[298]

While the *Gazette de Leyde* and *Courrier d'Avignon* continued to inform their readers about the developments in Pensacola, the news of the victory reached France in a curious way.[299] On July 27 the *Courrier d'Avignon* wrote that "we just have learned that Don Solano has returned to Havana, when a *Te Deum* has been sung for the conquest of Pensacola; it is surprising that we would not have been informed of such important news but for the celebrations on its behalf."[300] In its next issue the paper continued, "If we seemed surprised by the important news about the conquest of Pensacola coming to us by the *Te Deum* sung in Havana, the way our court was informed was no less unique. The governor of Cuba informed Philadelphia through an American ship, which upon its arrival met the ship *Neptune*, which was about to set sail for the Spanish coast, to which a detailed copy of the report of the governor was given, which we promise to publish in our next issue. This

French map published in 1782 as a result of the latest events in the war in North America and the Gulf of Mexico highlighting the importance of the Spanish conquest of Pensacola and the American and French victory at Yorktown. (Louis Brion de la Tour, *Suite du Théatre de la Guerre dans l'Amérique Septentrionale* . . . ; Prints and Photographs Division, Library of Congress, control no. 2006629304)

piece is full of such authenticity that the count of Montmorin, the French ambassador, sent it by special courier to Versailles."[301]

The news was later confirmed by the same newspaper in its August 7 issue and further expanded two weeks later.[302] One last detail: if the Spanish authorities wanted to keep the numerous problems between Bernardo de Gálvez and the navy private, they did not succeed, as the French press quoted the April 4 letter of Miguel de Alderete at length.[303] On August 21 the *Courrier d'Avignon* added, "Don Espeleta [Ezpeleta], brigadier of the army, has arrived in Havana with the official account of the conquest of Pensacola and the surrender of all of West Florida to Spanish arms, as well as the British settlements along the banks of the river San Juan. This brigadier accompanied the governor of Cuba, [who was] accused of not having fully backed Don Bernard Galvez and of being late in obeying his orders. It is reported that he is going to be court martialed."[304]

It has already been mentioned that the news of the victory arrived in the Spanish court in a curiously indirect way:[305] "The king has learned with the utmost joy and satisfaction of the happy conquest of Pensacola and its favorable circumstances. His Majesty has already shown his satisfaction for [illegible] letter from Havana brought by an American vessel, receiving the first news of this triumph of his arms. At that time the king ordered . . . that in celebration of the glories you have added to those of the Nation public [celebrations] would be done [crossed out in the original] solemn praises to the Lord of the Armies [were to be held], luminaries displayed magnificent illuminations during three days, and other public demonstrations to complete the joy."[306]

One witness, at least through hearsay, was a scholar from the Canary Islands, José Viera y Clavijo, who was visiting Madrid at the time.[307] In the same letter quoted above, José de Gálvez mentions the king's orders that the diary, the articles of capitulation, and the other reports be published "for all the public to be aware of the extraordinary and dangerous risks of the enterprise, and know how to judge the righteous reasons that prompted the King to give testimony so authentic of the appreciation that he has for it [crossed out in the original]."[308]

Starting in February 1781, both the *Gazeta de Madrid*, the official daily, and the *Mercurio Histórico y Político*, the official monthly, had been publishing news about the campaign against Pensacola.[309] A passage from the February 16 *Gazeta de Madrid* issue is noteworthy: "Days have passed since, thanks to *repeated royal orders* [italics mine], an expedition was prepared in that port [Havana] for the Gulf of Mexico."[310] That the royal orders had to be repeated proves that the court felt some impatience about the delays suf-

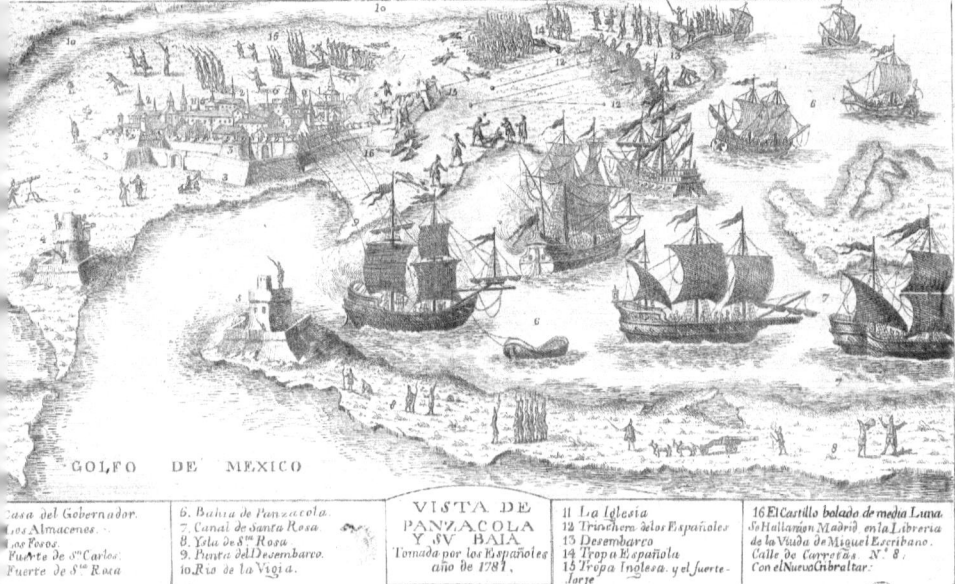

Engraving showing a view of Pensacola Bay conquered by the Spaniards in 1781. The low-cost image, which sacrifices all accuracy in favor of the depiction of as many ships and soldiers as possible, was sold in 1781 by a printer in Madrid who specialized in subjects appealing to the public. (*Vista de Panzacola y su Baia, Tomada por los Españoles año de 1781*, in Biblioteca Nacional de España, Madrid, MA00007568)

fered by Bernardo de Gálvez. Both the *Gazeta* and the *Mercurio* continued to publish accounts, reports, Bernardo de Gálvez's diaries, the articles of capitulation, and other documents during the next three months, which could have gone on longer if news of another very important Spanish victory—the conquest of Mahón, in the Balearic Islands—had not arrived.[311] The island of Minorca had been conquered by the British in 1708 during the Spanish War of Succession and had been a thorn in the Spanish side ever since.[312]

It is not easy to assess the real impact on the population of the news of the victory at Pensacola. Such a thing as public opinion did not exist in Europe at the time, and in Spain probably even less so, as is indicated by the fact that while in France and Britain a vibrant private press existed, in Spain it did not. Actually, by 1781 only one private newspaper was in circulation, the *Censor*, whose first issue appeared in February of that year. Since its main purpose was to spread scientific, technical, and cultural knowledge, it made no mention of Pensacola.[313] However, there is another way to evaluate the impression the news made on the public. On page 816 of the October 12, 1781, issue of the *Gazeta de Madrid* appeared the following small ad: "The three sites of Mahón, Gibraltar, and Pensacola on a new series of fans, in fine sheet. They can be found painted and unpainted in the Widow of Escribano's Bookshop, Carretas Street, number 8."[314] The bookshop specialized in publishing anything with good sales prospects. That same year the bookshop was selling prints of the three locations, along with other prints of a much less inspirational nature, such as *Authentic Portrait and Anatomical Account of the Girl with Two Heads and Four Arms, Born in Alfara, a Mile from the City of Valencia, on August 28 of the Present Year of 1781*.[315] In any case, the merchandise at sale indicates that the subject may have had a popular appeal. In the same vein, the appearance the same year, this time in Seville, of a pamphlet in verse under a long and tedious title suggests public familiarity with the subject.[316] Two years later another poet would publish his poetic musings on the victory at Pensacola.[317]

CONSEQUENCES OF THE CAMPAIGN AND THE VICTORY

I refer to the consequences of the campaign and the victory because certain effects were felt even before Pensacola was taken. On February 12, 1781, while yet another of many councils of war was taking place in Havana, José de Gálvez signed several important orders in El Pardo, where the royal court was located at the time. He reiterated that the conquest of Pensacola was of the utmost importance in expelling the English from the Gulf of Mexico; that after it fell into Spanish hands it must be defended, along with Mobile; that Bernardo de Gálvez would be supreme commander of all military operations in the region except "for the less important ones, to which you would appoint officers whom you trust to implement your orders"; and that concerning "harmony with the commanders in Havana . . . you are authorized to act without regard to future consequences, since [His Majesty] trusts that you will have no other aim but the glory and honor of the Royal Army, and the good and prosperity of the nation."[318]

On top of all that, José de Gálvez proceeded to write to the "commanders in Havana" that from that moment on, Bernardo de Gálvez was to be the supreme commander, and, even more important, that he was removing Victorio de Navia, Juan Bautista Bonet, and Diego José Navarro from their posts.[319] Probably because of his advanced age, Navarro was given the best exit and was posted as supreme military commander to Extremadura in the Iberian Peninsula.[320] Navia was kept between assignments for a time and afterward sent to Valencia to serve as acting military commander of that region, "during the sick leave granted to the Duke of Crillon."[321] Of the three, Bonet was punished the most. In 1783 he returned to European Spain and after a short time as second in command of the fleet under Admiral Luis de

Córdoba was sent to Cadiz, where he was never again given a command.[322] Not satisfied with this, José de Gálvez appointed José Solano as Bonet's replacement and Juan Manuel de Cagigal as provisional governor of Cuba. If there was still any doubt as to what was expected of them, he wrote to the latter that since his predecessor had delayed preparations for the expedition and did not recognize Bernardo de Gálvez's supreme command, he had incurred His Majesty's displeasure, so "it is expected that you, Sir, will never incur it in such excess."[323]

With a stroke of his pen, mightier than any general's or admiral's sword, José de Gálvez made all of Bernardo de Gálvez's enemies in Havana disappear. He also appointed him supreme commander to replace Navia and warned those in Havana that the transfer of command must take place immediately, regardless of Bernardo de Gálvez's whereabouts at the time the order arrived.[324] The reinforcement of Bernardo de Gálvez's powers went even further, as José de Gálvez detached Louisiana from its administrative dependency on Cuba while the war lasted and added to it all the newly conquered territories in Florida, "since that is demanded by the above mentioned general's decorum."[325] A last and important point, already made but worth repeating here, is that all of José de Gálvez's orders were issued before the fall of Pensacola but did not arrive there until its conquest was complete.[326]

Thus the consequences of the campaign; now those of the victory. Bernardo de Gálvez asked that those who had distinguished themselves during the siege and conquest of Pensacola be rewarded.[327] This request was to be almost fully granted by the king, with only minor adjustments.[328] The paperwork of the promotions, rewards, and so on, take up five separate large folders in the archives in Simancas and eleven full pages in the August issue of the *Mercurio Histórico y Político*.[329] Bernardo de Gálvez did not forget the French allies who fought alongside him and asked his king to intercede with theirs so that they, too, could be rewarded.[330]

As proof of His Majesty's utmost satisfaction with the conquest of this important stronghold and its fortunate circumstances, he promoted all of the top military commanders, not forgetting the supreme commander himself, whom he raised to the rank of *teniente general* (lieutenant general), the highest in the Spanish army at the time. With his promotion Bernardo de Gálvez became not only the youngest lieutenant general in the Spanish army—he just had turned thirty-five—but also the second-youngest man ever to attain this rank, surpassed only by the Duke of Wervik, who was promoted in 1747 at age twenty-nine. The average age for attaining the rank was fifty-three.[331] His promotion would not be his only reward. In August 1781 he was informed that the king also had decreed that the great Bay of Pensacola, which during Felipe II's reign was baptized Santa María Bay, "from now and forever would bear the name of *Santa María de Gálvez Bay* [underlined in the original], in honor of the most sacred Virgin and in memory of the conqueror who has reclaimed it for the crown."[332] He was also granted the prize money of 16,000 *pesos fuertes*, which Bernardo de Gálvez was grateful for, "because of the substantial losses I have suffered in the expeditions along the Mississippi and in Mobile and Pensacola, and to meet the high expenses I will face in equipping and presenting myself according to the rank of supreme commander of this operation."[333] The New Orleans Royal Treasury was instructed to pay him 31,200 pesos on account of his salary as general and for the time he had been acting governor of Louisiana.[334]

But as important as his promotion and other rewards were, the best was yet to come. On May 20, 1783, almost two years to the day after the conquest of Pensacola, King Carlos III signed in Aranjuez a *real cédula* (royal decree) awarding Bernardo de Gálvez the title of Count of Gálvez and Viscount of Gálvez-town [sic].[335] Becoming part of the titled aristocracy was not only a personal reward. It also meant the success of his entire family, the Gálvez clan of Macharaviaya. At that moment the clan had reached its zenith: his father, Matías, was viceroy of New Spain; his uncle José was minister of the Indies—and would be made Marquis of Sonora two years later—and Bernardo de Gálvez was a lieutenant general and a count.[336]

WEST FLORIDA RETURNS TO SPAIN

Before leaving Pensacola, Bernardo de Gálvez appointed as its commander Arturo O'Neill, lieutenant colonel of the Hibernia Regiment, whom he had known since the failed 1775 expedition against Algiers.[337] He needed someone there whom he could trust completely, since despite the clarity of the articles of capitulation, the situation in Pensacola was very delicate. The Floridas were a Loyalist bastion, especially West Florida. J. Leitch Wright has listed several reasons for this.[338] On the economic side, the cost of the colony (including royal officials' salaries, maintenance of the forts and barracks, and pay for army officers and troops) was far beyond what the local population paid in taxes. Thus, from this point of view, their independence would not be a wise decision. In addition, the commercial routes needed the protection of the Royal Navy. While in the thirteen colonies the presence of British troops was resented, the British and Anglo-American settlers in the Lower Mississippi valley, the Gulf Coast, and the Floridas welcomed them as a guarantee of protection against the threat of a Spanish invasion, a slave revolt, or an Indian attack. Besides, while British troops in the thirteen colonies were a

Coat of arms granted by King Carlos III to Bernardo de Gálvez as Count of Gálvez. Under the closed helmet with a count's crown, the coat of arms includes the heraldic symbols of Bernardo de Gálvez's family names and, in the lower right quarter, a reference to his victory at the battle of Pensacola: Gálvez wields his sword aboard the sloop *Galvezton*, which hoists a chief of squadron's banner under his motto, "Yo solo" (I alone). (In *Reales Cedulas en que El Rey Se Sirve hacer merced de Titulo de Castilla, con la Denominación de Conde de Gálvez, y la Adicion de una Flor de Lis de Oro en Campo azul, para el Escudo de sus Armas, 1783*; Madrid: imprenta de don Pedro Marin, 1783)

novelty, in this other region they had been part of day-to-day life since the very beginning. And finally, while in the thirteen colonies there were representative assemblies in which citizens could voice their complaints against British rule, the Floridas had no such institution, so any discontent did not have a way to be properly channeled. According to Joseph Barton Starr, the American Revolution was perceived in the Floridas as secondary to the clear and present danger of a Spanish attack.[339] In recently conquered Pensacola, the top priority was military, but other considerations also had to be dealt with, and Bernardo de Gálvez included them in his meticulous directions to Arturo O'Neill dated June 4. He instructed him on how to deal with the local population, why he should quickly repair the damage to the forts (especially the old Queen's Redoubt), where to correctly place a battery on top of the Red Cliffs, and how to attract the loyalty of the Indians, who had been so useful to the British in their defense of the place.[340]

As for the fate of the English-origin population of Pensacola after its conquest by Spain, although statistics are meager, they seem to indicate that while most of the people departed for other British territories in the Caribbean, part of them remained in the colony after the war.[341] Besides, some Loyalists sought and were granted protection by the Spanish Crown.[342] Of all the former subjects of His British Majesty, the case of Hamilton Chalmers and Guillermo Loende (*sic*: William Lawrence?), two Loyalist officers who deserted during the siege of Pensacola, stands out.[343] Both men volunteered for the Spanish army, and Bernardo de Gálvez agreed to sign them on, since both were Catholics. But they were later removed from service by the direct order of Alejandro O'Reilly on the grounds that their service would not be fair to his comrades in arms.[344] Nothing else has been found out about Loende's later life or career, but in the National Historic Archives in Madrid there is a letter from Chalmers to the Duke of Alcudia in Badajoz, Spain, dated 1793, offering his services as a secret agent in Europe or as a translator in the Ministry of Foreign Affairs.[345]

7. Objectives

JAMAICA, RETURN TO EUROPE, CUBA

Bernardo de Gálvez had planned to return directly to Cuba from Pensacola, but the news of a revolt in Natchez forced him instead to return to Louisiana. The immediate cause of the revolt was an appeal made by General John Campbell in early 1781 to the people of Natchez for their support in the defense of Pensacola. But already in late 1779, the Spanish authorities were concerned about their position in Natchez and worried about possible British intervention in the region. In November of that year the governor of Cuba had intercepted two letters "that proved the bad faith of the commanders of that nation [Britain], which is secretly promoting rebellion in this province."[1] In one of them, dated September 9, 1779, Campbell asked the population of Natchez "to join, in Manchac, Colonel Dickson and his company and the inhabitants of those districts, who would like to give proof of their fidelity and love of their King and Country against their perfidious and implacable enemies, the Spaniards."[2] Shortly afterward, another communication from Campbell to the justice of the peace in Natchez was intercepted wherein Campbell stated that "the only news I can give, Sir, is that we are ready for an expedition against New Orleans, where it is possible that we can soon meet.... We have made great preparations for an attack against the New Orleans *Dons** [underlined and explanatory note in the original]. *Expression referring to the way Spaniards address each other—Don Juan, Don Pedro."[3]

Bernardo de Gálvez was therefore justified in worrying about a British attack on Natchez while he commanded the siege of Pensacola. The attack never took place, but the revolt did. As pointed out by John Walton Caughey, "Stretching the truth, though perhaps without exaggerating his optimism, he [General Campbell] sent word to the population of Natchez that an English fleet was in the Gulf, that it would move against New Orleans, and he appealed to them to assist in the restoration of English control over Natchez. That this uprising might have the appearance of a regular military action, he sent a number of captain's commissions, . . . which were to be distributed among the leading settlers where they would do the most good."[4]

Believing that the British were about to win Pensacola, the population of Natchez attacked the Spanish garrison at Fort Panmure. On April 22, 1781, the fort surrendered under the unfounded assumption that it was about to be blown up. The news of the surrender quickly arrived in New Orleans and from there went to the Spanish encampment near Pensacola.[5] In the capital of Louisiana, preparations began immediately to send a force to suppress the revolt in Natchez,[6] but they were later dropped since more troops were thought necessary than were available in New Orleans.[7] While the siege of Pensacola was under way, there was little that Bernardo de Gálvez could do about Natchez,[8] but when the siege ended unexpectedly on May 8, his first impulse was to go to Natchez himself.[9] Later he decided to go to New Orleans instead and so postponed his departure for Cuba until the revolt was dealt with. The situation was less serious than he initially believed—in fact, it resolved itself almost on its own. It was enough for news of the British surrender in Pensacola to arrive in Natchez along with a very small detachment of Spanish troops for most of the rebels to lay down their arms while their leaders fled, fearing for their lives.[10] Their fear was exaggerated, since most of them were eventually pardoned, and the few who faced trial were punished only with fines.[11] So the revolt was over—but its consequences were not.

Viewing the revolt as a breach of the articles of capitulation, Bernardo de Gálvez was furious with the defeated British general John Campbell, to whom he wrote that since Natchez "is part of Western Florida, Natchez is mine [*Natchez me pertenece*]."[12] Gálvez also decided to keep the British officers captured in Natchez as hostages[13] "until the Court of London paid for the expenses incurred in sending a military detachment to reconquer Fort Panmure in Natchez."[14] The fate of the mayor James Campbell and naval captain Robert Deans would take years to be decided. In 1783 the folders of their cases were growing fatter.[15] The mayor's family name may have helped a bit, as he was the first hostage to be released in New Orleans, where, after he was freed, he was kept under surveillance. Robert Deans was not so lucky. He was sent to the Iberian Peninsula, where he sued the Spanish Crown for his travel expenses, of course without mentioning that as captain of HMS *Mentor* he had received prize money for the capture of six Spanish vessels.[16] After several requests from the British government to the Spanish ambassador in Paris, Deans was released and given between 4,000 and 5,000 *reales*, which José de Gálvez complained was more than enough, "since he would certainly find individuals in Spain and even in Madrid willing to satisfy his needs."[17]

Miniature depicting Bernardo de Gálvez on horseback. The painting accompanied the box containing a British flag captured during his campaigns in America. (*Portrait of Bernardo de Gálvez*; © Museo del Ejército)

Some of the leaders of the Natchez revolt decided not to return home and remained in Indian territory, where they threatened to attack Spanish settlements. According to Caughey, in most cases the threats failed to materialize, although sixty-year-old James Colbert, raised by the Chickasaw, led his Indian friends on some attacks as well as on an expedition to kidnap the wife of Francisco Cruzat, commander of Fort Saint Louis.[18] Joseph Barton Starr considers that even though the Natchez insurrection was the end of open

British fighting against the Spanish in what was once British West Florida, it by no means ended British intrigue in the area. According to him, the basis for this intrigue was the Loyalists' intention to speculate in land, their desire to retain their property now under Spanish control, and their plans, mostly little more than wishes, to unite British Canada with West Florida through the Ohio River Valley, so as to stop the advance of the American rebels.[19] The most ambitious of these intrigues was that of Lord John Murray, the Earl of Dunmore, ex-governor of Virginia. He proposed an attack on West Florida in order to provide a home for dispossessed and fleeing Loyalists and to allow West Floridians to regain their homes and possessions. Moreover, he sought to get hold of new lands for speculation in order to replace the four million acres he had lost in the Ohio Valley. From late 1781 to 1783, the Earl of Dunmore continued to push his scheme, which in the end did not receive the support of the government in London.[20]

Besides the Natchez rebellion, other British settlers decided to continue the war against Spain in the South. Of all of them, James Colbert was the one who succeeded in raising the most trouble for the Spaniards. Between 1782 and late 1783, when he died after a fall from a horse, Colbert carried out a succession of raids against Spanish outposts along the Mississippi River. The Spanish governor of Louisiana after the departure of Gálvez, Esteban Miró, avoided confrontations and was able to end the unrest through an *un trato suave* (gentle treatment).[21]

JAMAICA

Objectives and Preparations for the Campaign against Jamaica

Bernardo de Gálvez arrived in Havana at one o'clock on August 16, 1781.[22] The following day the governor in charge officially notified him of his appointment as supreme commander of the expedition against Jamaica.[23] The idea of attacking this British territory in the Caribbean was consistent with Spain's overall objective of expelling the British from the Gulf of Mexico.[24] As early as June 1780, a royal order had been issued to proceed against Jamaica immediately after the conquest of Pensacola.[25] One must remember, too, that José de Gálvez had already been deceived by a spy who offered to incite a slave revolt on the island so as to open the door to a peaceful Spanish invasion.[26]

Bernardo de Gálvez and his friend Francisco de Saavedra worked for many days on preparations for the expedition.[27] Since May Saavedra had been in Havana, on José de Gálvez's orders, working to ensure proper coordination of the expedition with Spain's French allies.[28] To this end he embarked in the French fleet under the command of the Chevalier de Monteil and headed to

Guarico, Haiti, where the fleet and troops were to be assembled.²⁹ In Guarico he had several meetings with the Count de Grasse, and they drew up and signed a joint plan along with a memorandum of understanding for implementing the alliance between their two countries for operations in the Caribbean. Obviously Saavedra's influence was considerable, but he had the intelligence to use it with the utmost discretion. He also advanced to Admiral Count de Grasse 100,000 of the 1 million pesos that French generals in Cuba were to receive for July and August. This amount proved to be insufficient, so Saavedra sailed to Havana to raise more funds through a public subscription for 500,000 pesos, which he accomplished in a very short time. During this period Bernardo de Gálvez arrived in Cuba, and both he and Saavedra decided that the latter should go to Mexico to raise more funds, since the amount they had on hand "did not even cover present debts."³⁰

Money was indispensable for the expedition, but so, too, were troops, ships, arms, ammunition, supplies, and information regarding the situation in Jamaica. The victory over British settlements on the Mississippi River may have been possible because of surprise and the victory in Mobile because of overwhelming force, but in Pensacola sheer luck had played an important role. However, for a successful attack on Jamaica, much more was needed. Port Royal had been under British domination for more than a century; its defenses were impressive; and, at least in theory, its garrison was sizable and well supplied. Gálvez desperately needed details about its real situation, so he continued to gather information from any source available. No documentation has been found about intelligence supplied by a Spanish prisoner of war who escaped the island, as well as that by two merchants, a Dutchman and a Frenchman.³¹ But the most famous Spanish agent sent to Jamaica was Francisco de Miranda. Under the cover of negotiating the exchange of several prisoners held on the island, he was directed to gather information about the strength and condition of British defenses.³² Miranda had arrived in Cuba on the orders of Juan Manuel de Cagigal, and on Cagigal's recommendation he was chosen for this delicate mission. His close relationship with his mentor would prove to be the source of many of his subsequent problems.³³ Despite the mystery in which Miranda cloaked his own life story and the tendency of most of his hagiographers to explain this episode with conspiracy theories, the fact remains that Miranda was accused of smuggling while carrying out his mission in Jamaica.³⁴ Although Bernardo de Gálvez had appointed him his aide-de-camp and, according to Miranda, had even promised to promote him to colonel, this prospect ended when Gálvez ordered the seizure of Miranda's papers as well as his arrest, which he barely escaped by fleeing to the United States.³⁵ The incident changed

Miranda's life forever. He later blamed, and hated, Gálvez for ending his career as an officer in the Spanish military.[36] The investigation that opened in 1782 against Cagigal and Miranda ended eighteen years later with their complete acquittals. But by this time it was too late for Miranda, as he had already chosen a new country: the Gran Colombia, which he had helped carve from his old homeland.[37]

In early 1781 Matías de Gálvez, Bernardo's father, deprived the British of the fortress of San Fernando de Omoa, today in Honduras but at the time under the *audiencia* of Guatemala. Matías needed reinforcements to continue his push against the enemy, so who better to ask for them than his own son?[38] Bernardo de Gálvez even began to gather troops for his father but was diverted by a much more important threat, which delayed the shipment of reinforcements until January of the following year: the revolt of the *comuneros* in Nueva Granada, a viceroyalty consisting of today's Colombia, Venezuela, Ecuador, and Panama.[39]

The news from Nueva Granada was confusing but seemed serious, so to get more information Bernardo de Gálvez dispatched Juan Tufiño, lieutenant colonel in the Guadalajara Regiment and "an officer of well-known intelligence, maturity, and resources." Tufiño returned in January 1782 to inform Gálvez that "everything in the kingdom of Santa Fe has been pacified."[40] Despite the initial alarm, which shook up the otherwise quiet daily routines of royal officials, the revolt had no lasting impact other than to delay implementation of the Bourbon reforms in the viceroyalty.[41]

The general plan for the attack on Jamaica was to proceed with an overwhelming joint force of 20,000 men and a fleet of more than thirty ships of the line.[42] Soldiers and ships would come from both America and Europe, and while waiting for the arrival of the latter, ships in the region would assemble in Guarico, Haiti. After they united they would all sail together against Jamaica.[43] The plan seemed simple enough, but its elements were sufficiently disparate that if just one of them failed, the entire operation could go up in smoke.

From Spain would come troops, ships, armament, ammunition, supplies, and money. From the Iberian Peninsula, three whole infantry regiments were expected.[44] Although most of the troops were already in America, transports were needed to ship them from Cuba, Puerto Rico, and Mexico to Guarico and then on to Jamaica. The main part of the Spanish fleet was to be made up of forces already in the Caribbean under the command of José Solano, reinforced with four men-of-war arriving from ports in the Iberian Peninsula. Transport of the Spanish troops from Havana to Guarico would not be completed until February 1782.[45] While this was going on, Bernardo de

Gálvez joined his men, who were encamped at the foot of the Príncipe Fort, near Havana. There he trained his troops in shooting, artillery fire, and siege warfare, the latter by opening a trench so that the engineers could practice.[46]

However, the arrival of supplies was delayed because of a confrontation between the quartermaster, Juan Ignacio de Urriza, and the governor in charge of Havana, Juan Manuel de Cagigal, which originated in the accusations of smuggling against Francisco Miranda. Bernardo de Gálvez himself had to intervene to calm the men down. He invited them both to dine with him in January 1782, when, according to Francisco de Saavedra, "their reconciliation took place," although it would prove to be short lived.[47]

Money was doubly needed to pay for the expenses of both allies. Madrid had promised Versailles 1 million pesos, which the French demanded in advance. Saavedra already had advanced money to Admiral Count de Grasse and then departed for Mexico to find more funds. He returned early in 1782 with 3 million pesos, "two for the navy and one for the army," as well as abundant supplies, "920 men from the New Spain Crown Regiment, [and] 250 forced laborers for the navy."[48]

The French contributed 6,000 men and fifteen men-of-war, mostly coming from Europe, since the condition of their forces in the Caribbean was precarious.[49] This deficit explains why the French commanders already in the Caribbean made constant demands for resources on Francisco de Saavedra. His diary is full of remarks about their incessant reminders of the Spaniards' need to fulfill their part of what had been agreed between the two courts in Europe.[50] To the 1 million pesos raised by Saavedra in Cuba, 2 or 2.5 million more—since it is not clear if the half-million already given was taken into account—were given to the French between October and December 1781 on Saavedra's orders, while he was still in Mexico.[51]

If, as was the case with the expedition against Pensacola, organizing a military operation with the ships and troops of just one country was not an easy task, it was even more complex under two flags. The orders received from Madrid mentioned only the need to keep the forces together to ensure comfortable numeric superiority over the British at all times. But everything else was left to the commanders on site.[52] The general terms were negotiated by Saavedra and Admiral Count de Grasse, but the plan of operation was worked out by Gálvez and the Chevalier de Monteil, while details were entrusted to the always competent Francisco de Saavedra, who succeeded in solving all problems in a very short time.[53]

Maintaining harmony between the two allies was not always easy, even among the top commanders. While in Havana, the Chevalier de Monteil complained to his minister of the navy of having been addressed in inappropriate language.⁵⁴ Several incidents happened in Guarico that demanded the full attention of the commanders to "maintain good harmony between the French and the Spaniards."⁵⁵ For example, in a report dated April 8, 1781, Bernardo de Gálvez informed his uncle that "shortly after the arrival of the three regiments from Cadiz, some problems occurred between our soldiers and those of the colony, one of which could have had serious consequences. However, Governor Bellecombe and I were constantly on guard to prevent and stop the angry mood by punishing by death those who would take up arms, either on the offensive or the defensive, and trying to make them be friends and aware of the need for union and good understanding among them all."⁵⁶

Despite the best efforts of Gálvez and Saavedra, on October 1, 1781, only about 5,000 men were ready for the expedition against Jamaica, very far from the 20,000 Spanish and French soldiers included in the attack plan (see appendix table 18). Bernardo de Gálvez had to surrender to facts and admit that the expedition would not be ready that year. He informed his uncle that "I have considered it more prudent to desist as of now in this attempt, which can only be accomplished by some unexpected event, which I will always be looking for, and to focus on the immediate campaign against [New] Providence," the main island of the Bahamas.⁵⁷

The Attack against New Providence

The first explicit mention of an expedition against New Providence occurs in the October 11, 1781, entry in Saavedra's diary.⁵⁸ But Bernardo de Gálvez must have suggested the idea earlier to his uncle, since otherwise it is hard to explain why, only one week after Saavedra's diary entry, José de Gálvez was already signing an order to the governor of Cuba to start organizing the expedition.⁵⁹ The governor immediately began preparing for an army of 1,000 men to go against the British island.⁶⁰ The idea of conquering New Providence was consistent with Spain's general objective in the American theater, which, as stated earlier, was to expel the British from the entire Gulf of Mexico.⁶¹ And while waiting for everything to be ready to capture the real prize of Jamaica, it seemed a good idea, "meanwhile," to take New Providence. "Meanwhile" is the word actually used by Saavedra in referring to the expedition, and it clearly conveys its purpose, which was to be a sort of training or rehearsal for Jamaica.⁶² Bernardo de Gálvez received strict orders from his uncle that, even though he was the supreme commander of all forces, he must appoint other officers for operations of "lesser importance."⁶³ But as Bernardo was tempted to lead his men this time, too, it took all of Francisco de Saavedra's skill to persuade him that a force of 1,000 men demanded a colonel, not a general, and that in his absence preparations for the expedition against Jamaica would inevitably suffer delay.[64] Gálvez reluctantly agreed and appointed Juan Manuel de Cagigal to be in charge of the attack against New Providence.[65] But when the men were ready, the ships were not, and so everything had to be postponed.[66] As time passed and the ships were nowhere to be found, Cagigal suggested accepting the offer of two American seamen, Alexander Gillon (or Alejandro Guillon) and William Cock (or Guillermo Cok, the name is uncertain), to provide an escort for the transport vessels, which had already been supplied by the Royal Treasury.[67] By mid-April 1782, in the words of quartermaster Juan Ignacio de Urriza, "after much work, and personally begging for resources from the merchants and inhabitants of the city [of Havana], I have everything ready to set sail, just awaiting a north wind."[68] The expedition against New Providence included a little more than 2,000 men, instead of the 1,000 initially planned, on board fifty-seven vessels, forty-five of which were Spanish and twelve American (see appendix, table 19).

On May 6 the fleet arrived in front of Nassau, the capital of New Providence.[69] This precise moment was chosen by Commodore Alexander Gillon, the commander of all of the U.S. ships and captain of the *South Carolina*, to inform Juan Manuel de Cagigal that "in case the general [Cagigal] signs the capitulations, one of his officers should be always present at the signing, [to demand] that his frigate be insured for 300,000 pesos, and that he be paid all costs incurred in making the ship ready, about sixty or seventy thousand pesos."[70] Gillon also threatened that if everything was not paid up on the spot, he would not move his ships, thereby blocking the entrance to the port for the rest of the squadron. At this point Francisco de Miranda began to shout insults at the American captain, while the rest of the officers were apparently deciding that there was no choice left but to return to Havana.[71] While negotiations between the American captain and the Spanish commanders continued, Miranda took a small ship to the British fort and issued the garrison an ultimatum: they had twelve hours to surrender or would be reduced to ashes. Miranda's bold move was successful, and Lieutenant Colonel John Maxwell—who, according to British sources, was in command of a garrison of only 170 men, most of them seriously ill—surrendered the fort immediately.[72]

The incident with Commodore Gillon had consequences, since both Havana and Madrid would seriously question "Anglo-American" participation in any Spanish military operation.[73] The problem had deeper implications than just an American captain with an attitude. If any operation were to be considered joint, it would contravene orders that stated specifically

A 1782 engraving published in London showing the British lion confronting its four enemies: Spain as a cocker spaniel, France as a fighting cock, America as a rattlesnake (first used as a satire by British cartoonists but soon embraced by Benjamin Franklin in his famous engraving titled *Join or Die* published in the *Pennsylvania Gazette* on May 9, 1754), and Holland as a pug dog. (*The British lion engaging four powers*, 1782, in Prints and Photographs Division, Library of Congress, control no. 2004673480)

that Spain was allied with France in the war against Britain, and while Spain shared a common enemy with the United States, the latter should not be considered an ally. In an *oficio reservadísimo* (secret instruction—the equivalent today of a top secret order) dated April 6, 1782, from José de Gálvez to Bernardo de Gálvez, José interpreted and developed a November 16, 1781, royal order by stating clearly that neither Bernardo de Gálvez nor José Solano— the latter on specific instructions from the minister of the navy—should "ever agree to use the army or the navy of His Majesty to help the war of the American colonists against their mother land. . . . [but] if in the course of the operation against Jamaica this is demanded by the French, such a request should not prevent them from working closely with the French generals."[74]

So, the Spanish were never to help the American rebels unless asked to do so by the French, in which case Solano and Gálvez must do everything possible to keep the joint force together. This was more easily said than done. Luckily for the two Spanish commanders, such a demand was never posed. With such a precedent, it is not surprising that Bernardo de Gálvez was asked about his reasons for not using the Spanish navy in the operation against New Providence. He received the inquiry from Madrid and passed it on to Juan Manuel de Cagigal to answer as commander of the expedition.[75] Confident in his victory, Cagigal did so with panache: for him the operation "was carried out with fortune and skill (not by the American chief, as the commander says, but by the Spanish, [who was] very much a Spaniard)."[76] That settled the matter.

Continuing Preparations for the Expedition against Jamaica

While the operation against New Providence was under way, Bernardo de Gálvez continued to work on preparations for the attack on Jamaica. Meanwhile the French fleet under Admiral Count de Grasse had begun the invasion of the island of Saint Kitts as a preliminary to the attack on Jamaica. The French attack met with a fierce resistance from the British garrison and the local militia, but rumors arrived in London about its fall in French hands. Panic spread not only among politicians but also among the powerful West India lobby, which feared the worst. According to Andrew Jackson O'Shaughnessy, the official confirmation of the loss of Saint Kitts arrived after Lord North resigned as prime minster.[77] This was precisely the Franco-Spanish objective behind the Jamaica offensive, to force Britain to sue for peace at the prospect of losing one of its most profitable American colonies still in its possession.

By February 1, 1782, Gálvez had 5,000 men in Havana. He decided to depart for Guarico, where he arrived at the end of the month,[78] with his men joining him a few days later.[79] These men were reinforced by a so-called garrison increase, also sent from Havana.[80] With the arrival of the troops sent from the Iberian Peninsula, he now, at the beginning of April 1782, had more than 9,000 men under his command.[81] This was a significant improvement but still far from the 20,000 men he had counted on. Thus everything depended upon the timely arrival of the French contribution to the joint force, but Gálvez had had no news of that fleet's whereabouts.[82] In early April the French fleet, with between thirty and thirty-five men-of-war under the command of the Count de Grasse, was already in Martinique, just a few days' sail from Cape French (today's Cap-Haïtien), the place for meeting up with the Spanish fleet. But as soon as those ships set sail for Cape French, a British fleet under the command of Admiral Sir George Rodney appeared in the vicinity. The first shots were fired on April 9, but the Battle of the Saints (or of the Saintes, since both spellings were, and still are, used), famous at the time, did not take place until three days later. It is not necessary to go into the details of the skirmish here—only to state that the French were roundly defeated.

The first rumors of the disaster reached Guarico on April 20.[83] Immediately Bernardo de Gálvez ordered the Spanish fleet to sail "to protect the French ships, which could be severely damaged."[84] On the other side of the Atlantic, news of the events arrived in mid-May. In addition to satisfaction in military and political circles, rampant enthusiasm marked the celebration of the English navy's victory in London. If a year earlier the surrender of Pensacola had been marked by the illumination of Madrid and the selling of prints and fans, on this occasion British patriotism (and the Britons' sense of commercial opportunity) completely surpassed that of the Spaniards. In London, excitement over the British victory in the naval Battle of the Saintes knew no bounds. In addition to the customary commemorative medals, there appeared a wide array of articles honoring Rodney's success.[85] Every English gentleman wanting to celebrate his country's victory could decorate his drawing room with at least eight original oil paintings and accompanying engravings, as well as a dioramic model of the battle; adorn himself with a pair of commemorative shoe buckles, three different kinds of golden badges, and a ring; pour his guests punch using a silver ladle into a goblet, a mug, or a bowl, all especially designed for the occasion; and even—and this list is far from complete—drink from a carved flask made from a coconut engraved with scenes of the battle.[86]

Little by little, details emerged about the magnitude of the disaster in Guarico. On April 23, 1782, Saavedra was summoned by Gálvez, who "told me that to him it seemed that all of our projects had come to an end; I told him that I felt that they had only been delayed for a time, that this moment required from us a show of even more determination and resolve, that two nations as powerful as France and Spain should not be dispirited by just one blow, that more than anything it was a lesson never to divide our forces, as we had done."[87]

It was crucial that the French defeat be presented as a surmountable obstacle.[88] Otherwise it would mean the dissolution of the expedition against Jamaica and therefore the end of Bernardo de Gálvez's supreme command. For this reason, the two men agreed that Francisco de Saavedra should go immediately to France "to arrange for urgent reinforcements to maintain our numerical superiority vis-à-vis the enemy."[89] In a letter from Bernardo de Gálvez that Saavedra would personally deliver to the Count of Aranda, he outlined a new plan, "provided reinforcements from both courts [are sent]."[90] This new plan required 3,000 to 4,000 men from French garrisons in the Isles du Vent (Windward Islands, today's Dominica, Martinique, Saint Lucia, Saint Vincent and the Grenadines, and Grenada) or Saint-Domingue (today's Haiti), which were to arrive by October. In the meantime, the consolidation of supplies and ammunition in Guarico would continue. Later, in December 1782 or January of the following year, after the arrival from Europe of a squadron of six men-of-war and transports with 5,000 men, they would attack the British islands of Antigua and Barbuda and then later in April sail for Haiti, and "if Jamaica has already been taken, all forces will be reunited" for a crossing of the Atlantic in early May to attack one of the main English ports, such as Portsmouth or Plymouth, and then immediately afterward occupy the Isle of Wight.

There was little Bernardo de Gálvez could do in Guarico other than offer some help and comfort to the crews of the battered French ships when they arrived there.[91] He tried to convince the commanders of the Spanish Royal Navy that, "since thirty ships could be assembled from French ships needing only slight repairs together with ours, it would be very advisable to sail with them and make ourselves respected by the enemy."[92] On top of being impractical, this idea was marked more by desperation than by intelligence and would not be implemented. After Saavedra's departure for France, Gálvez continued training his troops, sending reinforcements to Puerto Rico, and ensuring that both navies cooperated.[93] Twice that year he had to mediate with their commanders to ensure that no one departed from Guarico on other missions.[94]

Time in which nothing happens is time that passes most slowly, but luckily for Bernardo de Gálvez, while his military duties were a source of frustration, his private life compensated for every bitterness. On September 29, 1782, his son was born. Instead of awaiting her husband's return amid the comforts of her wealthy family in New Orleans, his wife, Feliciana, had decided to accompany him to the military camp in Guarico. On January 20, 1783, Miguel Matías Josef Luciano Antonio Bernardo de Gálvez y Saint-Maxent was solemnly baptized in Guarico.[95] An anonymous witness described the ceremony. The baby "exited the rooms accompanied by his elder sister. . . . At the entrance to the village a grenadier company presented arms, and a multitude of all classes of Spanish and French soldiers were in attendance."[96] Inside the church the infant was welcomed by General Gerónimo Girón and French and Spanish officers. After the baptism his baby clothes were changed for a grenadier's uniform from the New Spain Crown Regiment, "fulfilling my general's wish that the baby would be devoted to the service of His Majesty and His Royal Army." Representing the godfather was José Luciano de Villareal, corporal in the grenadiers of the regiment, "an old soldier with many years of service, a man of good will, and the most senior of his corps," to whom Bernardo de Gálvez granted a pension. Present on behalf of the godmother was the baby's half-sister, Adelaide. In the banquet that fol-

Portrait of Bernardo de Gálvez by Bartolomé Vázquez published in Madrid in 1782. Its likeness is uncertain because at the time the engraving was published, Gálvez had been living in America for several years. (Bartolomé Vázquez, *Retrato de Bernardo Gálvez*, engraving, Madrid: 1782; in Madrid: Biblioteca Nacional, inventory no. IH/3417/2)

lowed the religious ceremony, the proud parents "hosted about six hundred soldiers of both nations. . . . Two hundred more were seated in three splendidly set tables with the best wines and most exquisite food, beautiful ladies, brave generals, gallant officers, and happy civilians. . . . The rest of the day went in dancing, music, singing, and other amusements, which concluded with a splendid dinner. . . . With all of this the general sought to present the king with the small gift of his first-born son; to the regiment his appreciation of it as the one in which he began his military career; and to the troops his affection and satisfaction with them."[97]

The End of the War

Exactly the same day that Miguel de Gálvez y Saint-Maxent was baptized in Guarico, the preliminary articles of the peace between Spain and England were signed in Versailles. When news of the peace arrived in Guarico, Bernardo de Gálvez was not surprised, since he had been kept informed about developments by both his uncle and his friend Francisco de Saavedra. The peace was mainly the result of several parallel negotiations aimed at ending a war that was already too costly for all contestants. For Britain the public debt at the end of the war was double that of the previous decade.[98] For France the budgetary imbalance caused by the cost of the war was one of the reasons for its monarchy's downfall. On the Spanish side the last round of negotiations had started in May 1782. On May 29 the Spanish minister of foreign affairs, the Count of Floridablanca, sent instructions from Madrid to the Spanish ambassador to France in which he made several points directly related to the war in the American theater. The objective of expelling the British from the American continental lands on the Gulf of Mexico had been achieved. Spain was willing to accept the presence of a British colony north of Florida as a buffer zone, which, in the event of any problem, could be easily conquered. Floridablanca also mentioned that Jamaica could be returned to Britain in exchange for Minorca, Gibraltar, and other French claims.[99]

These were the instructions, but it may be useful to consider how such instructions were regarded, depending on one's viewpoint. For the capital, in the eighteenth as in the twenty-first century, instructions were a direct order issued after a global analysis of all issues, not just those in the hands of the embassies, which, in the capital's view, tended normally to focus too much on their relations with the host nation. On the other hand, embassies regarded instructions as a general framework issued by those who had no real knowledge of the situation on the ground. If, in addition to all this, we consider that in this particular instance, the two sides in the negotiations were represented by the strong personalities of Floridablanca and Aranda, it is not surprising that the negotiations were complex. In the end Gibraltar would remain in British hands, as it still does, but Spain would keep Minorca.[100] Concerning America, besides a solution to the old and nasty problem of Campeche, the British would regain New Providence, while Spain kept West Florida and acquired its eastern part, too.[101] Although the treaty closed a long chapter of confrontation between Spain and Britain on the new continent, it also created uncertainty about the security of Spain's North American territories. Without the British north of Florida to serve as a buffer between Spanish territories and the United States of America, the peace treaty opened the door to problems between the latter two countries. Several theories about this unavoidable clash have been advanced by both American and Spanish historians. In 1909 Ensor Chadwick wrote that "it was more than antiquity, more than an old civilization, which produced the differences which made it impossible for the North American Anglo-Saxon to live near his Spanish neighbor without friction. The chief cause was in the absolute racial unlikeness itself, and though racial differences are somewhat modified by more modern conditions, the basis of this unlikeness, this racial temperament, still has an influence over the relations of men, immeasurable in degree, and more potent, though so intangible than any other force in humanity."[102]

On the other side of the Atlantic, similar arguments were raised. In 1920 Manuel Conrotte, one of the first Spanish historians to study the role played by Spain in the American Revolutionary War, said that "the obstacle [to understanding Spain's role] was raised by the disparity of the conditions of both peoples, derived from the differences in the quality of their races: the Anglo-Saxon, democratic, tolerant, with no scruples about crushing anything on his way toward national progress, [and] the Iberian, not well endowed for the arts of administration and government, locked in abstract ideas, not inclined to feeling the human emotion derived from individual freedom, respectful of other peoples and mindful of harming their aspirations, could not understand each other in their public life."[103]

Leaving aside explanations based on national character and a certain degree of racism, it is relevant to briefly examine the consequences of U.S. independence for the Spanish monarchy. First, traditional historians on both sides of the Atlantic used to consider that the involvement of Spain in the American War of Independence was a mistake since the idea of a rebellion against a colonial power could be a dangerous example to follow for the Spanish possessions in America.[104] However, this approach has been contradicted by recent studies that consider that the independence of British and Spanish America was the result of very different historical processes. The American Revolution in British North America could be considered the result of a failed imperial reform, while the reforms carried out in the Spanish Empire were a success.[105] As Linda Colley has stated, London failed "to establish the kind of strong institutions of imperial control in North America that the Spanish had been able to construct in their Latin American colonies."[106] The Bourbon reforms were implemented in the Spanish Empire not without problems, but in its American territories the local elites joined the reformist project "to repair, not further tear, the bonds uniting the [Iberian] peninsula with the colonies."[107] In the case of the Spanish Empire in America, independence would come later, as a result of Napoleon's invasion of the Iberian Peninsula and caused by the absence, not the exercise of, royal authority.[108]

Second, traditional historians commonly assumed that the Spanish government at the time was wrong to contribute to the eradication of the British presence in America, since it only prepared the way for a conflict with the newly created United States. This line of thinking can be traced back to the famous secret report allegedly written by the Count of Aranda to King Carlos III, in which he stated that

> this federal republic has been born a pygmy, so to speak, and it needed the support and power of two states as powerful as Spain and France to win its independence. The day will come in which it grows and turns into a giant, even frightening, colossus in that region. It will then forget the benefits it has received from the two powers and will think only of its own expansion. Freedom of conscience, the ability to establish a new population in immense lands, as well as the advantages of a new government, will attract farmers and artisans from all nations. And within a few years we will see with real dismay the tyrannical existence of this colossus of which I am speaking. The first step for this power, once it has managed its rise to power, will be to take over Florida, in order to dominate the Gulf of Mexico. After harassing us and our relations with New Spain in this way, it will aspire to conquer this vast empire, which we will not be able to defend against a formidable power established in the very same continent as a neighbor of it.[109]

Count Aranda's report is considered the centerpiece of his ideas about America and proof of his premonitory abilities, since it predicts the power that the United States soon achieved. However, a recent study by José Antonio Escudero has questioned the authorship and the date of the document. On the basis of his investigation, it seems that the famous report was a forgery done in about 1825, at a time that the United States was already a major player in the Americas.[110] Aranda, or the forger, continued by offering a completely new vision of Spain's transatlantic relations, which was later called the Aranda Plan. He advised the king to "leave all American possessions, keeping only the islands of Cuba and Puerto Rico," and, so as to implement this "vast design in a way favorable for Spain, three sons of His Majesty should be sent to America: one as king of Mexico, the next of Peru, and the third as king of the rest of the territories . . . while Your Majesty keeps for himself the title of Emperor." Aranda's advice has been considered almost visionary and even a kind of precedent for the Manifest Destiny ideology, but at the time it seemed a little exaggerated. In any case, the fact was that after the signing of the peace treaty between Spain and Britain in Versailles on September 3, 1783, relations between the United States of America and Spain were under the shadow of three problems: the repayment of loans made by Spain to the United States, the drawing of Florida's border, and navigation along the Mississippi River.[111] To add more confusion, the two last issues, unresolved between Spain and the United States, had been settled by the peace treaty signed by Spain and Britain.[112]

The Spanish monetary contribution to the American Revolution has already been mentioned, so we need only point out that the question remained open for almost a decade, tainting all diplomatic communications between the two countries. As for the matter of the border, the issue was far from simple. During the peace negotiations, the proposals by Spain, France, and the United States for the new borders in North America were extremely different. Spain wanted the border drawn from the Gulf of Mexico following first the Apalachicola River and then the Flint River up to the Appalachian Mountains ending at Lake Erie. The French proposal followed the Spanish border from the South but went west to the Ohio River before continuing to Lake Erie. The United States, while leaving the Gulf Coast to Spain, was determined that the border would be over the Mississippi River. In theory, the question was supposed to be settled in the final peace treaty, but since Spain had not been a formal ally of the United States, the new republic felt free to agree to a treaty with the British without informing the Spanish negotiators. To further complicate the issue, the Anglo-American preliminary agreement of 1782 included a secret provision that stated that if Florida was to remain in British hands, the southern border of the United States would be drawn following the thirty-first parallel, the latitude just south of present-day Vicksburg. Although the provision would not be included in the final treaty between the United States and Britain, signed after the British had lost to Spain West Florida (which at the time reached up north to the 32° 28′ parallel), it would have an important effect on the treaty's implementation in the following years.[113]

According to Enrique San Miguel Pérez, Bernardo de Gálvez "masterfully interpreted King Carlos III's American policy . . . by stubbornly insisting that it should be traced following the thirty-fifth parallel and not the thirty-first."[114] For Bernardo de Gálvez the question was of the utmost importance. If the border were drawn to the north—today the thirty-fifth parallel is Tennessee's southern border with Mississippi, Alabama, and Georgia (with Mississippi and Alabama on the Spanish side and Georgia on the U.S. side)—then the territory would function de facto as a buffer zone that could absorb unavoidable tensions between the United States and the Spanish Floridas. If, on the contrary, the border were moved to the south—the thirty-first parallel divides southern Mississippi and Alabama from northern Louisiana and Florida—then U.S. territory would be only a few miles from New Orleans to the west and Pensacola to the east, and thus the stage for conflict would be set. Carmen de la Guardia Herrero describes the diplomatic clash that took place in Paris on August 3, 1782, between the Count of Aranda and John Jay in this way: "[Aranda's words]—John Jay came at ten in the morning and entering my studio I showed him a map of North America."[115] Aranda's surprise and devastation was enormous when John Jay put forward the American demands. "I asked Jay where he would draw the border," Aranda wrote, "—and while telling me that by a line along the Mississippi, he put his finger at its origin and went down almost to New Orleans."[116]

The problem was, as Bernardo de Gálvez wrote to his uncle in March 1784, that article 2 of the final peace treaty signed by the United States and Britain on September 30, 1783, had already established the border of Florida along the thirty-first parallel.[117] Esteban Miró was of the same opinion. In a letter to Bernardo de Gálvez from New Orleans that same month, he pointed out that a border on the thirty-first parallel was in direct contradiction to the articles of capitulation of Pensacola signed by General Campbell, which expressly determined that the whole province would be given to Spain.[118]

On the question of navigation along the Mississippi—which exceeds the scope of this book and, according to Sylvia Hilton, has been thoroughly studied by both American and Spanish historians—I will only mention Bernardo de Gálvez's opinion.[119] In a letter to Diego María de Gardoqui, who would become the first official Spanish representative to the United States, Gálvez clearly states that "the only rights that they [the United States] have along the Mississippi are those derived from their gratitude to us and not those of usurpation."[120] Even if in Bernardo de Gálvez's view the situation was crystal clear, from the perspective of international law it was otherwise. Navigation along the Mississippi had been regulated in the Peace of Paris, signed in 1763, which stated that navigation along the entire river would be free for all of the vassals of Britain and France.[121] Britain had ceded its right

His Excellency JOHN JAY *President of Congress & Minister Plenipotentiary from Congress at Madrid.*

John Jay was appointed minister to the Spanish court in September 1779 and lived in Spain for two years. Since Spain did not officially establish diplomatic relations with the United States until 1785, Jay was not recognized as an official envoy and was never formally received by the Spanish court. The lack of progress in his mission, the problems with some of his staff, and the cultural shock of late eighteenth-century Catholic Spain left Jay with sour memories of his years in Madrid. His wife, Sarah, a perceptive observer, recorded her feelings in a letter to her mother: "Excluded [from] the Society of our most intimate friends behold us in a Country whose customs, language & religion are the very reverse of our own, without connections, without friends, judge then if heaven could have bestowed a more acceptable present" (Sarah Livingston Jay to her mother, Madrid, August 28, 1780, in *Selected Letters of John Jay and Sarah Livingston Jay*, 90). (Pierre Eugène du Simitière, *His excellency John Jay . . .* ; Library of Congress, Library of Congress Prints and Photographs Division, control no. 2003689050)

to the Americans only in 1783.¹²² Despite Aranda's complaint that this had no precedent, in fact it could be argued that it was done according to international law in force at the time, which was quite different from today.¹²³ At the end of the eighteenth century, states' rights were conceived as absolute and without limit, so it was possible to transmit those rights without problem. It could also be argued that if the Mississippi River were not opened to the United States, its territories to the west of the river would be economically strangled by being deprived of their natural exit to open seas. In fact, the United States would cite the principles of natural law in its arguments with the Spaniards.¹²⁴

On top of all this, although Spain was interested in preventing the United States from using the river, it completely lacked the resources, both military and otherwise, to protect its interests in the region. Moreover, the United States had expressed its own views on multiple occasions. For example, in September 1779 the Continental Congress set forth its opinion about an eventual treaty with Spain. To lure Spain into declaring war against Britain, "if he [the king of Spain] shall obtain the Floridas from Great Britain, these United States will guarantee the same to his Catholic majesty; provided always, that the United States shall enjoy the free navigation of the river Mississippi into and from the sea."¹²⁵

It is true that the U.S. position suffered from certain oscillations over time. For example, while John Jay and Benjamin Franklin always took a strong position, the Continental Congress, in February 1781, informed Jay that it was willing to renounce navigation along the entire course of the Mississippi provided the Spaniards accepted the border at the thirty-first parallel.¹²⁶ Jay wrote back to Thomas McKean, then president of Congress, that "the cession of this navigation will, in my opinion, render a future war with Spain unavoidable."¹²⁷ Oliver Pollock, representative of the United States in New Orleans, with whom Bernardo de Gálvez worked closely, came to Jay's support.¹²⁸ In April 1782 Congress decided to cease all negotiations with Spain. In Benjamin Franklin's words, "Spain has taken four years to consider whether she should treat with us or not. Give her forty, and let us in the mean time mind our own business."¹²⁹

If, on the American side, Jay and Franklin were the hardliners, on the Spanish side Bernardo de Gálvez represented the hawks. Further on we shall see how Gálvez would be frequently consulted by the government as an expert on North American issues.¹³⁰ Spain's initial position was close to that of Gálvez and was reflected in the first set of instructions received by the chief Spanish negotiator, Diego María de Gardoqui.¹³¹ Later, the position would be softened with Spain's offer to the United States that the question of navi-

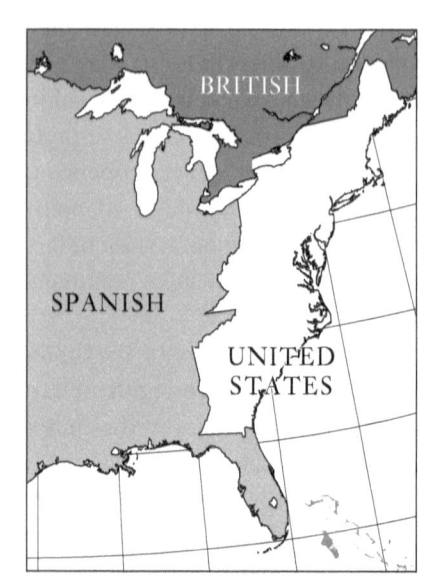
SPANISH PROPOSAL

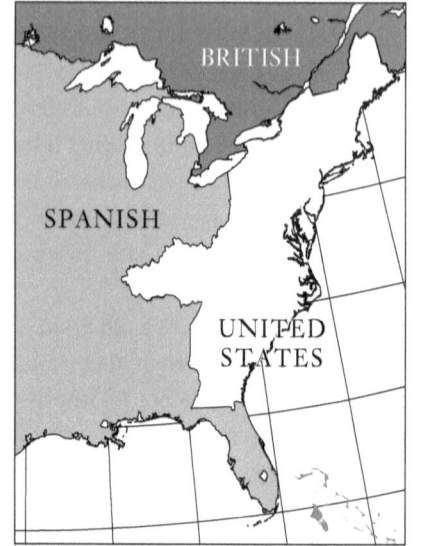
FRENCH PROPOSAL

U.S. PROPOSAL

TREATY OF PARIS, PROPOSALS

A cartoon by James Gillray published in April 1783 in London depicting the siege of Gibraltar in the background and, from right to left, America flying from Britain, while farting "poor John Bull! ha, ha, ha!"; Britain as John Bull, lamenting "'Tis lost! Irrecoverably lost!"; France as a snob courtesan, saying, "Ah, ah, me lord Angla, volez [sic] vous une pince de snuff, for the Diable will not give you back de Amerique"; Spain as a proud sixteenth-century knight, declaring "See Gibraltar! See Don Langara! By St. Anthony you have made me the laughing stock of Europe"; and a Dutchman complaining "De Donder take you, Monsieur, I think I have paid the Piper."
(James Gillray, *The Times, anno 1783*, in Prints and Photographs Division, Library of Congress, control no. 2004676762)

gation along the Mississippi be referred to a joint committee, while in the meantime U.S. vessels could gain access to the river by paying a 25 percent tax.[132] The issue would not be resolved until the final signing on October 27, 1795, of the Treaty of Friendship, Limits, and Navigation between Spain and the United States, in which article 4 states that "it is likewise agreed that the Western boundary of the United States which separates them from the Spanish Colony of Louisiana, is in the middle of the channel or bed of the River Mississippi from the Northern boundary of the said States to the completion of the thirty first degree of latitude North of the Equator; and his Catholic Majesty has likewise agreed that the navigation of the said River in its whole breadth from its source to the Ocean shall be free only to his Subjects, and the Citizens of the United States, unless he should extend this privilege to the Subjects of other Powers by special convention."[133]

Spain's complete acceptance of the U.S. position was proof of how much Spain and the world had changed in just a few years. Benjamin Franklin was wrong in his prediction. The United States had not needed forty but only thirteen years to achieve its goal in this matter.[134]

Bernardo de Gálvez received news about the signature of the preliminaries of the peace when it was brought by the French frigate *Astrea*.[135] He immediately halted his preparations for the attack on Jamaica and other British territories in the Caribbean.[136] Precisely at this moment Bernardo suffered an unknown illness, of which nothing is known other than it is mentioned by Francisco de Saavedra.[137] If, as is accurately pointed out by John Walton Caughey, making preparations for the attack on Jamaica "would prove as interesting as the usual description of military preparations, bereft, however, of the glamour that we read back into the preliminaries to successful adventures,"[138] even less appealing must have been the steps required for dismantling everything. For this reason, it is perhaps best to quote Bernardo de Gálvez himself as he describes the courteous visit paid by the Duke of Lancaster in early April 1783. The British fleet under the command of Admiral Hood was sighted near Guarico, and Gálvez sent a small ship to greet it, which returned with

> the *infante* [son or daughter of a king] Guillermo de Inglaterra, duke of Lancaster, who on the occasion of the ceasefire came ashore, where he has remained for more than 24 hours, and has been appropriately honored by the governor of this colony. The honors and distinctions I owe to His Royal Highness have been so above my merits that I can only judge them as bestowed upon the general in chief of the Spanish army here. This forced me to think of a response that would be worthy of our sovereign and of the army, and considering that the gift best suited to the pious character of Your Majesty and most agreeable to the English nation would be the pardon of their countrymen Juan Bloomart and the rest of his accomplices in the Natchez revolt, I decided to do it . . . writing everything in French since this prince spoke it.[139]

In his letter to the Duke of Lancaster, after apologizing for not having been able to order his troops to present arms because of the unexpected nature of his visit, Bernardo asks, "Would Your Highness accept the lives of these men in the name of the army and my sovereign?"[140] The duke accepted the gesture as one "that truly reflects a valiant nation such as Spain, and I consider this another proof to add to the many Your Excellency has given of the generosity of your behavior on all occasions that you have been presented with during the past war."[141]

Gálvez's fame had reached even his former enemies. Finished with courtesies, he returned to the unappealing business of dismantling the expedition. During this undertaking he wrote two letters to his uncle. In the first he says that "the signing of the peace (that as a good vassal I have celebrated for the general good of the nation) has deprived me of giving His Majesty proof that I have no other ambition in this world but to ensure that your orders are obeyed and your arms achieve the utmost glories."[142] In the second letter Bernardo acknowledges receipt of an order dated February 10 instructing him to present himself to the court and expresses gratitude that this will provide him with the opportunity to "kiss the royal hand that has so generously bestowed on me so many honors."[143]

Following orders, he sent one regiment to Buenos Aires and another to Lima, organized the garrison for St. Augustine in Florida, and appointed José de Ezpeleta provisional governor and military commander of both Louisiana and Florida.[144] He also gave Ezpeleta detailed instructions warning him that until the question of the borders was settled with the American colonies, it was "convenient, and even indispensable, to pay great care and attention in Louisiana, and have its forts ready so that the colonists [from the United States] respect them [that is, Spanish rights over the region]."[145] One of his last obligations as supreme commander of the expedition against Jamaica was to settle its accounts and pay off the debts of the navy and army. After promising all creditors that they would soon be paid, he prepared for his departure. And, in fact, the debts were paid only a month after Gálvez's embarkation, when the man-of-war *Santo Domingo* arrived from New Spain with 3 million pesos on board, of which 850,000 went to the merchants of Guarico.[146]

On May 8, 1783, Bernardo de Gálvez and his family embarked on the man-of-war *San Luis* and arrived in Havana on May 17.[147] During a short stay in Havana he continued to take care of the government of Louisiana—for example, by commissioning José de Evia to draw maps of West Florida and Pensacola, signing the appointment of Friar Cirilo de Barcelona as auxiliary bishop of New Orleans, and working on the budget of military expenses for the province.[148] He had shared with Francisco de Saavedra in October 1781 what is perhaps the best summary of his ideas about how Louisiana should be governed. Saavedra wrote, "He [Bernardo de Gálvez] showed me

French engraving published around 1784 depicting several battles of the American War of Independence. The central image, a winged victory blowing a trumpet, includes a banner with the names of the French and Spanish kings and those of the most relevant leaders, such as the Count de Vergennes, George Washington, the Count d'Estaing, D. Gálvez, and Lafayette. (N. Ponce, *Précis du traité de paix, signé à Versailles le 3 Septembre 1783*, in Prints and Photographs Division, Library of Congress, control no. 2004671468)

that the province should be governed by different rules than the others. The first thing is to allow them to trade with the French, since its inhabitants do not like other food or wines, or the wood and furs that are the sole products obtained by the Spaniards. Besides, it is a province that needs to be handled with extreme care, since it is close to the Americans, constantly deals with them, and is the first defense to our kingdom of Mexico, and if in revolt would be impossible to subdue, because of its situation and the courage of its inhabitants."[149]

On June 1, 1783, the army under Bernardo's command was officially disbanded, and with it he was discharged of his great responsibility. But he found himself encumbered with honors, since at that same time news arrived in Havana that he had been made Count of Gálvez. In a more practical vein, he was also awarded a salary as supreme commander until his arrival at the court, and his travel there was to be made on the king's behalf.[150] He also received the encomienda of Bolaños of the Order of Calatrava, which yielded an annual pension of 31,400 *reales de vellón* and was valued at 66,182 *reales de vellón*.[151] He would later lease the encomienda of Bolaños to a certain Luis de Valdelomar of Antequera.[152]

In Havana, Bernardo and Feliciana attended a ceremony presided over by Bishop Echeverría y Elguezua, at which son their Miguel was confirmed. Miguel's godfather and grandfather, Matías de Gálvez, was at the time viceroy of New Spain and at the confirmation was represented by Miguel's maternal grandfather, Gilberto Antonio Saint-Maxent.[153] With all matters settled, both personal and professional, and accompanied by his entire family (his wife, Feliciana; his stepdaughter, Adelaide, whom all witnesses agreed he considered as his own; and his own children, Matilde and Miguel), on June 16, 1783, Bernardo de Gálvez boarded the man-of-war *San Juan Nepomuceno* bound for Cadiz.[154]

EUROPE

On September 8, 1783, the Gálvezy Saint-Maxent family arrived in Cadiz, where they probably spent some time with Bernardo's uncle Antonio, who at the time was head of the port authority.[155] It is not known how long they stayed there but certainly not many days, as Bernardo de Gálvez would be eager to meet with his uncle José in Madrid to plan the next stage of his career. After staying a short while as his uncle's guests in a street called "of the Inquisition" (today known as García Molina), they moved to a *palacete* (which is not a small palace but a large townhouse) close to the palace of Buenavista, which the Duchess of Alba was building.[156] The house was apparently rented since when they later moved it was sublet.[157]

The impact of the U.S. War of Independence was not only political but also, important for Spain, economic. According to Jaume Vicens Vives, one of the most respected Spanish economic historians, "From the war came inflation and the bank of San Carlos. The rise in prices became unbearable."[158] I have mentioned that during his stay in Madrid, Bernardo de Gálvez was able to demonstrate his expertise in North American issues.[159] This fact was evident in orders received by Diego María de Gardoqui to correspond with the Count of Gálvez, "who can help you thanks to his ample knowledge on these matters," and in the advice Bernardo gave his uncle on trade regulations to apply to the Floridas' Native Americans.[160]

Spain would not be indifferent to European interest in the American Revolution. Besides the accounts by Bernardo de Gálvez himself, two other works of note appeared on the subject. The first account, published in Madrid in late 1778, bore the title *Noticia del establecimiento y poblacion de las colonias inglesas en la América Septentrional*. . . . (Notice on the settlement and population of the English colonies in North America. . . .). According to its title page, it was written by Don Francisco Álvarez, a native of the principality of Asturias. Its 196 pages are heavily indebted to previous works, mainly French. Its primary importance would seem to be that it proves a certain interest for the subject among Spanish readers of the time, but according to Francisco Aguilar Piñal, Francisco Álvarez was the pen name of José Olmeda y León.[161] The third son of the Marquis de los Llanos de Alguazas, he was one of the era's leading legal theorists and the author of the first international law manual published by a Spanish author (although he has been accused of borrowing too much from previous works without proper acknowledgment).[162] Both he and his father were members of the Economic Society of Friends of Madrid, of which both José and Miguel de Gálvez were founding members.[163] This connection may explain José Olmeda's sudden and unprecedented interest in a subject that he would never return to.

The second account, *Memorias históricas de la última guerra con la Gran Bretaña, desde 1774 hasta su conclusion: Estados Unidos de la América, año 1774 y 1775* (Historical memoirs of the late war with Great Britain, from 1774 until its end: United States of America, year 1774 and 1775), is the first and only volume published of several planned that appeared in Madrid in 1783.[164] The author, José de Covarrubias, was born in France but after 1771 worked in Madrid as a lawyer.[165] His fulsome dedication to the Count of Floridablanca was intended to gain his pardon for the scandal of a previous work, *Discurso sobre el estado actual de la abogacia en los tribunales de la nacion* (Discourse on the Present State of the Law Practiced in the Courts of the Nation), which harshly criticized the Madrid bar and was censored by the nation's law academy, the predecessor of the Royal Law Academy, whose president was Miguel de Gálvez, Bernardo's uncle.[166]

It may not be a coincidence that precisely at this time, these two authors with a certain relationship to members of the Gálvez clan decided to publish works about North America, a subject that neither of them had ever treated before and would ever treat again. Perhaps their interest was inspired directly or indirectly by José or Miguel de Gálvez.

Despite being consulted on North American affairs, writing letters that asked for rewards for the men who had suppressed the Natchez revolt, reiterating his gratitude for the French contribution to the victory in Pensacola, and adding his name to those of his father and uncles on a commemorative plaque in the Church of San Jacinto in Macharaviaya listing the family's accomplishments and generosity, the truth is that during his stay in Madrid, as he waited for his next assignment, Bernardo de Gálvez had more time on his hands than he had ever had before.[167] He tried to fill the time with a couple of hobbies.

Bernardo was the first member of the Gálvez clan to be given a title, and his uncle José followed him in 1785 when he was made Marquis of Sonora. It was at this time that Bernardo de Gálvez showed, for the first time, an interest in the family genealogy. Tensions between the old and new nobility during the reign of King Carlos III have been thoroughly studied. Since his rise to the aristocracy was made possible by social reforms implemented during the reign of King Carlos III—reforms that opened the ranks of the aristocracy to men of merit rather than of noble blood alone—perhaps Bernardo wanted to arm himself with arguments that proved that, beside his personal merits, his family tree was not devoid of important ancestors.[168] It is in this context that the letters he wrote to José Joaquín Domínguez Pareja-Obregón in late 1783 and early 1784 should be interpreted.[169] In the first letter he thanks him for the coming shipment and in the second for the arrival of a book published by Antonio Ramos in Malaga in 1781 on the genealogy of the house of Aguayo, which was remotely related to the Gálvez family.[170] That Bernardo de Gálvez took time to write two letters instead of just one to politely thank Domínguez suggests the degree of his interest in the subject.

His second hobby in Madrid was ballooning.[171] Bernardo's interest in this pastime was perfectly normal. First, by the end of the eighteenth century, ballooning was the latest fashion among the educated class. Balloon experiments carried out by the Montgolfier brothers in Paris in 1783 had a tremendous impact all over Europe, and in Spain the press published the latest news about them.[172] Public enthusiasm can be compared to the excitement during the late 1960s and early 1970s over the first moon landings, but with one important difference: the technology used in the 1780s was within the understanding of every enlightened person.[173]

Second, and very important, the military applications of the new invention strongly appealed to Bernardo de Gálvez.[174] In October 1783 André Giraud de Vilette, the second man to ascend on board a balloon, wrote in the *Journal de Paris* that while he was contemplating cities from above, he realized that "this ship, at little cost, could be very useful to an army for discovering the enemy's positions, movements, advances, and dispositions."[175] The anonymous author of a small work that appeared in Paris the following year under the title *L'art de la guerre changée par l'usage de machines aéro-*

Engraving representing the "aerostatic fish" flown over the Spanish city of Plasencia in March 1784, one of the multiple experiments with this type of machine that were popular during the last part of the eighteenth century. (C. Poisson Bresse, *Aerostàtique enlevé a Plazentia Ville d'Espagne* . . . ; Bibliothèque nationale de France, Département Estampes et photographie, FOL-IB-4 [2])

statiques (The art of warfare changed by the employment of the aerostatic machines) was even more precise.[176] The main challenge to military use of the new invention was lack of control over its navigation.[177] To solve this problem, the Science Academy of Lyon offered 1,200 livres for the best essay on "the most secure, the least costly, and the most efficient way to direct at will the aerostatic machines."[178] Two works were presented but the prize was not awarded. One year later, in his *History and Practice of Aerostation*, published in London, Tiberius Cavallo wrote about a series of unsuccessful devices designed for this purpose.[179] It was in this area that Bernardo de Gálvez hoped to make his contribution.

In volume 74 of the *Philosophical Transactions of the Royal Society of London* there is a report written in French and read by Sir Joseph Banks on July 1, 1784, titled "Sur un Moyen de Donner la Direction aux Machines Aérostatiques: Par M. Le Comte de Galvez." According to Sir Joseph, "On the afternoon of the first day of May 1784, in the channel of the Manzanares River, a boat twenty-five feet long and four and a half feet wide was prepared with a machine that he [Bernardo de Gálvez] had invented to prove his ideas."[180]

A revealing aspect is that for Bernardo de Gálvez it was not enough to design, build, and test his invention. He also staged a public demonstration, to which he invited a select group of scholars, both from Spain and abroad, who were asked to sign a certificate "to prove that the event in question had taken place in the way narrated, . . . as well as [to testify to] a plan of the mentioned machine."[181] The certificate was signed by José Viera y Clavijo, Agustín de Betancourt y Molina, Richard Worsley, Raim de S. Laurent, and Casimiro Gómez de Ortega. Each of the witnesses had been carefully chosen.

José de Viera y Clavijo, an intellectual born in the Canary Islands, was previously mentioned as a hearsay witness to Madrid's celebrations of the victory at Pensacola. He was a historian and a biologist who had a very important role as a publicist of scientific matters and whose lectures attracted "members of the aristocracy, including ladies, as well as some doctors and pharmacists, professors of physics, and other people who loved science."[182] Agustín de Betancourt was a respected military engineer behind the first balloon experiments performed in Spain, including the one in Madrid on December 15, 1785.[183] Casimiro Gómez de Ortega was a botanist, pharmacist, doctor, poet, and, from 1781, the first professor at Madrid's Royal Botanic Garden.[184] About Raim de S. Laurent, it has been impossible to find any information. Richard Worsley was a young member of the British Parliament who, in an attempt to forget the scandal surrounding his divorce, had departed on a long journey in Europe, during which he would amass a huge art and antiquities collection, for which he was later known.[185] Worsley's presence at Bernardo's demonstration was essential if the experiment on the Manzanares River was to attract the attention of the president of the Royal Society, Joseph Banks, who devoted his life to spreading scientific knowledge across Europe and America.[186] Underneath the polite wording of the report there is a question about the use of a "heavy and badly built boat, whose wings revealed no proportion at all," but it ended on a more positive note with the assertion that "this invention seemed to us deserving of the approval and praise of the Physics who, no doubt, will apply their efforts to supplying it with every perfection that the performance of its mechanism can achieve."[187] In other words, the idea could be interesting, but the experiment was not very well executed and much more work was needed. Banks's report, in French, was politely mentioned by other British and French publications, including *A New Review with Literary Curiosities, and Literary Intelligence* and the July issue of the *Journal Encyclopedique ou Universel*.[188]

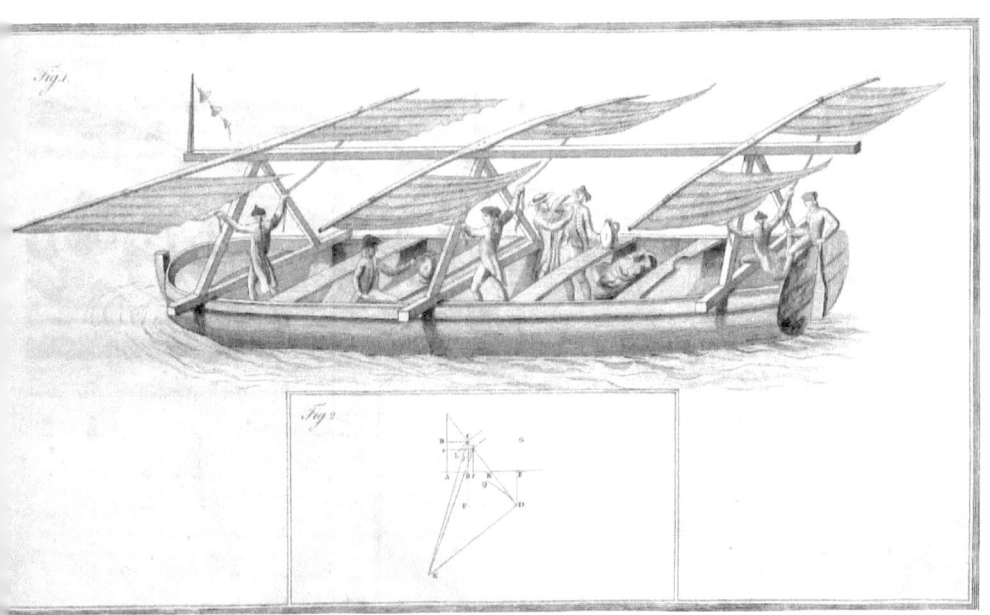

Engraving published in the *Philosophical Transactions of the Royal Society of London* showing the device invented by Bernardo de Gálvez that would allow one to direct hot-air balloons. (Banks, "Sur un Moyen de Donner la Direction aux Machines Aérostatiques")

Other reviews were less courteous. The *English Review, or, An Abstract of English and Foreign Literature for the Year 1789* stated that it was just "a frivolous expedient [sic], very inaccurately treated; and in the experiment relative to which the aerostatic machine was a boat!"[189] Even more critical was an article in the 1785 *Critical Review, or, Annals of Literature*, which, questioning the certificate, asked, "'We the undersigned certify'—What? That we *failed* on the canal of Manzanares *in a boat* [italics in the original] with very little wind, by the help of moveable sails like wings. Adieu Messrs. And, in return for your laborious certificate, and the very accurate plate which accompanies it,—may you receive a superior portion of discernment, and a little more philosophical accuracy!"[190]

Despite these criticisms, which Bernardo de Gálvez probably never learned about, the experiment was the focal point of a hobby that filled his otherwise long days at court. It is relevant to note that despite the publicity the experiment attracted in England and France, no trace of it has been found in the Spanish press at the time, even though everything related to balloons received much attention.[191] In any case, Bernardo de Gálvez's sojourn in Madrid was about to end. In January 1784 he was appointed *capitán general* (supreme military commander) of the two Floridas and the province of Louisiana, a huge territory: from the Mississippi to the Pacific Ocean plus the present state of Florida and southern parts of the present states of Alabama and Mississippi.[192] Of course, most of the land was sparsely populated and thus was only theoretically under the sovereignty of Spain, but nevertheless it was a very big territory under his command. Six months later, he was also appointed *capitan general* of Cuba. The accumulation of so many important jobs under one person can be explained both by his reputation as the victor in Pensacola, who had conquered the British Floridas for Spain, and by the trust that his uncle José placed in him. That all of these territories were governed by the same person created a unique set of difficulties.[193] In other words, Bernardo de Gálvez was the supreme authority over all Spanish territory in North and Central America and the Caribbean. And as if all of that authority was not enough, Bernardo de Gálvez was also appointed inspector general of all Spanish troops in America.[194]

Before leaving Madrid, Bernardo de Gálvez gave power of attorney to Diego Paniagua, so he could represent him during his absence from court.[195] In autumn 1784 he set sail for Cadiz, where he spent time inspecting the troops assembled there.[196] Among the affairs he had to deal with was a petition by Juan de San Martín, father of the liberator of Argentina, Chile, and Peru, to be promoted to the rank of lieutenant colonel. Bernardo backed the petition, but in the end the promotion never came about.[197] In Cadiz he also received news of his father's serious illness.[198] The Gálvez y Saint-Maxent family set sail for Cuba in late 1784 or early 1785.[199]

CUBA

On February 4, 1785, the family landed in Havana, and the same day Bernardo de Gálvez took office as governor and supreme military commander of the island.[200] According to Juan Bosco Amores Carredano, the island was experiencing a period of economic boom generated in part by its importance as a logistics center during the war with Britain, a time when more than 30 million pesos arrived, a rain of silver that benefited all.[201] During his governorship Bernardo de Gálvez did his best to consolidate and promote this economic expansion. As in Louisiana, he granted most demands of the local elite, including slave import permits.[202] He also appealed to wealthy locals' sense of self-importance by strongly and publicly backing their petitions to be awarded titles of nobility by the king.[203] With these actions and policies, by the end of his mandate there he was extremely popular among the Cuban elite, to the point that they asked from the king that their governor be given an estate "among the best lands to the west of the island."[204]

While in Havana, Gálvez had to deal with a scandal following allegations of corruption against Nicolás Arredondo, governor of the city of Santiago de Cuba. Arredondo was a prominent figure in Cuban society and one of the founding members of the Patriotic Society of Cuba. The allegations were based on certain murky dealings that Arredondo had had with two so-called merchants, the brothers Francisco and Tomás Creagh.[205] On March 17, 1785, Bernardo de Gálvez suspended Arredondo as governor of Santiago and sent him to prison while the investigation took place.[206] Some time later, the allegations were proved false and Arredondo was completely acquitted. He later had a brilliant administrative career as viceroy of the River Plate viceroyalty between December 1789 and March 1795.

As supreme military commander of Cuba, Bernardo de Gálvez continued with the reform of the corps stationed on the island that was begun under Alejandro O'Reilly. Bernardo's *Reglamento para las milicias de infantería y caballería de la isla de Cuba* (Regulations for the infantry and cavalry militias of the island of Cuba), issued on January 19, 1769, included items that were in fact concessions to the local elites, such as reserving certain commissions for their scions. In article 2, chapter 6, the regulations state that officers could be selected only from among "the most distinguished subjects, who have the quality of *ilustres* [a Spanish honorific, just below that of "Excellency"], . . . and sufficient means to support the rank decently, . . . [taking into account] the services they have rendered themselves as well as those rendered by their ancestors."[207] This provision accommodated members of the Cuban militias who had performed all of their duties with the utmost competence while the veteran troops were campaigning abroad during the war with Britain. Their performance proved the success of the military reform and even furthered it.[208] Bernardo de Gálvez had a great deal of respect for the Cuban militias, whose merits were comparable to those of any regular regiment.[209]

Gálvez did not have much time to govern Cuba, since on January 24, 1785, a royal decree was signed at the Royal Palace of El Pardo ordering him to move to New Spain to become its acting viceroy. At that time, the Spanish court was aware of the serious illness of the present viceroy, Matías de Gálvez, Bernardo's father. So Bernardo de Gálvez was sent to take charge "in case of his demise or if Don Matías is unable to perform his governmental duties."[210] The royal decree also determined that, since it was an acting appointment, Bernardo would be exempt from the usual formalities, and as a sign of the king's appreciation he would remain full *capitan general* and governor of Cuba, Louisiana, and both Floridas.[211] Nevertheless, it was impossible for him to deal personally with all of the matters related to these territories, and he was instructed to appoint Luis de Unzaga acting governor of Cuba or, if he was absent from the island at the time, to appoint his second in command, Bernardo Troncoso. It was also determined that he must suggest a successor in full. Bernardo de Gálvez put forward the name of his old and trusted friend José de Ezpeleta, who at that moment was under-inspector general of troops in New Spain.[212]

On May 16, 1785, little more than three months after their arrival in Cuba, Bernardo de Gálvez and his family boarded the man-of-war *Santa Águeda*, under the command of naval captain Rafael Orozco, and sailed for the port of Veracruz, Mexico.[213]

8. Viceroy of New Spain

Bernardo de Gálvez landed at Veracruz on May 25, 1785.¹ Fifteen years earlier he had arrived in Mexico under very different circumstances. Now he came as the new viceroy, representative of His Catholic Majesty in New Spain, and his arrival was a matter of state, with a complex protocol designed to make everyone aware of this important fact. The complexity of the pomp and circumstance surrounding the occasion emphasized Spanish power in America. Nothing was left to chance—each and every action was charged with deep meaning. From his landing in Veracruz to his triumphal entrance into Mexico City, as he followed the route taken by the conquistador Hernán Cortés in the early sixteenth century, his every step, according to Víctor Mínguez, symbolically represented the renewal of Spanish domination over the territory.²

His route and the stops he made on the way to the capital were described in detail by the official newspaper, the *Gazeta de México*.³ From the very beginning it was clear that Bernardo de Gálvez was not just another viceroy. According to an eyewitness, he altered not only the route but also all of the ceremonies.⁴ A modern historian has accused him of changing everything for no other reason than he wanted to do so.⁵ But other viceroys had done the same thing when they arrived not from Spain but from other assignments, as did Gálvez.⁶ While he certainly made changes according to his own desires, he also had important reasons for doing so. Altering the ceremonies was necessary because he arrived not as full but as acting viceroy and so, as the royal decree appointing him stated, was exempted from the usual formalities.⁷ To understand how and why he changed the traditional route, it is perhaps best to follow him on his way to Mexico City.

In Veracruz, where the new viceroy usually stayed for two weeks, Bernardo de Gálvez lingered only five days. He did not require much time to recover from the arduous, uncomfortable trip from the Iberian Peninsula, and since it was his third time in the city, there was no need for him to inspect the military installations, port, and other facilities.⁸ From Veracruz he followed

Mexico City's main square in 1769, representing the cortege of Viceroy Teodoro de Croix, under whom both José and Bernardo de Gálvez served. Through the apparent chaos of the market, full of merchants and products from all over the world, emerges the life of the biggest and richest city in the eighteenth-century Spanish Empire.
(J. Antonio Prado, *La Plaza Mayor de México en el siglo XVIII*, oil on canvas, circa 1769; Mexico: Museo Nacional de Historia, reproduction authorized by the Instituto Nacional de Antropología e Historia)

the viceroy's traditional route to Perote, about 100 miles to the north, where, instead of heading for Tlaxcala—usually the first important stop for a new viceroy, since its inhabitants' ancestors were the first allies of Cortés in his conquest of Mexico—he decided to go to Puebla. He had important reasons for making this change. Puebla had a population of 81,046 and was the capital of an *intendencia* or province with more than half a million people, while in the entire *intendencia* of Tlaxcala there were only 70,000 people.[9] Moreover, Puebla was the seat of an important bishopric, which between 1640 and 1648 had been occupied by Juan Palafoz y Mendoza, a proponent of the reformation of the Spanish Catholic Church to counteract the increasing power of the Jesuits. His beatification was strongly favored by King Carlos III.[10] And his final reason was that the "ruined, deserted, and miserable" city of Tlaxcala could not rival the vitality of Puebla, which, besides food industries, including mills and bakeries, also hosted armories, forges, and ceramics and blown glass production facilities.[11] By choosing to enter Puebla before Tlaxcala, Bernardo de Gálvez sent a strong message about the importance of economic development over tradition.

At Puebla's outskirts, the bishop and main local authorities greeted him. Instead of riding in on horseback, he decided to enter by coach, no doubt so that his wife could accompany him.[12] In Puebla he spent only three days instead of the traditional ten, and from there he proceeded to Tlaxcala, where, unsurprisingly, the population remained, according to a contemporaneous witness, a bit distant.[13] From Tlaxcala he continued through Hacienda Buenavista, Apan, San Juan de Teotihuacán, and San Cristóbal, to Guadalupe, sanctuary of the famous Virgin protectress of Mexico.

The stop in Guadalupe, the last before Mexico City, was rich with symbolism. It offered a clear message about the union of the church and the state and also about the renewal of the old covenant between the state and the indigenous communities of Mexico, which from the first had considered this Virgin and her image as their own. The story is that in 1531 the mother of Jesus had appeared before Juan Diego Cuauhtlatoatzin, an Indian, in Tepeyac, precisely where before the Spanish conquest there had been a temple consecrated to an Aztec deity, the mother goddess Tonantzin. Building new temples in already sacred soil was a strategy widely used by the Catholic Church in America, as it helped transfer the local population's religious beliefs to the new faith. In the case of Tepeyac, the transfer was especially easy, since the old mother goddess was simply replaced by a new one. If Bernardo's visit to Guadalupe was already important for this reason, it was made even more so by its timing during the reign of Carlos III. Throughout his reign the king and the state shared a common pulse with the church. According to Elisa Vargas Lugo, the Crown compensated for its expulsion of the Jesuits by reinforcing religious fervor through its exaltation of the Catholic dogma of the immaculate conception of the Virgin Mary.[14]

Finally, at eleven thirty on June 17, 1785, Bernardo de Gálvez entered Mexico City.[15] Until then it had been customary for the new viceroy to make two ceremonial entrances into the capital. However, Gálvez made only one because of a royal decree issued well before his arrival.[16] In addition, Gálvez wanted to quickly complete formalities to take up office and start working as soon as possible. This is exactly what he did on the same day that he entered the capital.[17]

A NEW STYLE OF GOVERNANCE

All contemporaneous accounts agree that a changed atmosphere arrived in Mexico with the new viceroy. Everything about him seemed different, but much of what appeared so novel actually had precedents in the long history of Spanish rule in New Spain.

The youthfulness of the viceregal couple was evident, especially when compared to the advanced age of Bernardo's predecessor, his father, Matías, who, at the time of his arrival as viceroy, was already sixty-six years old and seriously ill.[18] Similarly, other previous viceroys, including Martín de Mayorga (age fifty-eight), Antonio María de Bucareli (age fifty-four), and the Marquis de Croix (age sixty-seven), were far from young.[19]

The fact that Bernardo de Gálvez directly succeeded his father was a first. But, as José Ignacio Rubio Mañé has pointed out, there had already been cases of what he calls authentic "viceregal dynasties," or important noble families that supplied members for the viceroyalty, including the Dukes of Albuquerque during the seventeenth century.[20]

But despite being a count, Bernardo de Gálvez did not came from an old aristocratic family. This was not unusual, at least starting in the eighteenth century, when the new Spanish ruling dynasty, the Bourbons, opened the door to a new social class of families ennobled through their service in the army or the royal administration.[21] These new avenues to advancements were well illustrated by Bernardo and his uncle José. But it was precisely his lack of a social pedigree that was one of the first and few criticisms raised against Bernardo. In early August 1785, the people of Mexico City woke up to find the walls of their streets plastered with the following verse:

Yo te conocí pepita
Antes que fueras melón,
Maneja bien el bastón
Y cuida la francesita.

I knew you she-seed
Before you became a cantaloupe,
Handle the cane well
And take care of the little Frenchwoman.[22]

The first lines refer to an old Mexican saying about those who rise in life and forget their humble origins.[23] The *pepita* (she-seed) is presumably Bernardo de Gálvez when he arrived in Mexico fifteen years earlier as a young officer with no means or fortune of his own.²⁴ The cane has a double meaning, referring both to the marshal's or viceroy's baton and to the cane used to discipline one's wife—in this case, the *francesita* (little Frenchwoman). At the bottom of this attack there was nothing other than envy.

The Afrancesamiento of Bernardo de Gálvez

Afrancesamiento is a Spanish word with no direct equivalent in English. Its translation as "pro-French feeling" or "frenchification" does not fully convey its sense and implications in Spanish. In the late eighteenth century, the word was applied to Spaniards who were overly influenced by French culture—which is to say, the French Enlightenment. All enemies of the popular new philosophy became enemies of everything and anything French. Jacques Houdaille mentions that at the time in New Spain, there was a tendency to consider all foreigners as born heretics. Even though France was a Catholic country and the pope had awarded its king the title of "Most Christian King," French men and women were regarded as such. Houdaille adds that traditional Mexican society was shocked "by the broadminded way in which they [the French] interpreted the Sixth Commandment" and by the role the French played in spreading Enlightenment ideas through forbidden books and the promotion of Freemasonry in New Spain."²⁵ So *afrancesamiento* in Mexico during the decade of 1780 was not something new. According to José Miranda, the dissemination of Enlightenment ideas was accompanied by the adoption of French customs and usages among the elite.²⁶ For Enrique Florescano, most viceroys were enthusiastic supporters of the Enlightenment, and these men brought with them the political, social, religious, and economic ideas of the period and spread them through their courts and in the literary gatherings they frequently organized.²⁷

Of Bernardo de Gálvez's *afrancesamiento* there could be no doubt. He started his military career under the French flag in the Royal Cantabre Regiment. His fluent French was one reason Alejandro O'Reilly had chosen him as governor of Louisiana. His wife had been born French and remained one until she became a Spaniard in 1763, when Louisiana fell under Spanish rule. Most probably Bernardo de Gálvez spoke French when alone with Felicitas/Feliciana, and her Spanish, according to contemporaneous testimonies, always had a charming French accent.²⁸ Also, his uncle José was an *afrancesado* who had started his career as a lawyer at the French embassy in Madrid and had even married a second wife who was French.

In addition, the new viceroy's entourage was definitively pro-French. From New Orleans he brought his personal physician, Monsieur Saugrain, whom he sent to France to learn the latest advances in medicine and to collect a physics cabinet that could later be sent to Mexico.²⁹ He was accompanied by the husbands of his wife's two sisters, Juan Antonio de Riaño and Manuel Flon Tejada, who, according to Pablo Avilés Flores, were strongly influenced by French culture.³⁰ Also arriving with him were French-origin military officers as well as artists, artisans, gardeners, hairdressers, and cooks. There were even some Frenchmen from Europe who brought books that inspired local plays, operas, poetry, essays, and scientific books.³¹ French influence also permeated daily customs. According to Manuel Rivera Cambas, during Bernardo de Gálvez's time the first coffee shop in Mexico City opened, where a waiter invited passersby to enter and have a coffee and a madeleine in the style of France.³² Soon afterward this kind of locale attracted the suspicions of Spanish colonial authorities—as in 1790, when the viceroy at the time, the Count of Revillagigedo, labeled such shops as places where "the seeds of rebellion could be planted and nurtured."³³

Bernardo de Gálvez's role in introducing Enlightenment books to Mexico is difficult to assess, since no inventory of his private library has been found, unlike those of his uncle José and his friend Francisco de Saavedra.³⁴ At least part of his library was sold six months after his death in Mexico at a public auction, and some of his books later appeared in several private libraries.³⁵ Monelisa Pérez Marchand cites the testimony of a buyer who was surprised to find among his books several that were included on the index of forbidden books that circulated among the French residents of Mexico.³⁶ In an article about the problems of Juan Eugenio Santelises Pablo, a late eighteenth-century Mexican mine owner, René de León Meza mentions that he "had bought some works and books that had belonged to the viceroy, the count of Gálvez, among them a work in French under the title *Encyclopedia*, printed in Paris in 1773, in eight volumes, and the works of Moreli in five."³⁷ It is tempting to think that Bernardo de Gálvez owned the *Encyclopédie, ou dictionnaire raisonné des sciences, des arts et des métiers* by Diderot and d'Alembert, but the details registered about the set do not correspond to known editions of the *Encyclopedie*. The *Encyclopédie* had seventeen volumes of text, ten of engravings, and four supplements, none of them printed in 1773. Perhaps the details were miscopied or the mine owner Santelises had only those volumes related to his business, which was in fact the argument he used to justify his ownership of them.³⁸

The work by "Moreli" in five volumes has not been easy to identify. Assuming the author's name was misspelled, it could have been Robert Morel, a Benedictine monk who lived between 1656 and 1731 and whose ideas were considered dangerously close to Jansenism, a Christian theological trend that was condemned as heretical by Pope Innocent X in 1653. Morel's book *Effusions du cœur, ou entretiens spirituels et affectifs d'une âme avec Dieu, sur chaque verset des psaumes et des cantiques de l'Eglise* was forbidden in all Spanish territories after its inclusion on the 1747 edition of the *Index Expurgatorius*.[39] The *Index Expurgatorius* was an augmented update of the list of forbidden books published by the Catholic Church in Rome.[40] Another possibility is that the book mentioned by Santelises was the *Le grand dictionnaire historique ou Le mélange curieux de l'histoire sacrée et profane* by Louis Moreri, the 1712 edition of which was in five volumes.[41] It was partially included on the list of forbidden books because it suggested that the *Spiritual Exercises* of Saint Ignace of Loyola, the founder of the Jesuit Order, was merely an adaptation of a previous work by a Benedictine monk.[42] Bernardo de Gálvez's possession of possibly these and other forbidden books can be explained by the fact that those who needed them for professional reasons could obtain authorization to own them. For example, by the end of the eighteenth century in Lima, a total of fifty-two people, including twenty-seven clergy, nineteen lawyers, and four other professionals, had obtained such authorization.[43] The libraries of both José de Gálvez and Francisco de Saavedra also included forbidden books.[44]

Accusations of *afrancesamiento* against Bernardo de Gálvez also involved Freemasonry. According to Jacques Houdaille, one Felipe Faloris, an Italian who had lived in France, where he had joined the Grenoble Masonic Lodge, arrived in Veracruz in 1785. An artist by trade, he was commissioned to paint the viceroy's portrait, and therefore he had the opportunity to praise "the new sect" among Mexico's aristocracy.[45] This Felipe Faloris was actually Felipe Fabris, and the portrait mentioned was not of Bernardo de Gálvez but of the Count of Revillagigedo, viceroy between 1789 and 1794. Fabris was a minor painter from Venice who worked in Mexico, where, according to contemporaneous accounts, he "painted nudity, never prayed, always dined with his hat on, and someone heard him saying in Gibraltar that he read French books and admired Voltaire."[46] In 1787 he was sentenced by the Inquisition for the felony of Freemasonry and heretical propositions.[47] Bernardo de Gálvez's own relationship with Freemasonry is slippery terrain because of the obvious lack of documentation due to the secrecy of the movement and the "black legend" that has surrounded its study in Spain. One can only come to register contradictory assessments, one supporting his membership and the other completely denying it.[48]

In late August 1785, the same month in which the verse criticizing the new viceroy appeared, another one also covered the walls of Mexico City. This time it was in his favor.

El virey muy bueno,
La vireina major.
El inspector[49] *el Diablo,*
Y su muger . . . ¡peor!

The viceroy very good,
The vice queen even better.
The inspector a devil,
And his wife . . . the worst![50]

Months later, yet another new verse appeared, this time criticizing Bernardo de Gálvez for his lack of ardor in fulfilling his religious duties.

En todas partes te veo
Menos en el jubileo

Everywhere I see you
except attending mass[51]

Apparently Bernardo de Gálvez's schedule could be closely followed, since accounts of it have survived. His official schedule was subject to frequent comments by the official royal newspaper, *Gazeta de México*, while his private appointments can be traced with the help of the *Diario curioso de México de d. José Gómez, cabo de alabarderos* (Curious diary of Don José Gómez, corporal of the Alabardiers).[52] The Alabardiers Corps was a military unit in charge of ceremonial duties and the viceroy's protection. Membership in it was reserved for the scions of the most prestigious families, as was also the case with its fellow unit, the king's Royal Alabardiers at court. Because of his proximity to the viceroy, José Gómez was able directly to witness elements of Bernardo de Gálvez's life in Mexico. According to these two sources, it seems that during his first year as viceroy, in 1785, Bernardo and his wife devoted more time going to the theater and bullfights than to church: he attended seven solemn masses but went to eleven bullfights and four or five comedies.[53]

The Theater

Just four days after their arrival in Mexico City, the viceregal couple attended two plays: *Desdén con desdén* by Agustín Moreto and *La posadera feliz o el enemigo de las mujeres* by Carlo Goldoni.[54] Since both were "free and in their honor," it could be argued that their attendance was an official duty.[55] Nevertheless, Bernardo de Gálvez was much more than just a simple spectator. Aware of the importance of the theater as an instrument of popular education, in January 1786 he commissioned Silvestre Díaz de la Vega to draft new legislation for its regulation.[56] The *Reglamento para la dirección del Coliseo de Mexico* (Regulation for the direction of Mexico City's Coliseum), addressing its government, financing, and jurisdiction, was published on April 11 of the same year.[57] It called for tight censorship; revoked all previous authorizations to perform plays, so that applications had to be resubmitted; prohibited "all indecency and provocation that could cause the slightest scandal"; and allowed the performance only of Mexican traditional dances "under the precise and indispensable condition that they are performed with the utmost decency... forbidding any kind of addition such as those commonly known as *cuchillada* [literally, "the stab"], jumps, or provocative movements."[58] Gaspar Melchor de Jovellanos, one of the leading Spanish Enlightenment statesmen, ruefully asked "what our dances have come to be, but a pitiful imitation of the free and indecent dances of the lowest plebeians? While other nations stage the dances of gods and nymphs, we choose those of *manolos* [the plural of the name Manuel, applied to the lowest kind of mob] and fishwives."[59] To clarify the purpose of the theater, Bernardo de Gálvez ordered that the following verse be inscribed on the curtain of Mexico City's New Coliseum:

Es el drama mi nombre
y mi deber corregir al hombre
haciendo en mi ejercicio
amable la virtud, odioso el vicio.

Drama is my name
and my duty to improve men
making in my exercise
virtue loved, and vice hated.[60]

The 1786 *Reglamento para la dirección del Coliseo de Mexico* addressed not only the kind of plays and other performances deemed appropriate but also the management of the theater. It created a company by subscription formed "of dignitaries" in charge of everything related to the Coliseum. According to Juan Pedro Viqueira Albán, Gálvez's reforms were very modern and at the same time repressive and thus corresponded exactly to the Enlightenment's agenda for the theater.[61] Of all measures taken by Bernardo de Gálvez during his time as viceroy of Mexico, these regulations were the most long lasting. They remained in force until 1894, when the Republic of Mexico finally issued a new set of regulations.[62]

Bullfighting

Of all viceroys, Bernardo de Gálvez is considered the greatest aficionado of bullfighting.[63] As discussed earlier, during his previous stay in New Spain he delayed his departure on a mission against an Apache warrior until a bullfight in Chihuahua had ended.[64] Now as viceroy he had the opportunity to indulge his passion for bullfighting even more, but at the same time attending the fights must also have counted among his official duties. Despite an assertion by Viqueira Albán that by the end of the eighteenth century, bullfighting represented conservative or traditionalist principles while the theater represented the progressive trends of the Enlightenment, for Bernardo de Gálvez no such contradiction existed.[65] He used the bullfights, or corridas, as an opportunity to convey important political and social messages to the common people of Mexico.

In the late eighteenth century, on both the Iberian Peninsula and in Mexico, the corridas had a social function far beyond what football and baseball games mean for us today. All of these public performances serve as a kind of decompression valve for social and personal tensions, but the corridas were also an important source of revenue for the Royal Treasury.[66] This latter function was so important that Alberto González Troyano has argued that bullfighting survived the Enlightenment, which was ideologically against such a barbarous show, because the money it generated was so important to the always-needy royal coffers.[67]

Moreover, precisely during the second half of the eighteenth century a sort of revolution in the "art of bullfighting" took place and led to so-called serious bullfighting, with strict rules and customs that have survived into the twenty-first century.[68] This evolution in favor of regulations can be viewed as a consequence of the Enlightenment mentality, which, even if it was unsuccessful at totally suppressing this kind of spectacle, could constrain it in a civilized way. Despite this revolution, the truth is that a *corrida* in the 1780s had very little in common with a bullfight today. At that time, besides the actual fight with the bull, many kinds of "other entertainments" took place inside the bullring, including dogs fighting bulls, greyhound races, cockfights, and even the *cucaña* (greasy pole).[69]

Bernardo de Gálvez actively enjoyed all of these amusements. For the *cucaña* he donated generous prizes—for example, at the corrida on December 21, 1785, he gave 40 pesos for the winner, and the following day his gifts, according to José Gómez, were of unprecedented generosity and included "the best clothes, poultry, and animals, and even three silver trays."[70] He loved to see women bullfighters (*toreras*), and on November 15, 1785, he gave one a 100-peso prize, and on another occasion he cheered four *toreras* as they entered the bullring.⁷¹ He even sponsored one of the most famous ones.⁷²

Viqueira Albán mentions that by the second half of the eighteenth century, nobles no longer participated in bullfighting, which became the pastime of the plebeians.⁷³ But he adds that in New Spain, some of the aristocracy continued to take part, discreetly, either in the privacy of their haciendas or at public bullfights with their faces covered with masks. This was an instance of the so-called *tapados y preparados* (covered and prepared) that was in fashion between 1785 and 1786, during the time of Viceroy Bernardo de Gálvez, who encouraged a passion for bullfighting in New Spain society.⁷⁴ In so doing, Gálvez, knowingly or not, in fact helped close the gap between the common people and the aristocrats by encouraging them to share a common entertainment.

In addition, bullfights were a perfect way for Bernardo to show himself to the people of Mexico. The presence of the viceroy and other high officials at the fights was regulated by a strict protocol, which assigned each one a place according to his or her position in the New Spain social hierarchy.⁷⁵ But Bernardo de Gálvez was not satisfied with merely appearing in front of the people. He managed also to be among them, and if that meant breaking all rules of protocol, then so be it. During the bullfights celebrated a few days after his arrival in Mexico City, he strictly followed the rules, arriving in his box through a passage that led directly from the viceregal palace, or "in the state coach surrounded by his Alabardiers Corps, as is appropriate for His Majesty's representative."⁷⁶ Several months later, feeling much more comfortable in his new role, he started to give his appearances a personal touch. On November 14, 1785, there took place "the first corrida in the Volador bullring, to which the viceroy and his wife went in a *birloche* [a small topless four-wheeled carriage], and in the afternoon they went on foot."⁷⁷ Carlos María Bustamante, one of the most famous historians of the early Mexican Republic, comments that "when presenting himself driving a small carriage, with his wife at his side, the wind carried repeated and happy acclamations; perhaps the monarch of the Spains [sic] would not have received as many [cheers] as they did then in Mexico City's bullring."⁷⁸

At the December 20 corrida, after the performance of four *tapados* or noble bullfighters whose faces were hidden by masks, Bernardo de Gálvez threw them "four papers with four red bands with silver edges, and ... paper cones with *mascadas* [silk handkerchiefs], which had not been seen here before, and the afternoon was very entertaining."⁷⁹ Despite the apparent spontaneity of the viceroy's gesture, it was actually well thought out. Everything he threw to the *tapados* was a luxury item that he had purposely brought, while to the commoners participating in the *cucaña* he awarded money or food. On other occasions Bernardo de Gálvez let his enthusiasm show freely, as, for example, at the corrida that took place two days later, when "the viceroy had so much fun that he threw his handkerchief, then his wife's, and his daughter's, and it looked as if he was about to throw his uniform, too, and with all this the afternoon was very entertaining."[80]

Walking through Mexico City

Bernardo de Gálvez liked to walk through Mexico City as much as possible. Sometimes he did it alone, at other times with his wife or the rest of his family, but always with the least possible escort. These promenades were against all protocol and generated not a little anxiety among those in charge of his security.[81] Besides, at that time such a thing "had not yet been seen in this kingdom, at least not among the *señores* [that is, important people]."[82] Bernardo de Gálvez became increasingly uncomfortable with the protocol and security apparatus around him and his family, and twice he changed the rules governing the Alabardiers Corps, incorporating officers from various regular regiments in rotations of duty protecting the viceroy.[83] This was also "the first time such a thing was seen in Mexico."[84]

With his wife, Feliciana, he liked to take long walks through the garden known as the American *pensil* (literally, "beautiful garden") and later as the Mexican *pensil*. During the Enlightenment, gardens had become something very different from what they had been during the Baroque period. This is not the place to elaborate on their use as a means of appropriating nature or on their important connection to the development of botanical sciences.[85] But it is pertinent at least to mention that, according to María Dolores Muñoz Rebolledo and Juan Luis Isaza, late eighteenth-century gardens reflected a new sensibility toward nature, which was now considered a positive environment that complemented urban life.[86]

The Case of the Prisoners' Pardon

On April 8, 1786, José Gómez wrote in his diary that "today has been the most curious day in Mexico. It just so happened that on this day three prisoners were taken from the Acordada jail for execution, and by chance on their way from the jail to the gallows they crossed paths with the viceroy, the count of Gálvez, who was returning on horseback from the American *pensil*. Face to face with them, he pardoned them on behalf of the king our lord, for which the plebeians started shouting, 'Long live the viceroy.'"[87]

This episode has been singled out as an example of Bernardo de Gálvez's relentless appetite for popularity.[88] To assess if this allegation is true, it is necessary to take a closer look at it. Some historians excuse Gálvez's action this day as in line with an old tradition from Malaga, according to which a royal pardon was granted to some prisoners during Holy Week.[89] But in fact this tradition started well after Bernardo de Gálvez's death.[90] Moreover, if such tradition had existed at the time, certainly Bernardo de Gálvez would have mentioned it in a letter dated a few weeks later, when he reported the whole affair to his superior in Madrid.[91] He begins this letter by explaining that when he was returning from the *pensil*, where his family was recovering from illness, he suddenly encountered a crowd following the prisoners and, "not being able to retrace my steps, which could be unbefitting the dignity of my position," had to continue forward. Since "these king's vassals know that he [that is, the king] owns their lives, they also think that the viceroy who represents his royal person here also has all of his powers." The crowd started shouting demands for the prisoners' lives to be spared. Gálvez was in full sight of them, and "having no one to consult with in such predicament, I questioned, on one hand, whether I would surpass my authority by acquiescing to the demands of the crowd, or, on the other, whether in denying their requests . . . they would condemn me as heartless and destroy in a single blow the useful belief they have had in the dignity I embody." The letter continues with several references to the king's magnanimity, which are too unctuous, even for the elaborate language of the time, and ends by "humbly pleading that, if Your Majesty deigns to approve an action that has produced the best effect on these unhappy vassals, the life of these prisoners be spared."

From the details included in his explanations, the ingratiating language he uses (such as "having no one to consult with in such predicament"), his reiterated considerations of how useful the pardons have been, and the prudent silence about the affair maintained by the *Gazeta de México*, it is clear that Bernardo de Gálvez was worried. He himself admits that he had overstepped his powers as viceroy, as indeed, according to the law in force at the time, he had.[92] But he would have to wait until November 22 of that year for a resolution of the affair to arrive in Mexico City with the official mail. An August 5 royal order finally approved "Your Excellency's prudent action in suspending the execution of three prisoners" but added that from now on the judge should inform the viceroy about the date and time of executions, so that "Your Excellency can refrain from going outside the palace while prisoners are being taken to the gallows."[93]

Partying and Dancing

If going to bullfights and strolling through Mexico City gave Gálvez a chance to mingle, so did the parties and dances that he attended and hosted. Despite the anonymous accusation that "everywhere I see you / except attending mass," in fact according to José Gómez's accounts and those in the *Gazeta de México*, during his first year in office Bernardo attended only six parties, or one every two months.[94] Two of these could be considered official gatherings: an event on January 20 in honor of the king's birthday (at the time a sort of national day) and an event on March 19 in honor of Saint Joseph, patron saint of his uncle José (until very recently in Spain, birthday celebrations were less important than the parties given on one's name day, which is the feast day of one's patron saint).[95] Of the other gatherings Bernardo attended, two in particular stand out. The first was on October 12, 1785, when his son, Miguel, wore his new grenadier's uniform for the first time. That day, on the rooftop terrace of the viceregal palace, Bernardo gathered all of the officers and grenadiers of the New Spain Crown Regiment, to which his son belonged.[96] The other gathering took place in June 1786, when the whole family moved to San Agustín de las Cuevas in Tlapan, at the time a few miles from Mexico City. There, "such a trip had never been seen, not because it was fun but overwhelming: two days of bullfighting, cockfighting, fandangos in all the houses, squares, and streets, and lights everywhere; to the point that since the conquest of this kingdom, no such thing has been ever seen, nor any viceroy more applauded than the count de Gálvez."[97]

The Affair of the Funeral

Another episode that helps convey what has been called Gálvez's new style of governance and that also reveals a important facet of his personality took place on April 21, 1786. Again according to José Gómez's diary, that day "the viceroy went to the village of Chapultepec, and saw a dead man. He asked why he had not been buried. He was told that it was because the family had no money to pay for the priest's services. He asked for the priest and told him to bury the man, since he would pay for it himself. The priest answered him that he would do it some other day, since there were no singers. His Excellency retorted that it did not matter; since the man was to be buried that same afternoon, he himself would help in singing the anthems. In this way he attended the burial and helped with the singing and gave the widow sixteen pesos. This was the action of a very Christian prince."[98]

The importance of this anecdote goes beyond Gómez's comment about Gálvez being a "very Christian prince." Instead of pulling rank when faced with the insolence of the priest, he simply solved the problem by singing the anthems himself. Bernardo de Gálvez loved music, played the guitar, and liked to compose light tunes and funny songs, as his friend Francisco de Saavedra recorded in his diaries.[99] Music also relaxed him: for example, whenever he fell seriously ill he would always ask for music to be played while he was eating.[100] At the end of the burial, he gave some money to the widow and left. With such gestures it is not surprising that he was enormously popular among the Mexican people.

GÁLVEZ'S MILITARY MINDSET

Above all else, Bernardo de Gálvez was a soldier, and this experience greatly influenced the way he approached his position as viceroy. Of course he was neither the first nor the last member of the military to serve as New Spain's viceroy. But on multiple occasions he faced his challenges as viceroy in the same manner that he had previously faced challenges on the battlefield.

John Keegan calls "the imperative of example," the one that demands that the commander be physically present so the troops feel that he shares, at least in part, the dangers they face.[101] Time and again during his military career, Bernardo de Gálvez proved himself worthy of his men. In Algiers, despite his wounds, he did not retreat until the last of his men was safe; in the march toward Manchac he walked with them; and in Pensacola, he went alone inside the bay so as not to risk the life of a single man. As viceroy of New Spain he continued to govern with this kind of attitude.

Examples of his display of this attitude include the time he was the first to contribute to the fund for the relief of the hungry[102] and when he ordained that feeding people was more important than feeding horses and so moved through town in a small two-mule carriage instead of the six-horse state coach to which he was entitled as viceroy.[103] In February 1786, while visiting a hospice, it was not enough for him to see and touch the food given to the poor. Instead, "he tasted it himself to have a proper idea of it."[104] It was and still is a rule in the army that officers must taste the mess before their men.[105]

While in civilian life at the time bosses usually kept their contact with employees to a minimum, punishing the most serious mistakes or wrongdoings but almost never thinking about promotions, Royal Army regulations stipulated that officers had the duty to be aware of their subordinates' merits and faults, rewarding the former and punishing the latter.[106] Bernardo de Gálvez was doing exactly what he was used to doing in the army when, on October 11, 1785, in the midst of a serious crisis in New Spain, he issued an order to all royal officials with the promise that if it were executed with as much zeal as he himself would exert, they would be rewarded as they deserved, but if not, he would punish them severely.[107]

Maybe the best example of Bernardo de Gálvez's military mindset can be seen in his son Miguel's military career.[108] To describe Miguel's military career as "early" would be a huge understatement. As already seen, after receiving holy water from the priest during his baptism in Guarico, his parents changed Miguel into a little uniform of the grenadiers. Bernardo's unit, the New Spain Crown Regiment, was one of the most prestigious in all of New Spain and was also the one his father had served in during his campaigns in Mexico's northern provinces. "An old grenadier of long years of service, a good man, and the most senior of his corps" represented the godfather at the baptism and was promoted by Bernardo de Gálvez to the rank of captain in the Guanajuato Militias.[109] On October 12, 1785, a huge party took place at the viceregal palace on the occasion of Miguel's donning of a new uniform when he was only three.[110] Later I will return to criticism of the viceroy for allowing his first son to be passed arm to arm among the soldiers and grenadiers.[111] But among the troops, this kind of familiarity brought Bernardo de Gálvez huge popularity. A few months later, Miguel was promoted to second sergeant, and all of the noncommissioned officers from the New Spain Crown Regiment went to the palace to watch solemnly as he was pinned with his new stripes.[112] On October 1, 1786, Miguel received yet another promotion, this time to first sergeant.[113]

At the time, an early military career was not uncommon among aristocratic families with a military tradition, and having children wear uniforms in times of war was considered a patriotic gesture. For example, Thomas "Tad" Lincoln, Abraham Lincoln's fourth son, used to wear the Union uniform during the Civil War. In old European monarchies, it is still custom for the heir to the crown to start a military career at a very early age by being attached to one of the most prestigious regiments of his or her country. For example, on May 28, 1977, the Prince of Asturias, later King Felipe VI, was appointed honorary private in the King's Immemorial Regiment,[114] the oldest Spanish regiment and one of the oldest in the entire world.

A VICEROY PERHAPS TOO POPULAR

Bernardo de Gálvez's popularity among the people in Mexico was immense, and he also was well regarded by top royal officials. On May 26, 1786, the *royal audiencia*, the supreme administrative body of New Spain, whose members, significantly, were appointed not by the viceroy but by the king himself, wrote a letter to Carlos III. After pointing out some aspects of Bernardo's performance as viceroy, the members duly noted that "his humanity, his kindness, and natural cordiality that everybody welcomes, and his familiarity make the public content" and concluded that "this *royal audiencia*

Portrait of Miguel de Gálvez, second Count of Gálvez, Bernardo de Gálvez's only son and heir to his title. He served in the military from an early age but did not have a very distinguished career. After the execution of King Louis XVI, he and his mother, Feliciana or Felicitas, were suspected of being supporters of the French Revolution. During the French invasion of Spain, between 1808 and 1814, Miguel might have even served under the French occupation authorities. He died childless at the age of forty-two, and the title of Count of Gálvez passed to his older sister Matilde. Regrettably, no genuine portrait of Feliciana Saint-Maxent de Gálvez, widow Countess of Gálvez, has been found. (*Portrait of the count of Gálvez*, oil on canvas, late eighteenth century; Madrid: Museo del Prado, inventory no. P03734, © Madrid, Museo Nacional del Prado)

... assures Your Majesty that this North America will flourish, and will live happily under his [Gálvez's] hand for many years, as promised by this well-regulated, virtuous, and special beginning to the first year of his dignified and well-deserved viceregal government."[115] In his answer, the king, through his minister of the Indies, José de Gálvez, conveyed his satisfaction with the prudent, judicious, and active conduct of the Count of Gálvez, present viceroy of that kingdom, and offered to continue him in his present duties for the satisfaction and solace of his vassals of New Spain, "so long as he does not require him with more urgency for another assignment or commission."[116]

During Bernardo de Gálvez's mandate, at least two works appeared in Mexico celebrating his accomplishments. The first, written by Father José Joaquín Granados y Gálvez (who could have been a distant relative), was published in 1785 under the title *Elogios poéticos que a los insignes hechos del Excmo. Sr. Don Bernardo de Gálvez* (Poetic praises of the notable actions by His Excellency Señor Don Bernardo de Gálvez).[117] The other was by Francisco de Rojas y Rocha and bears the title *Poema épico: La rendición de Panzacola y conquista de la Florida occidental por el Excmo. Sr. Conde de Gálvez* (Epic poem: The surrender of Pensacola and the conquest of West Florida by His Excellency the Count of Gálvez).[118]

Gálvez's popularity also attracted critics, such as the early Mexican historian Carlos María Cavo Bustamante, who abandoned any pretense of historical objectivity when he showed his contempt for the viceroy by writing, "The count of Gálvez made great efforts to win a popularity hitherto unknown, and that tarnished, not to say prostituted, the dignity of the position of viceroy. What was this about pleasing the mob by wheeling his small coach inside a bullring, as Nero could have done in Rome, just to be applauded? What about sitting beside a slut woman bullfighter, offending public decency and even his own wife, who witnessed it? ... [The insults continue for several lines.] We can only believe that the viceroy had lost his mind, and that he needed the restraints supplied by the law on extravagant and dissipated young men."[119]

Bernardo de Gálvez's popularity was based not only on what I have called his new style of government. It also derived from some of his governmental actions as viceroy, which will be studied in the next section.

THE YEAR OF THE HUNGER

Only a few months after Bernardo de Gálvez was sworn in as viceroy, disaster struck Mexico. According to Alexander von Humboldt, "A very remarkable meteorological phenomenon contributed principally to the scarcity. The maize, after an extraordinary drought, was nipped by frost on the night of August 28, and, what is more remarkable, at an elevation of 1,800 meters. The number of inhabitants carried off by this fatal union of famine and disease throughout the whole kingdom was estimated at more than three hundred thousand."[120]

This was to be called "the year of the hunger."[121] By mid-September news of the famine began to reach Mexico City, and weeks later it was already clear that the situation was extremely serious.[122] After receiving several preliminary reports, Bernardo de Gálvez held two meetings with his top officials. After hearing them out, on October 11 he published a proclamation announcing the first of urgent measures to be taken.[123] In a letter to his uncle dated some two weeks later, he reassured him that he was fully aware of the enormous challenge ahead: "I think, Your Excellency, that during the time of my government, no other more important, serious, grave, delicate, or complex issue can occur; but also that no other will be faced with more concern, determination, care, and will to work."[124]

To have all possible information about the situation, Bernardo de Gálvez ordered royal officials, "without wasting a moment," to collect data from "all landowners in their respective departments" and compile this evidence into complete reports, to be sent to Mexico City by the first available post. In addition to information about the amounts of grain available, he demanded to know the prices of various grains in their markets and how much was needed for consumption in each department, so as to calculate the amounts that could be sent to other locations. It was also important to buy up as much grain as possible, so as to ensure that a sufficient supply of seeds would be available in the markets for the next harvest. For that purpose, money was needed—urgently. The bishop of Michoacán was the first to offer 30,000 pesos as a loan without interest.[125]

This was not enough—far from it—so Gálvez called together the "most distinguished citizens of all classes and states, and in a brief, elegant speech expressed to them their obligation to help the needy in this calamity."[126] To further encourage their generosity he publicly thanked them in the November 8 edition of the *Gazeta de México*, where a list of donors was published, and "to allow the public properly to show them their gratitude, and so their merit and generosity would be known, [of said merits] he [the viceroy] would immediately inform His Majesty."[127] That edition included a list of eighteen persons who made loans without interest, amounting to half a million pesos. In later editions of the *Gazeta de México* new donor lists appeared.[128] In another meeting Bernardo de Gálvez thanked the citizens for the funds already "donated" and went one step further by offering 12,000 pesos that remained from his father's estate and 1,000 more that he had to borrow.[129] This gesture was certainly grand, but in fact at that moment his inheritance from his father was out of his reach. At the end of their tenures, all Spanish high officials had to go through a so-called *juicio de residencia* or public investigation of their governments, during which their personal assets were frozen.[130] Even though in Matías de Gálvez's case the process was shortened, because of the important facts that he had died while on duty and his brother was who he was, at the time Bernardo de Gálvez made his offer the *juicio de residencia* was still under way and in fact would not end until September 1786. So his father's estate was not yet his to dispose of.[131] In any case, it is also true that he could easily have borrowed the 12,000 pesos or even 100,000 more. What banker would dare not lend money to the viceroy?

The proclamation of October 11, 1785, created a *junta de conferencias*, or sort of permanent committee, composed of representatives of the most important institutions (three from the civilian cabildo, two from the consulate, and two from the church cabildo) as well as some prominent private citizens (two ranchers, a military officer, a priest, two mine owners, four landowners, and three more persons with unidentified professions). This *junta* met every Monday in the city council office, and its main duty was to suggest any kind of measure to solve "this very serious issue."[132] Following Mexico City's example, *juntas* were created in other cities, including Puebla and Morelia.[133]

To keep the markets supplied, all landowners, "of whatever condition they might be," were ordered to assume responsibility for the transport of their products. To facilitate this, all taxes on the transit of the products were suspended.[134] This measure would later be extended to all taxes in general, once it became clear that the crisis made it almost impossible for most farmers to pay their taxes on time.[135] In a desperate attempt to reduce prices and increase the supply of grain, especially corn, for human consumption, it was ordered that none should be fed to animals. At the same time, all kinds of advice were offered on new ways to cook other produce, including a recipe for a "Dauphiné soup" by José Antonio de Alzate, one from the parish priest of Pénjamo for "making tortillas using ground *olote* with salt," "seven recipes for economic and satisfying cooking" from the bishop of Michoacán, and various tips appearing in the *Gazeta de México*, such as encouraging cattle to be fed with "*tejocotes*, alfalfa, and *olotes*" instead of corn.[136] To this same purpose, it was ordered that the number of mules and horses in carriage teams be reduced. Recall that Bernardo de Gálvez set the example by replacing the six-horse coach to which he was entitled as viceroy with a carriage pulled by two mules.[137]

These measures on the supply side aimed both to keep the markets open and to prevent "a rise in price of a first-necessity product for poor people."

One rise in price was blamed on those "who had closed their granaries and stopped the sale [of grain], causing grave damage to the poor, who even with money in their hands could find nowhere to buy their food." According to historian Laura Pérez Rosales, "In 1786 the price of one *fanega* was between 16 and 24 *reales* in Zacatecas [and] 24 to 28 in Nieves and Sombrerete ... while the average price for the period was no more than 12.2 *reales*."[138] The next step taken by the royal authorities was to establish public prices, with severe sanctions for black marketeers.[139] Another abuse suffered by the poorest was that instead of receiving part of their pay in cash and the rest in goods, as determined by the law, landowners began to pay them all in cash, and laborers could not afford to pay the new prices for food.[140]

An additional worry was population displacement resulting from thousands of country laborers flooding into the cities in search of food. To prevent this migration Bernardo de Gálvez ordered local officials to ensure that their villages were properly supplied, and if this was not possible, to "prevent such disasters in their jurisdictions, using their authority to keep inhabitants from moving out and foreigners from moving in." Orders in the October 11 proclamation were augmented with those published on March 8, 1786, which included "instructions to prevent poor Indians from abandoning their villages to go to the capital, and [to ensure that] in their daily food distribution the assistance centers paid attention that it was done with the utmost care."[141] Despite these efforts, it was impossible to contain the flood of hungry peasants into the cities, where their presence increased already serious supply problems.[142] In April 1786 another proclamation ordered "all beggars in the city to be sent to the hospice, [and] the able ones to labor in public works."[143] Later, when taking a look at Mexico City's Royal Hospice House, I will return to this subject.

The October 11 proclamation also included other medium-term measures, such as the immediate "sowing of corn, bean, and other seeds ... in the warmer lands" of Mexico to provide food and seed for the next harvest. The proclamation included obligations for almost everyone. Bernardo de Gálvez committed himself "to not sparing any effort that could contribute to ending the current need, and to reestablish abundance, and with it to ensure food for all inhabitants of this kingdom." Of public officials he demanded "punctual and exact implementation" of their orders, threatening them if they failed to do so. On landowners he imposed the responsibility of transporting their produce to local markets, supplying a certificate showing grain and seeds kept in their granaries, keeping their granaries and shops open so that "miserable Indians and poor people" could buy grain "at reasonable prices," and doing everything else stated in the proclamation, "for I do not want to be forced to take upon myself any serious action needed to help out these miserable people."[144]

According to Luz María Espinosa Cortés, Fabiola Rueda Arroniz, and Rosa María Andrade, during the year of the hunger a clear conflict between classes appeared, and tensions between landowners and the state also became more evident, especially as landowners had been pushing for the closure of the *alhóndigas* and *pósitos*, public grain storehouses, which they had considered an obstacle to the development of agriculture since the late seventeenth century.[145] It is precisely in this context that the October 11, 1785, proclamation needs to be understood. Tensions between royal officials and landowners only increased as the situation deteriorated. The privileges of Mexican hacendados during the late eighteenth century were not very different from those still evident in the 1930s, when the American journalist Henry Carr traveled though the country. In his book, *Old Mother Mexico*, he clearly describes how landowners managed their haciendas in more or less the same fashion that feudal lords had managed their estates in the Middle Ages.[146] Bernardo de Gálvez's fight against speculators and black marketeers was complemented by orders to public officials to be aware "of speculation by rich farmers and landowners, who sowed less this year than they usually did in previous years, so as not to lose money by harvesting crops that were overabundant."[147] They were also to pay special attention to what the hacendados "could say in private conversation . . . about the corn having a very low price if the next harvests were too abundant, and because of that decided to sow less than in past years."[148] Following the viceroy's orders, royal officials were extremely vigilant about any sign of hoarding or speculation. The archives are full of reports from all over Mexico informing the capital about this kind of abuse and the measures taken to correct and punish the perpetrators.[149]

The hunger was followed by a series of epidemics with a myriad of names: the *bola* (ball), intermittent fevers and pneumonia, malign fevers and spleen pains, measles, epidemic fevers, pleuritic pains, and *tabardillas* (a kind of typhus).[150] These diseases, combined with weakness caused by malnutrition, left thousands dead. Most probably the figure of 300,000 given by Alexander von Humboldt is exaggerated, but the scale of the disaster was unprecedented.[151]

Thousands of corpses had to be buried, including 50,000 in Nueva Galicia, in today's state of Jalisco, where new cemeteries had to be opened.[152] Medical practices at the time recommended preventing the spread of disease through such measures as "chasing pigs, dogs, and other filthy animals, and forcing garbage to be collected," and, later, killing all dogs and ensuring their quick burial to prevent the butchers from selling their meat.[153]

Masses, processions, and other kind of manifestations of religious fervor multiplied all over Mexico as the population was confronted with these disasters.[154] But the response of the church to the crisis was not to be limited to these religious activities. Among the first to be alert to the gravity of the situation were the bishops of Guanajuato, Guadalajara, and Michoacán.[155] The church was an extremely important source of information for royal officials, and Bernardo de Gálvez received detailed reports from the bishop of Puebla.[156] And the first person to advance money for the crisis was the bishop of Michoacán.[157] To the initial sum of 30,000 pesos he later added, among other sums, 70,000 for the city of Guanajuato, 40,000 for villages in Tierra Caliente, 9,000 for Pátzcuaro, and 4,000 for the village of Uruapan, to the point that, according to Jesús Romero Flores, by the end of 1785 the bishop had distributed 288,000 pesos.[158] Many pastors, priests, and other religious figures were very aggressive in the fight against speculation. Especially active was the bishop of Michoacán, who passed information to the viceroy about certain subjects in Tierra Caliente suspected of manipulating the price of corn and sent commissioners to gather information in different locations to prevent further speculation.[159]

In mid-1786 the situation started to improve. At the end of May, Bernardo de Gálvez wrote to his uncle that recent showers could be announcing that next year's harvest would be a good one, and since the epidemics were starting to ebb, he was confident that the following months would bring better news.[160] In his answer, José de Gálvez conveyed the king's satisfaction with the good news he had received, which was in large part a product of the "charitable zeal of the wealthy inhabitants of those parts."[161] During the following months Bernardo de Gálvez continued to inform the court of progress, sometimes not hiding the fact that if the weather forecasts of experts were not confirmed, the situation would grow even worse, since all available resources had already been spent.[162] In the end, the harvest was indeed extremely good, but problems did not end there, because profiteers "lock up and hide the [seeds and grain] they have, and sell them in small amounts . . . at a price determined by greed."[163] Bernardo de Gálvez's fury against these profiteers was registered in a letter dated September 1786, in which he complains about "the malice of those who inhumanely push for the high price of seeds not to go down . . . against whom I have taken, without any delay, all measures I have deemed necessary."[164]

It is important to emphasize that these measures, some of which have already been mentioned, contributed a great deal to increasing his already significant popularity among the less fortunate. Juan Antonio Flores, mayor of Metepec, said in a letter dated March 1786 that Bernardo de Gálvez's actions against these abuses earned him the favor of the local population.[165] But it seems that his concern for the people was not dictated merely by cold political calculation. He had a concept of society that could not tolerate such behavior by its richest members. Clearly stated in article 7 of his October 11, 1785, proclamation is that "these unhappy people, . . . although poor, are the ones who fatten the rich by giving with one hand what they receive with the other, and are the ones who enrich the kingdom with their arms through work, with their persons through war, and with the taxes they pay."[166] In another letter to his uncle he wrote, "It is they who make up the force and the nerve of the state, farming the land, breeding the livestock, working in the mines, and practicing all trades and arts."[167]

INDIAN POLICY

By the end of the eighteenth century, the Indian population of New Spain—which at the time was not only present-day Mexico but also most of what is now the southern United States as well as most of Central America—was about two and a half million people.[168] Taking into account that the total number of inhabitants of New Spain was between four and six million, Native Americans represented about two-fifths to nearly two-thirds of the population.[169] They were sufficiently numerous that a viceroy could not afford to ignore them or fail to engage with them. According to María del Carmen Galbis Díez, the constant interest of Bernardo de Gálvez in his people was shown by his efforts to better the living conditions of the Indians.[170] She offers two examples of this, concerning the Indian *gañanes* in the haciendas and the Indian *solicitadores*.

The Indian Gañanes in the Haciendas

In eighteenth-century Spanish, a *gañán* was the lowest kind of shepherd to work in the haciendas.[171] His work was devoid of the pejorative connotations that it has today. Although the haciendas functioned much like in a feudal state, as we have already seen, the origin of this particular kind of labor relation was specific to America. During the first decades of Spanish domination of the continent, the system of encomiendas regulated the work of the Native Americans for their new masters.[172] The model was prone to abuse and quickly developed into a system of de facto slavery until, in 1542, the so-called Leyes Nuevas (New Laws) abolished it. In its place a new system was introduced that, according to Demetrio Ramos Pérez, took into account the interests of the conquistadors and settlers while protecting the freedom and property of the natives, who had to work for their personal benefit as well as that of their communities and the whole society but could not be forced to work and had to be paid.[173] During the seventeenth century the system evolved into free contracts between employers and employees, based on salaries determined by law.[174] Nevertheless, abuses continued, especially against the least skilled laborers, such as the *gañanes*. In 1687, the *audiencia* issued a royal order emphasizing that their salaries should be paid in produce and clothing, to prevent their permanent servitude by a perverse system of loans.[175] The abuse was that the *gañanes* were paid with coupons that could be exchanged only in the haciendas' shops. Since the landowners controlled these shops, they determined the prices and kept them artificially high. By the end of the month it usually happened that the *gañanes*, through advances or loans against their salaries, owed more money than they had earned, so they had to remain working for the landowner until their debts were settled, which never happened. In fact, when the *gañán* died his children were burdened with their father's debt, and so a de facto system of slavery was perpetuated by this vicious circle.

The immediate origin of the particular case that Bernardo de Gálvez had to face dated back to February 1778, when the Indian Felipe Santiago, *gañán* in a hacienda in Tepeaca, presented an official complaint against his landowner so as to "be declared free to move out and to go work where he wanted, to which, with the approval of the district attorney, the viceroy agreed, but further ordering an investigation into the working conditions of all *gañanes* in the region." According to the file, the investigation found that Felipe Santiago's case was not unique—far from it, since in most of the haciendas the *gañanes* "were forced to work longer than from sunrise to sunset, [and were] punished for the slightest fault with lashes, blows, or incarceration; even their women were forced to work at hard tasks not suited to their weakness and the decency of their sex, without any kind of payment."[176] The case arrived before the then-viceroy, Matías de Gálvez, who issued a decree on March 28, 1784, that could not be published because of his serious illness, which ended with his death several months later. The *audiencia*, acting on behalf of the next viceroy, published a proclamation on June 3, 1785, that called for "preserving and taking care of the miserable Indians ... to respect their freedom, redeem them from vexations, and regulate their work."[177] An appeal by representatives of the landowners arguing that the former viceroy's decree had been suspended while the matter was referred to the courts in Madrid motivated Bernardo de Gálvez to take the problem into his own hands after he was sworn in as viceroy.[178] On November 23, 1785, the judge from Apan wrote him that "the unhappiness and misery of the poor Indian workers in this district is such that when at mid-day they take a rest from their work and should be eating something, some can only lie down with nothing to eat, and others have to go around the countryside in search of some wild herbs to eat, to partly satiate their hunger."[179] Confronted with such depictions, Bernardo de Gálvez answered with a proclamation that exclaimed, "What heart would not be moved by such a degree of calamity and misery!" He was clearly angered and frustrated, since

> it seemed that with these well thought-out decrees, if properly implemented by royal officials, nothing more would be needed, and the landowners would be well served and provided with hands to work their lands, and the Indians employed in this labor would have enough to eat, earned by their own sweat. Yet, despite all this, it does not happen in certain places, and I am forced to repeat, explain, and expand these precise and clear instructions. . . . I infer that Paragraph 8 of my October 11 proclamation is not being implemented, since if it were, the Indians would have enough corn to feed themselves. . . . Therefore I repeat and ratify the above-mentioned Paragraph 8 of my October 11 proclamation and instruct all royal officials to ensure that it is properly and fully implemented and [according to] the manner in which it has been already explained. . . . Be aware that proper measures will be taken to make myself obeyed in case of the slightest contravention.[180]

In essence, Gálvez reiterated what he had already ordered, that Indians should not be paid only in cash but also in goods and foods, since with price increases it would otherwise be impossible for them to feed themselves and their families. However, he changed this order a bit by authorizing advance payments to them of up to five pesos in cash, which the Indians could repay either in cash or with work, according to the customary salaries in a particular place.[181] Meanwhile, the appeal by the landowners continued its course in the courts, and in February 1788 the case reached the Council of the Indies, accompanied by a report from the Royal Treasury representative advising caution, since "excessive freedom [for the Indians] could end to their detriment." The representative suggested that a system similar to that already in place in the mines be implemented, which was basically to keep the Indians working until their entire debt was settled.[182] In the end the landowners won the argument.

The Indian Solicitadores

After several cases of abuses were brought to the viceroy's attention, Bernardo de Gálvez took steps to regulate Indians' access to the judicial system. At the time the Spanish judicial system had three kinds of legal professionals: *abogados* (lawyers), *procuradores* (attorneys), and *solicitadores* (solicitors).

The latter occupied the lowest rung on the ladder of justice. In charge of dealing directly with clients, they were responsible for writing down petitions, complaints, and other legal documents for a mostly illiterate population.[183] Bernardo's December 5, 1785, decree called "for better assistance, speed, and proper processing of the lawsuits and proceedings brought by Indians, by employees in charge of them."[184] The decree included such measures as an obligation clearly to display royal tariffs and the amount of gratuity for services to all poor clients, with a penalty of two pesos for the first sanction, four for repeated sanctions, and the loss of one's position if it happened again; a physical separation between two Indian solicitors, so they could not know the business the other was taking care of; admission of all documents submitted by Indians, even if they were not signed by a known lawyer, attorney, or solicitor, as long as their content could be verified by other means; an obligation to write down tariffs so there would be no confusion about them; the posting of working hours of royal officials in charge of Indian affairs; and, finally, an examination to become a solicitor, as was the case for both attorneys and lawyers.

The Northern Frontier and the Policy Regarding the "Barbaric Indians"

In describing Bernardo de Gálvez's campaigns against the Apache between 1769 and 1771, I transcribed some of his opinions about how the Crown should deal with the "barbaric Indians." The term "barbaric Indians" was the one employed at the time and is used by most present-day historians.[185] "Barbaric Indians" were those who lived mainly in the borderlands of the Spanish Empire and refused to be assimilated into its social structures. Now, as viceroy, Bernardo de Gálvez did not let the opportunity escape to put his ideas into practice, and he designed an entire policy regarding this complex issue.

Bernardo de Gálvez's *Instrucción formada en virtud de Real Orden de S.M.* (Instruction for governing the Interior Provinces of New Spain) was a set of orders and recommendations addressed to Jacobo de Ugarte y Loyola, general commander of the Interior Provinces of New Spain. It was drafted by Bernardo de Gálvez personally and signed in Mexico City on August 12, 1786.[186] Two days later it was presented to a committee of representatives of the main stakeholders—lawyers, landowners, and military officers—who unanimously approved it.[187] The *Instrucción* was an order enacted under his powers as viceroy, but Bernardo de Gálvez wanted it to be backed by the king himself, so he sent it to the royal court, which approved it in full by a royal order dated February 27, 1787.[188] With 216 articles, the *Instrucción* can be viewed as a set of measures for the pacification of the Interior Provinces, with "methodic and clear points" that Bernardo de Gálvez presents with the utmost candor and straightforwardness.[189] As he himself explains, it should not be considered a comprehensive program, which he was unable to draft because of "time [constraints] and other important issues" that demanded his attention.[190] The *Instrucción* was designed to be flexible and, in giving an important margin of maneuvering to Jacobo de Ugarte, adaptable to changing conditions on the ground. "If in certain parts of the provinces difficulties or inconveniences are found," wrote Bernardo, "its implementation can be suspended, [and] showing me the causes for it, I will have no problem changing my resolutions, or gladly embracing those offered to me for better service to the king, as well as for the welfare of those provinces."[191]

A New Model for Relations with the Apache

For the Spanish Crown to change its traditional policies about the "barbaric Indians" in general, and the Apache in particular, two factors were involved: the persistence, and in some cases the recrudescence, of old problems, and a new generation of royal officials and military officers, who dared to look at them from a new perspective.[192]

In 1786 Spanish authorities on both sides of the Atlantic were deeply worried about the situation on the northern frontier of New Spain. The "sorry state" of those lands had not changed in more than three centuries of Spanish rule.[193] Neither "the zeal nor the prudence" of Bernardo de Gálvez's predecessors had "remedied their misfortune," and "the preservation of the interior dominions costs the Royal Treasury millions of pesos." Bernardo de Gálvez estimated that while in 1723, with 734 *presidiales* (presidio troops) in the region, the cost was 283,930 pesos per year, in 1786, with nearly 4,000 *presidiales*, the cost was more than 1 million pesos.[194] Although "today its [that is, the Interior Provinces'] pacification presents even more difficulties than before," Bernardo de Gálvez decided to try to at least confront the problem with his usual zeal and enthusiasm.

From his own experience, Gálvez was perfectly aware of the difficulties of assessing the real situation on the ground. News and reports were abundant, but they were often contradictory. While some spoke of the total ruin of the region, others insisted that the problems were only minor or restricted to a specific area. For example, an account from an earlier period showed why catastrophic views had to be taken with a grain of salt. In 1673 a royal official named Mancera wrote to his superiors in Mexico City that "some news concerning minor hostilities by the Indians is so exaggerated that it could be about invasions by Vandals and Goths."[195] Bernardo de Gálvez was aware that this kind of exaggeration had to be approached with care, since it could be motivated by particular interests that were not always compatible with "the common interests of the rest of the inhabitants, the king's treasury, and his better service." In particular, testimonies and accounts from landowners had to be properly checked against the facts. According to Sara Ortelli, despite official discourse portraying the loosely controlled territory as marginal and isolated, that condition was extremely convenient for the landowners, since it allowed them to organize their productive and commercial activities with the greatest freedom, evade taxes, sell their products at higher prices, grab lands at lower ones, and control the region's main access routes.[196]

On top of this, it was common for the Apache to be accused of crimes that were actually committed by gangs of common criminals, who were responsible for most thefts of cattle, kidnappings, and murders.[197] To multiply his sources of information, Gálvez repeatedly ordered his officials to keep him up to date, not only about the progress of specific military operations but also about the general situation. He did not forget to ask them for eventual proposals for improvement.[198] In any case, Bernardo de Gálvez agreed with the landowners and most officials and officers on the ground that the greatest threat to peace on the northern frontier came from the Apache, who "are the real enemy." He believed that a solution could come only from "their voluntary or forced submission . . . or their total extermination." Since the first option was impossible "unless by God's miracle," and extermination was impracticable, forced submission was the only realistic choice. To achieve this, Gálvez designed a new policy clearly summarized in article 195 of the *Instrucción*: "Constant [war] against the declared enemy [that is, the Apache] will achieve their punishment, containment, and intimidation, to the point that they will leave our borders or ask for peace; this being granted, they will gently be attracted to the comforts of civilized life and to being dependent upon us by means of exchanges or trade and the proper gifts; if peace is broken either because of their whims or their insufferable treachery, we will return to constant and hard war, alternating this and peace as many times as is determined to be necessary by their arrogant or humble attitude."[199]

In other words, the possibility of a complete and total peace was to be abandoned and replaced by a low-intensity conflict, in which periods of calm would alternate, and even coexist, with military confrontation. While in the past the main instruments were military, now other tools, such as diplomacy and trade, would have an increasingly important role. The ultimate objective was to break the Apache groups' "vicious pillaging" of other communities simply through their acculturation. The new objective was not to defeat the Apache but to weaken them enough to force them into this new system. The first step, however, would be to make war "without interruption in all of the provinces and at all times against the Apache who have declared it on us." The idea was not to organize a general military campaign against them, as had been tried unsuccessfully during the late 1760s, but to confront only those Apache groups that directly defied Spanish rule, since "we must not deceive ourselves that even with the greatest number of veteran troops we will be able pacify the Interior Provinces." Even a local victory against the Apache would only push them against other Indian groups, Bernardo de Gálvez realized, and "the number of our enemies would be increased by those infidels who now live peacefully in the deep valleys of the same mountains, and by those who are unhappy in the mission's villages, and so hostilities would spread to the now peaceful regions of the viceroyalty, and no force would be able to confront the cruel attacks of this multitude of barbarians."

In line with his objective of weakening the Apache, Bernardo de Gálvez ordered military pressure to be combined with other kinds of actions, such as establishing alliances with certain of their enemies and fomenting divisions between different Apache groups. The policy of divide and conquer is as old as war itself: the Romans were masters at it, and the Spaniards implemented it successfully in America from the very start of the conquest. Gálvez himself mentions "the help of the Tlaxcaltecs, and progressively of most of the Indians of New Spain, which contributed to its [the Aztec Empire's] ruin." Applying the equally old principle that "the enemy of my enemy is my friend," the Spaniards welcomed Comanche attacks on the Apache.[200] Bernardo de Gálvez again recommended maintaining an alliance with the Comanche while remaining fully aware that the alliance was merely an instrument in the struggle against the Apache. The Spanish-Comanche alliance would be finally formalized in the Santa Fe agreement signed in 1786, which was almost a decade in the making and was possible only after the military defeat of the Comanche. In 1778, Juan Bautista de Anza, New Mexico's governor, carried out, according to James F. Brooks, the "single most successful military expedition in New Mexican history. His campaign's success derived from innovative tactics, fortunate timing, and probable internal dissension among the Comanches."[201] But since for the Spanish their alliance with the Comanche was an anti-Apache instrument, in regions where the Apache did not constitute a threat, the old alliance with the Yuta Indians was to be maintained for use against the Comanche and the Navajo. The divide-and-conquer maxim was to be mercilessly implemented, according to Bernardo de Gálvez, since the "defeat of the Gentiles [that is, non-Christians] [lies in] making them fight each other until they are completely destroyed. . . . [It] is achieved by encouraging, with efficient deception, disagreements among the various groups of each nation." As for the Apache, Gálvez instructed that the "bloody and vicious disunion between Lipanes and Mescaleros" should be encouraged while "peace should be kept with the Jicarillas against the Gileños." Everything had to be done with extreme caution or, in his words, "with the utmost skill . . . without us being openly involved in their grievances."

On the causes of the Apache Indians going to war, Gálvez clearly thought it was a matter of either necessity or vengeance. War, or the use of violence in their relations with other communities, was so deeply rooted in Apache culture that, according to James L. Haley, their word for "to explore" meant both to roam the country in search of food and to attack.[202] Bernardo de Gálvez admitted that the Apache thirst for vengeance could very well be justified by the abuses they had suffered under the Spaniards, "of which there are thousands of examples, both old and very new." To prevent and correct these abuses he warned that "I will consider it a most serious contravention of my orders if they are given even the slightest cause for complaint . . . and therefore I will make you responsible for problems caused directly or indirectly by any chief or officer, which prompts them to declare war on us."[203] He believed that peace would be sought by the Apache after they were pushed to the brink by the king's arms, and when they asked for it, it should always be granted. Bernardo de Gálvez even suggested the best methods for negotiating peace. In article 81 of the *Instrucción* he states that "it being customary to present the Indians with gifts when they appear with an intention to agree to a peace, I authorize the chiefs or commander in charge of such negotiations to present them with goods, tobacco, food, etc. . . . worth fifteen to twenty pesos, and also one or two pesos to each *gandul* [individual] for himself and his family." It is important to remember that peace was conceived as neither general nor total, since every peace applied only to those who committed to it within a specific region. Peace could also be somehow unstable and even accompanied by sporadic outbursts of violence, although it was peace nonetheless. Bernardo de Gálvez was very clear in stating that "a bad peace with all nations that asked for it would be better than the efforts of a good war." He ordered his subordinates to ignore small breaches of peace and to resort to war only when there was strictly no other choice. In his own words, they should "take no account of certain small defects derived from their ignorance, rough character, or bad habits, but severely punish the serious [defects], taking the opportunity to set an example, when the decorum of our armies can not be compromised."

Since the Apache resorted to war to fill their basic needs, he planned to change their behavior by "trading with them in goods that they like, are interested in, which at the end of the day will make them dependent on us." Trade would also have another positive benefit: "By satisfying their wishes, the king will spend much less than today." Trade as a tool for "civilizing" or "colonizing," depending one's point of view, is an idea that has venerable historical continuity. During the Enlightenment, writers and philosophers developed the idea, which was observed by other European colonial powers in their relations with Natives Americans living in territories claimed by or settled by European powers. The idea of trade as a civilizing tool was advanced by Montesquieu, who in his *De l'esprit des lois* (Spirit of the laws) said that "peace is the natural effect of trade" and its laws "polish and refine the most barbarous [morals]."[204] That this idea was already shared by many of Gálvez's contemporaries is evident in three examples. In 1799 Félix de Anzara shared with the then-viceroy the Marquis de Avilés his opinion about the colonization of the Chaco, who lived in the territory that is present-day Bolivia, Paraguay, and Argentina: "Under these circumstances what I find today is the best and actually the only course of action is to engage in good dealings and trade with these barbarians, so that by following their own interests they will preserve peace, as we see today in Paraguay among the Payaguas and Guanás, and in Buenos Aires with the Pampas."[205] A decade earlier, José Campillo y Cossío had argued that "the choice of domination over the advantages and benefits of trade and a friendly relation with the barbaric nations was the cause both of losing already conquered [peoples] and of not realizing others were as important."[206] And finally, in 1779 José de Gálvez had written to Viceroy Marquis de Croix that, "by this recommended manner of friendship, we will not only have all of the usual advantages [of conquest], but we will also completely dominate our presently relentless enemies without the slightest bloodshed."[207]

Although trade had been used before as a tool for colonization and civilization, what was now being suggested was radically new, both for the straightforwardness with which it was conceived—a clarity that some have considered almost cynical[208]—and for its scope, since the only supervision envisaged would be directed toward the prevention of possible abuses. Trade would include all kinds of products. Bernardo de Gálvez even listed the most popular ones: "horses, mares, mules, cattle, jerky, *piloncillo*, corn, tobacco, liquor, guns, ammunition, knives, clothes or rude fabrics, vermilion, mirrors, beads, and other *bujerias* [metal toys]." Among them several stand out—horses and mares, liquor, guns, and ammunition—because according to the Spanish law for America these items were totally or partially forbidden for the Indians to trade.[209]

Although in 1568 King Felipe II had forbidden the Indians to ride horses, in fact, as already seen, the horse became an integral part of northern Indian culture.[210] Even though this royal decree was, in theory, still in effect, no one thought of enforcing it.

As was previously mentioned, liquor was forbidden to the Indians, and their access to alcohol was limited to their traditional beverages, such as pulque in Mexico.[211] Bernardo de Gálvez considered the traditional policy a mistake, since liquor was in huge demand by the Indians and supplying them with it "would create a new need that would force them to depend on us." Moreover, in his words, its consumption "would be an instrument for controlling them, for discovering their deepest secrets, [and for] numbing them so they would not be able to think about or execute anything against us." In other words, alcohol was an instrument for their acculturation. Although the extent of liquor's impact in Native American cultures has been subject to debate, its effects would be devastating.[212]

The main change to the existing policy was in the trade of guns and ammunitions. At the time a law was still in effect that prohibited Indians from trading or owning guns.[213] This prohibition had been established long before and in theory applied to the entire American territory under the Spanish Crown. But at least one exception had already been made in the case of the Guaraní Indians, living in today's Paraguay, where Jesuit missionaries used Indian militias to defend them against attacks by *bandeirantes* coming in from Brazil. In the battle of Mbororé in 1641, the Guaraní militias defeated a *bandeira* of 450 Dutch and Portuguese soldiers, 700 canoes, and 2,700 Tupí Indians, and in 1790 they warded off an attack by Charrúa Indians, who were devastating the Guaraní and Spanish settlements on the Negro River.[214] We have seen that as governor of Louisiana, Bernardo de Gálvez traded guns and ammunition with the Indians. All of these instances could be considered exceptions to the general prohibition on guns for the Indians, but in fact Bernardo de Gálvez, as the supreme authority of New Spain, was putting a new policy into place. His main reasons for doing so were, first, that the Spaniards were not the only Europeans present in the northern provinces, so if the Indians were not supplied with guns by Spain, others powers would certainly do so; and, second, that one of the lessons he had learned during his campaigns against the Apache between 1769 and 1771 was that their arrows were dangerous.[215] The *Instrucción* is full of reminders about their accuracy and superior rate of fire.[216] So Gálvez concluded that it was better to supply them with guns, "which they anxiously desire," especially since guns require "great care to keep them ready." Moreover, their effective use requires "continuous training," and so it would be a long while before the

Indians could use them with the same expertise as Spanish soldiers. Finally, the need for replacement parts would force the Indians to keep trade open and remain on good terms with the Spaniards. Gálvez felt that the guns supplied to the Indians should be "long barreled, because they are the one the Indians prefer, and they also must have weak flintlocks and butts" and therefore need constant repair, which could be done only by Spanish gunsmiths. In addition, "their size would make them uncomfortable to ride with," and they would be "breaking constantly." Gálvez insisted that the Indians were also to be supplied with unlimited quantities of gunpowder and ammunition, so they "would prefer to use guns over bows and arrows so quickly that they will end up forgetting how to use them, in which case (as long as they do not declare war on us), when they ran out of ammunition, they will return to us." This was the theory, but the Apache would outwit Gálvez's policy not only by not giving up their bows but also by combining the use of both types of weapons. They would use their archers "to cover their musketeers so that they could load and fire in security."[217]

Trade would be complemented by money paid to individual Indian warriors and chiefs in exchange for their friendship, and for that purpose Gálvez sent funds to the authorities in the northern territories of the viceroyalty. According to Ned Blackhawk these allegiances "became cheaper to purchase than to lose, as New Mexico poured gifts and currency into former enemies' hands. Such forms of alliance created expectations of permanent beneficence."[218]

Some of the wording used by Bernardo de Gálvez in the *Instrucción* reflects his personality. Besides a clear proclivity to micromanage, already evident in the attention to detail he displayed time and again, he also showed a tendency to trust people more than structures. For him, being obeyed was not only a question of following the viceroy's orders but also of being personally loyal to him. In the foreword to the *Instrucción*, he states that Jacobo de Ugarte's command of the Interior Provinces was derived from his: "Your command, sir, derives from mine." Not satisfied with this single admonition, he repeats it at least four times in the text. His concept of the personal loyalty due to him becomes clear when he tells Ugarte that everything he does in the Interior Provinces will "acknowledge your immediate subordination to my orders, while I am in command of this viceroyalty."[219]

Having ensured Ugarte's personal attachment to him, Bernardo de Gálvez proceeded to restructure the Interior Provinces. Although Ugarte would remain general commander, the Interior Provinces would be divided into three separate units: Sonora and the Californias to the west, under the direct command of Ugarte; Nueva Vizcaya and New Mexico under José Rangel; and to the east, Texas, Coahuila, Nuevo León, and the colony of Nuevo Santander, under Juan Ugalde. To the heads of each of these new administrative units Gálvez gave separate and detailed instructions for its governance and pacification.[220] With this new structure Gálvez sought to respond faster and better to the situation on the ground. He was aware that "the vast expanse of the interior territories and their borders does not allow for frequent visits from you [Ugarte]; nor news about the war against the Indians to reach you in time, or their peace offers, or other important events; and last but not least, it is also impossible for your orders to be executed with the promptness demanded by unforeseen circumstances, which must be resolved without delay."[221]

He also ordered Ugarte to "give your full attention to military operations," and so that he would be able to do so, Gálvez discharged him from his responsibilities in matters of justice and the Royal Treasury, which Ugarte would merely supervise while the day-to-day work was carried out by people Ugarte would appoint. The military system for the defense of the Interior Provinces was also completely altered. The troops would now be divided into *presidial* companies, *volantes* companies, dragoons, and volunteers. The first were to be garrisons of the presidios, which, as seen before, was the Spanish name for what the United States would later call "forts" during the so-called conquest of the West. The *volantes* companies would not be attached to any particular fort but were to patrol certain areas and serve as reinforcements when more troops were needed to help a presidio or to conduct a specific military operation. The dragoons were cavalry soldiers who moved on horseback but fought on foot, and the volunteers were to be called up when needed, much like the militia replacing the *presidiales* when the latter were called for a specific military action. The volunteers were to receive proper military training, with their discipline and fair treatment assured by their officers and their armaments supplied by local authorities. The accounts of the presidios were to be kept with utmost care to prevent abuses. The officers of the regular military units—*presidiales*, *volantes*, and dragoons—had to be carefully selected. Their pay was to be raised, and their promotion was to be recommended according only to their individual merits. On the latter topic, Bernardo de Gálvez was adamant. He ordered that "neither his dark skin nor the circumstances of his birth should be relevant [for the appointment] of a sergeant or an officer, only his merits, fortitude, courage, knowledge, experience, and aptitude for war, and also his ability to command." Again and again he reiterated this idea, such as when he warned against the practice of "prostituting promotions by giving them to individuals who had not given constant proof of their courage and ability" or when he declared that "I would be very glad to recommend to His Majesty for promotion and other rewards all individuals of any class whatsoever, who have courageously distinguished themselves in combat." He always favored promotions based on merit rather than on simple seniority.

In addition to these reforms, Bernardo de Gálvez took great care to stress the importance of the new combat tactics that he wanted used. These tactics were adapted to the specificities of the terrain as well as to the manner in which the Apache fought. For Gálvez, the war against this kind of enemy "demanded, as do all wars, courage and resolve, but these qualities by themselves could also endanger the success of military operations if not accompanied by experience and first-hand knowledge of the mountains, wells, distances, tracks, ruses, rules, surprise attacks, skirmishes, and other specific abilities, which are part of a science or art not known by many, and learned only in practice."[222]

He emphasized time and again that practice makes perfect, and trusting the officers on the ground to command their troops to their best of their ability, he ordered Ugarte to leave them in "complete freedom, not limiting them in any way whosoever, so that in this way they will proceed without timidity." Bernardo de Gálvez also recommended trying always to use surprise against the Apache as the best way to conduct operations, and even when patrolling never to move along the same paths, with the same force, or at the same time of day, since this would ensure perfect targets for the enemy.

Before Bernardo de Gálvez's *Instrucción* was issued, the troops employed in the Interior Provinces were mainly *dragones de la cuera* (leather dragoons), so-called because of their leather breastplates.[223] The *dragones de la cuera* were heavy cavalry units encumbered with equipment and requiring six horses and a mule for every soldier. Gálvez considered these kinds of troops completely inadequate for the kind of war needed against the Apache, so he ordered them replaced by lighter troops who had greater mobility and needed fewer mounts per soldier. For him mobility and speed were of the utmost importance, almost an obsession. He recognized that large units were slowed down in their movements and that the clouds of dust they raised alerted enemies from miles away. He thus forbade contingents of more than 150 or 200 men. Apache attacks required a quick response, both because otherwise the enemy would be impossible to find, since they would have time to disappear, and because an immediate reaction would increase morale among the local population, who "would see our troops truly committed to their safety and protection." Bernardo de Gálvez added that all of his orders and recommendations must be implemented with "*prudencia mañosa"* (clever good sense) and adapted to the terrain and combat tactics of the Apache.

RESULTS AND ASSESSMENTS OF BERNARDO DE GÁLVEZ'S *INSTRUCCIÓN*

The *Instrucción formada en virtud de Real Orden de S.M.* of 1786 went much further than its predecessors of 1729[224] and 1772.[225] While previous attempts to pacify the Interior Provinces addressed specific challenges, such as excessive defense costs or the construction of a new line of presidios along their vast border, Bernardo de Gálvez's focus on the Apache menace actually resulted in the design of an entirely new policy for the northern frontier of New Spain. Its ambitious character was the source of one of its first problems. After Bernardo de Gálvez's death, the new viceroy, Manuel Antonio Flores Maldonado, considered the *Instrucción* too difficult to implement. But rather than abolishing it or even replacing it with another policy, he simply pushed it aside in favor of the much simpler and easier 1772 regulations.[226] However, Flores's vision, whose implementation would have ended Gálvez's policy, was not to be carried out, at least not completely. As has been seen, Bernardo de Gálvez insisted very much on the loyalty owed to him by Ugarte and other frontier officials and officers, and they did not betray his confidence in them. Even after Gálvez's division of the Interior Provinces into three parts was brushed aside, Ugarte remained their supreme commander, and despite the fact that he was a strong supporter of a policy of military confrontation with the Apache, he continued to implement, if not the letter, at least the general spirit of Bernardo de Gálvez's *Instrucción*. In fact, Viceroy Flores's replacement, Juan Vicente de Güemes Pacheco y Padilla, second Count of Revillagigedo, reinstated the *Instrucción*, if not in its entirety, at least in its main policy.[227] Thus Bernardo de Gálvez's Indian policy remained the official Spanish policy until the very end of Spain's dominion over North America. To evaluate its impact, it is relevant to turn to testimonies from the 1790s, which unanimously point out the peace and prosperity enjoyed by the region,[228] which refocused its government from a military to a policing purpose.[229]

Several assessments of Bernardo de Gálvez's Indian policy stress its practical and extremely candid approach to pacification of the provinces and confrontation with the Apache, concluding that it was cynical and subversive but distinctly utilitarian nevertheless, the intent being to subdue the Apache by promoting social disorganization and corrupting their will to fight. For nearly twenty-five years the new policy worked with moderate success.[230] But about its effectiveness all historians agree,[231] even on the point that, according to María Adelina Arredondo López, the policy introduced by Bernardo de Gálvez in the Interior Provinces made possible a relative peace from 1787 to 1831.[232]

Overall, the war with the Apache serves as a touchstone against which the general policy of the Spanish Crown toward the "barbaric Indians" can be assessed.[233] It is true that the Apache were not the only Native American group that resisted assimilation into the social scheme designed for Spanish America, but their tenacity was perceived by royal authorities as a threat that had to be properly and forcefully contained. For centuries the Spanish response had been partial and purely military in nature, but under Bernardo de Gálvez a new approach was applied. He personally had fought the Apache before becoming viceroy, and in order to defeat them he had studied their culture, customs, way of living, and combat tactics. Instead of blaming everything on the Apache, he understood the reasons for their aggressive behavior. Aware of the complex interplay of interests involved, he rarely accepted at face value the alarming news supplied by landowners and settlers and instead typically searched for other sources of information, so as to have a complete picture of the real situation on the ground. Conscious that a total victory against the Apache was impossible, he aimed at reducing the intensity of the conflict by combining controlled police actions with other political, diplomatic, and economic measures, such as the introduction of trade as the preferred instrument for resolving a problem that had previously had been considered solely from a military perspective. Furthermore, it is interesting to point out what Matthew Babcock has called the "several intriguing parallels" between Spanish and U.S. Indian policy in the late eighteenth and early nineteenth centuries. Although Bernardo de Gálvez and Thomas Jefferson had very different personalities, backgrounds, and careers, both were active members of the Enlightenment, and aside from embracing the myth of the noble savage, they shared the idea of demographic imperialism, which considered that hunting and gathering were to be replaced in favor of husbandry as the most productive use of land. For both, nomadic Native Americans had to become farmers in order to be "civilized," and they preferred to trade with them because it was a cheaper alternative to war, but nonetheless, they were willing to wage war simultaneously.[234]

GOVERNING MEXICO CITY

In the 1780s Mexico City not only was the most populated city in the viceroyalty of New Spain but also was the largest city in all of the Americas, and probably in the entire Spanish Empire. The 1790 census, conducted under the viceroy the Count of Revillagigedo, officially registered 104,740 inhabitants, but this figure has been questioned.²³⁵ Only one year later, José Antonio de Alzate criticized the way the census was carried out, since a great part of the population had deliberately hidden data from the authorities to evade their fiscal obligations or to avoid being drafted into the army. Comparing Mexico City's food consumption with that of Madrid's, Alzate estimated that the real population was around 213,000.²³⁶ In comparison, by the end of the eighteenth century, Havana had 80,000 and Lima 50,000 people, while in European Spain the most populous city was Madrid, with 147,543 inhabitants, followed by Barcelona with 115,000, Seville with 96,000, Valencia with 80,000, and Cadiz with 50,000.²³⁷ At about the same time, London had 750,000 people and Paris 500,000, while in North America in 1790, New York had 33,000 and Philadelphia 28,500.²³⁸

Besides being the largest city, Mexico City was also one of the richest, thanks to its location in the middle of a trade route from Europe to Asia and its role as the capital of a huge viceroyalty with very important resources, such as the silver mines in Zacatecas.²³⁹ It is interesting to note that the largest and probably richest city of the Spanish Empire was not its capital, Madrid, but a settlement in its colonies. This fact can be considered proof of how different Spanish colonization was from that of other European colonial powers—an issue that has been brilliantly studied by John H. Elliott in his *Empires of the Atlantic World: Britain and Spain in America, 1492-1830*.²⁴⁰ It is impossible to imagine a larger and richer city than Paris for the French Empire or London for the British.

A city as large as Mexico City demanded much of Bernardo de Gálvez's attention. Precisely at this time, during the Enlightenment, a concept of the science of policing emerged, which, according to Hira de Gortari Rabiela, was a global approach to the city and its administration, based on close observation of the urban territory and its inhabitants.²⁴¹ During the 1780s several important initiatives were introduced in Mexico City, including Viceroy Martín de Mayorga's division of the city into districts in 1782.²⁴² Two important works about the city's problems and needed reforms were also published: *Discurso sobre la policía de Mexico* (Discourse on the police of Mexico), attributed to Baltasar Ladrón de Guevara, and *Enfermedades políticas que padece la capital de esta Nueva España* (Political diseases suffered by the capital of this New Spain), by Hipólito Villaroel.²⁴³ The importance and impact of the latter work was such that it constitutes an excellent guide to some of the problems that Bernardo de Gálvez had to tackle during his tenure.

The Pulquerías

Pulquerías were taverns where pulque, the traditional native liquor, was sold. According to Villaroel, the "*pulquerías* should not be allowed to exist in their present state . . . [since they are] the source and encouragement of idleness, nudity, and neglect for both men and women."[244] As already seen, pulque was one of the traditional native liquors that Indians were allowed to consume. It was heavily taxed and in 1785 produced the significant sum of 946,000 pesos.[245] The landowners also made fortunes from it: "If the aristocracy of the Old World had old and renowned vineyards, why would that of New Spain not be able to own pulque haciendas?" And so "the great fortunes from mining and commerce were invested in the pulque industry."[246] The converging interests of the Indians to drink their pulque, the landowners to sell it, and the Royal Treasury to tax it determined that the regulation of pulque was aimed only at controlling the worst disorders produced by its consumption. An obsession with preventing private gatherings, gambling, and other vices meant that pulque had to be downed in a hurry while standing, which made customers appear as if they had no other purpose than to get drunk as quickly as possible.[247]

Public Street Lighting

According to Villaroel, "street lighting is necessary in this city for public convenience as well as the prevention of innumerable evils."[248] The matter had been regulated by viceroy Matías de Gálvez as well as during the transitional period after his death while the *audiencia* was in charge.[249] From Bernardo de Gálvez's time, a drawing of a street lamp that was to be placed on all main streets has survived.[250]

Forbidden Weapons

Hipólito Villaroel complained that every regulation forbidding the carrying of small arms was traditionally ignored in Mexico City.[251] Spanish legislation governing America always prohibited or restricted the use of swords and other small arms by Indians, mulattoes, blacks, slaves, and mestizos; limited the length of blades of knives and pocketknives; and required royal authorization to carry them.[252] In this particular area, Bernardo de Gálvez imposed even greater restriction by forbidding the import of pointed knives from Europe.[253]

Mexico City's Hospice

Villaroel wrote that hospices were "one of the most useful, pious, and best-suited institutions for Christian morals . . . but unfortunately their direction and administration has fallen into the hands of a well-intentioned priest with a charitable heart who has spent all of their resources."[254] The manner in which a society treats the groups that live on its margins, whether defined by class, morals, race, or ideology, tells more about the real priorities of that society than any formal declaration of principles or a bill of rights. In late eighteenth-century Spain, the authorities' concern for the poor focused on their two most visible aspects: begging and disturbing the public order. Before any solution could be formulated, the truly poor had to be separated from the merely idle, for the former could receive assistance whereas the latter would be prosecuted.[255] An example of the idle was reflected in the legislation approved by Bernardo de Gálvez concerning public order.[256] The general idea of the new law, according to Isabel Ramos Vázquez, was to help the poor and force the idle to work.[257] The matter became a priority during the year of the hunger, when thousands of famished peasants flooded into cities in search of assistance. On March 8, 1786, an order was given "with instructions that poor Indians should be prevented from leaving their villages for the capital, and assistance centers should distribute meals daily with appropriate discrimination."[258] Almost at the same time, the bishop of Michoacán was concerned with finding "a true and discreet way to distribute alms, while banishing idleness and vagabonds."[259] On April 10 of the same year, another proclamation appeared that ordered "all of the city's poor to be taken to the hospice, and the able-bodied to be sent to work in public works."[260] In another document from this period, Bernardo de Gálvez counseled practicing charity toward the poor, provided it would not be harmful and not push them into laziness.[261]

To employ "the lazy and the idle" and to provide resources to those displaced by the hunger, an ambitious program of public works was established. The idea came from the city of Guadalajara and was ardently implemented in Michoacán.[262] In Mexico City the road to Toluca was repaired and improved and some work was also performed at the palace at Chapultepec, which will be considered later at length.[263]

For the truly poor there were institutions such as the hospices. The Royal Hospice House for Poor Beggars was founded by Fernando Ortiz Cortés, a private citizen, and opened in 1774.[264] Originally it had four separate sections—for old men, old women, boys, and girls—but during the year of the hunger it also opened it doors to adult men and women.[265] Importantly, it had the first maternity ward in Mexico: its department of *partos ocultos* (secret births), according to María de los Ángeles Rodríguez Álvarez, took care of all pregnant woman who desired to keep their condition confidential, and after delivery the mothers could give their newborns up for adoption through the Royal Foundling House.[266] Despite its private origin, the Royal Hospice House was funded by the Crown, at first with 1,000 pesos per year from the official lottery. This amount was increased in 1781 during a food crisis.[267] During the year of the hunger, 1785–86, Bernardo de Gálvez assigned more funds to the Royal Hospice House by increasing from 2 to 3 percent the proportion of lottery proceeds allocated to it and by establishing a fine on gambling whose proceeds went directly to it.[268] In addition, Gálvez gave the hospice a grant of 8,000 pesos and asked the king for 12,000 more per year.[269] Gálvez also visited the hospice in February 1786, and "not satisfied enough with seeing and touching the food served to the poor, he tasted it himself to have a proper idea of it, and visited unescorted every sick person in bed, to be sure they were properly taken care of . . . and provided funding from his own pocket for the daily meals."[270]

The Palace at Chapultepec

During the year of the hunger an active program of public works was implemented to supply jobs to peasants arriving in the main cities.[271] In Mexico City, as mentioned earlier, the road to Toluca was repaired and improved.[272] Funds were also assigned for building the towers of its cathedral, repairing the Bucareli mall, and improving the palace at Chapultepec.[273] The case of the palace at Chapultepec reflects not only social and urban development policies but also, because of the personal involvement of Bernardo de Gálvez, a few of his important character traits.

Before the Spanish conquest of Mexico, Chapultepec Hill already hosted a palace and gardens begun by Aztec emperor Nezahualcóyotl in the second half of the fifteenth century. During his reign it was one of Moctezuma's favorites retreats.[274] In the seventeenth century, several royal houses were built on the hill to serve as holiday residences for the Spanish viceroys. In the following century these buildings were abandoned until, in April 1784, Viceroy Matías de Gálvez asked for funds to rebuild them so they could host the swearing-in ceremonies of all viceroys.[275] The expenditure was authorized in August of the same year.[276] After Matías de Gálvez's death the *audiencia* temporarily in charge of the viceroyalty tried to continue renovation of the royal houses but without real commitment or success.

Upon his arrival in Mexico, Bernardo de Gálvez "went in person to Chapultepec, and after carefully visiting everything I concluded that, since everything was in ruins, it was impossible to use anything there and would be better to start anew to build a simple country house."[277] To erect this "simple country house" he ordered engineer Lieutenant Colonel Francisco Bambiteli to draw up plans, "taking into account the decorum, solidity, and extension needed for this kind [of building], while avoiding superfluous ornamentation and costs." On December 23, 1785, "the first stone of the new palace was laid in a ceremony in which he [Gálvez] put with it some gold and silver coins."[278] Taking part in the construction was to be "a portion of the population, so they could provide for themselves through their work."[279] Soon it was clear that more funds were needed, so Bernardo de Gálvez wrote to his uncle explaining that, despite the previous authorization of 8,000 pesos along with the proceeds from two bullfights, the latter funds were already committed to cover the costs of the official ceremony on his entry into Mexico City as new viceroy.[280] Therefore he suggested that the Royal Treasury advance the money from the two bullfights that were to take place the following year. The answer was negative, although he did receive authorization to organize more than two bullfights to raise money for the building.[281]

The construction continued as long as the public works program was in operation, but the costs continued to rise and reached up to 3,000 pesos per week.[282] Faced with these expenses, the Council of the Indies, the supreme institution in charge of the administration of America, issued an unfavorable report, which, according to María del Carmen Galbis Díez, stated that since the building of the palace was his personal initiative, it was unacceptable that more than 123,000 pesos had already been spent during its first phase and work had not even started on the second phase.[283] Little was done while the *audiencia* was in charge of the viceroyalty immediately after the death of Bernardo de Gálvez, and nothing was done under viceroy Count of Revillagigedo.[284] The building was abandoned and its doors, windows, and glass sold.[285] When Alexander von Humboldt visited the palace in 1803, he found that "vandalism, which passes by the name of economy, has already much contributed to degrade an edifice on an elevation of 2,325 meters, which, in a climate so rude, is exposed to every impetuosity of the winds."[286]

In the General Archives of the Indies in Seville are five plans of the projected palace at Chapultepec.[287] Although the catalog states that the plans probably date from 1787, I believe they were part of the documentation that Bernardo de Gálvez likely submitted to the capital to gain approval for the construction. The plan of the ground floor of the Royal Palace of Chapultepec shows that the "decorum" of this "simple country house" included a main entrance; rooms for officers and troops of the viceregal guard and another for the alabardiers; a hall, an office, and a room for the secretariat; a waiting room, kitchens, a pantry, and a pastry pantry; rooms for the butlers, valets, grooms, pages, aide-de-camp, cook, and lackeys; a room for guests; and two staircases (the main staircase and another "reserved").[288] Another

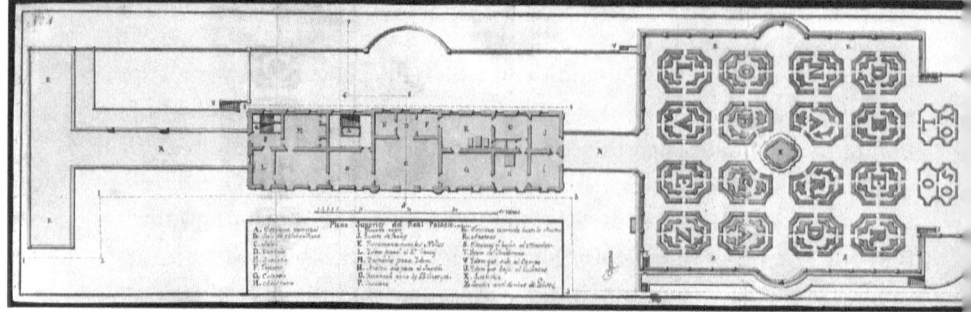

Blueprint of the second floor of the Royal Palace of Chapultepec, intended to be the summer residence of the viceroys of New Spain. The project was designed during Bernardo de Gálvez's tenure as viceroy with his direct involvement. Contrary to the customs of late eighteenth-century European aristocracy, the Gálvez couple shared their bedroom, and their children's apartments were just across their door. (*Plano Superior del Real Palacio de Chapultepec*, circa 1787, Archivo General de Indias, Mapas y Planos, Mexico 407; Ministerio de Educación, Cultura y Deporte, Archivo General de Indias)

plan shows the palace's facade in the purest neoclassical style, with a terrace for gardens.[289]

The plan of the second floor of the royal palace includes a hall for the alabardiers, a small corridor, an oratory, a sacristy, a reception hall for official ceremonies, a waiting hall, a wardrobe, a bath, the children's bedroom, a bedroom for the viceregal couple, the viceroy's study, and an exit to the gardens.[290]

A closer look at the disposition of rooms on the second floor is very revealing, as it shows how Bernardo de Gálvez imposed his own criteria and family needs on the usual design for this kind of official building. A room for the children was something the Gálvez y Saint-Maxent family needed but was of questionable value to most other viceroys, since they were usually appointed at a much older age. Not only that, but the children's room was directly adjacent to the main bedroom, which was unusual for the time. Actually, it was during the Enlightenment that new concepts of childhood and the family were born. Children started to be seen as individuals rather than as miniature adults, and the family was to be bound not only by duties (of both the parents and the children) but also by love.[291]

THE REFORM OF NEW SPAIN'S ARMY

One of the most important reforms in which Bernardo de Gálvez was involved during his governance of New Spain was the reform of its army. It has already been mentioned that the entire system of defense for the Spanish territories in America had been reconsidered in the 1760s. The reform started with the arrival of General Juan de Villalba in 1764, along with a group of officers and more than 700 men who were to be the backbone of a new army that would eventually have nine regiments.[292] However, the reforms were delayed by problems between Villalba and the viceroy the Marquis de Cruillas. For one reason or another, twenty years passed without any serious reform.[293] In 1783 Viceroy Matías de Gálvez decided to push the issue again by commissioning a new study from Colonel Francisco Antonio Crespo, at the time acting under-inspector general of troops in New Spain. Crespo had thirteen years' experience in Mexico, first as governor of Sonora during the war against the northern Indians and later in the Mexico City council, where he was an active member of the San Carlos Academy.[294] According to Christon I. Archer, unlike so many of his predecessors, who had drafted military plans without adequate knowledge of New Spain, Crespo understood the social, economic, and political barriers confronting those responsible for raising military forces.[295] María del Carmen Velázquez Chávez and María Luisa Rodríguez-Sala regard Crespo's *Project for the Arrangement of the Army of New Spain* the most complete and important late eighteenth-century document on this issue.[296] It was also the basis for Bernardo de Gálvez's reforms.

Bernardo de Gálvez believed it was necessary first to determine clearly the main objectives or priorities of the reforms. In his words, "New Spain has greedy neighbors who do not fit and are not happy within their present limits. The British have always tried to settle in Spanish American territories. On this coast we are familiar with the threatening presence of their fleets and convoys."[297] For confronting these "greedy neighbors" Spain had two very different kinds of troops. There were the regular troops, formed in 1784 from two regiments and several infantry companies; two cavalry regiments of dragoons; and two artillery companies, for a total of 4,389 men—a figure that Bernardo de Gálvez considered completely insufficient. By comparison, the British in 1775 had about 8,580 men in eighteen regiments in their American colonies.[298]

But the regular troops were not the only ones present. The provincial militias had 16,755 men; the urban militias totaled 1,841 men; the "non-organized Gulf and Caribbean militias" amounted to another 9,683 men; and 6,438 troops were under other "new and old units" (see appendix table 20). Thus the total number of troops was actually 39,106, but the condition of the non-regular troops was terrible, and these men were recruited from among "the most unhappy inhabitants."[299] The judgment of José de Ezpeleta was harsh:

"Confronted with the sad appearance of such a disfigured and confusing army . . . it would be better if [New Spain] had no troops at all."[300] To correct this, Bernardo de Gálvez considered it essential to formulate a "new military constitution" for New Spain. Its foundation would be Colonel Francisco Antonio Crespo's report, which had been sent to Madrid in January 1785.[301] From the court came the order that Bernardo de Gálvez should complete it with his own views, so he commissioned his close friend José de Ezpeleta, at the time inspector general of Mexico's troops, to write a new report, which was delivered in October of the same year.[302] Using both documents as guides, Bernardo de Gálvez wrote his own report, which was fully approved by the capital in January 1787.[303]

Bernardo de Gálvez believed that during peace a force of 16,000 men would be required, including 5,807 regulars or veterans, who in war could be increased to 9,319.[304] The rest of the force was to be formed by militias. Having militias represent two-thirds of the total force was an idea suggested by Crespo, and it went against all previous proposals that always assumed that the defense of the territory would be performed by veterans, which increased costs to the breaking point. The new veteran troops would be organized into four regiments. To the New Spain Crown Regiment already in place, three new regiments—Nueva España, Mexico, and Puebla—were to be added, along with a Veracruz volunteer battalion and two more companies. Because of the "possibilities of the Royal Treasury," instead of sending all troops to Mexico from European Spain, it was decided that only the core would be European-born soldiers, while the rest would be recruited in America. The core of the infantry would be 29 officers, 118 sergeants, 245 corporals, and 252 privates, while the cavalry would share some of the infantry officers and have 60 sergeants and 130 corporals and dragoons. Gálvez required all officers to be recruited from "among the army's best—those with the highest aptitude, intelligence, application, zeal, and behavior," while the noncommissioned officers (NCOs) and privates were to be "fit, honest, robust, of good appearance, . . . and not above thirty years old, and if possible some Germans should be included among them."[305] Gálvez explained this choice by stating that, "since these foreigners long to be allowed to move to America, they will be easily recruited. Once here they can be encouraged to marry local women and be sent to the Interior Provinces, where they can be very useful as settlers."[306]

The other two-thirds of the New Spain army was be recruited locally, which was unprecedented. Until this moment, the defense of America was presumed to rest on the shoulders of professional troops from European Spain, since Americans were considered inferior soldiers. This is an idea that

Christon I. Archer has labeled the dilemma of the *gachupín*.³⁰⁷ The *gachupines* in Mexico were Spaniards arriving directly from Europe who displayed a superior attitude toward the local populations. The discussion about the relative merits of European- and American-born soldiers continued until the very end of Spanish domination in America. Significantly, however, while the idea of European superiority was widespread, important voices disagreed. For example, although during the 1760s General Villalba considered the locals untrustworthy, the viceroy the Marquis de Cruillas knew that a large portion of the local population was perfectly prepared to become army officers.³⁰⁸ Bernardo de Gálvez's experience during his campaigns against the Apache made him an advocate for American soldiers. In contradiction to European-born soldiers, who believed that the "Americans lacked the spirit and generosity for [a career in] arms,"³⁰⁹ he considered them "no less brave than the Indians they fight."³¹⁰

His favorable opinion of Americans extended beyond their military qualities. During his government, a book by José de Castañeda was published in Madrid rather than in Mexico City under the self-explanatory title *Informe jurídico dirigido al Rey por la muy noble y muy leal ciudad de México, cabeza de la Nueva España, a favor de los españoles nacidos en la América para que se les prefiera en los empleos eclesiásticos, políticos y militares* (Legal report to the King by the most noble and most loyal city of Mexico, head of New Spain, in favor of Spaniards born in America to be preferred for church, political and military appointments).³¹¹ To Bernardo de Gálvez, European and American officers and soldiers were different: "In a word, the soldier who serves in America would not be good in Spain," since he "would miss the abundant food, would have to work much more to gain much less, would consider it impossible to suffer the lack of supplies common in our regiments, and especially would find it difficult to bear the treatment." On the other hand, the European arriving in America grew quickly accustomed to "the land's abundance, the freedom, the vices, and the tender manners of the locals, which are no different in big cities than in small villages. . . . Everywhere he is welcomed, the more so the fewer formalities he uses and if he embraces the uses and customs of the land."³¹²

Bernardo de Gálvez called not only for soldiers but also for officers who were American-born, since he believed it "essential to provide the American youth with an honorable occupation." Young Americans must be incorporated into the army by "winning the hearts of the people and using prudent and wise measures to attract them with a gentleness that inspires in them love for a military career, and shows them the honorable privileges they will be granted."³¹³ The privileges that Bernardo de Gálvez had in mind included the special legal status that the military had at the time, along with the social prestige attached to military service, both of which were powerful incentives in recruitment.[314] According to María Luisa Rodríguez-Sala, in New Spain under Gálvez, "the inhabitants were proud of their city, their military, and their viceroy. . . . All of this generated an unprecedented enthusiasm for everything related to the military."[315]

Among historians there is general agreement about the importance of the Americanization of the army, but there is still an open debate about its specific consequences. While some view it as having a direct impact on the rise of independence movements, others deny this link and stress the importance of other factors specific to each region.[316] According to Óscar Cruz Barney and Josefa Vega Juanino, the Crespo reform amounted to official recognition that the defense of the viceroyalty was impossible without the concurrence of the local population.[317] Carmen Losa Contreras points out that the army's Americanization could be at the origin of the Mexican tradition of the military's involvement in politics.[318] The regular army increased its percentage of American soldiers and officers, but the local militias were completely American. For a thorough reform of the militias, a reliable census was needed, which would indicate how much of the local population was considered fit for military service. While this information was being collected, Bernardo de Gálvez started to reform some existing militia units, including the Querétaro Provincial Cavalry Regiment, the Shopkeepers Infantry Regiment, and the cavalry companies of the guilds of bakers, pork butchers, and tanners of Mexico City.[319]

The total cost of the reform proposed by Crespo would have increased the annual budget by 155,624 pesos, but the new constitution proposed by Bernardo de Gálvez more than doubled this sum to 315,280 pesos, which, he asserted, was "the only possible way to secure the defense of this realm, so that my successors and I can answer to God and the king."[320]

The reports by Crespo and Ezpeleta along with Gálvez's comments were forwarded to the court by the end of February 1785 and were complemented by some additional remarks sent by Gálvez a year later.[321] In May 1786 Vicente Nieto, officer in the Michoacán militia, was directed to the Iberian Peninsula to start selecting the officers, NCOs, and soldiers to be sent to America.[322] The first part of the plan for the new constitution was approved on September 26, 1786, and the second part on April 13, 1787, but with an important caveat: the first group of officers, NCOs, and soldiers arriving in Mexico would be only half the number initially requested.[323]

PROMOTING THE ARTS AND SCIENCES

The promotion of the arts and sciences was essential for the Enlightenment, and Bernardo de Gálvez was actively involved in both areas through the Royal Academy of San Carlos of New Spain and several initiatives in the field of botany.

The Royal Academy of San Carlos of New Spain

The Royal Academy of San Carlos of New Spain was created by Matías de Gálvez in December 1783 but did not really start operations until November of the following year.[324] The November 8, 1785, issue of the *Gazeta de México* reported on its official opening ceremony. Once the viceroy and his wife were seated, a concert took place, followed by speeches by the academy's director and first secretary and remarks by one of the students on behalf of the alumni. After another musical interlude, the viceroy gave out prizes "much more precious for the kind words he addressed to each of the recipients than for their value."[325]

Among the prizes were those awarded to the winners of a competition for the design of a series of commemorative medals. The first design celebrated the founding of the academy and the second the establishment of the Court of Mining of Mexico.[326] The third was about the conquest of Pensacola. On the obverse side of the winning design for the medal is the bust of King Carlos III with the legend "*Carlos III el sabio y restaurador, Rey de España, Emperador de las Indias*" (Charles III the wise and the restorer, King of Spain, Emperor of the Indies). On the reverse is an image of Bernardo de Gálvez on horseback, with the forts of Pensacola behind him at the moment of their explosion along with the legend "*La sovervia y orgullo ynglés, avatido a España*" (The English pride and arrogance brought down by Spain). "On May 19, 1781, the Forts and City of Pensacola, Capital of West Florida, Surrendered to His Excellency Señor Don Bernardo de Gálvez."[327]

It is clear that promoting the arts in New Spain was perfectly compatible with Bernardo de Gálvez's self-promotion. Curiously, this third medal is not mentioned in the detailed account of the proceedings published in the *Gazeta de México*. The oversight was no doubt not random, but we can only speculate as to its causes. The design on the reverse of the third medal, by one of the best engravers at the time, Antonio Gil, is almost identical to an engraving published the same year in Paris and signed by Nicolás Ponce under the title *Prise de Pensacole* in a *Collection d'estampes représentant les évenemens de la guerre, pour la liberté de l'Amérique Septentionale*.[328]

Detail of the engraving depicting the medals awarded as prizes in a competition held by the Royal Academy of San Carlos in Mexico City. (Gil, *Medalla conmemorativa de la toma de Pensacola*; Ministerio de Educación, Cultura y Deporte, Archivo General de Indias)

The Promotion of Botany

The promotion of science was of the utmost importance to the Enlightenment, since it represented new knowledge against old traditions. But it was also an important instrument in the reform of both state and society.[329] Of all of the sciences, botany had a privileged position because of the immediate benefits to be obtained from it. According to Antonio González Bueno, botany had an important economic impact not only as a theoretical foundation for advances in agriculture, the tanning industry, or naval construction but also as an essential element in the inventory of colonial resources, which made it become a state science, a fashionable science, and a court science.[330]

During the last decades of the eighteenth century, several botanical expeditions were organized to study America's natural world, and the one sent to Mexico came about under the auspices of Bernardo de Gálvez. In September 1785, Gálvez wrote to his uncle that after several meetings with the renowned botanist Martín Sessé, he was persuaded to establish in Mexico a school for medicine, where professionals could be instructed on "the virtues and services of local plants" and continue the labor carried out during the past century by Dr. Francisco Fernández. Furthermore, so that all of the knowledge would not be buried "inside a book . . . it would also be advisable to establish a chair of botany, . . . which could be entrusted to Casimiro Ortega Gómez, first botanist of the royal court."[331] A month later he informed the capital of the implementation of a royal order to send to the court everything found in Mexico relevant to Dr. Fernández's work.[332] Dr. Fernández had made an expedition to New Spain at the end of the sixteenth and beginning of the seventeenth centuries, but all the specimens he gathered had been lost in a fire at the Royal Palace of El Escorial in 1761.[333]

Several years later, some of the papers from the expedition were found in one of the libraries seized from the Jesuits after their expulsion from Spain.[334] The finding attracted the interest of the government, which ordered the papers' immediate publication, but first all other relevant documents needed to be located. Bernardo de Gálvez commissioned "curious people and scholars to find out as much as they could about this issue."[335] Among them were the three most reputable intellectuals of New Spain: Martín Sessé, José Antonio Alzate, and José Ignacio Bartolache.[336] They could find no trace of Dr. Fernández's expedition, but their efforts gave them the opportunity to present to the viceroy an ambitious project for a new expedition, which would be accompanied by the establishment of a chair of botany and a botanical garden. Although the three initiatives would see the light of day only after Bernardo de Gálvez's death, according to José Luis Maldonado Polo, he was its enthusiastic protector, as his letters to the court backing the project show.[337] In one of the letters he supports the idea of a botanical garden in Mexico with the following arguments: "Such an institution in this capital could serve as perfect repository for the products of North America before their transport to the metropolis [that is, Madrid], where they will enrich not only the Royal Botanical Garden in Madrid but also the Royal Natural History Cabinet, which is one of the magnificent achievements that will render immortal the name of our sovereign."[338]

EVERYDAY BUSINESS

Besides tending to urgent and serious problems such as those arising during the year of the hunger and to specific issues such as the reform of the army and the reorganization of the Interior Provinces on the viceroyalty's northern border, Bernardo de Gálvez was also occupied with the everyday business of simply running New Spain. In and of itself this demanded a great deal of his working time. He had to deal with a wide range of issues concerning all aspects of the civilian and military administrations, since as viceroy he was the supreme civil authority and as captain general he was the supreme military commander.[339] He needed not only to sign important documents but also to oversee almost all promotions, pensions, awards, sanctions, fines, tax problems, conflicts between different authorities and officials, trade regulations and their implementation, trade permits, appointments and dismissals of royal officials, salaries, inventories, and so forth. Sometimes it must have seemed that everything needed his signature, as the indices of his official correspondence suggest. Since the indices were made on a monthly basis, they are also useful for following his workload during his tenure as viceroy, but one must keep in mind that they register only communications between Mexico City and the Iberian Peninsula and do not include correspondence going back and forth from New Spain's capital to the rest of the viceroyalty. It is also important to remember that they record communications of very different natures. Some matters demanded a huge amount of work on his part (such as the reorganization of the Interior Provinces), while others simply needed his signature (such as ordering the publication of the results of the royal lottery).

With this caveat in mind, from the moment he took office in mid-June 1785 until November of the following year, when he was forced to take a sick leave, Bernardo de Gálvez sent to the royal court a total of 939 communications, or an average of nearly two a day. As graph 3 shows, his work pace decreased significantly three times. The first decline was in November 1785,

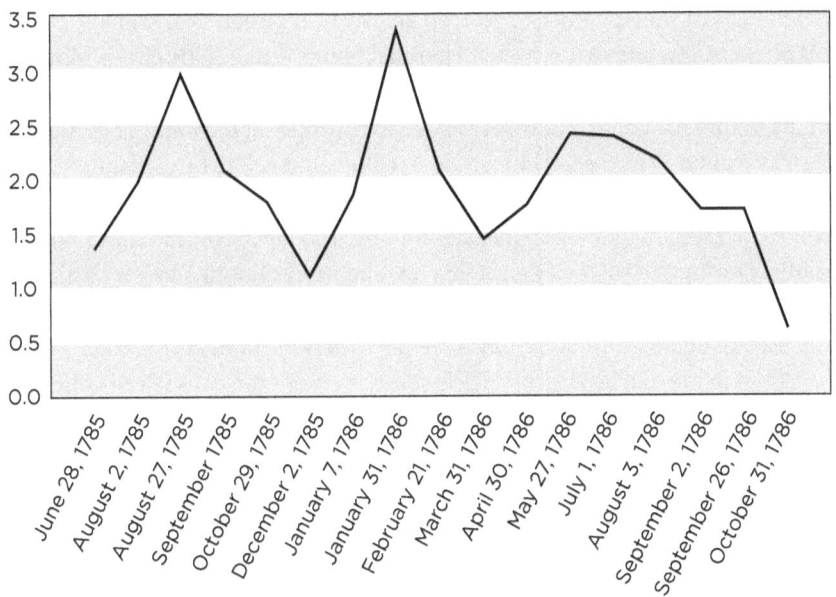

Graph 3. Daily Average of Dossiers Processed by
Bernardo de Gálvez as Viceroy of New Spain

Source: indexes of the official correspondence sent by Bernado de Gálvez to the court between June 28, 1785, and October 31, 1786, AGI, Mexico, 1513. See appendix table 21.

which coincides with the first mention of his absences from certain official functions because he was "a little indisposed."[340] The second decline occurred in March 1786. The accounts of his activities by the *Gazeta de México* and in the diary kept by José Goméz do not offer any particular reason, but it could have been that during this time he was completely devoted to solving the problems caused by the year of the hunger and this internal work is not accounted for in the indexes. The third decline, during the fall of 1786, was due to the initial phase of a serious illness (see also appendix table 21).

ILLNESS AND DEATH

Although he was only forty years old, Bernardo de Gálvez's health was already seriously impaired because of a lifetime spent fighting under the most extreme conditions. He had fought the Apache under the blazing sun of northern Mexico. He had marched before his men through the swamps of Louisiana and Florida. In New Orleans he fell so ill that he feared that his death would prevent him from fulfilling his marriage promise to Feliciana Saint-Maxent. He was just like Coriolanus: "The warlike service he has done, consider; think / Upon the wounds his body bears."[341] During his third campaign against the Apache he received an arrow in his left arm and a spear to his chest. A few days later he fell from his horse, striking his chest. Months later he had an accident while driving a carriage in an effort to reach his uncle before his departure from Mexico for Europe. At the landing in Algiers he was wounded in the leg but would not allow himself to be evacuated until the last of his men had safely retreated, and several months later he was still recovering in bed when his friend Francisco de Saavedra visited him in Cadiz. During the siege of Pensacola he received a shot in a finger of his left hand, a shot that also grazed his stomach. In February 1783, while preparing the assault against British Jamaica, he had a serious bout of malaria.

While in Mexico as viceroy, the first mention of problems with his health dates to September 1785, when he failed to attend a bullfight and a theater performance in his honor "because of being slightly indisposed."[342] The same thing happened in November.[343] At the end of July 1786 he did not attend a mass "because of being a little sick."[344] From that moment on, his health problems were increasingly frequent. In mid-August he went with his family to the village of San Ángel for a short rest, and a month later he tried to relax by listening to music during lunch, since he was "very ill."[345] His health continued to deteriorate to the point that on October 9, "a council of doctors met in the palace because the count of Gálvez was very ill."[346] Five days later he took communion in public. According to José Gómez, "The previous night the viceroy had a shave and in the morning on the day of communion he dressed in his lieutenant general's uniform and received His Majesty standing; it was eleven o'clock."[347] The majesty that Gómez talks about was not the king but the body of Christ that he received in communion. The October 24 issue of the *Gazeta de México* reported that "a solemn novena [a Catholic devotion consisting of nine consecutive days of prayer] was held in the San Hipólito Mártis Church for the important health of His Excellency the viceroy."[348]

By the end of the month he was so weak that the customary gun salutes at the burial of Captain José Luciano de Villareal, the veteran grenadier who had served as representative of the godfather at his son's baptism in Guarico, Haiti, were not performed so as not to disturb him.[349] On October 31 he departed for Tacubaya in search of a better climate that "could restore him to health, which we all hope will happen through the intervention of God, to whom all the population prays with the utmost fervor."[350] That same day, Bernardo de Gálvez wrote to his uncle that it was becoming increasingly difficult for him to continue to perform his "daily duties in such a vast government." He confided that he had been ill for the past months but had been able to continue to work until October 4, when he was confined to bed, where it was difficult for him even to sign documents. To fulfill his duties he put in place a system of "simplified signature," by which most documents would bear a note attesting that they had been approved by the viceroy but because of his "indisposition" had been signed by the competent official, while more important matters would be personally signed by him, although not with the usual full signature but with a simplified one.[351] Just a week later he was unable even to continue his duties under the simplified system, and he had no choice but to transfer his viceregal powers temporarily to the *audiencia*, keeping for himself decisions on all matters related to military affairs.[352] The *audiencia* immediately informed the court of its new powers and from October 10 began to discharge matters under its new authority.[353] The military affairs that Bernardo de Gálvez kept for himself started to suffer important delays.[354]

Aware that he was running out of time, on November 9 he dictated his last will and testament, which he completed with an addendum a couple of days later.[355] This document reflects his character and reveals important aspects of his private life. His main concern was to leave his family in the best possible situation. According to eighteenth-century standards, his family was not only the inner circle formed by his wife and children but also other relatives and dependents. For example, he included dispositions regarding his brother-in-law Juan de Riaño; his personal secretary Fernando de Córdoba; Francisco Carillo; and "the rest of the family who [with his death] would lose their present appointments" and on whose behalf he demanded of his uncle to "ask for the king's pity."[356] He freed his three personal slaves, Pierre, Barthelemy, and Barthelemy's wife, and left some money to several "dwarves" with a request that they be returned to their former owners.

To his wife, after pointing out that she "did not marry with any kind of dowry," he left her "the diamonds and pearl jewels." He asked his uncle to include her in the *montepío militar* (army pension system) since their "marriage was performed with a royal order only" and without official communication with the *montepío militar*. He also wanted "my children to go to Spain as soon as possible, to be educated with the utmost care under the supervision of their uncle José, the marquis of Sonora, and in case of his death, of my other uncle Don Miguel. The same will be done with the son or daughter to be born," since Felicitas was expecting. He also protected Adelaide, his wife's daughter from her previous marriage, leaving her a large sum. He added that "desiring that my wife does not separate from my children, I beg her to bear the sacrifice of not living among her own people and go with them to Spain as soon as possible and settle there to take care of them."

His estate was to be divided equally among all of his children, including the one yet to be born. The last will and testament does not include an inventory, but in one of the addenda he states that "my possessions are those I have acquired in Louisiana and on expeditions in those lands, and some trade I did there before marrying, and not being able to save anything from my salary, I believe my wife is not entitled to half of it," in accordance with Spanish law at the time. With this declaration Bernardo de Gálvez was probably trying to protect his estate from the *juicio de residencia*, which was demanded of all high royal officials after leaving their positions. But he also raised questions about his actions as governor of Louisiana. By mentioning the trade he conducted during his tenure as governor, he was in effect admitting that he had violated legal prohibitions against such activities.[357] During the decade following Gálvez's death, New Orleans's courts would be busy with a series of legal procedures concerning his estate that are proof of the depth of his economic involvement in the city.[358] And by leaving seventeen houses to the Ursuline convent in New Orleans, he further acknowledged the same contravention. In any case, no one was interested in tarnishing the reputation of such a beloved viceroy, and in January 1788 he was to be exonerated in his *juicio de residencia*, long after the death of his uncle.[359] Having settled all of his earthly affairs, on November 16 Bernardo de Gálvez bid farewell to his family "with a very emotional speech."[360] Two weeks later, on November 30, 1786, he died.[361]

Bernardo de Gálvez's plea to his uncle to take care of his family was soon answered. On February 27, 1787, the Count of Floridablanca informed José de Gálvez that "considering the distinguished services rendered by the late viceroy of New Spain . . . His Majesty has bestowed upon his widow an annual pension of 50,000 *reales*"; upon his son, Miguel, present Count of Gálvez, the encomienda of Bolaños in the Order of Calatrava; to the son to be born posthumously, an annual pension of 12,000 pesos (and 6,000 pesos in the case of a daughter); a pension of 6,000 pesos to his daughter, Doña Matilde de Gálvez; and a pension of 4,000 pesos to their half-sister, Doña Adelaide d'Estrehan.[362] The widow thanked the king for his generosity in a letter to José de Gálvez and asked him to transmit to His Majesty her and her children's deepest gratitude.[363]

Before continuing with the narration of the facts, just a few words about a legend. It has been suggested that his death could be attributed to poisoning. This is totally absurd, as no fact, document, or contemporaneous testimony even hints at such a possibility. Therefore the discussion of this conspiracy theory—which is not the only one about Bernardo de Gálvez—has been left to the "immortality of a footnote."[364] The debate about the specific illness that killed Bernardo de Gálvez can be considered closed thanks to the detailed study by Manuel Olmedo Checa, who with the help of several doctors has identified it as an amebiasis (amoebic dysentery), which in the era before antibiotics could be fatal.[365]

After his death, no *pliego de mortaja* (literally, "tender of shroud") was found.[366] The *pliego de mortaja* was the system whereby the acting successor of a viceroy who died during his tenure was chosen. Inside an envelope, labeled that it was to be opened only in the event of the viceroy's death, were five more envelopes, each marked with a number. The envelope bearing the number one was to be opened first, and if the person named in it was in the viceroyalty he would be appointed acting viceroy and the rest of the envelopes would be burned unopened. If he was not available, the second envelope would be opened, and so forth.[367] In cases where no *pliego de mortaja* was to be found, the law determined that the *audiencia* would serve as caretaker government while waiting for the appointment of a full or acting viceroy by the king.[368] So the situation was clear regarding civil administration, but for the supreme military command of the viceroyalty it was far different.[369] In fact, problems had already arisen after the death of Viceroy Bucareli in 1779 and emerged again on this occasion.[370] A nasty confrontation took place between the president of the *audiencia*, Eusebio Sánchez Pareja,[371] and the deputy military commander of the viceroyalty of New Spain, Pedro Mendinueta y Múzquiz.[372]

The death of the viceroy was announced by the *audiencia*. Bells tolled 100 times and three cannon shots were fired every half-hour while the body remained unburied.[373] The body was taken from Tacubaya to Mexico City, with "the whole road and street full of people crying for their loss." Dressed in "his lieutenant general uniform, the cape of the Royal Order of Carlos III, and the rest of his insignia," he remained for several days in the main hall of the viceregal palace, where alabardiers stood guard and priests prayed for his soul while the complex protocol for a viceregal burial was prepared.[374] The elaborate ceremony has prompted one historian to call the demise of a viceroy a "privileged death," which required several pages of the December 5 and 19 editions of the *Gazeta de México* to describe.[375]

In his last will, Bernardo de Gálvez expressed his desire for his body to lie with that of his father in the convent of the Church of San Fernando.[376] But since the grave was not ready the archbishop offered to host the body temporarily in the cathedral—a proposal that was accepted by the widow on the condition that "the bones of her deceased husband be taken later to the Church of San Fernando . . . while his heart and entrails remained in the cathedral."³⁷⁷ The practice of burying various parts of the body in different locations was common at the time and was done to better preserve the memory of the deceased.³⁷⁸

The burial ceremony took place on December 4, 1786. The funeral cortege departed from the viceregal palace at eight thirty in the morning. The pomp and circumstance of a viceroy's funeral was combined with that appropriate to the burial of a lieutenant general who had died in active service.³⁷⁹ The procession was so long that "to avoid having the first participants arrive at the cathedral before the last ones could leave the palace," the usual route was extended with the addition of four stops, where funeral orations were delivered.³⁸⁰ All of New Spain society was present. The military led the cortege with four field cannons each drawn by four horses, followed by two of the viceroy's horses, unmounted and wearing black velvet blankets embroidered with his coat of arms. There then appeared three high-ranking military officers on horseback brandishing unsheathed swords, followed by six grenadier companies and their *gastadores* (sappers in ceremonial uniform).

After them marched representatives of the people of Mexico, organized into their different fraternities, sororities, and guilds. Behind these mourners more than fifty priests and monks and the archbishop of Mexico preceded the viceroy's coffin, which rode on an artillery caisson covered by a black cloth embroidered with the Count of Gálvez's coat of arms. A detachment of the alabardiers' viceregal guard and representatives of the *audiencia*, the Court of Auditors, the New Spain Nobility Corps, and the Royal Medical Academy of Mexico escorted the coffin. The viceroy's family was represented by Don Manuel Flon Tejada, Bernardo's brother-in-law, since Felicitas was confined to bed by her advanced pregnancy. The procession continued with representatives of other institutions, royal officials, and military officers. All troops slowly moved to the beat of the drums with their drumheads loose (*cajas destempladas*), flags furled, and presented arms pointing down in mourning. On their arrival at the cathedral the coffin was laid upon a barrow covered with black velvet and escorted by the alabardiers. A solemn funeral mass was celebrated by the archbishop of Mexico, in which two choirs sang. In May of the following year another procession would take the coffin from the cathedral to the Church of San Fernando.³⁸¹

Exactly one week after the funeral the widow gave birth to a girl, who received all sorts of tributes.³⁸² The members of the city council decided unanimously to offer themselves as godfathers to the newborn.³⁸³ The problem was that the mother, following her dead husband's wishes, had already contacted Fernando José Mangino,³⁸⁴ but in the end an arrangement was agreed upon and the council members were godfathers for the baptism while Mangino was godfather for the confirmation.³⁸⁵ All of them competed to show their generosity to the baby and her mother. The City of Mexico presented Felicitas with a string of pearls valued at 11,000 pesos and another to the baby girl worth 4,000. The archbishop gave the baby a plate, spoon, fork, and knife, all of solid gold, as did Mangino. The mother reciprocated by giving the archbishop a box made of gold and a pectoral cross with diamonds, while to Mangino she gave two pieces of "very special cloth" and to the president of the city council a walking stick with golden grip garnished with diamonds.³⁸⁶

The baptism took place in the cathedral on December 19, and the baby girl was given the names of María, Guadalupe, Bernarda, Isabel, Felipa de Jesús, Juana Nepomuceno, and Felícitas, to which, in the ceremony of her confirmation immediately afterward, was added the name of Fernanda.³⁸⁷ Following an old Spanish tradition, the mother was not present at the ceremony, since it was considered bad luck for her to go out before the baby was baptized. Her first public appearance was not until March 7, when, with her two sisters and all of her children, she went to the sanctuary of Nuestra Señora de los Ángeles escorted by the viceregal alabardiers—an honor to which she was not entitled but accorded to her as a sign of respect for her deceased husband.³⁸⁸ Immediately afterward preparations for the departure of the Gálvez y Saint-Maxent family began.

On March 12 the auction of the former viceroy's possessions was started, and a few days later Felicitas received half of her husband's salary.³⁸⁹ The last official function attended by Felicitas was the solemn procession marking the removal of her husband's remains from the cathedral to the Church of San Fernando, which took place in May. On May 23 Felicitas wrote a farewell letter to the Mexico City council, in which she assured them that she would treasure her memories of their particular distinctions, which "I will do my best to have my children maintain as well . . . so my family will be forever thankful to the most noble, most loyal, imperial City of Mexico."³⁹⁰ Finally on May 25, 1787, the family left Mexico for Veracruz, from whence on June 9 they embarked for Cadiz on the man-of-war *El Astuto*.³⁹¹

Afterword

THE "BLACK LEGEND"

The oldest reference to Bernardo de Gálvez's "black legend" is by Alexander von Humboldt. In his *Political Essay on the Kingdom of New Spain*, first published in Paris in 1811, he says he heard during his travels in Mexico in 1803 that "Count Bernardo de Galvez [was] accused of having conceived the project of rendering New Spain independent from the peninsula."[1] Humboldt immediately rejected such an idea in no uncertain terms.

> I have seen men of respectability in the first situations who entertained this suspicion against the young viceroy. It is the duty of a historian, however, not to yield too easy an acquiescence to accusations of so grave a nature. The Count of Galvez belonged to a family that King Charles the Third had suddenly raised to an extraordinary degree of wealth and power. Young, amiable, and addicted to pleasures and magnificence, he had obtained from the munificence of his sovereign one of the first places to which an individual could be exalted; and consequently, it could not be becoming in him to break the ties, which for three centuries had united the colonies to the mother country [note by translator]. The Count of Galvez, notwithstanding his conduct was well calculated to gain the favor of the populace of Mexico, and notwithstanding the influence of the Countess of Galvez, as beautiful as she was generally beloved, would have experienced the fate of every European viceroy who aims at independence. In a great revolutionary commotion, it would never have been forgiven him that he was not born an American.[2]

Despite Humboldt's dismissal, the rumor was too good to allow truth to interfere, and it was immediately picked up and repeated. Among others was Humboldt's first English translator, John Black, who could not refrain from adding a note offering his own opinion on the subject: "(*Note by the English translator) What the intentions of Galvez were is another affair; but can the author seriously believe these circumstances really do away the suspicions which he has mentioned? No person was so likely to conceive a project of the sort as a man dazzled with the suddenness of his elevation, fond of magnificence, and eager for popularity. Alas! Gratitude is but a small obstacle in the way of ambition.—*Trans.*"[3]

Later on the rumor was repeated again and again by chroniclers, novelists, and even historians.[4] When dealing with conspiracy theories that Bernardo's death was caused by poisoning, I decided to confine them to the "immortality of a footnote." In this case, however, despite being tempted to do the same, I consider it worthwhile to subject the rumor of his alleged intention to become independent to more attention. Humboldt's argument for dismissing the rumors relies on the impossibility of success for an independentist movement, but it does not preclude the possibility that Bernardo de Gálvez could have had this intention or idea.

Before going further, it is relevant to remember that no documentation whatsoever backs up even the slightest suspicion that Bernardo de Gálvez desired to become the king of Mexico. But it is also clear that if such a conspiracy were in the making, the conspirators would have done everything possible to leave no written trace. Thus we are forced to enter the slippery terrain of signs, indications, and clues. All references to the conspiracy date from well after Bernardo de Gálvez's death, the first coming from Humboldt, who heard about it in 1803, nearly twenty years later, when Mexico was in a completely different political situation than in the 1780s. As much as we may want to trace the origins of Mexican independence back to that period, it is not possible to find an independentist feeling that was mature enough to appear during Bernardo de Gálvez's mandate as viceroy.[5] Thus the idea that he was working for the independence of Mexico must have been born well after his death, appearing not by coincidence precisely when Mexico was trying to find historical legitimacy for the independence it had already achieved. It is in this context that the interpretations offered by Carlos María Bustamante (1836), José María Lacunza (1845), and Lucas Alamán (1849) must be considered.[6]

Indications of some truth to the rumor could possibly be found in traces of tension between Bernardo de Gálvez and Spanish authorities on the other side of the Atlantic Ocean. But nothing of the sort is evident in the abundant official correspondence during his tenure as viceroy. On the contrary, all that Bernardo de Gálvez received from the government in Madrid were compliments, proof of the king's satisfaction with him and his actions, and important rewards and honors. The only reprimand he received was when he pardoned the prisoners sentenced to the gallows, and even in this instance royal displeasure was expressed in the softest terms possible.

Another element that could support the rumors was that Bernardo de Gálvez was a member in the Freemasons, as a couple of authors maintain.[7] These secret organizations have commonly been singled out as important contributors to the independence of Spain's American colonies. But again, no proof has been offered that the assertions about his membership are true. We must also question whether there were any benefits that could tempt Bernardo de Gálvez to take part in the Freemasons. One of the main reasons the organization existed was to offer members a means to acquire or reinforce a network of contacts, but Bernardo de Gálvez was already a prominent member of the Gálvez clan, and for contacts he did not need a secret organization.

Another hint of his independentist intentions could be in his total control of the army, and especially in its Americanization, which has already been mentioned. Bernardo de Gálvez's reform of the army of New Spain opened the military to Americans, and some historians see this as an important factor in Mexico's drive for independence. However, this reform was not limited to Mexico but took place throughout Spanish America. Furthermore, the reason behind it was economic—that is, an urgent need to cut the costs of America's defense by recruiting troops locally instead of relying heavily on units from the Iberian Peninsula, which were very expensive to raise and send to America.

Among other arguments employed to back up the black legend, his popularity is most often repeated. About his popularity there can be no doubt. It was partly due to his character, which is evident in his long walks through the city to mingle with locals, his enthusiastic support of bullfights, the enjoyment he derived from dances and parties, and his reaction to the priest who would not bury a poor dead man. It was also due to his government's actions during the year of the hunger, when he demonstrated profound sympathy for the governed, especially poorer people whom he tried to protect from the greed of the *hacendados* and rich merchants. The news of his death was received with public demonstrations of sorrow, which, although normal at the death of almost any ruler, in his case must be considered sincere.

Bernardo de Gálvez was not the only viceroy who died during his mandate, so it is useful to compare what happened in other instances. On both sides of the Atlantic it was traditional after the death of a viceroy or king to publish eulogies. After the death of Viceroy Bucareli in 1779, six eulogies appeared in Mexico during the year;[8] after the death of Viceroy Martías de Gálvez, two.[9] When King Carlos III died in 1789, three were published in Mexico.[10] But after the death of Bernardo de Gálvez, between November 1786 and the following year, twenty funeral eulogies were printed in Mexico as well as in Havana. The figure alone speaks to his popularity, but it is also relevant to mention some of their phrases in their titles to appreciate the feelings involved, which in several cases transcended official mourning to become very personal. Most of the eulogies spoke of the pain and sadness felt among Mexico's population: "tender sighs," "feelings of the America justly in pain," "America crying," "tearful Mexico," "cry with which Mexico responds," "American lamentations," "the tears of daybreak," "dignified cry of the Muses," and "pathetic woes of America." Others mentioned his government: "America saved during the government of His Excellency Don Bernardo de Gálvez" and "demonstration of the happy days [of his rule]." Three of the eulogies turned their attention to the young widow—for example, to her grief, which was expressed in the most elegant and noble manner as befit such a noble lady ("Poem in which Her Excellency Felicitas Maxan [sic] expresses her sentiment"), as well as to the birth of their daughter as a compensation for such a terrible loss ("Tearful Mexico and cheerful Mexico, sadness and joy, condolence and congratulations for the heartfelt death of His Excellency Don Bernardo de Gálvez, count of Gálvez, and for the happy birth of Doña Guadalupe Felicitas de Gálvez" and "Happiness of Mexico in its greater sorrow by the blessed birth of the second daughter of the Count of Gálvez").[11]

The construction of the Royal Palace of Chapultepec has also been scrutinized under the light of his supposed ambition to become king of Mexico. Again according to Alexander von Humboldt, "The plan of the edifice is very singular. It is fortified on the side of the city of Mexico. We perceive salient walls and parapets adapted for cannon, although these parts all have the appearance of mere architectural ornaments. Toward the north there are fosses and vast vaults capable of containing provisions for several months. The common opinion at Mexico is, that the house of the viceroy at Chapultepec is a disguised fortress . . . and it was supposed that the rock of Chapultepec was destined to serve as an asylum and defense for him in case of attack from European troops."[12]

Several authors insist on its fortress-like appearance.[13] Its location on the top of Chapultepec Hill was impressive, as an engraving published in New York in 1847 shows.[14] The official name of the residence in Spanish was Palacio Alcázar, "Palace Castle." Despite its military connotations, the word *alcázar* was used when referring to royal palaces to distinguish them from those that were not royal residences. In any case, even if Humboldt found a military purpose behind the "appearance of mere architectural ornaments," the plans sent by Bernardo de Gálvez to Madrid give no such impression.[15] What is obvious is that the construction of the Chapultepec palace was Bernardo de Gálvez's personal project. It has been already mentioned how its plans

Detail of the design for the gardens of the Royal Palace of Chapultepec, which includes Gálvez's name and motto. (*Plano Superior del Real Palacio de Chapultepec*, circa 1787, Archivo General de Indias, Mapas y Planos, Mexico 407; Ministerio de Educación, Cultura y Deporte, Archivo General de Indias)

reflected his personal and family needs, but now it is relevant to mention another important detail. The legend on one of the plans specifies that the letter Z corresponds to "the garden with the name of Gálvez." Turning the plan of the garden 90 degrees, the viceroy's name can clearly be seen, as can his motto above, "Yo Solo."[16]

Confronted with this feature, one would at least think that Bernardo de

Gálvez was preparing for a long mandate as viceroy of New Spain, since the palace would take some time to build and he obviously wanted to live in it as long as possible. The problem was that according to legislation at the time, the maximum length of time that a viceroy could serve was three years, and when he sent the plans he was already in his second year. However, it is also true that the legal limit was not always enforced, as happened with Viceroy Bucareli, who served nearly eight years.[17] The gardens of the palace at Chapultepec were not the only ego-boosting initiative taken by Bernardo de Gálvez during his tenure as viceroy of Mexico. In the previous chapter we have seen the designs for three medals awarded during the opening ceremony of the Royal Academy of San Carlos of New Spain, one dedicated to celebrating his conquest of Pensacola.[18]

To finish with the black legend of Bernardo de Gálvez, it is relevant to register what could be considered an irony of destiny. A decade after his death, Friars Jerónimo and Pablo de Jesús painted a portrait that must be regarded as an original in more than one sense of the word.

First, it was the product of a collaboration between two artists. In the bottom part of the portrait it is written that "Fray Jerónimo scratched it, Fray Pablo painted it." Second, it employed the unusual technique of sgraffito, "a technique in mural or ceramic decoration, in which the top layer of glaze, plaster, etc., is incised with a design to reveal parts of the ground."[19] It also used calligraphy to draw the viceroy's figure and his horse. So modern is its appearance that a reproduction of it is included in a book by Walter Hart Blumenthal, *Eccentric Typography*, which became the basis for a later exhibition under the auspices of UNESCO called *The Art of Writing*.[20] Bernardo de Gálvez's portrait is, according to Inmaculada Rodríguez Moya in her study of the iconography of viceregal power in Mexico, one of the few equestrian portraits of New Spain's viceroys. Actually, other authors maintain it is the only such portrait, and I have been unable to find another.[21] The position of the horse and rider immediately recalls Velazquez's royal portraits, but deducing from this, in a painting executed a decade after Bernardo de Gálvez's death, that he wanted to be presented in a regal posture is simply too far-fetched.

Between December 2011 and May 2012 an exhibition took place in the palace at Chapultepec titled *Treasures of the Royal Palaces of Spain: A Shared History*. The exhibition recreated the Salón de Acuerdos ("Throne Hall") of the Royal Palace of Mexico, and precisely "in the place where the king presided over the hall is exhibited a portrait of Viceroy Gálvez, who ordered the construction of what is today known as the Castle of Chapultepec."[22] In other words, 225 years after his death, Bernardo de Gálvez, or rather his portrait, effectively took the place reserved for the king.

THE FALL OF THE HOUSE OF GÁLVEZ

Probably the best way to describe what happened to the Gálvez clan after Bernardo de Gálvez's death is by borrowing a title from Edgar Allan Poe.[23] The founder of the clan, José de Gálvez, Bernardo's uncle, was growing old with no male descendants, and all of his hopes for perpetuating the family at the top of Spain's power ladder had been placed on Bernardo. His fame as a victorious military leader, his success in confronting the crisis in Mexico during the year of the hunger, and his enormous popularity had made him the perfect candidate to succeed his uncle as the next chieftain of the clan. Upon his death no one else could be found. Miguel, José's brother, died unmarried at the age of sixty-seven while returning from Prussia, where he had been posted as ambassador to the court of Frederick II. Antonio, the youngest brother, was a good-for-nothing, and his role in history was only to serve as adoptive father of María Rosa de Gálvez, a relatively famous poet and playwright.[24] Miguel de Gálvez y Saint-Maxent was not even five years old. Under these circumstances José de Gálvez would have needed twenty more years to transfer the power of the Gálvez clan to his grandnephew's generation. And power must be handed hot; otherwise, memories of favors already received will freeze.

In any case, José de Gálvez would not even be given the opportunity to try, since barely six months after his nephew's death he followed him to the grave. His death on June 17, 1787, like that of his nephew, was surrounded by rumors and legends also pointing to poison as the cause.[25] Others even relate a story, completely false, in which King Carlos III remonstrated José de Gálvez about the rumors that his nephew intended to proclaim himself king of Mexico, and the sadness and rage the minister felt caused his death shortly afterward.[26]

Miguel, Bernardo de Gálvez's only male descendant, despite his few years, was promoted to ensign before leaving New Spain.[27] In 1792, at nine years of age, he began his studies in the Real Seminario de Nobles (Royal School for Nobles) in Madrid, and five years later he was made ensign in the American Company of the Royal Guards of King Carlos IV, a prestigious military unit reserved for scions of the highest aristocracy.[28] In 1808 he was promoted to captain in the also prestigious King's Dragoons Regiment.[29] During Napoleon's invasion of Spain he must have shown insufficiently anti-French behavior. Eric Beerman even maintains that he joined the army of Joseph I, Napoleon's brother, who was king of Spain for a few years, but I have been unable to find any documentation supporting this claim.[30] After the French occupation he was submitted to a kind of trial to determine his true allegiance, which ended by declaring him clean and fit for service in the Royal

Spanish Army of Fernando VII.[31] He died young and a bachelor on April 3, 1825, and the title of Count of Gálvez went to his older sister, Matilde.[32]

Matilde, third Countess of Gálvez, married General Raimundo Minutolo de Capace in 1795 and moved to Naples.[33] In southern Italy she had a role in a conspiracy against the French invaders. She died in 1839 during a trip to Malaga. The title remained in Italy until mid-nineteenth century, when it was suppressed. It was rehabilitated and reclaimed in 1951.[34]

In 1792 Adelaide d'Estrehen, Matilde's and Miguel's half-sister, married Benito Pardo de Figueroa, a military officer and veteran of Pensacola who later became a diplomat under King Joseph I of Spain.[35]

Guadalupe, the posthumous daughter of Bernardo de Gálvez, lived with her mother and after her death moved to Malaga, where she lived with her aunt Isabel Saint-Maxent de Unzuaga.[36] She died in 1801.

Feliciana Saint-Maxent de Gálvez, widow Countess of Gálvez, accompanied her children to Madrid in accordance with her late husband's will.[37] A character in her own right, she was not easily confined to the limited role assigned to an aristocratic widow by Spanish standards of the time. After spending a short time in Cadiz, the family settled in Madrid in September 1787. Their address was 23 Corredera Baja de San Pablo, just across from the Church of San Antonio of the Portuguese, now known as San Antonio of the Germans.[38] There, according to Eric Beerman, she behaved like a "merry widow," but her home actually became the center of a French-style political and literary salon "that soon became popular for the importance of the invited as well as for her beauty and charm."[39] Feliciana's popularity would not last long, since the political environment was quickly changing. In less than two years, pro-French sentiments went from being fashionable to being highly suspicious, if not treasonous. The Spanish government that had embraced the Enlightenment became horrified by its child, the French Revolution. In June 1790 all foreigners were deported from Madrid, and although Feliciana was legally Spanish, both because Louisiana had been part of Spain since 1763 and because of her marriage, she became highly suspect. Her close friend Francisco de Cabarrús, a prominent banker of French origin, was thought to be sympathetic to the new French government and was closely followed by the police. In July Cabarrús asked Felicitas to deliver some jewels to the French embassy, with the result that he was accused of passing contraband and Felicitas's house was subjected to close surveillance. One of the police reports stated that at her residence a great number of foreigners and Spaniards met, where they ate, drank, and had coffee, and Cabarrús "remained most if not all nights well after dinner until one, since at twelve the gathering dispersed, while Cabarrús dined alone with the countess."⁴⁰ Other personalities invited to her house were the playwright Leandro Fernández de Moratín, the architect Francisco de Sabatini, and the politicians Count Aranda and Melchor Gaspar de Jovellanos.⁴¹

It was only a question of time before Feliciana attracted the attention of the authorities. On September 11 she was ordered to leave Madrid for Valladolid. There the police were instructed to keep a record of whom she met and to pay close attention to her conduct and conversations.⁴² From her exile Feliciana wrote to the king, the queen, and the Count of Floridablanca to proclaim her innocence. She suspected that the accusations against her originated with the Countess of Sonora, the widow of José de Gálvez, with whom she had an especially bad relationship. After some months in Valladolid she was allowed to move to Zaragoza, where she stayed until June 1793, when she was allowed to return to Madrid and was finally acquitted of any responsibility in the Cabarrús affair. There she received a visit by Alexander von Humboldt on his way to Mexico, and the scientist found her of "exceptional beauty and beloved by everyone."⁴³ Felicitas Saint-Maxent de Gálvez died in Aranjuez in May 21, 1799. Two alleged portraits of her have survived. The first one is a miniature about which no details are available, since it appears in a brief biography of the playwright Maria Rosa de Gálvez. The other is a pencil sketch of the entire Gálvez y Saint-Maxent family, with their names in French: Felicité, Michel, Adelaide, Matilde, Guadaloupe, and Benito. The presence of Benito, most probably son of Adelaide and Benito Pardo de Figeroa, could date the group portrait to about 1794.

None of the members of the Gálvez's clan would ever recover the power and influence they held during the times of Bernardo and José de Gálvez. As a contemporary pamphlet very accurately described it:

> The Galvezes dissolved,
> Like salt in water,
> And like sparks in the forge
> Phosphorus disappeared.
> Down they went as up they went
> As an exhalation;
> God grants them pardon,
> Without us forgetting their crossing,
> That this world plays tricks
> On the ones who worship it.⁴⁴

Appendix

TABLE 1. *British Prisoners Taken during the Mississippi Campaign, 1779–1780*

		Lieut. Col.	Capt.	Lieut.	2nd Lieut.	Ensigns	Serg.	Corp.	Drumm.	Privates	Surg.	Other
Baton Rouge	Artillery			1				1		9		
	16th Reg.	1	1	2	1	1	7		6	120	1	1
	60th Reg.			1						4		
	Waldeck Reg.		2	3			8		6	176	3	3
	Indep. comp.		1			1	1			14		
	Garrison										2	1
Manchac	16th Reg.						1			4		
	60th Reg.			1			1			11		
	Indep. comp.			1			1			4		
Thompson's Creek	16th Reg.						1			4		
	Waldeck Reg.									8		
Amite River	60th Reg.						3		1	7		
	Indep. comp.									1		
Miss. River	16th Reg.									1		

Lakes										1
16th Reg.	1	5	9	1	2	3	1	14	2	1
Waldeck Reg.									49	6
									414	6

Officers	18
NCOs	27
Privates	428
Surgeons	6
Other	6
TOTAL	485

Source: London Gazette, March 28–April 1, 1780.

TABLE 2. *Forces under the Command of Bernardo de Gálvez, January 1780*

	1st Manuscript	2nd Manuscript	Diary
España Regiment	670	600	600
Príncipe Regiment	43	43	43
Havana Fixed Inf. Reg.	90	90	90
Louisiana Fixed Inf. Reg.	141	141	141
Artillerymen	14	14	14
Carabineers	26	26	26
White militia	223	223	323
Black and mulatto militia	107	107	107
Slaves			24
Anglo-American volunteers	26	26	26
Total	1,340	1,270	1,394

Sources: First manuscript, "Relación de la toma de la Mobila por las armas del Rey de España verificada en 14 de marzo de 1780," Archivo General de Simancas, SGU, LEG 6912, 2; second manuscript, a copy of the previous one; diary, "Diario que yo, d. Bernardo de Gálvez, brigadier de los Reales Ejércitos, gobernador de la provincia de la Luisiana y encargado por S.M. de la expedición contra Panzacola y Mobila, formé de los acontecimientos que ocurren en ella," Archivo General de Simancas, SGU, LEG 6912, 2.

TABLE 3. *Ships under the Command of Bernardo de Gálvez, January 1780*

Type of Ship	Name	Cannons	Crew	Commander	Year Built	Building Yard
Spanish Royal Navy frigate	*Volante*	20		Navy lieutenant Luís Lorenzo de Terrazas	1754	Havana
Spanish Royal Navy packet boat	*Kaulicán*	12		Ramón Bertendona	1764	Havana
Private armed corsair packet boat	*Galveztown, Galvezton,* or *Gálvez*	20	21 officers and specialists, 18 artillerymen and 64 sailors	Pedro Rousseau		Former HMS *West Florida*
Private frigate	*La Misericordia*					
Pink	*San Vicente Ferrer*					
	San Francisco de Paula					
	La Merced					
	?					
Galeota	*Valenzuela*	1		Juan Antonio de Riaño		New Orleans?
Brig	*San Salvador de Orta*					
	?					
Packet boat	*Rosario*	16			1728	

Sources: "Diario que yo, d. Bernardo de Gálvez, brigadier de los Reales Ejércitos, gobernador de la provincia de la Luisiana y encargado por S.M. de la expedición contra Panzacola y Mobila, formé de los acontecimientos que ocurren en ella," Archivo General de Simancas, SGU, LEG 6912, 2; "Año 1779. Lista de la tripulación del bergantín nombrado Galvezton," Archivo General de Indias, Seville, Papeles de Cuba, 648; Beerman, "El diario de Bernardo de Gálvez," 127–28; *Ocho libros de asientos de las tripulaciones de navíos*, 469; Ortega Pereyra, *El Real Arsenal de La Habana*, 99.

TABLE 4. *First Ships at Mobile from Havana, February 1780*

Type of Ship	Name	Cannons	Commander	Year Built	Building Yard
Sloop	*Terrible*				
	?				
Frigate	*San Jose, alias el Caiman*	30	Navy commander Miguel de Goicoechea	1770	Havana
Packet boat	*San Pío*	16		1777	El Ferrol
Brig	*Santa Teresa*	12		1780	Havana
	San Juan Nepomuceno, alias Renombrado	14 to 16	Nicolás Díaz de Mayorga y Martínez	1770s	Bought by the Spanish Royal Navy
Schooner	?				
	?				

Sources: "Diario que yo, d. Bernardo de Gálvez, brigadier de los Reales Ejércitos, gobernador de la expedición contra Panzacola y Mobila, formé de los acontecimientos que ocurren en ella," Archivo General de Simancas, SGU, LEG 6912, 2; J. M. Torres, *Lo que fuimos y lo que somos*, 111; Blanco Nuñez, *La construcción naval en Ferrol*, 44; González-Aller Hierro, "Relación de buques de la Armada," 470; Caughey, *Bernardo de Gálvez in Louisiana*, 176–77.

TABLE 5. *Spanish Forces Ready in Havana to Join the Pensacola Expedition under the Command of Bernardo de Gálvez, January 5, 1780*

Infantry Units	Capts.	Lts.	Under-lts.	Ensigns	Soldiers	Staff
Príncipe Reg.	14	14	16	0	620	Lt. Col. Blas Martín Romero
Navarra Reg.: grenadiers' company	1	1	1	0	70	4 ADCs
Navarra Reg.: light infantry company	1	0	1	0	51	2 chaplains
Artillery	1	1	1	0	42	2 surgeons
Louisiana Fixed Inf. Reg.: light infantry company	1	1	0	0	51	2 gunsmiths
Catalonia Reg.: light infantry company	1	1	1	1	100	1 drummer
Free Brown (*Pardos Libres*) Reg.: grenadiers' company	1	1	1	0	88	2 waiters
Free Brown (*Pardos Libres*) Reg.: light infantry company	1	1	0	0	51	
Free Black (*Morenos libres*) Reg.: grenadiers' company	1	1	1	0	88	Several engineers
Free Black (*Morenos libres*) Reg.: light infantry company	1	1	0	0	51	
Pardos' artillery militia	1	1	0	0	50	
Morenos' artillery militia	1	1	0	0	50	
Engineers (*Gastadores libres de fortificación*)	0	0	0	0	100	
Total	24	24	22	1	1,412	

Source: Plan que manifiesta el estado de fuerza de que se compone la expedición, que está pronta a salir de este puerto con destino, y a las órdenes del gobernador de la Luisiana, brigadier d. Bernardo de Gálvez, in Diego José Navarro to José de Gálvez, confidential letter no. 101, Havana, January 5, 1780, Archivo General de Indias, Seville, Santo Domingo, 2082.

TABLE 6. *Troops aboard at Havana's Port for the Expedition under the Command of Bernardo de Gálvez, February 16, 1780*

			Totals	
Units	Officers	Soldiers	Officers	Soldiers
Príncipe Reg.: two battalions	42	604		
Navarra Reg.: first battalion	31	689		
Havana Fixed Inf. Reg.: one light infantry company	2	51		
Catalonia Reg.: light infantry	4	100	83	1,488
Artillery	2	42		
White ADCs and waiters for the command of *pardos* and *morenos*	2	2		
Pardos: grenadiers and light infantry	5	139		
Morenos: grenadiers and light infantry	5	139	16	517
Pardos and *morenos* militia	4	139		
Siege workers	2	100		
Total			99	2,005

Source: Noticia de la tropa embarcada en el Puerto de La Habana el día 15 de este mes en 11 buques de guerra y 19 de transporte para la Expedición que se destina a las órdenes del Brigadier Don Bernardo de Gálvez, Gobernador de la Provincia de la Luisiana, Havana, February 16, 1780, Archivo General de Indias, Seville, Santo Domingo, 2082.

TABLE 7. *Troops aboard the Fleet in Havana for the Pensacola Expedition under the Command of Bernardo de Gálvez, March 7, 1780 (Note: several ships of different types had the same name.)*

WARSHIPS

Ship Type	Name	Cannons	Commander	Men Aboard
Ship of the line	*San Gabriel*	70	Navy captain Joaquín de Cañaveral	600
	San Juan Nepomuceno	70	Navy captain José Perea	551
	San Ramón	64	Navy captain José Calvo de Irazábal	577
Frigate	*Ntra. Sra. de la O*	42	Navy captain Gabriel de Aristizábal	284
	Santa Matilde	36	Navy commander Miguel de Alderete	265
	Santa Marta	36	Navy commander Andrés Valderrama	271
	El Caymán	22	Navy commander Miguel de Goicoechea	177
Packet boat	*San Pío*	18	Navy lieutenant Pedro Obregón	141
Brig	*Santa Teresa*	14	Navy lieutenant Manuel Bilbao	101
	El Kaulicán	14	Navy lieutenant Ramón Bertendona	99
	El Renombrado	18	Navy lieutenant José María Chacón	110
	San Francisco Xavier	10	Captain Juan Vicente Carta	24
	San Juan Baptista	10	Captain Pedro Imán	24
Saic	*San Peregrino*	10	Navy lieutenant Juan de Herrera	44
Sloop	*Ntra. Sra. del Carmen*	14	Lieutenant Miguel de Sapiain	88

TABLE 7. *Continued*

TRANSPORT SHIPS

Ship Type	Name	Cannons	Commander	Men Aboard
Frigate	*El Corazón de Jesús*	1	José María Mongioti	24
	San Juan Baptista	8	Juan Gamindes	23
	Ntra. Sra. del Carmen	8	Francisco Pruna	19
	San Ignacio de Loyola	6	José Magarola	21
	La Luisiana	9	Claudio Chabot	29
Saic	*El Santo Cristo del Calvario*	6	Jaime Espárrago	19
	Ntra. Sra. del Carmen	4	Jaime Fornell	16
	San Cayetano	7	Cristóbal Rosell	21
	San Francisco de Paula	5	Jaime Tremoll	16
	Jesús, María y José	8	Rafael Ferret	19
	Santa Rosalía	8	José Antion Gatell	19
	El Ángel de la Guarda	6	Francisco Pruna	18
	El Santo Cristo del Calvario	8	Félix Grau	19
	La Pura y Limpia Concepción	4	José Soler	16
	Ntra. Sra. de los Remedios	5	José Barrera	13
	Ntra. Sra. de los Desamparados	2	José Blanch	14
Packet boat	*San Magín*		José Robira	24
Brig	*Santa Eulalia*	4	Mariano Fontrodona	13
	San Juan Baptista	4	Juan Vilaró	13
	Ntra. Sra. del Carmen		Antonio Morales	13

MAIL SHIPS

Ship Type	Name	Cannons	Commander	Men Aboard
Schooner	*La Pureza de María*	8	Militia lt. Tomás del Manzano	9
	Ntra. Sra. de la Concepción		Melchor Rodríguez	6
	Ntra. Sra. de la Merced		Juan de Aranda	8
Sloop	*La Pastora*		Felipe Camacho	9
	Ntra. Sra. del Carmen		Andrés Caval	6
Guairo	*Ntra. Sra. de Regla*		Juan Rosales	5

TABLE 7. *Continued*

SUMMARY OF FORCES

Captains and officers	90
Sergeants, drummers, and soldiers	1,781
Artillerymen (*pardos* and *morenos*)	106
Siege workers	100
Surgeons and hospital personnel	16
HQ	31
Logistics	4
Artillery guard	1
Supplies	4
Gunsmiths, carpenters, coopers, cart wrights, and blacksmiths	15
Total men in arms	2,148
War navy officers and crews	3,346
Merchant navy captains and crews	410
Total men departed from Havana	5,904

TROOPS FROM MOBILE ARRIVED AT NEW ORLEANS

España Reg.: second battalion	717
Detachments from Príncipe Reg. and Havana Fixed Inf. Reg.	60
Companies from Louisiana Fixed Inf. Reg.	122
New Orleans' militia	400
Total troops from Mobile	1,299
Total men under Gálvez's command	7,203

Sources: Estado de la Expedición Militar que por orden superior comunicada al Excmo. Sr. Teniente General Don Diego José Navarro, Gobernador y Capitán General de la Isla de Santiago de Cuba con residencia en esta ciudad de La Habana, y ha salido de su puerto contra el de Panzacola, dominación inglesa, los navío y fragatas de guerra de la Escuadra del mando del Excmo. Sr. Don Juan Bautista Bonet y las demás embarcaciones de transporte a incorporarse con las de Nueva Orleans, y seguir al Ejército a las órdenes del Sr. Brigadier y Gobernador de la Provincia de la Luisiana D. Bernardo de Gálvez, cuyo pormenor es a saber, Havana, March 7, 1780, Biblioteca Nacional, Madrid, MS, 17.616; Estado de la Expedición Militar que por virtud de Real orden se ha aprobado por el Excmo. Sr. D. Diego José Navarro, Caballero de la orden de Santiago, Teniente General de los Reales Ejércitos, Gobernador y Capitán General de esta isla de Cuba, y embarcado en este puerto sobre los navíos de guerra de la Escuadra del mando del Excmo. Sr. D. Juan Bautista Bonet, y otras embarcaciones particulares, con destino a incorporarse en la Nueva Orleans con las tropas que allí se hallan a las órdenes del Brigadier D. Bernardo de Gálvez, que debe mandar el jefe y proceder a la expugnación de los estados de S.M.B. en la Mobila y Panzacola, Havana, March 6, 1780, Archivo General de Simancas, SGU, LEG, 6912.

TABLE 8. *Navy Squadron and Troops for the Pensacola Expedition under the Command of Don Bernardo de Gálvez, October 16, 1780 (Note: several ships of different types had the same name.)*

ESCORT

Type	Name	Commander	Offic.	Men	Unit
Ship of the line	Guerrero	Navy captain Fidel Eslava			
	Velasco	Navy captain S. Muñoz de Velasco			
	Dragón	Navy captain Pedro Autrán			
	San Juan Nepomuceno	Navy captain José Perea			
	San Ramón	Navy captain José Calvo de Irazábal			
	San Genaro	Navy captain Félix Tejada			
	Astuto	Navy commander Estanislao Velasco			
Frigate	Santa Matilde	Navy commander Miguel Alderete	6	70	Navarra Reg.
	Santa Rosalía	Navy commander Andrés Tacón	6	65	Havana Fixed Inf. Reg.
	Nuestra Señora de la O	Navy captain Gabriel de Aristizábal	5	89	Príncipe Reg.
	Santa Cecilia	Navy commander Miguel de Goicoechea	6	84	España Reg.
	Caymán	Navy commander José de Rada	4	70	King's Reg.
Packet boat	San Pío	Navy commander Pedro Obregón	1	30	King's Reg.
		Total escort	28	408	

TABLE 8. *Continued*

CONVOY

	Type	Name	Troops Aboard		Unit
			Offic.	Men	
1st Division	Frigate	*La Paz*	4	152	King's Reg.
	Packet boat	*San Juan Baptista*	6	125	España Reg.
	Saic	*El Ángel de la Guarda*	6	110	España Reg.
		Santa Rosalía	5	107	España Reg.
	Frigate	*Príncipe de Asturias*	8	157	España Reg.
	Saic	*Los Desamparados*	4	90	España Reg.
	Brig	*Carmen, de Pascual*	5	80	España Reg.
		Concepción de Ferrer	5	100	España Reg.
	Frigate	*Luisiana*	—	—	Hospital
	Packet boat	*Conde de Aranda*	8	114	Havana Fixed Inf. Reg.
	Saic	*Paula, de Tremoll*	5	104	Havana Fixed Inf. Reg.
		San Cayetano	4	99	Havana Fixed Inf. Reg.
		Jesús, María y José	3	53	Dragoons
	Packet boat	*Paula, de Genes*	3	105	Cataluña Reg.
	Saic	*San Felipe*	3	101	Cataluña Reg.
	Packet boat	*Rosario*	3	110	Cataluña Reg.
	Frigate	*Merced*	4	139	*Morenos*
2nd Division	Frigate	*La Luz*	7	135	Navarra Reg.
		San Ignacio de Loyola	5	100	Navarra Reg.
	Saic	*Los Remedios*	4	100	Navarra Reg.
		Carmen, de Fornell	5	116	Navarra Reg.
		Padua, de Bru	3	80	Navarra Reg.
		Calvario, de Cala	3	97	Navarra Reg.
	Packet boat	*Jesús Nazareno*	4	80	Navarra Reg.
	Pink	*San Vicente Ferrer*	4	116	Navarra Reg.
	Brig	*San José*	—	—	Hospital
	Frigate	*Santa Rosalía*	7	116	Príncipe Reg.
	Saic	*El Calvario, de Espárrago*	4	97	Príncipe Reg.

TABLE 8. *Continued*

CONVOY

	Type	Name	Troops Aboard Offic.	Men	Unit
2nd Division	Saic	Ntra. Sra. del Mar	4	44	Príncipe Reg.
		Carmen, de Graciós	4	86	Príncipe Reg.
	Polacre	San Francisco de Paula			Dragoons and their horses
	Saic	Buen Viaje			Dragoons and their horses
		Santo Cristo del Calvario			Dragoons and their horses
	Brig	Baptista, de Vadillo	4	139	Pardos
3rd Division	Saic	Concepción	3	87	Artillery
		Calvario	3	100	Pardos and morenos
	Brig	Pura y Limpia	—	100	Engineers (*gastadores*)
		Ntra. Sra. de la Merced	—	—	Gunpowder
	Sloop	Industris	—	—	Gunpowder
		Ntra. Sra. del Toro	—	—	Gunpowder
		Pastora	—	—	Gunpowder
		Poder de Dios	—	—	Gunpowder
		Carmen	—	—	Gunpowder
		Ntra. Sra. del Rosario	—	—	Gunpowder
		Rosario, de Piña	—	—	Gunpowder
		Santa Inés	—	—	Gunpowder
		San José y Ánimas	—	—	Gunpowder
		Jesús Nazareno	—	—	Gunpowder
		San Pedro, de Vitori	—	—	Gunpowder
		Los Remedios	—	—	Gunpowder
	Brig	San Juan Baptista	1	23	Light infantry
		Total transports	169	3,770	

Source: Escuadra del mando del Señor Don José Solano, Jefe de esta clase de la real Armada, y buques de su convoy que transportan la tropa del Ejército a las órdenes del Mariscal de campo el Señor Don Bernardo de Gálvez, aboard the *San Juan Nepomuceno*, at sea close to Havana's port, October 16, 1780, Archivo General de Simancas, Marina 420.

TABLE 9. *Ships and Men Lost after the Storm of October 18–23, 1781*

Havana		Campeche		New Orleans		Mobile		Total	
Offic.	Men	Offic.	Men	Offic.	Men	Offic.	Men	Offic.	Men
48	862	75	1,771	28	831	13	365	164	3,829

Sources: Estado general que manifiesta los oficiales y tropa que se embarcó en la expedición del mando del mariscal de campo d. Bernardo de Gálvez, que dio vela de este puerto el 16 de octubre de 1780, y parajes a que han arribado hasta hoy día de la fecha a resultas del temporal que experimentó desde el 18 al 23 del mismo mes, in Diego José Navarro to José de Gálvez, official letter no. 894, Havana, November 20, 1780, Archivo General de Indias, Seville, Santo Domingo, 2082; Diego José Navarro to José de Gálvez, official letter no. 898, Havana, November 28, 1780, Archivo General de Indias, Santo Domingo 2082; José de Ezpeleta to Pedro Piernas, official letter, Mobile, November 6, 1780, Archivo General de Indias, Cuba 2.
Note: The ships lost were the packet boat *San Francisco de Paula* in Campeche; the brig *Ntra. Señora del Carmen*; and the saic *San Antonio de Padua*, abandoned in Campeche. There was no news from the saics *Santa Rosalía*, *Jesús, María y José*, or *San Francisco de Paula*, nor from the schooners *Divina Pastora*, *El Poder de Dios*, *Santa Inés*, or *San Pedro*.

TABLE 10. *Expedition for the Relief of Mobile and the Conquest of Pensacola, February 28, 1781 (Note: several ships of different types had the same name.)*

WARSHIPS

Ship		Commander				
Type	Name	Rank	Commander Name	Crew	Units Aboard	Men
Ship of the line	*San Ramón*	Navy captain	José Calvo de Irazábal	410	King's Reg.: 1st company of grenadiers	63
Frigate	*Santa Clara*	Navy commander	Miguel de Alderete	292	Navarra Reg., 1st company of grenadiers	43
	Santa Cecilia		Miguel de Goicoechea	283	King's Reg.: 2nd company of grenadiers	30
Chambequín (type of frigate)	*Caymán*		José Serrato	154	Navarra Reg., 2nd company of grenadiers	20
Packet boat	*San Pío*	Navy lieutenant	José María Chacón	110	King's Reg.: 2nd company of grenadiers	33
			Total	1,249	Total	189

TRANSPORTS

	Ship Type	Name	Captain	Crew	Unit/Cargo Aboard	Men
3rd Division	Frigate	*La Victoria*	Álvarez	21	—	—
		Santa Rosalía	Virgili	20	España Reg., 1st company of grenadiers	63
		El Vizcayno	Butrón	13	Guadalajara Reg.	77
					Hibernia Reg.	35
		Ntra. Sra. del Carmen	Crosa	18	Soria Reg.	110
		Ntra. Sra. de la Merced	Río	25	Soria Reg.	103
	Packet boat	*San José y San Joaquín*	Miranda	12	Hibernia Reg.	90
		Ntra. Sra. del Camino	Lezama	13	Hibernia Reg.	80
		San Juan Baptista	Peynado	16	Príncipe Reg., 1st company of grenadiers	63
	Polacre	*El Conde de Aranda*	Pont	12	Flanders Valon Reg.	57
	Total			150	Total	678
1st Division	Polacre	*La Concepción*	Mausat	25	Flanders Valon Reg.	100
		San José	Clausell	18	Aragon Reg.	77
					Soria Reg.	21
	Saic	*Ntra. Sra. de la Merced*	Bobera	20	Soria Reg.	100
	Brig	*La Pura y Limpia*	Arrate	10	Flanders Valon Reg.	90
		San José y las Ánimas	Rodrígez	16	Flanders Valon Reg.	60

TABLE 10. Continued

TRANSPORTS

	Ship Type	Name	Captain	Crew	Unit/Cargo Aboard	Men
1st Division	Sloop	*Ntra. Sra. del Carmen*	Columba	8	Salt, liquor, bricks	—
		La Begoña	Allende	12	Artillery	50
					Engineers (*Gastadores de fortificación*)	102
	Packet boat	*Santa Catalina*	Landiburu	12	Provisions for Mobile	—
	Brig	*El Marqués de Narros*	Murruta	13	Provisions for Mobile	—
	Total			134	Total	600
2nd Division	Packet boat	*Jesús Nazareno*	Valderas	17	Supplies for artillery	—
		El Conde de Aranda	Antoniano	16	Supplies for artillery	—
	Polacre	*Virgo Potens*	Dodero	16	Provisions for the expedition	—
	Sloop	*Ntra. Sra. del Carmen*	Morell	7	Provisions for the expedition	—
	Schooner	*La Concepción*	Masas	5	Salt, liquor, bricks	—
	Frigate	*Western Norland*	Ninstec	20	Hospital	—
	Sloop	*Ntra. Sra. del Toro*	Morell	7	—	—
		El Rosario	Meyreles	5	Provisions for the expedition	—
		Prudencia	Fabre	10	—	—
	Total			103		

SUMMARY OF TROOPS ABOARD

Unit	Capts.	Lts.	Under-lts.	Serg.	Drums	Corporals and Soldiers	Total Men (Excluding Officers)
King's Reg.	2	2	2	4	2	120	126
Príncipe Reg.	—	1	—	2	1	60	63
España Reg.	1	1	1	2	1	60	63
Navarra Reg.	—	1	—	2	1	60	63
Soria Reg.	3	3	3	9	6	216	231
Guadalajara Reg.	1	1	1	3	2	72	77
Hibernia Reg.	5	4	4	12	8	288	308
Aragon Reg.	1	1	1	3	2	72	77
Flanders Valon Inf. Reg.	4	4	4	12	9	287	307
Artillery	—	—	1	2	1	47	50
Engineers (*Gastadores de fortificación*)	—	—	—	—	—	102	102
Total	17	18	17	51	33	1,384	1,467
General staff							25
Army							1,543
Navy							1,249
Transports							387
Total							3,179

Sources: Estado que manifiesta los Buques de Guerra y Comboy [*sic*], del mando del Capitán de Navío, Don José Calvo de Irazábal en el que se conduce el Ejército que, a las órdenes del Sr. Don Bernardo de Gálvez, Mariscal de Campo, se dirige al socorro de la Movila y conquista de Panzacola, Havana, February 17, 1781, Archivo General de Simancas, Marina 421; Estado que manifiesta los Buques en que se han embarcado las tropas destinadas a las órdenes del mariscal de Campo D. Bernardo de Gálvez, que dieron vela el día de la fecha, Havana, February 28, 1781, Archivo General de Indias, Seville, Santo Domingo, 2083A; Tropa que se ha embarcado a la orden del Mariscal de Campo Don Bernardo de Gálvez en Havana, February 28, 1781, Archivo General de Indias, Seville, Cuba, 1377.

TABLE 11. *British Forces at the Siege of Pensacola, February–May 1781*

Units	Men	Commander
3rd Waldeck Reg.	310	Lt. Col. Albrecht von Horn
16th Infantry Reg.	282	Lt. Col. Alexander Dickson
60th Infantry Reg.		Lt. Col. William Stiell
Pennsylvania and Maryland Loyalists	273	Maj. John McDonald
Royal Foresters	41	Adam Chrystie
Officers	54	
Subtotal	960	
Indians	400–500	
Blacks	50	
Armed civilians	107	
Total	1,517–1,617	
Royal Navy	139	Maj. Friedrich Pentzel

Sources: B. Gálvez, *Diario de las operaciones . . .* , Biblioteca de Palacio Real / Biblioteca Nacional, Madrid; Coker, *Siege of Pensacola 1781 in Maps*, 118–19.

TABLE 12. *Troops Sent to Pensacola from Mobile, March 1781.*

Units	Ships
Carabineers	Barge of the general
Gastadores (sappers)	*Bercha* [sic] (small ship?)
Artillery	
1st half of the fusiliers with their captain and under-lieutenant	Long boat from the *Santa Rosalía*
	Boat of Mr. Colon
Príncipe Regiment	Long boat from the brig *Cañonero*
	Sloop of Mr. Parent
Navarra Regiment	Long boat from the frigate
	Long boat of the packet boat
	Long boat from the pink
	Sloop of Narbona
	Sloop of Trouillet
	Sloop of Orbane
Havana Fixed Infantry Regiment	Long boat from the saic *Paula*
	Schooner of Mme. Agustín
	Sloop of Florentin
España Regiment	Long boat from the *Ángel de la Guarda*
	Schooner of Mr. Alexandre
	Schooner of Mr. Favre
	2nd *bercha* [sic] (small ship) (if it returns on time)
	Boat of Mr. Delivois
	Boat of Mr. Ward
	Boat of Mr. La Forre
2nd half of the fusiliers	Long boat from the brig *San Juan Baptista*
	Sloop of Marcelino
Total troops arrived to Pensacola from Mobile	905

Sources: Orden para el día 10 de marzo de 1781, Órdenes dadas al destacamento de la Mobila desde el día 4 de marzo hasta el 22 del mismo de 1781, Archivo Ezpeleta, Seville, Papeles de Panzacola, in Medina Rojas, *José de Ezpeleta*, 718–19; Francisco de Miranda, "Diario de lo mas particular ocurrido desde el día de nuestra salida del puerto de La Habana," s.l., s.a., Archivo Francisco de Miranda, Caracas, Venezuela, Viajes, t. 3, España, América, ff. 70–75.

TABLE 13. *Troops Sent to Pensacola from New Orleans, March 1781 (Note: several ships of different types had the same name.)*

TROOPS ARRIVED BY SEA

Units			Ships	
Name	Offic.	Men	Type	Name
King's Reg.	7	132	Frigate	Ntra. Sra. de la Paz
Príncipe Reg.	3	60	Saic	Santa Rosalía
España Reg.	1	40		
Soria Reg.	2	55	Packet boat	San Gil
Soria Reg.	3	51	Saic	San Francisco de Paula, de Escardó
Guadalajara Reg.	1	53		San Francisco de Paula, n. 99
Aragon Reg.	2	55	Saic	
Navarra Reg.	4	101	Saic	Ntra. Sra. del Carmen
Navarra Reg.	5	120	Frigate	Ntra. Sra. de la Luz
Navarra Reg.	3	59	Polacre	San Josef or San José
America's Dragoons	1	30		
Catalonia Volunteers	2	89	Packet boat	El Rosario
Havana Fixed Inf. Reg.	3	57	Polacre	San Miguel
España Reg.	1	20		
Grenadiers of the Louisiana Reg.	5	48	Polacre	San Francisco de Paula
Louisiana's Dragoons	3	40		
Louisiana Regiment Light Infantry	5	77	Saic	Ntra. Sra. de la Merced

Name	Offic.	Men	Type	Name
Pardos' Grenadiers and Light Infantry	5	138	Brig	*San Juan Baptista*
Morenos' Grenadiers and Light Infantry	5	123	Frigate	*Ntra. Sra. de la Merced*
Subtotal	61	1,348		
Sick/unfit for service		31		
Total		1,379		
TROOPS ARRIVED BY LAND				
Artillery		4		
America's Dragoons		25		
Carabineers		11		
Militias		32		
Free *Pardos* (mullatos) and Free		90		
Morenos (blacks)				
Black Armed Slaves		75		
Total		237		
Total troops sent from New Orleans to Pensacola		1,616		

Sources: B. Gálvez, *Diario de las operaciones...*, Biblioteca de Palacio Real / Biblioteca Nacional, Madrid; "Diario de las operaciones..." (first manuscript), Archivo General de Simancas, SGU, 6913, Ex3; Estado de los oficiales y tropa que, al mando de d. Cayetano de Salla, teniente coronel del Regimiento de Soria, sale de esta Plaza para la Expedición a Panzacola con expresión de presentes y enfermos, New Orleans, February 28, 1781, Archivo General de Indias, Cuba 563; Estado que manifiesta los oficiales y tropa que de la Nueva Orleans, salieron el 3 de este mes al mando del teniente coronel d. Cayetano de Salla, con expresión de los que quedan en aquel hospital y buques en que va cada uno, a bordo de la saetía San Francisco de paula de Escardó, March 23, 1781, Archivo General de Indias, Cuba 81.

TABLE 14. *Troops Sent to Pensacola from Havana, April 9, 1781*

Units	Offic.	Men
Soria Reg.	12	250
Guadalajara Reg.	14	291
Hibernia Reg.	10	250
Aragon Reg.	10	256
Catalonia Reg.	10	242
Flanders Valon Inf. Reg.	7	186
Artillery	4	62
Totals	67	1,537

Sources: Noticia de los señores oficiales y tropa de Ejército que manda el Excmo. Sr. D. Victorio de Navia, embarcadas en los Navíos de Guerra, con expresión de lo que va por dotación de dichos Navíos y lo que va destinado para el Destacamento que manda el Mariscal de Campo D. Juan Manuel de Cagigal, Havana, April 10, 1781, Archivo General de Indias, Santo Domingo 2086; Saavedra, *Diario*, entry from April 9, 1781, 163.

TABLE 15. *Spanish and French Squadron Sent to Pensacola from Havana, April 8, 1781*

Division	Type of Ship	Name	Nationality	Commander
2nd	Ship of the line	L'Intrepide / Intrépido	France	Duplessis Pafcau
		Astuto	Spain	Estanislao de Velasco y Coello
		San Nicolás	Spain	Francisco Morales
		San Francisco de Asís	Spain	José Domás y Valle*
		San Francisco de Paula	Spain	
	Frigate	La Licorne / Unicornio	France	Señor de San Ours
	Brig	Renombrado	Spain	
1st	Ship of the line	Le Triton / Tritón	France	Didier de Pierrefeu
		Magnánimo	Spain	Carlos Torres*
		San Luis	Spain	
		Le Destin / Destino	France	Maitz de Goimpy
		Guerrero	Spain	
	Cutter-brig	Le Serpent / Serpiente	France	Lalonne
	Frigate	L'Andromaque / Andrómaca	France	Caballero de Ravenel
3rd	Ship of the line	Gallardo	Spain	Francisco Morales
		San Gabriel	Spain	
		Le Palmier / Palmier	France	Caballero de Monteil
		Dragón	Spain	Pedro Autrán
		Arrogante	Spain	Felipe López de Carrizosa
	Frigate	Ntra. Sra. de la O	Spain	
	Brig	Levrette / Lebrel	France	
	Frigate	Mexicana	Spain	

Sources: Orden de batalla de la escuadra combinada. Aboard the San Luis en el Puerto de Havana el 8 de April de 1781, in D. José Solano, *Diario del Jefe de la Escuadra D. José Solano, Toma de Panzacola, April y May 1781*, Archivo General de Simancas, Marina 422. For the French commanders, see Lacou-Gayet, *La marine militaire de la France*, 347–48. For the Spanish ones, see www.todoababor.es and www.threedecks.org (accessed September 20, 2015).
* Not confirmed.

TABLE 16. *Total Spanish and French Forces at the Siege of Pensacola, April 23, 1781*

	Units	Men
1st Brigade	King's Reg.	419
	Príncipe Reg.	257
	Navarra Reg.	672
	Havana Fixed Inf. Reg.	244
	1st Brigade total	1,592
2nd Brigade	Soria Reg.	495
	Hibernia Reg.	467
	Flanders Valon Inf. Reg.	424
	2nd Brigade total	1,386
3rd Brigade	Guadalajara Reg.	328
	España Reg.	482
	Aragon Reg.	287
	Louisiana Fixed Inf. Reg.	149
	Dragoons	97
	3rd Brigade total	1,343
4th Brigade	Navy and other	1,323
	Brigades total	5,644
1st Division	2nd company of Catalonia Reg.	228
Campo Volante (reserve)	Havana Fusiliers Company	78
	Havana Colored Militia	262
	New Orleans Colored Militia	173
	1st Division total	741
2nd Division French Division	2nd Division total	509
3rd Division Artillery	From the Spanish navy	80
	From the French navy	108
	From the French army	74
	From the Spanish army	209
	3rd Division total	471
	Divisions total	1,721
HQ	Carabineers	13
	Engineers (*gastadores de fortificación*)	107
	HQ total	120
Total		7,485

Source: Orden para 23 de abril, ordenes dadas desde el 22 hasta el 25 de marzo a los Destacamentos de La Habana y Movila, desde dicho día hasta el 21 de abril a los dos expresados y el de Orleans, y desde el 22 en que se reunió el refuerzo último hasta la rendición de Panzacola, Archivo Ezpeleta, Seville, Papeles de Panzacola, in Medina Rojas, *José de Ezpeleta*, 766–67.

TABLE 17. *Spanish and French High-Ranking Officers at the Siege of Pensacola, April 23, 1781*

HQ	Supreme commander	Bernardo de Gálvez
	ADCs to the supreme commander	Barón de Kessel
		Esteban Miró
		Pedro Rodríguez
		Arturo O'Neill
	Second supreme commander	Juan Manuel de Cagigal
	ADCs to the second supreme commander	Francisco Miranda
		Francisco Montalvo
		Juan Cagigal
	Major general	José de Ezpeleta
	ADCs to the mayor general	Benito Pérez
		Juan de Urbina
		Veremundo Ramírez
	Quartermaster general	Francisco de Nava
	Artillery commander	Vicente Risel
	Trench commander (*mayor de trinchera*)	José Urraca
1st Brigade	Brigadier (Col.) Jerónimo Girón	
	Lt. Col. Joaquín Mayone	
	Sargento mayor, Capt. Joaquín Pérez Isava	
2nd Brigade	Brigadier Col. Manuel Pineda	
	Lt. Col. Barón de Carondelet	
	Sargento mayor Casimiro Bofarull	
3rd Brigade	Brigadier Col. Francisco Longoria	
	Lt. Col. Cayetano de Salla	
	Sargento mayor, Capt.-Lt. Col. [sic] Manuel Márquez	
4th Brigade	Brigadier navy captain Felipe López de Carrizosa	
	Col. José Pereda	
	Col. José Zabala	
	Sargento mayor, Capt. Juan de Alcázar	
1st Division	Col. Pablo Figuerola	
Campo Volante	Lt. Col. Gilberto Maxent	
(reserve)	First ADC Antonio Juárez	
2nd Division	Commander, navy captain Mr. Boiderut	
French Division	Sargento mayor capt. Mr. D'Amariton	
	ADC Mr. De Renty	
3rd Division Artillery	Commander, Lt. Col. Vicente Risel	

Source: Orden para 23 de abril, ordenes dadas desde el 22 hasta el 25 de marzo a los Destacamentos de La Habana y Movila, desde dicho día hasta el 21 de abril a los dos expresados y el de Orleans, y desde el 22 en que se reunió el refuerzo último hasta la rendición de Panzacola, Archivo Ezpeleta, Seville, Papeles de Panzacola, in Medina Rojas, *José de Ezpeleta*, 766–67.

TABLE 18. *Army Assembled for the Expedition against Jamaica, October 1, 1781*

Regiments	Fit for Service		Sick and Convalescent in Havana		Missing/ Absent without Leave	
	Offic.	Sold.	Offic.	Sold.	Offic.	Sold.
Soria	92	925	8	94	2	44
Guadalajara	94	829	9	90	0	14
Hibernia	48	679	7	108	4	29
Aragon	49	991	7	109	9	196
Second of Catalonia	44	741	1	98	0	89
Flanders	46	612	9	92	1	49
Artillery	4	87	0	9	0	1
Pardos (mullatos) and *Morenos* (blacks)	0	129	0	9	0	0
Totals	377	4,993	41	609	16	422

Plus 33 officers assigned to HQ

Source: Estado de la fuerza con que se halla el ejército de operación, hoy día de la fecha con expresión de los presentes y en estado de hacer servicio, enfermos y convalecientes en Havana, ausentes en varios destinos y la alta y baja ocurrida en el mes próximo pasado, signed by Jose de Ezpeleta, Havana, October 11, 1781, in Archivo General de Indias, Santo Domingo, 2084.

TABLE 19. *Expedition against the Island of New Providence under the Command of Juan Manuel de Cagigal, April–May 1782*

Nationality	Type	SHIPS Name/Number	Commander
United States	Frigate	*Carolina del Sur* [*South Carolina*]	Commodore Alejandro [Alexander] Guillón [Gillon]
	Schooner	*Boetsi* [sic]	Guillermo [William] Cok [Cock?]
	Frigate	2	
	Brig	5	
	Schooner	2	
	Sloop	1	
	Total U.S. ships	12	
Spain	Frigate	5	
	Packet boat	2	
	Brig	6	
	Saic	7	
	Polacre	1	
	Gunboat	10	
	Longboat	3	
	Schooner	7	
	Sloop	4	
	Total Spanish ships	45	
Total		57	

TABLE 19. *Continued*

ARMY

Guadalajara, España, and Corona de Nueva España Regiments, plus artillery, light infantry, and others	
Officers at HQ	21
Lieutenant colonels	2
Sergeant majors	1
Captains	24
Lieutenants	31
Under-lieutenants	33
Chaplains	3
Surgeons	3
Gunsmiths	3
Sergeants	75
Drummers	55
Corporals and soldiers	1,790
Total	2,041

Source: Estado que manifiesta los oficiales y tropa de que se compone la expedición al mando del Excmo. Sr. D. Juan Manuel de Cagigal, con expresión de los barcos cañoneros, sus comandantes, número de cañones, morteros, obuses y bombas con sus calibres, Archivo General de Indias, Santo Domingo, 2084.

TABLE 20. *Military Forces in New Spain, 1784*

REGULAR ARMY

Infantry	Zamora Reg.	1,377
	Corona de la Nueva España Reg.	1,377
	Two companies in San Juan de Ulúa	240
	One company in Acapulco	105
Dragoons	España Reg.	522
	Mexico Reg.	522
Artillery	Two companies	246
	Total	4,389

PROVINCIAL MILITIA

Infantry	Mexico Reg.	1,464
	Tlaxacala and Puebla Reg.	1,464
	Córdoba and Jalapa Reg.	1,464
	Toluca Reg.	1,464
	Oaxaca Batt.	758
	Valladolid Batt.	732
	Infantry from the Príncipe Legion	758
	Infantry from the San Carlos Infantry	928
	Mexico's *pardos* (brown) Batt.	758
	Puebla's pardos Batt.	758
Dragoons	Puebla Reg.	588
	Valladolid (Michoacán) Reg.	588
Cavalry	Querétaro Reg.	588
	Veracruz Lancers	400
	Cavalry from the Príncipe Legion	1,446
	Cavalry from the San Carlos Legion	2,597
	Total	16,755

URBAN MILITIA

Infantry	Mexico's Commerce Reg.	810
	Puebla's Commerce Reg.	328
	Mexico's Company *de Orfebres* (goldsmiths)	79
	Veracruz's *blancos* (whites) two companies	226
	Veracruz's *pardos* (brown) and *morenos* (blacks) two companies	270
Cavalry	Mexico's Gilds companies	128
	Total	1,841

TABLE 20. *Continued*

	NON-ORGANIZED MILITIAS FROM THE GULF COAST AND THE CARIBBEAN	
Infantry	San Blas' Batt.	766
	82 separate companies	5,218
Cavalry	83 separate companies	3,699
	Total	9,683

	NEW AND OLD MILITIA UNITS	
Infantry	Guadalajara Reg.	1,557
	18 separate companies	1,448
Cavalry	47 separate companies	3,433
	Total	6,438
	Total military forces in New Spain	39,106

Sources: McAlister, *El fuero militar en la Nueva España*, app. 1, 105–6; Proyecto del Coronel D. Francisco Antonio Crespo, inspector interino de las tropas, para el arreglo del Ejército de Nueva España, dictámenes e informes sobre el mismo de D. José de Ezpeleta y del Virrey Conde de Gálvez, apoyo al proyecto del virrey D. Manuel Antonio Flórez e informe del subinspector D. Pedro Mendinueta, Mexico, 1784–1787, Archivo General de Simancas, SGU, LEG, 6985, 1; Proyecto de arreglo del Ejército de Nueva España del coronel inspector D. Francisco Antonio Crespo, dictámenes e informes, Mexico, 1785–1786, Archivo General de Simancas, SGU, LEG, 6985, EXP.12.

TABLE 21. *Official Correspondence Dispatched by Bernardo de Gálvez between June 28, 1785, and October 31, 1786*

Date Sent	Reference Numbers	Number of Working Days	Number of Dossiers	Average Number of Dossiers Handled Daily
June 28, 1785	1 to 16	12	16	1.333
August 2, 1785	17 to 83	35	67	1.914
August 27, 1785	88 to 155	25	72	2.880
September 1785	156 to 217	30	62	2.067
October 29, 1785	218 to 276	33	59	1.788
December 2, 1785	277 to 315	34	39	1.147
January 7, 1786	316 to 380	36	65	1.806
January 31, 1786	381 to 460	24	80	3.333
February 21, 1786	461 to 502	20	42	2.100
March 31, 1786	503 to 557	38	55	1.447
April 30, 1786	558 to 612	31	55	1.774
May 27, 1786	613 to 676	27	64	2.370
July 1, 1786	677 to 756	34	80	2.353
August 3, 1786	757 to 826	32	70	2.188
September 2, 1786	827 to 877	30	51	1.700
September 26, 1786	878 to 918	24	41	1.708
October 31, 1786	919 to 939	34	21	0.618
Totals		499	939	1.882

Source: Indexes of the official correspondence sent by Bernado de Gálvez to the court between June 28, 1785, and October 31, 1786, Archivo General de Indias, Mexico 1513.

Acknowledgments

While it is customary to include in the acknowledgments a list of the people and institutions that have helped the author to research, write, and publish his book, I have to confess that my previous experience with this section is not a very good one. In the list of acknowledgments included in my first book, published in 2002, either by error or by a kind of Freudian slip, I forgot to include an in-law, and all hell broke loose within my family circle. Thus, I decided not to include an acknowledgment section in my following books and just to dedicate them to my wife and two sons. Furthermore, I strongly believe that a book is the product not only of all those who helped the author but also, and in no small measure, of those who hindered him. I have always found more revealing of a person's character not the list of his friends and supporters but the one of his foes, the latter usually much larger than the former. Accordingly, I was initially inclined not to include either of them, because my friends and those who have helped me already know it, and as for the foes, I think it's enough that I know who they are.

Nevertheless, and after some common sense was hammered into me, I realized it would be unfair not to acknowledge in this book the following persons and institutions.

Professor Sylvia. L. Hilton of the Complutense University in Madrid is the first person I wish to thank. As one of the leading scholars in early United States–Spain relations, she pointed me in the direction of Bernardo de Gálvez, a suggestion I have never regretted. After traveling together the always-uncharted waters of academic research, I'm proud to count her among the small number of my friends.

As English is my second language, most if not all of the credit of improving my first English manuscript goes to Marilyn Wyatt, a comrade from hard times in distant lands. Her diligence, patience, and good sense of humor made my work not only possible but also very enjoyable.

My thanks go to the directors, librarians, researchers, and staffs of libraries, archives, and documentation centers I frequented, without whose diligence, and sometimes courtesy, my work would have been impossible: Archivo General de Simancas; Archivo General de Indias in Seville; Real Academia de la Historia, Archivo Histórico Nacional, Museo Naval, Museo de América, Biblioteca Hispánica, and Biblioteca Nacional in Madrid; Museo del Ejército in Toledo; the Museo de las Cortes de Cádiz; the Sociedad Económica de Amigos del País de Málaga; the Library of Congress, and its magnificent Hispanic Division under the direction of Georgette Dorn (whom I sincerely admire), the National Archives, and the Museum of the American Indian in Washington, D.C.; the Bibliothèque nationale de France in Paris; the Widener Library and the Harvard Map Collection at Harvard University, Cambridge; the Milton S. Eisenhower Library at Johns Hopkins University, Baltimore; and the National Archives in Kew, Richmond, United Kingdom.

I am grateful to Kathleen DuVal for her generosity in allowing me the honor to write with her an article on Bernardo de Gálvez for the *Proceedings of the 2015 Sons of the American Revolution Annual Conference: The Marquis de Lafayette and the European Friends of the American Revolution* and for her encouragement and support in the long and winding road leading to the publication of this book.

I thank former president of the Sons of the American Revolution Joe Dooley, the force behind the annual conference of the Sons of the American Revolution, to whom I owe an apology for contributing in turning around what was supposed to be a commemoration of the Marquis de Lafayette in 2015 into a celebration of Bernardo de Gálvez.

The Fundación Consejo España-Estados Unidos, with its chairman, José Manuel Entrecanales, and its secretary general, Manuel Lejarreta, have been actively promoting a better knowledge of the common history between the U.S. and Spain.

Gabriel Paquette has offered support and friendship since we first met. His bonhomie and profound knowledge of the eighteenth-century Portuguese and Spanish empires in the Americas have enriched my historical views and research. His active involvement in finding the right publisher for this book and other endeavors—such as assisting in my appointment as visiting scholar at the Johns Hopkins University, which proved crucial for the completion of the last stages of my research—has made me count him among my closest friends.

My gratitude toward David Armitage stems from his support in finding the appropriate university press to publish this book; he has also become an indispensable ally in promoting academic ties between the United States and Spain.

My meticulous and thorough editor at the University of North Carolina Press at Chapel Hill, Charles Grench, has patiently endured my natural tendency to go full speed ahead, damn the torpedoes. The book has also been much improved by Jad Adkins, who helped me in finding the right illustrations. My editor, Julie Bush, made the original manuscript into a much better book.

The Fundación Rafael del Pino granted me a fellowship to study at Harvard University. The Rafael del Pino's staff; its president, María del Pino y Calvo-Sotelo (the embodiment of politeness and efficiency combined); former director, Amadeo Petitbò (with whom I enjoyed the pleasures of numerous intelligent conversations that have cemented a strong friendship); and Vicente José Montes, current director (in whom I found a partner in all sorts of projects and initiatives), have been of most valuable assistance. Being a fellow at the Weatherhead Center for International Affairs at Harvard University allowed me not only to hugely improve my knowledge but also to meet and learn from some of the leading scholars in the history field. Especially enlightening were Joyce Chaplin's Proseminar on Early American History and Charles S. Maier and Sven Beckert's Seminar on Approaches to Global History. Michèle Lamont, Weatherhead Center director; Kathleen Molony, director of the Fellows Program; Heather Conrad, coordinator of the executive office and Fellows Program; and the rest of the staff helped me to fully squeeze my year at Harvard. I appreciate the other fellows at the Weatherhead Center—Danielle Barnes, Ayesha Dawood, Sebastian Domzalski, Kirk Dorr, Ifigenia Kanara, Moshik Lipetz, Dan O'Bryant, Marzena Rogalska, Ludger Siemes, and Philippe Tremblay—for their always-interesting contributions during our weekly breakfast meetings. After having the opportunity to meet Tamar Herzog at Harvard University, my initial admiration for her work evolved into an enriching friendship. Manuel Muñiz, director of the program on transatlantic relations, has been not only the perfect guide to navigate my way through Anglo-Saxon academia but also the perfect partner in different projects and initiatives.

The book has also benefited from the experiences from several lectures and talks at different institutions, especially those at Rice University on the battle of Pensacola, at the Society of the Cincinnati on the Spanish role in the American Revolutionary War, at the Library of Congress on Bernardo de Gálvez, and at the Transatlantic Seminar at the Weatherhead Center for International Affairs on the American Revolutionary War in a global context.

George Washington's Mount Vernon institution has been crucial in expanding my understanding of certain aspects of the Revolutionary War. I'm especially thankful to Barbara B. Lucas and Sarah Miller Coulson, former and current regents of the Mount Vernon Ladies Association; Curt Viebranz, president and CEO of the Mount Vernon Ladies Association (whose Spanish is much better than he would admit); and Douglas Bradburn, founding director of the magnificent Fred W. Smith National Library for the Study of George Washington at Mount Vernon (whose depth of knowledge about the intellectual and legal debates on early American citizenship is matched by his intelligent and active leadership of the library).

The Daughters of the American Revolution have a long tradition in promoting a better knowledge of this crucial historical period by embracing the profound diversity of the different contributions to American independence. Their Forgotten Patriots Project is an example to be followed and has been of immense value in my research. My special thanks go to Lynn Forney Young and Ann T. Dillon, former and present presidents general, and to the always courteous staff at the magnificent DAR headquarters in Washington, D.C.

I am indebted to Raimundo Pérez-Hernández, current director of the Ramón Areces Foundation in Madrid, who patiently accepted my intellectual pursuits amidst our frenzied work in Madrid and to whose family's clan I'm a proud adopted member. Ramón Gil-Casares, who understood the relevance of Bernardo de Gálvez for the diplomatic relations between the United States and Spain and whose friendship I treasure.

Antonio Campos, mayor of Macharaviaya, welcomed me to his beautiful village and guided me through the stories and legends about the Gálvez family. Elias Bendodo, president of the Diputación de Málaga, has made it his mission to keep alive the memory of Bernardo de Gálvez. The passion about Bernardo of the members of the Granaderos y Damas de Gálvez is so contagious that sometimes they make it very difficult for a historian to keep his necessary objectivity.

My lifelong admiration for the work of the Omohundro Institute, one of the most prestigious institutions for the study of early American history, is now complemented with my gratitude for helping me find the right publisher for this book, especially to its director, Karin Wulf.

My thanks go to Andrew Jackson O'Shaughnessy for his encouragement to write in English a biography of Bernardo de Gálvez; to William Di Giacomantonio for his interest in making Bernardo de Gálvez a household name in the history of the American Revolutionary War; to my lifelong friends Florentino Carreño and Carlos Moreiro, who have never failed to be there for me; and to Graciela Vargas for her contagious enthusiasm.

Before ending the list of acknowledgments, I would like to mention some people who have influenced me beyond measure: my grandfathers Professor Salvador Quintero Delgado and Ambassador José Saravia; my father, Salvador Quintero Saavedra, who always was afraid that his son's intellectual pursuits would condemn him to the same fate as his father's but nevertheless supported me in every possible way; my uncle Ramón (Moncho) whom I miss every day; and Santiago Vargas Rocha, whom I had the opportunity to know only through the loving memory of his daughter.

Last, and certainly not least, I thank Elisa, Salvador, and Santiago, without whom nothing would make sense, and of course my mother, Zarina.

Notes

ABBREVIATIONS
AE   Archivo Ezpeleta, Seville, Spain
AFM   Archivo Francisco de Miranda, Caracas, Venezuela
AGI   Archivo General de Indias, Seville, Spain
AGMG   Archivo General Municipal de Guadalajara, Jalisco, Mexico
AGNM   Archivo General de la Nación de México, Mexico D.F., Mexico
AGS   Archivo General de Simancas, Simancas, Spain
AHM   Archivo Histórico Militar, Madrid, Spain
AHN   Archivo Histórico Nacional, Madrid, Spain
ANF   Archives Nationales de France, Pierrefitte-sur-Seine, Paris and Fontainebleau, France
BN   Biblioteca Nacional, Madrid, Spain
BPR   Biblioteca de Palacio Real, Madrid, Spain
DF   *Expediente* (dossier)
LoC   Library of Congress, Washington, D.C., United States
ms   manuscript
NAL   National Archives, London, United Kingdom
PRO   Public Record Office (formerly British Public Record Office), National Archives, London, United Kingdom
r.   recto (front of the leaf of paper)
RLI (1681) *Recopilación de Leyes de los Reynos [sic] de las Indias: Mandadas imprimir, y publicar por la magestad católica del rey Don Carlos II, nuestro señor.* Madrid: Julián de Paredes, 1681.
RLI (1774) *Recopilación de Leyes de los Reinos de las Indias.* 3rd ed. Madrid: Antonio Pérez de Soto, 1774.
v.   verso (back of the leaf of paper)
WPA   Works Progress Administration by Louisiana State Museum

INTRODUCTION

1. Saavedra, *Diario*, entry of May 6, 1781, 185.

2. Britain had acquired Florida in 1763, after the Seven Years' War. *"Artículos de Capitulación convenidos y acordados entre el Señor D. Bernardo de Gálvez . . . (Articles of Capitulation between His Excellency Don Bernardo de Galvez . . .)* s.l., s.a., BPR, III/6526 (2), and BN, 2/12654; "Diario de las operaciones . . ." (first manuscript), AGS, SGU, 6913, Ex3; *Scots Magazine* 43 (1781).

3. H.J. Res. 105 Joint Resolution, conferring honorary citizenship of the United States on Bernardo de Gaalvez [sic Gálvez, changed in the rest of the document] y Madrid, Viscount of Galveston and Count of Gálvez, approved December 16, 2014, https://www.congress.gov/bill/113th-congress/house-joint-resolution/105/text (accessed September 10, 2016).

[387]

4. For the increasing attention devoted by American historians, especially early American historians, to regions and groups not previously considered by traditional historiography, see A. Taylor, *American Colonies*, ix–xvii; DuVal, *Native Ground*; Fenn, "Whither the Rest of the Continent?"; Chaplin, "Expansion and Exceptionalism"; Hinderaker and Horn, "Territorial Crossings"; Saunt, "Go West"; Mapp, *Elusive West*, 1–26; and Mapp, "Interpretative Implications of a Continental Approach." For the need to incorporate the Spanish-American empire into the field of early American history, see Elliott, "Britain and Spain in America"; and Cañizares-Esguerra, *How to Write the History of the New World*, 1–59.

5. Thomas Stackhouse, *North America: In its present Divisions, agreeable to the Peace* (London, c. 1783), BN, NE, MR/4/I serie 26/003.

6. Armillas Vicente, "El nacimiento de una gran nación"; Reparaz, *Yo Solo*; Yela Utrilla, *España ante la independencia de los Estados Unidos*; Conrotte, *La intervención de España en la independencia*. Also see the works by Olmedo Checa and Vázquez de Acuña (see bibliography). For the term "gift" applied to the Spanish participation in the war, see Chávez, *Spain and the Independence of the United States*.

7. Gálvez's experiment was reported in volume 74 of the *Philosophical Transactions of the Royal Society of London*, read by Sir Joseph Banks on July 1, 1784.

8. For the concept of negotiated authority, see Greene, "Negotiated Authorities."

9. B. Gálvez, *Noticia y reflexiones*, 42–43.

10. DuVal and Quintero Saravia, "Bernardo de Gálvez."

CHAPTER 1

1. Genealogists tend to be as creative as their subjects' power and wealth allow. When Bernardo de Gálvez was made count and his uncle José became marquis, the Spanish Crown's official genealogist, at the time called "King of Arms," traced the origins of the Gálvez family back into the Middle Ages. In 1964, another genealogical treatise about the Gálvez family by the Marquis of García del Postigo (literally, "García of the shutter") mentioned historians who trace the Gálvez ancestry back to a Tartessian warlord who fought the Carthaginians. Vázquez de Acuña, *Historial de la Casa de Gálvez*, 1115.

2. García de Segovia, "The Shepherds of Macharaviaya: Eclogue on the Death of His Excellency Joseph de Gálvez, Marquis of Sonora" (poem) in *Los Pastores de Macharavialla* [sic], mentioned in *Memorial instructivo y curioso de la corte de Madrid*.

3. López-Cordón Cortezo, "Secretarios y secretarías en la edad moderna."

4. Ensenada's *Catastro* registered seventy-four as the number of *vecinos* (residents). The conversion from *vecino* to the total inhabitants is not easy. According to Antonio Domínguez Ortiz, *vecino* usually designated a family, and at that time families were all those who lived in the same house, including servants. Both classic (Braudel and Kamen) and recent (Martín Galán and Bustelo García del Real) historiography recommend multiplying *vecinos* by 4 or 4.5 to obtain the total number of inhabitants. Domínguez Ortíz, *Sociedad y Estado*, 60; Braudel, *La méditerranée*, 36In3; Kamen, *War of Succession*, 367n16; Martín Galán, "Nuevos datos," 593–633; Bustelo García del Real, "La transformación de vecinos," 154–64; Ensenada's census, in AGS, *Catastro de Ensenada*, dirección General de Rentas, 1st Remesa (batch), Catastro de Ensenada, Respuestas Generales, Libro 296, fols. 541v–542r.

5. Bernardo de Gálvez's certified copy of baptism signed by Friar Thomás de San Julián. Macharaviaya's Parish Book of Baptisms, year 1746, f. 131v, in *Pruebas hechas a instancia del sr. Coronel don Bernardo de Gálvez para la Cruz de la Real y Distinguida Orden Española de*

Carlos III, AHN, Estado-Carlos III, DF 49, f. 11v. For the biography of José de Gálvez, see Claret, *José de Gálvez*; Rodas de Coss, "José de Gálvez Gallardo," xxix; and Vázquez de Acuña, "El Ministro de Indias."

6. Death certificate of María Magdalena de Grimaldo, deceased June 13, 1749, *Libro de entierros de la parroquia de Santa Cruz de Madrid*, f. 195, in Rodas de Cos, "José de Gálvez Gallardo," xxix, 106.

7. Matías de Gálvez and María Josefa de Madrid marriage certificate, *Libro de esponsales de 1745*, f. 42, in *Pruebas hechas a instancia del sr. Coronel don Bernardo de Gálvez para la Cruz de la Real y Distinguida Orden Española de Carlos III*, AHN, Estado-Carlos III, DF 49, fols. 12r-12v.

8. Lynch, *La España del siglo XVIII*, 177.

9. Recaño and Torrens, "Algunos apuntes," 17; Reher and González-Quiñones, "Do Parents Really Matter?"

10. Alemán Illán, "Actitudes colectivas," 7.

11. Miranda, *Colombeia*, 5:117.

12. Rumeu de Armas, *Piraterías y ataques navales*, vol. 3, pt. 2, 738, mentioned in Rodríguez del Valle and Conejo Díaz de la Cortina, "Matías de Gálvez," 227.

13. Royal decision of Felipe V, March 12, 1738, quoted in Morales Moya, "Milicia y nobleza," 125.

14. Connell and Mack, *Naval Ceremonies*, 108.

15. Peter Young, *Blücher's Army*, 8; Henderson, *Blücher and the Uprising*, 133.

16. Quintero Saravia, *Blas de Lezo*, 45-53.

17. Kroener, "L'État moderne," 255.

18. Marquis de Croix to Juan Gregorio Muniain, Minister of War, Mexico, March 5, 1769, AGI, Mexico, 2429; Bernardo de Gálvez. Empleos, AGS, SGU, leg. 1, and AGS, SGU, leg. 7220, 2, fols. 4-8, f. 1r.

19. Although in Spain, France, and Britain the conflict bears the name of the Seven Years' War, in the United States it used to be referred to as the French and Indian War; in Germany and Austria, the Third Silesian War; in Sweden, the Pomeranian War; and in India, the Third Carnatic War. Füssel, *Der Siebenjährige Krieg*, 7.

20. Thackeray, *Luck of Barry Lyndon*, 1:115.

21. The name by which this war is known in Britain has its origin, as related by Winston Churchill, in the following incident: "A captain trading with the Spanish possessions, one Jenkins, was brought before the House of Commons to produce his ear in a bottle, and to maintain that it had been cut off by Spanish coastguards when his ship was searched. 'What did you do?' he was asked. 'I commended my soul to God and my cause to my country,' was the answer put in his mouth by the Opposition. Jenkins' ear caught the popular imagination and become the symbol of agitation. Whether it was in fact his own ear or whether he had lost it in a seaport brawl remains uncertain, but the power of this shriveled object was immense." Churchill, *History of the English-Speaking Peoples*, 3:101. During this war, Lawrence Washington served as captain. On his return, he decided to name his plantation in honor of his former commander, Vice Admiral Edward Vernon. At his death in 1752, Mount Vernon went to his younger half-brother, George Washington. For the origins of the war, also see Quintero Saravia, *Blas de Lezo*, 194-208.

22. Ferrer del Río, *Historia del reinado*, 1:207.

23. *Ordonnance . . . portant création d'un régiment d'infanterie de troupes légères*.

24. Definition of *Cantabres ou Cantabriens* in Moreri, *Le grand dictionnaire*, 3:139; definition of *Cantabria* in Covarrubias, *Tesoro de la lengua castellana*, 189.

25. Pajol, *Les guerres sous Louis XV*, 7:223.

26. Araneder and Etchegoyhen, "Pierres de Soule," 160.

27. The Chevalier de Béla had very little luck as an author. Not only did he never publish his magnum opus, "History of the Basque People," but it also was extensively copied without attribution by Barthélémy Jean-Baptiste Sanadon in his *Essay on the Nobility of the Basque People*, published in Pau in 1785 and translated into Spanish the following year. Chevalier de Béla, "Histoire des Basques," ms, Bibliothèque nationale de France, Paris, France, Département des manuscrits, Document en français, Nouvelles acquisitions françaises, NAF 20053–20055; Sanadon, *Essai sur la noblesse des Basques*.

28. *Ordonnance . . . portant augmentation dans le régiment des Cantabre*.

29. *Ordonnance . . . portant une nouvelle réforme dans le régiment Royal-Cantabre; Ordonnance . . . pour réformer une partie des compagnies à cheval du régiment Royal-Cantabre; Ordonnance . . . au sujet du régiment Royal-Cantabre; Ordonnance . . . portant rétablissement du régiment Royal-Cantabre*.

30. Order of July 8, 1757, in *État militaire de la France 1758 pour l'année 1758*, 186–87.

31. Pajol, *Les guerres sous Louis XV*, 6:129.

32. Ibid., 133. On July 21, an inspection of the French troops took place in Valladolid. Of the 7,900 men that in theory formed the army group, only 6,764 were fit for service. Ibid., 138.

33. Charles Juste de Beauvau-Craon, prince of Beauvau to the Duke of Choiseul, August 10, 1762, D.G., 3619, 26, partially in Pajol, *Les guerres sous Louis XV*, 6:138–39.

34. Duke of Choiseul to the prince of Beauvau, Paris, September 28, 1752, D. G., 3619, 61, partially in ibid., 6:147; prince of Beauvau to the Duke of Choiseul, Castel-Branco, October 23, 1762, D. G., 3619, 81, partially in ibid., 6:151.

35. The regimental uniform was predominantly sky blue, and its most curious feature was its headgear: a sky-blue beret *à la béarnaise* with white buttons and tassels. Mouillard, *Armée française*, chap. 8; Susane, *Histoire de l'ancienne infanterie française*, 8:336.

36. Susane, *Histoire de l'ancienne infanterie française*, 8:336.

37. Anderson, *Crucible of War*, xxi.

38. Ibid., 745.

39. Calleja Leal and O'Donnell y Duque de Estrada, *1762*; Entick, *General History of the Late War*; Albino, "Cevallos, la colonia del Sacramento."

40. Céspedes del Castillo, *América Hispánica (1492–1898)*, 324.

41. Carlos III became king of Spain after the death of his two half-brothers, Luis I (who reigned between January 15 and August 31, 1724, but died at the age of seventeen; after his death his father, who had abdicated and retired, became king for a second time until 1746) and Fernando VI (king between 1746 and 1759, who also died childless). Before becoming Carlos III of Spain he was Carlos VII of Naples.

42. Céspedes del Castillo, *América Hispánica*, 324.

43. During the more than three centuries that the Spanish convoys crossed the Atlantic, they were either captured or sunk only three times: twice by the English and once by the Dutch. Pérez-Mallaína Bueno, "Generales y almirantes"; Albi de la Cuesta, *La defensa de las Indias*, 9.

44. Marchena Fernández, "El ejército de América."

45. Albi de la Cuesta, *Banderas olvidadas*, 40–86.

46. Marchena Fernández, *Oficiales y soldados*, 83; Kuethe, "Las milicias disciplinadas de América." (2005).

47. Kuethe, "Las milicias disciplinadas de América," (2005) 109.

48. Ibid., 108.

49. *Processo formado de orden del Rey N. Señor por la Junta de Generales*;

Confession del Coronel de Dragones de Edimbourg Don Carlos Caro; *Declaraciones recibidas en Cadiz*; *Satisfacción del Mariscal de Campo D. Juan de Prado*; *Satisfacción del Coronel D. Balthasar Ricaud de Tirgale*; *Satisfacción de Don Alexandro Arroyo de Rozas Coronel del Regimiento fixo de La Habana*; *Satisfacción de Don Juan Antonio de la Colina*; Pedro Pablo Abarca de Bolea, Conde de Aranda, *Carta y consulta al Rey por el Conde de Aranda, Presidente en la Junta formada para entender en la causa de Juan de Prado y consortes . . . (sobre la pérdida de La Habana, con los cargos de que le acusaban)*, ms, 1765, BN, MSS/1687; *Copia de la Resolución de Carlos III, sobre la sentencia contra el Mariscal de Campo Juan de Prado y otros, por haber entregado La Habana a los ingleses y varias diligencias para su cumplimiento*, ms, 1765, BN, MSS/18755/44; *Decreto de Carlos III, aprobando la sentencia contra Don Juan de Prado, Gobernador de La Habana y otros, por haberse entregado a los ingleses*, El Pardo, ms, March 4, 1765, BN, MSS/11265/74.

50. Navarro García, *Hispanoamérica en el siglo XVIII*, 172-73.

51. Gutiérrez, *Fortificaciones en Iberoamérica*, 36.

52. Segovia Salas, *Las fortificaciones de Cartagena de Indias*, 22.

53. *Defensa de La Habana y sus Castillos por el Brigadier e Ingeniero director d. Silvestre Abarca, Empezado en 1763 y concluido en 1774*, Real Academia de Historia, Madrid, catalog number 2, 1, 6, no. 8.

54. Gutiérrez, *Fortificaciones en Iberoamérica*, 36.

55. Fernández Duro, *Armada española*, 7:117-18.

56. The transfer of Louisiana from France to Spain was done through a secret diplomatic pact between the two Bourbon monarchs in late 1762.

CHAPTER 2

1. On the history and legal precedents of the general visit, see Priestley, *Jose Galvez*, 83-134; and Céspedes del Castillo, "La visita como institución indiana."

2. Solórzano Pereira, *Política indiana*, 4:159-77; Holy Bible, New International Version.

3. *Recopilación de las Leyes de estos Reynos [sic], hecha por mandado de la Majestad Católica del Rey don Phelippe Segundo nuestro Señor (1581)*. Laws 16 and 17, title 4, book 2; *Recopilación de Leyes de los Reinos de las Indias* (1774). Title 34 of book 2 includes forty-seven laws, and title 31 of book 2 has thirty-two laws.

4. Céspedes del Castillo, "La visita como institución indiana," 986.

5. Priestley, *Jose Galvez*, 84.

6. Marquis de Esquilache, partially in Varela Marcos, "Los prolegómenos de la visita," 454.

7. Francisco de Armona to the Marquis de Esquilache, Aranjuez, June 12, 1764, in ibid., 454.

8. Varela Marcos, "Los prolegómenos de la visita," 458.

9. Instruction from the Council of Indies to José de Gálvez, Madrid, March 14, 1765, and March 16, 1765, in Priestley, *Jose Galvez*, 413-17; Julián de Arriaga to José de Gálvez, El Pardo, March 14, 1765, in ibid., 123-28; *Secret Instruction which Don Francisco de Armona must follow in New Spain, by the marquis de Esquilache*, San Ildefonso, July 30, 1765, AGI, Mexico, 1245, in Varela Marcos, "Los prolegómenos de la visita," 463-65.

10. Varela Marcos, "Los prolegómenos de la visita," 463-64.

11. J. Gálvez, *Informe general que el Excmo. Sr. Marqués de Sonora siendo Visitador General de este reyno*, 26.

12. Claret, *José de Gálvez*, 79.

13. J. Gálvez, *Informe general que el Excmo. Sr. Marqués de Sonora siendo Visitador General de este reyno*, 10.

14. Claret, *José de Gálvez*, 88-89.

15. Antolín Espino, "El virrey marqués de Cruillas," 163.

16. Julián de Arriaga to the Marquis de Croix, San Lorenzo, November 5, 1765, AGI, Mexico, 1508.

17. Antolín Espino, "El virrey marqués de Cruillas," 147–50.

18. Navarro García, "El virrey marqués de Croix," 171.

19. Marquis de Croix to the king, Mexico, September 26, 1766, in Croix, *Correspondance du marquis de Croix*, 200–201.

20. Teodoro de Croix, Acapulco, January 17, 1767, in Croix, *Correspondance du marquis de Croix*, 204.

21. J. Gálvez, *Informe general que el Excmo. Sr. Marqués de Sonora siendo Visitador General de este reyno*.

22. St. Clair Segurado, *Expulsión y exilio*, 62.

23. Pragmática-Sanción, El Pardo, February 27, 1767, in *Colección general de las providencias*, 1:5–6.

24. Alberto Gil Novales summarizes the reasons traditionally mentioned for the expulsion of the Jesuit order: the king's personal ones related to the slander campaign allegedly carried by the Jesuits against him; the accusation that they were the authors of seditious pamphlets; their role in the bishop Palafox's case; their alleged participation in the Esquilache mutiny; their political doctrines that justified regicide; some colonial issues (their missions in Paraguay and their attitude in the Philippines during the British occupation of Manila); their allegiance to a foreign power (the papacy) above their loyalty to their king; and the most serious one, that they were a state within the state, a sort of ecclesiastical Trojan horse. Gil Novales, "Política y sociedad," 231. Salvador de Madariaga argues that with the expulsion of the Jesuits, "Spain severed the strongest bond that united its Crown with the kingdoms in America." Madariaga, *El auge y el ocaso*, 2:307.

25. St. Clair Segurado, "La participación del ejército," 511.

26. *Colección general de las providencias*, 1:15.

27. *Adicción a la instrucción sobre el estrañamiento de los jesuitas*, 19.

28. Marquis de Croix, Mexico, June 30, 1767, in Croix, *Correspondance du marquis de Croix*, 207.

29. The whole proclamation in N. Martín, *Instrucciones del virrey marqués de Croix*, 22–23; and in Navarro García, "El virrey marqués de Croix," 264–65.

30. Zahino Peñafort, *Iglesia y sociedad en México*, 199.

31. Marquis de Croix to Julián de Arriaga, Mexico, December 3, 1767, AGI, Mexico, 2778, in Zahino Peñafort, *Iglesia y sociedad en México*, 203.

32. J. Gálvez, *Informe sobre las rebeliones populares de 1767*, 26.

33. Ibid., 28–30.

34. J. Gálvez, *Informe general que el Excmo. Sr. Marqués de Sonora siendo Visitador General de este reyno*, 139.

35. Hackel, *Children of Coyote*, 50–51.

36. The term "barbaric Indians" was applied during the eighteenth century to those indigenous groups that resisted being absorbed into the social scheme established by Spain for the Indies. Its use has been established by leading scholars such as David J. Weber and Luis Navarro García. Weber, *Bárbaros, Spaniards and Their Savages*; Navarro García, "El ilustrado."

37. Navarro García, *José de Gálvez y la comandancia general*, 144.

38. *Dictionary.com Unabridged*, s.v. "golilla," http://dictionary.reference.com/browse/golilla (accessed September 8, 2014).

39. Andrés-Gallego, *El motín de Esquilache*, 324.

40. Lynch, *La España del Siglo XVIII*, 265.

41. According to Federico González Súarez, Espejo strongly denied being the

author of the satire called *Portrait of a Golilla*, and no evidence was found, but most people were convinced he was behind it. Santa Cruz y Espejo, *Escritos del doctor Francisco Javier Eugenio Santa Cruz y Espejo* 2, no. 7, xviii.

42. Ortelli, *Trama de una guerra conveniente.*

43. Navarro García, *Hispanoamérica en el siglo XVIII*, 172–73.

44. Marín Leoz, "El gobierno interino de la Audiencia," 1105–6.

45. Navajas Josa, "El padre Kino y la Pimería," 51–54.

46. Calles Montaño, "Territorio, cristiandad y rebelión," 144.

47. Medina Bustos, "El Gobierno indígena en los Pueblos de Misión," 67.

48. Expedición a Sonora por José de Gálvez, AGI, Guadalajara, 416.

49. *Plan de una compañía de accionistas para fomentar el beneficio de las minas de Sonora y Cinaloa* [sic], *y restablecer las pesquerías de perlas en el Golfo de California*, AHN, Diversos-Colecciones, 28, N.43.

50. Marquis de Croix to Julián de Arriaga, Mexico, March 26, 1767, AGI, Guadalajara, 416, mentioned in Navarro García, *José de Gálvez y la comandancia general*, 149.

51. Cuentas de la expedición a Sonora, 1775, AGI, Mexico, 2479.

52. Navarro García, *José de Gálvez y la comandancia general*, 149–50.

53. "Demanda por pago de pesos de Doña Rosalía y doña Manuela Barcina y Zarate, residentes de la ciudad de puebla, contra don Juan Manuel Varela, regidor perpetuo de la villa de Atlixco, por 1,600 pesos más réditos, por escritura otorgada," dated March 24 and October 29, 1795, AGNM, GD66 Judicial, vol. 43, DF 8, fols. 201–8.

54. Rodríguez García, *El fiscal de Real Hacienda*, 75; Zepeda Cortés, "El *socio incómodo* del ministro."

55. Suárez Argüello, "De caminos, convoyes y peajes," 226.

56. Appointement of Francisco Gil as *alcalde mayor* (judge) of Cuautla Amilpas, July 1770, ms, AGNM, Alcaldes mayores, 1, fols. 131–32, mentioned in Borah, "Alguna luz sobre el autor," 58.

57. Noticia breve de la expedición Militar de Sonora y Cinaloa, su éxito feliz, y ventajoso estado en que por consecuencia de ella se han puesto ambas Provincias, Mexico, June 17, 1771, AHN, Diversos-Colecciones, 28, N.44, 1–2, and in BPR, I/F/33 (60).

58. Hernández Sánchez-Barba, *La última expansión española*, 227–28.

59. Ibid., 230.

60. José de Gálvez to the Marquis de Croix, Los Álamos, June 2, 1769, in *Documentos para la historia de México*, 2:40; D. Joseph de Galvez, del Supremo Consejo y Camara de Indias . . . Declaro à todos los habitantes de estas provincias de Cinaloa, y Sonora, al desembarcarme en su districto, que por ser el principal objeto . . . proveer à su tranquilidad, y bien publico, que han perturbado, y destruido los enemigos Seris y Pimas . . . les intimo por este edicto . . . admiten el arrepentimiento . . . y concedo el termino . . . de quarenta dias . . . a fin de que se me presenten todos los sublevados ó caudillos . . . , Santa Bárbara, May 8, 1769, BPR, I/F/33 (55).

61. D. Joseph de Galvez, del Supremo Consejo y Camara de Indias . . . Declaro à todos los habitantes de estas provincias de Cinaloa, y Sonora, al desembarcarme en su districto, que por ser el principal objeto. . . , Santa Bárbara, May 8, 1769, BPR, I/F/33 (55).

62. José de Gálvez to Juan de Pineda and Domingo Elizondo, Los Álamos, July 7, 1769, In *Documentos para la historia de México*, 2:54–55; José de Gálvez to Juan de Pineda, Los Álamos, July 15, 1769, in ibid., 60–61.

63. Sentence given by José de Gálvez, San Luis de la Paz, July 18, 1769, in ibid., 62–64.

64. José de Gálvez to the Marquis de Croix, July 23, 1769, where he writes

that he had been in bed for seven days, in ibid., 65-66; Marquis de Croix to José de Gálvez, Mexico, October 24, 1769, in ibid., 26.

65. Elizondo, *Noticia de la expedición militar*, 59.

66. Manifiesto de la conducta observada por don Eusebio Ventura Beleña en las comisiones puestas a su cargo en esta Nueva España por los señores excelentísimo virrey marqués de Croix e ilustrísimo visitador general don José de Gálvez, 1772, AGI, Guadalajara, 416, f. 1060, mentioned in Río, "Autoritarismo y locura," 119-20.

67. Gabriel Antonio de Vildósola to the Marquis de Corix, pueblo de Ures, January 29, 1770, AGNM, Provincias Internas, 70, 1, fols. 206r-206v, mentioned in Río, "El noroeste novohispano," and in Ortega Noriega, *Historia general de Sonora*, 218.

68. Two copies of Juan Manuel de Viniegra's testimony have been found. One was found by Mario Hernández Sánchez-Barba in Spain's National Library in Madrid (see Hernández Sánchez-Barba, *La última expansión española*, 229), *Expedición de Gálvez a California, Sonora y Nueva Vizcaya, relatada por su secretario don Juan Manuel de Viniegra*, Madrid, October 10, 1771, BN, ms, 4.494, Varios, fols. 411-530. See *Inventario general de manuscritos de la Biblioteca Nacional*, 10: 277. The second is in the Bancroft Library: Viniegra, *Varios papeles escritos después de practicado el viaxe a Californias, Sonora y Nueva Vizcaia por el visitador general del reino de Mexico por don Josef de Galvez año de 1773*, Bancroft Library, University of California, Berkeley, Banc Mss 86/87 cm, f. 50 r.

Ignacio del Río mentions a third (*Apunte instructivo de la expedición que el ilustrísimo señor don José de Gálvez . . . hizo a la península de California, provincias de Sonora y Nueva Vizcaya . . . por Juan Manuel de Viniegra . . .*, 1773, AHN, Estado 2845, DF 1), but in the National Historic Archive, Madrid, under that reference there is a document (*Expediente sobre el reconocimiento por Luis XV de Francia del título "Su Majestad Imperial de Todas las Rusias," creado por Pedro I el Grande, y sus implicaciones en el ceremonial de las Cortes rusa y francesa"*) that does not correspond to José de Gálvez. Río, "Autoritarismo y locura," 122-23.

69. Foucault, *Historia de la locura*, 25-27. For contemporary medical treatises, see Plater, *Praxeos medica*; Boissier de Sauvages de Lacroix, *Nosologie méthodique*; and Linneo, *Genera morborum*.

70. Priestley, *Jose Galvez*, 278-82; Navarro García, *José de Gálvez y la comandancia general*, 170-205; Navarro García, "El virrey marqués de Croix," 324-27; Hernández Sánchez-Barba, *La última expansión española*, 250.

71. Hernández Silva, *La expedición del visitador José de Gálvez*, 35. On their part, Salvador Bernabéu Albert and Ignacio del Río insist that the whole episode should be read in the context of the tensions generated in Mexico by the Bourbons' plan of reforms. Bernabéu Albert, "La venganza de Sancho Panza"; Río, "Autoritarismo y locura."

72. Marquis de Croix to José de Gálvez, Mexico, December 2, 1769, AGI, Guadalajara, 416, fols. 651r-654v; Marquis de Croix to Julián de Arriaga, Mexico, December 20, 1769, ibid., 656r-657r.

73. Isidoro Vázquez de Acuña wrote that Bernardo arrived with an expedition under the command of General Juan de Villalba (Vázquez de Acuña, "El Conde de Gálvez," 53), but his name does not appear among its members (*Relación de la tropa del general Juan de Villalba*, AGI, Contratación, 5507, N.2, R.26). María Isabel Pérez de Colosía Rodríguez maintains that he was assigned as a captain to what she calls an infantry fixed regiment (*regimiento fijo de infantería*) (Pérez de Colosía Rodríguez, "Rasgos biográficos," 92). The problem with this claim is that in New Spain at the time there were several fixed regiments (Gómez Ruiz and Alonso

Juanola, *El ejército de los borbones*, vol. 3/1, 8-120). Finally, both Sebastián Souviron and Isidoro Vázquez de Acuña place Bernardo in the Crown Regiment, Regimiento de la Corona (Souviron, *Bernardo de Gálvez*, 31; Vázquez de Acuña, *Historial de la Casa de Gálvez*, 1238). But in 1764 the Crown Regiment was posted to Buenos Aires. However, there also was a New Spain Crown Regiment, Regimiento de la Corona de Nueva España, in which Bernardo nominally served (Sotto, *Historia Orgánica*, vol. 8, 48-49, and vol. 11, 455-56).

74. Priestley, *Jose Galvez*, 135.
75. Regimiento Infantería de la Corona de Nueva España, Empleos, AGS, SGU, leg. 7220, 5; estado que manifiesta la fuerza de las cuatro compañías de voluntarios . . . arreglado a la revista pasada hoy, día de la fecha, fechado en Hacienda de los Dolores, April 4, 1769, AGI, Guadalajara, 416.
76. Navarro García, *José de Gálvez y la comandancia general*, 189; Lope de Cuéllar to José de Gálvez, Chihuahua, April 28, 1769, AGI, Guadalajara, 416.
77. Marquis de Croix to Juan Gregorio Muniain, Minister of War, Mexico, March 5, 1769, AGI, Mexico, 2429; *Bernardo de Gálvez. Empleos*, AGS, SGU, leg. 1; and SGU, leg. 7220, 2.
78. Real Academia Española, *Diccionario de la lengua castellana*, 9th ed., 497.
79. Jacinto Espinosa to the Marquis of Grimaldi, Mexico, February 9, 1765, AHN, leg. 2330, mentioned in Priestley, *Jose Galvez*, 135.
80. Marquis de Croix to Juan Gregorio de Muniain, Mexico, July 27, 1768, where Croix informs that he has granted the request made by Lope de Cuéllar, captain in the Regiment de la Corona, that his brother, Francisco de Cuéllar, ensign in the Regiment of America, be assigned under his [Lope de Cuéllar's] command, AGNM, Instituciones Coloniales, Gobierno Virreinal, Correspondencia de Virreyes, 036, vol. 17.

81. For Bernardo de Gálvez's appointment as active lieutenant, Aranjuez, June 4, 1769, see *Bernardo de Gálvez. Empleos*, AGS, SGU, leg. 1, SGU, leg. 7220, 2. See also Militares, concede el grado de teniente a don Bernardo de Gálvez, June 18, 1769, AGNM, Instituciones Coloniales, Gobierno Virreinal, Reales Cédulas Originales y Duplicadas (100), Reales Cédulas Originales, vol. 94, 128. And see Nombramiento, el virrey de Nueva España comunica a don Julián de Arriaga, que ha dirigido a don Bernardo Gálvez, el despacho donde se le concede grado y sueldo de teniente de infantería, 2nd series, Mexico, October 12, 1769, AGNM, Instituciones Coloniales, Gobierno Virreinal, Correspondencia de Virreyes (036), vol. 13.
82. J. D'W. W., *Diccionario militar*, 293.
83. Ibid., 398.
84. Terrón, *Ejército y política*.
85. See article 2, title 6, treaty 2, and article 2, title 10, treaty 2 of the 1768 Royal Army Regulations (*Ordenanzas de S.M. para el régimen, disciplina, subordinación y servicio de sus Exércitos*). Definition of the term "promotion" (*ascenso*), first part, *Correo de Madrid*, Saturday, August 16, 1788, no. 190, 1139-41; second part, August 20, 1788, no. 191, 1147-45; third part, August 23, 1788, no. 192, 1155-57.
86. Regimiento Infantería de la Corona de Nueva España, Empleos, AGS, SGU, leg. 7220, 5.
87. Ibid.
88. Batallón y Regimiento de la Corona de Nueva España, Hojas de servicios, 1779, AGI, Mexico, 2431A.
89. Regimiento Infantería de la Corona de Nueva España, Empleos, AGS, SGU, leg. 7220, 5. See also Milicias, el virrey de Nueva España comunica a don Juan Gregorio de Muniain, que en vista de la Real Orden del 4 de June de este año, en que Su Majestad se ha servido conceder a don Bernardo de Gálvez el sueldo de teniente de infantería vivo, y mandar se le tenga presente para compañía, ya ha sido propuesto para la compañía vacante del

segundo batallón del regimiento de infantería de la corona del reino, 2nd series, Mexico, October 26, 1769, and Marquis de Croix to Juan Gregorio de Muniain, Mexico, October 26, 1769, AGNM, Instituciones Coloniales, Gobierno Virreinal, Correspondencia de Virreyes (036), vol. 17.

90. Oficios y cédulas de nombramientos en el Regimiento de Dragones de México para Joseph Aldasoro al mando de una Compañía, así como Antonio de Barrios al mando de otra Compañía, a Joseph Manuel Ravago como Teniente, a Juan María de Barrios al mando de otra Compañía, a Manuel Bustillos al mando de otra Compañía; y para el Regimiento de Infantería de la Corona, a Bernardo de Gálvez al mando de una Compañía, a Joseph de Blengua como subteniente de Bandera, a Ignacio de la Ronade como Teniente Coronel de Infantería, a Luis Godro como Capitán de Infantería, y a Alonso Raphan como subteniente de Infantería, Madrid, December 1769, AGNM, Instituciones Coloniales, Indiferente Virreinal, Cajas 6000–6743, Caja 6028, 054 (Indiferente de Guerra Caja 6028).

91. For *diné*, see Worcester, *Apaches*, 7; for *dné*, see Babcock, *Apache Adaptation to Hispanic Rule*, xvii; for *tin-ne-áh*, see Haley, *Apaches*, 9.

92. For the different theories on the origin of the term "Apache," see Haley, *Apaches*, 9.

93. Hodge, *Handbook of American Indians*, 63; Worcester, "Apaches in the History of the Southwest," 25.

94. Haley, *Apaches*, 9; Hodge, "Early Western History," 442, quoted by Haley, ibid., 9. B. Davis, *Truth about Geronimo*, 1, mentions that the term "apachureros [sic] de huesos" (bone crushers) may refer to the Apache way of torturing prisoners.

95. Basso, "Western Apache," 462.

96. On the much-needed criticism of nonnative sources, see Evans-Pritchard, *Anthropology and History*, 5; Sturtevant, "Anthropology, History, and Ethnohistory," 16–17; Walker, "Ethnology and History," 27–29; and Axtell, "Ethnohistory of Early America," 118.

97. Fenton, *American Indian and White Relations*, 21–22; Fenton, "Field Work," 75.

98. The assertion is commonly attributed to Winston Churchill, but, as with a great deal of Churchilliana, there is no documentation to support it. The most reliable source is Nehru, *Discovery of India*, 287. The origins of the idea behind writing the history from the point of view of the defeated could be traced to Miguel León-Portilla, while Howard Zinn has applied it to the history of the Americas. Foucault, *Il faut défendre la société*; León-Portilla, *El reverso de la conquista*; León-Portilla, *Crónicas indígenas*; Zinn, *People's History of the United States*.

99. Worcester, *Apaches*, 4; Opler, "Apachean Culture Pattern," 368; Palmer, *Apache Peoples*, 47. Hugo de O'Conor, in his report about the situation in the Interior Provinces written between 1771 and 1776, mentions *chiricagui, gileños, mimbrerenos, mezcaleros, faraones, rancherías de Pasqual*, from *El Ligero*, from *Alonso*, from *capitán Vigotes*, and from *del Natagé* (O'Conor, *Informe de Hugo de O'Conor sobre el estado de las Provincias Internas*, 77). Nicolás de Lafora, arround 1772, stated that "the Apache nation is one and the same, but with the denominations of *gileños, garlanes, chilpaines, xicarillas, pharaones, mezcaleros, natuges, lipanes*, etc." (Lafora, "Viaje a los presidios internos," 273–74). Antonio Cordero, in his 1796 *Descripción de los apaches*, divides them into *tontos, chiricaguis, gileños, mimbreños, faraones, mescaleros, llaneros, lipanes*, and *navajos* (336).

100. B. Gálvez, *Noticia y reflexiones*.

101. *Instrucción formada en virtud de Real Orden de S.M.* [Instruction for governing the Interior Provinces of New Spain].

102. Opler, "Apachean Culture Pattern," 370.

103. Ibid., 368.

104. Moorhead, *Apache Frontier*, 3; Babcock, *Apache Adaptation to Hispanic Rule*, 5.

105. Catlin, *Last Rambles*, 189, mentioned in Haley, *Apaches*, 11.

106. Haley, *Apaches*, 11.

107. *Shipwrecks* was the title given to Alvar Núñez Cabeza de Vaca's account of his successful expedition first published in 1555 under the less appealing title *Account and Commentaries*. Núñez Cabeza de Vaca, *La relacion y comentarios del gouernador*; Haley, *Apaches*, 24; Worcester, "Early Spanish Accounts of the Apache Indians," 308.

108. Worcester, *Apaches*, 9.

109. Forbes, *Apache, Navaho, and Spaniard*.

110. For playing cards, see Calloway, *New Worlds for All*, 47–48; Wayland, Wayland, and Ferg, *Playing Cards of the Apaches*, 53; and Opler, *Apache Life-Way*, 299. For the horse, see Hämäläinen, "The Rise and Fall of Plains Indian Horse Cultures"; and Schroeder, "Shifting for Survival," 297. The introduction of the horse has been called the "technological revolution for the Great Plains," Oberg, *Native America*, 80.

111. Carlisle, "Spanish Relations with the Apache Nations," 2; Wissler, "Diffusion of Horse Culture," 254–56.

112. *Real cédula* of November 30, 1647, to the governor of Nueva Vizcaya, ordering him to comply with all the royal orders (*cédulas*) that absolutely forbade that under any circumstance the Indians should be enslaved, AGI, Guadalajara, 230, L.3, f. 44v-45v.

113. John, *Storms Brewed in Other Men´s Worlds*, 271–72.

114. La Vere, *Texas Indians*, 137.

115. Hämäläinen, *Comanche Empire*.

116. Navarro García, *José de Gálvez y la comandancia general*, 78.

117. Important contemporaneous accounts about the "Apache problem" are those of Pedro de Rivera, Hugo de O'Conor, Antonio Bonilla, José Cortés, Nicolás de Lafora, and Bernardo de Gálvez himself. Alessio Robles, "Diario y derrotero de lo caminado . . . Pedro de Rivera"; O'Conor, *Informe de Hugo de O'Conor sobre el estado de las Provincias Internas*; Bonilla, *Breve compendio*; Cortés, *Views from the Apache frontier*; La Vere, *Texas Indians*, 4; Lafora, "Viaje a los presidios internos"; B. Galvéz, *Noticia y reflexiones*.

The so-called Apache problem was a high priority in the political agenda of the viceroyalty of New Spain, under three different headings: the frontier, the Internal Provinces (*provincias internas*), and the pacification of the "barbaric Indians."

The contributions of Frederick Jackson Turner's "frontier," Herbert E. Bolton's "borderlands," and the "new Western history" have had a profound impact on the study of the Apache in the Internal Provinces of New Spain and of other indigenous groups in other regions (Turner, *Frontier in American History*; Bolton, "Epic of Greater America"; Bolton, *Spanish Borderlands*; Limerick, *Legacy of Conquest*; R. White, *"It's Your Misfortune and None of My Own"*; R. White, *Middle Ground*). On the frontier, the first bibliographical repertoire was published in 1943, and today more than one thousand works deal with the subject (Coker et al., "Research in the Spanish Borderlands"; Deeds, "New Spain's Far North"; Hilton, "Spanish Colonies in North America"; Steck, *Tentative Guide*; Weber, *Spanish Frontier*; Weber, *Bárbaros, Spaniards and Their Savages*).

On the Internal Provinces of New Spain during the eighteenth-century, the classic studies are those by Herbert Ingram Priestley, María del Carmen Velázquez Chávez, and Luis Navarro García. Also relevant are more recent works by Salvador Bernabéu Albert and Alfredo Jiménez Núñez, as well as several studies that address specific aspects or regions (Priestley, *Jose Galvez: Visitor-General*; Velázquez Chávez, *El estado de guerra en Nueva España*; Navarro García, *José de Gálvez y la comandancia general*; Bernabeu Albert, *El Septentrión novohispano*; Jiménez Núñez, *El gran norte de México*; Brinckerhoff and Faulk, *Lancers for the King*; Hernández Sánchez-Barba, *La última expansión española en América*; Velázquez Chávez, *Tres estudios sobre las Provincias Internas*).

On the pacification of the "barbarian Indians" in the borderlands of the Spanish Empire, much has been written in several of the works already mentioned. These studies are complemented by the work of other important authors on specific aspects (Berry, "Indian Policy of Spain"; Bushnell, "Spain's Conquest by Contract"; Kinnaird, "Spanish Treaties with Indian Tribes"; Lázaro Ávila, "Los tratados de paz con los indígenas"; Levaggi, "Los tratados entre la Corona y los indios"; Levaggi, "Aplicación de la política española de tratados"; Levaggi, *Diplomacia hispano-indígena en las fronteras de América*; Park, "Spanish Indian Policy"; Roulet, "Con la pluma y la palabra").

On the Apaches' history, there is a very complete bibliography that considers their interactions with the Spaniards in general and their situation during the eighteenth century. For their interactions with the Spaniards, see Basso, "Western Apache"; B. Davis, *Truth about Geronimo*; Ewers, *Plains Indian History and Culture*; Haley, *Apaches*; Hodge, "Early Western History," 442; Hodge, *Handbook of American Indians*; Hook, *Apaches*; John, *Storms Brewed in Other Men's Worlds*; Cortés, *Views from the Apache frontier*; La Vere, *Texas Indians*; Opler, "Apachean Culture Pattern"; Opler, "Chiricagua Apache"; Opler, "Mescalero Apache"; Worcester, "Apaches in the History of the Southwest"; and Worcester, *Apaches*. For the Apaches' situation in the eighteenth century, see Moorhead, *Apache Frontier*; Navarro García, "El ilustrado"; Ortelli, "Las reformas borbónicas vistas desde la frontera"; Ortelli, *Trama de una guerra conveniente*; and Worcester, "Early Spanish Accounts of the Apache Indians."

118. P. Powell, "Chichimecas," 315-16.

119. For the Pueblo revolt, see Knaut, *Pueblo Revolt of 1680*; Weber, *Spanish Frontier*, 133-41.

120. In 1741 two Russian ships were sighted in North American Pacific Ocean waters, the *Sviatoi Piotr* (Saint Peter) and the *Sviatoi Pavel* (Saint Paul) from the so-called Great Expedition under the command of Vitus Bering. Ortega, "Ross," 123; Pritchard, "Joint Tenants."

121. Navarro García, "El norte de Nueva España," 16.

122. Navarro García, *José de Gálvez y la comandancia general*, 25-28; Jiménez Núñez, *El gran norte de México*, 126-25; Weber, *Spanish Frontier*, 135-41.

123. In 1723, Colonel Pedro de Rivera was ordered by the viceroy Casafuerte to inspect the presidios and to report on the state of the defenses of northern New Spain.

124. Moorhead, *Presidio*, 27.

125. In Alessio Robles, "Diario y derrotero de lo caminado . . . Pedro de Rivera," 99-196.

126. *Reglamento para todos los presidios de las Provincias internas de esta Governación*.

127. Instrucción para formar una línea o cordón de quince presidios sobre las Fronteras de las Provincias Internas de este Reino de Nueva España, y Nuevo Reglamento del número y calidad de Oficiales y Soldados que estos y los demás han de tener, Sueldos que gozarán desde el día primero de enero del año próximo de mil setecientos setenta y dos, y servicio que deben hacer sus Guarniciones, Mexico, 1771, AGI, Guadalajara, 273. Once approved by the king it was published as *Reglamento e Instrucción para los Presidios. . . . Instrucción formada en virtud de Real Orden de S.M., que se dirige al señor Comandante General de las Provincias internas Don Jacobo Ugarte y Loyola para el gobierno y puntual observancia*

de este Superior Gefe y de sus inmediatos Subalternos, Mexico, August 26, 1786 por el virrey de la Nueva España, Conde de Gálvez, original copies in AGI, Guadalajara, 268, and Ultramar, 714, and AGS, Guerra Moderna, 7041. Published as B. Gálvez, *Instrucción formada en virtud de real orden de S.M., que se dirige al señor comandante general de provincias internas* . . .

128. Velázquez Chávez, *Tres estudios*, 27.

129. Ortelli, *Trama de una guerra conveniente*, 34.

130. Carvajal, *Testamento politico*, in Artola, "América en el pensamiento," 59.

131. Captain José de Berrotarán to the viceroy Count of Villagigedo [*sic* Revillagigedo], report, Mexico, April 17, 1748, copy in AGI, Guadalajara, 513, mentioned in Moorhead, *Presidio*, 48.

132. The viceroyalty of Nueva Granada was initially created in 1717 but suppressed in 1724; it was finally reestablished in 1740. The viceroyalty of Rio de la Plata was provisionally created on August 1, 1776, permanently on October 27, 1777.

133. In the Library of Madrid's Royal Palace are two almost identical copies of the project. The first one is under the title *Proyecto sobre el establecimiento de un virreinato en la Nueva Vizcaya, cuya capital es Durango* . . . , Madrid, May 12, 1760, BPR, Miscelánea de Ayala, vol. 54, 2872, fols. 203-27. The second one is *Idea que manifiesta las ventajas que resultarían a la seguridad de los reinos de Nueva España, fomento de sus minas y frutos con la erección de un nuevo virreinato en la ciudad de Durango, capital de la Nueva Vizcaya, separado del de México* . . . , Madrid, December 18, 1760, BPR, Miscelánea de Ayala, vol. 10, 2824, fols. 30-41v. See Navarro García, *José de Gálvez y la comandancia general*, 90-94.

134. José de Gálvez was appointed *secretario de estado de la secretaría del Despacho Universal de Indias* (minister of the Indies) by a royal order dated January 30, 1776. By royal decree dated May 16, 1776, Teodoro de Croix was appointed governor and commander in chief of the provinces of Nueva Vizcaya, Sonora, Sinaloa, and the Californias. The *real cédula* of August 22, 1776, contained Croix's instructions. Gerhard, *La frontera norte de la Nueva España*, 29; Navarro García, *José de Gálvez y la comandancia general*, 278.

135. The classic study is Hanke, *La humanidad es una*.

136. Luque Alcaide, "Debate sobre el indio"; Zahino Peñafort "La cuestión indígena."

137. See Gerbi, *La disputa del nuevo mundo*, 47-65.

138. Lafora, "Viaje a los presidios internos," 277.

139. Cordero, *Descripción de los apaches del coronel Antonio Cordero incluida en sus Notas sobre la nación apache compuestas en 1796*, 339. According to Matson and Schroeder, the original is in the Bancroft Library, but we have been unable to find it.

140. Cortés, *Views from the Apache frontier*, 17.

141. Weber, *Bárbaros, Spaniards and Their Savages*, 147.

142. For their cruelty, see O'Conor, *Informe de Hugo de O'Conor sobre el estado de las Provincias Internas*. For the opposite view, see Cortés, *Views from the Apache frontier*, 8-30.

143. Among them: *Representación que las provincias de Sonora, Ostimuri y Sinaloa hicieron al ingreso de D. Juan Pineda en su gobierno, lamentando . . . las crueles y diarias hostilidades de los indios seris, pimas y hiaquis*, BPR, Mss, BiII/2824, fols. 60 r.-66 v. vol.; *Informe que en el año de 1763 hizo D. Juan de Pineda al virrey de Nueva España del infeliz estado de las provincias de Sonora y Ostimuri que estaban abandonadas y despobladas por el terror que habían infundido a sus moradores las continuas irrupciones de los indios seris y pimas* . . . , San Miguel de Horcasitas, December 20, 1763, BPR, Mss, BiII/2824,

fols. 67 r.–69 v. vol.; *Dictamen de D. Juan Bautista de Anza al gobernador de Sonora Don Juan de Pineda en que para contener el arrojo de los indios seris y pimas que intentan destruir las provincias de Ostimuri y Sonora propone la fundación de un presidio en el parage de Buena Vista . . . uno en San Joseph de los Pimas y otro en Mazatan . . .* , Real Presidio de Tubac, November 15, 1763, BPR, Mss, BiII/2824, fols. 70 r.–72 r. vol; *Norma que da Don Bernabé de Urea al gobernador de Sonora para contener los pérfidos insultos de los indios seris y pimas en la provincia de Ostimuri . . .* , Real Presidio de Santa Gertrudis del Altar y November 12, 1763, BPR, Mss, II/2824, fols. 75 r. –77 r.; *Arbitrio de Don Gabriel de Vildesola al gobernador de Sonora Don Juan de Pineda en que para sujetar la rebeldía de los indios pimas bajos y hiaquis propone la unión de las dos compañías del Altar y San Miguel en el Pitio . . .* , Presidio de Fronteras, November 16, 1763, BPR, Mss, II/2824, fols. 78 r.–80 r.

144. Ortelli, *Trama de una guerra conveniente*, 51.

145. Moorhead, *Presidio*, 49.

146. Navarro García, *José de Gálvez y la comandancia general*, 337.

147. Hernández Sánchez-Barba, *La última expansión española*, 178.

148. Ortelli, *Trama de una guerra conveniente*, 61.

149. Teodoro de Croix to Antonio Bucareli, Mexico, August 22, 1777, in *La administración de d. Frey Antonio María Bucareli y Ursúa*, 1:364.

150. Antonio Bucareli to Teodoro de Croix, Mexico, 27 August 1777, in ibid., 1:372.

151. Borges, "Primero hombres," 522.

152. Solórzano Pereira, *Política indiana*, vol. 1, 94.

153. *Real cédula* to the Audiencia of Guatemala, November 19, 1787, mentioned in Weber, *Bárbaros, Spaniards and Their Savages*, 95.

154. Weir, "Ruin of Ruins," 41.

155. Haley, *Apaches*, 116.

156. Carlisle, "Spanish Relations with the Apache Nations," 3.

157. Weber, *Bárbaros, Spaniards and Their Savages*, 143.

158. Moorhead, *Presidio*, 270.

159. Méndez Beltrán, "Trabajo indígena en la frontera," 249, quoted in Weber, *Bárbaros, Spaniards and Their Savages*, 169.

160. Jiménez Núñez, *El gran norte de México*, 279.

161. Ordenanzas de Felipe II sobre descubrimiento, nueva población y pacificación de las Indias, July 13, 1573, in Morales Padrón, *Teoría y leyes de la conquista*, 493.

162. Bonilla, *Breve compendio*, 39.

163. Title 10, article 1, of the *Reglamento e instrucción para los presidios que se han de formar en la línea de fronteras de la Nueva España*, San Ildefonso, September 10, 1772.

164. Marquis de Croix to Juan Gregorio Muniain, Minister of War, Mexico, March 5, 1769, AGI, Mexico, 2429; *Bernardo de Gálvez. Empleos*, AGS, SGU, leg. 1, SGU, leg. 7220, 2.

165. Bernardo de Gálvez's appointment as active lieutenant, Aranjuez, June 4, 1769, *Bernardo de Gálvez. Empleos*, AGS, SGU, leg. 1, SGU, leg. 7220, 2.

166. Lope de Cuéllar to José de Gálvez, Chihuahua, April 28, 1769, AGI, Guadalajara, 416.

167. José Fainí y Gálvez, AGI, Contratación, 5511B, N.1, R.14.

168. Dossier for the admission of José Fainí y Gálvez into the Order of Santiago, AHN, Órdenes Militares, Caballeros Santiago, DF2816; Vázquez de Acuña, *Historial de la Casa de Gálvez*, 1130.

169. José de Fainí to Julián de Arriaga, minister of the Indies, Durango, June 11, 1771, AGNM, Reales Cédulas Duplicados, 107, fols. 75r–76v, in Mirafuentes Galván, *Movimientos de resistencia*, 2:61.

170. José de Fainí to Julián de Arriaga, Chihuahua, June 26, 1770, AGI, Guadalajara, 416.

171. Navarro García, *José de Gálvez y la comandancia general*, 191.

172. José de Gálvez, Real de los Álamos, July 15, 1769, in *Documentos para la historia de México*, 2:59.

173. Juan Manuel de Viniegra, *Varios papeles escritos después de practicado el viaxe a Californias, Sonora y Nueva Vizcaia por el visitador general del reino de Mexico por don Josef de Galvez año de 1773*, the Bancroft Library, University of California, Berkeley, Banc Mss 86/87 cm, f. 50r, f. 67r.

174. Juan Manuel de Viniegra stated that Bernardo signed, probably as a witness, several letters that Viniegra and Matías de Armona sent to Viceroy Croix about the madness of the visitor-general, November 6 and 22 and December 16, 1769. Nota de los papeles que exhibieron judicialmente don Juan Manuel de Viniegra y don Miguel José de Armona; hecho de orden del virrey marqués de Croix por el ayudante mayor de dragones de España don Juan Velázquez. Los cuales documentos llevaban desde la provincia de Sonora a México para hacer ver al señor virrey los informes ya dirigidos el grado infeliz en que estuvo por su enfermedad el Ilmo. Sr. D. José de Gálvez, in Viniegra, *Varios papeles escritos*, f. 50r, f. 72r.

175. Viniegra, *Varios papeles escritos*, f. 50r, f. 53v.

176. Ibid., fols. 55v–56r.

177. Río, "Autoritarismo y locura," 126.

178. Viniegra, *Varios papeles escritos*, f. 50r, f. 54v.

179. Roy Porter, *Flesh in the Age of Reason*, 305–7.

180. Viniegra, *Varios papeles escritos*, f. 50r, f. 56v.

181. "Minuta de un célebre pasaporte, dictado por su ilustrísima y escrito por su sobrino d. Bernardo Gálvez y Azanza, que debió darse al criado Juan Espejo por resultar de haberle nombrado su ilustrísima *Gobernador del Nuevo Reino de Californias* [underlined in ink in the original]." Nota de los papeles que exhibieron judicialmente don Juan Manuel de Viniegra y don Miguel José de Armona, in Viniegra, *Varios papeles escritos*, f. 50r, f. 77r.

182. Viniegra, *Varios papeles escritos*, f. 50r, f. 63r.

183. Bartra, "Doce historias de melancolía," 46.

184. Viniegra, *Varios papeles escritos*, f. 50r, f. 58v.

185. "Apunte instructivo de la expedición que el Ilmo. Sr. D. José de Gálvez, visitador general de Nueva España, hizo a la península de California, provincias de Sonora y Nueva Vizcaya, desde que la resolvió y emprendió hasta que volvió a México. Comprehende las ocurrencias y hechos más notables, con referencia a papeles y documentos originales que deben existir en la Secretaría del virreinato de Nueva España, y a sucesos hechos públicos y notorios en aquellas partes. Dispuesto por orden superior de don Juan Manuel de Viniegra, secretario de dicho sr. Ministro y de la expedición que siguió y sirvió hasta su vuelta a México," in ibid., f. 50r, f. 57v.

186. Ramos Vázquez, "La represión de los delitos atroces," 264.

187. Alonso Romero, "El proceso penal en la Castilla moderna," 214–15.

188. Clavero, "Delito y Pecado."

189. *Las Siete Partidas del Rey Don Alfonso el sabio*, law 1, title 30, partida 7; ibid., 3:701.

190. Río, "Autoritarismo y locura," 131.

191. McCarty, "La educación de un virrey," 100.

192. Ibid.

193. Río, "Autoritarismo y locura."

194. Juan Manuel de Viniegra, Miguel José de Azanza, and Juan Antonio Gómez de Argüello to José de Gálvez, Havana, February 6, 1774, in Viniegra, *Varios papeles escritos*, f. 50r, fols. 12v–13r and 23v–24r.

195. National Library of Spain and Bancroft Library.

196. *Manifiesto de la conducta observada por don Eusebio Ventura Beleña en las comisiones puestas a su cargo en*

esta Nueva España por los señores excelentísimo virrey marqués de Croix e ilustrísimo visitador general don José de Gálvez . . . , 1772, AGI, Guadalajara, 416; *Expedición a Sonora por José de Gálvez*, AGI, Guadalajara, 416.

197. *Graciosas especias que se le ocurrieron al visitador general Don José de Gálvez antes de partir a la expedición de Sonora y California* . . . , in Diversos documentos sobre Nueva España, AGI, Estado, 42, N.3.

198. Concepción, *Historia general de Philipinas*, 367–68. Faveau was the author of several maps, among them *Chart of Balabac*.

199. Galbis Diez, "El virrey don Miguel José de Azanza," 4–5.

200. "Especies ridículas y ráfagas notorias que produjo el figurón [sic] del visitador general de Nueva España don José de Gálvez, mientras corrió soñando los áridos desiertos de Californias, y por la provincias de Sonora y Nueva Vizcaya. Exíbense para deducir por ellas su carácter, y con la mira de satisfacer plenamente el gusto de un caballero que ha mandado extenderlas," in Viniegra, *Varios papeles escritos*, f. 95v.

201. According to Viniegra, "Don Quixote was nothing compared to Gálvez from Malaga." Ibid., f. 110r.

202. *Expediente de información y licencia de pasajero a Indias de Juan Manuel de Viniegra, tesorero oficial real de las Cajas de Portobelo, con su criado Millán Pérez Ibarreta, natural del Pedroso, hijo de Francisco Pérez Hernández y de Josefa Ibarreta Navarro, a Tierra Firme*, AGI, Contratación, 5519, N.2, R.27.

203. Juan Manuel de Viniegra, Miguel José de Azanza, and Juan Antonio Gómez de Argüello to José de Gálvez, Havana, February 6, 1774, in Viniegra, *Varios papeles escritos*, f. 50r, fols. 12v–13r.

204. José de Fainí to the Marquis de Croix, Chihuahua, August 24, 1770, AGI, Guadalajara, 512.

205. *Expedición a Nueva Vizcaya. Solicitud. El virrey de Nueva España envía a don Julián de Arriaga, la relación de las últimas noticias de la segunda campaña contra los bárbaros apaches de Nueva Vizcaya realizada por el capitán don Bernardo de Gálvez, para quien solicita el grado y el sueldo de teniente coronel del ejército*, 2nd series, Mexico, June 27, 1771, AGNM, Instituciones Coloniales, Gobierno Virreinal, Correspondencia de Virreyes (036), vol. 14, fols. 318r–326v.

206. Vicente Rodríguez, Derrotero, from November 1 to December 2, 1775, AGNM, Provincias Internas, 24, mentioned in Weddle, "Galvez Crossings on the Pecos River."

207. McCarty, "La educación de un virrey," 101.

208. Marquis de Croix to Julián de Arriaga, Mexico, December 26, 1770, AGI, Guadalajara, 416, in Navarro García, *José de Gálvez y la comandancia general*, 193.

209. McCarty, "La educación de un virrey," 101–2.

210. Marquis de Croix to Julián de Arriaga, Mexico, 31 January 1771, AGNM, CV, 2nd series, 14, no. 839, fols. 71r–72v, in Mirafuentes Galván, *Movimientos de resistencia*, 1:67; Navarro García, *José de Gálvez y la comandancia general*, 194.

211. Bernardo de Gálvez to the Marquis de Croix, varia correspondencia informando del éxito obtenido en las dos primeras salidas contra los Apaches e incluyendo sus diarios, Chihuahua, from April 26, 1769, to December 14, 1770, AGNM, Provincias Internas, 97, 1, fols. 1r–254v, in Mirafuentes Galván, *Movimientos de resistencia*, 1:66; Bernardo de Gálvez, *Diario*, from October 9 to November 20, 1770, AGNM, Provincias Internas, 97, Dolph Briscoe Center for American History, University of Texas at Austin.

212. Marquis de Croix to Julián de Arriaga, Mexico, June 27, 1771, no. 1028, Mexico, 1269, in Navarro García, *José de Gálvez y la comandancia*, 195.

213. Marquis de Croix to Juan Gregorio

de Muniain, Mexico, September 19, 1771, AGI, Mexico, 1269.

214. Hugo O'Conor to Antonio Bucareli, Chihuahua, December 20, 1771. In *Boletín del Archivo General de la Nación* 30, no. 3 (1959); and in Piñera Ramírez, *Visión histórica de la frontera norte*, 2:84–85.

215. Bernardo de Gálvez to Antonio Bucareli, Chihuahua, October 18, 1771, AGI, Guadalajara, 512; Hugo O'Conor to Antonio Bucareli, Chihuahua, December 20, 1771. In *Boletín del Archivo General de la Nación* 30, no. 3 (1959); and in Piñera Ramírez, *Visión histórica de la frontera norte*, 2:84–85.

216. Bernardo de Gálvez to the Marquis de Croix, Chihuahua, November 29, 1771, AGI, Guadalajara, 512.

217. Although several Spanish spellings of his family name can be found in contemporary documents (sometimes even transcribed as Oconór) we have kept the most common Spanish spelling instead of the original O'Connor.

218. Alejandro O'Reilly to Antonio Bucareli, Madrid, September 25, 1772, AGI, Mexico, 1242.

219. Dossier for the admission of Hugo O'Conor Orrian into the Order of Calatrava, July 1763, AHN, Órdenes Militares, Expedientillos, N.12257; pruebas para la concesión del Título de Caballero de la Orden de Calatrava de Hugo O'Conor y Orrian Doyle y Nangel, natural de Dublín, Reino de Irlanda, Capitán de Infantería destinado al Ejército de América, 1763, AHN, Órdenes Militares, Caballeros Calatrava, DF1819.

220. Santiago, *Red Captain*, 8–33.

221. Antonio Bucareli to Alejandro O'Reilly, Mexico, October 27, 1771, AGI, Mexico, 1242, partially in Navarro García, *José de Gálvez y la comandancia*, 211.

222. Rubio Mané, "Itinerario del teniente coronel."

223. Cutter, *Defenses of Northern New Spain*; Manjarrez Cuellar, "Aproximación a la representación del espacio," 99–100.

224. Vigness, "Don Hugo O'Conor," 36.

225. García Hernán and Recio Morales, *Extranjeros en el Ejército*; Recio Morales, *La presencia irlandesa en los ejércitos*.

226. Akenson, *Irish History of Civilization*, 1:187.

227. Recio Morales, "When Merit Alone Is Not Enough," 121.

228. Request in Antonio Bucareli to Hugo O'Conor, Mexico, October 27, 1771. In the letter Bucareli mentions José de Gálvez's request that his nephew Bernardo could accompany him on his return to the Iberian Peninsula, AGI, Mexico, 1242. Request granted in Licencias, la concede a don Bernardo de Gálvez, para que acompañe a su tío el visitador, May 17, 1772, AGNM, Instituciones Coloniales, Gobierno Virreinal, Reales Cédulas Originales y Duplicados (100), Reales Cédulas Originales, vol. 100, 163.

229. Several dispatches, dated from October 16, 1771, to July 23, 1773, AGNM, H, 24, 3, fols. 135–94, in Mirafuentes Galván, *Movimientos de resistencia*, 1:67–68; Antonio Bucareli to Julián de Arriaga, Mexico, February 23, 1772, AGI, Guadalajara, 512; Antonio Bucareli to Julián de Arriaga, Mexico, 22 February 1772, AGI, Mexico, 1246; Antonio Bucareli to Julián de Arriaga, Mexico, 24 February 1772, AGI, Mexico, 1246.

230. José de Echeveste to Antonio Bucareli y Ursua, solicitando los documentos de los gastos de la nota que anexa, pues como apoderado del Capitán Bernardo de Gálvez, tiene que justificar la cuentas de la última campaña que comandó éste ante el real Tribunal y Audiencia de cuentas, 1772, AGNM, Instituciones Coloniales, Indiferente Virreinal, Cajas 4000–4999, Caja 4806, 002 (Tribunal de Cuentas Caja 4806).

231. José de Gálvez to Julián de Arriaga, Havana, March 4, 1772, AGI, Mexico, 1246.

232. Ibid., Cádiz, May 20, 1772; Priestley, *Jose Galvez*, 310–11; Navarro García, "El virrey marqués de Croix," 379–80.

233. *Noticia breve de la expedición Militar de Sonora y Cinaloa, su éxito feliz, y ventajoso estado en que por consecuencia de ella se han puesto ambas Provincias*, Mexico, June 17, 1771, AHN, Diversos-Colecciones, 28, N.44, 10–11, and in BPR, I/F/33 (60).

234. Ibid.

235. D. Powell, "Addition of Rare Southwestern Historical Items," 26; Jiménez Núñez, *El gran norte de México*, 377.

236. A copy of the original report by José de Gálvez under the title "Memoria de d. Josef Galvez sobre el estado de América. Mejico [sic]" is to be found in the Archivo General de Indias. It has been published twice, in 1867 and 2002. *Informe del Visitador general de Nueva España, Don José de Gálvez a Don Antonio Bucarely, nombrado Virrey de dicho reino, sobre los asuntos que ha tenido a su cargo, dado en virtud de R.O. de 24 May 1771, copia simple*, AGI, Estado, 34, N.35; *Informe general que el Excmo. Sr. Marqués de Sonora siendo Visitador General de este reyno*; Suárez Argüello, *Informe general que en virtud de real orden instruyó y entregó el excelentísimo señor Marqués de Sonora*.

237. Suárez Argüello, *Informe general que en virtud de real orden instruyó y entregó el excelentísimo señor Marqués de Sonora*, xi.

238. Marquis de Croix to Julián de Arriaga, Mexico, March 26, 1771, Extracto de Noticias de Sonora, AGI, Guadalajara, 416, mentioned in Navarro García, *José de Gálvez y la comandancia general*, 183–84.

239. *Expedición a Nueva Vizcaya. Solicitud. El virrey de Nueva España envía a don Julián de Arriaga* . . . (see note 205 above).

240. Antonio Bucareli to Alejandro O'Reilly, Mexico, October 27, 1771, AGI, Mexico, 1242, partially in Navarro García, *José de Gálvez y la comandancia general*, 211.

241. Alejandro O'Reilly to Antonio Bucareli, February 22, 1772, AGI, Mexico, 1242.

242. Antonio Bucareli to Julián de Arriaga, Mexico, December 21, 1771, AGI, Indiferente General, 512.

243. Hugo O'Conor, report, Mexico, July 22, 1777, in Cutter, *Defenses of Northern New Spain*, and partially in Manjarrez Cuellar, "Aproximación a la representación del Espacio," 100.

244. Royal order of June 27, 1782; Navarro García, *José de Gálvez y la comandancia general*, 376–77; Ramírez Meza, "La comandancia general de las Provincias Internas," 46.

245. Expedición en Nueva Vizcaya, el virrey de nueva España envía a don Julián de Arriaga, noticias relacionadas a los progresos de las expediciones contra los barbaros y rebeldes en la Nueva Vizcaya, bajo el mando del capitán de infantería don Bernardo de Gálvez, quien se ha distinguido en todas las líneas [Campaign in Nueva Vizcaya, the viceroy of New Spain send to Julián de Arriaga news related to the progress in the campaign against the barbarians and rebels in Nieva Vizacaya], 2nd series, Mexico, December 26, 1770, AGNM, Instituciones Coloniales, Gobierno Virreinal, Correspondencia de Virreyes (036), vol. 14; Apaches. Enterado de los progresos conseguidos por nuestras armas bajo la conducta del capitán de infantería don Bernardo Gálvez [Acknowledging the progress made by our armies under the command of Infantry Captain don Bernardo de Gálvez], Mexico, March 23, 1771, AGNM, Instituciones Coloniales, Gobierno Virreinal, Reales Cédulas Originales y Duplicados (100), Reales Cédulas Originales, vol. 98, 78; Expedición de Sonora, el virrey de Nueva España envía a don Julián de Arriaga, las noticias comunicadas por don Bernardo de Gálvez, respecto al estado de los indios rendidos en Sonora y situación en que se mantienen aquellas provincias [Campaign in Sonora, the viceroy of New Spain sends to don Julián de Arriaga the news received from don Bernardo de Gálvez about the condition of the Indians

who have surrendered and on the situation in this province], 2nd series, Mexico, September 19, 1771, AGNM, Instituciones Coloniales, Gobierno Virreinal, Correspondencia de Virreyes (036), vol. 14; Velázquez, "Los apaches y su leyenda," 164–70; Porro, "La defensa y consolidación," 22; B. Gálvez, *Noticia y reflexiones*.

246. Two copies of Gálvez's *Noticia y reflexiones* have survived. One is in the Navy Museum in Madrid (*Noticia y reflexiones sobre las guerras que se mantiene con los indios apaches en la N.E.*, Museo Naval, ms, 567, Virreinato de Méjico, vol. 1, doc. 11, fols. 246r–270r, no author listed). About this copy, Belén Navajas Josa argues that, according to the museum's index cards, the author of the copy could have been Antonio de Pineda, a naval officer, but other sources point to Bernardo de Gálvez. A couple of lines translated into English were the clues that helped to identify the author. On the Navy Museum's index card is written "it looks like Pineda's handwriting—the same as in the previous document," and indeed, both could be the work of the same person. Although throughout the document there are three different handwriting examples, most seem to be Pineda's ("Informes sobre las Provincias Internas por el Ingeniero Lafosa [*sic* Lafora]," Museo Naval, ms, 567, Virreinato de Méjico, vol. 1, doc. 9, fols. 205r–241r). On the other hand, a fragment of the text has been quoted by Weber, who states that, according to Elizabeth A. H. John in her article "Bernardo de Gálvez on the Apache Frontier," the author is Bernardo de Gálvez (Weber, *La frontera española en América del Norte*, 297; Weber, *Spanish Frontier*; John, "Bernardo de Gálvez on the Apache Frontier"). Therefore, for Navajas Josa it is possible that Pineda's text could be a copy made around 1790 of the original text written by Bernardo de Gálvez around 1762 [*sic* 1772] (Navajas Josa, "El padre Kino y la Pimería," 34).

The second copy of the *Noticia y reflexiones* was found within a group of manuscripts by Blas de Osés in the Steiner Collection of the Hill Museum and Manuscript Library at Saint John's University in Collegeville, Minnesota (Osés, *Documentación varia*, ms, Mexico, 1817, the Hill Museum and Manuscript Library, Steiner Collection, Bush Centre, St. John's University, Collegeville, Minn., Steiner 27, Blas Osés, Manuscritos, No. 2, 35–66). In the second volume of the manuscript, between pages 35 and 66, is the transcription of the *Noticia y reflexiones*. Blas de Osés was a lawyer and law professor at the University of Mexico who around 1820 was commissioned by the liberal government in Madrid to explore the possibility of establishing commercial relations with the recently independent Mexico (Moreno de los Arcos, *La primera cátedra*, 876–79). The mission ended when Fernando VII was reinstated into absolute power in 1823. For his classes at the university, Osés visited several archives, copying what he considered to be the most important documents. In copying the *Noticia y reflexiones* he stated that this account was copied from the original in volume two of Various Papers from the Library of the Ecclesial Cabildo of Mexico (Osés, *Documentación varia*). Regarding the author, he wrote on page 66, after recording the acronym "B. d. G.," which according to him appeared in the original document: "Warning. According to the initial and previous note, this memory was written by D. [Don] Bernardo de Gálvez, viceroy of this no. [New] Spain . . . , and at that time he travelled through the Internal Provinces and was awarded the comandancia of Chihuahua. After the year 1785, he succeeded his father in the viceroyalty, and he died the following year" (Osés, documentación varia, 66). Felipe Teixidor, Elizabeth A. H. John, and David J. Weber attribute the document to Bernardo de Gálvez's hand. Elizabeth A. H. John first (1984) was skeptical about the authorship by Bernardo de

Gálvez but later (1988) accepted it without reserve. Teixidor, "Noticia y reflexiones sobre la guerra"; John, "Cautionary Exercise in Apache Historiography"; John, "Bernardo de Gálvez on the Apache Frontier"; Weber, *Spanish Frontier*, 290.

247. Hernández Sánchez-Barba, *La última expansión española*, 178.

248. B. Gálvez, *Noticia y reflexiones*, 39.

249. Blyth, *Chiricahua and Janos*, 20.

250. B. Gálvez, *Noticia y reflexiones*, 42-43.

251. Ibid., 65.

252. Ibid.

253. "Temperamento, f. N, La constitución, y disposición de los mixtos con la proporción de sus calidades." Real Academia Española, *Diccionario de la lengua castellana* (1734), 240; B. Gálvez, *Noticia y reflexiones*, 37.

254. B. Gálvez, *Noticia y reflexiones*, 38.

255. Ibid., 65-66.

256. Ibid., 39-40.

257. Ibid., 38-39.

258. Barr, *Peace Came in the Form of a Woman*, 5. Pritzker, *A Native American Encyclopedia*, 327-58.

259. B. Gálvez, *Noticia y reflexiones*, 39.

260. Ibid., 45, 43.

261. Ibid., 44, 46.

262. Ibid., 45.

263. Ibid., 47.

264. Starkey, *European and Native American Warfare*, 22.

265. B. Gálvez, *Noticia y reflexiones*, 51.

266. Ibid., 52.

267. Ibid., 49.

268. Ibid., 52.

269. Starkey, *European and Native American Warfare*, 20.

270. Crosby, *Throwing Fire*, 104-5.

271. Latham and Paterson, *Saracen Archery*, 138-42.

272. Duffy, *Military Experience*, 207.

273. B. Gálvez, *Noticia y reflexiones*, 56.

274. Ibid., 51-52.

275. Moorhead, *Presidio*, 178.

276. B. Gálvez, *Noticia y reflexiones*, 41.

277. Ibid., 40-41.

278. Ibid., 59.

279. Ibid., 60-61.

280. Ibid., 56-57.

281. Ibid., 57.

282. Ibid., 59.

283. Ibid.

284. Ibid., 60.

285. Ibid., 49.

286. Ibid., 53-54.

287. Ibid., 63-64.

288. Today *guapo* could be translated as "handsome," but during the eighteenth century meant to be courageous, bold, or aggressive. Real Academia Española, *Diccionario de la lengua castellana* (1734), 4:87.

289. B. Gálvez, *Noticia y reflexiones*, 62.

290. Ibid.

291. Ibid., 55.

292. Ibid.

293. General Murray's opinon about the Arab revolt in the movie *Lawrence of Arabia*. Lean, *Lawrence of Arabia*.

294. McCarty, "La educación de un virrey."

CHAPTER 3

1. A recurrent error places Bernardo de Gálvez in France during these years. Boeta, *Bernardo de Gálvez*, 42; Díaz Nogueras, "Bernardo de Gálvez," 755-56; Caughey, *Bernardo de Gálvez in Louisiana*, 67; Pérez de Colosía Rodríguez, "Rasgos biográficos," 91-92; Souviron, *Bernardo de Gálvez*, 30; Vázquez de Acuña, "El Conde de Gálvez," 53; Vázquez de Acuña, *Historial de la Casa de Gálvez*, 1238; Wilson and Fiske, *Appleton's Cyclopaedia of American Biography*, 2:584.

2. Captain Bernardo de Gálvez Military Record (*hoja de servicios*), AGS, ID Persona 10032, Secretaría de Guerra, 2653, DF 8; *Estado militar de España año de 1769*, 21.

3. Royal ordinance of February 28, 1707, mentioned in Sotto, *Historia Orgánica de las Armas*, vol. 9, 401.

4. Sotto, *Historia Orgánica de las Armas*, vol. 9, 401.

5. Regimiento de infantería de Sevilla, AGS, Secretaría de Guerra 2653.

6. Captain Bernardo de Gálvez Military Record, AGS, ID Persona 10032, Secretaría de Guerra, 2653, DF 8, f. 18.

7. Reximiento de Ynfantería de Sevilla, Relación de los oficiales, primeros sargentos y cadetes que tiene este reximiento según la antigüedad que gozan a 1 de enero de 1775, AGS, Secretaría de Guerra, 2653, DF 8.

8. Carramolino, *Historia de Ávila*, 3:392–93; Navarro Loidi, "Las matemáticas en la Academia Militar de Ávila"; Martínez Paricio, "La Real Escuela Militar"; Sotto, *Memoria histórica de las academias*, 57–64.

9. Royal order, January 31, 1774, mentioned in Sotto, *Memoria histórica de las academias*, 57–64.

10. Terrón Ponce, *Ejército y política*, 28; Alejandro O'Reilly, *Relación sucinta que explica el método y reglas bajo las cuales prosiguen sus estudios los oficiales que concurren a la Escuela Militar de Ávila, que ha erigido S.M. en el año de 1774, fiándome la dirección de ella*, Archivo General Militar de Madrid, formerly known as Archivo Central del Servicio Histórico Militar, Madrid, Colección Conde de Clonard, leg. 10 (hereafter *Relación sucinta*).

11. Sotto, *Memoria histórica de las academias*, 63.

12. The quote is from Alejandro O'Reilly to José de Gálvez, Puerto de Santa María, May 7, 1776, AGI, Santo Domingo, 2586, fols. 927r–928v. See also *Estado militar de España año de 1774*, 4.

13. Gómez Ruiz and Alonso Juanola, *El ejército de los borbones*, vol. 4, 468.

14. Martínez Paricio, "La Real Escuela Militar"; Shafer, *Economic Societies*; Paquette, *Enlightenment*, 142–45.

15. Elorza, *Socialismo utópico español*, 104; Elorza, "Peñaflorida."

16. Martínez Paricio, "La Real Escuela Militar," 53.

17. O'Reilly, *Relación sucinta*.

18. Simpson, *Elements of plane geometry*.

19. O'Reilly, *Relación sucinta*.

20. Ibid.

21. Guibert, *Essai général de tactique*; Saavedra, *Los Decenios*, 74.

22. Ortíz de Urbina Montoya, "Un gabinete numismático," 211.

23. Euclides, *Los seis primeros libros*; Bails and Capmany, *Tratados de Mathematica*; Aguirre, *Indagación y reflexiones*.

24. Valdelvira González, *Los militares ilustrados*, 23.

25. O'Reilly, *Relación sucinta*.

26. Saavedra, *Los Decenios*, 74.

27. O'Reilly, *Relación sucinta*.

28. Saavedra, *Los Decenios*, 76.

29. Navarro Loidi, "Las matemáticas en la Academia Militar de Ávila," 315–16; Saavedra, *Los Decenios*, 73; Beerman, "¿Quién era el General Urrutia que Goya retrató?," 198.

30. Fernández Fraile, *La enseñanza del francés*, 95; Chantreau, *Arte de hablar bien francés*.

31. O'Reilly, *Relación sucinta*.

32. Count de Ricla, Informe sobre cadetes de Infantería, Archivo General Militar de Madrid, formerly known as Archivo Central del Servicio Histórico Militar, Madrid, Colección conde de Clonard, leg. 8, mentioned in Terrón Ponce, *Ejército y política*, 31.

33. Terrón Ponce, *Ejército y política*, 34.

34. Dalrymple, *Travels through Spain*, 57.

35. Saavedra, *Los Decenios*, 73.

36. Papeles en verso y prosa, que han salido en esta Corte, al triste succeso de las Armas catholicas en la expedición del día 8 de julio de este año de 1775, contra los argelinos, mandando dicha expedición el theniente general Conde Orreylli, por lo respectivo a tierra, y por mar el theniente general Don Pedro Castexón, BN, MSS 10935, mentioned in Terrón Ponce, *Ejército y política*, 31.

37. Terrón Ponce, *Ejército y política*, 44.

38. Ibid.

39. Saavedra, *Los Decenios*, 73.
40. O'Reilly, *Relación sucinta*.
41. Saavedra, *Los Decenios*, 79.
42. V. Fuente, *Historia de las Universidades*, 4:207.
43. Saavedra, *Los Decenios*, 80.
44. Ibid., 81.
45. Ibid., 80.
46. Cantillo, *Tratados*, 505.
47. Martínez Carreras, "El africanismo español," 357-58.
48. Epalza, "Intereses árabes," 11-12.
49. Voltes Bou, *Carlos III y su tiempo*, 127.
50. Lynch, *Bourbon Spain*, 294.
51. *Gazeta de Madrid*, supplement, April 4, 1775, in Danvila y Collado, *Reinado de Carlos III*, 201-2.
52. Jover Zamora, *España en la política internacional*, 89-90.
53. López Delgado, "Estado de la cuestión," 14.
54. Fernán-Núñez, *Vida de Carlos III.*, 251.
55. Ferrer del Río, *Historia del reinado*.
56. Martínez Peñas, *El confesor del rey*, 644-45.
57. García Lasaosa, "La política exterior," 309.
58. Both spellings are found in contemporary documents.
59. Sánchez Doncel, *Presencia de España*, 273-74.
60. Braudel, *La méditerranée*, 2:291.
61. Plans of the city and port of Algiers: Plano en grande que representa el frente de la ciudad y muelle de Argel con parte de la playa hasta el Río, parte de la costa de Poniente y castillos en ella situados con el proyecto de un bombardeo y operaciones que deberá practicar el comandante de la esquadra . . . ; plano y perfil de una porción de la calzada que baja de la ciudad al muelle . . . y perfil cortado según la línea 2.3. que cruza por medio muelle, Lorieri fecit, map ms, AGS, MPD, 10, 018; Conrotte, *España y los países musulmanes*, 160-61.
62. Count of Aranda to the Marquis of Grimaldi, Paris, April 10, 1775, Archivo General de la Administración, Alcalá de Henares, Madrid, Spain, Estado, 4351, in Danvila y Collado, *Reinado de Carlos III*, 195. The meaning of the expression is not easy to translate. The general idea is that if Spain kept under its dominion only certain enclaves in North Africa, that would show the Moroccans that Spain was interested only in those posts that were vital to it.
63. Plan de la ville et environs d'Alger ou sont compris les chateaux, forts, et batteries qui defendent les aproches de cette place, por Ricardo de Tirgalle, map ms, AGS, MPD, 22, 014.
64. Plan for the conquest of Algiers by Francisco Ricaurd (Proyecto de tomar Argel por Francisco Ricaurd), AGS, SGU, leg. 2010.
65. Memoria que presentó para forzar a los argelinos a que en adelante guarden la fe de los tratados y plan de operaciones militares por Francisco Ricaud, AGS, SGU, leg. 2004; plan de la ville et environs d'Alger oú sont compris les chateaux, forts et batteries et environs, por Francisco Ricaud de Tirgale, map ms, AGS, MPD, 10, 077.
66. *Estado militar de España año de 1774*, 3, 6, 56; *Estado militar de España año de 1775*, 6 and 73.
67. Torres Ramírez, *Alejandro O'Reilly*, 10.
68. Saavedra, *Los Decenios*, 80.
69. For the translation of the different kinds of ships, see Terry y Rivas, *Diccionario maritime*; *Dos expediciones españolas contra Argel*, 87; and Fernández Duro, *Armada española*, 7:170.
70. *Kalendario manual . . . 1774*, 56, 59; *Kalendario manual . . . 1775*, 57, 61; Espinosa de lo Monteros y Abadía, *Plano topographico de la Villa y Corte de Madrid: al Excmo. Sr. Conde de Aranda Capitán General de los Exércitos y Presidente del Consejo, por Antonio Espinosa de los Monteros, Académico de la Real de las Nobles Artes, escala de 1200 pies Castellanos*, equi-

valente a 400 Varas Castellanas, 1769, in BN, GMG/1365, MR/8/II serie 13/044 and MV/13 14087-3001, sheet 6, city block 143.

71. Sotto, *Historia Orgánica de las Armas*, vol. 9, 401. There are three copies of the order of battle for the attack against Algiers: Orden de Batalla del Exercito de S.M. destinado a la Expedición para África que ha hecho a la vela del Puerto de Cartagena, AGS, MPD, 38, 068; AGS, MPD, 38, 069; and AGS, MPD, 38, 070.

72. J. D'W. W., *Diccionario militar*, 166.

73. Blanch, *De la ciencia militar*, mentioned in C. Varona, *Apuntes para un libro*, 386.

74. Fernán-Núñez, "Diario de la expedición contra Argel," 2:119-220; ibid. *Vida de Carlos III.*, 250.

75. Originally in Moltke, *Militarische Werke*, vol. 2, part 2, 33-40, taken from Hughes, *Moltke on the Art of War*, 45-47.

76. *Dos expediciones españolas contra Argel*, 91-92.

77. Ataque a la Ciudad de Argel, acompaña a una carta de Andrés Boleda al Conde de Ricla, Barcelona, April 13, 1776; Relación del modo que se había de tener para el desembarco en Argel; Descripción de la ciudad de Argel y sus fortalezas; and Memorial de Matías del Vao, Madrid, December 1775, solicitando exponer cómo se han de hacer las baterías en España y llevarlas a Argel, AGS, MPD, 12, 096.

78. Report by the Marquis de la Cañada, August 10, 1775, AGS, Guerra Moderna, 2004, partially quoted in *Dos expediciones españolas contra Argel*, 115-16.

79. Report by Victorio de Nava Osorio about the expedition against Algiers, September 11, 1775, AGS, Guerra Moderna, 2004, in *Dos expediciones españolas contra Argel*, 117.

80. Fernández de Castro y Pedrera, "La expedición contra Argel," 15.

81. Odriozola y Añativia, *Compendio de artillería*, 157.

82. On the cavalry tactics when attacking infantry at the battle of Waterloo, see Keegan, *Mask of Command*, 153-56.

83. In the "Ideal plan of the city of Algiers" (*Plano ideal que manifiesta la ciudad de Argel*), the position occupied by the light infantry (*cazadores*) is marked with a number 4. Attached to this plan is a paper with a drawing of the Spanish positions after the disembarkation, with the redoubt mentioned. Plano ideal que manifiesta la ciudad de Argel con sus baterías y campamentos en la disposición que se hallaron el día 30 de junio de 1775, que llegó a su rada el ejército de S.M. mandado por el Exmo. Sr. Conde de O'Reilly con el proyecto para su ataque y lo que sucedió el día 8 de julio del mismo año por D. Silvestre Abarca en la bahía de Argel a 12 de julio de 1775, map, ms, AGS, MPD, 13, 020. Also see Ataque a la Ciudad de Argel, plan attached to the letter from Andrés Boleda [sic] to the Count of Ricla, Barcelona, April 13, 1776; Relación del modo que se había de tener para el desembarco en Argel; Descripción de la ciudad de Argel y sus fortalezas; and Memorial de Matías del Vao, Madrid, December 1775, solicitando exponer cómo se han de hacer las baterías en España y llevarlas a Argel, AGS, MPD, 12, 096.

84. Alejandro O'Reilly to José de Gálvez, Puerto de Santa María, May 7, 1776, AGI, Santo Domingo, 2586, folder 11, fols. 927r-928v.

85. List of dead and wounded officers in "Relación de Oficiales muertos y heridos en la función del día 8 de julio de 1775," in *Relación puntual de lo acaecido con motivo de la Expedición dispuesta contra Argel en el año de 1775*.

86. Black, *Warfare in the Eighteenth Century*, 167.

87. Plano ideal que manifiesta la ciudad de Argel, con sus baterías y campamentos en la disposición que se hallaron el día 30 de junio de 1775, que llegó a su rada el exército de S.M. mandado por el Exmo. Sr. Conde de O'Reilly, con el proyecto para su ataque y lo que sucedió el día 8 de julio del mismo año, rubricado por Silvestre Abarca, AGS, MPD, 07, 160.

88. *Dos expediciones españolas contra Argel, 1541 y 1775*, 124-25.
89. *Chroniques de la régence d'Alger*, 192.
90. Ibid., 188.
91. Galindo y de Vera, *Historia, vicisitudes y política*, 324.
92. Plano en grande que representa el frente de la ciudad y muelle de Argel con parte de la playa hasta el Río, parte de la costa de Poniente y castillos en ella situados con el proyecto de un bombardeo y operaciones que deberá practicar el comandante de la esquadra . . . ; Plano y perfil de una porción de la calzada que baja de la ciudad al muelle . . . y perfil cortado según la línea 2.3. que cruza por medio muelle, Lorieri fecit, map ms, AGS, MPD, 10, 018.
93. Lynch, *La España del Siglo XVIII*, 294.
94. Count O'Reilly to King Carlos III, report, aboard the ship of the line *Velasco*, July 9, 1775, in *Dos expediciones españolas contra Argel*, 125-26.
95. Among other documents, see Papeles que han salido con motivo de los funestos sucesos de la expedición dirigida por España contra Argel, año 1775, BN, ms, 1959; and *Inventario general de manuscritos de la Biblioteca Nacional*, 5:382.
Satirical poems about the expedition against Algiers of July 8, 1775: Interrogatorio: Se defendió? / Con arrojo . . . f. 32v; Carlos despierta / mira que te engañan . . . (wall poster), f. 33v; Razonamiento de España con la nobleza en interrogatorio: Que has hecho, nobleza fiel? / De tantos héroes nobles . . . fol. 34, 15; Octava sobre la Expedición de Argel: Nunca vio el mundo tropa semejante / por la mayor nobleza dirigida . . . f. 61, BN, ms, 2901; *Inventario general de manuscritos de la Biblioteca Nacional*, 9:108-9.
Critical history and contemporaneous accounts on the expedition against Algiers of July 1775: (1) An epic satirical poem, fols. 159-81, BN, ms, 3733; *Inventario general de manuscritos de la Biblioteca Nacional*, 10:167. (2) A comedy, fols. 182-86, BN, ms, 3733; *Inventario general de manuscritos de la Biblioteca Nacional*, 10:167. (3) Expedición de Argel del año de 1775, a cargo de los Tenientes Generales Conde de O'Reylli [sic] . . . y D. Pedro Castejón . . . Colección de varios papeles y poesías producidos con motivo del desgraciado éxito de las armas cathólicas . . . y lamentable victoria de los Mahometanos en el día 8 de Julio del referido año, BN, ms, 3750; *Inventario general de manuscritos de la Biblioteca Nacional*, 10:171.
Papers in prose and verse about the expedition against Algiers in 1775 and its commander the Count O'Reilly: (1) El Marqués más conturbado y Jefe de la injusticia; La sociedad antihispana, poema épico; Junta anual de la Sociedad antihispana en el día de Inocentes de 1776. (2) Relación y súplica que el Alexandro Argelino hace al Rey; La conquista de Argel, comedia; Poesías sobre el mismo asunto. (3) Diario de la expedición; Funciones de Irlanda; El segundo Atila en África. (4) Testamento satírico de O'Reilly en prosa y verso; Poesías varias referentes al mismo asunto. All in BN, ms, 4087-4090; and *Inventario general de manuscritos de la Biblioteca Nacional*, 10:263-54.
Other compositions: several comedies about the Algiers expedition (*comedias sobre la desgraciada expedición a Argel del Conde O'Reilly*), in *Inventario general de manuscritos de la Biblioteca Nacional*, 9:200; a satirical composition, *Carta historrélica* [sic] *que la Fortuna escribió al Conde de O'Reylly* [sic]. *Argel, 15, julio, 1775*, fols. 71-83v., BN, ms, 6692, *Inventario general de manuscritos de la Biblioteca Nacional*, 9:241.
96. Ferrer del Río, *Historia del reinado*, 3:134.
97. Fernández Duro, *Armada española*, 7:179.
98. Gil Novales, "Política y sociedad," 243.
99. Saavedra, *Los Decenios*, 97.

100. Ibid., 99.
101. *Gazeta de Madrid*, no. 5, January 30, 1776; Saavedra, *Los Decenios*, 99.
102. *Gazeta de Madrid*, no. 5, January 30, 1776, 43-46.
103. Ibid., February 20, 1776, 70.
104. Marchena Fernández, *Oficiales y soldados*, 147-48.
105. Alejandro O'Reilly to José de Gálvez, Puerto de Santa María, May 7, 1776, AGI, Santo Domingo, 2586, folder 11, fols. 927r-928v.
106. Bernardo de Gálvez's appointment as colonel of the Louisiana Fixed Infantry Regiment (*regimiento de infantería fijo de la Luisiana*), in ibid., fols. 930r-v.

CHAPTER 4

1. Bernardo de Gálvez's appointment as colonel of the Louisiana Fixed Infantry Regiment (Regimiento de infantería fijo de la Luisiana), AGI, Santo Domingo, 2586, folder 11, fols. 930r-v; Marquis de la Torre, governor and captain general of Cuba, to José de Gálvez, Havana, December 1, 1776, AGI, Santo Domingo, 1211.
2. Article 36 of the Constitutions (regulations) of the Royal and Distinguished Spanish Order of Carlos III, *Constituciones de la Real y Distinguida Orden Española de Carlos Tercero*, 22.
3. Martínez, *Genealogical Fictions*, 283; Siete Iglesias, "¿Qué es nobleza de sangre?," 105-6; Larios Martín, "Ciencias complementarias de la nobiliaria," 29; Lira Montt, "La prueba de hidalgía en el derecho indiano," 131-32.
4. Villalba Pérez, "La Orden de Carlos III"; Sánchez de Rivera y Alfaro, "La Real y distinguida Orden de Carlos III"; Cadenas y Vicent, *Extracto de los expedientes de la Orden de Carlos III*; Morales Moya, "Movilidad social en la España del siglo XVIII"; Domínguez Ortiz, "Política nobiliaria de la Ilustración"; Cárdenas Piera, *Propuestas, solicitudes y decretos*. María Isabel Pérez de Colosía Rodríguez states that Bernardo was already a member of the Caballeros Hijosdalgo de Madrid, a sort of society formed by aristocrats, but we have been unable to find any documentation to back her assertion. Pérez de Colosía Rodríguez, "Rasgos biográficos," 94.
5. Luis de Unzaga y Amezaga (1721-1792), was a military officer who, before being appointed as Lousisiana's governor, was the colonel of the Fixed Infantry Regiment of Havana. Coutts, "Martin Navarro," 62n 1; Holmes, *Honor and Fidelity*, 20-21; Sucre, *Gobernadores y Capitanes*, 290-91.
6. José de Gálvez to Bernardo de Gálvez, Madrid, November 25, 1776, AGI, Cuba, 174.
7. D. Fisher, *Washington's Crossing*, 81-83.
8. Ibid., 137.
9. For the British strategy, see Wilcox, *Portrait of a General*, 42-43, 94-97.
10. Middlekauff, *Glorious Cause*, 333.
11. Paine, "American Crisis," 49.
12. D. Fisher, *Washington's Crossing*, 369.
13. On George Washington's decision to launch this attack, see Freeman, *George Washington*, vol. 4, 306, no. 15; and C. Ward, *War of the Revolution*, 1:292.
14. For the battles of Trenton and Princeton, see D. Fisher, *Washington's Crossing*.
15. Ruigómez de Hernández, *El gobierno español*, 176-77.
16. Count of Aranda to the Marquis of Grimaldi, Paris, May 3, 1776, AGS, Estado, 4602, in Ruigómez de Hernández, *El gobierno español*, 185.
17. José de Gálvez to the governor of Cuba, 1776, AGI, Cuba, 1227.
18. Ibid.
19. For Charles Lee's life, see Fredericksen, *American Military Leaders*, 419-20. For his campaigns in the South, see Alden, *General Charles Lee*, 108-10; and Carlos [*sic*: Charles] Lee to José de Gálvez, Williamsburg, May 1776, AHN, Estado 4224. Although the letter is filed as ad-

dressed to José de Gálvez, it was actually sent to the Spanish governor of Florida (Bernardo de Gálvez had arrived that same month to New Orleans). In Ruigómez de Hernández, *El gobierno español*, 187; see also Carlos [*sic*: Charles] Lee to Luis de Unzaga, May 1776, AGI, Cuba, 2370.

20. Ruigómez de Hernández, *El gobierno español*, 189-90.

21. Royal order to the governor of Louisiana, September 28, 1775, AGI, Papeles de Cuba, 174A.

22. Abbey, "Efforts of Spain," 57.

23. Keegan, *Intelligence in War*, xv.

24. Lowental, *Intelligence*.

25. Jomini, *Précis de l'art de la guerre*, 188.

26. Lowental, *Intelligence*, 55.

27. Martín Navarro to Bernardo de Gálvez, New Orleans, May 7, 1781, AGI, Papeles de Cuba, 83.

28. José de Gálvez to the governor of Cuba, official letter, El Pardo, March 18, 1780, AGI, Santo Domingo, 2082; José de Gálvez to the Marquis de la Torre, May 23, 1777, AGI, Papeles de Cuba, 1227.

29. Diego José Navarro to José de Gálvez, letter no. 666, Havana, December 28, 1779, AGI, Santo Domingo, 2082.

30. Bernardo de Gálvez to Juan Delavillebreuve, official letter draft copy, New Orleans, May 18, 1778, AGI, Papeles de Cuba, 112.

31. British letter dated October 7, 1779, intercepted by the Spanish, included in Diego José Navarro to José de Gálvez, official letter no. 634, Havana, November 11, 1779 (1st of this date), AGI, Santo Domingo, 2082.

32. José de Gálvez to the governor of Cuba, confidential letter, El Pardo, January 11, 1780, in ibid.

33. Narrett, *Adventurism and Empire*, 86.

34. Bernardo de Gálvez to Francisco Cruzat, official letter draft copy, New Orleans, August 25, 1777, AGI, Papeles de Cuba, 112.

35. James, "Spanish Influence," 199.

36. Bernardo de Gálvez to José de Gálvez, official letter no. 63, New Orleans, July 10, 1777, AGI, Santo Domingo, 2596.

37. Order, August 28, 1777, AGI, Santo Domingo, 1598 A and B.

38. Bernardo de Gálvez to José de Gálvez, confidential letter no. 1421, April 5, 1777, AGI, Santo Domingo, 1598 A and B; Bernardo de Gálvez to José de Gálvez, confidential letter no. 116, November 8, 1777, in ibid.

39. Bernardo de Gálvez to José de Gálvez, confidential letter no. 129, New Orleans, March 11, 1778, AGI, Santo Domingo, 2596.

40. Caughey, "Panis Mission," 481.

41. Peter Chester to Bernardo de Galvez, April 7, 1778, AGI, Cuba, 191, in Caughey, "Panis Mission," 485.

42. Jacinto Panis to Bernardo de Gálvez, report, New Orleans, July 5, 1778, AGI, Cuba, 112; Bernardo de Gálvez to José de Gálvez, confidential letter no. 175, New Orleans, July 28, 1778, AGI, Santo Domingo, 2596.

43. Bernardo de Gálvez to Diego Joseph Navarro, confidential letter no. 201, New Orleans, August 17, 1779, AGI, Papeles de Cuba, 2351.

44. Caughey, "Panis Mission," 488-89.

45. Report by Sergeant Felipe Jorge on the situation of Pensacola's defenses, letter draft copy, Mobile, September 26, 1780, AGI, Papeles de Cuba, 19; news given by Roberto Holms, resident and planter of Pensacola, apprehended three leagues from Mobile on the 5th of this month, Havana, February 15, 1780, AGI, Santo Domingo, 2082; information by several deserters, Mobile, August 11, 1780, AGI, Papeles de Cuba, 2; English deserters inform on the defenses of Pensacola, Mobile, September 27, 1780, AGI, Papeles de Cuba, 2; English deserters inform on the defenses of Pensacola, in José de Ezpeleta to Bernardo de Gálvez, official letter, Mobile, December 30, 1780, AGI, Papeles de Cuba, 2; plan of Pensacola supplied by

an Englishman, in M. Huet to Bernardo de Gálvez, AGI, Papeles de Cuba, 114.

46. José de Gálvez to Bernardo de Gálvez, official letter draft copy, February 22, 1777, AGI, Santo Domingo, 1598 A and B.

47. Bernardo de Gálvez to José de Gálvez, letter no. 61, June 2, 1777, in ibid.

48. Ibid., letter no. 75, August 9, 1777.

49. Ibid., letter no. 116, December 30, 1777.

50. Ibid., confidential letter no. 251, New Orleans, February 25, 1779; Diego José Navarro to José de Gálvez, letter no. 485, Havana, April 14, 1779, AGI, Santo Domingo, 1598 A and B.

51. Diego Joseph Navarro to José de Gálvez, confidential letter no. 45, Havana, July 16, 1778, AGI, Santo Domingo, 1598 A and B; ibid., confidential letter no. 63, Havana, February 9, 1779; ibid., confidential letter no. 65, Havana, April 15, 1779.

52. Bartolomé Fernández Armesto, copy of the very confidential official letter from José de Gálvez to the governor of Santo Domingo, Isidro Peralta y Rojas, where José de Gálvez informs about the offer made by the spy Bartolomé Fernández Armesto, El Pardo, March 12, 1780, AGI, Santo Domingo, 2082.

53. José de Gálvez to the governor of Santo Domingo, Isidro Peralta y Rojas, in the letter from José de Gálvez to the governor of Cuba, copy of the very confidential official letter, El Pardo, March 12, 1780, in ibid.

54. José de Gálvez to the governor of Cuba, El Pardo, March 12, 1780, in ibid.

55. José de Gálvez to the governor of Puerto Rico, Isidro Peralta y Rojas, confidential official letter draft copy, El Pardo, March 22, 1780, in ibid.

56. Juan Manuel de Cagigal to Bernardo de Gálvez, confidential letter no. 1, Havana, November 17, 1781, AGI, Indiferente General, 1584; ibid., confidential letter no. 2, Havana, November 26, 1781; ibid., confidential letter, Havana, March 26, 1782.

57. José de Gálvez to the governor of Cuba, March 16, 1782, AGI, Santo Domingo 2083, A.

58. Bernardo de Gálvez to José de Gálvez, confidential letter no. 40, Guarico, May 18, 1782, AGI, Santo Domingo, 2549.

59. Pablo Figuerola, Colonel of the Regiment Cataluña, to Bernardo de Gálvez, official letter, Port-au-Prince, June 6, 1782, AGI, Indiferente General, 1580; news about Jamaica by Jacobo Spitrionis, Dutch spy, in Pablo Figuerola, colonel of the Regiment Cataluña, to Bernardo de Gálvez, official letter, Port-au-Prince, June 23, 1782, AGI, Indiferente General, 1580.

60. Marlborough, "Case and Vindication," in Lediard, *Life of John, Duke of Marlborough*, 2:370–80.

61. Expenses in spies during October 1778, Bernardo de Gálvez to José de Gálvez, confidential letter no. 203, New Orleans, October 24, 1778, AGI, Santo Domingo, 2596; list of indispensable expenses made in secret commissions, Bernardo de Gálvez to José de Gálvez, dispatch 203, New Orleans, October 24, 1778, AGI, Santo Domingo, 2547; expenses made and ways to conceal them, Bernardo de Gálvez to José de Gálvez, confidential letter no. 254, New Orleans, February 25, 1779, AGI, Santo Domingo, 2596; remittance of 400,000 pesos to Bernardo de Gálvez for secret commissions, Juan Ignacio de Urriza to José de Gálvez, letter no. 896, Havana, January 19, 1782, Santo Domingo, 1659.

62. Calloway, *Scratch of a Pen*; Greene, "Negotiated Authorities"; Certeau, *L'invention du quotidien*, 54.

63. Din, "Spanish Control over a Multiethnic Society." The adaptation to the local population in order to ensure their fidelity to a new country (this time Britain) also took place in western Florida between 1781 and 1821; see McMichael, *Atlantic Loyalties*.

64. Bouligny, "Noticia del estado actual del comercio y población de la Nueva Orleans y Luisiana Española," Madrid, August 16, 1776, BN, 19265, men-

tioned in Din, "La defensa de la Luisiana española," 164.

65. Din, "La defensa de la Luisiana española," 156.

66. Caughey, *Bernardo de Gálvez in Louisiana*, 8.

67. Torres Ramírez, *Alejandro O'Reilly*, 98, 110.

68. Instructions to Alejandro O'Reilly, AGI, Cuba, 2357, in Torres Ramírez, *Alejandro O'Reilly*, 99–100.

69. Torres Ramírez, *Alejandro O'Reilly*, 130.

70. Din, "La defensa de la Luisiana española," 163.

71. Alejandro O'Reilly to Julián de Arriaga, letter no. 3, New Orleans, October 17, 1769, BN, Colección de la Luisiana, 1, fols. 1–9, in Din, "La defensa de la Luisiana española," 159.

72. Bernardo de Gálvez to José de Gálvez, New Orleans, March 21, 1777, AGI, Santo Domingo, 2656.

73. Bernardo de Gálvez to José de Gálvez, New Orleans, June 2, 1777, in Serrano y Sanz, *Documentos históricos*, 314.

74. Bernardo de Gálvez to José de Gálvez, New Orleans, May 12, 1777, quoted in José de Gálvez to Bernardo de Gálvez, letter no. 80, San Ildefonso, August 15, 1777, AGI, Papeles de Cuba, 114.

75. Marquis de la Torre to Bernardo de Gálvez, Havana, June 1, 1777, in Din, "La defensa de la Luisiana española," 166.

76. José de Gálvez to Bernardo de Gálvez, letter no. 80, San Ildefonso, August 15, 1777, AGI, Papeles de Cuba, 114.

77. Din, "La defensa de la Luisiana española," 163.

78. Sabatini, report on Louisiana, Madrid, August 15, 1794, Archivo General de la Administración, Alcalá de Henares, Madrid, Spain, 5-1-7-7, in Cabrero, "Francisco Sabatini," 147.

79. Bernardo de Gálvez's appointment as colonel of the Louisiana Fixed Infantry Regiment, AGI, Santo Domingo, 2586, folder 11, fols. 930r-v.

80. "Year of 1767," "Luysiana, Órdenes expedidas para enviar tropas a esta colonia y formación de un batallón que la guarnezca," AGI, Santo Domingo, 2656, quoted in Din, "La defensa de la Luisiana española," 156–57.

81. Holmes, *Honor and Fidelity*, 17–18; Osorio, *El Regimiento de la Luisiana*.

82. Article 1, title 1, treaty 1, *Ordenanzas de S.M. para el régimen, disciplina, subordinación y servicio de sus Exércitos*, 2.

83. Andreu Ocariz, "Militares catalanes," 2:207.

84. Bernardo de Gálvez to José de Gálvez, letter no. 171, New Orleans, June 12, 1778, AGI, Papeles de Cuba, 184A. Estado de fuerza Batallón Luisiana, in Bernardo de Gálvez to José de Gálvez, letter no. 170, New Orleans, June 9, 1778, AGI, Santo Domingo 2596.

85. Estado de fuerza Batallón Luisana, May 8, 1779, AGI, Papeles de Cuba, 159A.

86. Rumeu de Armas, *Piraterías y ataques navales*, vol. 3, pt. 2, 738, quoted in Rodríguez del Valle and Conejo Díez de la Cortina, "Matías de Gálvez," 227.

87. Instrucción dada por Matías Gálvez a los oficiales encargados del reclutamiento para el Regimiento de Infantería de Luisiana, AGI, Santo Domingo, 2.661.

88. Bernardo de Gálvez to José de Gálvez, New Orleans, letter no. 304, July 7, 1779, AGI, Papeles de Cuba, 223B; Molina Martínez, "La participación canaria," 157.

89. Holmes, *Honor and Fidelity*, 25.

90. Bernardo de Gálvez to José de Gálvez, letter no. 304, New Orleans, July 7, 1779, AGI, Papeles de Cuba, 223B.

91. Holmes, *Honor and Fidelity*, 25.

92. Bernardo de Gálvez to Martín Navarro, AGI, Papeles de Cuba, 83, in Din, "For Defense of Country," 14.

93. McFarlane, "Los ejércitos coloniales," 238.

94. Bravo, "Las élites militares," 507; Marchena Fernández, "La expresión de la guerra"; Suárez, *Las milicias*, 156.

95. Article 1, title 18, treaty 2, *Ordenanzas de S.M. para el régimen, disciplina,*

subordinación y servicio de sus Exércitos, 236.

96. The battalion's (later regiment's) first uniform was a white dress coat with blue lining and white buttons, blue pants, cuffs, and collar. Gómez Ruiz and Alonso Juanola, *El ejército de los borbones*, vol. 3/2, 126.

97. The dragoons were not strictly cavalry but mounted troops. They traveled on horseback but fought on foot.

98. Albi and Stampa, "La caballería española en ultramar," 121. The uniform of the Company of Louisiana or New Orleans's Dragoons was blue with red facings and golden buttons. Gómez Ruiz and Alonso Juanola, *El ejército de los borbones*, vol. 3/2, 126.

99. Gómez Ruiz and Alonso Juanola, *El ejército de los borbones*, vol. 3/2, 126.

100. Din, "La defensa de la Luisiana española," 159.

101. Alejandro O'Reilly to the Marquis of Grimaldi, New Orleans, September 30, 1770, AGI, Santo Domingo, 86, in Kinnaird, *Spain in the Mississippi Valley*, 183–86.

102. Caughey, *Bernardo de Gálvez in Louisiana*, 137–38.

103. Marchena Fernández, "El ejército de América," 72.

104. Certified copy of the census sent by Bernardo de Gálvez, New Orleans, May 12, 1777, AGI, Cuba, 2351.

105. Estado de fuerza, New Orleans, January 1, 1779, AGI, Santo Domingo, 2662.

106. Gómez Ruiz and Alonso Juanola, *El ejército de los borbones*, vol. 3/2, 127. For its uniform, see Spring, *Las compañías de Infantaria* [sic], 59. The uniform was blue with red facings and golden buttons.

107. Holmes, *Honor and Fidelity*, 17–18, 24.

108. Its uniform was the same as the New Orleans Infantry Militia Batallion. Gómez Ruiz and Alonso Juanola, *El ejército de los borbones*, vol. 3/2, 126–27.

109. Both militias wore white uniforms, but the *pardos*' uniforms had green facings and silver buttons while the *morenos*' uniforms had red facings and golden buttons. Ibid., 127.

110. Hanger, "Privilege and Honor," 391.

111. Gómez Ruiz and Alonso Juanola, *El ejército de los borbones*, vol. 3/2, 127–30.

112. This is the unit's name in the official record sent to Madrid by Louisiana's governor Baron of Carondelet on March 20, 1797. Carabineros de Nueva Orleáns, AGS, SGU, 7292, 5. Other authors mention a slightly different one: Distinguished Company of New Orleans Carabineros. See Gómez Ruiz and Alonso Juanola, *El ejército de los borbones*, vol. 3/2, 131; Martínez Laínez and Canales Torres, *Banderas lejanas*, 422; and "Da cuenta de haber formado una compañía con la denominación de Carabineros de la Luisiana y ofreciendo remitir el diseño de su uniforme solicita la correspondiente aprobación de S.M. y el completo del armamento que expresa," Bernardo de Gálvez to José de Gálvez, letter no. 288, New Orleans, June 5, 1780, AGI, Santo Domingo, 2547.

113. Holmes, *Honor and Fidelity*, 17–18, 23.

114. The uniform consisted of a flea- or brownish-color coat, white trousers and facings, buttonholes with golden braid, and golden buttons. Gómez Ruiz and Alonso Juanola, *El ejército de los borbones*, vol. 3/2, 131; Bueno Carrera, *Tropas virreinales*.

115. Caughey, "Bernardo de Gálvez and the English Smugglers," 46.

116. Fabel, "Anglo-Spanish Commerce," 35.

117. Caughey, "Bernardo de Gálvez and the English Smugglers," 49.

118. Gayarré, *History of Louisiana*, 3:46.

119. Quoted in Villiers du Terrage, *Les dernières années*, 352.

120. Quoted in ibid., 354.

121. Martín Navarro, *Reflexiones políticas sobre el estado actual de la provincia de la Luisiana*, 1782, BN, Manuscritos de

Ultramar, 13, in Serrano y Sanz, *Documentos históricos*, 366.

122. José de Gálvez to Bernardo de Gálvez, Madrid, November 25, 1776, AGI, Cuba, 174.

123. Instruction que devra observer le Gouverneur de la Louisiane relativement à l'exportation du bois, des vivres et des fruits que Sa Majesté a bien voulu permettre pour le temps qu'elle le jugera à propos pour secourir les Isles françaises Sous le Vent, Madrid [Instructions to be followed by the governor of Louisiana for the export of wood, food, and fruits that His Majesty has allowed for the time he would deem necessary for the recovery of the French isles of Sous le Vent], July 8, 1776, in Villiers du Terrage, *Les dernières années*, 353–54.

124. Leroy-Beaulieu, *De la colonisation*, 32–33, quoted in Whitaker, "Commerce of Louisiana," 219.

125. Whitaker, "Commerce of Louisiana," 219–22.

126. Order, October 29, 1778, Cedulario vol. 31, fol. 52v. and no. 50, "Por la que se autoriza al gobernador de la Luisiana a que siempre que lo necesite pueda enviar barcos a comerciar libremente con el puerto de Veracruz," in Ayala, *Diccionario de gobierno*, 7:117.

127. Report by Villars y Fabre, New Orleans, March 30, 1777, in Gayarré, *History of Louisiana*, 3:106.

128. Bernardo de Gálvez to José de Gálvez, New Orleans, May 12, 1777, AGI, Santo Domingo, 2596.

129. James, "Spanish Influence," 198–99; Fabel, "Anglo-Spanish Commerce," 37.

130. Thomas Lloyd to Bernardo de Gálvez, April 1777, AGI, Cuba, 188-C.

131. Bernardo de Gálvez to Captain Thomas Lloyd, New Orleans, May 11, 1777, Public Record Office, America and West Indies 269, fols. 355–59, in Historical Manuscripts Commission, *Report on American Manuscripts*, 1:109.

132. Caughey, *Bernardo de Gálvez in Louisiana*, 72–73.

133. Din, "Protecting the 'Barrera.'"

134. James, "Spanish Influence," 199.

135. British merchants of New Orleans to Thomas Lloyd, New Orleans, April 26, 1777, AGI, Cuba, 188-C.

136. Narrett, *Adventurism and Empire*, 78.

137. British merchants of New Orleans to Thomas Lloyd, New Orleans, April 26, 1777, AGI, Cuba, 188-C.

138. Letter attributed to the British merchants in the Mississippi (circa May 1777), in Historical Manuscripts Commission, *Report on American Manuscripts*, 1:112–13.

139. Order, May 20, 1779, Cedulario vol. 35, fol. 158 v., no. 150, "12. Que de las producciones de la Isla (Cuba) que se extrajesen para la Luisiana no se exigiese más que el 2 por ciento del almojarifazgo que previene la ley 13, título 15, libro 8 de la Recopilación de Indias, exceptuando las harinas y legumbres que nada debían pagar por regularse aquella provincia dependiente de Havana," in Ayala, *Diccionario de gobierno*, 3:351.

140. Report by the commissioners Villars y Favre d'Aunoy to Paris, New Orleans, July 18, 1778, in Gayarré, *History of Louisiana*, 3:117–18.

141. Lieutenant Colonel Coronel William Stiell to General Sir William Howe, Pensacola, June 3, 1777, in Historical Manuscripts Commission, *Report on American Manuscripts*, 1:115–16.

142. Fabel, "Anglo-Spanish Commerce," 41–43.

143. Caughey, "Bernardo de Gálvez and the English Smugglers," 58.

144. Alejandro O'Reilly to José de Gálvez, Puerto de Santa María, May 7, 1776, AGI, Santo Domingo, 2586, folder 11, fols. 927r–928v.

145. Weber, *Spanish Frontier*, 228.

146. Solórzano Pereira, *Política indiana*, book 2, chapter 6, number 1, p. 170.

147. Levaggi, "República de indios," 427.

148. Ibid., 426.

149. Although Gary B. Nash has con-

vincingly argued that the different European policies toward the Indians have more to do with local conditions than with previous conceptions or ideas, the fact remains that the outcome would be different policies. Nash, *Red, White, and Black*, 310-19.

150. Elliott, *Empires of the Atlantic World*, 269; Elliott, "Britain and Spain in America."

151. González López-Briones, "Reacciones diferentes ante una política similar," 121; Trigger and Swagerty, "Entertaining Strangers."

152. Marston, *French-Indian War*, 16-17.

153. Calloway, *One Vast Winter Count*, 360-61.

154. Nasatir, *Borderland in Retreat*, 15.

155. Bolton, *Athanase de Mézières*, 2:71-72.

156. Bernardo de Gálvez to José de Gálvez, dispatch 3, New Orleans, January 28, 1777, AGI, Santo Domingo, 2547, Duplicados de Gobernadores e Intendentes.

157. Bernardo de Gálvez to José de Gálvez, New Orleans, October 24, 1778, in West, "Indian Policy of Galvez," 100-101.

158. Bernardo de Gálvez to José de Gálvez, dispatch 3, New Orleans, January 28, 1777, AGI, Santo Domingo, 2547, Duplicados de Gobernadores e Intendentes.

159. Bernardo de Gálvez to José de Gálvez, dispatch 204, New Orleans, October 24, 1778, in ibid.

160. "No se pueden rescatar, ni dar á los Indios armas ofensivas, ni defensivas, por los inconvenientes, que pueden resultar," law 24, title 1, book 6, *RLI* (1681); "Que no se puedan vender armas á los Indios, ni ellos las tengan," law 31, ibid.

161. "Sobre la bebida del pulque, usada por los indios de la Nueva España," law 37, ibid..

162. "Que no se consientan estancos de vino, y carnicerías en Tlaxcala," law 43, ibid.

163. For the importance of trade and gifts in shaping Indian support in the Anglo-Spanish war, see Holland Braund, *Deerskins and Duffels*, 168; Cashin, *William*, 224-25; and R. White, *Roots of Dependency*, 79-82.

164. Mauss, *Gift*, 1.

165. Bernardo de Gálvez to José de Gálvez, dispatch 3, New Orleans, January 28, 1777, AGI, Santo Domingo, 2547, Duplicados de Gobernadores e Intendentes.

166. Vargas Machuca, *Indian Militia*, 2:13.

167. Bernardo de Gálvez to José de Gálvez, dispatch 29, Pensacola, May 26, 1781, AGI, Santo Domingo, 2548, Duplicados de Gobernadores e Intendentes, fols. 22r-23r.

168. Ibid.

169. Ibid.

170. Ibid.

171. The so-called Indian peace medals have been studied from the numismatic perspective, i.e. as objects. See J. Adams, "Peace Medals of George III"; Belden, *Indian Peace Medals*; Lopez, "Indian Peace Medals"; Pickering, *Peace Medals*; and Prucha, *Indian Peace Medals in American History*. From the historical perspective, see the works cited in this section.

172. Betts, *American Colonial History Illustrated*, 32.

173. For the medals coined in honor of Santa Rosa de Lima, see Medina, *Medallas europeas relativas a América*, 277-80.

174. Ibid., 37-38.

175. Obverse: the legend HONOS ET VIRTUS with the image of two warriors shaking hands, one dressed as a Roman, representing France, and the other one representing its Indian allies. Betts, *American Colonial History Illustrated*, 82.

176. Nute, "Indian Medals and Certificates," 266.

177. Betts, *American Colonial History Illustrated*, 82.

178. Usner, "American Indians in Colonial New Orleans" in *Powhatan's Mantle*, 172.

179. Villena, "The First Spanish Military Decorations."

180. Ewers, "Symbols of Chiefly Authority."

181. Ewers, *Plains Indian History and Culture*, 106–7; Weber, *Bárbaros, Spaniards and Their Savages*, ill. no. 25, 187.

182. DuVal, "The Education of Fernando de Leyba."

183. Letters from Bernardo de Gálvez to José de Gálvez dated 1777 and 1778, AHN, Estado 3884 bis, DF 7, ns. 1–8.

184. The design by Tomás Francisco Prieto, official engraver of His Catholic Majesty, is very similar to the old design, the main difference being that the bust of King Carlos III is adorned with the insignia of the Order of the Toisón de oro ("Golden Fleece") and the medal bears the signature of the artist (AHN, Fondos Contemporáneos Ministerio de Hacienda, Madrid, 7870, DF3, mentioned in Cox, "Rare Spanish Carlos III"). This new medal is commonly called the large *al mérito* medal, first coined in April 1778 (medal *Al mérito de tamaño grande*; see Tayman, Lopez, and Liechty, "Tomás Prieto's al Mérito Spanish Indian Peace Medals," 19–31). Although few have survived, one is in the Lázaro Galdiano Museum in Madrid and another was auctioned by Stack's Bowers Galleries in New York in 2009, selling for $17,250. On the obverse of the golden silver medal is a bust of the king's profile to the right and the legend CARLOS III. REY DE ESP. EMP DE LAS INDIAS (Charles the Third. King of Spain and Emperor of the Indies). On the back is AL MERITO surrounded by a laurel wreath. It is signed T. PRIETO under the bust. The diameter is 56 mm. (2.126 inches), and the medal has been uncirculated. Museum Lázaro Galdiano, Madrid, Medal Collection, inventory no. 5213; Stack's, 123 W. 57th St., New York, the Americana Sale, December 1, 2009, Lot no. 5012, http://legacy.stacks.com/Lot/ItemDetail/25474 (accessed September 6, 2016). A couple of historians have mentioned the possible existence of other *al mérito* medals that could have been coined in Mexico, although they both admit that no documentary evidence has been found (Medina, *Medallas coloniales Hispano-Americanas*, 24). C. Willys Betts even refers to a medal supposedly given by the Spanish governor Francisco de Cruizat to Huisconsin, a Mitasse chief of the Sauks and Foxes, which was part of the numismatic collection of the Wisconsin Historical Society (Betts, *American Colonial History Illustrated*, 239). Unfortunately, no such medal has been found among the inventory of this institution (Wisconsin Historical Society, http://www.wisconsinhistory.org [accessed September 10, 2016]).

185. Bernardo de Gálvez to Gilberto Antonio Maxent, Havana, July 7, 1783, in Levaggi, "Aplicación de la política española de tratados," 236.

186. For the different terms applied, see Roulet, "Con la pluma y la palabra," 315. The term "treaty" is the one most commonly used, both in studies in English and Spanish (Berry, "The Indian Policy of Spain"; Charles Gibson, "Conquest, Capitulation, and Indian Treaties"; Kinnaird, "Spanish Treaties with Indian Tribes"; Lázaro Ávila, "Los tratados de paz con los indígenas"; Levaggi, "Los tratados entre la Corona y los indios"; Levaggi, *Diplomacia hispano-indígena*). Although for David J. Weber the question of the name used for these agreements is little more than a legal technicality, it is relevant to point out that the use of "treaty" implies certain equality among the parties, an equality that was never intended by the Spanish Crown (Weber, *Bárbaros, Spaniards and Their Savages*, 208). For a recent discussion on the subject, see Herzog, *Frontiers of Possession*, 258–66.

187. Bushnell, "Spain's Conquest by Contract," 302.

188. Charles Gibson, "Conquest, Capitulation, and Indian Treaties," 2; Levaggi, "Los tratados entre la Corona y los indios," 90.

189. Levaggi, "Los tratados entre la Corona y los indios," 90.

190. Weber, *Bárbaros, Spaniards and Their Savages*, 205.

191. Treaty of the governor of Pensacola, Arturo O'Neill, with the Talapuches, Pensacola, June 14, 1781, AGI, Cuba, 36, in Levaggi, *Diplomacia hispano-indígena*, 281–82.

192. Bernardo de Gálvez to José de Gálvez, dispatch 90, New Orleans, September 1777, AGI, Santo Domingo, 2547, Duplicados de Gobernadores e Intendentes.

193. The names of the Native American groups used by the eighteenth-century Spaniards do not correspond to the ones employed by the British or the French at that time, and even less to the names by which these groups are known today. When possible, and certain, we have translated the Spanish name to its English equivalent; when uncertain or impossible, we have kept the Spanish denomination.

194. Bernardo de Gálvez to José de Gálvez, dispatch 90, New Orleans, September 1777, AGI, Santo Domingo, 2547, Duplicados de Gobernadores e Intendentes.

195. Ibid.

196. Ibid.

197. Francisco Cruzat to Bernardo de Gálvez, report, San Luis de Ylinneses [*sic*: Ilinueses] (St. Louis), December 6, 1777, in Houck, *The Spanish Regime in Missouri*, 1:141–48.

198. Bernardo de Gálvez to José de Gálvez, dispatch 109, New Orleans, December 30, 1777, AGI, Santo Domingo, 2547, Duplicados de Gobernadores e Intendentes.

199. Ibid., dispatch 134, March 24, 1778.

200. For the Indian slavery in British North America, see Gallay, *Indian Slave Trade*.

201. For the analysis of the different slavery models (Spanish, French, and British), see further in the text while considering Louisiana's slave population.

202. Last will and testament of Queen Isabel la Católica, in Solórzano Pereira, *Política indiana*, book 1, chapter 23, number 15.

203. Papal bull *Sublimis Deus*, given by Pope Paulo III, June 2, 1537; in Céspedes del Castillo, *Textos y documentos de la América Hispánica*, 229–30. For the study of the debate about the humanity of the Indians, see the classic work of Lewis Hanke, *All Mankind Is One*.

204. Law 23, title 10, book 6, *RLI* (1681).

205. B. Casas, *Apologética histórica*; Zabala, *Ideario de Vasco de Quiroga*; Aiton, review of *Ideario de Vasco*; Castañeda Delgado, *Don Vasco de Quiroga*; Lockhart, review of *Gobierno del Peru*; Matienzo, *Gobierno del Perú*.

206. Law 1, title 2, book 6 of the *RLI* (1681) determined that "es nuestra voluntad y mandamos, que ningún Adelantado, Gobernador, . . . no otra persona, . . . sea osado de cautivar indios naturales de nuestras Indias, Islas, y Tierrafirme del Mar Océano, descubiertas, ni por descubrir, ni tenerlos por esclavos . . . excepto en los casos, y naciones, que por las leyes de este título estuviere permitido." Law 37, title 18, book 2, "Que los fiscales tengan por obligación particular el acudir a la libertad de los Indios," given by Carlos V, Valladolid, August 11, 1553. Law 65, title 3, book 3, "Que los Virreyes conozcan en primera instancia de las causas de los indios con apelación a sus Audiencias," by Felipe II, Madrid, April 9, 1591. Law 14, title 6, book 6, "Que los eclesiásticos, y Seglares avisen a los Protectores, Procuradores, y Defensores, si algunos indios no gozan de libertad," by Carlos V. Real Cédula al Gobernador de la Margarita que informe que los indios de la provincia de Guayana hay en aquella isla y si se sirve de ellos como esclavos, Madrid, December 20, 1609; Real Cédula al Presidente de la Audiencia de la Isla Española sobre la libertad de ciertos indios traídos del Brasil, San Lorenzo, August 18, 1617; Real Cédula al obispo de Guadalajara sobre las penas impuestas a las personas

que hicieren esclavos a los indios que se cogieren en guerras, Madrid, February 10, 1674. Law 1, title 3, book 1, *Cedulario de Alonso de Zurita*, published in 1574, by the emperor [Carlos V] and his mother, Lady Juana, Granada, November 9, 1526. Real Cédula que se cumplan las Cédulas que prohíben la esclavitud de los Indios, Madrid, April 2, 1676.

207. For the Mindanaos in the Philippines, see *Las Siete Partidas del Rey Don Alfonso el sabio*, law 1, title 21, partida 4; law 12, book 6, title 2, *RLI* (1681); *Real Cédula de 29 de Mayo de 1620*, Cedulario vol. 39, fol. 168, no. 152, in Ayala, *Diccionario de gobierno*, 6:29; and Solórzano Pereira, *Política indiana*, book 2, chapter 1, number 36. For the Caribe Indians, see law 12, book 6, title 2 of the *RLI* (1681); and Sepúlveda, *Historia del Nuevo Mundo*, 39–43, 57, 61–62. For certain tribes in Chile, see Enquiry to the Consejo de Indias, November 17, 1607, about whether the Indians captured in the war in Chile could be enslaved; *real cédula*, Ventosilla, May 26, 1608, authorizing the enslavement of the Indians captured in the war in Chile; *real cédula*, Madrid, April 9, 1662, about the committee to be responsible for dealing and setting the conditions for the enslavement of the Indians captured in the war in Chile; law 14, book 6, title 2, *RLI* (1681), on the freedom of the Indians of Chile, ordering their immediate freedom, combining the orders issued by Felipe III on May 26, 1608, by Felipe IV on April 13, 1625, and April 9, 1662, and by Carlos II and the queen governor on August 1 and 5, 1663; law 16, book 6, title 2, *RLI* (1681), which reiterates the order for the freedom of the Indians and dictates new ones for those of Chile, Carlos II, Madrid, June 12, 1679. For the River Plate Indians, see *real cédula* for the governors of the Río de la Plata and the Province of la Guayra authoring them to pursue, capture, and enslave some war Indians, Madrid, April 16, 1618. The authorization was revoked by another *real cédula* in law 7, title 2, book 6, *RLI* (1681). For the Pijaos, see *real cédula* to the president of the audience of Quito about the manner that the expeditions against the Pijao Indians should be conducted, July 8, 1598, annulling a previous authorization for their enslavement.

208. Maduell, *Census Tables*, 16–27.

209. Cetified copy of the census sent by Bernardo de Gálvez, New Orleans, May 12, 1777, AGI, Cuba, 2351.

210. Maduell, *Census Tables*, 16–27; Webre, "Problem of Indian Slavery,", 117–35, also in Din, *Louisiana Purchase*, 353.

211. DuVal, "Indian Intermarriage," 273.

212. Din, *Spaniards, Planters, and Slaves*, 147; Webre, "Problem of Indian Slavery."

213. Usner, *Indians Settlers and Slaves*, 132.

214. Lauber, *Indian Slavery in Colonial Times*, 57–59; Usner, "American Indians in Colonial New Orleans" (2nd ver.), 298; Webre, "Problem of Indian Slavery."

215. Foley, "Slave Freedom Suits." *Marguerite, a free woman of color vs. Chouteau, Pierre, Sr.*, July 1825, St. Louis Circuit Court Records, Missouri Historical Society (St. Louis, Mo.), http://stlcourtrecords.wustl.edu (acccesed March 16, 2016).

216. Almaraz, "Social Interaction," 28.

217. Bernardo de Gálvez to José de Gálvez, dispatch 204, New Orleans, October 24, 1778, AGI, Santo Domingo, 2547, Duplicados de Gobernadores e Intendentes.

218. Ibid.

219. See Vinson, *Bearing Arms for His Majesty*.

220. Data from Marichal and Souto Mantecón, "Silver and Situados."

221. Tepaske, "Economic Problems of Florida Governors"; Holmes, "Some Economic Problems," 522.

222. Coutts, "Martín Navarro," 118, 128, 139.

223. Order, February 24, 1780, Cedulario vol. 35, fol. 293v. and no. 271, "Nombramiento de intendente de la Real hacienda a d. Martín Navarro," in Ayala, *Dicciona-*

rio de gobierno, 8:79. On Martín Navarro, see Coutts, "Martin Navarro."

224. Din, "Spanish Control over a Multiethnic Society," 50.

225. Coutts, "Martin Navarro," 142–43.

226. Creté, *La vie quotidienne en Louisiane*, 50–51.

227. Acosta Rodríguez, "Crecimiento económico desigual," 757.

228. Solano Acosta, "La emigración acadiana," vol. 2, 85.

229. Acosta Rodríguez, *La población de Luisiana*, 283.

230. Solano Acosta, "La emigración acadiana," 85.

231. Kinnaird, "American Penetration," 225.

232. B*** D*** [sic], *Voyage à la Louisiane*, 216; certified copy of the census sent by Bernardo de Gálvez, New Orleans, May 12, 1777, AGI, Cuba, 2351.

233. Din, "Spanish Control over a Multiethnic Society," 49.

234. Gitlin, "On the Boundaries of Empire," 77–78; Armillas Vicente, "Nueva Orleans."

235. José de Gálvez a Bernardo de Gálvez, Madrid, November 25, 1776, AGI, Cuba, 174.

236. Din, "Spanish Control over a Multiethnic Society," 50.

237. Creté, *La vie quotidienne en Louisiane*, 106; Tallant, *Romantic New Orleanians*; Saxon, *Gumbo Ya-Ya*, 140.

238. Din, "Spanish Control over a Multiethnic Society," 50.

239. Hanger, "Almost All Have Callings," 414.

240. Cetified copy of the census sent by Bernardo de Gálvez, New Orleans, May 12, 1777, AGI, Cuba, 2351.

241. "*Code Noir*: Edit du Roi, touchant l'Etat & la discipline des esclaves négres de la Louisiane, donné à Versailles au mois de mars de 1724," 135–36.

242. Malagón Barceló, *Código Negro Carolino*, xxxiii.

243. Ibid.

244. Order, May 22, 1765, Cedulario vol. 12, fol. 140, no. 149, "Que no se innovase en su régimen y en nada se sujetase a las leyes y prácticas de los dominios de Indias," in Ayala, *Diccionario de gobierno*, 7:68.

245. Proclamation by Alejandro O'Reilly, New Orleans, August 27, 1769, BN, ms, 19246, 13, in Lucena Salmoral, *Los Códigos negros*, 51, no. 9.

246. Lucena Samoral, *Los códigos negros de la América española*, 6. Extracto del Código Negro de Francia para el gobierno de los negros esclavos de la provincia y colonia de la Luisiana, mandado observar por Real Decreto, dado en Versalles en el mes de marzo de 1724, y cuyas ordenanzas se citan al margen del extracto formado del Código de la isla Española [Excerpt of the French Code Noir for the government of the slaves of the province of Louisiana, published by royal decree, signed in Versailles in the month of March 1724, which is quoted in the margins of the excerpt of the Code for the Island of Hispaniola], BN, ms, 8734, Varios referentes a Indias 7, fols. 97–104, in *Inventario general de manuscritos de la Biblioteca Nacional*, 13:88.

247. Tannenbaum, *Slave and Citizen*, 43–65 and 8; Sio, "Reviewed Interpretations of Slavery," 291.

248. Hevia Bolaños, *Laberinto de comercio*, book 1, chapter 1, section 6.

249. Código Negro de Santo Domingo de 1784, in Lucena Salmoral, *Los Códigos negros*, law 1, chapter 24, p. 227. For comparative studies of the *code noir*, see Hadden, "Fragmented Laws"; and Peabody, "Slavery, Freedom, and the Law."

250. D. Davis, *Problem of Slavery*. Alejandro de la Fuente and Ariela Gross have studied the evolution of comparative historical research on slavery, from the traditional legal approach, through the revisionist/social historian view, to a new view from the legal perspective but from the bottom up "through slaves' claims in court, trial-level adjudications, and interactions among ordinary people and

low-level government officials." Quoted in Herzog, "Colonial Law"; Herzog, *Frontiers of Possession*, 263. Also see Fuente and Gross, "Comparative Studies"; A. Fuente, "Slave Law and Claims-Making"; A. Watson, *Slave Law in the Americas*;

251. Hanger, "Avenues to Freedom." Quoted in Ingersoll, "Free Blacks in a Slave Society: New Orleans, 1718–1812," 181.

252. Lucena Salmoral, "El derecho de coartación," 357.

253. Ibid., 362.

254. Ingersoll, "Free Blacks in a Slave Society," 180–82.

255. Ibid., 174.

256. Spear, *Race, Sex, and Social Order*, 100–101.

257. The PBS program *History Detectives* broadcast a series dedicated to investigating family memorabilia with possible historical significance. In episode 10 ("The Gálvez Papers") of the eighth season, aired for the first time on August 30, 2010, Michael Nolden Henderson asked for the program's help in finding out about an old document that gave freedom to one of his ancestors. After a certain amount of suspense—much needed in the television program—the experts determined that the document was a copy of an original in the Municipal Archives of New Orleans, signed by Bernardo de Gálvez on December 16, 1779. The story had a happy TV ending when more than two hundred years later, the descendant, Michael Nolden Henderson, was accepted as the first African American member of the Georgia chapter of the Sons of the American Revolution (Paul, "Michael Nolden Henderson").

258. Cole, "Capitalism and Freedom," 1013–15.

259. Law 1, title 5, book 7, *RLI* (1681).

260. Law 10, ibid.; law 19, ibid.

261. Order, March 8, 1776, Cedulario, vol. 27, fol. Y, no. 214, Confirma la Real Cédula de 20 de marzo de 1775 que "prohíbe a los vecinos de Nueva Orleans la transportación y venta de los negros esclavos de aquella isla [Cuba] u otra cualquiera," in Ayala, *Diccionario de gobierno*, 1:258.

262. Houck, *History of Missouri*, 1:305; edict by Bernardo de Gálvez, New Orleans, November 21, 1777, Bancroft Library, Berkeley, Louisiana Collection, in Caughey, *Bernardo de Gálvez in Louisiana*, 77.

263. Lachance, "Politics of Fear," 195.

264. Hall, *Africans in Colonial Louisiana*, 278.

265. Din and Harkins, *New Orleans Cabildo*, 159.

266. Ordinance for the restraint of slaves (Ordenanzas para la sujeción de esclavos) of 1535, 1542, and 1545 by the Cabildo of Santo Domingo, AGI, Santo Domingo, 1034. Traslado del Libro de Ordenanzas del Cabildo de Santo Domingo sacado por don Francisco Rendón Sarmiento, Secretario de Cámara y de Gobierno, por orden de la Real Audiencia dominicana y a petición del Fiscal, intitulado "Testimonio de las Ordenanzas antiguas de la Ciudad de Santo Domingo de la Isla Española," May 19, 1768, and signed by the above-mentioned Secretario de Cámara, in Lucena Salmoral, *Los Códigos negros*, 46–52.

267. Law 21, title 5, book 7, *RLI* (1681).

268. Article 32 of the "*Code noir*: Edit du Roi, touchant l'Etat & la discipline des esclaves négres de la Louisiane, donné à Versailles au mois de mars de 1724."

269. Lucena Salmoral, *Los Códigos negros*, 59.

270. Case of the slave María Juana, in Din and Harkins, *New Orleans Cabildo*, 161, no. 17.

271. Din and Harkins, *New Orleans Cabildo*, 162; Nunemaker, "Documents."

272. Royal decree, September 24, 1750, ordering the freedom of all black slaves of the English and Dutch colonies who fled to the viceroyalty of New Spain in order to become Catholics, in Lucena Salmoral, *Regulación de la esclavitud*, 215.

273. Bernardo de Gálvez to Francisco

Collell, Francisco Cruzat, Juan Delavillebeuvre, Carlos de Grand Pré, and Baltasar de Villiers, letters and drafts, New Orleans, September 24, 1779, AGI, Papeles de Cuba, 112.

274. Spear, *Race, Sex, and Social Order*, 103. For the contemporary views on the "moderation" of Spanish policies regarding slavery, see Nicolás María Vidal to the cabildo, October 24, 1800, Cabildo Records, 4:28, and appeal of the cabildo, July 23, 1790, in Gayarré, *History of Louisiana*, 4:301–5.

275. Bouligny, *Noticia del estado actual del comercio y población de la Nueva Orleans y Luisiana española, y los medios de adelantar aquella provincia que presenta a S.M. Católica* . . . , 1776, BN, Mss 19265.

276. Carlos III, *Instrucción reservada que la Junta de estado*, 191.

277. Ibid., 191; José de Gálvez to Bernardo de Gálvez, Madrid, November 25, 1776, AGI, Cuba, 174.

278. Merrill, *Germans of Louisiana*, 19–20.

279. L'Isle, *Carte de la Louisiane*.

280. Merrill, *Germans of Louisiana*, 32.

281. Leblanc, "Acadian Migrations," 523–35; Faragher, *Great and Noble Scheme*.

282. Arsenault, *Histoire des Acadiens*, 309.

283. Griffiths, *L'Acadie*, 97.

284. Solano Acosta, "La emigración acadiana," 90–91.

285. Houck, *Spanish Regime in Missouri*, 1:152, 154, 156; Aron, *American Confluence*, 79, 81.

286. Chandler, "Ulloa's Account." Certificación del intendente de Nueva Orleans, Don Esteban Gayarre, de lo acaecido en la sublevación de los franceses, New Orleans, October 30, 1768, AHN, Estado 3889-c; tradducción del diario de los sucesos de la Luisiana, November 1768 to March 1769; José Melchor de Acosta, *Relación diaria, verídica, y circunstanciada de todos los acaecimientos en la colonia de la Luisiana y ciudad del Nuevo Orleans*. . . . The last three documents are in Serrano y Sanz, *Documentos históricos*, 272–95.

287. Solano Acosta, "La emigración acadiana," 89.

288. Bernardo de Gálvez to the inhabitants of the colony of Louisiana, order draft copy, New Orleans, March 3, 1778, AGI, Cuba, 112.

289. Bernardo de Gálvez to Baltasar de Villiers, official letter no. 43, New Orleans, January 2, 1779, AGI, Cuba 112.

290. Bernardo de Gálvez to the commanders of the Mississippi River, Punta Colorada, and Manchac, letter draft copy, July 14, 1778, AGI, Cuba, 112; Bernardo de Gálvez to John Ferguson, certified copy of the letter, New Orleans, May 15, 1778, AGI, Cuba, 1232.

291. Ekkberg, *Colonial St. Genevieve*, 430.

292. Aron, *American Confluence*, 79, 81.

293. By 1785, 12,000 Loyalist refugees fleeing from the Carolinas and Georgia were living in the Floridas (about 5,000 whites and 8,000 slaves). Most of them departed to British territories in the Caribbean and the Bahamas. For the estimated number of Loyalists in West Florida, see Caughey, *East Florida*, 120–21; and Troxler, "Loyalist Refugees."

294. Jasanoff, *Liberty's Exiles*, xii.

295. Martínez Laínez and Canales Torres, *Banderas lejanas*, 252.

296. Calloway, *Scratch of a Pen*.

297. Bouligny, *Noticia del estado actual del comercio y población de la Nueva Orleans y Luisiana española, y los medios de adelantar aquella provincia que presenta a S.M. Católica* . . . , 1776, BN, Mss 19265, partially in Morales Folguera, *Arquitectura y urbanismo*, 299.

298. Molina Bautista, *Historia de Alhaurín de la Torre*, 203.

299. Nunemaker, "Documents."

300. Castillo Meléndez, "La aventura americana," 109–10.

301. The original Spanish measures

are in *quintales*. Conversion according to Romero García, "Medidas antiguas españolas," 67; Merino Navarro, *La Armada española*, 78.

302. Morales Padrón, "Las Canarias," 230.

303. Rumeu de Armas, Antonio, *Piraterías y ataques navales*, vol. 3, pt. 2, 738.

304. José de Gálvez to Matías de Gálvez, Aranjuez, August 4, 1777, AGI, Santo Domingo, 2661.

305. Santana Perez and Sánchez Suárez, *Emigración por reclutamiento*.

306. Hoffman, *Luisiana*, 154.

307. Martínez Gálvez and Medina Rodríguez, "La aportación de las familias malagueñas," 99.

308. Samper and Hernández, "La Luisiana," 76.

309. Din, *Canary Islanders*, 13–14.

310. Tornero Tinajero, "Emigración canaria a América," 348–49.

311. Molina Martínez, "La participación canaria," 156.

312. Acosta Rodríguez, *La población de Luisiana*, 140; Bernardo de Gálvez to José de Gálvez, New Orleans, July 7, 1779, AGI, Santo Domingo, 2662.

313. Hoffman, *Luisiana*, 156.

314. Carlos III, *Instrucción reservada que la Junta de estado*, 191.

315. Morales Folguera, *Arquitectura y urbanismo*, 299–300.

316. Morales Folguera, "Fundación de ciudades," 1534.

317. Houck, *History of Missouri*, 1:304–5.

318. Arena, "Land Settlement Policies," 60.

319. Bernardo de Gálvez to José de Gálvez, dispatch 233, New Orleans, January 19, 1779, AGI, Santo Domingo, 2547.

320. Scramuzza, "Galveztown," 41.

321. Villa de Galvez, Louisiana, 1778, LoC, MaLC, G4014, G224 1778, P5 Vault.

322. Din, *Canary Islanders*, 28–29.

323. Morales Folguera, *Arquitectura y urbanismo*, 141.

324. Plan of the terrain for the Spanish families in Galveztown (Plano de los terrenos destinados para las familias españolas de Galveztown, las que empiezan a 350 toesas del ángulo [a] del fuerte de San Carlos de Baton Rouge), AGI, Mapas y Planos, Florida-Luisiana, 230.

325. Sternberg, "In Search of Galveztown."

326. Bernardo de Gálvez to José de Evia, instruction draft copy, Havana, July 14, 1783, AGI, Indiferente General 1580; José de Evia to Bernardo de Gálvez, Havana, July 31, 1783, AGI, Cuba, 2360. For the role played by Gálvez in geographic expeditions, see González-Ripoll Navarro, "Idea y representación," 86–87; Holmes, *José de Evia*; Martín Merás, *Cartografía marítima Hispana*, 191; and Weddle, *Changing Tides*, 168–84.

327. See the documentation annexed to Nunemaker, "Documents."

328. Molina Bautista, *Historia de Alhaurín de la Torre*, 205.

329. Morales Folguera, *Arquitectura y urbanismo*, 307.

330. Map of the land close to the Mississippi for the new settlers of Valenzuela (Mapa de los terrenos dados junto al Misisipi a los nuevos pobladores de Valenzuela), map ms, AGI, Mapas y Planos, Florida-Luisiana, 92; Morales Folguera, *Arquitectura y urbanismo* 308.

331. Acosta Rodríguez, *La población de Luisiana*, 400.

332. Morales Folguera, *Arquitectura y urbanismo*, 312.

333. Ibid., 311; López Estrada, *Tomás Moro y España*; Chul, "La república utópica."

334. Cervantes, *Don Quijote*, 4:36.

335. Ibid., 1:30.

336. Din, *Canary Islanders*, 47–63.

337. Morales Folguera, *Arquitectura y urbanismo*, 311.

338. For the language, see Alvar López, *El dialecto canario de Luisiana*; Alvar López, "El dialecto canario de la Luisiana"; Armistead, "Tres dialectos españoles de Luisiana"; Armistead, "Coplas

tradicionales"; Lipski, "Reducción de 's' y 'n' en el español"; Lipski, "El dialecto español"; Neumann-Holzschuh, "Español vestigial"; and Pratt, "El español del noroeste." For the dress, see MacUrdy, "Los 'isleños' de la Luisiana."

339. Morales Folguera, *Arquitectura y urbanismo*, 314.

340. Ibid., 132, 133.

341. Castillo Meléndez, "La aventura americana," 109–10.

342. Blume, "El cultivo de la caña," 102–3.

343. Ibid.

344. José de Gálvez to Bernardo de Gálvez, Madrid, November 25, 1776, AGI, Cuba, 174.

345. Lavedan, *Tratado de los usos*, 27, 78.

346. Canga Argüelles, *Diccionario de Hacienda*, 5:160.

347. González Enciso, "En torno al contrabando," 199.

348. Testimonio de expediente a consecuencia de real orden sobre fábrica de cigarros con hoja de maíz y traer tabacos de la Luisiana, 1775, AGI, Mexico, 1622; Coutts, "Boom and Bust," 230; Grupo de Estudios del Tabaco, "El consumo del Tabaco," 317.

349. In this meeting, held in June 1777, Gálvez informed the Louisiana planters about the Order, April 24, 1776, Cedulario, vol. 27, f. 67, no. 60, in Ayala, *Diccionario de gobierno*, 13:126.

350. Caughey, *Bernardo de Gálvez in Louisiana*, 77.

351. Report by Villars y d'Aunoy, New Orleans, circa 1778, in Gayarré, *History of Louisiana*, 3:107.

352. Solbes Ferri, "Los comerciantes extranjeros," 648.

353. Coutts, "Boom and Bust," 230–37.

354. B*** D*** [sic], *Voyage à la Louisiane*, 214–15; Din, "Spanish Control over a Multiethnic Society," 64.

355. Baudier, *Catholic Church*, 180.

356. Armillas Vicente, "Organización eclesiástica," 30.

357. Brasseaux, "Moral Climate."

358. Bispham, "Contest for Ecclesiastical Supremacy," 184–85; Armillas Vicente, "Organización eclesiástica," 30.

359. Armillas Vicente, "Organización eclesiástica," 52.

360. Consejo de Indias to the bishop of Cuba, Madrid, 1778, AGI, Santo Domingo, 2586, in Cebrián González, "El obispado de Nueva Orleans," 780; Consejo de Indias to the bishop of Cuba, Madrid, 1778, AGI, Santo Domingo, 2586, in Cebrián González, "El obispado de Nueva Orleans," 781.

361. Mills, "Quintanilla's Crusade," 278.

362. Bolton, *Athanase de Mézières*, 2:134–35.

363. Lemmon, "Spanish Louisiana," 521.

364. Cebrián González, "El obispado de Nueva Orleans," 781–82.

365. Greenleaf, "Inquisition in Spanish Louisiana" (1996), 543; Gannon, "Church Influence."

366. Curley, *Church and State*, 166; Greenleaf, "Inquisition in Spanish Louisiana" (1975), 48.

367. Armillas Vicente, "La educación femenina."

368. Ibid., 1275.

369. Bernardo de Gálvez to Antonio Bentura [sic: Ventura], New Orleans, December 30, 1777, AGI, Santo Domingo, 2547, no. 2 and 3.

370. Clark, *Masterless Mistresses*, 128–29. Also see Clark, *Voices from an Early American Convent*, 1–19.

371. Caughey, *Bernardo de Gálvez in Louisiana*, 165–68.

372. Armillas Vicente, "La educación femenina," 1275.

373. Francisco Luis Héctor de Carondelet, Baron de Carondelet, to Eugenio de Llaguno, New Orleans, May 31, 1796, AGI, Santo Domingo, 2565, no. 20.

374. Pitot, *Observations*, 32–33.

375. Arístegui, *Misión en Managua*, 19.

376. Pontalba, *Memoir on Louisiana*, 206.

377. Soniat du Fossat, *Synopsis of History of Louisiana*, 29.

378. For a study of Saint-Maxent and his family, see Coleman, *Gilbert Antoine de St. Maxent*; and Ezquerra, "Un patricio colonial."

379. Beerman, "The French Ancestors."

380. Translation of the diary on Lousiana's events from November 1786 to March 1769 (Traducción del diario de los sucesos de la Luisiana, Noviembre de 1768 a Marzo de 1769 incluida en la Certificación del intendente de Nueva Orleans, don Esteban Gayarre, de lo acaecido en la sublevación de los franceses), New Orleans, October 30, 1768, AHN, Estado 3889C, in Serrano y Sanz, *Documentos históricos*, 272–85.

381. Acosta, *Relación diaria, verídica, y circunstanciada de todos los acaecimientos habidos en la colonia de la Luisiana y ciudad del Nuevo Orleans*, 285–95.

382. Ezquerra, "Un patricio colonial," 111.

383. Nunemaker, "Documents"; Armillas Vicente, "El criollismo luisianés," 182.

384. Ezquerra, "Un patricio colonial," 112–13.

385. Law 47, title 2, book 5 "Que la prohibición de tratar, y contratar comprende a los gobernadores, corregidores, alcaldes mayores y sus tenientes" que refiere su castigo a las disposiciones de tít. 16, lib. II. *RLI* (1681), vol. 1, 151v. Law 55, title 16, book 2. "Que los oidores, alcaldes y fiscales no tengan casas, chacras, estancias, huertas, ni tierras." *RLI* (1681), vol. q, 222r.

386. Last will and testament of Bernardo de Gálvez, in Fernández-Carrión, "Vida privada del Virrey," 468; Beerman, "Last Will and Testament," nos. 2–4; Souviron, *Bernardo de Gálvez*, 21–105.

387. Proceedings against Gilberto Antonio Maxent (Sobre diligencias practicadas contra el Coronel Gilberto Antonio Maxent sobre extracción y embarque de 28,000 pesos para Jamaica, arresto y embargo de todos sus bienes), 1784–1788, in "Expedientes de Real Hacienda e instancias de partes," AGI, Santo Domingo, 2642; Diligencias practicadas contra los bienes del coronel D. Gilberto Antonio de Maxent, 1784, in "Causas civiles," AGI, Papeles de Cuba, 171A.

388. Ezquerra, "Un patricio colonial."

389. Alexander von Humboldt to engineer Miguel Constanzó, Mexico, November 22, 1803. In Moncada Maya, *El ingeniero Miguel Constanzó*, 332. Also see Beerman, "La bella criolla Felicitas," 296; Beerman, "Governor Bernardo de Galvez's New Orleans Belle," 41; Puig-Samper, "Humboldt," 335.

390. Ostendorf, "Creole Cultures," 111.

391. *Gone with the Wind*, directed by Victor Fleming.

392. Orwell, *English People*, 6.

393. Guy Soniat du Fossat was a Frenchman who arrived in Louisiana in 1751. He was twice New Orleans's mayor and the author of the first history of Louisiana. Caulfield, *French Literature of Louisiana*, 4–5.

394. Soniat du Fossat, *Synopsis of History of Louisiana*, 29.

395. Darby, *Geographical Description*, 276–77.

396. "Le mot femme est le secret de l'art. C'est à tort qu'on représente la poésie sous la forme d'un ange. . . . La Créole, c'est une houri moins le Coran, une Sultaine pour la beautë mais moins le sérail; un file de Smyrne ou de Georgie, qui ne vous répond pas, Allah est grand Mahomet est son prophète! Quand vous liu dites bonjour; C'est un ange aux ailes de feux. . . . Mais qui parle français. On dirait lire les poètes qu'ils sont tous nés sur les bords du Mississippi. Ils peignent d'après l'original, alors même qu'ils ne crioient faire que des protraits de fantasie: les chimères de l'-bas son des réalites ici: ici, elles on leur nom de famille et leur extrait de baptême; Cet idéal chéri qu'il pursuivent à traver les nécessités de

la vie, au grand galop de leur pensée, ils l'atteindraient surement á l'aide des navires." Hains Boussuge, French original in the first number of the magazine *Louisiana Creole; Gazette des salons, des arts et des modes*, in Domínguez, *White by Definition*, 121.

397. Martínez y Gálvez, "La mujer y la vida familiar," 1381.

398. Morlas, "La Madame et la Mademoiselle," 32–33; Martín Gaite, *Usos amorosos en el dieciocho en España*.

399. Porras Muñoz, "Acta de matrimonio," 281.

400. Solórzano states that this kind of marriage "nam licet negari non possit, matrimonium etiam in articulo mortis validum esse . . ." Solórzano Pereyra, *De Indiarum Iure*, book 2, chapter 20, number 19, quoted in Dougnac Rodríguez, *Esquema del Derecho de Familia*, 13.

401. Copy of the original appointment of Bernardo de Gálvez as full governor of Louisiana: Nombramiento Bernardo de Gálvez como gobernador en propiedad de la Luisiana, Aranjuez, May 8, 1779, AGS, Títulos de Indias, Dirección General del Tesoro, Inventario 24, leg. 186, f. 52; law 44, title 2, book 5, *RLI* (1774), vol. 2, 151r.

402. Numbers 130 to 133 of the royal ordinance of December 18, 1701, and book 1, title 17 of the Ordenanzas of June 12, 1728, on the marriage of officers and soldiers, in Diez Muñiz, "El matrimonio de militares," 58–59.

403. The *tocas* was the right that an officer's widow had to claim a certain amount of money to be paid in full once in a lifetime, as opposed to the widow's pension, which was paid periodically. Rubió y Bellvé, *Diccionario de ciencias militares*, 3:856. HM's *ordenanza* about the prohibition for officers to marry without his royal permission (prohibición de casamientos de oficiales sin su real permiso), *real cédula*, October 30, 1760, determined that "the officer who marries without Royal Permission would be removed, and his wife would not have pension rights." *Recopilación de penas militares con arreglo a ordenanza y reales órdenes hasta el día*, Madrid: Pedro Sanz, 1834, 57.

404. Certificate by Doctor don Santiago José de Echeverría y Elguezúa, bishop of the Holy Cathedral of Santiago de Cuba, Havana, July 2, 1783. Pruebas para la concesión del Título de Caballero de la Orden de Calatrava de Miguel de Gálvez y Sant-Maxent, natural de Guarico (Haíti), Conde de Gálvez y Cadete de la Compañía Americana de Reales Guardias de Corps, AHN, Órdenes Militares, Caballeros Calatrava, 1009.

405. Vázquez de Acuña, "El Ministro de Indias," 471.

406. Certificate by Doctor don Santiago José de Echeverría y Elguezúa, bishop of the Holy Cathedral of Santiago de Cuba, Havana, July 2, 1783. Pruebas para la concesión (see in n. 405 above).

407. Beerman, "La bella criolla Felicitas," 294.

408. Birth registry of Matilde Bernarda Felipa Isabel Juana Felicitas y Fernanda de Gálvez y Saint Maxent, in *Records of the American Catholic Historical Society of Philadelphia*, vol. 86–90 (1977–79): 41.

409. *Ocho libros de asientos de las tripulaciones de navíos*, AGI, Papeles de Cuba, 648.

410. Armillas Vicente, "El criollismo luisianés," 177; Armillas Vicente, "Nueva Orleans."

411. Poydras, *Le dieu et les nayades*; Poydras, *Épître a Don*; Tinker, *Les écrits de langue française*, 2.

412. Dunbar-Nelson, "People of Color in Louisiana."

413. Kein, "Louisiana Creole Food Culture," 249.

414. S. White, "'Wearing Three or Four Handkerchiefs around His Collar,'" 532. For references to the use of the Spanish mantilla or shawl by New Orleans's ladies, see Field, McLaughlin and McLaugh-

lin, *Louisiana Voyages*, 147; Durell, *New Orleans as I Found It*, 28; and Seebold, *Old Louisiana Plantation Homes*, 11.

415. Bernardo de Gálvez to José de Gálvez, dispatch no. 320, New Orleans, October 16, 1779, AGI, Santo Domingo, 2586.

416. José de Gálvez to Bernardo to Gálvez, El Pardo, January 12, 1780, AGI, Santo Domingo, 2586.

CHAPTER 5

1. "Guerra con toda la tierra y paz con Inglaterra." The origin of the axiom is not clear. Richard Ford, an English traveler through Spain in the mid-nineteenth century, recorded having heard it as a popular saying (R. Ford, *Handbook for Travellers in Spain*, 2:595). Other authors have attributed it to very different origins. John Elliott states that it was the king-emperor Carlos V to first formulate it (Elliott, "Paz y Guerra"). It has also been attributed to King Carlos II (Maura, *Carlos II y su corte*, 1:66); Fernando VI (Aldama, *Historia general de España*, 12:234); Carlos IV (Godoy, *Memorias de don Manuel Godoy*, 1:277); and even to Carlos III, who allegedly said something similar to the English ambassador during an audience (Alcalá Galiano, *Historia de España*, 5:269).

2. Rodríguez Casado, "Política exterior de Carlos III," 233.

3. Hilton, "España y Norteamérica," 35.

4. Becker, *España e Inglaterra*; Marfil García, *Relaciones entre España y la Gran Bretaña*, 130; Yela Utrilla, *España ante la independencia de los Estados Unidos*, 1:484.

5. Villacañas Berlanga, "Resumen del Seminario," 12.

6. Voltes Bou, "La tentativa de mediación," 318.

7. M. Rodríguez, *La revolución americana*.

8. Abol-Brasón y Álvarez-Tamargo, "El conde de Floridablanca," 96; Hernández Sanchez-Barba, "El americanismo del conde de Floridablanca," 45-48; Lynch, *La España del Siglo XVIII*, 265-66;

Rodríguez Casado, "Política exterior de Carlos III"; Vaca de Osma, *Carlos III*, 290.

9. Hernández Sanchez-Barba, "El bicentenario de 1776."

10. Ruigómez de Hernández, *El gobierno español*, 225; Hernández Franco, *La gestión política*, 334.

11. Batista González, "Significación político-estratégica," 81; Comellas, *Historia de España Moderna*, 217; Avilés Fernández, *Carlos III*, 73.

12. Count of Floridablanca "Memorial presentado al rey Carlos III," 310.

13. Voltes Bou, "La tentativa de mediación."

14. See delegates of Rhode Island to William Greene, Philadelphia, December 8, 1778, in Smith et al., *Letters of Delegates to Congress*, 11:304-5; and Gouverneur Morris to the Journal Pennsylvania Packet, February 27, 1779, in ibid., vol. 12: 115-21.

15. Committee of Commerce to Bernardo de Gálvez, Philadelphia, July 19, 1779, in ibid., 25:658.

16. Alonso Baquer, "Los ministros de Carlos IV," 82.

17. Bernardo de Gálvez to the inhabitants of the colony of Louisiana, order draft copy, New Orleans, March 3, 1778, AGI, Cuba, 112.

18. Bernardo de Gálvez to Baltasar de Villiers, official letter no. 43, New Orleans, January 2, 1779, in ibid.

19. Caughey, *Bernardo de Gálvez in Louisiana*, 102-34; *Pictorial History of the Marines*, 17-18. For Willing's raid, see Narrett, *Adventurism and Empire*, 79-88.

20. Bernardo de Gálvez to José de Gálvez, confidential letter no. 130, New Orleans, March 11, 1778, AGI, Santo Domingo, 2596.

21. Narrett, *Adventurism and Empire*, 72.

22. Oliver Pollock to Committee of Congress, [April] 1777, Pollock Papers, Library of Congress, quoted in Narrett, *Adventurism and Empire*, 72, 285.

23. See Abbey, "Peter Chester's De-

fense"; Abbey, "Intrigue of a British Refugee."

24. Bernardo de Gálvez to John Ferguson, certified copy of the letter, New Orleans, May 15, 1778, AGI, Cuba, 1232.

25. Bernardo de Gálvez to the commanders of the Mississippi River, Punta Colorada, and Manchac, letter draft copy, July 14, 1778, AGI, Cuba, 112.

26. Narrett, *Adventurism and Empire*, 86.

27. Secret Committee to Bernardo de Gálvez, Philadelphia, June 12, 1777, in Smith et al., *Letters of Delegates to Congress*, 25:624–25.

28. Committee of Commerce to Bernardo de Gálvez, Pennsylvania, October 24, 1777, in ibid., 635–38; Committee of Commerce to Bernardo de Gálvez, Pennsylvania, November 21, 1777, in ibid., 638–39.

29. Continental Congress, minutes of the October 31, 1778, session, in *Journals of the Continental Congress*, 12:1083–84.

30. The war debts stemming from American independence have been studied by historians from the United States, France, and Spain from very different angles. In the United States, the focus has been on the impact of the total debt on the finances of the new nation. In France, the emphasis has been on the size of its contribution and its consequences on the unstable financial situation that the country had to face after the end of the war against Britain. In Spain, till very recently, the tone has been much of a complaint about how its contribution has not been sufficiently recognized, neither by historians nor by the U.S. government or its society. This attitude had much to do with a certain inferiority complex that Spain developed vis-à-vis the United States after the war in Cuba (1898). For the image of Spain in the United States and vice versa, see Powell, *Tree of Hate*.

31. Diego María Gardoqui to the Duke of Alcudia, dispatch, October 26, 1794, AHN, Estado 3884, in Fulton, *Relaciones diplomáticas*, 54.

32. The exact amount rendered by the Count of Aranda was 5,634,910 *reales de vellón*. Socorros dados a los Estados Unidos de América por medio del Sr. Conde de Aranda, Embajador de España en aquel tiempo [Aid given to the United States through the Count of Aranda, Ambassador of Spain at that time], AHN, Estado 3889 bis, exp. 15, in Armillas Vicente, "Ayuda secreta y deuda oculta," 187.

33. Bemis, *Pinckney's Treaty*, 334. Also see Armillas Vicente, "Nuevas consideraciones"; and Ribes-Iborra, Vicente, "La era Miralles," 165. The translation of historical currencies into modern equivalents is extremely complicated, but in order to supply the reader with a rough idea, we have followed the conversions offered by Larrie D. Ferreiro complemented by other studies. Ferreiro, *Brothers at Arms*, 340; Lepore, *Mercado y empresa en Europa*; McKusker, *Money and Exchange in Europe and America*; Maddison, "Historical Statistics for the World Economy."

34. In his 1926 article, Samuel Flagg Bemis determined the amount of the Spanish financial aid to the United States as $13,551,888 ($397,230 nonrefundable and $248,098 in loans), which converted in French livres would be 3,387,972, and in Spanish *reales de vellón* 13,551,888. See Bemis, *Pinckney's Treaty*, 93; Perkins, "Bemis Regit!"; and Dull, *Diplomatic History*. For the conversion of the French currency to the Spanish one, see Bails, *Arismética [sic] para negociantes*, 286, 305, and 372.

35. Aulard, "La dette Américaine," 331–32. The exact amount of the French financial assistance to the American Revolution in Spanish currency was 166,980,000 *reales de vellón*; see Armillas Vicente, "El nacimiento de una gran nación."

36. Armillas Vicente, "Ayuda secreta y deuda oculta," 188–92.

37. José de Gálvez to the *intendente*

of Havana, to the governor of Santo Domingo, to the governor of Puerto Rico, to the *intendente* of Caracas, to the governor of Yucatán, to the governor of Caracas, and to the governor of Cuba, confidential official letter draft copy, San Ildefonso, August 29, 1782, AGI, Santo Domingo, 2188; Juan Ignacio de Urriza, *intendente* of Havana, to José de Gálvez, letter no. 670, Havana, April 21, 1780, AGI, Santo Domingo, 1657; Martín Navarro to Arturo O'Neill, letter no. 90, New Orleans, June 27, 1782, AGI, Cuba, 83; Luis de Unzuaga to Bernardo de Gálvez, official letter no. 134, Havana, May 24, 1783, AGI, Indiferente General, 1583.

38. Diego José Navarro to José de Gálvez, letter no. 365, Havana, October 23, 1778, AGI, Santo Domingo, 1598 A and B.

39. Calderón Cuadrado, "Alianzas comerciales hispano-norteamericanas," 214.

40. Armillas Vicente, "Ayuda secreta y deuda oculta," 185.

41. James, *Oliver Pollock*, 174–76; McDermott, *Spanish in the Mississippi Valley*, 329–31.

42. The exact amount is 1,507,670 *reales de vellón*. Razón de los préstamos o socorros en dinero que en la Nueva Orleans y en La Habana se han dado a los colonos americanos por disposición de sus respectivos gobernadores, deducida de la correspondencia de éstos desde fin de diciembre de 1776 hasta junio de 1779 [Detail of the loans and grants in cash given to the American colonists by the governors of New Orleans and Havana, taken form their correspondence from December 1776 to June 1779], New Orleans, September 13, 1780, AHN, Estado 3884, DF 4, no. 74, in Armillas Vicente, "Ayuda secreta y deuda oculta," 187 and 194.

43. The exact figure is 431,282,000 *reales de vellón*.

44. Canga Argüelles, *Diccionario de Hacienda*, 4:43–44.

45. Teijeiro de la Rosa, "La financiación de la guerra," 102.

46. E. Hamilton, *El florecimiento del capitalismo*, 140–41.

47. Tedde de Lorca, "La Real Hacienda de Carlos III," 228.

48. Ibid., 228–33.

49. On the role played by the San Carlos Bank, see Calderón Quijano, "El banco de San Carlos," 43–44; Torres Sánchez, "Crecimiento y expansión," 145; Ferreiro, *Brothers at Arms*, 340; Lepore, *Mercado y empresa en Europa*; McKusker, *Money and Exchange in Europe and America*; and Maddison, "Historical Statistics for the World Economy."

50. Treaty of Alliance between the Crowns of Spain and France against that of England (Tratado de alianza defensiva y ofensiva celebrado entre las coronas de España y Francia contra la de Inglaterra), Aranjuez, April 12, 1779, in Cantillo, *Tratados*, 552–54.

51. José de Gálvez to Diego José Navarro, confidential letter, San Ildefonso, August 29, 1779, AGI, Cuba, 1290.

52. Longchamps, *Historia de la última guerra entre la Inglaterra*, 76.

53. *Mercurio Histórico y Político*, Madrid, July 1779, 274.

54. Diego José Navarro, memorandum included in an official letter copy, Havana, June 27, 1779, AGI, Santo Domingo, 2082.

55. Diego José Navarro to José de Gálvez, confidential official letter no. 105, Havana, February 26, 1780, AGI, Santo Domingo, 2082.

56. José de Gálvez to Diego José Navarro, Aranjuez, May 21, 1780, AGI, Santo Domingo, 2082.

57. José de Gálvez to Bernardo de Gálvez, most confidential official letter draft copy, San Lorenzo, November 16, 1781 (third of this date), AGI, Indiferente General, 1578.

58. For general considerations on the Spanish strategy, see Chávez, "Spanish Policy and Strategy."

59. Scott, *British Foreign Policy in the Age of the American Revolution*, 277.

60. Reeve, "British Naval Strategy," 86. Also see Dull, *French Navy*, 111; and Rodger, *Command of the Ocean*, 136.

61. José de Gálvez to Bernardo de Gálvez, letter no. 124, May 18, 1779, AGI, Cuba, 569.

62. Diego José Navarro to Bernardo de Gálvez, Havana, letter no. 550, July 28, 1779, AGI, Santo Domingo, 2082.

63. José de Gálvez to Diego José Navarro, confidential letter, San Ildefonso, August 29, 1779, AGI, Cuba, 1290; governor of Cuba requests from Bernardo de Gálvez a plan for the attack against Pensacola and Mobile, in Diego José Navarro, governor of Cuba, to Bernardo de Gálvez, copy of the letter, Havana, July 18, 1779, AGI, Santo Domingo, 2543, and Cuba, 2; plans to attack the English in the Mississippi, in Juan Bautista Bonet to José de Gálvez, Havana, September 11, 1779, AGI, Santo Domingo, 2081.

64. On June 1, 1778, the Louisiana Fixed Infantry Battalion had 431 men; on January of the following year, 500. Estado de fuerza del batallón de infantería de la Luisiana, signed by Bernardo de Gálvez, New Orleans, June 1, 1778, AGI, Santo Domingo, 2547; estado de fuerza del batallón de infantería de la Luisiana, signed by Bernardo de Gálvez, New Orleans, January 1, 1779, AGI, Santo Domingo, 2662.

65. The minutes of this Council of War and others are in Bernardo de Gálvez to José de Gálvez, dispatch, New Orleans, October 16, 1779 (second of this date), AGS, SGU, leg. 6912, 1. Unless otherwise stated, the quotations in this section are from this document. There is another version of the "Account of the expedition against the English settlements along the Mississippi" (Relación de la expedición contra los establecimientos ingleses del Misisipi) but written in third person in a manuscript in Madrid's National Library (Serrano y Sanz, *Documentos históricos*, 343-52) that, with certain variations, was published in the issue 106 of the *Gazeta de Madrid*, December 12, 1778. It is also interesting to compare Bernardo's own manuscript with the excerpt by Diego José Navarro sent to José de Gálvez (Extracto de lo acaecido en la expedición hecha por el brigadier d. Bernardo de Gálvez, gobernador de la provincia de Luisiana, contra los establecimientos y fuertes que tenían los ingleses sobre el río Mississippi, que consiguió tomarles desalojándolos enteramente), in Diego José Navarro to José de Gálvez, official letter no. 633, Havana, November 11, 1779 (first of this date), AGI, Santo Domingo, 2082B.

66. A reference to this letter from Lord George Germain to Frederock Haldimand is made in Colonel Patrick Sinclair, governor of Makinac [sic], to Captain Diedrich Brehm, Michilimackinac, February 15, 1780, in Thwaites, "Papers from de Canadian Archives," 145.

67. Bernardo de Gálvez appointment as full governor of New Orleans, Aranjuez, May 8, 1779 (Nombramiento Bernardo de Gálvez como gobernador en propiedad de la Luisiana, May 8, 1779), AGS, Títulos de Indias, Dirección General del Tesoro, Inventario 24, leg. 186, f. 52.

68. Suetonio, *Las vidas de los doze cesares*, 25.

69. Statement made by Lieutenant Colonel Alexander Dickson about the reason to withdraw toward Baton Rouge, September 22, 1779, *Louisiana Historical Quarterly* 12 (1929): 263-64, in Caughey, *Bernardo de Gálvez in Louisiana*, 155.

70. Frederick II of Prussia, "Des marches d'armée," 110.

71. The Army Regulations (Reales Ordenanzas) of Carlos III determined that during training the marches with full equipment "in good terrain, would be six thousand four hundred *varas* [about 5.6 km or 3.48 miles] per hour" (article 55, title 17, treaty 2 of the *Ordenanzas de S.M.*

para el régimen, disciplina, subordinación y servicio de su Exércitos, vol. 1, 227; Romero García, "Medidas antiguas españolas," 67).

72. Bernardo de Gálvez to General John Campbell, copy of the letter, New Orleans, August 23, 1779, AGI, Cuba, 182.

73. Caughey, *Bernardo de Gálvez in Louisiana*, 154.

74. Gayarré, *History of Louisiana*, 3:127.

75. Caughey, *Bernardo de Gálvez in Louisiana*, 155.

76. *London Gazette*, no. 12070, March 28-April 1, 1780; *London Magazine*, April 1780, 189-90.

77. Bernardo de Gálvez to José de Gálvez, dispatch, New Orleans, October 16, 1779 (second of this date), AGS, SGU, leg. 6912, 1.

78. Diego José Navarro to José de Gálvez, letter no. 578, Havana, August 11, 1779, AGI, Santo Domingo, 2082.

79. Marquis de González de Castejón, Minister of the Navy, to José de Gálvez, answering a previous from the latter, San Lorenzo, October 23, 1779, AGI, Santo Domingo, 2082.

80. See Juan Bautista Bonet to José de Gálvez, Havana, August 12, 1779, AGI, Santo Domingo, 2081.

81. A reference to the letters from General Campbell is made in Lieutenant Colonel Alexander Dickson to General John Campbell, Baton Rouge, December 15, 1779, in the *London Magazine*, April 1780, 189-90.

82. Examples of these oaths: oaths taken by Lieutenant Colonel Alexander Dickson made at Pensacola and by several British officers, AGI, Cuba, 1550; oath by British officers Jas. [sic] Wilson (May 20, 1780) and August Alberti (July 5, 1780), AGI, Cuba, 193.

83. Pittman, *Plan of Fort Rosalia*.

84. Oliver Pollock to the inhabitants of the Natchez district, copy of the letter, September 23, 1779, AGI, Cuba, 192, in Caughey, *Bernardo de Gálvez in Louisiana*, 158.

85. Juan Delavillebeuvre to Bernardo de Gálvez, Fort Panmure, December 12, 1779, AGI, Cuba, 107, in Delavillebeuvre, "Fort Panmure."

86. Haynes, *Natchez District*, 124.

87. Dart, "West Florida," 260-61.

88. Meyers, *History of Baton Rouge*, 43; W. Miller, *Spanish Commandant of Baton Rouge*, 19-20, quoted in Meyers, *History of Baton Rouge*, 43.

89. J. P. Jones, *John Paul Jones' Memoir*, 111; Rea, "Florida and the Royal Navy's Floridas," 197.

90. Vicente Rillieux's promotion to lieutenant, El Pardo, January 12, 1780, AGS, SGU, leg. 6912, 2.

91. The king rewards Fernando de Leyva and Francisco Cartabona for their valiant defense of St. Louis (San Luis de Ilionenses), in *Gazeta de Madrid*, no. 14, February 16, 1781.

92. Caughey, *Bernardo de Gálvez in Louisiana*, 164-67.

93. Martín Navarro to José de Gálvez, New Orleans, August 18, 1780, in Thwaites, *Collections of the State Historical Society*, 406-10.

94. Extracto de lo acaecido en la expedición hecha por el brigadier d. Bernardo de Gálvez, gobernador de la provincia de Luisiana, contra los establecimientos y fuertes que tenían los ingleses sobre el río Mississippi, que consiguió tomarles desalojándolos enteramente, in Diego José Navarro to José de Gálvez, official letter no. 633, Havana, November 11, 1779 (1st of this date), AGI, Santo Domingo, 2082B.

95. Mill, *Considerations on Representative Government*, 44-45.

96. Contreras, *Compendio de los veinte libros*, vol. 2, 145.

97. José de Gálvez to Diego José Navarro, confidential letter, San Ildefonso, August 29, 1779, AGI, Cuba, 1290.

98. Beerman and Din, "Victory on the Mississippi," 200; Reparaz, *Yo Solo*, 21; Thomas, "Gálvez Campaigns," 41; C. Ward, *War of the Revolution*, 678.

99. Beerman and Din, "Victory on the Mississippi," 200.

100. Caughey, *Bernardo de Gálvez in Louisiana*, 163; Chávez, *Spain and the Independence of the United States*, 172.

101. William Campbell, governor of Pensacola, to Captain Anthony Forstel, Pensacola, September 9, 1779; Charles Stewart to Captain Anthony Forstel, October 1, 1779; Elias Bunnford to Judge William Hicorn, October 2, 1779; artillery captain William McJohnstone to unknown, October 2, 1779, all in AGI, Santo Domingo, 2082.

102. Mr. Gordon to Thompson & Campbell, merchants in Jamaica, Pensacola, November 18, 1779, in Historical Manuscripts Commission, *Report on American Manuscripts*, 2:63.

103. José de Gálvez to Diego José Navarro, confidential letter, San Ildefonso, August 29, 1779, AGI, Cuba, 1290.

104: Extracto de lo acaecido en la expedición hecha por el brigadier d. Bernardo de Gálvez, gobernador de la provincia de Luisiana, contra los establecimientos y fuertes que tenían los ingleses sobre el río Mississippi, que consiguió tomarles desalojándolos enteramente, in Diego José Navarro to José de Gálvez, official letter no. 633, Havana, November 11, 1779 (1st of this date), AGI, Santo Domingo, 2082B.

105. Article 19, title 16, treaty 2 of the *Ordenanzas de S.M. para el régimen, disciplina, subordinación, y servicio de su Exércitos*, vol. 1, 205.

106. Martín Navarro to José de Gálvez, New Orleans, September 20, 1779, AGS, SGU, leg. 6912, 2.

107. José de Gálvez to Bernardo de Gálvez, El Pardo, January 10, 1780, in ibid.

108. Martín Navarro to José de Gálvez, New Orleans, September 20, 1779, in ibid.

109. Din, *Francisco Bouligny*, 104.

110. Bernardo de Gálvez to José de Gálvez, dispatch, New Orleans, October 16, 1779 (second of this date), AGS, SGU, leg. 6912, 1.

111. Poydras, *La Prise du morne du Bâton Rouge*; Tinker, *Louisiana's Earliest Poet*; Pearl, "Capture of the Blufols."

112.
Je l'ai vu ce Héros, qui cause tes allarmes,
Il resemblait un Dieu, revêtu de ses armes,
Son Panache superbe, alloit au gré du vent,
Et ses cheveux épars lui servoient d'ornement.
Un maintien noble et fier annonçoit son courage,
L'héroïque vertu, brilloit sur son visage.

113.
Tant que dans nos Climats, ce généreux Vainqueur,
D'un Peuple qu'il chérit, fera tout le bonheur;
Le Dieu l'interrompant, laisse éclater sa joie,
Je le vois, lui dit-il, c'est le Ciel qui l'envoie.
Qu'il vive dans le sein de la prospérité,
Qu'il goûte le plaisir, de se voir adoré.
Que ses grandes vertus, soient par tous célébrées,
Que ses belles actions, obtiennent des Trophées.

114. José de Gálvez to Diego José Navarro, dispatch, Aranjuez, April 30, 1780, AGS, SGU, leg. 6912, 2.

115. *Gazeta de Madrid*, no. 106, December 31, 1779; military service record of Captain José Valière, AGS, SGU, leg. 7291, in Marchena Fernández, Caballero Gómez, and Torres Arriaza, *El ejército de América*.

116. Bernardo de Gálvez to José de Gálvez, dispatch, New Orleans, October 16, 1779 (third of this date), AGS, SGU, leg. 6612, 2.

117. Noticia de los oficiales y varios otros individuos que de resultas de la expedición se considera deben ser ascendidos, Bernardo de Gálvez, dispatch, New Orleans, October 27, 1779, AGS, SGU, leg. 6912, 2. Also see Relación de Oficiales

de milicias que se han hallado en la expedición del coronel don Bernardo de Gálvez, in ibid.; Relación de los oficiales veteranos de los distintos cuerpos que se han hallado en la expedición al mando del coronel Bernardo de Gálvez, Nueva Orleans, October 16, 1779, in Bernardo de Gálvez to José de Gálvez, dispatch, New Orleans, October 16, 1779 (third of this date), in ibid.

118. José de Gálvez to Miguel de Muzquiz, El Pardo, February 6, 1779, in ibid.; Miguel Muzquiz to José de Gálvez, dispatch, El Pardo, February 7, 1780, in ibid.

119. *Relación de los individuos de los cuerpos militares, y de los empleados de la Real Hacienda a quienes S.M. se ha dignado conceder ascenso de resultas de la expedición hecha contra los establecimientos ingleses del río Mississippi*, El Pardo, January 10, 1780, in ibid.

120. José de Gálvez to Bernardo de Gálvez, dispatch, El Pardo, February 16, 1781, in ibid., 4; José de Gálvez to Bernardo de Gálvez, dispatch, Madrid, January 6, 1780, in ibid., 2.

121. José de Gálvez to Diego José Navarro, confidential letter, San Ildefonso, August 29, 1779, AGI, Cuba, 1290.

122. José de Gálvez to the governor of Cuba, confidential letter, El Pardo, January 11, 1780, AGI, Santo Domingo, 2082.

123. Ribes, "Nuevos datos biográficos"; Fernández y Fernández, "Juan de Miralles"; Matzke McCadden, "Juan de Miralles"; Pradells Nadal, *Diplomacia y comercio*; Portell Vila, *Juan de Miralles*; Portell Vila, *Los "otros extranjeros."*

124. George Washington to Anne Cesare, Chevalier de la Luzerne, May 11, 1780; George Washington to Diego Jose de Navarro, March 4, 1779; George Washington to Anne Cesare, Chevalier de la Luzerne, April 27, 1780; George Washington to Maria Elirio [*sic*: Elixio or Eligio] de la Puente, October 13, 1780, *The George Washington Papers at the Library of Congress*, Library of Congress, https://memory.loc.gov/ammem/gwhtml/gwhome.html (accessed January 5, 2017).

125. James Lovell to Samuel Adams, March 31, 1780, in Smith et al., *Letters of Delegates to Congress*, 14:397–98.

126. Juan de Miralles to José de Gálvez, March 12, 1780, AGI, Santo Domingo, 2598.

127. *Papers of the Continental Congress, 1774–1789*, item 137, I, f. 345.

128. George Washington to Juan de Miralles, Cuartel General de Morristown, February 27, 1780, in Sparks, *Writings of George Washington*, 6:476–77.

129. *Gazeta de Madrid*, no. 106, December 31, 1779, 945–50; *Suplemento de la Gazeta de Madrid*, January 14, 1779.

130. José de Gálvez to Diego José Navarro, confidential letter, San Ildefonso, August 29, 1779, AGI, Cuba, 1290.

131. Bernardo de Gálvez to José de Gálvez, confidential letter no. 129, New Orleans, March 11, 1778, AGI, Santo Domingo, 2596; Jacinto Panis to Bernardo de Gálvez, report, New Orleans, July 5, 1778, AGI, Cuba, 112; Bernardo de Gálvez to José de Gálvez, confidential letter no. 175, New Orleans, July 28, 1778, AGI, Santo Domingo, 2596.

132. Bernardo de Gálvez to Diego Joseph Navarro, confidential letter no. 201, New Orleans, August 17, 1779, AGI, Cuba, 2351.

133. Caughey, "Panis Mission," 488–89.

134. Jacinto Panis to Bernardo de Gálvez, New Orleans, July 5, 1778, AGI, Cuba, 112.

135. Bernardo de Gálvez to Diego José Navarro, confidential letter no. 201, New Orleans, August 17, 1779, AGI, Cuba, 2351.

136. Caughey, *Bernardo de Gálvez in Louisiana*, 173.

137. Caughey, "Panis Mission," 487.

138. Ibid., 486.

139. Bernardo de Gálvez to Diego José Navarro, confidential letter no. 228, New Orleans, October 16, 1779, AGI, Cuba, 2351.

140. Luis Huet to Bernardo de Gálvez, Havana, November 20, 1779, in ibid.

141. Diego José Navarro to Bernardo de Gálvez, Havana, November 20, 1779, in ibid.

142. Bernardo de Gálvez to Esteban Miró, New Orleans, December 31, 1779, AGI, Santo Domingo, 2543, and Cuba, 2.

143. "Relación de la toma de la Mobila por las armas del Rey de España verificada en 14 de marzo de 1780" (Account of the taking of the Mobile by the arms of the King of Spain verified on March 14, 1780), AGS, SGU, leg. 6912, 2. Diario formado por Don Esteban Miró, Teniente Coronel Graduado y Sargento Mayor del Regimiento Fijo de la Luisiana para dar cuenta al señor Don Bernardo de Gálvez, Brigadier de los Reales Ejércitos y Gobernador de la Provincia de la Luisiana de cuanto ocurre en esta plaza de La Habana relativo a la comisión que puso a su cuidado, Havana, February 10, 1780, AGI, Santo Domingo, 2543, and Cuba, 2.

144. The first account of the expedition is in a manuscript (with a large amount of corrections) titled "Relación de la toma de la Mobila por las armas del Rey de España verificada en 14 de marzo de 1780," AGS, SGU, leg. 6912, 2. The second account, bearing the same title, is a fair copy of the previous one, in ibid. The third account is the official and final diary, under the title "Diary that I, d. Bernardo de Gálvez, brigadier of the Royal Armies, governor of the province of Louisiana, and entrusted by His Majesty with the expedition against Pensacola and Mobile, made about the events that occurred during it" ("Diario que yo, d. Bernardo de Gálvez, brigadier de los Reales Ejércitos, gobernador de la provincia de la Luisiana y encargado por S.M. de la expedición contra Panzacola y Mobila, formé de los acontecimientos que ocurren en ella"), in ibid.

145. Vegas, *Diccionario geográfico universal*, 4:293.

146. Fernández de Navarrete, *Diccionario marítimo español*; "BARRA. Banco de arena, y a veces interpolado de bajos de piedra, que se extiende en la boca o entrada de los ríos y rías, haciéndola difícil y peligrosa, especialmente en las mareas bajas. . . . A veces suelen también dársela los nombres de *bajo fondo, pasa y broa*, o se equivoca con ellos," 85–86. "PASA. Canal estrecho o canalizo por donde pueden pasarse catre bajos. Dícese también *pasage* y *paso*, y en algunos escritos se encuentra como equivalente a *barra* y *bajo fondo*," in ibid., 405–6. Unless otherwise stated, the quotes in this section are from Gálvez's diary, "Diario que yo, d. Bernardo de Gálvez, brigadier de los Reales Ejércitos, gobernador de la provincia de la Luisiana, y encargado por S.M. de la expedición contra Panzacola y Mobila, formé de los acontecimientos que ocurren en ella," AGS, SGU, leg. 6912, 2.

147. Manuscript version: "Diario que yo, d. Bernardo de Gálvez . . . ," AGS, SGU, leg. 6912, 2. Published version: "Diario que yo, d. Bernardo de Gálvez, brigadier de los Reales Ejércitos, gobernador de la provincia de la Luisiana, y encargado por S.M. de la expedición contra Panzacola y Mobila, formé de los acontecimientos que ocurren en ella," in *Mercurio Histórico y Político*, 105 and 198–226.

148. Gayarré, *History of Louisiana*, 3:135–36; Hamilton, *Colonial Mobile*, 253; Martin, *History of Louisiana*, 2:52; Fortier, *A History of Louisiana*, 2:70–71; Caughey, *Bernardo de Gálvez in Louisiana*, 176.

149. Jerónimo Girón Moctezuma to the king, Seville, January 24, 1789, AGS, SGU, leg. 6915, 13.

150. Depauger, *Plan (et profil) du fort Condé projeté a faire a la Mobille*, May 29, 1724, map ms, Archives Nationales d'Outre-Mer, Aix-en-Provence, France, Dépôt des Fortifications des Colonies, FR CAOM 04DFC121A; Pauger [sic: Depauger], Plan profil et élévation du fort Condé de la Mobille pour faire voir le revetement en maçonnerie de briques qu'il convient de faire pour soutenir le terreplain du corps de la place au lieu de

charpente comme il était projetté, March 23, 1725, map ms, in ibid., FR CAOM 04DFC125C.

151. Quesada, *Spanish Colonial Fortifications*, 32–33.

152. McConnell, *Army and Empire*, 50, 90.

153. Coker and Coker, "Siege of Mobile," 166.

154. The fort contained six twelve-pounder cannons, two nine-pounders, eight six-pounders, seventeen four-pounders, three two-pounders, and thirteen half-pounders (6 cañones de a 12, 2 de a 9, 8 de a 6, 17 de a 4 y 3 de a 2 y 13 pedreros de a 1/2). Relación de la artillería, montajes y municiones, y demás efectos que se han hallado en el fuerte de la Mobila de resulta de su toma, verificada el 14 de mes de la fecha, cuya existencia es la misma que se manifiesta en este inventario formado por mi, Don Juan de los Remedios, Subteniente del Real Cuerpo de Artillería, nombrado a este fin por Don Julián Álvarez, Comandante de la de esta expedición, con asistencia de Don Josef María de la barba, Guarda Almacén de la misma, Mobile, March 19, 1780, AGS, SGU, leg. 6912.

155. Bernardo de Gálvez to Elias Durnford, River de los Perros, March 1, 1780. The copies of the letter written in French in English and Spanish archives are identical. For the first one, see "Diario que yo, d. Bernardo de Gálvez . . . ," AGS, SGU, leg. 6912, 2. For the British version, see, NAL, Record Office, Colonial Records, America and West Indies, Floridas 1702–1782, no. 533, in Beer, "Surrender of Fort Charlotte," 697.

156. See Nunemaker, "Documents."

157. Elias Durnford to General John Campbell, Mobile, March 2, 1780, NAL, Record Office, Colonial Records, America and West Indies, Floridas 1702–1782, no. 533, in Beer, "Surrender of Fort Charlotte," 697.

158. Ibid., 698.

159. Elias Durnford to Bernardo de Gálvez, Mobile, March 1, 1780. The Spanish and English versions are identical. For the first one, see "Diario que yo, d. Bernardo de Gálvez . . . ," AGS, SGU, leg. 6912, 2. For the British version, see, NAL, Record Office, Colonial Records, America and West Indies, Floridas 1702–1782, no. 533, in Beer, "Surrender of Fort Charlotte," 697.

160. Depending on the source, the size of the British garrison varies from 162 (Return of the Killed, Wounded and Prisoners of the Garrison of Forte Charlotte, Mobile, Surrendered to Spain by Capitulation the 14th day of March 1780, Pensacola, August 26, 1780, PRO, CO:5/597) to around 300 (Hamilton, *Colonial Mobile: An Historical Study*, 252). The Spanish sources mention 126 men: 113 soldiers and 13 officers (Relación de los oficiales, tropas y demás individuos hechos prisioneros de guerra en el sitio de la Mobila, Mobile, March 20, 1780, AGI, Cuba, 2351).

161. Elias Durnford to General John Campbell, Mobile, March 1, 1780, NAL, Record Office, Colonial Records, America and West Indies, Floridas 1702–1782, no. 533, in Beer, "Surrender of Fort Charlotte," 698.

162. In the original French text the word *cigalles* appears, but it is probably a transcription error; the word must be *cigarres* (cigars).

163. Bernardo de Gálvez to Elias Durnford, Punta Chawtaw, March 5, 1780, "Diario que yo, d. Bernardo de Gálvez . . . ," AGS, SGU, leg. 6912, 2.

164. Account of the attack and conquest of Mobile by Captain José Sastre, Trinidad, August 19, 1784, in ibid., 10.

165. "Mais si je vous promets de ne pas s'établir de batterie derrière aucune maison, quoiques [sic] le peu qui restent sont déjà hors de la porté de canon, et les d'autres motifs on pourrai peut être trouver des expédients pour sauver les maisons de malheureux habitants sans nous compromettre ni moins ni plus." Bernardo de Gálvez to Elias Durnford, Punta

Chawtaw, March 5, 1780, "Diario que yo, d. Bernardo de Gálvez...," in ibid., 2.

166. Elias Durnford to Bernardo de Gálvez, Mobile, March 7, 1780, "Diario que yo, d. Bernardo de Gálvez...," in ibid.

167. Caughey, *Bernardo de Gálvez in Louisiana*, 179.

168. Bernardo de Gálvez to Elias Durnford, Mobile, March 7, 1780, "Diario que yo, d. Bernardo de Gálvez...," AGS, SGU, leg. 6912, 2.

169. Taitt, *Plan of part of the rivers Tombecbe, Alabama, Tensa, Perdido*.

170. "Carta de D. Bernardo de Gálvez fecha en la Mobila a 20 de marzo de 1780, al Excmo. Sr. D. Joseph de Gálvez, Secretario de Estado y del Despacho de Indias," in *Mercurio Histórico y Político*, Madrid, June 1780, 194-98; Bernardo de Gálvez to José de Gálvez, Mobile, March 20, 1780, in ibid. (no page).

171. General John Campbell to General Sir Henry Clinton, Pensacola, February 12, 1780, PRO, America and West Indies, 137, f. 241; Historical Manuscripts Commission, *Report on American Manuscripts*, 2:89; Caughey, *Bernardo de Gálvez in Louisiana*, 180.

172. "Carta de D. Bernardo de Gálvez fecha en la Mobila a 20 de marzo de 1780, al Excmo. Sr. D. Joseph de Gálvez, Secretario de Estado y del Despacho de Indias," in *Mercurio Histórico y Político*, Madrid, June 1780, 194-98; Bernardo de Gálvez to José de Gálvez, Mobile, March 20, 1780, in ibid. (no page).

173. Duffy, *Military Experience*, 293.

174. *Articles of Capitulation, Mobile* ("Artículos de Capitulación propuestos por D. Elías [sic] Durnford, Esq. Teniente de Gobernador de la provincia de la Florida del Oeste, capitán de ingenieros y comandante de las tropas de Su Majestad Británica en el fuerte Charlota de la Mobila, acordados por el Sr. D. Bernardo de Gálvez, caballero pensionado de la Real y Distinguida Orden de Carlos Tercero, Brigadier de los ejércitos de Su Majestad, Inspector, Intendente y Gobernador General de la provincia de la Luisiana y General de la expedición"), Campo de la Mobila, March 13, 1780, In *Mercurio Histórico y Político*, July, 1780, 315-22. "Diario que yo, d. Bernardo de Gálvez...," AGS, SGU, leg. 6912, 2.

175. Duffy, *Military Experience*, 293.

176. Krebs, "Making of Prisoners of War"; Black, *European Warfare*, 37.

177. Sanz, *Diccionario militar*, 72.

178. Elias Durnford to John Campbell, Fort Charlotte, Mobile, March 14, 1780, PRO, America and West Indies 155, f. 601; Historical Manuscripts Commission, *Report on American Manuscripts*, 2:102.

179. Caughey, *Bernardo de Gálvez in Louisiana*, 185.

180. "Diario que yo, d. Bernardo de Gálvez...," AGS, SGU, leg. 6912, 2.

181. Inventario de lo capturado en Mobila, Juan Antonio Gayarre, comisario y ministro de hacienda de la expedición de Mobila to José de Gálvez, official letter, New Orleans, June 6, 1780, AGI, Santo Domingo, 2572; Juan Antonio Gayarre, comisario y ministro de hacienda de la expedición de Mobila to José de Gálvez, official letter, New Orleans, June 7, 1780, AGI, Santo Domingo, 2572. This Manuel González should not be confused with the colonel of the Regiment España with the same name, "Relación de la campaña que hizo D. Bernardo de Gálvez, contra los ingleses, en la Luisiana," September 1779, BN, Manuscritos que fueron de la Biblioteca de Ultramar no. 14, in Serrano y Sanz, *Documentos históricos*, 374. Bernardo de Gálvez to José de Gálvez, Mobile, March 1780, AGS, 6912, 2.

182. José de Gálvez to Bernardo de Gálvez, June 22, 1780, AGS, 6912, 2.

183. Bernardo de Gálvez's proposal of promotions and rewards to the officers who participated in the conquest of Mobile was granted by the king on February 9, 1781. Bernardo de Gálvez to José de Gálvez, Havana, November 28, 1780, AGS, 6912, Ex4.

184. *Gazeta de Madrid*, supplement, June 20, 1780, 450-51.
185. *Estado Militar de España para el año 1781*, 12.
186. Beerman, "Aztec Emperor's Descendant."
187. Pedro Piernas to José de Gálvez, New Orleans, May 6, 1780, AGI, Cuba, 147A.
188. John Adams to the president of Congress, Paris, July 19, 1780, in Wharton, *Revolutionary Diplomatic Correspondence*, 3:870.
189. John Adams to the Count de Vergennes, Paris, July 13, 1780, in ibid., 849.
190. *Journals of the Continental Congress*, 17:523, 700; *Papers of the Continental Congress, 1774-1789*, National Archives, National Archives and Records Service, General Services Administration, 1959, Washington, D.C., item 41, fols. 8:114-16.
191. William C. Houston to William Livingston, Philadelphia, June 5, 1780, in Smith et al., *Letters of Delegates to Congress*, 15:252-53.
192. *Journals of the Continental Congress*, 17:600-601; *Papers of the Continental Congress*, National Archives, National Archives and Records Service, General Services Administration, 1959, Washington, D.C., item 50, fols. 120, and 371-72.
193. *Caledonian Mercury* (Midlothian, Scotland), March 29, 1780.
194. Ibid., August 16, 1780.
195. By date: *Caledonian Mercury*, March 29, 1780, 3; *Derby Mercury* (Derbyshire, England), July 7, 1780, 4, and July 14, 1780, 2; *Norfolk Chronicle* (Norfolk, England), July 15, 1780, 2; *Oxford Journal* (Oxfordshire, England), July 15, 1780, 1; *Caledonian Mercury*, July 15, 1780, 2-3; *Hampshire Chronicle* (Hampshire, England), July 17, 1780, 3; *Northampton Mercury* (Northamptonshire, England), July 17, 1780, 1; *Leeds Intelligencer* (West Yorkshire, England), July 18, 1780, 1; *Norfolk Chronicle*, July 22, 1780, 1; *Derby Mercury*, August 4, 1780, 1; *Oxford Journal*, August 5, 1780, 2; *Hampshire Chronicle*,

August 7, 1780, 2; *Reading Mercury* (Berkshire, England), August 7, 1780, 2; *Derby Mercury*, August 11, 1780, 2; *Reading Mercury*, August 14, 1780, 3.
196. *Derby Mercury*, August 4, 1780, 1; *Reading Mercury*, August 7, 1780, 1.
197. *Journal Politique, ou Gazette des Gazettes*, second fortnight July 1780, 19-21; ibid., first fortnight August 1780, 22-26.
198. *Journal Historique et Littéraire*, second fortnight August 1780, 545-47. Includes a copy of the letter from Bernardo de Gálvez to José de Gálvez. Quote from *Courrier d'Avignon* (Avignon, France), July 4, 1780, 2.
199. José de Gálvez to Bernardo de Gálvez, Aranjuez, June 22, 1780, AGI, Cuba, 175, in Caughey, *Bernardo de Gálvez in Louisiana*, 186.
200. José de Gálvez to Bernardo de Gálvez, Aranjuez, June 23, 1780, AGS, 6912, EX2.
201. Bernardo de Gálvez to José de Gálvez, Mobile, March 20, 1780 (ms version), in ibid.
202. José de Gálvez to Diego José Navarro, confidential letter, Aranjuez, April 20, 1780, AGI, Santo Domingo, 2082.
203. Ibid.
204. Ibid.
205. Martínez Laínez and Canales Torres, *Banderas lejanas*, 505; Quesada, *Spanish Colonial Fortifications*, 32-33.
206. Caughey, *Bernardo de Gálvez in Louisiana*, 187.
207. Plan que manifiesta el estado de fuerza de que se compone la expedición, que está pronta a salir de este puerto con destino, y a las órdenes del gobernador de la provincia de la Luisiana, brigadier d. Bernardo de Gálvez, in Diego José Navarro to José de Gálvez, confidential letter no. 101, Havana, January 5, 1780, AGI, Santo Domingo, 2082.
208. Instrucción que yo el Brigadier Don Bernardo de Gálvez doy al Teniente Coronel Don Esteban Miró para que, en presencia de ella, pueda cumplir con los distintos encargos que son objeto de

su comisión, New Orleans, December 31, 1779, AGI, Santo Domingo, 2543, and Cuba, 2.

209. Saavedra, *Los Decenios*, 76.

210. Diario formado por Don Esteban Miró, Teniente Coronel Graduado y Sargento Mayor del Regimiento Fijo de la Luisiana para dar cuenta al señor Don Bernardo de Gálvez, Brigadier de los Reales Ejércitos y Gobernador de la Provincia de la Luisiana de cuanto ocurre en esta plaza de La Habana relativo a la comisión que puso a su cuidado, Havana, February 10, 1780, AGI, Santo Domingo, 2543, and Cuba, 2.

211. Palma, "Cortar el revesino," 239.

212. José de Gálvez to Diego José Navarro, confidential letter, Aranjuez, April 24, 1780, AGI, Santo Domingo, 2082.

213. Medina Rojas, *José de Ezpeleta*, 10.

214. Juan Bautista Bonet to Diego José Navarro, Havana, February 22, 1780, AGI, Santo Domingo, 2082.

215. Ibid.

216. José de Ezpeleta to his father, Joaquín de Ezpeleta y Dicastillo, Havana, February 21, 1780, AE, Papeles de Panzacola, in Medina Rojas, *José de Ezpeleta*, 11–12.

217. Diario formado por Don Esteban Miró, Teniente Coronel Graduado y Sargento Mayor del Regimiento Fijo de la Luisiana para dar cuenta al señor Don Bernardo de Gálvez, Brigadier de los Reales Ejércitos y Gobernador de la Provincia de la Luisiana de cuanto ocurre en esta plaza de La Habana relativo a la comisión que puso a su cuidado, Havana, February 10, 1780, AGI, Santo Domingo, 2543, and Cuba, 2.

218. Estado Mayor del Ejército destinado para la conquista de la plaza de Panzacola, Castillo de la Mobila, April 1, 1780, AE, Papeles de Panzacola; Medina Rojas, *José de Ezpeleta*, 22.

219. Juan Bautista Bonet to Bernardo de Gálvez, letter no. 14, March 15, 1780, AGI, Santo Domingo, 2543, and Cuba, 2.

220. Bernardo de Gálvez to Juan Bautista Bonet, letter no. 16, March 22, 1780, in ibid.

221. Correspondence between Bernardo de Gálvez and Miguel de Goicoechea, Mobile, April 6, 1780, in ibid.; Medina Rojas, *José de Ezpeleta*, 24.

222. Bernardo de Gálvez to the commanders of the warships at Mobile Bay, copy of the enquiry, Mobile, April 6, 1780, AGI, Santo Domingo, 2543, and Cuba, 2.

223. Bernardo de Gálvez to Miguel de Goicoechea, letter no. 1, April 13, 1780, in ibid.; Caughey, *Bernardo de Gálvez in Louisiana*, 190.

224. Enrique Grimarest's appointment as governor of the fort of Mobile and civil governor of its district (Nombramiento de Enrique Grimarest como gobernador del castillo de la Mobila y comandante civil de su distrito), Mobile, March 16, 1780, AGI, Cuba, 113; testimonio de la jura de Enrique Grimarest como gobernador del castillo de la Mobila y comandante político de su distrito, Mobile, March 17, 1780, AGI, Cuba, 81.

225. Juan Bautista Bonet to Bernardo de Gálvez, aboard the *San Gabriel*, April 6, 10, and 17, 1780, AGI, Cuba, 113.

226. Medina Rojas, *José de Ezpeleta*, 26; Bernardo de Gálvez to Gabriel de Aristizábal, aboard the *Galvezton*, May 2, 1780, AGI, Santo Domingo, 2543, and Cuba, 2; Gabriel de Aristizábal to Bernardo de Gálvez, aboard the *Galvezton*, May 2, 1780, AGI, Santo Domingo 2543, and Cuba, 2.

227. War Council (Junta de Guerra), May 4, 1780, AGI, Cuba, 177A.

228. Ibid.

229. Bernardo de Gálvez to Juan Bautista Bonet, May 4, 1780, AGI, Santo Domingo, 2543, and Cuba, 2; Medina Rojas, *José de Ezpeleta*, 28.

230. Representación que ha hecho el mariscal de campo don Bernardo de Gálvez, gobernador de la Luisiana, en que expone individualmente y justifica con documentos las ocurrencias verificadas con los generales de La Habana, desde antes de la declaración de guerra hasta el

27 de noviembre de 1780 sobre las expediciones de la Movila y Panzacola, recibida el 27 de enero de 1781 y dada cuenta al Rey en 29 del mismo. Nota. El principal se quemó por orden del sr. D. Josef de Gálvez el 29 de junio por estar muy maltratado, AGS, SGU, leg. 6912, EX3.

231. Bernardo de Gálvez to José de Ezpeleta, Mobile Bay, May 3, 1780, AGI, Cuba, 1377; Bernardo de Gálvez to Enrique Grimarest, Mobile Bay, May 3, 1780, AGI, Cuba, 81.

232. Representación que ha hecho el mariscal de campo don Bernardo de Gálvez..., AGS, SGU, leg. 6912, EX3.

233. John Campbell to Henry Clinton, Pensacola, May 13, 1780, in Historical Manuscripts Commission, *Report on American Manuscripts*, 2:121–22.

234. John Campbell to Sir Henry Clinton, May 18, 1780, PRO, Carleton Papers 30/55; Historical Manuscripts Commission, *Report on American Manuscripts*, 2:124; Rush, *Spain's Final Triumph*, 21.

CHAPTER 6

1. Fidelity oath, Mobile, March 22, 1780, AGI, Cuba, 193B.

2. Serment de fidélité prêté par provision par les habitants anglais de la Mobile, le 17 Mars 1780 à trois heures de l'après-midi, AGI, Cuba, 200.

3. Bernardo de Gálvez to John Campbell, Punta de la Mobila, April 6, 1780, AGI, Cuba, 193B.

4. Narrett, *Adventurism and Empire*, 87.

5. Charles Stuart's report on his visit to the Choctaw country, July 1, 1778, PRO, Colonial Office, Series 5/79, fols. 109–202, in O'Donnell, *Southern Indians*, 74.

6. Bernardo de Gálvez to José de Gálvez, letter no. 116, New Orleans, December 30, 1777, AGI, Santo Domingo 1598, A and B, and Santo Domingo, 2547, Duplicados de Gobernadores e Intendentes, dispatch 109; Bernardo de Gálvez to José de Gálvez, New Orleans, March 24, 1778, AGI, Santo Domingo, 2547, Duplicados de Gobernadores e Intendentes, dispatch 134.

7. Alexander Cameron to George Germain, October 31, 1780, PRO, Colonial Office, Series 5/82, f. 111, in O'Donnell, *Southern Indians*, 104.

8. Medina Rojas, *José de Ezpeleta*, 53.

9. Atkin, *Appalachian Indian Frontier*, 62, 68.

10. Charles Stuart to Alexander Cameron, December 20, 1779, PRO, Colonial Office, Series 5/81, f. 47, in O'Donnell, *Southern Indians*, 92. Jackson, "John Stuart: Superintendent of Indian Affairs for the Southern District."

11. Crane, "Origin of the Name."

12. Bernardo de Gálvez mentions the following groups by their Spanish names: Alibamones, Arkansas, Atacapas, Avoyelles, Bayagoulas, Bicategueny, Bilosocis, Carcouay, Chactas, Chatimachais de la Grande Tierra, Chetimachas del Rio, Houmais, Mobilienoes, Nilchez, Ofogoulars, Opeluzan, Tinzais, Tonicas, and Ylinois. Bernardo de Gálvez to José de Gálvez, New Orleans, September 1777, AGI, Santo Domingo, 2547, Duplicados de Gobernadores e Intendentes, dispatch 90.

13. Medina Rojas, *José de Ezpeleta*, 56.

14. Swanton, *Indian Tribes*, 252–56.

15. Ibid., 184–85.

16. Calloway, *American Revolution*, xii.

17. Hart, "Unsettled Periphery," 31.

18. Sheehan, "Indian-White Relations."

19. Schmidt, "Blacks and Indians," 40.

20. Rindfleisch, "Rebels and Indians," 4.

21. Starkey, *European and Native American Warfare*.

22. O'Donnell, *Southern Indians*, viii.

23. Calloway, *American Revolution*, 26.

24. For Samuel Kirkland, see Merritt, "Native Peoples," 240. For William and Guy Johnson, see Allen, *His Majesty's Indian Allies*, 22–39, 40–56. For John Stuart, see Hamer, "John Stuart's Indian Policy." For Thayendanegea or Joseph Brant, see Kelsay, *Joseph Brant*. For Athanase de Mézières, see Bolton, *Athanase de Mézières*.

25. Merritt, "Native Peoples," 241.

26. A. Davis, "Employment of Indian Auxiliaries," 713.

27. Washburn, "Indians and the American Revolution."

28. John Stuart to Lord Dartmouth, March 28, 1775, PRO, Colonial Office, Series 5/76, f. 89, in O'Donnell, *Southern Indians*, 18.

29. Starr, *Tories, Dons, and Rebels*, 73-74.

30. Boyd and Navarro Latorre, "Spanish Interest in British Florida," 130.

31. Alexander McGillivray to Arturo O'Neill, January 1, 1784, in Caughey, *McGillivray of the Creeks*, 65.

32. Starr, *Tories, Dons, and Rebels*, 74.

33. John Stuart to Alexander Cameron, December 16, 1775, PRO, Colonial Office, Series 5/77, in Starr, *Tories, Dons, and Rebels*, 76.

34. John Campbell to Lord George Germain, December 15, 1779, in Osborn, "Relations with the Indians," 267.

35. John Campbell to Sir Henry Clinton, July 18, 1780, British Headquarters Papers, 2919, reel 10, in Starr, *Tories, Dons, and Rebels*, 177.

36. Alexander Cameron to Sir Henry Clinton, Pensacola, July 18, 1780, in Historical Manuscripts Commission, *Report on American Manuscripts*, 2:159-60.

37. O'Brien, "Choctaw Defense," 124-25.

38. Starr, *Tories, Dons, and Rebels*, 179.

39. Caughey, *McGillivray of the Creeks*, 16.

40. A. Davis, "Employment of Indian Auxiliaries," 719.

41. Ibid.

42. George Washington to Major-General Schuyler, New York, April 19, 1776, in W. Ford, *Writings of George Washington*, 4:31.

43. Declaration of Independence, Philadelphia, July 4, 1776.

44. A. Davis, "Employment of Indian Auxiliaries," 726.

45. Bernardo de Gálvez to José de Gálvez, letter no. 116, New Orleans, December 30, 1777, AGI, Santo Domingo, 1598 A and B, and Santo Domingo, 2547, Duplicados de Gobernadores e Intendentes, dispatch 109; Bernardo de Gálvez to José de Gálvez, New Orleans, March 24, 1778, AGI, Santo Domingo, 2547, Duplicados de Gobernadores e Intendentes, dispatch 134; documents presented and read in the Council of War on July 15, 1778 (Documentos presentados y leídos en la Junta de Guerra que el Sr. D. Bernardo de Gálvez, Gobernador de esta Provincia, mandó celebrar y presidió en su casa el día 15 de julio de este año de 1778), AGI, Cuba, 182A; Medina Rojas, *José de Ezpeleta*, 68-69.

46. Calloway, *One Vast Winter Count*, 319.

47. Bernardo de Gálvez to John Campbell, Punta de la Mobila, April 6, 1780, AGI, Cuba, 193B.

48. Osborn, "Major-General John Campbell," 333; instructions to the governor of Mobile (Instrucción que deberá observar el Gobernador Interino del Castillo de la Mobila y Comandante Civil de su Distrito), Mobile, April 15, 1780, AGI, Cuba, 113; Medina Rojas, *José de Ezpeleta*, 41.

49. Enrique Grimarest to Bernardo de Gálvez, Mobile, April 24, 1780, AGI, Cuba, 4A.

50. José de Ezpeleta to Bernardo de Gálvez, Mobile, June 7, 1780, AGI, Cuba, 113; José de Ezpeleta to Antonio Pascual, official letter, Mobile, June 13, 1780, in ibid.; José de Ezpeleta to Bernardo de Gálvez, Mobile, 16 June 1780, in ibid.

51. John Campbell to Bernardo de Gálvez, Pensacola, April 20, 1780, in ibid., and also in Campbell Papers, Record Office, London, partially in Osborn, "Major-General John Campbell," 333.

52. List of merchandises needed in this post for gifts to the Indians (Relación de efectos que se necesitan en este destino para regalos de indios . . .), Mobile, May 22, 1780, AGI, Cuba, 2; Relación de los géneros y efectos que en el día nos

hacen más falta . . . , Mobile, May 31, 1780, AGI, Cuba, 81.

53. José de Ezpeleta to Bernardo de Gálvez, Mobile, May 10, 1780, AGI, Cuba, 81. This association is still evident in the last edition of the official Spanish dictionary, published in 2014 by the Real Academia Española de la Lengua (Spanish Royal Academy of Language), and has been strongly contested by members of the Roma community, who have threatened to sue the academy for racism. "El colectivo gitano denunciará a la RAE ante el Tribunal de Derechos Humanos [The gypsy associations would sue the Royal Spanish Academy in the European Court of Human Rights]," *El Pais*, November 8, 2014.

54. Alexander Cameron to George Germain, October 31, 1780, PRO, Colonial Office, Series 5/82, f. 111, in O'Donnell, *Southern Indians*, 158–59.

55. Bernardo de Gálvez to José de Ezpeleta, New Orleans, May 19, 1780, AGI, Cuba, 81; ibid., May 27, 1780, Cuba, 2; ibid., May 30, 1780, Cuba, 1377.

56. Medina Rojas, *José de Ezpeleta*, 365.

57. Ibid., 372.

58. Adelberg, *The American Revolution in Monmouth County*, 7; "Asymmetric Warfare"; Axelrod, *Real History*, 302; Chace, "Defining Asymmetric Warfare"; Skelton, "America's Frontier Wars."

59. Medina Rojas, *José de Ezpeleta*, 383; Kinnaird, *Spain in The Mississippi Valley*, 419.

60. Bernardo de Gálvez to José de Ezpeleta, Havana, November 20, 1780, AGI, Cuba, 1377.

61. Medina Rojas, *José de Ezpeleta*, 530.

62. José de Ezpeleta to Bernardo de Gálvez, Mobile, January 22, 1781, AGS, SGU, leg. 6912, 4.

63. According to Spanish reports, the casualties amounted to 200 regular soldiers and between 300 and 500 Indians. José de Ezpeleta to Bernardo de Gálvez, Mobile, January 19 and 22, 1781, in ibid.; John Campbell to Lord George Germain, Pensacola, January 5, 1781, PRO, Colonial Office, Series 5/597; John Campbell to Sir Henry Clinton, January 5, 1781, British Headquarters Papers, 9899, reel 27, in Starr, *Tories, Dons, and Rebels*, 187, and in PRO, Colonial Office, Series 30:55/89.

64. HMS *Mentor* is discussed in more detail below. HMS *Hound* was a small ship built in Deptford in 1776 and was in service up to 1784. See The Age of Nelson website, http://www.ageofnelson.org (accessed September 10, 2016).

65. José de Ezpeleta to Bernardo de Gálvez, Mobile, January 22, 1781, AGS, SGU, leg. 6912, 4.

66. José de Ezpeleta to Bernardo de Gálvez, Mobile, January 19 and 22, 1781, in ibid.

67. Medina Rojas, *José de Ezpeleta*, 537.

68. José de Ezpeleta to Bernardo de Gálvez, Mobile, January 22, 1781, AGS, SGU, leg. 6912, 4.

69. John Campbell to Dalling, Pensacola, January 9, 1781, PRO, Colonial Office, Series 137/80. Return of the killed and wounded, Village opposite Mobile, January 7, 1781, PRO, Colonial Office, Series 5/597, in Medina Rojas, *José de Ezpeleta*, 544, no. 25.

70. José de Ezpeleta to Bernardo de Gálvez, Mobile, January 19, 1781, AGS, SGU, leg. 6912, 4; José de Ezpeleta to Bernardo de Gálvez, Mobile, January 15, 1781, in ibid.; Relación de los muertos, heridos y prisioneros en el ataque del destacamento de la Aldea el 7 de enero de 1781, in ibid.

71. Benjamin Baynton to Peter Baynton, Pensacola, February 2, 1781, Pennsylvania State Archives, MG 19, Sequestered Baynton, Wharton and Morgan Papers, 1725-1827, part 3, Baynton Family Papers, 1770-1827, Correspondence of Benjamin Bayton, 1777-1785, On-Line Institute for Advanced Loyalist Studies, http://www.royalprovincial.com (accessed September 10, 2016).

72. José de Ezpeleta to Bernardo de Gálvez, Mobile, January 19, 1781, AGS, SGU, leg. 6912, 4.

73. Estado de fuerza del Regimiento Inmemorial del Rey, Havana, August 28, 1780, AGI, Santo Domingo, 2082.

74. Estado que manifiesta el número de oficiales y tropa que se compone la Expedición encargada al mando del Mariscal de Campo D. Bernardo de Gálvez, August 29, 1780, AGI, Cuba, 134A.

75. Copias de cartas intercambiadas en Bernardo de Gálvez y Victorio de Navia in Diego José Navarro to José de Gálvez, Havana, October 17, 1780, AGI, Santo Domingo, 2082.

76. Both diaries had been extensively quoted by Max von Eelking in his history on the German troops under the British flag during the Revolutionary War. Eelking, *German Allies*, 14. Eelking does not provide the date in which Captain Teutzel's diary ends.

77. John Campbell to Sir Henry Clinton, April 9, May 7, and May 12, 1781, PRO, Carleton Papers 30/55, in Rush, *Spain's Final Triumph*, 93-96, 96-100, 100-108.

78. The manuscript of James A. Mathews's diary is extensively quoted by J. F. H. Claiborne, who regrettably does not give any more details. Mathews, "Journal of the Siege," 1:126n; Farmar, "Journal of the Siege of Pensacola"; Rea, *Major Robert Farmar*, 143-45.

79. "A Journal of the siege of Pensacola West Florida 1781 by Robert Adulphus Farmar," copy in AFM, Viajes, vol. 3, fols. 104-12.

80. Lettres du chevalier de Monteil, commandant le *Palmier*, de la Havane, devant Pensacola, du Cap, puis montant le Languedoc, du Cap, ANF, Fonds Marine sous-série B/4: Campagnes; Mar/B/4/184, 1781-1782 (2 pièces de 1787), fols. 206r-298v, 1781; M. de Champmeslin, chef d'escadre, rend compte au Conseil de Marine de la prise des forts de Pensacola et de Sainte-Rose, ANF, Fonds Marine,

sous-série B/4: Campagnes; Mar/B/4/1 à Mar/B/4/203, 1571-1785 [1787], F°418-1720; Lettres du général don Bernardo de Galvez et du chef d'escadre don Solano et lettre du major général Campbell, de Pensacola / Relation française de la prise de Pensacola / Articles de la capitulation. ANF, Fonds Marine sous-série B/4: Campagnes; Mar/B/4/184, 1781-1782 (2 pièces de 1787), fols. 278r-298v, 1781.

81. *Diario del Jefe de la Escuadra D. José Solano, Toma de Panzacola, April y May 1781*, AGS, Marina 422.

82. W. S. Robertson, *La vida de Miranda*, 21-22; Valery, *Miranda en Pensacola*, 60-61.

83. *Diario de lo más particular ocurrido desde el día de nuestra salida del puerto de La Habana*, AFM, Viajes, vol. 3, fols. 70-75 and fols. 99-102.

84. *Diario de lo ocurrido en la escuadra, y tropas, que al mando del Jefe de Escuadra Don Josef Solano; y del Mariscal de Campo Don Juan Manuel de Cagigal, salieron de La Habana el 9 de Abril de 1781, para socorrer al ejército español, que atacaba la plaza de Panzacola. . . . Sitio de dicha plaza. . . . Su rendición &a*, in ibid., fols. 80-98. There is an English translation: Worcester, "Miranda's Diary of the Siege of Pensacola."

85. Farmar, "A Journal of the siege of Pensacola West Florida 1781," AFM, Viajes, vol. 3, fols. 104-12. Britain had acquired Florida in 1763, after the Seven Years' War. *Articles of Capitulation Between his Excellency Don Bernardo de Galvez, Knight Pensioner of the Royal and Distinguished order of Charles III . . . ; Diario de las operaciones de la expedición contra la Plaza de Panzacola concluida por las Armas de S.M. Católica bajo las órdenes del Mariscal de Campo D. Bernardo de Gálvez*, s.l., s.a., BPR, III/6526 (2), and BN, 2/12654 (hereafter *Diario de las operaciones . . .* , BPR/BN); "Diario de las operaciones . . ." (first manuscript), AGS, SGU, 6913, Ex3 (hereafter referred to as "first

manuscript"); *Scots Magazine*, 43 (1781); AFM, Viajes, vol. 3, fols. 117–20, http://www.franciscodemiranda.org/colombeia (accessed September 10, 2016).

86. Saavedra, *Diario*, 124–200; Saavedra, *Los Decenios*.

87. Medina Rojas, *José de Ezpeleta*, 829.

88. "Diario de las operaciones de la expedición contra la Plaza de Panzacola concluida por las Armas de S.M. Católica bajo las órdenes del Mariscal de Campo D. Bernardo de Gálvez," Bernardo de Gálvez to José de Gálvez, official letter, Pensacola, May 12, 1781, AGS, SGU, 6913, Ex3.

89. "Diario de las operaciones que ejecuta la expedición del mariscal de campo comandante general de ella del 9 de marzo al desembarco en la isla de Santa Rosa," s.l, s.a., no signature, in ibid., Ex12.

90. Among those who think it was published in Havana in 1781 are Antonio Palau y Dulcet, Pedro Vindel, and Charles Leclerc. Joseph Sabin and Obadiah Rich maintain it was printed in Madrid. Others, like José Toribio Medina, Donald E. Worcester, Fred Cubberly, and José Porrúa Turanzas, believe it was in Mexico City. To conclude, N. Orwin Rush offers the possibility of being printed in Pensacola or New Orleans. Palau y Dulcet, *Manual del librero hispano-americano*, vol. 6, item 96980; Vindel, *Catálogo de la Librería*, vol. 1, ítem 2173; Leclerc, *Bibliotheca Americana*, item 2526, 663; Sabin, *Dictionary of Books*, 7:144; Rich, *Bibliotheca Americana Nova*, 1:300; Medina, *La imprenta en México*, 6:324; Worcester, "Miranda's Diary of the Siege of Pensacola," 164; Cubberly, "Fort George (St. Michael) Pensacola"; B. Gálvez, *Diario de las operaciones contra la plaza de Panzacola 1781*, ed. Porrúa Turanzas; Rush, *Spain's Final Triumph*, 40.

91. *Diario de las operaciones . . .* , BPR/BN.

92. (1) Plano del Puerto de Panzacola, situado su boca en la Latitud no. de 30 grados y 14 minutos, y Longitud de 288 grados 4 minutos Meridiano de Tenerife, circa 1780, in Servicio Geográfico del Ejército, *Cartografía de Ultramar*, 370 and plate no. 93, and *Cartoteca histórica*, 16. (2) Francisco de Miranda, "Diario de lo mas particular ocurrido desde el día de nuestra salida del puerto de La Habana," s.l., s.a., AFM, Viajes, vol. 3, España, América, fols. 80–98, entry of April 29, 1781. (3) Huet, Plano de la villa de Pansacola [*sic*] en WE Florida del Fuerte Jorge y de las fortificaciones adyacentes últimamente construidas para la defensa y seguridad de dicha plaza por la nación Británica, y atacada por las fuerzas españolas al mando del mariscal de campo dn. Bernardo de Gálvez: rendida en 8 de mayo de 1781, Pensacola, May 19, 1781, map ms, AGI, Mapas y Planos—Florida Luisiana 247. (4) Planas, Plano de la villa de Panzacola, Fuerte Jorge, y fortificaciones adyacentes últimamente construídas por la Nación Británica, atacadas por las Fuerzas Españolas al mando del Mariscal de Casmpo D. Bernardo de Gálvez y rendidas el 8 de mayo de 1781, map ms, Servicio Geográfico del Ejército, in Servicio Geográfico del Ejército, *Cartografía de Ultramar*, 371–72, plate no. 94, and *Cartoteca histórica*, 16. (5) Plano de la Población de Pansacola [*sic*] conquistada por las Armas Españolas al mando del mariscal de campo D. Bernardo de Gálves [*sic*] en 8 de mayo de 1781 con el campamento y ataque para su rendición, map ms, s.l., s.a., in Servicio Geográfico del Ejército, *Cartografía de Ultramar*, 373, plate no. 95, and *Cartoteca histórica*, 16. (6) Plano de la villa de Panzacola, Fuerte Jorge, y Fortificaciones adyacentes últimamente construidas por la Nación Británica, atacadas por las fuerzas españolas, al mando del mariscal de campo don Bernardo de Gálvez, y rendidas el 8 de mayo de 1781, escala de 100 varas reales, map ms, s.l., s.a., Ministère de la Guerre, Archives Historiques, Vincennes, État Major 7C 224. (7) Plano de Panzacola, sus

Fuertes y ataques, map ms, s.l., s.a., Ministère de la Guerre, Inspection du Génie, Bibliothèque, Vincennes, 15-3. (8) Plan de la ville de Pensacola dans la West Floride, ms, s.l., s.a., Bibliothèque de la Service Hydrographique, Vincennes, 4044C-67. (9) Poruntilo y Labaggi, Plano de la Fuerte Plaza de Panzacola y de su Bahía situada al Norte del seno Mexicano, en la lat. De 30° y 30' y en la long. De 287° y 20' según el Meridiano de Tenerife. Conquistada a los Ingleses en 8 de Mayo de 1781 por las Armas del Rey Ntro. Sr. Mandadas por el valor y acierto del Excmo. Sr. D. Bernardo de Gálvez, conde de Gálvez, caballero pensionado de la Distinguida orden de Carlo 3° [sic], Comendador de Bolaños en la Calatrava, Teniente Gral. de los Reales Ejércitos y Comandante General de el de observación en América, map ms, Sevilla, 1783, AGS, MPD, 12, 090. (10) Toma de la Plaza de Panzacola y con ella la rendición de la Florida Occidental a las armas del Rey Carlos Tercero, Año de 1781, map ms, s.l., s.a., 6-A-20, in Martín Merás, "La toma de Pensacola a través de los mapas." (11) *Plano de los Ataques, y de las Fortificaciones de la plaza de Panzacola; la que rindieron los españoles el 8 de mayo de 1781.* (12) Joaquín de Peramar, Plano de la Bahía de Santa María de Gálvez, copia manuscrita de un plano inglés, map ms, in Servicio Geográfico del Ejército, *Cartografía de Ultramar*, 374, plate no. 96, and *Cartoteca histórica*, 16. (13) Heldring, *Map of the Harbour of Pensacola in West Florida*, map ms, s.l., 1781, University of Michigan Library, William L. Clements, Maps 5-J-9. (14) Plan of the siege of Fort George and works adjacent at Pensacola in West Florida, by Henry Heldring capt. lieut: in the 3th Regmt of Waldeck, & acting engineer at Pensacola, map ms, s.l., 1781, William L. Clements Library, University of Michigan, Maps 5-J-10. (15) Plan of Fort George and adjacent works at Pensacola in West Florida by Henry Heldring capt. 3d. Regt of Waldeck & engineer at Pensacola, map ms, s.l., 1781, William L. Clements Library, University of Michigan, Maps 5-J-11.

93. See Juan Manuel de Cagigal's intervention in the council of war held on November 30, 1780, AGI, Santo Domingo, 2082.

94. Bernardo de Gálvez's diary (*Diario de las operaciones . . .* , BPR/BN). The quotes in this section are from this document.

95. Medina Rojas, *José de Ezpeleta*, 651-69.

96. Bernardo de Gálvez to Diego José Navarro, Havana, December 10, 1780, AGI, Santo Domingo, 2083B.

97. Medina Rojas, *José de Ezpeleta*, 651-69; Saavedra, *Diario*, entry of January 22, 1781, 128-29.

98. Saavedra, *Diario*, 45.

99. Ibid., entry of February 4, 1781, 140.

100. Copy of the votes presented by the members of the Council of War held on November 30, 1780, as to whether the expedition against Pensacola should and could be tried again (Copia de los votos presentados por los señores vocales de la junta de generales en la celebrada el día 30 de noviembre de 1780, sobre si debía y se podía intentar de nuevo la expedición a Panzacola), Council of War, Havana, November 30, 1780, AGI, Santo Domingo 2082. Unless otherwise stated, the quotes in this section refer to this document.

101. Saavedra, *Diario*, entry of January 23, 1781, 134.

102. Ibid., February 9, 1781, 145.

103. Chevalier de Monteil to the French minister of the navy, aboard the *Palmier*, Havana, March 31, 1781, ANF, Fonds Marine sous-série B/4: Campagnes; Mar/B/4/184, fols. 219r-217v; ibid., April 4, 1781, fols. 222r-2225v.

104. Saavedra, *Diario*, entry of January 23, 1781, 129, and January 31, 1781, 136.

105. Ibid., February 5, 1781, 140-42.

106. Caughey, *Bernardo de Gálvez in Louisiana*, 200.

107. "Diario de las operaciones . . ." (second manuscript), AGS, SGU, 6913,

Ex12 (hereafter referred to as "second manuscript").

108. John Campbell to Sir Henry Clinton, January 5, 1781, British Headquarters Papers, 9899, reel 27, in PRO, Colonial Office, Series 30:55/89, in Osborn, "Major-General John Campbell," and in Faye, "British and Spanish Fortifications of Pensacola," 278.

109. "Diario de las operaciones..." (second manuscript).

110. José Calvo to Diego José Navarro, copy of the letter, s.l., s.a., included in the one from Diego José Navarro to José de Gálvez, Havana, April 6, 1781, AGI, Santo Domingo, 2083.

111. Francisco de Miranda, "Diario de lo mas particular ocurrido desde el día de nuestra salida del puerto de La Habana," s.l., s.a., AFM, Viajes, vol. 3, España, América, fols. 70–75.

112. The quotes in this section are from the correspondence exchanged between Gálvez and naval captain José Calvo between March 12 and 17, 1781, AGS, SGU, 6913, 2: Bernardo de Gálvez to José Calvo, Campo de la Isla de Santa Rosa, March 12, 1781; José Calvo, Miguel de Aldetere, Felix Goycoechea, José Zerrato, and José María Chacón to Bernardo de Gálvez, on board the *San Ramón*, March 13, 1781; Bernardo de Gálvez to José Calvo, Campo de la Isla de Santa Rosa, March 13, 1781; José Calvo to Bernardo de Gálvez, on board the *San Ramón*, March 14, 1781; José Calvo, Miguel de Aldetere, Felix Goycoechea, José Zerrato, and José María Chacón to Bernardo de Gálvez, on board the *San Ramón*, March 14, 1781; José Calvo to Bernardo de Gálvez, on board the *San Ramón*, March 15, 1781; Bernardo de Gálvez to José Calvo, Campo de la Isla de Santa Rosa, March 15, 1781; José Calvo to Bernardo de Gálvez, on board the *San Ramón*, March 16, 1781 (first of this date); Bernardo de Gálvez to José Calvo, Campo de la Isla de Santa Rosa, March 16, 1781; José Calvo to Bernardo de Gálvez, on board the *San Ramón*, March 16, 1781 (second of this date); Bernardo de Gálvez to José Calvo, Campo de la Isla de Santa Rosa, March 17, 1781.

113. Plano del Puerto de Panzacola, situado su boca en la Latitud no. de 30 grados y 14 minutos, y Longitud de 288 grados 4 minutos Meridiano de Tenerife, map ms, circa 1780, in Servicio Geográfico del Ejército, *Cartografía de Ultramar*, 370 and plate no. 93, and *Cartoteca histórica*, 16.

114. "Diario de las operaciones que ejecuta la expedición del mariscal de campo comandante general de ella desde el 9 de marzo que desembarcó en esta Isla de Santa Rosa," AGS, SGU, 6913, Ex12.

115. Francisco de Miranda, "Diario de lo mas particular ocurrido desde el día de nuestra salida del puerto de La Habana," s.l., s.a., AFM, Viajes, vol. 3, España, América, fols. 70–75.

116. José Calvo to the Marquis de González de Castejón, aboard the *San Ramón*, Havana, March 28, 1781, AGS, Marina, 421.

117. "Diario de las operaciones..." (second manuscript).

118. According to the equivalence between the ranks in the Spanish navy and those of the army (Correspondencia de las clases de oficiales de la Armada con los del Ejército), the rank of *mariscal de campo* (one star general) in the army was equivalent to *jefe de escuadra* (rear admiral) in the navy. *Ordenanzas de su Magestad* [sic], article 1, title 1, treaty 3, 103–4; ibid., article 5, title 3, treaty 3, 129.

119. The brig *Galvezton* and the *galeota Valenzuela*, named in honor of the third wife of his uncle José, were under direct command of Bernardo de Gálvez as governor of Louisiana. It is also relevant to mention that other two ships, with no documented relation with Gálvez (most probably the owners chose the names to try to ingratiate themselves with the Spanish authorities), would sail North American waters during the last part of the eighteenth-century. The brig

Don Galvez, owned by Joseph Hawkins of Boston, would be involved in illegal trade in South Carolina, Martinique, and Cuba, carrying slaves from the African Gold Coast (McMillin, *Final Victims*, 2:37; the Trans-Atlantic Slave Trade Database, http://www.slavevoyages.org [accessed April 15, 2017]; *House of Lords Sessional Papers*, 200). The *Countess de Galvez*, under Captain James Hoskins, was also involved in slave trade between the Gold Coast and Jamaica in the 1790s. In 1794, in its return to London from Jamaica, the *Countess de Galvez* was driven ashore and wrecked at Shoeburyness, Essex (Trans-Atlantic Slave Trade Database, http://www.slavevoyages.org [accessed April 15, 2017]; *Lloyd's List*, London, Friday, October 10, 1794). The ship called *La Joven Feliciana*, owned by Francisco Mayronne, was taking slaves into Galveston in 1790 (Francisco Mayronne suit against Domingo Assareto [sic: Assoret], January 15, 1790, London Metropolitan Archives, Records of Lloyd's of London RG 2, WPA 2358, Sp 1897).

120. Caughey, *Bernardo de Gálvez in Louisiana*, 203.

121. In this paragraph, Bernardo de Gálvez changes from the first to the third person.

122. "Diario de las operaciones..." (second manuscript).

123. *Ordenanzas de S.M. para el régimen, disciplina, subordinación y servicio de sus Exércitos. Ordenanzas de su Magestad [sic] para el Govierno [sic] Militar, Político, y Económico de su Armada Naval*.

124. Caughey, *Bernardo de Gálvez in Louisiana*, 198; José de Gálvez to Juan Manuel Cagigal, official letter draft copy, El Pardo, February 12, 1781 (first of this date), AGI, Santo Domingo, 2083 B.

125. Saavedra, *Diario*, entry of May 26, 1781, 200.

126. Juan Manuel de Cagigal to José de Gálvez, letter no. 18, Havana, June 14, 1781, AGI, Santo Domingo, 2083 B.

127. *Ordenanzas de su Magestad [sic] para el Govierno [sic] Militar, Político, y Económico de su Armada Naval*, article 1, title 1, treaty 3, 103–4.

128. Juan Bautista Bonet to José Calvo Irazábal, official letter, Havana, February 6, 1781, in *Diario de las operaciones...*, BPR/BN, 2.

129. *Ordenanzas de su Magestad [sic] para el Govierno [sic] Militar, Político, y Económico de su Armada Naval*, article 36, title 5, treaty 1, 77.

130. Caughey, *Bernardo de Gálvez in Louisiana*, 202.

131. Beerman, *Yo Solo*; Beerman, "Yo solo not solo"; Reparaz, *Yo Solo*; Victoria, *España contrataca*; Esparza, "Bernardo de Gálvez"; Villarejo and Villatoro, "Gálvez"; Mena, *Yo Solo*; King Juan Carlos I, speech in honor of Bernardo de Gálvez, Washington, D.C., June 3, 1976, http://www.casareal.es/noticias/news/1291-ides-idweb.html (accessed September 10, 2016).

132. Francisco de Miranda, "Diario de lo mas particular ocurrido desde el día de nuestra salida del puerto de La Habana," s.l., s.a., AFM, Viajes, vol. 3, España, América, fols. 70–75; "Diario de las operaciones que ejecuta la expedición del mariscal de campo comandante general de ella desde el 9 de marzo que desembarcó en esta Isla de Santa Rosa," s.l., s.a, AGS, SGU, 6913, 12; "Diario de las operaciones..." (second manuscript).

133. Real Cédula, Aranjuez, May 20, 1783, BN, ms, 10.639; Asiento de decreto de gracia a nombre de Bernardo Gálvez, sobre merced de título de Castilla para sí, sus hijos y sus sucesores, con revelación de lanzas y media annata para sola su persona, AHN, Consejos 2753, a. 1783, n. 4.

134. Bernardo de Gálvez to Pedro Rousseau, Guarico, April 15, 1782, certified copy by Gilberto Leonard and Manuel González, New Orleans, December 5, 1803, Rosemonde E. & Emile Kuntz Collection: Spanish Colonial Period, 1769–1803, Manuscripts Collection 600, Tulane University, Object File Name 600.3.83, http://specialcollections.tulane.edu

/archon/index.php?=collections/control card&id=785 (accessed November 20, 2015).

135. "Diario de las operaciones..." (second manuscript); "Diario de las operaciones..." (first manuscript); *Diario de las operaciones...*, BPR/BN.

136. Francisco de Miranda, "Diario de lo mas particular ocurrido desde el día de nuestra salida del puerto de La Habana," s.l., s.a., AFM, Viajes, vol. 3, España, América, fols. 70–75.

137. Ibid.

138. José Calvo to the Marquis de González de Castejón, aboard the *San Ramón*, Havana, March 28, 1781, AGS, Marina, 421.

139. Francisco de Miranda, "Diario de lo mas particular ocurrido desde el día de nuestra salida del puerto de La Habana," s.l., s.a., AFM, Viajes, vol. 3, España, América, fols. 70–75; *Diario de las operaciones...*, BPR/BN.

140. John Campbell to Lord George Germain, November 26, 1780, PRO, Colonial Office, Series 5/597, in Starr, *Tories, Dons, and Rebels*, 186.

141. Instructions from Bernardo de Gálvez to Arturo O'Neill, Pensacola, June 4, 1781, AGI, Cuba, 2359.

142. Francisco de Miranda, "Diario de lo mas particular ocurrido desde el día de nuestra salida del puerto de La Habana," s.l., s.a., AFM, Viajes, vol. 3, España, América, fols. 70–75.

143. José Calvo to Diego José Navarro, copy of the letter, s.l., s.a., included in the one from Diego José Navarro to José de Gálvez, Havana, April 6, 1781, AGI, Santo Domingo, 2083.

144. Saavedra, *Diario*, entry of April 5, 1781, 160.

145. Francisco de Miranda, "Diario de lo mas particular ocurrido desde el día de nuestra salida del puerto de La Habana," s.l., s.a., AFM, Viajes, vol. 3, España, América, fols. 70–75.

146. Ibid.

147. Miguel Alderete to José Calvo, aboard the frigate *Santa Clara*, Pensacola, March 22, 1781, AGS, Marina, 421.

148. José Calvo to the Marquis de González de Castejón, aboard the *San Ramón*, Havana, March 28, 1781, AGS, Marina, 421.

149. Ibid., Havana, June 25, 1781.

150. Fernández Duro, *Armada Española*, 7:397.

151. "Poema sobre la prudencia militar, deducida y fundada de los sucesos que presentan las historias sagradas y profanas, por las cuales se advierten las verdaderas causas de las pérdidas de los generales, batallas e imperios," mentioned by Fernández de Navarrete, *Biblioteca Marítima Española*, 2:50; "La impiedad de este siglo combatida en diferentes metros en defensa de la virtud y de la Religión," BN, ms, 5599, in *Inventario General de Manuscritos de la Biblioteca Nacional*, 10:421.

152. "It is extremely difficult to state the exact number of troops needed for the successful siege of an enemy's stronghold. But when there is no danger that enemy forces will come to its rescue, the number can be calculated the following way. In general, an army of twenty-four or twenty-five thousand men can surround a stronghold with six redoubts, and keep its garrison inside.... However, this calculation is given only as a comparison and never as a rule." Noizet de Saint-Paul, *Elementos de fortificación*, 178, no. 2.

153. Deiler, "German Waldeck Regiment," 202–7; Ingrao, "'Barbarous Strangers'"; Eelking, *German Allies*.

154. For the uniform of the Pennsylvania Loyalists, see Chartrand, Embleton and Embleton, *American Loyalist Troops*, 14; and Siebert, *Loyalists of Pennsylvania*.

155. For its uniform, see Chartrand, *American Loyalist Troops*, 12–13.

156. Osborn, "Major-General John Campbell," 319–20.

157. Cannon, *Historical Record of the Sixteenth*, 18–20.

158. Wallace, *Regimental Chronicle*, 9–12.

159. John Campbell to Sir Henry Clinton, February 19, 1779, British Headquarters Papers, 1737, reel 7, in Starr, *Tories, Dons, and Rebels*, 133.

160. Starr, *Tories, Dons, and Rebels*, 140.

161. Lord George Germain to the Lords of the Admiralty, January 6, 1776, PRO, Colonial Office, CO 5/123, in Starr, *Tories, Dons, and Rebels*, 51.

162. Minutes of the local council of Pensacola, September 7, 1776, PRO, Colonial Office, Series 5/634, in Starr, *Tories, Dons, and Rebels*, 54, no. 50.

163. John Campbell to Sir Henry Clinton, February 19, 1779, British Headquarters Papers, 1737, reel 7, in Starr, *Tories, Dons, and Rebels*, 133.

164. Ibid., 133.

165. Ibid., 134.

166. Sir Henry Clinton to John Campbell, October 21, 1780, British Headquarters Papers, 3079, reel 11, in Starr, *Tories, Dons, and Rebels*, 162.

167. Fort George was demolished years after the Revolutionary War, and the city of Pensacola grew on top of its remains. In 1976 a small part was reconstructed, which today stands in the corner between Palafox and Jackson Streets. Coker, "Pensacola, 1686-1821," 44–45. Also see Manuel, *Pensacola Bay*, 9–10; Quesada, *History of Florida Forts*, 38; and *Diario de las operaciones* . . . , BPR/BN.

168. Quesada, *Spanish Colonial Fortifications*, 22–23.

169. In March 1780 the *Mentor* captured the *Concepción* and the *San Joseph*; in May, the *El Santísimo Sacramento*; in August, the *Baton Rouge*; in October, the *Jesús, María y José*; and in March 1781, the *Santo Servando*. The descriptions of the captures by the *Mentor* are in its captain's report to Admiral Peter Parker in Jamaica, PRO, Admiralty 1/242, in Servies, *Log of H.M.S. Mentor*, 11–14, 22, 57n21; and Owsley, review of *The Log of H.M.S. Mentor*.

170. Log of the HMS *Mentor*, entry of April 14, 1781, in Servies, *Log of H.M.S. Mentor*, 176.

171. Bernardo de Gálvez to John Campbell, island of Santa Rosa, March 20, 1781, in *Diario de las operaciones* . . . , BPR/BN, and "Diario de las operaciones . . ." (first manuscript).

172. Juan [sic John] Campbell to Bernardo de Gálvez, Cuartel general de Pensacola, March 20, 1781, in *Diario de las operaciones* . . . , BPR/BN, and "Diario de las operaciones . . ." (first manuscript).

173. John Campbell to Bernardo de Gálvez, Cuartel General de Pensacola, March 21, 1781, in *Diario de las operaciones* . . . , BPR/BN, and "Diario de las operaciones . . ." (first manuscript).

174. Peter Chester to Bernardo de Gálvez, Pensacola, March 21, 1781 (second of this date), in *Diario de las operaciones* . . . , BPR/BN, and "Diario de las operaciones . . ." (first manuscript).

175. Starr, *Tories, Dons, and Rebels*, 34.

176. Rush, *Spain's Final Triumph*, 18.

177. John Campbell to Sir Henry Clinton, March 10, 1779, British Headquarters Papers, 1815, reel 7, in Starr, *Tories, Dons, and Rebels*, 139.

178. John Campbell to Sir Henry Clinton, May 18, 1780, PRO, Carleton Papers 30/55, in Historical Manuscripts Commission, *Report on American Manuscripts*, 2:124, and in Rush, *Spain's Final Triumph*, 21.

179. John Campbell to Sir Henry Clinton, September 18, 1780, PRO, Carleton Papers 30/55, in Historical Manuscripts Commission, *Report on American Manuscripts*, 2:124, and in Rush, *Spain's Final Triumph*, 22.

180. John Campbell to Sir Henry Clinton, April 9, 1781, PRO, Carleton Papers 30/55, in Historical Manuscripts Commission, *Report on American Manuscripts*, 2:124, and in Rush, *Spain's Final Triumph*, 95.

181. John Campbell to Sir Henry Clinton, May 7, 1781, PRO, Carleton Papers

30/55, in Historical Manuscripts Commission, *Report on American Manuscripts*, 2:124, and in Rush, *Spain's Final Triumph*, 100.

182. John Campbell to Sir Henry Clinton, May 12, 1781, PRO, Carleton Papers 30/55, in Historical Manuscripts Commission, *Report on American Manuscripts*, 2:124, and in Rush, *Spain's Final Triumph*, 106.

183. Minutes of the local council of Pensacola, February 17, 1780, PRO, Colonial Office, Series 5/635, in Starr, *Tories, Dons, and Rebels*, 182.

184. John Campbell to Lord George Germain, December 15, 1779, PRO, Colonial Office, Series 5/597, in Starr, *Tories, Dons, and Rebels*, 159.

185. James Bruce to John Pownal, October 16, 1777, PRO, Colonial Office, Series 5/155, in Starr, *Tories, Dons, and Rebels*, 65.

186. Bernardo de Gálvez to John Campbell, island of Santa Rosa, March 21, 1781, in *Diario de las operaciones* . . . , BPR/BN, and "Diario de las operaciones . . ." (first manuscript); Bernardo de Gálvez to Peter Chester, island of Santa Rosa, March 21, 1781, in *Diario de las operaciones* . . . , BPR/BN, and "Diario de las operaciones . . ." (first manuscript).

187. Bernardo de Gálvez to John Campbell, island of Santa Rosa, March 21, 1781, in *Diario de las operaciones* . . . , BPR/BN, and "Diario de las operaciones . . ." (first manuscript); Bernardo de Gálvez to Peter Chester, island of Santa Rosa, March 21, 1781, in *Diario de las operaciones* . . . , BPR/BN, and "Diario de las operaciones . . ." (first manuscript).

188. *Diario de las operaciones* . . . , BPR/BN; "Diario de las operaciones . . ." (first manuscript).

189. Bernardo de Gálvez to John Campbell, island of Santa Rosa, March 22, 1781, in *Diario de las operaciones* . . . , BPR/BN, and "Diario de las operaciones . . ." (first manuscript). This letter was accompanied by another to the governor of Pensacola with very similar content, Bernardo de Gálvez to Peter Chester, island of Santa Rosa, March 22, 1781, in *Diario de las operaciones* . . . , BPR/BN, and "Diario de las operaciones . . ." (first manuscript).

190. "Diario de las operaciones . . ." (second manuscript).

191. John Campbell to Bernardo de Gálvez, Pensacola, March 22, 1781, in *Diario de las operaciones* . . . , BPR/BN, and "Diario de las operaciones . . ." (first manuscript).

192. Noizet de Saint-Paul, *Elementos de fortificación*, 178, no. 2; Noizet de Saint-Paul, *Traité complet de fortification*.

193. Saavedra, *Diario*, entry of February 27, 1781, 149.

194. *Diario de las operaciones* . . . , BPR/BN; "Diario de las operaciones . . ." (first manuscript).

195. Ibid.

196. Ibid.

197. Lieux, "Malaria in Florida."

198. *Diario de las operaciones* . . . , BPR/BN; "Diario de las operaciones . . ." (first manuscript).

199. *Diario de las operaciones* . . . , BPR/BN; "Diario de las operaciones . . ." (first manuscript).

200. Quoted in Tsouras, *Warrior's Words*, 243.

201. Saavedra, *Diario*, entry of February 1, 1781, 137.

202. In a letter to his superiors in Paris, the commander of the French fleet informed them that he had no choice but to submit to the demands of the Spanish generals in Havana to form a joint fleet with the Spanish navy. The Chevalier de Monteil to the French minister of the Navy, on board the *Palmier* anchored before Pensacola, May 16, 1781, ANF, Fonds Marine sous-série B/4: Campagnes; Mar/B/4/184, fols. 240r–243v, f. 240r. The commander of the French fleet complained several times about the lack of cooperation from the Spanish authorities in Havana to refit and provision his

ships. See Chevalier de Monteil to the *Junta* of Havana, on board the *Palmier* anchored in Havana's port, February 10, 1781, in ibid., fols. 206r–208v; Chevalier de Monteil to the French minister of the Navy, on board the *Palmier* anchored in Havana's port, February 6, 1781, in ibid., fols. 210r–213r; Chevalier de Monteil to the *Junta* of Havana, on board the *Palmier* anchored in Havana's port, March 3, 1781, in ibid., fols. 214r–215v; Chevalier de Monteil to the *Junta* of Havana, on board the *Palmier* anchored in Havana's port, March 25, 1781, in ibid., fols. 216r–217v; and Saavedra, *Diario*, entries of February 11, 1781, 145–46, and March 13, 1781, 153–54.

203. Chevalier de Monteil to the French minister of the Navy, on board the *Palmier* anchored in Havana's port, March 28, 1781, ANF, Fonds Marine sous-série B/4: Campagnes; Mar/B/4/184, f. 218v.

204. Saavedra, *Diario*, entry of March 30, 1781, 158.

205. Ibid., April 1, 1781, 159.

206. Ibid., April 7, 1781, 162.

207. Lista de oficiales franceses que bajaron a tierra de la escuadra del caballero de Monteil. Hace presente en dicha lista se expresan las gracias que los unos esperan de su soberano por la intercesión de nuestro monarca y que los otros se recomienda [sic] a las que SM se sirva dispensarles, in Bernardo de Gálvez to José de Gálvez, dispatch no. 25, Pensacola, May 26, 1781 (first of this date), AGI, Santo Domingo, 2548, and AGS, SGU, leg. 6913, 4.

208. *Diario de las operaciones . . .* , BPR/BN; "Diario de las operaciones . . ." (first manuscript).

209. Saavedra, *Diario*, entry of April 22, 1781, 172.

210. John Campbell to Sir Henry Clinton, May 12, 1781, PRO, Carleton Papers 30/55, in Rush, *Spain's Final Triumph*, 100.

211. Eelking, *German Allies*, 14.

212. Saavedra, *Diario*, entry of April 21, 1781, 171.

213. Mathews, "Journal of the Siege," 1:126n.

214. The Aragon Regiment (Regimiento de Aragón), known as "The Formidable," was created in 1711 under the name Sagunto Dragoons and from 1715 was known as the Regiment of Aragon. In 1775 it participated in the failed attack on Algiers in which Bernardo de Gálvez also fought. In 1780 two of its battalions with 287 men were assigned to the expedition under the command of General Victorio de Navia for the relief of Pensacola. In 1783 it returned to Cadiz, Spain, and later garrisoned in Cartagena, Spain. Sotto, *Historia Orgánica de las Armas*, 11:374–419; Gómez Ruiz and Alonso Juanola, *El ejército de los borbones*, vol. 3/2, 46; *Estado militar de España para el año 1781*.

The Catalonia Volunteers Light Infantry Regiment (Regimiento de Infantería Ligera Voluntarios de Cataluña) had its origins in two battalions raised in 1762. It also fought in the 1775 expedition against Algiers. Its first battalion of 228 men was assigned to the Pensacola expedition. In 1783 three of its companies were detached for Havana's garrison, others for the Louisiana Fixed Infantry Regiment, and the rest returned to European Spain and were sent to Extremadura. Sotto, *Historia Orgánica de las Armas*, 13:399–417; *Estado militar de España para el año 1781*; Andreu Ocariz, "Militares catalanes."

The Spain Regiment (Regimiento de España), known as "The Martyr," was created in 1663 under the name Portugal Tercio and from 1718 bore the name Spain. In 1776 the entire regiment arrived in Havana, and one year later its first battalion was sent to Louisiana, where it fought in the campaign against the British settlements on the Mississippi. In 1780 its second battalion fought in Mobile, and the following year 482 men from the first and second battalions distinguished themselves at Pensacola. That same year it participated in the conquest of Providence Island. In 1784 it returned to Havana, where it stayed for a year before returning to European Spain. Sotto, *Historia Orgánica de las Armas*, 10:33–81; *Estado militar de España para el año 1781*.

The Flanders Valon Infantry Regiment (Regimiento de Infantería Valona de Flandes) was one of the four regiments from Flanders under the Spanish flag. Its origins dated back to 1596, but its name was not awarded until 1718. Some 424 of its men fought in Pensacola. In 1792 it was dissolved and its soldiers assigned to the Naples Regiment. *Estado militar de España para el año 1781*; Pérez Frías, "Unidades extranjeras en el Ejército borbónico," 636–37; Borreguero Beltrán, "Extranjeros al servicio del Ejército español."

The Guadalajara Regiment (Regimiento de Guadalajara), known as "The Tiger," had origins going back to 1657. In 1780 it sailed to Havana, from whence 328 of its men were assigned to the expedition against Pensacola. That same year they participated in the conquest of Providence Island. Sotto, *Historia Orgánica de las Armas*, 9:1256–318; Gómez Ruiz and Alonso Juanola, *El ejército de los borbones*, vol. 3/2, 46; *Estado militar de España para el año 1781*.

The Havana Fixed Infantry Regiment (Regimiento de Infantería Fijo de La Habana), or "The Noble," was one of the first military units to serve in Cuba in the sixteenth century. It was officially created in 1710, when a battalion was formed; it became a regiment in 1753. In 1769 one of its battalions served in New Orleans, and in 1779, under the command of Gálvez, that battalion of the Havana Fixed Infantry Regiment fought in the campaign against the British settlements on the Mississippi. The following year 244 of its men sailed with Gálvez from Cuba to Pensacola. Sotto, *Historia Orgánica de las Armas*, 11: 420–49; *Estado militar de España para el año 1781*; Gómez Ruiz and Alonso Juanola, *El ejército de los borbones*, vol. 3/2, 46.

The Hibernia Regiment (Regimiento de Hibernia), known as the Hibernian Column, had origins in the early eighteenth century, when five Irish infantry corps served under Philip V, the first Spanish king of the house of Bourbon. In 1717 it was named the First Irish Infantry Regiment. In honor of Ireland's patron, Saint Patrick, its uniform had green facings. In 1780 it was assigned to the expedition under Victorio de Navia and sailed to Cuba. In 1781 a company of grenadiers and seven companies of fusiliers sailed to Pensacola. They returned to Havana and the following year took Saint Augustine in Florida. In 1783 they were stationed in Havana until returning to Cadiz in 1788. Sotto, *Historia Orgánica de las Armas*, 11: 315–50; Pérez Frías, "Unidades extranjeras en el Ejército borbónico," 641; *Estado militar de España para el año 1781*; Murphy, "Irish Brigade"; Borreguero Beltrán, "Extranjeros al servicio del Ejército español."

The Mallorca Regiment (Regimiento de Mallorca), or "The Invincible," dated from 1682. In 1779 it sailed from Coruña to Havana and the following year, under Gálvez's command, took part in the campaign on the Mississippi. Four companies of its first battalion and two companies of grenadiers fought at Pensacola. In 1783 some of its members were reassigned to the Louisiana Fixed Infantry Regiment, and the rest embarked for Cadiz. Sotto, *Historia Orgánica de las Armas*, 10:82–136; *Estado militar de España para el año 1781*.

The Navarra Regiment (Regimiento de Navarra), or "The Triumphant," was created in 1705 under the name Tercio de Navarra. Its name was changed two years later to the Navarra Regiment. In 1775 it fought in Algiers and was garrisoned in Avila, where Francisco de Saavedra and Bernardo de Gálvez studied at the Royal Military Academy. In 1778 it sailed from Ferrol to Havana and two years later fought in Mobile, where it remained at its garrison under the command of José de Ezpeleta. In 1780, 360 of its men accompanied Ezpeleta to Pensacola. Later that same year a grenadier company and five companies of fusiliers were sent to suppress the revolt in Natchez. After 1783 most of its members were reassigned to other units, and the rest were discharged. Sotto, *Historia Orgánica de las Armas*, 11: 237-82; Gómez Ruiz and Alonso Juanola, *El ejército de los borbones*, vol. 3/2, 46; *Estado militar de España para el año 1781*.

The Prince's Regiment (Regimiento del Príncipe), or "The Bold," had origins in the early sixteenth century and changed its name in 1776. In 1769 it was posted to Caracas, Venezuela, and later that same year embarked for Cuba. In 1779 one of its companies was sent to Louisiana, where it fought in Mobile. Some of its units remaining in Havana were later sent to Pensacola. In 1782 it returned to European Spain. Sotto, *Historia Orgánica de las Armas*, 7:423-523; Gómez Ruiz and Alonso Juanola, *El ejército de los borbones*, vol. 3/2, 46; *Estado militar de España para el año 1781*.

The King's Regiment (Regimiento del Rey), or "The Brake," dated back to 1632 and received its name in 1766. In 1780 it embarked for Cuba under the command of Victorio de Navia. A small detachment, two grenadier companies, three fusiliers, and three smaller groups fought at Pensacola. In 1782 some of its members took part in the conquest of Providence and others in the rescue of Puerto Rico, and the rest occupied Saint Augustine, Florida. Sotto, *Historia Orgánica de las Armas*, 9:5-95; *Estado militar de España para el año 1781*.

The Soria Regiment (Regimiento de Soria), or "The Bloody," was founded as the Bravant Tercio in 1591 and changed its name several times until it was baptized Soria in 1715. In 1781, 495 of its troops participated in the conquest of Pensacola. In 1783 it was reinforced with soldiers from the Navarra Regiment and sent to the viceroyalty of Peru to repress Tupac Amaru's revolt. Sotto, *Historia Orgánica de las Armas*, 8:455-516; *Estado militar de España para el año 1781*.

America's Dragoons (Dragones de América) had origins in the King's Irish Dragoons Regiment created in 1754. In 1761 two of its squadrons were sent to Cuba, where they fought against the British attack. The Irish Dragoons were suppressed in 1763, and their cavalrymen, along with those of the Merida Dragoons, formed the America Dragoons. In 1781 ninety-seven cavalrymen sailed from Havana to join the attack against Pensacola. Sorando Muzás, *Banderas*; *Mercurio de España*, January 1781, 102-3.

The Havana Fusiliers Company (Compañía de Fusileros de La Habana) was a company of seventy-eight men from the Havana Fixed Infantry Regiment, created by Alejandro O'Reilly in July 1763. Gómez Ruiz and Alonso Juanola, *El ejército de los borbone*, vol. 3/2 11-12; Orden para 23 de abril, ordenes dadas desde el 22 hasta el 25 de marzo a los Destacamentos de La Habana y Movila, desde dicho día hasta el 21 de abril a los dos expresados y el de Orleans, y desde el 22 en que se reunió el refuerzo último hasta la rendición de Panzacola, AE, Papeles de Panzacola, in Medina Rojas, *José de Ezpeleta*, 766-67.

The Battalion of Havana Free Blacks (Batallón de morenos libres de La Habana) was identified as Havana's Colored Militias in Bernardo de Gálvez's list of troops under his command. Its strength in Pensacola was 262 men. Gómez Ruiz and Alonso Juanola, *El ejército de los borbones*, vol. 3/2 22-24; Orden para 23 de April . . . , in Medina Rojas, *José de Ezpeleta*, 766-67.

The New Orleans Colored Militia (Milicias de color de New Orleans) was represented by 173 of its men at Pensacola. Orden para 23 de April . . . , in Medina Rojas, *José de Ezpeleta*, 766-67.

215. Order for April 23 . . . , in Medina Rojas, *José de Ezpeleta*, 766-67.

216. José Solano to the Marquis de Castejón, Pensacola, May 18, 1781, copy included in the correspondence of Chevalier de Monteil, ANF, Fonds Marine sous-série B/4: Campagnes; Mar/B/4/184, f. 281.

217. Bernardo de Gálvez to the Marquis de Castejón, Pensacola, May 26, 1781, copy included in the correspondence of Chevalier de Monteil, in ibid., f. 284; Chevalier de Monteil to the French minister of the Navy, on board the *Palmier*, Pensacola, April 27, 1781, in ibid., fols. 232r–233v, f. 232r.

218. For further details about the French participation in the siege and conquest of Pensacola, see Quatrefages, "La participación militar de Francia."

219. Order for April 23 . . . , in Medina Rojas, *José de Ezpeleta*, 766–67.

220. The d'Agenois Regiment, after its return from Savannah in September 1779, was garrisoned in Martinique. Two of its companies fought at Pensacola. Lieutenant Alexandre-Claude-Louis-Mellon Soret de Boisbrunet, who was also at Yorktown, left an interesting diary of both campaigns. Susane, *Histoire de l'acienne infanterie française*, 3:383–87; Dawson, "New Record"; Dawson, "Les 2112 Français morts aux États-Unis."

The Cambresis Regiment was garrisoned in Haiti, from which two companies fought in Pensacola. Susane, *Histoire de l'acienne infanterie française*, 4:46–48.

The Poitou Regiment, like the Cambresis, was posted to Haiti and had a small detachment present in Pensacola, while the rest of its men were assigned to the French naval squadron under the command of the Count de Guishen. Susane, *Histoire de l'acienne infanterie française*, 4:46–48.

For the French seamen, see Bernardo de Gálvez to the Marquis de Castejón, Pensacola, May 26, 1781, copy in the correspondence of the Chevalier de Monteil, ANF, Fonds Marine sous-série B/4: Campagnes; Mar/B/4/184, f. 284; and Chevalier de Monteil to the French minister of the navy, on board the *Palmier*, Pensacola, April 27, 1781, in ibid., fols. 232r–233v, f. 232r.

221. Trentian, *French Regiments*.

222. Chevalier de Monteil to the French minister of the Navy, on board the *Palmier*, Pensacola, April 27, 1781, ANF, Fonds Marine sous-série B/4: Campagnes; Mar/B/4/184, fols. 232r–233v, f. 232r.

223. The Vauban method was first mentioned in 1688 in *Nouvelle manière de fortifier les Places*. Vauban's manuscript, with thirty-five drawings, plans, and illustrations, is in the Mazarin Library in Paris. Vauban, "Traité de l'attaque et de la deffense [sic] des places," ms, Bibliothèque Mazarin ms, 3772 y Conservatoire national des arts et métiers-Conservatoire numérique des Arts & Métiers, CNAM FOL RES QE 2, http://cn.cnam.fr/CGI/redir.cgi?FOLRESQE2 (accessed September 10, 2016). (There is a facsimile edition: Vauban. *Le triomphe de la méthode ou le Traité de l'attaque des places de monsieur de Vauban, ingénieur du roi*, edited by Nicolas Faucherre and Philippe Prost [Paris: Découvertes-Gallimard, 1992]. The first edition of Vauban's work would not be published until twenty-five years after his death: Vauban, *De l'Attaque et de la défense des places, par M. de Vauban* (Bibliothèque nationale de France, Paris, FRBNF39316942). Only the first part of this work could be attributed without doubt to Vauban; the second part seems to be a new edition of the "Discours sur la défense des places, présenté à Louis XIV en 1675" by Guillaume de La Fon de Boisguérin, msr. de Deshoulières (L'institut de la Gestion Publique et du Développement Économique, "Un dossier bio-bibliographique sur Sébastien Le Prestre, Marquis de Vauban," http://www.comite-histoire.minefi.gouv.fr/sections/igpde [accessed September 10, 2016]). The first Spanish translation appeared in 1743, *Tratado de la defensa de las plazas que escrivio [sic] Mr. de Vauban . . . para la instrucción del . . . Duque de Borgoña; traducido

de francés en español por Don Ignacio Sala...; y augmentado con algunas reflexiones, y addiciones...

224. *Diario de las operaciones...*, BPR/BN; "Diario de las operaciones..." (first manuscript).

225. Farmar, "Journal of the Siege of Pensacola," entry of April 22, 1781, 169.

226. Francisco de Miranda, "Diario de lo mas particular ocurrido desde el día de nuestra salida del puerto de La Habana," s.l., s.a., AFM, Viajes, vol. 3, España, América, fols. 70-75, entry of April 24, 1781; Saavedra, *Diario*, entry of April 24, 1781, 174.

227. *Diario de las operaciones...*, BPR/BN; "Diario de las operaciones..." (first manuscript); Saavedra, *Diario*, entry of April 25, 1781, 175-76.

228. Farmar, "Journal of the Siege of Pensacola," entry of April 24, 1781, 169.

229. As examples of this feu de joie, see *Reflexions sur le Feu de Joye*. See also *Diario de las operaciones...*, BPR/BN; "Diario de las operaciones..." (first manuscript).

230. Saavedra mentions two trenches, one of 500 *toesas* and the other of 700 (Saavedra, *Diario*, entry of April 29, 1781, 179). Medina Rojas calculates the total length of the trenches to be 700 *varas* (Medina Rojas, *José de Ezpeleta*, 768). Heldring says the trenches measured 2,600 feet (Heldring, *Map of the Harbour of Pensacola in West Florida*).

231. Saavedra, *Diario*, entry of May 4, 1781, 182.

232. Francisco de Miranda, "Diario de lo mas particular ocurrido desde el día de nuestra salida del puerto de La Habana," s.l., s.a., AFM, Viajes, vol. 3, España, América, fols. 70-75, entry of May 4, 1781.

233. *Diario de las operaciones...*, BPR/BN; "Diario de las operaciones..." (first manuscript).

234. Saavedra, *Diario*, entry of May 6, 1781, 185.

235. John Campbell to Sir Henry Clinton, May 7, 1781, PRO, Carleton Papers 30/55, in Rush, *Spain's Final Triumph*, 100.

236. Francisco de Miranda, "Diario de lo mas particular ocurrido desde el día de nuestra salida del puerto de La Habana," s.l., s.a., AFM, Viajes, vol. 3, España, América, fols. 70-75, entry of May 8, 1781.

237. *Artículos de capitulación* [Articles of Capitulation Between his Excellency Don Bernardo de Galvez, Knight Pensioner of the Royal and Distinguished order of Charles III, Major-General of the armies of his Catholic Majesty, Inspector, Intendant, and Governor General of the Province of Louisiana, and General of the Expedition &c. &c. &c. and His Excellency Peter Chester Esq; Captain-General, Governor, and Commander in Chief in and over his Majesty's province of West Florida, Chancellor and Vice Admiral of the same, &c. &c. &c. and his Excellency Major-General John Campbell, Commander of His Majesty's forces in the said province of West Florida]; *Scots Magazine*, 43 (1781).

238. *Diario de las operaciones...*, BPR/BN; "Diario de las operaciones..." (first manuscript).

239. *Diario de las operaciones...*, BPR/BN; "Diario de las operaciones..." (first manuscript). In his diary, Bernardo de Gálvez mentions 105 dead but does not include the wounded. The data shown here is from Coker, *Siege of Pensacola*, 120-21, drawn from original British official sources, PRO, Colonial Office, Series 5/597, f. 354. In his official report, General Campbell states a different number: 90 dead, 46 wounded, 23 deserters, and 1,030 prisoners (139 from the Red Cliffs garrison; 32 from Fort George; 73 from the civil branch of the ordinance; 149 from the navy; 11 from HQ; 30 officers; 7 servants; 10 Royal Artillery corps; 43 sergeants; 38 corporals; 31 fifes and drums; 466 soldiers; plus General Campbell himself). *London Magazine or Gentleman's Monthly Intelligencer*, 50, October 1781, 499-501; *Diario de las operaciones...*, BPR/BN; "Diario de las operaciones..." (first manuscript).

240. Chevalier de Luzerne to the Continental Congress, including a memorial by Francisco Rendón, Philadelphia, September 24, 1781, in Wharton, *Revolutionary Diplomatic Correspondence*, 4:728-29.

241. *Pennsylvania Gazette* (Philadelphia), August 8, 1781; *New-York Gazette*, July 16, 1781; *Weekly Mercury* (Philadelphia), July 16, 1781.

242. Summary of the arms and ammunition found in the forts and town of Penscola (Resumen de las armas y municiones que se han encontrado en los Fuertes y Plaza de Panzacola), in *Diario de las operaciones . . .* , BPR/BN. The full inventory is in "Inventario general hecho por d. Julián Álvarez, capitán graduado de aruntilería con asistencia del sr. D. Thomás del Rey, auditor de guerra de la presente Expedición y con intervención de d. Francisco Javier Navarro, guarda parque de la misma, de la artillería, montajes, carruajes, armas y demás utensilios de guerra que se han hallado y siguen en esta Plaza de Panzacola y Fuertes de ella de resultado de la toma por el Ejército de S. C. M. mandado por el sr. D. Bernardo de Gálvez, caballero pensionado de la distinguida Real orden de Carlos III, mariscal de campo de los Reales Ejércitos, y por disposición del sr. D. José Fajardo y Covarrubias, intendente de esta Expedición, que se verificó el día diez de mayo de este año," in "Diario de las operaciones . . ." (first manuscript).

243. José de Ezpeleta, list of dead and wounded of the army under General Gálvez from its disembarkation in the island of Santa Rosa to the surrender of Pensacola (Relación de los muertos y heridos que ha tenido el ejército a las órdenes del mariscal de campo el sr. D. Bernardo de Gálvez, desde su desembarco en la isla de Sta. Rosa hasta el día 8 de mayo, en que se rindió la Plaza de Panzacola), Pensacola, May 12, 1781, in *Diario de las operaciones . . .* , BPR/BN; and "Diario de las operaciones . . ." (first manuscript).

244. For the numbers and role of Choctaw and Creek fighters in Pensacola, see Holland Braund, "Anglo-Spanish Contest," 98-101; O'Donnell, "Hamstrung by Penury," 82-87; and Green, "Creek Confederacy," 69-72.

245. *Diario de las operaciones . . .* , BPR-BN; "Diario de las operaciones . . ." (first manuscript).

246. "Relación de las fortificaciones, provisionales, cuarteles, pabellones, casa de gobierno político, almacenes y demás edificios que pertenecen al Rey, y de la estimación prudencial de cada uno según el actual estado," signed by Antonio Fernández Trevejo, Pensacola, May 19, 1781, AGS, SGU, 6913, Ex3; "Inventario general hecho por d. Julián Álvarez, capitán graduado de aruntilería con asistencia del sr. D. Thomás del Rey . . . ," in "Diario de las operaciones . . ." (first manuscript).

247. Bernardo de Gálvez to Diego José Navarro, Pensacola, May 15, 1781, AGI, Santo Domingo, 1232.

248. Ibid.

249. Diego José Navarro to José de Gálvez, Havana, May 28, 1781, in Reparaz, *Yo Solo*, 203-6.

250. Bernardo de Gálvez to José de Gálvez, Pensacola, May 26, 1781 (third of this date), AGS, SGU, 6913, Ex3.

251. The estimated value of the constructions and forts at Pensacola was 1,440,900 pesos. "Relación de las fortificaciones, provisionales, cuarteles, pabellones . . . ," signed by Antonio Fernández Trevejo, Pensacola, May 19, 1781, AGS, SGU, 6913, Ex3.

252. *Mercurio Histórico y Político*, Madrid, July 1781, 291-92.

253. Diego José Navarro to José de Gálvez, Havana, May 28, 1781, in Reparaz, *Yo solo*, 203-6.

254. Petition of the Province of Louisiana to King Carlos III (Petición de la Provincia de Luisiana al Rey Carlos III), in *Representaciones al Rey Carlos III por el Consejo Superior en Nueva Orleans*, BN, Papeles sobre Luisiana, vol. 3, MS19248, hh. 36-46; *real cédula* of May 20, 1783,

BN, ms, 10.639; Petition by New Orleans' Notables to King Carlos III (Petición de los notables de Nueva Orleans al Rey Carlos III), New Orleans, October 12, 1781, AHN, Estado 4233, partially in Holmes, "Bernardo de Gálvez," 174.

255. Petition from the population of Lousiana to the king, in Esteban Miró to José de Gálvez, New Orleans, March 18, 1782, AGI, Santo Domingo, 2548.

256. *New Jersey Gazette* (Trenton), July 4, 1781, 3; *Pennsylvania Gazette*, July 4, 1781, 3; *New-York Gazette*, July 16, 1781; *Weekly Mercury*, July 16, 1781.

257. Samuel Huntington to Bernardo de Galvez, Philadelphia, June 23, 1781, in Smith, *Letters of Delegates to Congress*, 17: 344-45.

258. George Washington to Francisco Rendón, headquarters in front of York, June 8, 1781, in W. Ford, *Writings of George Washington*, 9:345.

259. George Washington to Francisco Rendón, headquarters in front of York, October 12, 1781, in W. Ford, *Writings of George Washington*, 9:379.

260. Samuel Huntington to George Washington, Philadelphia, July 3, 1781, in Smith, *Letters of Delegates to Congress*, 17: 366-67.

261. Narrett, *Adventurism and Empire*, 101.

262. Edmund Jennings to John Adams, Brussels, March 4, 1782, in *Adams Papers*. Richard Potts to Samuel Hughes, July 24, 1781, in Smith, ed., *Letters of Delegates to Congress*, 17:440-41.

263. *Royal American Gazette* (New York), September 21, 1780, 1.

264. *Maryland Journal*, published as *La Prensa* (Baltimore), November 21, 1780, 2; *New-Jersey Gazette*, December 6, 1780, 3; *Providence Gazette and Country Journal* (R.I.), December 20, 1780, 3; *Thomas's Massachusetts Spy Or, American Oracle of Liberty* (Worcester), December 21, 1780, 3.

265. *Pennsylvania Journal*, May 23, 1781, 3.

266. *The Connecticut Journal* (New Haven), May 31, 1781 2; *Pennsylvania Packet, or the General Advertiser* (Philadelphia), June 12, 1781, 2; *New Jersey Gazette*, June 13, 1781, 2; *Connecticut Journal*, June 28, 1781, 3.

267. *New-York Gazette, and Weekly Mercury* (New York), June 4, 1781, 2.

268. *Royal Georgia Gazette* (Savannah), June 21, 1781, 2.

269. *Freeman's Journal: or, The North-American Intelligencer* (Philadelphia, Pa.), July 18, 1781, 1, 2; *Royal American Gazette*, July 19, 1781, 2; *Pennsylvania Packet, or the General Advertiser*, July 21, 1781, 1; *Providence Gazette and Country Journal*, August 11, 1781, 1.

270. *New-Hampshire Gazette State Journal, and General Advertiser* (Portsmouth), July 30, 1781, 1.

271. Debate of May 21, 1781, in *Parliamentary Register*, 3:358-72.

272. "A bill to direct the payment into the Exchequer of the respective balances remaining in the hands of the several persons therein to be named, for the use and benefit of the public; and for indemnifying the said respective persons, and their representatives in respect of such payments, and against all future claims relating hitherto, and for other purposes therein to be mentioned."

273. Tory MP for Reigate between 1747 and 1784. Between 1772 and 1782, Sir Charles Cocks was clerk of the ordnance, a sort of secretary of the Board of Ordnance, the institution in charge of arms and ammunition supplies for the army and the navy.

274. Between November 1775 and February 1782, Lord Germaine was secretary of state for America. Lord Germaine was secretary of state for America and in Lord North's Tory cabinet.

275. Debate of May 21, 1781, in *Parliamentary Register*, 3:358-72.

276. *London Gazette*, August 7, 1781, 1-3.

277. Ibid., August 9, 1781, 1-4.

278. *Courrier d'Avignon*, July 31, 1781, 1.

279. *Gazeta de Madrid*, May 18, 1781.
280. Ibid., June 29, 1781.
281. Ibid., August 24, 1781.
282. See http://www.britishnewspaperarchive.co.uk (accessed September 10, 2016).
283. *Northampton Mercury*, May 7, 1781; *Leeds Intelligencer*, May 29, 1781; *London Magazine or Gentleman's Monthly Intelligencer*, May 1781, 240-41.
284. *Bath Chronicle and Weekly Gazette* (Somerset, England), June 14, 1781; *Hampshire Chronicle*, June 18 and 25, 1781; *Leeds Intelligencer*, June 26, 1781; *Caledonian Mercury*, June 27, 1781; *Norfolk Chronicle*, June 30, 1781; *Scots Magazine*, July 1, 1781; *Hampshire Chronicle* (Hampshire), July 2, 1781; *Leeds Intelligencer*, July 3, 1781; *Oxford Journal*, July 7, 1781; *Hereford Journal* (Herefordshire, England), July 12, 1781; *Derby Mercury*, July 19, 1781; *Hereford Journal*, July 26, 1781; *Newcastle Courant* (Tyne and Wear, England), July 28, 1781; *Northampton Mercury*, July 30, 1781.
285. *Newcastle Courant*, July 21, 1781; *Northampton Mercury*, July 23, 1781; *London Chronicle*, July 19-21, 1781.
286. *Derby Mercury*, July 26, 1781.
287. *Scots Magazine*, August 1, 1781; *Bath Chronicle and Weekly Gazette*, August 2, 1781; *Hereford Journal*, August 2, 1781; *Caledonian Mercury*, August 4, 1781; *Hampshire Chronicle*, August 6, 1781; *Reading Mercury*, August 6, 1781; *London Chronicle*, August 9-August 11, 1781; *Newcastle Courant*, August 11, 1781; *Northampton Mercury*, August 13, 1781.
288. *Leeds Intelligencer*, August 14, 1781; *Hereford Journal*, August 16, 1781; *Hampshire Chronicle*, August 20, 1781; *Derby Mercury*, August 30, 1781; *Derby Mercury*, September 6, 1781; *Hampshire Chronicle*, September 10, 1781; *Caledonian Mercury*, September 12, 1781; *Oxford Journal*, September 15, 1781; *Bath Chronicle and Weekly Gazette*, September 20, 1781; *Derby Mercury*, September 20, 1781; *Newcastle Courant*, September 22, 1781; *Norfolk Chronicle*, September 29, 1781; *Oxford Journal*, September 29, 1781; *Northampton Mercury*, October 1, 1781; *Scots Magazine*, December 2, 1781, *Leeds Intelligencer*, December 4, 1781.
289. *Bath Chronicle and Weekly Gazette*, August 16, 1781, and October 18, 1781; *Caledonian Mercury*, October 17, 1781, and October 31, 1781; *Derby Mercury*, November 15, 1781, October 11, 1781, and October 25, 1781; *Hampshire Chronicle*, August 20, 1781; *Ipswich Journal*, August 18, 1781, and October 6, 1781; *Leeds Intelligencer*, October 30, 1781, and October 9, 1781; *London Magazine or Gentleman's Monthly Intelligencer*, August 1781, 398-99, and October 1781, 499-501; *Newcastle Courant*, August 18, 1781, November 3, 1781, and October 20, 1781; *Norfolk Chronicle*, August 18, 1781, and November 3, 1781; *Northampton Mercury*, August 20, 1781, August 27, 1781, and October 22, 1781; *Oxford Journal*, August 18, 1781, and November 10, 1781; *Reading Mercury*, September 17, 1781; *Scots Magazine*, May 1, 1782, and October 1, 1781.
290. *Norfolk Chronicle*, September 15, 1781; *Reading Mercury*, September 17, 1781.
291. *London Magazine or Gentleman's Monthly Intelligencer*, 307-8, 336-37.
292. Relation fraçaise des operations relatives à la prise de Pensacola, s.l., s.a., ANF, Fonds Marine sous-série B/4: Campagnes; Mar/B/4/184, fols. 285r-287r, f. 287r.
293. Ibid., f. 286v; Chevalier de Monteil to the French minister of the navy, on board the *Palmier*, Pensacola, April 27, 1781, in ibid., fols. 232r-233v, f. 232; Chevalier de Monteil to the French minister of the navy, on board the *Palmier*, Pensacola, May 16, 1781, in ibid., fols. 234-37r, f. 234r.
294. *Les gazettes européennes du 18e siècle*, http://www.gazettes18e.fr (accessed September 10, 2016).
295. *Courrier d'Avignon*, June 1, 1781, 1-2; *Gazette de Leyde* (France), June 1, 1781, 7.

296. *Courrier d'Avignon*, June 22, 1781, 1–2; *Gazette de Leyde*, June 22, 1781, 1–2.

297. *Courrier d'Avignon*, June 26, 1781, 3; June 29, 1781, 2; July 20, 1781, 3.

298. Ibid., July 3, 1781, 1.

299. *Gazette de Leyde*, July 6, 1781, 5; *Courrier d'Avignon*, July 10, 1781, 1; *Gazette de Leyde*, July 17, 1781, 4–5.

300. *Courrier d'Avignon*, July 27, 1781, 2; *Gazette de Leyde*, July 31, 1781, 3.

301. *Courrier d'Avignon*, July 31, 1781, 1.

302. Ibid., August 7, 1781, 1; August 24, 1781, 2–3; September 7, 1781, 1–3.

303. Ibid., July 6, 1781; *Gazette de Leyde*, July 20, 1781, 5–6.

304. *Courrier d'Avignon*, August 21, 1781, 2.

305. *Mercurio Histórico y Político*, July 1781, 291–92; *Gazeta de Madrid*, August 10, 1781.

306. José de Gálvez to Bernardo de Gálvez, San Ildefonso, August 9, 1781 (first of this date), AGS, SGU, leg. 6913, 2.

307. José Viera y Clavijo to the Count de Aguilar, Spanish ambassador to Vienna, July 19, 1781, in Fernández Hernández, *Algunas cartas familiares*, 172–73.

308. José de Gálvez to Bernardo de Gálvez, San Ildefonso, August 9, 1781 (first of this date), AGS, SGU, leg. 6913, 2.

309. *Gazeta de Madrid*, May 11, 18, June 5, 29, 1781; *Mercurio Histórico y Político*, June 1781, 195–205, and July 1781, 291–92.

310. *Gazeta de Madrid*, February 16, 1781.

311. Ibid., August 10, 1781; *Diario de las operaciones...*, BPR/BN; *Gazeta de Madrid*, August 24, 1781; *Mercurio Histórico y Político*, August 1781, 386–409, and September 1781, 93–112.

312. The importance of reclaiming the island was such that January 6, the date of the Spanish attack, was and still is celebrated by the Spanish military as its day, the Pascua Militar. On that day, the Spanish head of state hosts a formal reception in Madrid's royal palace to honor members of the military.

313. See http://hemerotecadigital.bne.es/details.vm?q=id:0003829198&lang=es (accessed September 10, 2016); Cases, "El Censor."

314. *Gazeta de Madrid*, October 12, 1781.

315. *Nueva vista de Gibraltar*; *Ultima vista del castillo de S. Felipe y Mahón*, engraving; *Vista de Panzacola y su Baia*; *Verdadero retrato y relación anatómica*, engraving; Torres Pérez, "Pliego suelto fechado en 1781," 147–59.

316. *Noticiosa, verica, triunfante, y victoriosa relación que declara* (also in New York Public Library, New York, KF 1781).

317. Dueñas, *Rasgo épico en obsequio del excelentísimo señor don Bernardo de Gálvez, por la conquista de Panzacola*.

318. José de Gálvez to Juan Manuel Cagigal, official letter draft copy, El Pardo, February 12, 1781 (first of this date), AGI, Santo Domingo, 2083 B; José de Gálvez to Juan Manuel de Cagigal, El Pardo, February 12, 1781 (second of this date), AGI, Santo Domingo, 2082.

319. José de Gálvez to Juan Manuel Cagigal, official letter draft copy, El Pardo, February 12, 1781 (first of this date), AGI, Santo Domingo, 2083 B; José de Gálvez to the *intendente* of Havana, confidential letter, El Pardo February 12, 1781, AGI, Santo Domingo, 2082.

320. *Mercurio Histórico y Político*, November 1781, 273.

321. Ibid., June 1789, 186–87.

322. *Estado Militar de España del año 1783*, 74.

323. José de Gálvez to Juan Manuel de Cagigal, El Pardo, February 12, 1781 (second of this date), AGI, Santo Domingo, 2082.

324. José de Gálvez to Juan Manuel Cagigal, official letter draft copy, El Pardo, February 12, 1781 (first of this date), AGI, Santo Domingo, 2083 B; José de Gálvez to the *intendente* of Havana, El Pardo, confidential letter, February 12, 1781, AGI, Santo Domingo, 2082.

325. José de Gálvez to Juan Manuel

Cagigal, official letter draft copy, El Pardo, February 12, 1781 (first of this date), AGI, Santo Domingo, 2083 B.

326. Saavedra, *Diario*, entry of May 26, 1781, 200.

327. Relación de los oficiales, sargentos y cadetes que recomiendo a la piedad del Rey de resultas de la expedición de Panzacola, con expresión de Cuerpos, Clases, méritos y ascensos a que los considero acreedores, Pensacola, May 26, 1781, AGS, SGU, leg. 6913; relación de los individuos el Cuerpo de Ingenieros que se han hallado en la conquista de Panzacola y que considero acreedores de las gracias que para ellos solicito de la Real piedad, Pensacola, May 26, 1781, in ibid.; relación de los individuos del Real Cuerpo de Aruntilería que se han hallado en la conquista de Panzacola y que considero acreedores de las gracias que para ellos solicito de la real piedad, Pensacola, May 26, 1781, in ibid.; relación de los individuos del estado eclesiástico, Real Hacienda y Justicia que se han hallado en la expedición al mando del mariscal de campo Don Bernardo de Gálvez destinada a la conquista de Panzacola y recomiendo a la piedad del Rey, Pensacola, May 26, 1781, in ibid.

328. Comunica gracias y ascensos a los jefes de la expedición, José de Gálvez to Bernardo de Gálvez, San Ildefonso, August 8, 1781, in ibid.; relación de los oficiales, sargentos y cadetes del ejército que más se han distinguido en la conquista de Panzacola, y por lo mismo han merecido la Piedad del Rey los premios siguientes, San Ildefonso, August 9, 1781, in ibid.; comunica gracias a los individuos de los cuerpos de infantería, artillería e ingenieros, José de Gálvez to Miguel de Muzquiz, San Ildefonso, August 13, 1781, in ibid.; variaciones que ha habido en los cuerpos comprendidos en la promoción, s.l., s.a., in ibid.

329. Gracias solicitadas por Bernardo de Gálvez por la conquista de Pensacola, 1781, in ibid., 7, 8, 9, 10, and 12; *Mercurio Histórico y Político*, August 1781, 399–409.

330. Bernardo de Gálvez to José de Gálvez, dispatch no. 25, Pensacola, May 26, 1781 (first of this date), AGI, Santo Domingo, 2548, and AGS, SGU, leg. 6913, 4. On August 5, José de Gálvez sent a note to the Count of Floridablanca asking him to "give the appropriate order to our Ambassador in Paris in order for him to ask [from the king of France] for a suitable reward for those French officers [who participated in the Pensacola siege]." José de Gálvez to the Count of Floridablanca, August 5, 1781, in ibid. On August 9, the Count of Floridablanca instructed the Spanish ambassador in Paris accordingly, San Ildefonso, August 9, 1781, in ibid.

331. The data for the promotions are from *Estado Militar de España año de 1782*, 7–9. For the birth and death dates, see *Mercurio Histórico y Político* between 1782 and 1799.

332. José de Gálvez to Bernardo de Gálvez, San Ildefonso, August 9, 1781 (second of this date), AGS, SGU, leg. 6913, 5. The Red Cliffs fort was renamed San Carlos, and Fort George as San Miguel, for it surrendered on San Miguel's day.

333. Bernardo de Gálvez to José de Gálvez, Havana, October 26, 1781 (fourth of this date), AGI, Santo Domingo, 2083 B.

334. Bernardo de Gálvez to José de Gálvez, Havana, December 31, 1781, AGI, Santo Domingo, 2548.

335. Real cédula, Aranjuez, May 20, 1783, BN, ms, 10.639; Asiento de decreto de gracia a nombre de Bernardo Gálvez, sobre merced de título de Castilla para sí, sus hijos y sus sucesores, con revelación de lanzas y media annata para sola su persona, AHN, Consejos 2753, a. 1783, n. 4.

336. On August 14, 1782, Matías de Gálvez had been appointed acting viceroy of New Spain, and exactly one year later he was made full viceroy. Rodríguez del Valle and Conejo Díez de la Cortina, "Matías de Gálvez," 232–33.

337. Orden para 23 de April . . . , in Medina Rojas, *José de Ezpeleta*, 766–67.
338. Wright, "British East Florida."
339. Starr, "Left as a Gewgaw," 18.
340. Instructions from Bernardo de Gálvez to Arturo O'Neill, Pensacola, June 4, 1781, AGI, Cuba, 2359.
341. Troxler, "Loyalist Refugees."
342. Starr, "Left as a Gewgaw," 25.
343. Hamilton Chalmers had been ensign in the New Jersey Volunteers, a Loyalist unit. Morris, *The Papers of Robert Morris*, 55. The Guillermo Loende [sic] that appears in the Spanish documents could be William Lawrence, an ensign in the First Battalion of the New Jersey Volunteers. On-Line Institute for Advanced Loyalist Studies, http://www.royalprovincial.com (accessed September 10, 2016).
344. Alejandro O'Reilly, ruling, August 20, 1784, AGS, GM, Suplemento, 7; Borreguero Beltrán, "Extranjeros al servicio del Ejército español," 91.
345. Hamilton Chalmers to the Duke de Alcudia, Badajoz, June 3, 1793, AHN, Diversos-Colecciones, 18, n. 1681.

CHAPTER 7

1. British letters intercepted by the Spanish, dated September 9 and October 7, 1779, in Diego José Navarro to José de Gálvez, official letter no. 634, Havana, November 11, 1779 (second of this date), AGI, Santo Domingo, 2082.
2. British letter dated September 9, 1779, intercepted by the Spanish, ibid.
3. In Diego José Navarro to José de Gálvez, letter no. 666, Havana, December 28, 1779, AGI, Santo Domingo, 2082.
4. Caughey, *Bernardo de Gálvez in Louisiana*, 215.
5. "Información de una negra [sic] sobre el bloqueo del rebelde Blomart a Natchez," Martín Navarro to Bernardo de Gálvez, New Orleans, May 7, 1781, AGI, Cuba, 83; "Rendición del fuerte Natchez," official letter draft copy de Enrique Grimarest, New Orleans, May 13, 1781, AGI, Cuba, 114.
6. Martín Navarro to Bernardo de Gálvez, New Orleans, May 1, 1781, AGI, Cuba, 83.
7. Ibid.
8. Ibid., May 13, 1781; Bernardo de Gálvez to Esteban Miró, official letter, Pensacola, May 15, 1781, AGI, Cuba, 83; "Noticias de la rebelión de Natchez y operaciones que se están llevando a cabo para reducirla," Carlos de Grand-Pré, commander of Punta Cortada to Pedro Piernas, acting-governor of Louisiana, copy of the letter no. 155, Pointe Coupée, May 16, 1781, AGI, Cuba, 9A; Esteban Miró to Diego José Navarro, New Orleans, May 25, 1781, AGI, Santo Domingo, 2083 B.
9. Bernardo de Gálvez to Gerónimo Girón, Pensacola, May 26, 1781, AGI, Cuba, 2; Juan Manuel de Cagigal to José de Gálvez, letter no. 26, Havana, June 22, 1781, AGI, Santo Domingo, 2083 B.
10. "Condiciones para la capitulación de Natchez," Mr. Blommart to the governor of Louisiana, letter copy, Fort Panmure, June 2, 1781, AGI, Cuba, 8. For details about Natchez's revolt, see Caughey, *Bernardo de Gálvez in Louisiana*, 215–42; Siebert, "Loyalists in West Florida"; "Testimonio del Proceso," AGI, Santo Domingo, 2548; report on Natchez's revolt, Jorge Rapalie to Esteban Miró, Natchez, June 18, 1781, AGI, Cuba, 8; Bernardo de Gálvez to José de Gálvez, letter no. 462, New Orleans, July 19, 1781, AGI, Santo Domingo, 2083 B; Bernardo de Gálvez to Martín de Mayorga, viceroy of New Spain, official letter draft copy, July 23, 1781, AGI, Santo Domingo, 2085 A; Bernardo de Gálvez to José de Gálvez, letter no. 48, Havana, January 18, 1782 (first of this date), AGI, Santo Domingo, 254.
11. Esteban Miró to Mr. Hutchins, official letter copy, June 6, 1781, AGI, Cuba, 8.
12. Bernardo de Gálvez to John Campbell, June 3, 1781, AGI, Santo Domingo, 2548.

13. Bernardo de Gálvez to José de Gálvez, letter no. 29, Havana, October 26, 1781 (second of this date), AGI, Santo Domingo, 2548.

14. Miguel de Muzquiz to the Count of Floridablanca, Aranjuez, April 30, 1783, AGS, SGU, leg. 6913, 11.

15. Expediente sobre los oficiales ingleses Deans y Campbell retenidos por el teniente general don Bernardo de Gálvez en calidad de rehenes de resultas de la conquista de Panzacola, AGS, SGU, leg. 6913, 11.

16. In March 1780, the HMS *Mentor* captured the Spanish brig *Concepción* and the schooner *San Joseph*; in May, *El Santísimo Sacramento*; in August, the sloop *Baton Rouge*; in October, the *Jesús, María y José*; in March 1781, the schooner *Santo Servando*. For the report of the captain of the HMS *Mentor* to Admiral Peter Parker, see PRO, Admiralty 1/242, in Servies, *Log of H.M.S. Mentor*, 11–14, 22, 57n21.

17. Count of Floridablanca to José de Gálvez, San Lorenzo, December 26, 1782, AGS, SGU, leg. 6913, 11; royal decision, March 31, 1783, in the margin of the letter from Fernando de Rojas [?] to José de Gálvez, Valladolid, March 8, 1783, in ibid.; note by José de Gálvez in the margin of a letter from the Count of Floridablanca to José de Gálvez, Aranjuez, May 3, 1783, in ibid.

18. Caughey, *Bernardo de Gálvez in Louisiana*, 228–30.

19. Starr, "Left as a Gewgaw," 23.

20. For Dunmore's plans, see Robert Ross, "Observations on the Importance of Lousiana to Great Britain, with a state of the force now actually in it, & some hints which may be useful, should an attempt be made to reduce the Colony & try to annex it to His Majesty's Domnisons" [1782], PRO, 30/55/52; and Earl of Dunmore to George Germain, March 30, 1782, PRO/Colonial Office, Series 5/175. Also see Starr, "Left as a Gewgaw," 23. For detailed a study of Dunmore's plans, see Wright, "Lord Dunmore's Loyalist Asylum."

21. Din, "Loyalist Resistance after Pensacola"; Corbitt, "James Colbert"; Atkinson, *Spledid Land*; Haynes, *Natchez District*; Esteban Miró to Bernardo de Gálvez, New Orleans, June 5, 1782, Archivo Nacional de Cuba, Fondo Floridas, 3, 4.

22. Saavedra, *Diario*, entry of August 16, 1781, 208.

23. Juan Manuel de Cagigal to Bernardo de Gálvez, Havana, August 17, 1781, AGI, Santo Domingo, 2082.

24. José de Gálvez to Diego José Navarro, confidential letter, San Ildefonso, August 29, 1779, AGI, Cuba, 1290.

25. Acknowledgment of receipt of the order of June 19, 1780, which ordered Bernardo de Gálvez to attack Jamaica after conquering Pensacola, in Bernardo de Gálvez to José de Gálvez, confidential official letter no. 129, November 27, 1780, AGI, Santo Domingo, 1233.

26. "7. Pero si se verificase en la misma Isla de Jamaica la sublevación de los negros del palenque de ella y pidiesen auxilios para sostenerla, es preciso dárselos a toda costa, acudiendo con preferencia a aquel objeto como el de mayor importancia y consecuencia para facilitarnos una paz honrosa y ventajosa ... y finalmente suscitar a estos por todas partes cuantos embarazos y oposiciones sean posibles para distraerles y hacerles más difícil la defensa de la enunciada isla." José de Gálvez to Bernardo de Gálvez, confidential official letter draft copy, El Pardo, February 12, 1781, AGI, Santo Domingo, 2083 A.

27. Saavedra, *Diario*, entry of August 20, 1781, 209.

28. Ibid., May 31, 1781, 201.

29. El Guárico, alias, el cavo francés, es una de las colonias y puertos qe. posseen los franceses en la parte occidental de la Ysla Española, una de las de Barlosto. en la América septemtrional., situada en 19p0s44′ ms. de latd. no. y en 303p0s57′ mts. de longd. desde Tenerife en la vanda

del Norte de la ysla, 17 legs. al O. 1/4 SO del Monte Christo y 25 legs. al E. del Co. Sn. Nicolás, map ms, LoC Geography and Map Division, control no. 90683830.

30. Saavedra, *Diario*, entries of July 21, 1781, 204; July 25, 1781, 204; August 1-16, 1781, 206-8; and September 12, 1781, 214.

31. Diego José Navarro to José de Gálvez, confidential letter no. 133, Havana, January 15, 1781, AGI, Santo Domingo, 2083 B; Juan de Aysa, prisoner in Jamaica sends information, in Diego José Navarro to José de Gálvez, letter no. 934, Havana, January 27, 1781, in ibid.; consignment of 400,000 pesos to Bernardo de Gálvez for secret commissions, in Juan Ignacio de Urriza to José de Gálvez, letter no. 896, Havana, January 19, 1782, AGI, Santo Domingo, 1659; news on Jamaica from an escaped prisioner, in Pablo Figuerola, colonel of the regiment Cataluña, to Bernardo de Gálvez, Puerto Príncipe, June 6, 1782, AGI, Indiferente General, 1580; news on Jamiaca given by Jacobo Spitrionis [sic], Dutch spy, in Pablo Figuerola, colonel of the regiment Cataluña, to Bernardo de Gálvez, Port-au-Prince, June 23, 1782, AGI, Indiferente General, 1580; Saavedra, *Diario*, entry of September 6, 1781, 213.

32. "Se dirigirá VM con la posible brevedad por el Puerto del Batabanó [sic] al de Kingston en la Jamaica, para pactar, establecer, y concluir con su Gobernador, y Capitán General un cartel de canje formal entrc los súbditos de su Majestad Católica, y los de su Majestad Británica, que se hallan prisioneros en esta isla [Cuba], y la de Jamaica." Diego José Navarro, captain general of Cuba, to Francisco de Miranda, confidential instruction, Havana, August 9, 1781, AFM, Viajes vol. 3, fols. 128-44; Juan Manuel de Cagigal to H.E. the governor and captain general of Jamaica, Havana, August 9, 1781, in ibid.; Juan Manuel de Cagigal to vice admiral Pedro [Peter] Parker, commander general of the British naval forces in Jamaica, Havana, August 9, 1781, in ibid.

The exchange of prisioners was verified after the signature of the agreement (Convenio para el Canje de Prisioneros entre el Mariscal de Campo D. Juan Manuel de Cagigal, Gobernador de la Havana y Capitán General por Su Majestad Católica de la isla de Cuba y sus dependencias, etc., etc.; Su Excelencia el Mayor General Dalling, Capitán General, Gobernador y Comandante en Jefe por Su Majestad Británica de la isla de Jamaica; y el Caballero Pedro Parker, Vicealmirante de la Escuadra Blanca y Comandante en Jefe de los navíos y embarcaciones de Su Majestad Británica, empleados y por emplear en dicha isla de Jamaica y en el golfo de México desde el río Misisipi hasta el Cabo de Florida), Santiago de la Vega, aboard the ship of the line *Ramillies*, at the Bay of Puerto Real [Kingston], Jamaica, November 18, 1781, AFM, Viajes vol. 3, fols. 128-44.

"Informe presentado por el General Cagigal a Don José de Gálvez, ministro de Indias, sobre los servicios prestados por Francisco de Miranda en la Isla de Jamaica y su misión secreta, incluyendo recomendaciones en su favor," Havana, January 22, 1782, AFM, Viajes, vol. 4, fols. 57-63.

33. This interpretation is sustained by the letters sent from Juan Manuel de Cagigal to Bernardo de Gálvez, all in AFM, Viajes vol. 4: Havana, September 6, 1782, f. 101; Havana, September 7, 1782, f. 99; Havana, March 6, 1782, f. 67; Guarico, August 8, 1782, fols. 96-97; Havana, May 30, 1783 (version B), fols. 233-34. In http://www.franciscodemiranda.org/colombeia (accessed September 10, 2016).

34. See *History of Don Francisco de Miranda's Attempt to Effect a Revolution in South America*, 281; Bohórquez Morán, *Francisco de Miranda*, 90-92; Carrasco, *Francisco de Miranda*, 460-61; and Rumazo González, *Francisco de Miranda*, 51-52. The whole file of the inquiry against Francisco de Miranda can be found in Procesos y sentencias, Contrabando,

AGS, SGU, leg. 6844, 135. See also the following letters from Juan Ignacio de Urriza to Juan Manuel de Cagigal, all in AFM, Viajes, vol. 4: Havana, December 17, 1781, fols. 35-46; Havana, December 22, 1781, fols. 35-46; Havana, December 24, 1781, fols. 35-46; Havana, January 13, 1782, fols. 35-46; Havana, January 21, 1782, fols. 35-46.

35. Francisco de Miranda to King Carlos III through the Count of Floridablanca, London, April 10, 1785, in Miranda, *Documentos fundamentales*, 29.

36. Ibid., 30.

37. Francisco de Miranda to Juan Manuel de Cagigal, Allsops Buildings, near London, April 9, 1800. The letter contains the partial transcription of the sentence with the exculpatory verdict. Juan Manuel de Cagigal to Francisco de Miranda, Valencia, December 10, 1799, both in Antepara, *Miranda y la emancipación suramericana*. See also Bohórquez, *Francisco de Miranda*, 270-74.

38. Saavedra, *Diario*, entries of August 27 and 28, 1781, 210-11.

39. Ibid., January 28, 1782, 264-65.

40. Ibid., September 13, 1781, 214; September 22, 1781, 216; and January 26, 1782, 263-64.

41. McFarlane, *Colombia before Independence*, 252-71.

42. José de Gálvez to Bernardo de Gálvez, official letter draft copy, Aranjuez, April 6, 1782 (first of this date), AGI, Santo Domingo, 2084; Juan Ignacio de Urriza to José de Gálvez, Havana, April 9, 1782 (second of this date), in ibid.

43. The plans of the French-Spanish joint attack against Jamaica are in the following documents: (1) Francisco de Saavedra to José de Gálvez, confidential letter no. 5, Havana, February 16, 1781, AGI, Indiferente General, 1578; (2) Planes navales franceses transmitidos por Francisco de Saavedra a José de Gálvez, in Francisco de Saavedra to José de Gálvez, official letter, Havana, August 23, 1781 (second of this date), AGI, Indiferente General, 1599;

(3) José de Gálvez to Bernardo de Gálvez, confidential official letter draft copy, San Ildefonso, September 27, 1781, AGI, Santo Domingo, 2083 B; (4) Planes contra Jamaica de acuerdo con los franceses, in José de Gálvez to Bernardo de Gálvez, official letter draft copy, San Lorenzo el real, November 16, 1781 (first of this date), AGI, Santo Domingo, 2083 A; (5) José de Gálvez to Bernardo de Gálvez, most confidential official letter draft copy, San Lorenzo, November 16, 1781 (fourth of this date), AGI, Indiferente General, 1578; (6) José de Gálvez to Bernardo de Gálvez, official letter draft copy, Madrid, December 14, 1781 (second of this date), AGI, Santo Domingo, 2083 A; (7) Juan Ignacio de Urriza to José de Gálvez, confidential letter, Havana, April 9, 1782 (first of this date), AGI, Santo Domingo, 2084; (8) Plan de operaciones conjunto de España y Francia para atacar Jamaica, in Bernardo de Gálvez to José de Gálvez, confidential letter no. 40, Guarico, May 18, 1782 (second of this date), AGI, Santo Domingo, 2549; (9) Plan de operaciones francés para la toma de Jamaica, in Bernardo de Gálvez to José de Gálvez, extremely confidential letter no. 33, Guarico, May 18, 1782 (first of this date), AGI, Indiferente General, 1578, and Santo Domingo, 2549.

44. "Ha resuelto SM enviar desde Cádiz 4 navíos y 3 regimientos de infantería con destino al Guarico para que allí se unan a nuestra escuadra y ejército de Havana al mismo tiempo que las fuerzas francesas," in José de Gálvez to Bernardo de Gálvez, confidential official letter draft copy, San Ildefonso, September 27, 1781, AGI, Santo Domingo, 2083 B.

45. Saavedra, *Diario*, entry of February 1, 1782, 266.

46. Ibid., October 9, 1781, 222; October 13, 1781, 223; October 19, 1781, 226.

47. Ibid., January 22, 1782, 262.

48. Ibid., November 21, 1781, 240; December 9, 1781, 252-53.

49. "Propuso el rey a SM Cristianísimo que auxiliase en la empresa, y que

habiendo ofrecido hacerlo a fines de diciembre o primeros de enero con 15 navíos y 6000 hombres," in José de Gálvez to Bernardo de Gálvez, confidential official letter draft copy, San Ildefonso, September 27, 1781, AGI, Santo Domingo, 2083 B. See also the following from ANF, Fonds Marine sous-série B/4: Campagnes; Mar/B/4/184: Chevalier de Monteil to the Spanish generals junta in Havana, on board the *Palmier* at Havana's port, February 10, 1781, fols. 206r–208v; Chevalier de Monteil to the French minister of the Navy, on board the *Palmier* at Havana's port, February 6, 1781, fols. 210r–213r; Chevalier de Monteil to the *Junta* of Spanish generals in Havana, on board the *Palmier* at Havana's port, March 3, 1781, fols. 214r–215v.

50. Saavedra, *Diario*, entries of May 21, 201; July 22, 204; July 24, 204; July 26, 205; July 30, 205–6; September 24, 217, all from the year 1781.

51. Funds for the French navy, 1,000,000 and 500,000 pesos, in Juan Ignacio de Urriza to José de Gálvez, letter no. 861, Havana, October 26, 1781, AGI, Santo Domingo, 1657; 2,000,000 pesos for the French, in Juan Ignacio de Urriza to José de Gálvez, official letter no. 1038, Havana, December 20, 1782, AGI, Indiferente General, 1583.

52. Orders to Bernardo de Gálvez instructing him not to divide his forces from the French in order to always have a numeric superiority against the British, in José de Gálvez to Bernardo de Gálvez, Aranjuez, April 6, 1782 (second of this date), AGI, Santo Domingo, 2084; coordination of Spanish and French naval operations for the invasion of Jamaica, in José de Gálvez to Bernardo de Gálvez, El Pardo, January 24, 1782, AGI, Santo Domingo, 2084; coordination of plans with France for the conquest of Jamaica, in José de Gálvez to Bernardo de Gálvez, Madrid, December 14, 1781 (first of this date), AGI, Santo Domingo, 2083 A; plans for the attack against Jamaica in coordination with the French, in José de Gálvez to Bernardo de Gálvez, San Lorenzo, November 16, 1781 (second of this date), AGI, Santo Domingo, 2083 A.

53. Spanish sources: Plan de operaciones conjunto de España y Francia para atacar Jamaica, in Bernardo de Gálvez to José de Gálvez, confidential letter no. 40, Guarico, May 18, 1782 (second of this date), AGI, Santo Domingo, 2549; Plan de operaciones francés para la toma de Jamaica, in Bernardo de Gálvez to José de Gálvez, very confidential letter no. 33, Guarico, May 18, 1782 (first of this date), AGI, Indiferente General, 1578, and Santo Domingo, 2549. French sources: Chevalier de Monteil to the French minister of the navy on board the *Palmier* at Havana's port, April 8, 1781, ANF, Fonds Marine sous-série B/4: Campagnes; Mar/B/4/184, fols. 230r–231v; French naval plans sent by Francisco de Saavedra to José de Gálvez, in Francisco de Saavedra to José de Gálvez, Havana, August 23, 1781 (first of this date), AGI, Indiferente General, 1599. See also Saavedra, *Diario*, entries of May 31, 1781, 201; and July 18–26, 1781, 203–5.

54. Chevalier de Monteil to the French minister of the Navy on board the *Palmier* at Havana's port, March 31, 1781, ANF, Fonds Marine sous-série B/4: Campagnes; Mar/B/4/184, fols. 219r–217v.

55. Chevalier de Monteil to the French minister of the Navy on board the *Palmier* at Pensacola's port, April 27, 1781, in ibid., fols. 232r–233v, f. 232r; Chevalier de Monteil to the French minister of the Navy on board the *Palmier* at Penscola's port, May 16, 1781, in ibid., fols. 234–237r, 237r; Saavedra, *Diario*, entries of February 25, 1782, 272; March 18, 1782, 280; and March 29, 1782, 286–87.

56. Bernardo de Gálvez to José de Gálvez, dispatch no. 28, Guarico, April 8, 1782, AGI, Santo Domingo, 2549.

57. Ibid., very confidential no. 2, Havana, October 26, 1781 (first of this date), 2084 and 2549.

58. Saavedra, *Diario*, entry of October 11, 1781, 222–23.

59. Plan to attack New Providence, in José de Gálvez to Diego José Navarro, governor of Cuba, San Lorenzo, October 18, 1780, AGI, Santo Domingo, 2082.

60. Juan Ignacio de Urriza to José de Gálvez, confidential letter no. 81, Havana, November 18, 1781, AGI, Santo Domingo, 2084.

61. José de Gálvez to Diego José Navarro, confidential letter, San Ildefonso, August 29, 1779, AGI, Cuba, 1290.

62. Saavedra, *Diario*, entry of October 11, 1781, 222.

63. José de Gálvez to Bernardo de Gálvez, confidential official letter draft copy, El Pardo, February 12, 1781, AGI, Santo Domingo, 2083 A.

64. Saavedra, *Diario*, entry of October 11, 1781, 222–23.

65. Bernardo de Gálvez to Juan Manuel de Cagigal, Havana, January 20, 1782, AGI, Santo Domingo, 2085.

66. Juan Ignacio de Urriza to José de Gálvez, confidential letter no. 86, Havana, January 17, 1782, AGI, Santo Domingo, 2084.

67. Juan Manuel de Cagigal to Bernardo de Gálvez, Havana, March 14, 1782, AGI, Cuba, 1318.

68. Juan Ignacio de Urriza to José de Gálvez, confidential official letter no. 97, Havana, April 12, 1782, AGI, Santo Domingo, 2084.

69. On the military operations in New Providence, see the map Croquis de las inmediaciones a la villa de Nasso [*sic*: Nassau] en la isla de Providencia, de su puerto y sondeo de los canales que forman su callos, of which there are three identical copies: AGI, Mapas y Planos, Santo Domingo, 472; AGI, Mapas y Planos, Santo Domingo, 472bis; and Mapas y Planos, Mexico, 388. See also the map Mapa de la Ysla de Providencia, AGI, Mapas y Planos, Santo Domingo, 470.

70. Juan Martin Galiano, *ministro principal* of the Royal Treasury for the expedition [aganist New Providence] to Juan Ignacio de Urriza, New Providence, May 19, 1782, AGI, Santo Domingo, 2084.

71. Ibid.

72. Southey, *Chronological History of the West Indies*, 2:538; New Providence's articles of capitulation (Artículos de capitulación estipulados en Nassau de Nueva Providencia el 8 de mayo de 1782 entre el Excmo. sr. D. Juan Manuel de Cagigal, capitán general y comandante en jefe de Havana y el Excmo. Sr. D. Juan Maxwell esqr. Capitán general y comandante jefe de las islas de Bahama, canciller vicealmirante y primado de dichas islas y teniente coronel del ejército de SMB), in Juan Ignacio de Urriza to José de Gálvez, letter no. 965, Havana, June 10, 1782, AGI, Santo Domingo, 2084.

73. Juan Dabán, acting governor of Cuba, to José de Gálvez, letter no. 240, Havana, May 27, 1782, AGI, Santo Domingo, 2085 B; Bernardo de Gálvez to José de Gálvez, letter no. 133, Guarico, June 30, 1782, in ibid.

74. José de Gálvez to Bernardo de Gálvez, extremely confidential order, Aranjuez, April 6, 1782 (third of this date), AGI, Santo Domingo, 2084.

75. Bernardo de Gálvez to José de Gálvez, letter no. 264, Havana, June 7, 1783, AGI, Santo Domingo, 2549.

76. Juan Manuel de Cajigal to Bernardo de Gálvez, Havana, May 30, 1783 (version A), in ibid.

77. O'Shaughnessy, *Empire Divided*, 237.

78. Saavedra, *Diario*, entry of February 26, 1782, 272.

79. "Acaba salir felizmente de este puerto para el de Guarico la expedición que se estaba preparando al convoy de la escuadra del Tte. General José Solano, compuesta de los navíos de guerra *San Luis*, *San Nicolás*, *El Magnánimo*, *San Genaro*, *San Francisco de Paula*, *San Francisco de Asís* y *San Ramón*; corbetas *San Gil* y *la Liebre*; fragata el *Galveston* [*sic*] y bergantines el *Renombrado* y *El*

Galgo" (61 transportes: 23 fragatas, 11 paquebotes, 18 bergantines, 9 saetías y 3 goletas ligeras destinadas para correo), "En los barcos de transporte se ha embarcado la tropa . . . reducida a 372 oficiales, 59 cadetes, 12 capellanes, 11 cirujanos y 5288 soldados." Also see Noticia de la fuerza con que el ejército de operación al mando del mariscal de campo d. Gerónimo Girón se ha embarcado hoy día de la fecha en los navíos de guerra y transportes con expresión de las familias y criados (104 familiares y 74 criados), signed by Juan Ignacio de Urriza, Havana, March 2, 1782, all the documents in Juan Ignacio de Urriza to José de Gálvez, confidential letter no. 89, Havana, March 5, 1782, AGI, Santo Domingo, 2084.

80. "Noticia de la tropa del ejército de operación del mando del Excmo. sr. D Bernardo de Gálvez que ha fondeado en este puerto a las ordenes del mariscal de campo d. Jerónimo Girón," signed by Francisco Mendieta, Guarico, April 8, 1782, AGI, Santo Domingo, 2549.

81. No details have been found about his arrival except for a reference to the subject, in Bernardo de Gálvez to José de Gálvez, Guarico, dispatch no. 28, April 8, 1782, in ibid.

82. Bernardo de Gálvez to José de Gálvez, confidential official letter no. 23, Guarico, March 24, 1782, AGI, Santo Domingo, 2084; information about the delay in the departure of the French fleet, in José de Gálvez to Bernardo de Gálvez, El Pardo, January 15, 1782, in ibid.; waiting for the arrival of the French fleet, in Bernardo de Gálvez to José de Gálvez, confidential letter no. 19, Guarico, March 24, 1782, in ibid.; information on the reasons why he has not been able to attack Jamaica, in Bernardo de Gálvez to José de Gálvez, confidential official letter no. 23, Guarico, March 24, 1782, in ibid.

83. Saavedra, *Diario*, entry of April 20, 1782, 299–300.

84. Ibid., April 21, 1782, 301.

85. Cast for the commemorative medal of the Battle of the Saints, 1782, plaster cast, circa 1782, Object ID: SEC0959, National Maritime Museum, Greenwich, London.

86. All objects in this note can be found in the National Maritime Museum, Greenwich, London, and on its website: http://www.rmg.co.uk/national-maritime-museum. Captions in quote marks are taken from the website. Oil paintings: (1) Anon., *The Battle of the Saints, 1782*, oil on canvas, circa 1782. Object ID: BHC0447. (2) Nicholas Pocock, *The Battle of the Saints, 12 April 1782*, oil on canvas, circa 1782. Object ID: BHC0444. (3) Thomas Luny, *The Battle of the Saints, 12 April 1782*, oil on canvas, circa end of the eighteenth century and beginning of the nineteenth, Object ID: BHC0701. (4) Thomas Luny, *The Battle of the Saints, 1782*, oil on canvas, circa 1782. Object ID: BHC0439. (5) Thomas Luny, *The Battle of The Saints, 12 April 1782*, oil on canvas, 1782. Object ID: BHC0438. (6) Thomas Mitchell, *The Battle of the Saints, 12 April 1782*, oil on canvas, 1782. Object ID: BHC0441, Caird Collection. (7) Thomas Whitcombe, *The Battle of the Saints, 12 April 1782: Surrender of the "Ville de Paris,"* oil on canvas, 1783. Object ID: BHC0446. (8) Thomas Whitcombe, *The Battle of the Saints, 12 April 1782: End of the Action*, oil on canvas, 1782. Object ID: BHC0445, Caird Collection.

Dioramic model: Richard Paton, model of "Admiral Rodney's victory at the Battle of the Saints (1782) after an (engraved) 1783 painting by Richard Paton, with Admiral Sir George Rodney's flagship 'Formidable' on the left and Hood's 'Barfleur' on the right. The model combines false perspective and painting on glass, fitted into a gilded wooden case with concave metal panels painted 'en grisaille' inserted at each end." Object ID: MDL0011.

Shoe buckle: E. S. Thomason, "One of a pair of shoe buckles (JEW0007-0008) with a plain silver frame. The buckle has an iron chape with pitchfork prongs on an iron crossbar and a two-pronged iron roller. The inside of the buckle is inscribed with the words 'Victory over the French, Admiral Rodney & Admiral Hood 1782 12th of April.'" Object ID: JEW0008.

Badges: (1) Badge commemorating the Battle of the Saints, 1782. Perforated badge of oval form showing on either side *La Ville de Paris* under sails (two on fore, one on main and mizzen), flying the British above the French ensign at the stern, the Union flag crossed with the Royal standard above. Obverse: legend RODNEY FOR EVER 12 APRIL 82 A PROUD DAY FOR OLD ENGLAND. Below ship, LA VILLE DE PARIS. Reverse: legend STRUCK TO THE MAN WHO HAS HUMBLED SPAIN HOLLAND & FRANCE. Below ship, FORMIDABLE. Object ID MEC1141. (2) Badge commemorating the Battle of the Saints, 1782. Perforated badge of oval form showing *La Ville de Paris* under sails (one on fore and mizzen, three on main), flying the British above the French ensign at the stern. Obverse: legend, RODNEY FOR EVER 12 APRIL 82 A PROUD DAY FOR OLD ENGLAND. Below ship, LA VILLE DE PARIS. Reverse: legend, STRUCK TO THE MAN WHO HAS HUMBLED SPAIN HOLLAND & FRANCE. Below ship, FORMIDABLE. Object ID: MEC1140. (3) Badge commemorating the Battle of the Saints, 1782. Uniface. A pierced badge of oval form showing *La Ville de Paris* under main and mizzen topsails, flying the British above the French ensign at the stern, surrounded by a ribbon. Legend, VILLE DE PARIS TAKEN BY S G B RODNEY IN THE GLORIOUS ACTION 12 APRIL 1789. The property of a daughter of King George III. Object ID: MEC1139.

Ring: "Gold ring set with a mauve glass intaglio. The ring has an oval bezel and the design is contemporary. The intaglio is decorated with a depiction of a foul anchor and bears the inscription '12 Apl 1782 RODNEY L'ESPERANCE REALISÉE.'" Object ID: JEW0184.

Silver ladle: "Silver punch ladle commemorating the Battle of the Saints, 12 April 1782. The ladle has a semi-circular silver bowl with slight husk pattern on the flared collar and a pouring lip. . . . The underside of the bowl has an engraving of a French first rate wearing French fleurs de lys flags, and above it the inscription: 'The Ville de Parie taken ye 12 April 1782.'" Object ID: ZBA0483.

Goblet: John Schofield, "Silver goblet presented by the people of Martinique to Admiral George Brydges Rodney (1718?-92) to commemorate his victory at the Battle of the Saints, 12 April 1782. Plain goblet, gilded inside, standing on a circular foot with a beaded rim. Engraved with a scene of the French Admiral the Comte de Grasse handing the French colours to Britannia with the Flagship 'VILLE DE PARIS' in the background and Neptune standing with his trident. A putto above the figures plays a trumpet with the inscription '12 Apr 1782.' On the other side a crest of 'a dolphin naiant embowed, devouring a fish both proper' is that of Captain John Symonds, Rodney's flag captain of the 'Formidable.'" Object ID: PLT0081.

Mugs: (1) "Brown marbled mug, with three applied reliefs—an oval medallion of a ship inscribed 'VILLA DE PARIS' [*sic*] between two full length figures with banners behind inscribed 'LORD HOOD' and 'LORD RODNEY.'" Object ID: AAA4369. (2) Edward Withers (attrib.), "Chelsea-Derby porcelain jug commemorating the battle of the Saints, the lip modelled as the head of Admiral Sir George Brydges Rodney (1719-92), inscribed in gilt below: 'April the 12th 1782.' The jug is hand painted in natural colours, with coloured flower sprays on both sides and under the liIt has gilt rims and blue borders at the top and bottom and a glass base." Object ID: AAA4361.

Bowls: (1) "Ch'ien Lung Chinese export porcelain punch bowl with a deep foot, decorated on the outside with a grisaille painting of the Battle of the Saints

1782 after the published engraving by Robert Dodd. On one side are the arms of Sir Charles Douglas Bt [sic] (d. 1789), Rodney's Captain of the Fleet at the Saints. His motto is inscribed as: 'Lock Sicker' (be sure)—the Douglas family motto. The inner rim of the bowl is bordered with a pattern of green and gold, and there is a small floral motif on the bottom." Object ID: AAA4357. (2) "Ch'ien Lung punch bowl painted in grisaille with a depiction of the Battle of the Saints, 1782 after Robert Dodd. On the other side is a caricature based on 'Politeness' by James Gillray (a seated Englishman and Frenchman exchanging abusive remarks). Inscribed above the Englishman 'You be Damm'd,' his dog's collar is inscribed 'CTAS.' Above the Frenchman 'Vous etes une Bête' (you are a brute). There is a gilt lattice work border inside, and a circular floral pattern in the centre." Object ID: AAA4358.

Flask: "A carved flask made from a coconut depicting naval operations against the French in the West Indies during the American War of Independence. The eyes at the top of the nut have been formed into a bearded mask, with one enlarged into a mouth. The base is carved with a flaming sun. The sides are divided into two panels covering the entire surface. One side depicts the landing of troops at St. Kitts in January 1782 and Hood's fleet. It is inscribed: 'Landing ye, 28 & 69 Regs. on St. Kitts 28 Jan. 82,' 'the Frigates covering the Troops in landing,' 'THE ENGLISH LINE OF 22 SAIL.'" Object ID: OBJ0481.

87. Saavedra, *Diario*, entry of April 23, 1782, 303.

88. Bernardo de Gálvez to José de Gálvez, confidential letter no. 30, Guarico, April 26, 1782 (first of this date), AGI, Santo Domingo, 2084.

89. Bernardo de Gálvez to José de Gálvez, Guarico, April 26, 1782 (second of this date), AGI, Santo Domingo, 2549; Saavedra, *Diario*, entry of April 23, 1782, 303;

Bernardo de Gálvez to José de Gálvez, confidential letter no. 30, Guarico, April 26, 1782 (first of this date), AGI, Santo Domingo, 2084.

90. Copy of the letter from Bernardo de Gálvez to the Count of Aranda, in Bernardo de Gálvez to José de Gálvez, very confidential letter no. 33, Guarico, May 18, 1782 (first of this date), AGI, Indiferente General, 1578, and Santo Domingo, 2549.

91. Bernardo de Gálvez to José de Gálvez, confidential letter no. 44, Guarico, June 20, 1782, AGI, Santo Domingo, 2084.

92. Saavedra, *Diario*, entry of April 24, 1782, 304.

93. Bernardo de Gálvez to José de Gálvez, confidential letter no. 99, Guarico, December 20, 1782, AGI, Santo Domingo, 2549.

94. Bernardo de Gálvez to José de Gálvez, Guarico, June 23, 1782, in ibid.; Bernardo de Gálvez to José de Gálvez, confidential letter no. 60, Guarico, December 22, 1782, in ibid.

95. Cerified copy of Miguel de Gálvez's baptism certificate, in Autos de las pruebas para caballero de la orden de Calatrava que pretende Don Miguel de Gálvez y Satmagent [sic], cadete de la compañía Americana de Reales Guardias de Corps, aprobado en May de 1797, AHN, Órdenes Militares, Caballeros Calatrava, DF1009, fols. 47v–48v; pruebas para la concesión del Título de Caballero de la Orden de Calatrava de Miguel de Gálvez y Sant-Maxent, natural de Guarico (Haíti), Conde de Gálvez y Cadete de la Compañía Americana de Reales Guardias de Corps, in ibid.

96. Anonymous, *Guarico, 21 January 1783*.

97. Ibid.

98. The British national foreign debt almost doubled over the decade and by the end of the war amounted to £231,843,631. See Morales Lezcano, "Diplomacia y política financiera," 541, 563.

99. Cantillo, *Tratados*, 579–80.

100. Article 2 of the preliminary

articles (*artículos preliminares*) and article 4 of the final peace treaty (*tratado definitivo de paz*).

101. Articles 4, 5, and 3 of the preliminary articles and articles 6, 7, and 5 of the final peace treaty.

102. Chadwick, *Relations of the United States and Spain*, 4.

103. Conrotte, *La intervención de España en la independencia*, 8–9.

104. As an example of this traditional view, see J. H. Elliott's *Empires of the Atlantic World*, chapters 10 and 11.

105. Brewer, *Sinews of Power*, 175; Drayton, *Nature's Government*, 91–92; Paquette, "Image of Imperial Spain."

106. Colley, *Britons*, 135; Tucker and Hendrickson, *Fall of the British Empire*.

107. Paquette, *Enlightenment*, 150.

108. The traditional view on the impact of the Bourbon reforms of the Spanish Atlantic Empire that took place during the second half of the eighteenth century was that they opened the gates for the later independence of Spanish America in the early nineteenth century. The main argument behind this interpretation was that the reforms strengthened royal authority and metropolitan control over the American territories at the expense of the power and autonomy of the local American societies, especially the creole elites. However, recent contributions question this interpretation. Now the Spanish monarchy of the late eighteenth and early nineteenth centuries is no longer viewed as an empire at the verge of collapse but as an integrated ensemble with a high degree of administrative unity, and the origins of Spanish American independence not in the Bourbon imperial reforms but in the French invasion of the Iberian Peninsula in 1808. Eastman, "Sacred Mantle," 4; Guerra, *Modernidad e independencies*; Breña, *El primer liberalismo*; Breña, *El imperio de las circunstancias*; Breña, "Emancipation Process," 43; Echeverri, *Indian and Slave Royalists*, 10. On the evolution of the historiography on this subject, see Paquette, "Dissolution of the Spanish Atlantic Monarchy"; Varela Tortajada, "Nación"; Wasserman, "El concepto de nación"; Herzog, "Los americanos frente a la Monarquía"; and Donézar, "De las naciones-patrias."

109. Escudero, *El supuesto memorial del conde de Aranda*; Count of Aranda, Dictamen reservado que el Excelentísimo Señor Conde de Aranda dio al Rey Carlos III sobre la independencia de las colonias inglesas después de haber hecho el tratado de paz ajustado en París en el año 1783, AGI, Estado 91, no. 55 (a).

110. Escudero, *El supuesto memorial del conde de Aranda*.

111. Final peace treaty signed at Versailles, September 3, 1783, in Cantillo, *Tratados*, 586–90; Armillas Vicente, "Ayuda secreta y deuda oculta"; Carreño, *La diplomacia extraordinaria entre México y Estados Unidos*, vol. 1, 46, quoted in C. Ward, *War of the Revolution*, 63–93.

112. Preliminary articles of peace, November 30, 1782, in H. Miller, *Treaties and Other International Acts*, vol. 2, docs. 1–40, 1776–1818; the Paris Peace Treaty of September 30, 1783, in ibid.

113. For the border between the United States and Spain, see, DuVal, *Independence Lost*, 229–38; Bemis, *Diplomacy of the American Revolution*, 54–60; Wright, *Florida in the American Revolution*, 117–24; and Morris, *Peacemakers*, 441–43.

114. Armillas Vicente, "Ayuda secreta y deuda oculta," 195; San Miguel Pérez, "La crisis de la estrategia política," 31.

115. Count of Aranda to the Count of Floridablanca, Paris, August 10, 1782, AHN, Estado, leg. 3885, DF1.

116. Guardia Herrero, "Hacia la creación de la República Federal," 55.

117. Bernardo de Gálvez to José de Gálvez, Madrid, March 2, 1784, AHN, Estado 3885, DF 24, no. 2.

118. Esteban Miró to Bernardo de Gálvez, New Orleans, March 12, 1784, AHN, Estado 3885, ex18, no. 9; Artículos de capitulación convenidos y acordados

entre el Señor D. Bernardo de Gálvez, Caballero Pensionado de la Real y distinguida Orden de Carlos Tercero, Mariscal de Campo de los Reales Ejércitos de S.M. Católica, Inspector, Superintendente y Gobernador General de la Provincia de la Luisiana, y Comandante General de la Expedición; y los Excelentísimos Señores D. Pedro Chester, Escudero, Capitán General, Gobernador Comandante en Jefe, Canciller y Vice-Almirante por S.M. Británica de la Provincia de West-Florida, y Comandante General de las Tropas de S.M. Británica en dicha Provincia, in *Diario de las operaciones* . . . , BPR/BN; "Diario de las operaciones . . ." (first manuscript). See also Sáchez-Fabres, *Situación histórica de las Floridas*, 49.

119. Hilton, "El Missisippi y la Luisiana," 196–98.

120. Quoted in Reparaz, *Yo Solo*, 24.

121. Article 7 of the final treaty between the kings of Spain and France and the king of Great Britain signed in Paris, February 10, 1763, in Cantillo, *Tratados*, 486–94.

122. Article 8 of the final treaty between the United States of America and Great Britain, September 30, 1783, in ibid.

123. San Miguel Pérez, "La crisis de la estrategia política," 33.

124. Sáchez-Fabrés, *Situación histórica de las Floridas*, 49.

125. September 28, 1779, session, in Wharton, *Revolutionary Diplomatic Correspondence*, 3:344; and in *Journals of the Continental Congress*, 15:1168–69.

126. John Jay to Benjamin Franklin, San Ildefonso, September 8, 1780, in Jay, *Correspondence and Public Papers of John Jay*, 1:404–5; Benjamin Franklin to John Jay, Passy, France, October 2, 1780, in ibid., 432–34; Continental Congress, February 15, 1781, session, in *Journals of the Continental Congress*, 19:152–53.

127. John Jay to the president of the Continental Congress, San Ildefonso, October 3, 1781, in Jay, *Correspondence and Public Papers of John Jay*, 2:75–93;

also see John Jay to the president of the Continental Congress, Madrid, April 25, 1782, in ibid., 21–22.

128. Oliver Pollock to the president of the Continental Congress, October 15, 1781, in James, "Oliver Pollock," 345.

129. Benjamin Franklin to John Jay, Passy, France, April 22, 1782, in Franklin, *Writings of Benjamin Franklin*, 9:211–12.

130. Caughey, *Bernardo de Gálvez in Louisiana*, 252.

131. Instruction on the limits of the Floridas and Louisiana and on the navigation along the Mississippi, San Ildefonso, July 29, 1784, AHN, Estado 3384; see also Sáchez-Fabrés, *Situación histórica de las Floridas*, 52–54.

132. The 25 percent tax is a complicated issue. In 1787 the Spanish court approved a provisional tax of 25 percent on downriver shipments by Kentucky settlers, but a royal order of December 1, 1788, contained a more explicit policy measure, establishing a duty of 15 percent on goods shipped down the Mississippi to Louisiana by Kentucky residents and those settlers in bordering U.S. frontier regions, as a privilege offered to those living along the rivers emptying into the Ohio (Din, "Pierre Wouves D'Argés in North America"). Count of Floridablanca to Diego de Gardoqui, draft copy no. 4, San Ildefonso, September 5, 1787, AHN, Estado 3893 bis, no. 174, in Sáchez-Fabrés, *Situación histórica de las Floridas*, 57–58; explanation of the 1787 plan, Madrid, 1787, AHN, Estado 3889, ex1, no. 1.

133. Treaty of Friendship, Limits, and Navigation between Spain and the United States, October 27, 1795. In http://avalon.law.yale.edu/18th_century/sp1795.asp (accessed September 23, 2017).

134. Benjamin Franklin to John Jay, Passy, France, April 22, 1782, in Franklin, *Writings of Benjamin Franklin*, 9:211–12.

135. Bernardo de Gálvez to José de Gálvez (probably first months of 1783), AGI, Santo Domingo, 2549.

136. Accounts of the Expeditionary

Army (Cuentas del Ejército de Operaciones), AGI, Cuba 462, leg. 462.

137. Saavedra, *Diario*, entry of February 15, 1783, 345.

138. Caughey, *Bernardo de Gálvez in Louisiana*, 244.

139. Bernardo de Gálvez to José de Gálvez, Guarico, letter no. 230, April 6, 1783, AGI, Santo Domingo, 2549, and in AGI, Indiferente General 1578.

140. Copy of the letter from Bernardo de Gálvez to the Duke of Lancaster, in Bernardo de Gálvez to José de Gálvez, letter no. 242, Guarico, April 25, 1783, AGI, Santo Domingo, 2549. Other copies in AGI, Cuba, 9A and 116.

141. Duke of Lancaster to Bernardo de Gálvez, aboard the *Barfleur* at the Port of Jamaica, April 15, 1783, in Bernardo de Gálvez to José de Gálvez, letter no. 242, Guarico, April 25, 1783, AGI, Santo Domingo, 2549.

142. Bernardo de Gálvez to José de Gálvez, confidential letter no. 68, Guarico, April 9, 1783, in ibid.

143. Bernardo de Gálvez to José de Gálvez, confidential letter no. 73, Guarico, April 26, 1783, in ibid.

144. Instrucción de lo que deberá observar el brigadier D. José de Ezpeleta, Havana, June 10, 1783, AGI, Indiferente General, 1580, in Amores Carredano, "La capitanía general de Cuba," 787.

145. Bernardo de Gálvez to Juan Ignacio de Urriza, Havana, June 9, 1783, AGI, Indiferente General, 1579; Bernardo de Gálvez to José de Ezpeleta, instruction draft copy, Havana, July 10, 1783, in ibid., 1580; Porras Muñoz, "El fracaso de Guarico," 605–6.

146. Juan Ignacio de Urriza to Bernardo de Gálvez, Havana, June 26, 1783, AGI, Indiferente General, 1579; Porras Muñoz, "El fracaso de Guarico," 606.

147. Bernardo de Gálvez to José de Gálvez, Havana, May 26, 1783, AGI, Indiferente General, 1578.

148. Bernardo de Gálvez to José de Evia, instruction draft copy, Havana, July 14, 1783, in ibid., 1580; José de Evia to Bernardo de Gálvez, Havana, July 31, 1783, AGI, Cuba, 2360. Later we will consider the role played by Bernardo de Gálvez in promoting the geographical expeditions. See González-Ripoll Navarro, "Idea y representación," 86–87; Holmes, *José de Evia*; Martín Merás, *Cartografía marítima Hispana*, 191; Weddle, *Changing Tides*, 168–84; Paredes, *Plano de la bahía de Pansacola*; bishop of Cuba to Bernardo de Gálvez, Havana, January 18, 1783, AGI, Indiferente General, 1580; budget for the defense of Louisiana, Pensacola, and Mobile, New Orleans, November 7, 1783, AGI, Cuba, 116.

149. Saavedra, *Diario*, entry of October 5, 1781, 220.

150. Porras Muñoz, "El fracaso de Guarico," 605.

151. Proceso concedido sobre título de vizconde de Gálvez Tosón [*sic*: Galveztown or Galvezton] a Bernardo de Gálvez, May 2, 1783, AHN, 5085, mentioned in Porras Muñoz, "El fracaso de Guarico," 607. The value of the encomienda de Bolaños was 66,182 *reales de vellón*. In "Valor líquido en reales de vellón de la encomienda de Bolaños de la Orden de Calatrava," *Estado Militar de España, año de 1784*, 105.

152. Don Diego Paniagua, como apoderado de don Bernardo de Gálvez, conde de Gálvez, da en arriendo la encomienda de Bolaños, a don Luís de Valdelomar, Madrid, June 30, 1785, Protocolo notarial (public notary archives number) 21.385, mentioned in Matilla Tascón, *Catálogo de documentos notariales*, 206; *Mercurio histórico y político*, March 1793, 307.

153. Pruebas para la concesión del Título de Caballero de la Orden de Calatrava de Miguel de Gálvez y Sant-Maxent, natural de Guarico (Haíti), Conde de Gálvez y Cadete de la Compañía Americana de Reales Guardias de Corps, AHN, Órdenes Militares, Caballeros Calatrava, 1009; expediente sobre concesión del título de Castilla y de la encomienda de

Bolaños de la Orden de Calatrava, contiene: Título de Vizconde de Gálvez - Town [sic], cancelado, blasón y genealogía de la casa de los Gálvez, de Macharaviaya, y relación de méritos, AHN, Consejos 5085, a. 1783, DF2.

154. Beerman, "Governor Bernardo de Galvez's New Orleans Belle"; Beerman, "La bella criolla Felicitas"; Ezquerra, "Un patricio colonial"; Porras Muñoz, "Hace doscientos años"; Bernardo de Gálvez to José de Gálvez, Cádiz, September 9, 1783, AGI, Indiferente General, 1578.

155. Bernardo de Gálvez to José de Gálvez, Cádiz, September 9, 1783, AGI, Indiferente General, 1578; Stein and Stein, *El apogeo del imperio*, 220.

156. *Kalendario manual . . . 1784*, 55; *Kalendario manual . . . 1785*, 73; *Kalendario manual . . . 1786*, 77; Beerman, "Governor Bernardo de Galvez's New Orleans Belle," 43.

157. Don Diego Paniagua, como apoderado de don Bernardo de Gálvez, conde de Gálvez, da en subarriendo la casa que habitaba en Madrid dicho conde, Madrid, December 13, 1784. Protocolo notarial (public notary archives number) 21.384, f. 278, mentioned in Matilla Tascón, *Catálogo de documentos notariales*, 206.

158. Vicens Vives, *Historia de España y América*, 547.

159. Armillas Vicente, "Ayuda secreta y deuda oculta"; Caughey, *Bernardo de Gálvez in Louisiana*, 252; Reparaz, *Yo Solo*, 24; San Miguel Pérez, "La crisis de la estrategia política," 31; Bernardo de Gálvez to José de Gálvez, Madrid, March 2, 1784, AHN, Estado 3885, DF 24, no. 2; Esteban Miró to Bernardo de Gálvez, New Orleans, March 12, 1784, AHN, Estado 3885, ex18, no. 9.

160. The order to Gardoqui is mentioned in Sáchez-Fabrés, *Situación histórica de las Floridas*, 54; Bernardo de Gálvez to José de Gálvez, December 20, 1783, in Whitaker, *Documents Relating to the Commercial Policy*, 38–41; Vicente Manuel de Zéspedes to the Count de Gálvez, letter no. 22, Saint Augustine, Florida, September 21, 1784, AGI, Santo Domingo, 2543; Vicente Manuel de Zéspedes to the Count de Gálvez, letter no. 28, Saint Augustine, Florida, October 21, 1784, AGI, Santo Domingo, 2543.

161. Aguilar Piñal, *Bibliografía de autores españoles*, no. 1.191, 192–93, and no. 1.119, 149.

162. Olmeda y León, *Noticia del establecimiento*; Nussbaum and García Arias, *Historia del Derecho Internacional*, 486.

163. Lesen y Moreno, *Historia de la Sociedad Económica*, 111.

164. Covarrubias, *Memorias históricas*.

165. On José de Covarrubias, see Mariluz Urquijo, "Gestiones en torno de la formación," 237–49.

166. The original file of the censorship proceedings concerning the manuscript is in Madrid's Archivo Histórico Nacional, Consejos, Impresiones 5544, exp. 100. The work would be finally published twenty years later in a very modified version, Covarrubias, *Memorias históricas*.

167. Bernardo de Gálvez to José de Gálvez, Madrid [?], December 10, 1783, AGI, Santo Domingo, 2535; Bernardo de Gálvez to the Count of Floridablanca, Madrid, March 15, 1784, AGI, Cuba, 1373, in Porras Muñoz, "El fracaso de Guarico," 608–9. The plaque reads,

> Reinando Carlos III y siendo
> Obispo de Málaga el Ilmo. Sr.
> D. José Molina, a instancia de los
> ilustres hijos de esta villa D. Matías,
> D. José, D. Miguel, D. Antonio y
> D. Bernardo de Gálvez, el primero
> teniente general de los Reales
> Ejércitos y Virrey de Nueva España,
> el segundo Regidor Perpetuo de
> la Ciudad de Málaga, caballero
> Gran Cruz de la Real distinguida
> Orden de Carlos III, Consejero de
> Estado, gobernador de Indias y
> Secretario del Despacho Universal
> de este Departamento; el tercero

Regidor Perpetuo de dicha Ciudad de Málaga, caballero pensionado de la misma Real Orden y Consejero de Guerra; y el cuarto caballero pensionado de la misma Real Orden, Coronel de Infantería y comandante general de la bahía de Cádiz, y el quinto Conde de Gálvez, caballero de dicha Real Orden, comandante de Bolaños en la de Calatrava, teniente general de los reales ejércitos, gobernador y capitán general de la isla de Cuba, de la Luisiana y ambas Floridas. Se construyó de orden del rey esta Iglesia, sus capillas, altares, bóvedas y panteón a costa respectiva del fondo de su fábrica del de la Real de Naipes y del caudal de dichos señores patricios, bajo la dirección del Sr. D. José Ortega y Monroy, presbítero. Por el arquitecto D. Miguel del Castillo. Año 1785.

168. On the social mobility in Spain during the eighteenth century, see Soria Mesa, *La Nobleza en la España Moderna*, 245-47.

169. José Joaquín Domínguez Pareja-Obregón y Atienza, Baron de Gracia Real granted by King Carlos IV, royal dispatch, September 17, 1798, in Atienza y Navajas, *Nobiliario español*, 376; Bernardo de Gálvez to José Joaquín Domínguez Pareja-Obregón, San Lorenzo de El Escorial, November 20, 1783, BPR, II/4583 (1); Bernardo de Gálvez to José Joaquín Domínguez Pareja-Obregón, Madrid, January 4, 1784, BPR, II/4583 (2).

170. Ramos, *Descripción genealógica de la casa de Aguayo*. The family relation between the Gálvez and the Saavedra families was far from close. Miguel Pérez de Saavedra, godfather of Miguel de Gálvez (Bernardo's uncle), was probably the brother of Francisco de Saavedra, second Marquis of Rivas. See "Transcripción de la comparencia de Miguel de Gálvez ante el notario mayor Jorge del Águila," November 23, 1747, in Expediente de pruebas de caballero de la orden de Carlos III de Miguel de Gálvez y Gallardo, AHN, Estado-Carlos III, DF60, fols. 8r. and 8v.

171. Olmedo Checa, "Bernardo de Gálvez," 247.

172. "Paris, August 29, 1783—a hot-air balloon called Montgolfier was made," a description of the events during the presentation of the balloon is in *Gazeta de Madrid*, no. 74, September 16, 1783, 774. "Paris, October 14, 1783—Mr. Mongolfier would try to make new discoveries with his hot-air balloon," ibid., no. 87, October 31, 1783, 923-24. "Paris, November 21, 1783—report of an experiment with the hot-air balloon," ibid., no. 98, December 9, 1783, 1032-34.

173. Yajima et al., *Scientific Ballooning*, 3.

174. To the testimonies from André Giraud de Vilette and from the unknown author of the book *On the Art of War*, published in Paris in 1784, also see those of William Cooke and Benjamin Franklin. Cooke, *Air Balloon*; Benjamin Franklin to John Ingenhausz, January 16, 1784, in *Complete Works of Benjamin Franklin*, 8:432-33. Also see Haydon, *Military Ballooning*, 2-4.

175. Letter from André Giraud de Vilette to the editor, *Journal de Paris*, October 20, 1783.

176. Anonymous, *L'art de la guerre changée par l'usage de machines aérostatiques*, mentioned by Haydon, *Military Ballooning*, 3.

177. Robène, *L'homme à la conquête de l'air*, 63-70.

178. "Indiquer la maniére plus súre, la moins dispendieuse et la plus efficace de diriger a volonté les machines aérostatiques," in Delandine, *Manuscrits de la bibliothèque de Lyon*, 2:185-86.

179. Cavallo, *History and Practice of Aerostation*, 290-97.

180. Banks, "Sur un Moyen de Donner la Direction aux Machines Aérostatiques," 469.

181. Ibid. 470.

182. Vega González, *Ciencia*, 160.

183. Ibid., 138.

184. Mansilla Legoburo and Vidal Casero, "Casimiro Gómez Ortega."

185. Worsley, *Museum Worsleyanum*.

186. Gascoigne, "Joseph Banks and His Abiding Legacy."

187. Banks, "Sur un Moyen de Donner la Direction aux Machines Aérostatiques," 470.

188. Maty, *New Review*, 116; *Journal Encyclopedique ou Universel*, October 1785, vol. 7, part 1, 17.

189. *English Review*, 38.

190. *Critical Review, or, Annals of Literature*, 21.

191. No mention of Gálvez's aerostatic experiment has been found in the Spanish press of the time. Other news about hot-air balloons: Madrid, January 13, 1784. "Representación del famoso globo aerostático, se halla en las librerías de la viuda de Escribano," *Gazeta de Madrid*, January 13, 1784, 48; Antwerp, March 9, 1784. "Llegó a Warneton [sic] un globo aerostático," ibid., March 30, 1784, 282; Madrid, March 30, 1784. "Demostración de hacer el globo aerostático," ibid., March 30, 1784, 288; Madrid, June 1, 1784. "Diálogo sobre el globo aerostático y nave atmosférica entre un Abate y una Dama, de D. Fermín Jávaga Denia," ibid., June 1, 1784, 475–76; Madrid, September 3, 1784. "Experiencias hechas con el globo aerostático en Barcelona, se halla en la librería de Fernández," ibid., September 3, 1784, 746; "Escriben de Milán haberse hecho allí varios experimentos conformes a los executados en Paris con la máquina aerostática . . . ," *Mercurio de España*, January 1784, 1:39; "Canto en elogio de la brillante invención del globo aerostático y famosos viajeros aéreos, ejecutados por los célebres viajeros franceses en los días 21 de noviembre y 1 de diciembre de 1783, escribía Cipariso, labrador asturiano en las frondosas riberas del río Narcea. Se vende en dichas librerías," *Mercurio de España*, February 1785, Imprenta Real, Madrid, 180.

192. José de Gálvez to several American authorities, official letter copy, El Pardo, January 23, 1784, AGI, Indiferente General, 1948. On the border between the United States and Spain, see Bowen, *Correct map of the United States*; Kneass, *Map of the United States*; McMurray and Scot, *United States According to the Definitive Teatry* [sic]; and Pownall, *New map of North America*.

193. Luis de Las Casas to the Count de Campo de Alange, official letter no. 171, Havana, March 30, 1792, AGS, Guerra Moderna, 1, 6916; Zaro [sic], official letter draft copy, February 19, s.a. [1795?], in ibid., 6929, quoted in Andreu Ocariz, "Los intentos de separación de la capitanía general," 418.

194. Galbis Díez, "Bernardo de Gálvez," 332; Porras Muñoz, "Bernardo de Gálvez," 615.

195. Poder otorgado por don Bernardo de Gálvez, conde de Gálvez, teniente general de los Reales Ejércitos, y electo gobernador y capitán general de la isla de Cuba, Provincia de la Luisiana, Panzacola, las Floridas y demás agregados, a favor de don Diego Paniagua, Madrid, August 2, 1784. Protocolo notarial (public notary archives number) 21.384, f. 278, mentioned in Matilla Tascón, *Catálogo de documentos notariales*, 206.

196. *Mercurio de España*, September 1784, Imprenta Real, Madrid, 75–76.

197. Torre Revello, *Don Juan de San Martín*, 18.

198. Isidoro Váquez de Acuña says that the news arrived while Bernardo de Gálvez was in La Guaira, during a stop on his way to Havana, but due to its importance we believe that the news should have been sent directly from Mexico. Vázquez

de Acuña, "El capitán general," and Ibid. "El Conde de Gálvez," 82–83.

199. Galbis Díez, "Bernardo de Gálvez," 332.

200. *Gazeta de México*, February 22, 1785, in A. Valdés, *Historia de la Isla de Cuba*, 256; Vázquez de Acuña, "El Conde de Gálvez," 82–83.

201. Amores Carredano, "La elite cubana," 146.

202. Ibid.

203. During the time when Bernardo de Gálvez was governor in Havana, several nobility titles were under process (Nieto y Cortadellas, *Dignidades nobiliarias en Cuba*): Count de Casa-Barreto (Royal decree March 4, 1787, 107); Marquis de Casa-Calvo (Royal decree December 17, 1785, 128); Marquis de Casa-Peñalver (Royal decree February 28, 1790, 155); Count de Pozos-Dulces (Royal decree June 24, 1790, 395); Marquis de Prado-Ameno (Royal decree October 10, 1787, 400); Count de Santa Cruz de Mompox (Royal decree March 1, 1795, 520); Count de Santa María de Loreto (Royal decree January 15, 1787, 533). See also Gómez de Olea y Bustinza, *La Nobleza Titulada*, 44, no. 38.

204. José de Ezpeleta to José de Gálvez, Havana, August 7, 1786, AGI, Cuba, 1409; Amores Carredano, "La elite cubana," 146.

205. Pezuela, *Ensayo histórico de la isla de Cuba*, 308; Pezuela, *Diccionario geográfico*, 1:200.

206. Pezuela, *Historia de la Isla de Cuba*, 3:200.

207. Article 2, chap. 6, *Reglamento para las milicias de infantería y caballería de la isla de Cuba*.

208. Kuethe, "Development of the Cuban Military," 704.

209. Bernardo de Gálvez to Diego Navarro, New Orleans, August 17, 1779, AGI, Cuba, 2351.

210. *Real cédula*, January 24, 1785, AGI, Mexico, 1512.

211. Ibid.

212. Royal order, June 22, 1785, AGI, Mexico, 1417.

213. *Gazeta de México*, June 7, 1785.

CHAPTER 8

1. *Gazeta de Mexico*, June 7, 1785; Bernardo de Gálvez, Count de Gálvez, to the king, June 28, 1785, AGI, Mexico, 1287.

2. Mínguez, "Héroes clásicos," 62.

3. "Route that H.E. the Count of Gálvez, viceroy of New Spain, decided to take on his way to Mexico City" ("Derrotero que determinó seguir en su viaje a Mexico el Excmo. Sr. Conde de Gálvez, virrey de esta Nueva España"), *Gazeta de Mexico*, June 7, 1785.

4. García Panes, *Diario particular del camino*, 117.

5. Chiva Beltrán, "El ocaso de un ceremonial," 7.

6. The two previous viceroys, Martín de Mayorga (arrived in 1779) and Matías de Gálvez (arrived in 1783), had changed the tradicitional itinerary because they had arrived in New Spain from their previous postings as governors of Guatemala. Ibid.

7. *Real cédula*, January 24, 1785, AGI, Mexico, 1512.

8. Gómez, *Diario curioso de México*, 7:209.

9. Carlos Contreras Cruz and Claudia Patricia Pardo Hernández give slightly smaller figures than those of the 1790 census in "La ciudad de Puebla de los Ángeles," 556–68. See also table 87, "Población total del país por intendencia en 1790 y 1895; tasas de incremento medio anual por intendencias de los periodos 1742–1790 y 1790–1895," in Dirección General de Estadística, *1er Censo de población de la Nueva España*, 159.

10. Moriones, "Historia del proceso de beatificación."

11. García Panes, *Diario particular del camino*, 100; Cuenya, *Puebla de los Ángeles*, 89.

12. For details about the protocol while

entering Puebla and Tlaxcala, see García Panes, *Diario particular del camino*, 118–19; Chiva Beltrán, *El triunfo del virrey*; and Cárdenas Gutiérrez, "Las insignias del rey," 193–216.

13. Chiva Beltrán, *El triunfo del virrey*, 222, 97; García Panes, *Diario particular del camino*.

14. Vargas Lugo, "Imágenes de la inmaculada concepción," 78.

15. *Gazeta de Mexico*, June 21, 1785.

16. Copy of *real cédula*, El Pardo, March 14, 1785, AGI, Mexico, 1815, mentioned in Flores Moscoso, "Protocolo del cabildo secular," 464.

17. Audiencia gobernadora to José de Gálvez, letter no. 197, Mexico, June 28, 1785, AGI, Mexico, 1512; Gómez, *Diario curioso de México*, 7:210.

18. García Panes, *Diario particular del camino*, 117.

19. For details about the viceroys, see Calderón Quijano, *Los virreyes de la Nueva España en el reinado de Carlos III*; Rubio Mañé, *El virreinato*, 251.

20. Rubio Mañé, *El virreinato*, 249–52.

21. Ibid., 269–70.

22. In Gómez, *Diario curioso de México*, 7:213; Guzmán Wolffer, "Entrevista con Rafael Barajas"; Peña, *Dos siglos de risa mexicana*, 17; Zuno, *Historia de la Caricatura*, 16.

23. J. A. Torres, *Al buen entendedor*, 115.

24. Gómez, *Diario curioso de México*, 7:206.

25. Houdaille, "Frenchmen and Francophiles."

26. J. Miranda, *Humboldt y México*, 17–22.

27. Florescano and Gil Sánchez, "La época de las reformas borbónicas," 184.

28. Bernardo's wife's given name was Felicitas, but after their marriage she used its Spanish version: Feliciana. Beerman, "La bella criolla Felicitas."

29. Joseph Ignace Guillotin to Benjamin Franklin, Paris, June 18, 1787, *Papers of Benjamin Franklin*, http://franklinpapers.org/franklin/framed Volumes.jsp?vol=45&page=060 (accessed September 10, 2016).

30. Juan Antonio de Riaño, married to Victoire de Saint Maxent, was a naval officer whom Gálvez appointed mayor of Valladolid de Michoacán in 1786. Martínez y Gálvez, "La mujer y la vida familiar," 1394; see also Ezquerra, "Un patricio colonial." Lieutenant Colonel Manuel de Flon, Count de la Cadena, was married to Mariana de Saint Maxent. Gálvez would appoint him acting governor of the city of Puebla; see *Gazeta de Mexico*, January 24, 1786; Martínez y Gálvez, "La mujer y la vida familiar," 1394; and Ezquerra, "Un patricio colonial."; Avilés Flores, "La imagen de la independencia de México en Francia."

31. Avilés Flores, "La imagen de la independencia," 283–84.

32. Rivera Cambas, *Historia antigua y moderna*, 148.

33. Count of Revillagigedo to Antonio Valdés, Mexico, January 14, 1790, in *Precursores ideológicos*, 1:8, mentioned in Leonard, "1790 Theater Season," 107.

34. Solano, "Reformismo y Cultura Intelectual"; Molina Martínez, "Ilustración y reforma."

35. The auction of Gálvez's state started on June 21, 1787, *Gazeta de Mexico*, June 19, 1787.

36. Pérez Marchand, *Dos etapas ideológicas*, 110, 167.

37. León Meza C., "Ideas y lecturas," 136.

38. Ibid.

39. Morel, *Effusions du cœur*; Moreno Cebada, *Las herejías*, 4:478–79; *Index librorum prohibitorum*; Carbonero y Sol, *Índice de los libros prohibidos*, 454–55.

40. Luque Talaván, *Un universo de opiniones*, 176–79.

41. Moreri, *Le grand dictionnaire*, vol. 3.

42. Carbonero y Sol, *Índice de los libros prohibidos*, 455.

43. Maeder, "Libros, bibliotecas, control," 17; Millar Corbacho, "La Inquisición de Lima."

44. Solano, "Reformismo y Cultura Intelectual," 19; Molina Martínez, "Ilustración y reforma."

45. Houdaille, "Frenchmen and Francophiles," 10.

46. Esparza Castillo, "El retablo perpetuo," 17, 153; Rodríguez Moya, *El retrato en México*, 98–99; Suárez Fernández, *Historia general de España*, 13:610; Rojas, *La nueva sociabilidad política*, 29.

47. Castro Olivas, "Sociedades secretas," 106–7. On the Masonic activities of Felipe Fabris in Mexico, see Desdevises de Dezert, "L'Inquisition aux Indes Espagnoles," 106–7; Ferrer Benimeli, *La masonería española*, 293; Ferrer Benimeli, *La Masonería española*, 42; Martínez Moreno, "El establecimiento de las masonerías," 154–56; and Navarrete, *La masonería*, 28.

48. Sanchez Casado, *Los altos grados de la masonería*, 128–29; Aceves Pastrana, "La difusión de la ciencia"; Porras Muñoz, "Hace doscientos años," 323.

49. At the time, José de Ezpeleta was New Spain's general inspector of troops.

50. Gómez, *Diario curioso de México*, 214.

51. Ibid., 217.

52. Ibid., 106; *Kalendario manual . . . 1793*; Gómez Ruíz and Alonso Juanola, *El ejército de los borbones*, vol. 3/1, 9.

53. Gómez, *Diario curioso de México*, 210–28.

54. Moreto, *Comedia famosa*; Goldoni, *La posadera feliz*.

55. Chiva Beltrán, *El triunfo del virrey*, 106.

56. Díaz de la Vega, *Discurso sobre el objeto de los dramas*, in Solano, *Las voces de la ciudad*, 128; "Reglamento para la dirección del Coliseo de Mexico en lo gubernativo, económico y jurisdiccional, mandado observar por el virrey conde de Gálvez en 11 de April de 1786," Mexico, AGNM, Bandos 14, 62, in Solano, *Las voces de la ciudad*, 20. Also see Viqueira Albán, *¿Relajados y reprimidos?*, 228.

57. Peña, "El teatro novohispano," 167.

58. Jovellanos, "Memoria para el arreglo de la policía"; proclamation, April 11, 1786, Mexico, AGNM, Ramo Historia, vol. 473, ex16, fols. 77r–90v, Ramo Correspondencia de Virreyes, vol. 1, fols. 139–402, and Ramo Bandos, vol. 14, DF 24, fols. 62–75, in Mañón, *Historia del Teatro Principal de México*, 21–33.

59. Jovellanos, "Memoria para el arreglo de la policía," 293.

60. Viqueira Albán, *¿Relajados y reprimidos?*, 75; Galí i Boadella, *Historias del bello sexo*, 296.

61. *Reglas de gobierno de la sociedad de suscriptores del teatro de la ciudad de Mexico*, in Solano, *Las voces de la ciudad*, 62; Viqueira Albán, *¿Relajados y reprimidos?*, 59.

62. Olavarría y Ferrari, *Reseña histórica del teatro*, 1:53–63.

63. Viqueira Albán, *¿Relajados y reprimidos?*, 45; Rangel, *Historia del toreo en México*, 183.

64. McCarty, "La educación de un virrey," 101–2.

65. Viqueira Albán, *¿Relajados y reprimidos?*, 131.

66. Flores Hernández, "Organización de corridas de toros," 503; Rangel, *Historia del toreo en México*, 105, 55–56.

67. González Troyano, "Algunos libros de toros," 187.

68. Sánchez Álvarez-Insúa, "Toros y sociedad," 902–4.

69. The *cucaña* was a greased pole with prizes on the top. This entertainment took place during bullfight intermissions. On all kinds of "other entertainments" during or between bullfights, see Rangel, *Historia del toreo en México*.

70. Gómez, *Diario curioso de México*, 7:227.

71. Porras Muñoz, "Bernardo de Gálvez," 619; Gómez, *Diario curioso de México*, 7:222, 223.

72. Gómez, *Diario curioso de México*, 7:223.

73. Viqueira Albán, *¿Relajados y reprimidos?*, 40.

74. Ibid.; Gómez, *Diario curioso de México*, 7:226–27.
75. Viqueira Albán, *¿Relajados y reprimidos?*, 36–39.
76. Rangel, *Historia del toreo en México*, 185.
77. Gómez, *Diario curioso de México*, 7:222.
78. Cavo and Bustamante, *Los tres siglos de México*, 3:57.
79. Gómez, *Diario curioso de México*, 7:227.
80. Ibid.
81. Ibid., 226, 228.
82. Ibid., 219.
83. In March and May 1786. Gómez, *Diario curioso de México*, 7:234, 238.
84. Ibid., 238.
85. Schama, *Landscape and Memory*.
86. Muñoz Rebolledo and Juan Luis Isaza L., "Naturaleza, jardín y ciudad," 9.
87. Gómez, *Diario curioso de México*, 7:236.
88. Boeta, *Bernardo de Gálvez*, 120; Cavo and Bustamante, *Los tres siglos de México*, 3:62; Valle-Arizpe, *Virreyes y virreinas*, 155.
89. Fernández-Carrión, "Vida privada del Virrey," 465.
90. Clavijo García, *La Semana Santa malagueña*, 7, mentioned in Mapelli, "La liberación de un penado," 163.
91. Extraordinario caso ocurrido con motivo de haberse encontrado el virrey inesperadamente el sábado de Ramos por la mañana con tres reos de la Acordada que llevaban al último suplicio, In Bernardo de Gálvez to José de Gálvez, Mexico, April 28, 1786, in Valle-Arizpe, *Virreyes y virreinas*, 153–55; Cavo and Bustamante, *Los tres siglos de México*, 3:62–64.
92. Law 27, title 3, book 3, *RLI* (1774), vol. 2, 17; law 60, ibid., 21–22.
93. Royal order, August 5, 1786, to the viceroy of New Spain, AGI, Mexico, 1513.
94. On October 12, 1785 (Gómez, *Diario curioso de México*, 7:217–18); November 12, 1785 (ibid., 222); December 1, 1785 (ibid., 225); January 20, 1786 (230); March 19, 1786 (233); and June 1, 1786 (239–40).
95. Gómez, *Diario curioso de México*, 230, 233.
96. Ibid., 217–18.
97. Ibid., 240.
98. Ibid., 236–37.
99. Saavedra, *Los Decenios*, 97.
100. Gómez, *Diario curioso de México*, 7:246.
101. Keegan, *Mask of Command*, 329.
102. *Suplemento a la Gazeta de Mexico*, October 18, 1785, in M. Valdés, *Gazetas de Mexico*, 411–18.
103. A *pragmática-sanción* (royal decree) issued on November 9, 1785, determined that only the carriages of the king, the royal family, and the viceroys could have six-horse teams. Galán Domingo, "De las Reales Caballerizas," 229. See also the anonymous poem on an imagined travel of Don Quixote and Sancho Panza to Mexico published in Mexico City between 1770 and 1780, under the title "Oportuno encuentro del valiente manchego don Quijote con su escudero Sancho Panza en las riberas de Mexico. Obra póstuma de los dos, e instrucción de la presente historia. Guardada del público para su duración, un apasionado del asunto," BN, ms, 12930/24, Poesías varias, in Rodilla, "Diálogo satírico de don Quijote," 274 and 293; proclamation, November 7, 1785, AGNM, Bandos 13, 418, in Solano, *Las voces de la ciudad*, 44, and in *Gazeta de Mexico*, November 22, 1785.
104. *Gazeta de Mexico*, February 28, 1786.
105. Article 11, title 6, treaty 2, of the *Ordenanzas de S.M. para el régimen, disciplina, subordinación y servicio de sus Exércitos*, vol. 1, 144; articles 1 and 2, title 28, treaty 2, ibid., 303–4.
106. For the captain's duties, see article 4, title 10, treaty 2; for the colonel's, article 1, title 16, treaty 2, ibid., 157, 196–97.
107. Order, October 11, 1785, in Ventura Beleña, *Recopilación Sumaria*, 1–5.

108. Service record of Miguel de Gálvez, AGS, Secretaría de Guerra, 7270, exX, f. 34.

109. Anonymous, Guarico, January 21, 1783, in A. Valdés, *Historia de la Isla de Cuba*, 1:280–82.

110. Gómez, *Diario curioso de México*, 7:217–18.

111. Cavo and Bustamante, *Los tres siglos de México*, 3:62.

112. Gómez, *Diario curioso de México*, 7:246.

113. Service record of Miguel de Gálvez, AGS, Secretaría de Guerra, 7270, exX, f. 34.

114. The Spanish newspaper *ABC* reported on the ceremony in which the heir of the Spanish throne was appointed honor soldier in 1977, "El Príncipe de Asturias, soldado de honor," *ABC*, May 29, 1977. See also García, "El Príncipe de Asturias."

115. Regent and *oidores* (judges) of the Real Audiencia of Mexico to the king, Mexico, May 22, 1786, signed by all the ten members of the Real Audiencia, AGI, Mexico, 1513.

116. José de Gálvez to the regent and *oidores* of the Real Audiencia of Mexico, San Ildefonso, August 18, 1786, AGI, Mexico, 1513.

117. On José Joaquín Granados y Gálvez, see Gómez Montoya, "José Joaquín Granados," 1–29; Granados y Gálvez, *El Andaluz Perseo: Elogios poéticos que a los insignes hechos del Excmo. Sr. Don Bernardo de Gálvez, escribía el P. Fray Joaquín Granados y Gálvez, franciscano observante, a un amigo suyo*; Medina, *La imprenta en México*, 6:557; Beristain, *Biblioteca Hispano americana septentrional*, 2:50, quoted in Estrada, *Obras completas*, 2:256.

118. Rojas y Rocha, *Poema épico*.

119. Cavo and Bustamante, *Los tres siglos de México*, 3:62.

120. Humboldt, *Essai politique sur le royaume*, 1:91.

121. Carbajal López, "Los años del hambre," 57; Bravo Ugarte, *Historia sucinta de Michoacán*, 226; Charles Gibson, *Los aztecas bajo dominio español*, 471; Maldonado López, "Temblores de tierra," 22; Malvido, "Factores de despoblación"; Molina del Villar, "Comportamiento y distribución," 138; Canales Guerrero, "Propuesta metodológica," 99.

122. The *Gazeta de Mexico* of September 20, 1785, reported news from Valladolid, Guadalajara, and Guanajuato but nothing on the reaction of the viceroyal authorities in the capital.

123. Order, October 11, 1785, in Ventura Beleña, *Recopilación Sumaria*, 2:1–5. Unless otherwise stated, the following quotations are from this document.

124. Bernardo de Gálvez to José de Gálvez, Mexico, October 28, 1785, AGI, Mexico, 1418, no. 262.

125. Fray Antonio de San Miguel, bishop of Michoacán, to Bernardo de Gálvez, Sala Capitular de Valladolid de Michoacán, October 8, 1785, in *Gazeta de Mexico*, October 18, 1785, 406–47.

126. *Suplemento a la Gazeta de Mexico*, October 18, 1785, in M. Valdés, *Gazetas de Mexico*, 415.

127. *Gazeta de Mexico*, November 8, 1785.

128. Ibid., December 27, 1785.

129. *Suplemento a la Gazeta de Mexico*, October 18, 1785, in M. Valdés, *Gazetas de Mexico*, 415–16.

130. Law 49, title 15, book 5, *RLI* (1774), vol. 2, 1187–88.

131. "Edicto del oidor don Eusebio Ventura Beleña, avisando de la dispensa concedida al Sr. Matías de Gálvez, virrey ya fallecido, para no exigírsele la residencia y emplazando a quienes tengan algo que demandar lo hagan en el plazo de cuarenta días," AGNM, Bandos 13, 390, in Solano, *Las voces de la ciudad*, 51. See also *Gazeta de Madrid*, September 19, 1786, 615. The news was published in Mexico in *Gazeta de Mexico*, January 16, 1787, 227. See also *Mexico. Año de 1785. Testimonio de los Autos formados en virtud de Real*

Orn. De 26 de Marzo de este año, dispensando por ella S.M. del Juicio de Residencia al Exmo. S. Virrey que fue de esta no. E. D. Matias de Galvez, pero previniendo se publique un Edicto en todas las Provincias de este Virreinato por si algunos tuvieren que pedir contra SE y que se reciba una Información completa sobre su Conducta, Gobierno, y Providencias, Mexico, 1785, in Diego Mallén, "El juicio de residencia del virrey Matías de Gálvez martes," entry of August 4, 2009, http://diegomallen.blog spot.com.es (accessed September 10, 2016).

132. *Suplemento a la Gazeta de Mexico*, October 18, 1785, in M. Valdés, *Gazetas de Mexico*, 416.

133. Order, January 16, 1786, Universidad Autónoma de Puebla, Microfilms r. 6, in García Acosta, Pérez Zevallos, and Molina del Villar, *Desastres agrícolas en México*, 354; Comunicación de haberse formado la juntas de ciudadanos, Puebla, January 16, 1786, Universidad Autónoma de Puebla, Microfilms r. 6, in ibid.; minutes of the city council of Morelia, Archivo Histórico Municipal de Morelia, Actas de cabildo, l. 58, s.a., in ibid.

134. Order, October 11, 1785, and proclamation of July 3, 1786, AGNM, Bandos 14, 84; Solano, *Las voces de la ciudad*, 35; *Gazeta de Mexico*, July 25, 1786.

135. The temporary tax exemption was granted after hundreds of petitions arrived at the capital. García Acosta, Pérez Zevallos, and Molina del Villar, *Desastres agrícolas en México*; Florescano, *Fuentes para la historia*.

136. Alzate Ramírez, *Consejos útiles para socorrer*, 7, 45; Solano, *Las voces de la ciudad*, 214; the Mexican Pamphlet Collection, 1605–1888, from the holdings of the Sutro Library, California State Library, 22; Pérez Verdía, *Historia particular del estado de Jalisco*, 1:377; Romero Flores, *Historia de Michoacán*, 378–90; "Tequesquite (from the náhuatl *tequizquitl*, efflorescent stone) . . . Méx. Salitre de tierras lacustres," *Diccionario de la lengua española*, Real Academia Española, 2001, http://lema.rae.es/drae (accessed September 10, 2016); *Gazeta de Mexico*, January 10, 1786.

137. Proclamation, November 7, 1785, AGNM, Bandos 13, 418, in Solano, *Las voces de la ciudad*, 44; *Gazeta de Mexico*, November 22, 1785.

138. A *fanega* was a Spanish grain measurement of about 2.57 bushels. Pérez Rosales, *Familia, poder, riqueza*, 118; Carbajal López, "Los años del hambre," 65–66.

139. See part 10 of the royal order of October 11, 1785.

140. Part 8 of the royal order of October 11, 1785; proclamation, June 3, 1785, "por el que se publica el decreto de 12 de 22 de marzo de ese año promovido en tiempos del virrey Matías de Gálvez sobre gañanías para la conservación y cuidado de los miserables indios . . . mantener a los infelices indios en su libertad, redimirlos de vejaciones, y reglar sus trabajos, igualmente cooperar al fomento de la agricultura en que estriba la subsistencia de todo el público," in Ventura Beleña, *Recopilación Sumaria*, 193–99.

141. Notice, March 8, 1786, "con instrucciones para impedir que los indios pobres abandonen sus pueblos para irse a la capital, y para que los centros asistenciales distribuyan comidas diariamente lo hagan con el discernimiento que corresponde," AGNM, Bandos 14, 50, in Solano, *Las voces de la ciudad*, 217.

142. For Guadalajara, see Pérez Verdía, *Historia particular del estado de Jalisco*, 1:80; Archivo General Municipal de Guadalajara, Jalisco, Actas de cabildo, 1785, leg. 8, fols. 76r–78v, in García Acosta, Pérez Zevallos, and Molina del Villar, *Desastres agrícolas en México*, 343; and Archivo General Municipal de Guadalajara, Jalisco, Actas de cabildo, 1786, leg. 32, fols. 100r–100v, in García Acosta, Pérez Zevallos, and Molina del Villar, *Desastres agrícolas en México*, 358. For Morelia in Michoacán, see Rivera Cambas, *Mexico*

pintoresco, 3:379, in Romero Flores, *Historia de Michoacán*, 367.

143. Proclamation, April 10, 1786, AGNM, Bandos 14, 59, in Solano, *Las voces de la ciudad*, 217.

144. Quoted in Rosenzweig et al., *Breve historia del Estado de México*, 302.

145. Espinosa Cortés, Rueda Arroniz, and Andrade, *Cronología de hambrunas*, 119.

146. Carr, *Old Mother Mexico*, 63–71; Ouweneel, "Eighteenth-Century Mexican Peonage," 23.

147. AGNM, Impresos oficiales, vol. 15, e. 7, fols. 21–25, in García Acosta, Pérez Zevallos, and Molina del Villar, *Desastres agrícolas en México*, 355.

148. AGNM, Alhóndigas, vol. 10, e. 1, s.a., in ibid.

149. Just to mention a few documented examples: In Tlaxcala, landowners were threatened with the seizure of their crops if they did not obey; see Archivo General del Estado de Tlascala, C. 140, cuad. 57, f. 20, in García Acosta, Pérez Zevallos, and Molina del Villar, *Desastres agrícolas en México*, 329. For Tlalpujahua, see Florescano, *Fuentes para la historia*, 402. For the report by the Dominican friars of Azcapotzalco, see Florescano, *Fuentes para la historia*, 366. For the complaints of the mayor of Morelia against certain rich farmers, see Archivo Histórico del Municipio de Morelia, Actas del cabildo de Morelia, vol. 58, s.a., in García Acosta, Pérez Zevallos, and Molina del Villar, *Desastres agrícolas en México*, 336. In the Valley of Santa Rosa in Coahuila, the local local authorities banned the sale of crops for profit; see Archivo Municipal de Muzquiz, Coahuila c. 6, l. 5, e. 5, 3 fols., in García Acosta, Pérez Zevallos, and Molina del Villar, *Desastres agrícolas en México*, 33. For the problems of Antonio Flores, mayor of Merepec, with Eduardo Bracamonte, who kept grains in his warehouse and refused to sell them at the official prices, see Archivo General de Notarías del Estado de Mexico, Sección histórica, vol. 123, l. 4, fols. 663–65, in García Acosta, Pérez Zevallos and Molina del Villar, *Desastres agrícolas en México*, 341. For the investigation of several rich landowners in Querétaro for not having contributed to the remedy of the crisis, see Florescano, *Fuentes para la historia*, 341. For the provisons by the city council of Morelia against the abuses commited by the bakers, see Archivo Histórico del Municipio de Morelia, Actas del cabildo, l. 58, s.a., in García Acosta, Pérez Zevallos, and Molina del Villar, *Desastres agrícolas en México*, 361. For other actions by the same cabildo against those who were artificially increasing the prices, see Archivo Histórico del Municipio de Morelia, Actas del cabildo, l. 58, s.a., in García Acosta, Pérez Zevallos, and Molina del Villar, *Desastres agrícolas en México*, 366, 368.

150. The *bola*: Vos, *Vivir en frontera*, 64; Archivo del Centro de Estudios Mayas, Instituto de Investigaciones Filológicas, Universidad Nacional Autónoma de México, Mexico D.F., Documentos correspondientes al Archivo General de Centroamérica, 1, 1, e. 18, in García Acosta, Pérez Zevallos, and Molina del Villar, *Desastres agrícolas en México*, 350. Intermittent fevers and pneumonia: Cavo and Bustamante, *Los tres siglos de México*, 3:57. Malign fevers and spleen pains: AGNM, Actas de Cabildo, 1785, paq. 7, leg. 8, fols. 95r–96v, in García Acosta, Pérez Zevallos, and Molina del Villar, *Desastres agrícolas en México*, 331. Measles: AGNM, Tributos, vol. 47, e. 10, fols. 180r–210v, in García Acosta, Pérez Zevallos, and Molina del Villar, *Desastres agrícolas en México*, 331. Epidemic fevers: Galbis Díez, "Bernardo de Gálvez," 335. Pleuritic pains: Archivo Judicial de Puebla, e. 5121, in García Acosta, Pérez Zevallos, and Molina del Villar, *Desastres agrícolas en México*, 362. *Tabardillas*: Bernardo de Gálvez to José de Gálvez, Mexico, September 26, 1786, AGI, Mexico, 1513; Florescano, *Fuentes para la historia*, 175–76.

151. Reher, "¿Malthus de nuevo?"

152. For Nueva Galicia: Munguía Cárdenas, *Panorama histórico de Sayula*, 48. For Jalisco: AGMG, Actas de cabildo, 1787, l. 6, fols. 26r-37v, in García Acosta, Pérez Zevallos, and Molina del Villar, *Desastres agrícolas en México*, 356.

153. Minutes of the city council of Guadalajara, March 29, 1785, AGMG, Actas de cabildo, 1785, paq. 7, leg. 8, fols. 95r-96v, in García Acosta, Pérez Zevallos and Molina del Villar, *Desastres agrícolas en México*, 331; minutes of the city council of Guadalajara, November 11, 1786, AGMG, Actas de cabildo, 1786, l. 32, fols. 76r-v, in García Acosta, Pérez Zevallos, and Molina del Villar, *Desastres agrícolas en México*, 368-69.

154. For examples of religious ceremonies, see AGNM, Actas de cabildo, 1785, leg. 8, f. 22, in García Acosta, Pérez Zevallos, and Molina del Villar, *Desastres agrícolas en México*, 331; AGMG, Instituto Dávila Garibi, Guadalajara, leg. 25, paq. 7, f. 9; minutes of the city council of Mexico City, May 10, 1785, Archivo Histórico de la Ciudad de Mexico, Actas cabildo, 105A, in García Acosta, Pérez Zevallos, and Molina del Villar, *Desastres agrícolas en México*, 332; and Archivo Histórico Municipal de Morelia, Michoacán, Actas de cabildo, vol. 58, s.a., in García Acosta, Pérez Zevallos, and Molina del Villar, *Desastres agrícolas en México*, 336. For religious ceremonies in San Luis de Potosí, see Florescano, *Fuentes para la historia*, 175-76; and minutes of the city council of Mexico City, March 20, 1786, Archivo Histórico de la Ciudad de Mexico, Actas de cabildo 106A, in García Acosta, Pérez Zevallos, and Molina del Villar, *Desastres agrícolas en México*, 359. For "Súplicas al Señor Sacramentado" in San Luis de Potosí, see Florescano, *Fuentes para la historia*, 155. For *Novena* in Mexico City in May 1786, see AGNM, Correspondencia virreyes, c. 12, f. 144, in García Acosta, Pérez Zevallos, and Molina del Villar, *Desastres agrícolas en México*, 363. For rogations to the Virgin in Cadereyta, Querétaro, see Florescano, *Fuentes para la historia*, 352-53.

155. Bravo Ugarte, *Historia sucinta de Michoacán*, 226; Pérez Verdía, *Historia particular del estado de Jalisco*, 1:377; Romero Flores, *Historia de Michoacán*, 158, 368-74.

156. Bishop of Puebla to Bernardo de Gálvez, reports, s.a., Archivo del Ayuntamiento de Puebla, Reales cédulas, 12, f. 51, in García Acosta, Pérez Zevallos, and Molina del Villar, *Desastres agrícolas en México*, 353.

157. Fray Antonio de San Miguel, bishop of Michoacán, to Bernardo de Gálvez, Sala Capitular de Valladolid de Michoacán, October 8, 1785, in *Gazeta de Mexico*, October 18, 1785, 406-47.

158. Romero Flores, *Michoacán histórico y legendario*, 186.

159. Minutes of the city council of Michoacán, November 11, 1785, Archivo Histórico Municipal de Michoacán, Actas de cabildo, vol. 58, s.a., in García Acosta, Pérez Zevallos, and Molina del Villar, *Desastres agrícolas en México*, 342; Romero Flores, *Michoacán histórico y legendario*, 158.

160. Bernardo de Gálvez to José de Gálvez, letter no. 667, Mexico, May 27, 1786 (first of this date), AGI, Mexico, 1420.

161. José de Gálvez to Bernardo de Gálvez, San Ildefonso, August 17, 1786, AGNM, Reales órdenes, vol. 3, e. 75, f. 143, in García Acosta, Pérez Zevallos, and Molina del Villar, *Desastres agrícolas en México*, 363.

162. Bernardo de Gálvez to José de Gálvez, letter no. 754, Mexico, July 1, 1786, AGI, Mexico, 1420; ibid., letter no. 826, August 3, 1786, AGI, Mexico, 1419.

163. Medina Rubio, *La Iglesia*, 247.

164. Bernardo de Gálvez to José de Gálvez, Mexico, September 26, 1786, AGI, Mexico, 1513.

165. Juan Antonio Flores, mayor of Metepec, to Bernardo de Gálvez, Metepec, March 1786, Archivo General de Notarías del Estado de Mexico, Sección histórica,

vol. 125, l. 5, fols. 309r–318v, *asunto* (matter) 4, in García Acosta, Pérez Zevallos, and Molina del Villar, *Desastres agrícolas en México*, 357.

166. Order, October 11, 1785, in Ventura Beleña, *Recopilación Sumaria*, 1–5, 3.

167. Bernardo de Gálvez to José de Gálvez, letter no. 262, Mexico, October 29, 1785 (second of this date), AGI, Mexico, 1418.

168. López Sarrelangue, "Población indígena," 521.

169. According to the census of 1790, the total population of New Spain was 4,636,074 inhabitants, but Nicolás Sánchez-Albornoz has pointed out that the census was severely flawed since it did not take into account a big part of the total population. According to Sánchez-Albornoz the real population of New Spain at the time would have been closer to six million. In Dirección general de estadística, *1er Censo de población de la Nueva España*, 106; Sánchez-Albornoz, "La población," 20.

170. Galbis Díez, "Bernardo de Gálvez," 344–45.

171. Real Academia Española, *Diccionario de la lengua castellana compuesto por la Real Academia Española reducido a un tomo para su más fácil uso* (1803), 506.

172. One of the best short descriptions of the encomienda system is the one given by the *Encyclopedia Britannica*: "As legally defined in 1503, an encomienda (from *encomendar*, "to entrust") consisted of a grant by the crown to a conquistador, soldier, official, or others of a specified number of Indians living in a particular area. The receiver of the grant, the encomendero, could exact tribute from the Indians in gold, in kind, or in labour and was required to protect them and instruct them in the Christian faith. The encomienda did not include a grant of land, but in practice the encomenderos gained control of the Indians' lands and failed to fulfill their obligations to the Indian population. The crown's attempts to end the severe abuses of the system with the Laws of Burgos (1512–13) and the New Law of the Indies (1542) failed in the face of colonial opposition and, in fact, a revised form of the repartimiento system was revived after 1550." *Encyclopedia Britannica Online*, s.v. "encomienda," accessed October 25, 2015, http://www.britannica.com/topic/encomienda. Also see Lockhart, "Encomienda and Hacienda"; and Keith, "Encomienda, Hacienda, and Corregimiento."

173. Ramos Pérez, *Historia de América*, 9:37.

174. Ibid., 39.

175. Real cédula a la Audiencia de Mexico mandando se cumplan las ordenanzas del virrey duque de Alburquerque que regulaba los salarios de los indios gañanes de las haciendas y prohibiendo que se les pagase con efectos y ropas, a fin de evitar que por deudas se perpetuase el indio en la estancia, Madrid, June 4, 1687, Biblioteca Nacional de México, Mexico D.F., Mexico, ms, 13.332, fols. 14–16, in Solano, *Cedulario de tierras*, 368–69.

176. Testimonio del expediente de las quejas de los indios gañanes de las haciendas, AGI, Mexico, 1739, in Galbis Díez, "Bernardo de Gálvez," 345–46.

177. Real Audiencia, proclamation, June 3, 1785, in Ventura Beleña, *Recopilación Sumaria*, 193–99.

178. Testimonio del expediente de las quejas de los indios gañanes de las haciendas, AGI, Mexico, 1739, in Galbis Díez, "Bernardo de Gálvez," 345–46.

179. Proclamation, March 28, 1786, AGNM, Bandos 14.

180. The "well thought-out decrees" mentioned here refer to the decree of March 28, 1784 (during Bernardo's father's tenure as viceroy), and the proclamation by the *audiencia gobernadora* of June 3, 1785. Proclamation, March 28, 1786, AGNM, Bandos 14.

181. Proclamation, March 28, 1786, AGNM, Bandos 14.

182. Testimonio del expediente de las quejas de los indios gañanes de las haciendas, AGI, Mexico, 1739. In Galbis Díez, "Bernardo de Gálvez," 344-45.

183. Borah, *Justice by Insurance*, 445.

184. Decreto para mejor asistencia, breve y buen despacho de las causas y negocios de los indios por los subalternos a quienes toca, December 5, 1785, in Ventura Beleña, *Recopilación Sumaria*, 199-203.

185. The term *indios bárbaros* (barbaric Indians) was the eighteenth century's name for those Native Americans who lived in the borderlands of the Spanish Empire and resisted being incorporated and assimilated into the Spanish colonial society. The term is also used by contemporary historians as Luis Navarro García and David J. Weber. Navarro García, "El ilustrado"; Weber, *Bárbaros, Spaniards and Their Savages*.

186. *Instrucción formada en virtud de Real Orden de S.M.* [Instruction for governing the Interior Provinces of New Spain], Mexico, August 26, 1786 por el virrey de la Nueva España, Conde de Gálvez, original document in AGI, Guadalajara, 268; idem. Ultramar, 714; and in AGS, Guerra Moderna, 7041.

187. Navarro García, *José de Gálvez y la comandancia general*, 454-55; Navarro García, "El ilustrado," 10.

188. Marquis de Sonora [José de Gálvez] to Jacobo de Ugarte, copy of the letter, El Pardo, February 27, 1787, AGNM, Provincias Internas, 77, DF 8, mentioned in Moorhead, *Apache Frontier*, 132.

189. *Instrucción formada en virtud de Real Orden de S.M.*, preamble, 2; Navarro García, "El ilustrado," 11.

190. Instruction of August 26, 1786, article 213, 59; López Alanís, "Mecanismos de violencia militar."

191. Instruction of August 26, 1786, article 216, 60.

192. Picazo Muntaner, "El impacto de las guerras nativas," 17-18.

193. Instruction of August 26, 1786. Unless otherwise stated, all quotes in this section are from this document.

194. Ibid., article 25, 9-10.

195. Mancera to Veragua [sic], October 22, 1673, mentioned in Porras Muñoz, *La frontera con los indios*, 91.

196. Ortelli, "De vándalos," 22.

197. Ortelli, "Enemigos internos," 469.

198. Instruction of August 26, 1786, article 136, 38; article 148, 41-42; article 155, 43-44; article 157, 44; article 170, 47; article 191, 52.

199. Unless otherwise stated the quotations in this section are from Gálvez's *Instrucción formada en virtud de Real Orden de S.M.* [Instruction for governing the Interior Provinces of New Spain], Mexico, August 26, 1786 por el virrey de la Nueva España, Conde de Gálvez, original document in AGI, Guadalajara, 268; idem. Ultramar, 714; and in AGS, Guerra Moderna, 7041.

200. Calloway, *One Vast Winter Count*, 377.

201. Brooks, *Captives and Cousins*, 74.

202. Haley, *Apaches*, 116; Phone, Olson, and Martínez, *Dictionary of Jicarilla Apache*.

203. Porro, "La defensa y consolidación," 22; Vázquez, "Los apaches y su leyenda."

204. Montesquieu, *De l'esprit des lois*, vol. 2, book 20, chapters 1-3, 12-13.

205. Félix de Anzara to the viceroy the Marquis de Avilés, report on the colonization of the Chaco, Buenos Aires, February 19, 1799, in Angelis, *Colección de obras y documentos*.

206. Campillo y Cossío, *Nuevo Sistema de govierno [sic] económico para la América*, 14.

207. José de Gálvez to Teodoro de Croix, El Pardo, February 22, 1779, Archivo Franciscano, in Weber, *Bárbaros, Spaniards and Their Savages*, 178.

208. Haley, *Apaches*, 40-41.

209. *RLI* (1681).

210. Law 33, title 1, book 6, *RLI* (1681), forbidding Indians to ride on horses, by

Felipe II, Madrid, July 19, 1568, and Córdoba, March 1, 1570.

211. Ibid., law 43, forbidding wineshops in Tlaxcala, by Felipe II, Poblete, April 17, 1585; ibid., law 37, "sobre la bebida del pulque, usada por los indios de la Nueva España."

212. Vachon, "L'eau de vie"; Dailey, "Role of Alcohol"; MacAndrew and Edgerton, *Drunken Comportment*; Lurie, "World's Oldest On-Going Protest Demonstration"; Mancall, *Deadly Medicine*.

213. Law 24, title I, book 6, *RLI* (1681), "no se pueden rescatar, ni dar a los Indios armas ofensivas, ni defensivas, por los inconvenientes, que pueden resultar . . . ," by Emperador D. Carlos, Burgos, September 6, 1521, in Valladolid, June 6, 1523, and in Toledo, May 21, 1534; ibid., law 31, "que no se puedan vender armas a los Indios, ni ellos las tengan," by Felipe IV, Madrid, August 1, 1633.

214. Quarleri, "Gobierno y liderazgo jesuítico-guaraní," 103; Weber, *Bárbaros, Spaniards and Their Savages*, 176-77.

215. B. Gálvez, *Noticia y reflexiones*, 51-52.

216. Instruction of August 26, 1786, article 40, 14; article 68, 21; article 69, 21; article 72, 21-22; article 73, 22; article 74, 22; article 75, 22.

217. Carlisle, "Spanish Relations with the Apache Nations," 28; Vigness, "Nuevo Santander," 489-91.

218. Blackhawk, *Violence over the Land*, 106.

219. Instruction of August 26, 1786, article 148, 41-42; article 171, 47-48.

220. Instruction of August 26, 1786. For Sonora and California: articles 105 to 116, 30-33; for Nueva Vizcaya: articles 117 to 161, 33-45; for New Mexico and the village of El Paso: articles 162 to 170, 46-47; for Texas, Coahuila, Nuevo León, and Nuevo Santander: articles 171 to 191, 47-52.

221. *Instrucción formada en virtud de Real Orden de S.M.* [Instruction for governing the Interior Provinces of New Spain], Mexico, August 26, 1786 por el virrey de la Nueva España, Conde de Gálvez, original document in AGI, Guadalajara, 268; idem. Ultramar, 714; and in AGS, Guerra Moderna, 7041.

222. Ibid.

223. Albi de la Cuesta, "La caballería en América," 178.

224. *Reglamento para todos los presidios de las Provincias internas de esta Gobernación* (1729).

225. Instrucción para formar una línea o cordón de quince presidios sobre las Fronteras de las Provincias Internas de este Reino de Nueva España, y Nuevo Reglamento del número y calidad de Oficiales y Soldados que estos y los demás han de tener, Sueldos que gozarán desde el día primero del Enero del año próximo de mil setecientos setenta y dos, y servicio que deben hacer sus Guarniciones, Mexico, 1771, AGI, Guadalajara, 273. Once approved by the king it was published under the title *Reglamento e Instrucción para los Presidios que se han de formar en la Línea de frontera de la Nueva España* (1772).

226. Moorhead, *Presidio*, 108.

227. Moorhead, *Apache Frontier*, 211-69.

228. Matson and Schroeder, "Cordero's Description of the Apache," 336; Jacobo de Ugarte to Count of Revillagigedo, viceroy of New Spain, report, Chihuahua, September 1, 1790, Archivo General y Público de la Nación, Mexico, Provincias internas, tomo 84, exped. 1. The very positive report could be accused of partiality since Ugarte was interested in presenting his achievements in a favorable light, but his assessment was corroborated by the viceroy in Count of Revillagigedo, viceroy of New Spain, to Jacobo Ugarte, copy of the letter, Mexico, January 26, 1791, Archivo General y Público de la Nación, Mexico, Provincias internas, tomo 159, exped. 6, mentioned in Moorhead, *Apache Frontier*, 281-82.

229. Park, "Spanish Indian Policy," 317-36.

230. Basso, "Western Apache," 466.

231. Arredondo López, "Andanzas de un pueblo," 551; Basso, "Western Apache," 466; Bancroft, *History of Arizona and New Mexico*, 378; Greenleaf, "Nueva Vizcaya Frontier"; Haley, *Apaches*, 40-41; Hook, *Apaches*, 21; Lamar and Truett, "Greater Southwest," 72, 79-80; Moorhead, *Apache Frontier*, 289; Moorhead, *Presidio*, 109; Ortelli, *Trama de una guerra conveniente*, 58-59; Spicer, *Cycles of Conquest*, 240; Worcester, *Apaches*, 33-34.

232. Arredondo López, "Andanzas de un pueblo," 551.

233. González Cruz, "Represión y trato a los indígenas."

234. Babcock, *Apache Adaptation to Hispanic Rule*, 8.

235. Table 3, "Nueva España, población de localidades mayores de 10.000 habitantes, por sexo y actividades, 1790," in Dirección general de estadística, *1er Censo de población de la Nueva España*, 106.

236. José Antonio de Alzate to the Count of Revillagigedo, March 10, 1791, AGNM, Historia, vol. 74, 4-13, in Dirección general de estadística, *1er Censo de población de la Nueva España*, 16.

237. Anes, "La América virreinal," 212. Data from the so-called Count of Floridablanca's census done between 1787 and 1788, Estado General de la Población de España en el año de 1787, Real Academia de Historia, Madrid, Departamento de Cartografía y Artes Gráficas, C-Atlas E, II, 3, no. reg. 966. According to this census the population of the Spanish Peninsula (including Ceuta, Orán, and other Spanish territories in North Africa) was 10,268,150. Vicens Vives, *Historia de España y América*, 8-10.

238. Campbell Gibson, "Table 2. Population of the 24 Urban Places: 1790"; Lemon, "Colonial America in the Eighteenth Century," 133.

239. Pérez Herrero, "El crecimiento económico novohispano."

240. Elliott, *Empires of the Atlantic World*.

241. Gortari Rabiela, "La ciudad de México de finales," 117.

242. *Ordenanza de la división de la nobilísima ciudad de Mexico en cuarteles.*

243. Ladrón de Guevara, *Discurso sobre la policía de Mexico*; González-Polo, "La ciudad de México"; Gortari Rabiela, "La ciudad de México de finales," 118; López Sarrelangue, "La policía de la ciudad de México," 227-35. The original manuscript of the *Enfermedades políticas que padece la capital de esta Nueva España* (Political diseases suffered by the capital of this New Spain), by Hipólito Villaroel, is in the Hubert Howe Bancroft Collection at the University of Berkeley, California (Banc Mss M-M 245; M-M 246; M-M 247; M-M 248). One copy is in Mexico's National Library and another one is in the National Library in Madrid (BN, ms, 19663, vol. 1; 19664, vol. 2; 19665, vol. 3; 19666, vol. 4). In 1830, a partial edition was published, followed in 1930 by a complete one that was reprinted in 1979. Arnaiz Amigo, "Estudio preliminar"; Borah, "Alguna luz sobre el autor"; Estrada, "El México de Villaroel"; "Introducción a las Enfermedades políticas de la Nueva España de Hipólito Villaroel," v-xii; Hernández Sorelo, "Hipólito de Villarroel."

244. Villaroel, *Enfermedades políticas*, 263.

245. Viqueira Albán, *¿Relajados y reprimidos?*, 173, 181.

246. Ibid.

247. Ibid., 204-6.

248. Villaroel, *Enfermedades políticas*, 229.

249. Proclamation, May 8, 1784, AGNM, Bandos 13, 72, in Ventura Beleña, *Recopilación Sumaria*, 353-55, and in Solano, *Las voces de la ciudad*, 44; proclamation, January 29, 1785, reiterating the proclamation of May 8, 1784, AGNM, Bandos 13, 299, in Ventura Beleña, *Recopilación Sumaria*, 355, and in Solano, *Las voces de la ciudad*, 44.

250. Bernardo de Gálvez to José de

Gálvez, Mexico, July 28, 1785, AGI, Mexico, 1873; Diseño de un farol para el alumbrado de las calles de Mexico, July 28, 1785, AGI, Mapas y Planos, Mexico, 401.

251. Villaroel, *Enfermedades políticas*, 177.

252. See the following in *RLI* (1774). Legislation banning the use of arms by the Indians: "No se las den," law 24, title 1, book 6, vol. 2, f. 190; "No las tengan," law 31, f. 191.

Forbidding the use of arms by the mulattoes: Forbidding "traer armas a los mulatos," law 14, title 5, book 7, vol. 2, f. 287.

Forbidding the use of arms by the black people: "Prohibiendo a los negros traer armas," law 15, title 5, book 7, vol. 2, f. 287; law 16, title 5, book 7, vol. 2, f. 287, "que los mulatos y zambaygos no traigan armas, y los mestizos las puedan tener con licencia." To those in Cartagena de Indias, law 17, title 5, book 7, vol. 2, f. 287, and law 18, title 5, book 7, vol. 2, f. 287.

Partially forbidding the use of arms by the mestizos: "Que los mulatos y zambaygos no traigan armas, y los mestizos las puedan tener con licencia," law 16, title 5, book 7, vol. 2, f. 287.

Regulations on the type of arms allowed and forbidden: "Estoques, verdugos o espadas de más de cinco cuartas de cuchilla," law 9, title 8, book 7, vol. 2, f. 296; law 12, title 5, book 3, "que no se lleven armas a las Indias sin licencia del Rey, pena de perderlas," vol. 2, f. 29, originally by Felipe II, Madrid, December 10, 1566, and El Escorial, July 1, 1568.

253. Proclamation, October 26, 1785, "prohibiendo la importación de cuchillos flamencos o españoles con punta, por considerarse arma prohibida," AGNM, Bandos 14, 48, in Solano, *Las voces de la ciudad*, 35.

254. Villaroel, *Enfermedades políticas*, 225.

255. Arrom, "Vagos y mendigos."

256. Sacristán, "Filantropismo," 23.

257. Ramos Vázquez, "Policía de vagos para las ciudades," 217.

258. Notice, March 8, 1786, AGNM, Bandos 14, 50, in Solano, *Las voces de la ciudad*, 217.

259. Antonio de San Miguel, bishop of Michoacán, to the justicia y regimiento (judicial authorities and police) of Valladolid, Morelia, October 1785, in Aguilar Ferreira, "Fray Antonio de San Miguel."

260. Proclamation, April 10, 1786, AGNM, Bandos 14, 59, in Solano, *Las voces de la ciudad*, 217.

261. Notice by the Count de Gálvez, Mexico, March 1786, AGNM, Impresos oficiales, vol. 15, e. 11, fols. 35r-37v, in García Acosta, Pérez Zevallos, and Molina del Villar, *Desastres agrícolas en México*, 356.

262. Minutes of the city council of Guadalajara, November 15, 1785, AGMG, Actas del cabildo, 1785, leg. 8, fols. 76r-78v, in ibid., 343, and in *Gazeta de Mexico*, November 8, 1785.

263. Repairs on the road from Mexico City and Toluca, AGNM, Caminos y calzadas, vol. 11, e. 4, fols. 112r-127v, in García Acosta, Pérez Zevallos, and Molina del Villar, *Desastres agrícolas en México*, 346.

264. Arrom, *Containing the Poor*; Morales Rodríguez, "Para contener al pueblo"; "Testimonio de las constituciones formadas para el régimen y gobierno del Hospicio de Pobres de Mexico," 1785, AGI, Mexico, 1791, ex16a, fols. 37-38v, reiterated by a decree of February 23, 1799, AGNM, Bandos 10, in Arrom, *Containing the Poor*, 320; D. Peza, *La beneficencia en México*, 63-71.

265. Cossío, *Datos históricos sobre las propiedades*, 28-30.

266. Rodríguez Álvarez, *Usos y Costumbres Funerarias*, 186; Aguilar, *Los hospitales de México*, 63.

267. Cordoncillo Samada, *Historia de la Real Lotería*, 61.

268. Galbis Díez, "Bernardo de Gálvez," 342.

269. Bernardo de Gálvez to José de

Gálvez, Mexico, AGI, Mexico, 1420, mentioned in ibid.

270. *Gazeta de Mexico*, February 28, 1786.

271. Suárez Argüello, "De caminos, convoyes y peajes," 224.

272. AGNM, Caminos y calzadas, vol. 11, e. 4, fols. 112r-127v, in García Acosta, Pérez Zevallos, and Molina del Villar, *Desastres agrícolas en México*, 346.

273. Álvarez Noguera, *José Damián Ortiz de Castro*, 20; Torre Villar and Navarro de Anda, *Instrucciones y memorias*, 2:1513; Muñoz Rebolledo and Isaza L., "Naturaleza, jardín y ciudad," 15.

274. Moreno Cabrera, "La arqueología de Chapultepec," 26.

275. Matías de Gálvez to José de Gálvez, Tacubaya, April 26, 1784, in Cavo and Bustamante, *Los tres siglos de México*, 3:48-49.

276. Bernardo de Gálvez to José de Gálvez, Mexico, July 27, 1785 (fourth of this date), in ibid., 3:59-61.

277. Ibid.

278. Gómez, *Diario curioso de México*, 7:228.

279. Bernardo de Gálvez to José de Gálvez, January 24, 1786, AGI, Mexico, 1884; minutes of the city council of Guadalajara, November 15, 1785, AGMG, Actas del cabildo, 1785, leg. 8, fols. 76r-78v, in García Acosta, Pérez Zevallos, and Molina del Villar, *Desastres agrícolas en México*, 343.

280. Bernardo de Gálvez to José de Gálvez, Mexico, July 27, 1785 (second of this date), AGI, Mexico, 1884.

281. Royal order, January 3, 1786, AGI, Mexico, 1884.

282. Galbis Díez, "Bernardo de Gálvez," 344.

283. Ibid.

284. *Audiencia gobernadora* to José de Gálvez, letter no. 97, Mexico, January 26, 1787, enclosing a certification about the construction and present state of the palace at Chapultepec, AGI, Mexico, 1884; Amerlinck de Corsi, "Los grandes proyectos," 224.

285. Fernández, *Chapultepec*, 68; Moreno Cabrera, "La arqueología de Chapultepec," 26; Romero Flores, *Chapultepec en la historia de México*, 69.

286. Humboldt, *Essai politique sur le royaume*, 2:105.

287. Bernardo de Gálvez to José de Gálvez, letter no. 91, Mexico, July 27, 1785 (third of this date), AGI, Mexico, 1884. The five plans are all found in AGI, Mapas y Planos, Mexico: Plano de la antigua fábrica de Chapultepec, Palacio que fue de los Excmos. Señores Virreyes de Nueva España y después Cárcel de acordada, circa 1787, 404; Plano de la antigua fábrica de Chapultepec, Palacio que fue de los Excmos. Señores Virreyes de Nueva España y después Cárcel de acordada, circa 1788, 411; Plano inferior del Real Palacio de Chapultepec, circa 1787, 405; Varios perfiles y diseños de la fachada del Palacio de Chapultepec, Mexico, circa 1787, 406; Plano Superior del Real Palacio de Chapultepec, circa 1787, 407.

288. Plano inferior del Real Palacio de Chapultepec, circa 1787, AGI, Mapas y Planos, Mexico, 405.

289. Varios perfiles y diseños. . . . , AGI, Mapas y Planos, Mexico, 406.

290. Plano superior del Real Palacio de Chapultepec, in ibid., 407.

291. C. Adams, *Taste for Comfort and Status*, 21. Also see Flandrin, *Families in Former Times*, 135-40; Trumbach, *Rise of the Egalitarian Family*; Traer, *Marriage and the Family*; Medick and Warren, introduction to *Interest and Emotion*.

292. McAlister, "The Reorganization of the Army"; Navarro García, *Hispanoamérica en el siglo XVIII*, 172-73.

293. Archer, *Army in Bourbon Mexico*, 38.

294. Rodríguez Baena, "El virrey Manuel Antonio Flórez [sic]," 1:33.

295. Archer, *Army in Bourbon Mexico*, 38.

296. Rodríguez-Sala, *Los cirujanos del ejército*, 55.

297. Bernardo de Gálvez to José de Gálvez, confidential letter no. 481, Mexico, February 24, 1786 (first of this date), AGS, SGU, leg. 6958, 1.

298. May, *British Army in North America*, 5.

299. Bernardo de Gálvez to José de Gálvez, confidential letter no. 481, Mexico, February 24, 1786 (first of this date), AGS, SGU, leg. 6958, 1.

300. José de Ezpeleta to Bernardo de Gálvez, Mexico, August 5, 1785, AE, Papeles de Mexico, no. 40, in Medina Rojas, "La reforma del ejército," 319.

301. *Audiencia regente* to José de Gálvez, confidential letter no. 194, Mexico, January 27, 1785, AGI, Mexico, 1415.

302. Royal order, February 22, 1785, in Bernardo de Gálvez to José de Gálvez, confidential letter no. 481, Mexico, February 24, 1786 (first of this date), AGS, SGU, leg. 6958, 1; Informe del Inspector sobre el Dictamen general que instruyó el coronel don Francisco Antonio Crespo encargado interinamente de la Inspección para el mejor establecimiento y arreglo del ejército de Nueva España, Mexico, October 24, 1785, AE, Papeles de Mexico, in Medina Rojas, "La reforma del ejército," 322.

303. Royal order, January 24, 1787, mentioned in *audiencia regente* to José de Gálvez, letter no. 13, Mexico, May 23, 1787, AGI, Mexico, 1421.

304. Proyecto del Coronel D. Francisco Antonio Crespo, inspector interino de las tropas, para el arreglo del Ejército de Nueva España, dictámenes e informes sobre el mismo de D. José de Ezpeleta y del Virrey Conde de Gálvez, apoyo al proyecto del virrey D. Manuel Antonio Flórez [sic Flóres] e informe del subinspector D. Pedro Mendinueta, Mexico, 1784–1787, AGS, SGU, leg. 6985, 1; Proyecto de arreglo del Ejército de Nueva España del coronel inspector D. Francisco Antonio Crespo, dictámenes e informes, Mexico, 1785–1786, AGS, SGU, leg. 6985, DF12.

305. Bernardo de Gálvez to José de Gálvez, confidential letter no. 481, Mexico, February 24, 1786 (first of this date), AGS, SGU, leg. 6958, 1; Bernardo de Gálvez to José de Gálvez, confidential letter no. 613, Mexico, May 22, 1786, AGI, Mexico, 1420.

306. Bernardo de Gálvez to José de Gálvez, confidential letter no. 613, Mexico, May 22, 1786, AGI, Mexico, 1420.

307. Archer, *Army in Bourbon Mexico*, 23–58.

308. Rodríguez-Sala, *Los cirujanos del ejército*, 41. About the high opinion that the Marquis de Cruillas had about the *criollos*, see Navarro García, "Nobleza criolla."

309. B. Gálvez, *Noticia y reflexiones*, 41.

310. Ibid., 40–41.

311. Castañeda, *Informe jurídico dirigido al Rey*, 57–58; Luque Taraván, *Un universo de opiniones*, 372.

312. Bernardo de Gálvez to José de Gálvez, confidential letter no. 481, Mexico, February 24, 1786 (first of this date), AGS, SGU, leg. 6958, 1.

313. Ibid.

314. Brading, "Government and Elite"; Bravo, "Las élites militares," 507; Marchena Fernández, "La expresión de la guerra"; Suárez, *Las milicias*, 156.

315. Rodríguez-Sala, *Los cirujanos del ejército*, 57.

316. Among those who consider that the "Americanization" of the Spanish army in America was a relevant factor for later independence movements are Albi de la Cuesta, *La defensa de las Indias*, 189; Brading, "Government and Elite"; Garavaglia and Marchena, *América Latina de los orígenes*, 2:310; González Batista, *La estrategia española en América*, 137; Jane, *Liberty and Despotism*, 84; Losa Contreras, "La formación de la milicia urbana," 195; McAlister, *El fuero militar*, app. 1, 22; J. Rodríguez, *Independence of Spanish America*, 29–30; and Semprún Bullón, "El esfuerzo bélico realista," 42.

Among those who consider that the impact depended more on regional and local conditions are Bethell, *Historia de América latina*, 9; Lynch, "El reformismo borbónico e Hispanoamérica," 47-48; Lynch, "Los factores estructurales de la crisis," 42; Lynch, *Las revoluciones hispanoamericanas*, 17; Marchena Fernández, *La institución militar*, 157; Marchena Fernández, *Ejércitos y milicias*; Marchena Fernández, "El ejército de América"; and Ossa Santa Cruz, "La criollización," 415.

317. Cruz Barney, "Las milicias en la Nueva España," 80; Vega Juanino, *La institución militar*, 27.

318. Losa Contreras, "La formación de la milicia urbana," 195; Fernández de Velasco, "El militarismo en la vida del mexicano."

319. Estado y providencias tomadas respecto al establecimiento del regimiento de caballería provincial de Querétaro, in Bernardo de Gálvez to José de Gálvez, letter no. 170, Mexico, September 23, 1785, AGI, Mexico, 1417; Informe de Francisco Antonio Crespo sobre la necesidad de arreglo de compañías de los gremios de la ciudad de Mexico, y la conveniencia de formar un escuadrón de caballería urbana con ellas [Report by Francisco Antonio Crespo about the need to reform Mexico City's Guilds militia's companies, and on the need to form with them a urban (*sic*) cavalry squadron], 1784, AGS, Guerra Moderna, Secretaría Consejo de Guerra, 6988, DF 5, leg. 1, in Losa Contreras, "La formación de la milicia urbana," 196-205.

320. Bernardo de Gálvez to José de Gálvez, confidential letter no. 481, Mexico, February 24, 1786 (first of this date), AGS, SGU, leg. 6958, 1.

321. Bernardo de Gálvez to José de Gálvez, confidential letter no. 650, Mexico, May 26, 1786, AGI, Mexico, 1420.

322. Bernardo de Gálvez to José de Gálvez, confidential letter no. 613, Mexico, May 22, 1786, AGI, Mexico, 1420.

323. Archer, *Army in Bourbon Mexico*, 45; *audiencia regente* to José de Gálvez, letter no. 13, Mexico, May 23, 1787, AGI, Mexico, 1421.

324. On the Royal Academy of San Carlos of New Spain, see Báez Macías, "La Academia de San Carlos"; Brown, *La Academia de San Carlos*; Carrillo y Gariel, *Datos sobre la Academia de San Carlos*; Charlot, *Mexican Art*; Donahue-Wallace, "El grabado en la Real Academia de San Carlos"; Estrada, *Algunos papeles para la historia de las bellas artes*; Ruíz Gomar, "Grabado y numismática." Royal order, December 25, 1783, in *Gazeta de Mexico*, March 24, 1784.

325. *Gazeta de Mexico*, November 8, 1785.

326. Gil, *Medalla conmemorativa del Tribunal de Minería de Mexico*.

327. Gil, *Medalla conmemorativa de la toma de Pensacola*.

328. Ponce, *Collection d'estampes représentant les événemens de la guerre*.

329. González Bueno and Rodríguez Nozal, "Conocimiento científico y poder"; Lafuente, "Las expediciones científicas."

330. González Bueno, "Plantas y luces," 109; González Bueno and Rodríguez Nozal, "Conocimiento científico y poder," 490-91.

331. Bernardo de Gálvez to José de Gálvez, letter no. 181, Mexico, September 25, 1785, AGI, Mexico, 1417, enclosing the "Testimonio de expediente sobre establecer un jardín botánico d. Martín Sessé, en la huerta de San Pedro y San Pablo," Mexico, September 17, 1785.

332. Bernardo de Gálvez to José de Gálvez, letter no. 268, Mexico, October 29, 1785 (first of this date), AGI, Mexico, 1418; Bernardo de Gálvez to José de Gálvez, letter no. 771, Mexico, July 22, 1786 (second of this date), AGI, Mexico, 1419.

333. Pardo-Tomás, "El Protomédico Francisco Hernández"; Somolinos, "Vida y obra de Francisco Hernández."

334. Maldonado Polo, "La expedición botánica," 6-7.

335. Bernardo de Gálvez to José de Gálvez, letter no. 771, Mexico, July 22, 1786 (second of this date), AGI, Mexico, 1419.

336. López Piñero, "La obra botánica de Cavanilles"; Díaz, "El Jardín Botánico"; Maldonado Polo, "La expedición botánica," 9; Hernández Luna, *José Antonio Alzate*; Moreno de los Arcos, *La primera cátedra*; Peset, "José Antonio Alzate"; Fernández del Castillo, *La facultad de medicina*.

337. Maldonado Polo, "La expedición botánica," 19.

338. Bernardo de Gálvez to José de Gálvez, letter no. 181, Mexico, September 25, 1785, AGI, Mexico, 1417.

339. For the list of legislation, orders, and other documents processed by Bernardo de Gálvez during his tenure as viceroy of New Spain, see Rodriguez García, *El fiscal de Real Hacienda*, 295, 310.

340. Gómez, *Diario curioso de Mexico*, 7:224.

341. Shakespeare, *Coriolanus*, act 2, scene 2.

342. Gómez, *Diario curioso de Mexico*, 7:216.

343. Ibid., 224.

344. Ibid., 244.

345. Ibid., 245, 246.

346. Ibid., 248.

347. Ibid.

348. *Gazeta de Mexico*, October 24, 1786.

349. Gómez, *Diario curioso de Mexico*, 7:248.

350. *Gazeta de Mexico*, November 7, 1786.

351. Bernardo de Gálvez to José de Gálvez, Mexico, October 31, 1786, copy of the letter sent that same day, AGI, Mexico, 1512.

352. Decree by Bernardo de Gálvez, Tacubaya, November 8, 1786, AGI, Mexico, 1512; Bernardo de Gálvez to Francisco Fernández de Córdoba, certified copy, ibid.

353. *Audiencia de Mexico* to José de Gálvez, letter no. 1, Mexico, November 8, 1786, including a copy of the decree from the viceroy where he entrusted the *audiencia* with the government, AGI, Mexico, 1512; and Audiencia de Mexico to José de Gálvez, Mexico, November 26, 1786, in ibid.; list of the dossiers processed by the *audiencia* between November 10, 1786, and May 8, 1787, AGI, Mexico, 1742.

354. Francisco Fernández de Córdova to José de Gálvez, Mexico, December 2, 1786, AGI, Mexico, 1513.

355. The original copy of the notes dictated on November 9, 1786, by Bernardo de Gálvez for his last will and testament with two additions made two days later is in the Archives of the Ministry of Justice in Madrid and has been published three times: Souviron, *Bernardo de Gálvez*, 95–97; Beerman, "Last Will and Testament of Bernardo de Gálvez"; and Fernández-Carrión, "Vida privada del Virrey." The quotes in this section are from Bernardo de Gálvez's last will.

356. The mail that arrived in Mexico by the end of February contained his choice of appointments to superintendant of the royal mint as well as attaché to the Secretaría de Indias. Gómez, *Diario curioso de México*, 7:260.

357. Law 54, title 3, book 3, *RLI* (1774), vol. 2, f. 23; law 53, title 16, book 2, ibid., vol. 1, f. 221; law 54, title 3, book 3, ibid., vol. 2, f. 23.

358. For example: Juan Ventura Morales, agent for the succession of Bernardo de Gálvez, vs. Luis Toutant Beauregard, April 22, 1790, proceedings instituted to compel defendant to liquidate his business accounts with Gálvez, Louisiana State Museum, New Orleans, Black Book 146, WPA 2474, box 58, file 27; Juan Ventura Morales, agent for the succession of Count de Gálvez, vs. Pedro Rousseau, May 5, 1790, proceedings instituted to compel defendant to pay 200 pesos, defendant claimed the money was needed to pay the crew of the vessel that took the Countess de Gálvez to Havana, Louisiana State Museum, New Orleans, Black Book 147, WPA 2494, box 58, file 25.

359. Royal order, January 20, 1788, El Pardo, in *Gazeta de Mexico*, June 17, 1788. Also see proclamation by Viceroy Manuel Antonio Flóres, June 10, 1788, "avisando haberse concedido dispensa de residencia al difunto virrey conde de Gálvez," AGNM, Bandos 14, 342, in Solano, *Las voces de la ciudad*, 51. Viceroy Flóres informed about a proclamation containing the royal order that exempted the Count de Gálvez from his *juicio de residencia*, May 16, 1788, Library of the University of Texas at San Antonio, catalog no. 1225. After the death of José de Gálvez, the ministry of the Indies was divided in two departments: Gracia y Justicia de Indias (entrusted to Antonio Porlier) and Hacienda y Guerra de Indias (provisionally ascribed to the minister for the navy, Antonio Valdés y Bazán). In Navarro García, "La crisis del reformismo borbónico," 5.

360. Gómez, *Diario curioso de Mexico*, 7:251.

361. *Gazeta de Mexico*, December 5, 1786; testimonio del expediente formado por el fallecimiento del Excmo. Sr. Conde de Gálvez, "a las cuatro y cuarto de la mañana de este día ha fallecido en el pueblo de Tacubaya, y a mi presencia (como lo certifico) el Excmo. Sr. Conde de Gálvez," in Juan Fernández de Córdoba to José de Gálvez, Mexico, November 30, 1786, AGI, Mexico, 1512.

362. Count of Floridablanca to José de Gálvez, El Pardo, February 27, 1787 (first and second of this date), AGI, Mexico, 1512.

363. Countess of Gálvez to the Marquis of Sonora, Mexico, May 23, 1787 (second and first of this date), in ibid.

364. The expression "immortality of a footnote" has been borrowed from the *Economist* ("George Bert, Obituary"). The first mention of the rumor about the poisoning of Bernardo de Gálvez appeared in 1836, and despite its having no support, neither by facts nor by evidence, it has been repeated ever since. Cavo and Bustamante, *Los tres siglos de México*, 2:65; Rivera Cambas, *Los gobernantes de México*, 1:457; Alcázar Molina, *Los virreinatos*, 82; Rubio Argüelles, quoted in Olmedo Checa, *Bernardo de Gálvez*, xxx; Galbis Díez, "Bernardo de Gálvez," 353-54; Marañón Moya, "Bernardo de Gálvez," 91; Castañeda Iturbide, *Gobernantes de la Nueva España*, 2:100; Villalpando, *El Virrey*; Ocampo Alfaro, *Diccionario de escritores mexicanos*, 256: Rodríguez Moya, *La mirada del virrey*, 147; Porras Muñoz, "Hace doscientos años," 324.

365. Olmedo Checa, *Bernardo de Gálvez*, xxix.

366. José de Gálvez to the *audiencia gobernadora*, El Pardo, February 21, 1787, AGI, Mexico, 1512; *Gazeta de Mexico*, December 5, 1786.

367. Ots y Capdequí, *Instituciones*, 59-50, 261-62.

368. Law 3, title 15, book 2, by Felipe III, Madrid, January 3, 1600, *RLI* (1681); Solórzano Pereira, *Política indiana*, book 5, chapter 2, no. 42, vol. 4, 50-51.

369. Marín Leoz, Juana, "El gobierno interino de la Audiencia," 1108.

370. "El virreinato debe recaer en la Audiencia con la calidad de que el ministro que haga las veces del capitán general se aconseje en lo correspondiente a las armas se aconseje en lo perteneciente a las armas con el jefe de la tropa, procurando ambos buena correspondencia y armonía, cuidando dicho jefe no se divulgase en lo público copias de sus representaciones por los inconvenientes que podían resultar," royal order, July 29, 1780, in Cedulario, tomo 38, f. 100r-v, no. 78 and 79, in Ayala, *Diccionario de gobierno*, vol. 13, 366; in AGS, Secretaría de Guerra 7011, ex1, r. 1, f. 2v; and in Marín Leoz, "El gobierno interino de la Audiencia," 1109; Royal order, May 20, 1785, AGS, Secretaría de Guerra 7011, ex1, r. 1, f. 23r.; Testimonio del expediente formado en consecuencia del oficio del Excmo. Sr. Virrey conde de Gálvez comprehensivo de la real orden de 10 de enero último en que deben entenderse las facultades de los subinspectores

en calidad de cabos subalternos de los señores virreyes cuando por fallecimiento de estos recaiga al gobierno en las reales Audiencias, Mexico, November 8, 1786. It was approved on February 19, 1787, AGI, Mexico, 1512. Royal order, Aranjuez, January 10, 1786, AGS, Secretaría de Guerra 7011, ex1, r. 1, f. 3; Instrucción de Vicente de Herrera y de Rivero del supremo consejo de Indias deja a su sucesor en la regencia de Mexico Eusebio Sánchez Pareja, Mexico, November 6, 1786, AGI, Mexico, 1742.

371. "El día 8 llegó aquí d. Eusebio Sánchez Pareja sin esperara a su sucesor en Guadalajara, como parece correspondía en virtud de la real cédula de 20 de February de 1786, y en el día inmediato tomó posesión a tiempo que el Excmo. Conde de Gálvez había entregado el gobierno a la Audiencia por haberle agravado sus males. Le ha dado la instrucción correspondiente, . . . y he asistido al Tribunal hasta su venida, y dejado todo corriente sobre lo de el día, y nada sin providencia . . . y en los 4 años y 2 meses que he servido la Regencia resultan de exceso más de 3.000 pleitos y expedientes despachados sobre el quinquenio de mayor número de los quince años últimos." Vicente de Herrera to the king, Mexico, November 15, 1786, AGI, Mexico, 1742.

372. Recibo del despacho de subinspector general para el brigadier Pedro de Mendinueta, in Bernardo de Gálvez to José de Gálvez, letter no. 185, Mexico, September 25, 1785, AGI, Mexico, 1417.

373. *Gazeta de Mexico*, December 5, 1786. Unless otherwise stated the quotes in this section are from this document.

374. Ibid., December 19, 1786.

375. Rodríguez Álvarez, *Usos y Costumbres Funerarias*, 191–226; Porras Muñoz, "Hace doscientos años."

376. "Apuntes que [Bernardo de Gálvez] doy a don Ramón Posada para que con arreglo a ellos extienda mi testamento, dados en Tacubaya el 9 de noviembre de 1786," in Fernández-Carrión, "Vida privada del Virrey," 468.

377. Archbishop of Mexico to José de Gálvez, Mexico, December 2, 1786, AGI, Mexico, 1512.

378. González Obregón, "El funeral de los virreyes," 129.

379. The honors and ceremony for the funerals of high-ranking military officers who died during their service was regulated in title 5, treaty 3, of the *Ordenanzas de S.M. para el régimen, disciplina, subordinación y servicio de sus Exércitos*, 1: 357–83; see also Reder Gadow and Pérez-Frías, "La regulación social de la muerte."

380. Porras Muñoz, "Hace doscientos años," 318; Rodríguez Álvarez, *Usos y Costumbres Funerarias*, 91.

381. *Gazeta de Mexico*, May 22, 1787.

382. Ibid., January 3, 1787.

383. Ibid. Unless otherwise stated the quotations in this section are from this document.

384. Donahue-Wallace, "El grabado en la Real Academia de San Carlos," 50.

385. Gómez, *Diario curioso de México*, 7:253.

386. Ibid.

387. *Gazeta de Mexico*, January 3, 1787.

388. Gómez, *Diario curioso de México*, 7:261. This honor had been previously granted to the widow of Matías de Gálvez, Bernardo's father. *Audiencia gobernadora* to José de Gálvez, Mexico, November 21, 1784, AGI, Mexico, 1512.

389. The auction of Gálvez's estate started on June 21, 1787, *Gazeta de Mexico*, June 19, 1787. Fernando José Grangino [sic], superintendent of the Royal Treasury, to José de Gálvez, Mexico, May 27, 1787, AGI, Mexico, 1512.

390. Countess de Gálvez to the city council of Mexico City, Mexico, May 23, 1787, in *Gazeta de Mexico*, June 5, 1787. The city council would reply the following day, city council of Mexico City to the Countess de Gálvez, Mexico, May 24, 1787, in ibid., June 5, 1787.

391. Archbishop Alonso Núñez de Haro to José de Gálvez, Mexico, June 22, 1787, AGI, Mexico, 1512. The archbishop had been appointed acting-viceroy by royal order, February 27, 1787. Jose de Gálvez to the *audiencia gobernadora*, El Pardo, February 27, 1787, AGI, Mexico, 1513.

AFTERWORD

1. John Black translated the original French "on accusa" as "was accused," but it is better translated "on accusa" as "has been accused." Humboldt, *Essai politique sur le royaume*, 2:203, English trans., *Political Essay on the Kingdom of New Spain*, trans. John Black, 2:103.

2. Humboldt, *Essai politique sur le royaume de la Nouvelle-Espagne*, 2:203, and *Political Essay on the Kingdom of New Spain*, 2:103.

3. Ibid.

4. Cavo and Bustamante, *Los tres siglos de México*, 2:65; Lacunza, *Discursos Históricos*, 528; Alaman, *Disertaciones sobre la historia*, 3:75-76, app.; Gayarré, *History of Louisiana*, 3:166; Bancroft, *History of Mexico*, 397-98; Rivera Cambas, *Los gobernantes de México*, 1:457; Caughey, *Bernardo de Gálvez in Louisiana*, 254-55; Vázquez de Acuña, *Historial de la Casa de Gálvez*, 1276; Vázquez de Acuña, "El Conde de Gálvez," 85; Claret, *José de Gálvez*, 249; Boeta, *Bernardo de Gálvez*, 130; McCarty, "La educación de un Virrey," 101; Pérez de Colosía Rodríguez, "Rasgos biográficos de una familia ilustrada," 103-4; Porras Muñoz, "Hace doscientos años," 324.

5. Hamnett, "Problemas interpretativos."

6. Lacunza, *Discursos Históricos*; Alamán, *Disertaciones sobre la historia*.

7. Sánchez Casado, *Los altos grados de la masonería*, 128-29; Aceves Pastrana, "La difusión de la ciencia."

8. Solano, *Las voces de la ciudad*, 205-6.

9. Carrillo, *Llanto de México en la muerte*, in Solano, *Las voces de la ciudad*, 206; Fernández de Uribe, *Solemnes exéquias*, in ibid.

10. Solano, *Las voces de la ciudad*, 207.

11. Alaniz Calderón, *Llanto del Melpomene*, in ibid., 206; Olmedo Checa, *Bernardo de Gálvez*, 247-49; Medina, *La imprenta en México*, 6:442; Barea, *Oración fúnebre*; Castro Osores [sic: Ozores], *Tiernos suspiros con que se procura explicar*, in Solano, *Las voces de la ciudad*, 206; Olmedo Checa, *Bernardo de Gálvez*, 225-27; Medina, *La imprenta en México*, 6:451; Castro, *Sentimientos de la América*; Conde y Oquendo, *Oración fúnebre*; Fernández de San Salvador, *La América llorado por la temprana muerte de su amado*; González de la Vega, *México llorosa y México risueña*; Larrañaga, *La América socorrida*; Lizararrás, *Lamentos americanos*; *Llanto con que responde México*, in Medina, *La imprenta en México*, 6:414; Monte, *Rendido y fiel obsequio en festiva demostración*; Pacheco Martínez, *Las lágrimas*; Quirós y Campo-Sagrado, *Condigno llanto*, in Medina, *La imprenta en México*, 6:459; Reygadas, *Liras que la Excma. Señora dña. Felicitas Maxan* [sic]; Santa María y Sevilla, *Suspiros que en la muerte del virrey de México*; Ubiella, *Demostración*, in Medina, *La imprenta en México*, 6:488; M. Valdés, *Apuntes de algunas de las gloriosas acciones*; Vargas, *Carta de pésame*, in Solano, *Las voces de la ciudad*, 207; Villegas de Echeverría, *Felicidad de México*, in Olmedo Checa, *Bernardo de Gálvez*, 293-95; Villegas de Echeverría, *Coloquio tierno*.

12. Humboldt, *Essai politique sur le royaume*, 2:202-3, and *Political Essay on the Kingdom of New Spain*, 2:102-3.

13. Vázquez de Acuña, *Historial de la Casa de Gálvez*, 1276; Claret, *José de Gálvez*, 249; Boeta, *Bernardo de Gálvez*, 130.

14. Campos, *Chapultepec*, plates no. 1 to 5.

15. Plano inferior del Real Palacio de Chapultepec, circa 1787, AGI, Mapas

y Planos, Mexico, 405; varios perfiles y diseños de la fachada del Palacio de Chapultepec, Mexico, circa 1787, in ibid., 406; plano superior del Real Palacio de Chapultepec, circa 1787, in ibid., 407.

16. Plano superior del Real Palacio de Chapultepec, circa 1787, in ibid., 407. Although the plans have been dated circa 1787, we consider that they should have been dated a couple of years earlier since it seems logical that they were drawn previous to the start of the construction on December 1785.

17. Law 71, title 3, book 3, *RLI* (1774), vol. 2, 22r, established three years as the term of office for the viceroy. The law was originally published on March 10, 1555, and four times repeated, in 1659, 1653, 1660, and 1663. Despite this legal limit, many viceroys surpassed it.

18. Gil, *Medalla conmemorativa de la toma de Pensacola*.

19. *Webster's Third New International Dictionary*.

20. Fuentes, *El Alma de México*; Blumenthal, *Eccentric Typography*; "El arte de la escritura."

21. Rodríguez Moya, *La mirada del virrey*, 97; Pérez Vejo and Quezada, *De novohispanos a mexicanos*, 18.

22. *Tesoros de los Palacios Reales de España*.

23. Poe, "Fall of the House of Usher."

24. On the unconventional life of María Rosa de Gálvez, see J. R. Jones, "María Rosa de Gálvez: Notes," and "María Rosa de Gálvez, Rousseau." On her works, see García Lorenzo, *Autoras y Actrices*, 108–14.

25. Anonymous, "Honras que a la muerte del Excmo. Señor Don Joseph de Galvez, Ministro del Despacho Universal de Yndias, hizo un sacerdote de Apolo, en este año de 1787," *Papeles curiosos manuscritos*, vol. 72, h. 123v–124v., BN, Mss/10956; anonymous, "A la repentina muerte," in Guillén Robles, *Historia de Málaga*, 601, and in Vázquez de Acuña, *Historial de la Casa de Gálvez*, 1208.

26. Vázquez de Acuña, *Historial de la Casa de Gálvez*, 1276.

27. Military record of Miguel de Gálvez, Regimiento de Infantería de la Corona de la Nueva España, December 1789, AGS, Secretaría de Guerra, leg. 7270, ex10X, f. 34.

28. Genealogía del alumno del Real Seminario de Nobles de Madrid: Miguel Gálvez Maxent y Gallardo, Conde de Gálvez, Natural de Guarico (Venezuela), 1783, Hijo de D. Bernardo de Gálvez, teniente general de los Reales Ejércitos, caballero pensionado de la Real Orden de Carlos III, comandante general del Ejército de operaciones en América, Partida de bautismo del seminarista y testimonio de nobleza de 1792, Madrid, June 26, 1792, AHN, Universidades, 665, DF 4; Pruebas para la concesión del Título de Caballero de la Orden de Calatrava de Miguel de Gálvez y Sant-Maxent, natural de Guarico (Haíti), Conde de Gálvez y Cadete de la Compañía Americana de Reales Guardias de Corps, 1797, AHN, Ordenes Militares, Caballeros Calatrava, 1009; Artacho y Pérez-Blázquez, "Cofradías," 92.

29. Expediente del conde de Gálvez y marqués de la Sonora, 1823, Sección de Guerra, expedientes personales de miembros del ejército, AHN, Estado 44B.

30. Beerman, "Governor Bernardo de Galvez's New Orleans Belle," 44.

31. Expediente del conde de Gálvez y marqués de la Sonora, 1823, Sección de Guerra, expedientes personales de miembros del ejército, AHN, Estado 44B.

32. Vázquez de Acuña, *Historial de la Casa de Gálvez*, 1288.

33. Beerman, "Governor Bernardo de Galvez's New Orleans Belle," 44.

34. The title of Count de Gálvez was rehabilitated in 1991 by Pedro María Alarcón de la Lastra y Romero, order of October 3, 1991, "por la que se manda expedir, sin perjuicio de tercero de mejor derecho, Real Carta de Sucesión en el título de Conde de Gálvez a favor de don Pedro María Alarcón de la Lastra y Romero,"

Madrid: Boletín Oficial del Estado, November 5, 1991, 35540.

35. In official Spanish documents the spelling of her family name could be "de Etrehans" or "Destrehans." Count de Floridablanca to José de Gálvez, El Pardo, February 27, 1787, AGI, Mexico, 1512. For Benito Pardo de Figueroa's biography, see *Notas genealógicas que para tomar el Hábito de Santiago*, also in BPR, CAJ/FOLL-FOL/120 (16). Benito Pardo de Figueroa, ambassador of José I Bonaparte [king of Spain] to Russia, to the Minister of Foreign Affairs, Saint Petersburg, s.a., AHN, Estado 3004, DF47.

36. Beerman, "Governor Bernardo de Galvez's New Orleans Belle," 44.

37. On the life of the Countess de Gálvez, see Beerman, "El conde de Aranda," and "La bella criolla Felicitas."

38. Today La Puebla Street.

39. Beerman, "Governor Bernardo de Galvez's New Orleans Belle"; Beerman, "El conde de Aranda," 351.

40. Destierro de la condesa de Gálvez y familia, extracto de las diligencias practicadas en las inmediaciones a la casa de la condesa viuda de Gálvez, September 10, 1790, AHN, Hacienda leg. 4828, in Beerman, "El conde de Aranda," 356.

41. Beerman, "El conde de Aranda," 351.

42. Ibid., 362.

43. Alexander von Humboldt to Miguel Constanzó, Mexico, November 22, 1803, in Moncada Maya, *El ingeniero Miguel Constanz*, 332; Puig-Samper, "Humboldt," 335; Ferrer Benimeli, Sarasa, and Serrano, "El conde de Aranda."

44.
Los Gálvez se deshicieron,
Como la sal en el agua,
Y como chispas de fragua
Fósforos desaparecieron.
Bajaron como subieron
A modo de exhalación;
Dios le concede el perdón,
Sin que olvidemos el paso,
Que este mundo dá cañazo
A quién le da adoración.

Anon., *Décimas a la repentina muerte de d. José de Gálvez*, in Guillén Robles, *Historia de Málaga*, 601.

Bibliography

ARCHIVES

Note: the full details of all manuscript primary sources are given when quoted in the endnotes.

Archives Nationales de France, Pierrefitte-sur-Seine, Paris and Fontainebleau, France
Archives Nationales d'Outre-Mer, Aix-en-Provence, France
Archivo del Centro de Estudios Mayas, Instituto de Investigaciones Filológicas, Universidad Nacional Autónoma de México, Mexico D.F., Mexico
Archivo Ezpeleta, Seville, Spain
Archivo Francisco de Miranda, Caracas, Venezuela
Archivo General de Indias, Seville, Spain
Archivo General de la Administración, Alcalá de Henares, Madrid, Spain
Archivo General de la Nación de México, Mexico D.F., Mexico
Archivo General de Simancas, Simancas, Spain
Archivo General Militar de Madrid, formerly known as Archivo Central del Servicio Histórico Militar, Madrid, Spain
Archivo General Municipal de Guadalajara, Jalisco, Mexico
Archivo Histórico Militar, Madrid, Spain
Archivo Histórico Nacional, Madrid, Spain
Biblioteca de Palacio Real, Madrid, Spain
Biblioteca Nacional, Madrid, Spain
Biblioteca Nacional de México, Mexico D.F., Mexico
Bibliothèque nationale de France, Paris, France
British Public Record Office, London, United Kingdom
Library of Congress, Washington, D.C., United States
Louisiana State Museum, New Orleans, United States
Museo Naval, Madrid, Spain
National Archives, Kew, Richmond, United Kingdom
National Maritime Museum, Greenwich, London, United Kingdom
New York Public Library, New York, United States
Real Academia de la Historia, Madrid, Spain

MAPS, PLANS, AND ENGRAVINGS

Note: the full details of all manuscript maps and sketches are given when quoted in the endnotes.

Bellin, Jacques Nicolas. *Carte du Canal de Bahama*. Map. Paris: Didot, 1768.

———. *Carte reduite des costes de la Louisiane et de la Floride*. Map. Paris: Didot, 1764.

Berteaux, Lausan (drawing), and Ponce, Nicolás (engrav.). *Prise de Pensacola*. Engraving. In Nicolás Ponce, *Collection d'estampes représentant les événemens de la guerre, pour la liberté de l'Amérique Septentionale*. Paris: Chez M. Ponce, graveur de

Mr. le comte d'Artois, rue Ste. Hyacinthe, no. 19. et chez M. Godefroy, graveur de sa majesté impériale, rue des Francs-Bourgeois, porte St. Michel, 1784[?].

Bowen, Thomas. *A correct map of the United States of North America; including the British and Spanish territories, carefully laid down agreeable to the treaty of 1784*. Map. London [circa 1784]. Library of Congress, Washington, D.C., Geography and Map Division, catalog number 74692103.

Bresse, C. *Poisson Aerostàtique enlevé a Plazentia Ville d'Espagne situé au milieu des Montagnes, et dirigé par Dom Joseph Patinho jusqu'a la Ville de Coria aur bort de la Riviere d'Arragon, éloigné de 12 lieues de Plazentia le 10 mars 1784*. Paris: chez Chereau, 1784. Bibliothèque nationale de France, département Estampes et photographie, FOL-IB-4 (2).

Brieva, Simón. *Retrato de Bernardo Galvez*. Engraving. Madrid: 1781. Biblioteca Nacional, Madrid, IH/3417/1. In Ángel María de Barcia, *Catálogo de los Retratos de personajes españoles que se conservan en la sección de estampas y de bellas artes de la Biblioteca Nacional*, 347-48. Madrid: Viuda é hijos de M. Tello impresor de cámara de S.M., 1901.

Britania [sic] and Her Daughter—A Song. Engraving. London: I. Mills, March 8, 1780. Washington, D.C.: Library of Congress Prints and Photographs Division, control no: 2004673374.

The British Lion Engaging Four Powers. Engraving. London: J. Barrow, June 14, 1782. Washington, D.C.: Library of Congress, Library of Congress Prints and Photographs Division, control no. 2004673480.

Demostración de la baia de Argel, en la que se manifiestan los castillos, baterías y acampamentos de su Dey y del Bey de Constantina y Damasco; el parage por donde executó el desembarco la tropa de S. M. el día 8 de julio de 1775; la situación de la esquadra y convoy. Y assimismo la colocación de los navíos, fragatas, xaveques, bombardas y galeotas destinadas para batir los fuertes y barrer la playa para proteger el desembarco de la tropa. Archivo General de Simancas, Secretaría de Guerra, Legajos, 02010, accompanying a letter from Francisco Sabatini to the Count de Ricla, Madrid, October 23, 1775.

Durnford, Elias (draw.), Canot, C. and Morris, T. (engrav.). *A view of the market place in the city of the Havana = Vue de la place du marché dans la ville de la Havane prise = Vista de la plaza del mercado en la Ciudad de la Havana*. London: John Bowles, [1768]. Library of Congress, Washington D.C.: Library of Congress control no: 2009633664.

Espinosa de los Monteros y Abadía, Antonio. *Plano topographico de la Villa y Corte de Madrid: Al Excmo. Sr. Conde de Aranda Capitán General de los Exercitos y Presidente del Consejo, por Antonio Espinosa de los Monteros, Académico de la Real de las Nobles Artes, escala de 1200 pies Castellanos, equivalente a 400 Varas Castellanas*. Map. Madrid: Antonio Espinosa de los Monteros y Abadía, 1769. Biblioteca Nacional, Madrid, GMG/1365; MR/8/II series 13/044 and MV/13 14087-3001, page 6, city block 143.

Expulsion et embarquement des Jésuites des états d'Espagne, par ordre de S. M. C. le 31 mars 1767. Paris: circa 1788. Bibliothèque nationale de France, RESERVE QB-201 (106)-FOL.7.

Faveau, Antonio. *Chart of Balabac and part of the east coast of Palawan or Paragua by Don Antonio Faveau Quasada*. 1753, map, publ. by A. Dalrymple; Mr. Smith, sculp., Bibliothèque nationale de France, Paris, département Cartes et plans, CPL GE DD-2987 (7539).

George, B. *A Chart of the bay and Harbour of Pensacola in the Province of West Florida. Surveyed by George Gauld*. Map. London: a.m., J. F. W. Des Barres, 1780. Library of Congress, Washington, D.C., Maps of North America, 1750-1789, 1663, G3932.P45 1780.G3 Vault.

Gil, Jerónimo Antonio. *El Excmo. Sr. Don José de Gálvez, Marqués de Sonora*. Engraving, in Santiago Magro y Zurita and Eusebio Ventura Beleña, *Elucidationes ad quatuor libros Institutionum Imperatoris Justiniani*. México: Felipe Zúñiga Ontiveros, 1787.

———. *Medalla conmemorativa de la toma de Pensacola*. Engraving. Archivo General de Indias, Seville, Mapas y Planos, Monedas 6.

———. *Medalla conmemorativa del establecimiento de la Academia de San Carlos*. Engraving. Archivo General de Indias, Seville, Mapas y Planos, Monedas 6.

———. *Medalla conmemorativa del Tribunal de Minería de México*. Engraving. Archivo General de Indias, Seville, Mapas y Planos, Monedas 6.

———. *Retrato de Miguel de Gálvez y Saint Maxent*. Engraving. Biblioteca Nacional, Madrid, IH/3424. In Eusebio Ventura Beleña, *Recopilación Sumaria de todos los autos acordados de la Real Audiencia y Sala del Crimen de esta Nueva España y providencias de su Superior Gobierno: De varias Reales Cédulas y Órdenes que, después de publicada la Recopilación de Indias, han podido recogerse, así de las dirigidas a la misma Audiencia ó Gobierno, como de algunas otras que por sus notables decisiones convendrá no ignorer*, vol. 1, i. México: Felipe de Zúñiga y Ontiveros, 1787.

Gillray, James. *The Times, anno 1783*. London: W. Humphrey, 14 April 1783. Washington, D.C.: Library of Congress, Library of Congress Prints and Photographs Division, control no. 2004676762.

Green V. (engrav.). *General Washington, after a portrait by Trumbull, J. Esqr. of Connecticut, 1780*. London: published by appointment of M. De Neufville . . . by V. Green, January 15, 1781. Washington, D.C.: Library of Congress, Library of Congress Prints and Photographs Division, Control Number 2004666688.

Heldring, Henry. *Map of the Harbour of Pensacola in West Florida*. Map, s.a., William A. Clements Library, University of Michigan, Ann Arbor. Mentioned in William S. Coker, *The Siege of Pensacola 1781 in Maps, with Data on Troop Strength, Military Units, Ships, Casualties and Related Statistics*, 76. Pensacola: Perdido Bay Press, 1981.

Jefferys, Thomas. *A Description of the Spanish Island and Settlements on the Coast of the West Indies: Compiled from authentic Memoirs, Revised by Gentlemen . . . and Illustrated with Thirty-Two Maps and Plans*. Map (2nd ed.). London: Printed for Faden and Jefferys, Geographer to the King . . . , 1774.

Kneass, William. *A map of the United States and part of Louisiana*. Map, s.l. [circa 1784]. Library of Congress, Washington, D.C., Geography and Map Division, catalog number 74692963.

L'Isle, Guillaume de. *Carte de la Louisiane et du cours du Mississipi [sic]: Dressée sur un grand nombre de mémoires entrautres sur ceux de Mr. le Maire*. Map. Paris: Chez de L'Isle, 1718.

Major. d'après P. B. de la Rue. *Cantabres Volontaires*. Engraving, Paris, F. Chereau, 1747. In *Nouveau recueil des troupes légères de France* . . .

McMurray, William, and Robert Scot. *The United States According to the Definitive Teatry [sic] of Peace signed at Paris Septr. 3d., 1783*. Map, s.l. [circa 1784]. Biblioteca Nacional, Madrid, MR/8/II series 28/061.

Nueva vista de Gibraltar: Año de 1781: Grabada por la última lamina fina que se anunció en la Gazeta del martes 22 de Mayo de 1781, que contiene la línea, el Espaldon,

Caminos cubiertos, nuevas Baterías de la Plaza, Barcas Cañoneras y otras cosas que en él se expresan. Engraving. Madrid: Viuda de Escribano, 1781. Biblioteca Nacional, Madrid, invent/34570.

Paredes. *Plano de la bahía de Pansacola.* Map, s.l., 1782. Library of Congress, Washington, D.C., Geography and Map Division, catalog number 75693014.

Pittman, Capt. Philip. *Plan of Fort Rosalia.* Map. London: J. Nourse, 1770.

Plan de la ville de Pensacola dans la West Floride. Map, s.l., s.n., s.a. In Bibliothèque de la Service Hydrographique, 4044C-67.

Plano de la Población de Pansacola [sic] conquistada por las Armas Españolas al mando del mariscal de campo D. Bernardo de Gálves [sic] en 8 de Mayo de 1781 con el campamento y ataque para su rendición. Map. Ms., s.l., s.n., s.a. In Servicio Geográfico del Ejército, *Cartografía de Ultramar. carpeta II: Estados Unidos y Canadá*. Madrid: Servicio Geográfico e Histórico del Ejército, 1953 373, plate 95. Also in Servicio Geográfico del Ejército, *Cartoteca histórica, Índice de mapas y planos históricos de América*, 16. Madrid: Servicio Geográfico del Ejército, 1974.

Plano de los Ataques, y de las Fortificaciones de la plaza de Panzacola; la que rindieron los españoles el 8 de mayo de 1781. Map. Mss., s.l., s.n., s.a. MN 6-A-21. In María Luisa Martín Merás, "La toma de Pensacola a través de los mapas," in *Bernardo de Gálvez y su tiempo*, edited by Manuel Olmedo Checa, 38–53. Málaga: Colegio Oficial de Ingenieros Técnicos Industriales de Málaga, 2007.

Plano del Puerto de Panzacola, situado su boca en la Latitud N. de 30 grados y 14 minutos, y Longitud de 288 grados 4 minutos Meridiano de Tenerife. Map. Ms. [circa 1780]. In Servicio Geográfico del Ejército, *Cartografía de Ultramar. carpeta II: Estados Unidos y Canadá*, Madrid: Servicio Geográfico e Histórico del Ejército, 1953, 370, plate 93. Also in Servicio Geográfico del Ejército, *Cartoteca histórica, Índice de mapas y planos históricos de América*, 16. Madrid: Servicio Geográfico del Ejército, 1974.

Plano del río de la Movila en latitud de 30 grados y 10 minutos, cuya conquista e igualmente la de su fortificación y habitaciones se ha echo por el brigadier y comandante general de la provincia de la Luisiana el 12 de marzo de 1780, Dn Bernardo de Gálvez. Archivo General de Simancas, MPD, 15, 006.

Ponce, Nicolás. *Prise de Pensacola.* Engraving. In *Collection d'estampes représentant les événemens de la guerre, pour la liberté de l'Amérique Septentionale.* Paris: Chez M. Ponce, graveur de Mr. le comte d'Artois, rue Ste. Hyacinthe, no. 19. et chez M. Godefroy, graveur de sa majesté impériale, rue des Francs-Bourgeois, porte St. Michel, 1784 [?].

Portillo y Labaggi, José. *Plano hidrográfico de la Costa de la Florida Occidental desde el Río Misisipi hasta el Cabo de S. Blas. Conquistada a los Yngleses baxo la Dirección del Excmo. Sr. Dn. Bernardo de Gálvez, conde de Gálvez con la toma del castillo y bahía de Movilla en 14 de Marzo de 1780; la importante Plaza y Bahía de Panzacola en 8 de Mayo de 1781 delineado por Dn José Portillo y Labaggi.* Sevilla: May 8, 1783. Archivo General de Simancas, MPD, 22, 017.

Pownall, Thomas. *A new map of North America, with the West India Islands. Divided according to the preliminary articles of peace, signed at Versailles, 20, Jan. 1783. Wherein are particularly distinguished the United States and the several provinces, governments &ca. which compose the British dominions.* Map. London: Robt. Sayer, Map, Chart & Printseller, 1786. Library of Congress, Washington, D.C., Geography and Map Division, catalog number 74693113.

Simitière, Pierre Eugène du. *His excellency John Jay, president of congress & minister plenipotentiary from congress at Madrid.* Engraving. London: R. Wilkinson, May 15, 1783. Washington, D.C.: Library of Congress, Library of Congress Prints and Photographs Division, control no. 2003689050.

Taitt, David. *A plan of part of the rivers Tombecbe, Alabama, Tensa, Perdido, & Scambia in the province of West Florida; with a sketch of the boundary between the nation of upper Creek Indians and that part of the province which is contiguous [sic] thereto, as settled at the congresses at Pensacola in the years 1765 & 1771 . . .* Map, s.l. [circa 1771]. Library of Congress, Washington, D.C., Geography and Map Division, G3971.P53 1771.T3 Vault.

Tour, Louis Brion de la. *Suite du Théatre de la Guerre dans l'Amérique Septentrionale y Compris le Golphe du Méxique.* Paris: Esnauts et Rapilly, 1782. Washington, D.C.: Library of Congress, Library of Congress Prints and Photographs Division, control no. 2006629304.

Ultima vista del castillo de S. Felipe y Mahón con la salida de los Ingleses, el Desembarco, Campo de los Franceses y Nuevas Disposiciones, según ultimas Noticias Expresadas en las Gazetas de Madrid. Madrid: Viuda de Escribano, s.a. Biblioteca Nacional, Madrid, MV/12.

Vázquez, Bartolomé. *Retrato de Bernardo Gálvez.* Engraving. Madrid: 1782, Biblioteca Nacional, Madrid, IH 3417-2. In Ángel María de Barcia, *Catálogo de los Retratos de personajes españoles que se conservan en la sección de estampas y de bellas artes de la Biblioteca Nacional,* 347-48. Madrid: Viuda é hijos de M. Tello impresor de cámara de S.M., 1901.

Verdadero retrato y relación anatómica de la niña de dos cabezas y cuatro brazos, nacida en el lugar de Alfara, distante una legua de la ciudad de Valencia, el día 28 de agosto de este presente año de 1781. Engraving. Madrid: Viuda de Escribano, 1781. Archivo Histórico Nacional, Consejos, 50698, no. 38.

A view of Pensacola, in West Florida Vue de Pensacola dans le Floride occidental. Print. London: G. Gauld, 177? Washington, D.C.: Library of Congress, Library of Congress Prints and Photographs Division Library of Congress, control no. 2004672419.

Vista de Panzacola y su Baia: Tomada por los españoles año de 1781. Madrid: Viuda de Escribano, 1781. Biblioteca Nacional, Madrid, MA00007568.

Walker, James (attrib.). *The Storming of Chapultepec, Sept. 13th 1847.* Engraving of a lost painting, National Museum of American History, Washington, D.C., catalog number 60.2602.

BOOKS, ARTICLES, PAMPHLETS, WALL POSTERS,
AND OTHER PRINTED MATERIAL

Abbey, Kathryn Trimmer. "Efforts of Spain to Maintain Sources of Information in the British Colonies before 1779." *Mississippi Valley Historical Review* 15, no. 1 (June 1928): 56-68.

———. "The Intrigue of a British Refugee against the Willing Raid, 1778." *William and Mary Quarterly,* 3rd ser., 1, no. 4 (October 1944): 397-404.

———. "Peter Chester's Defense of the Mississippi after the Willing Raid." *Mississippi Valley Historical Review* 22, no. 1 (June 1935): 17-32.

Abol-Brasón y Álvarez-Tamargo, Manuel de. "El conde de Floridablanca y la política de su época." In *José Moñino y Redondo, conde de Floridablanca (1728-1808): Estudios en el bicentenario de su muerte,* edited by Jesús Menéndez Peláez, 55-178. Gijón: Fundación Foro Jovellanos del Principado de Asturias, 2009.

Aceves Pastrana, Patricia Elena. "La difusión de la ciencia en la Nueva España en el siglo XVIII: La polémica en torno a la nomenclatura de Linneo y Lavoisier." *QUIPU-Revista latinoamericana de historia de las ciencias y la tecnología* 4, no. 3 (1987): 357–86.

Acosta, Joaquín. *Compendio Histórico: Descubrimiento y colonización de la Nueva Granada*. Paris: Imprenta de Beau, 1848.

Acosta, José Melchor de. *Relación diaria, verídica, y circunstanciada de todos los acaecimientos en la colonia de la Luisiana y ciudad del Nuevo Orleans, desde el 1º de noviembre de 1768 que salió de ella su gobernador y capitán general don Antonio de Ulloa, hasta 20 de abril de 1769 que salió de la fragata de mi mando nombrada El Bolante, La Habana, 22 mayo 1769*. In *Documentos históricos de la Florida y la Luisiana: Siglos XVI al XVIII*, edited by Manuel Serrano y Sanz, 272–95. Madrid: Librería General de Victoriano Suárez, 1913.

Acosta Rodríguez, Antonio. "Crecimiento económico desigual en la Luisiana española." *Anuario de Estudios Americanos* 34 (1977): 735–57.

———. *La población de Luisiana Española (1763–1803)*. Madrid: Ministerio de Asuntos Exteriores, 1979.

Adams, Christine. *A Taste for Comfort and Status: A Bourgeois Family in Eighteenth-Century France*. Pennsylvania: Pennsylvania State University Press, 2000.

Adams, J. W. "The Peace Medals of George III." In *The Medal in America*, edited by A. M. Stahl, 2:1–15. New York: American Numismatic Society, 1999.

Adams Papers. Founding Families: Digital Editions of the Papers of the Winthrops and the Adamses, edited by C. James Taylor. Massachusetts Historical Society, Boston, 2007. https://www.masshist.org/adams/adams-family-papers (accessed March 2, 2017).

Adelberg, Michael S. *The American Revolution in Monmouth County: The Theatre of Spoil and Destruction*. Charleston, S.C.: History Press, 2010.

Adelman, Jeremy, and Stephen Aron. "From Borderlands to Borders: Empires, Nation-States, and the Peoples in between in North American History." *American Historical Review* 104 (June 1999): 814–41.

Adicción a la instrucción sobre el estrañamiento de los jesuitas de los dominios de S.M. por lo tocante a Indias e islas Filipinas, Section 11. In *Colección general de las providencias hasta aquí tomadas sobre el estrañamiento y ocupación de temporalidades de los Regulares de la Compañía que existían en los dominios de S.M. de España, Indias, e Islas Filipinas á consequencia del Real Decreto de 27 de Febrero, y Pragmática-Sanción de 2 de Abril de 1767*, 1:17–23. Madrid: Imprenta Real de la Gazeta, 1767.

La administración de d. Frey Antonio María Bucareli y Ursúa, cuadragésimo sexto virrey de México. México: Secretaría de Gobernación de los Estados Unidos Mexicano— Publicaciones del Archivo General de la Nación, 1936.

Aguilar, Gilberto. *Los hospitales de México*. México D.F.: Bayer, 1936.

Aguilar Ferreira, Melesio. "Fray Antonio de San Miguel anuncia la construcción del acueducto de Morelia." *Anales del Museo Michoacano* 4 (1946): 79–81.

Aguilar Piñal, Francisco. *Bibliografía de autores españoles del siglo XVIII*. Madrid: Consejo Superior de Investigaciones Científicas, 1983.

Aguirre, Manuel de. *Cartas y discursos del militar ingenuo al Correo de los Ciegos de Madrid*. Edited by Antonio Elorza. San Sebastián: Izarra, 1973. First published 1785.

———. *Indagación y reflexiones sobre la Geografía, con algunas noticias previas e indispensables*. Madrid: Joachin Ibarra, 1782.

Aiton, Arthur S. "The Diplomacy of the Louisiana Cession." *American Historical Review* 36 (1931): 701-20.

———. Review of *Ideario de Vasco de Quiroga*, by Silvio Zabala, Colegio de México, México D.F., 1941. *Hispanic American Historical Review* 22, no. 4 (November 1942): 708-9.

Akenson, Donald Harman. *An Irish History of Civilization*. London: Granta Books, 2005.

Alaman, Lucas. *Disertaciones sobre la historia de la República Mejicana desde la época de la conquista*. México D.F.: Lara, 1849.

Alaniz Calderón, Miguel. *Llanto del Melpomene por la sensible muerte del Excmo. Sr. Conde de Gálvez, virrey de la Nueva España*. México: Rangel, 1786.

Alarcón, Justo S. "La presencia histórica del hispano en Estados Unidos: Don Bernardo de Gálvez." *Culturadoor* 19 (1995): 1-10.

Alarios Trigueros, Milagros, and María del Camino Represa Fernández. *Documentos relativos a la independencia de Norteamérica existentes en archivos españoles, vol. II, Archivo General de Simancas: Secretaría de Guerra: Florida y Luisiana (años 1779-1802)*. Madrid: Ministerio de Asuntos Exteriores, 1985.

Albi de la Cuesta, Julio. *Banderas olvidadas: El ejército realista en América*. Madrid: Ediciones de Cultura Hispánica, 1990.

———. "La caballería en América." In *La caballería española: Un eco de clarines* by Julio Albi de la Cuesta, Leopoldo Stampa Piñeiro, and Juan Silvela Milans del Bosch, 165-96. Madrid: Tabapress, 1992.

———. *La defensa de las Indias (1764-1799)*. Madrid: Ediciones Cultura Hispánica, 1987.

Albi de la Cuesta, Julio, and Leopoldo Stampa. "La caballería española en ultramar." *Revista de Historia Militar*, year 29, no. 59 (1985): 107-22.

Albino, Oscar C. "Cevallos, la colonia del Sacramento y la primera invasión inglesa al Río de la Plata." *Boletín del Centro Naval* 810 (January-April 2005): 41-50.

Alcalá Galiano, Antonio. *Historia de España desde los tiempos primitivos hasta la mayoría de la Reina doña Isabel II, redactada y anotada con arreglo a la que escribió en inglés el doctor Dunham*. Madrid: Sociedad Literaria y Tipográfica, 1845.

Alcázar Molina, Cayetano. *Los virreinatos en el siglo XVIII*. Barcelona: Salvat, 1945.

Aldama, Dionisio S. de. *Historia general de España desde los tiempos primitivos hasta fines del año 1860, inclusa la gloriosa guerra de África*. Madrid: Manuel Tello, 1864.

Alden, John Richard. *General Charles Lee: Traitor or Patriot?* Baton Rouge: Louisiana University Press, 1951.

Alemán Illán, Anastasio. "Actitudes colectivas ante la muerte en Murcia durante el siglo XVIII." PhD diss., Universidad de Murcia, 1992.

Alessio Robles, Vito, ed. "Diario y derrotero de lo caminado, visto y observado en la visita que hizo a los presidios de la Nueva España Septentrional el Brigadier don Pedro de Rivera." *Archivo Histórico Militar Mexicano* 2 (1946): 199-234.

Allen, Robert S. *His Majesty's Indian Allies: British Indian Policy in the Defence of Canada, 1774-1815*. Toronto: Dundurn Press, 1992.

Almaraz, Félix D., Jr., "Social Interaction between Civil, Military and Mission Communities in Spanish Colonial Texas during the Height of the Bourbon Reforms, 1763-1772." *Revista Complutense de Historia de América* 21 (1995): 11-28.

———. "An Uninviting Land: El Llano Estacado, 1535-1824." In *Spain and the Plains: Myths and Realities of Spanish Exploration and Settlement on the Great Plains*, edited by Ralph H. Vigil, Frances W. Kaye, and John R. Wunder, 70-89. Niwot: University Press of Colorado, 1994.

Alonso Baquer, Miguel. "Los ministros de Carlos IV frente a la revolución francesa." *Revista de Historia Militar* 14, no. 29 (1970): 79-99.

Alonso Romero, María Paz. "El proceso penal en la Castilla moderna." *Estudis: Revista de Historia Moderna* 22 (1996): 199-215.

Álvarez Barrientos, Joaquín. "Representaciones de la Ilustración. ¿Cómo se vio, cómo la vieron, cómo la vemos?" In *Ilustración, ilustraciones*, edited by Jesús Astigarraga Goenaga, María Victoria López-Cordón Cortezo, and José María Urquia Echave, 1:101-28. Donostia-San Sebastián: Real Sociedad Bascongada de Amigos del País / Sociedad Estatal de Conmemoraciones Culturales, 2009.

Álvarez Noguera, José Rogelio. *José Damián Ortiz de Castro: Maestro mayor de la catedral de México, 1787-1793*. México D.F.: Consejo Nacional para la Cultura y las Artes, 2008.

Álvarez y Baena, Joseph Antonio. *Hijos de Madrid, ilustres en santidad, dignidades, armas, ciencias y artes, diccionario histórico por el orden alfabético de sus nombres*. Madrid: Benito Cano, 1790.

Alvar López, Manuel. "El dialecto canario de la Luisiana." *Catharum: Revista de ciencias y humanidades* 1 (2000): 9-11.

———. *El dialecto canario de Luisiana*. Las Palmas de Gran Canaria: Universidad de Las Palmas de Gran Canaria, 1998.

Alzate Ramírez, José Antonio de. *Consejos útiles para socorrer a la necesidad en tiempo que escasean los comestibles*. México: Felipe de Zúñiga y Ontiveros, 1786.

———. *Memorias y Ensayos*. México D.F.: Universidad Nacional Autónoma de México, 1985.

Amerlinck de Corsi, María Concepción. "Los grandes proyectos de arquitectura y urbanismo." In *México en el mundo de las colecciones de arte, Nueva España* 2, 183-226. México D.F.: Secretaría de Relaciones Exteriores / Universidad Nacional Autónoma de México / Consejo Nacional para la Cultura y las Artes, 1994.

Amo, Bruno del (Recortes). "La Tauromaquia en el siglo XVIII." *Cuadernos Taurinos* 1 (1951): 10-25.

Amores Carredano, Juan Bosco. "La capitanía general de Cuba y la defensa de Luisiana y Florida ante el expansionismo norteamericano (1783-1789)." In *Actas del VII Congreso Internacional de Historia de América*, edited by José Antonio Armillas, 787-97. Zaragoza: Gobierno de Aragón, 1998.

———. "La elite cubana y el reformismo borbónico." In *Reformismo y sociedad en la América borbónica: In memoriam Ronald Escobedo*, edited by Pilar Latasa, 133-54. Pamplona: Ediciones Universidad de Navarra S.A., 2003.

Anderson, Fred. *Crucible of War: The Seven Years' War and the Fate of Empire in British North America, 1754-1766*. New York: Knopf, 2000.

Andrés-Gallego, José. *El motín de Esquilache, América y Europa*. Madrid: Fundación Maphre Tavera / Consejo Superior de Investigaciones Científicas, 2003.

Andreu Ocariz, Juan José. "Los intentos de separación de la capitanía general de Luisiana de la de Cuba." *Estudios: Zaragoza* (1978): 397-431.

———. *La Luisiana española*. Zaragoza: Pedro Cerbuna, 1975.

———. "Militares catalanes en Luisiana." In *Primer Congrés d'Història Moderna de Catalunya*, 2:205-13. Barcelona: Universitat de Barcelona, 1984.

Anes, Gonzalo. "La América virreinal y los procesos de independencia." *Boletín de la Real Academia de Historia* 203, no. 3 (2006): 209-26.

———. *El siglo de las luces*. In *Historia de España*, edited by Miguel Artola, vol. 4. Madrid: Alianza Editorial, 1996.

Angelis, Pedro de. *Colección de obras y documentos relativos a la Historia Antigua y Moderna de las provincias del Río de* La Plata. vol. 4, Buenos Aires: Imprenta del Estado, 1836.

Anonymous. "A la repentina muerte de D. José de Gálvez, ministro de Indias, Décimas." In F. Guillén Robles, *Historia de Málaga y su provincial*, 601. Málaga: Imp. Rubio y Cano, 1874.

Anonymous. *L'art de la guerre changée par l'usage de machines aérostatiques.* Paris, 1784.

Anonymous. *Guarico, 21 January 1783.* In Antonio J. Valdés, *Historia de la Isla de Cuba y en especial de La Habana*, 1:280-82. La Habana: Oficina de la Cena, 1813.

Anonymous. "Mintió la Gaceta el martes, . . ." Wall poster, Madrid, 1775. In Cesáreo Fernández Duro, *Armada española, desde la unión de los reinos de Castilla y Aragón*, 7:179. Madrid: Museo Naval, 1972-73. First published 1895-1903.

Anonymous. "Que por fin todo se errase, . . ." Wall poster, Madrid, 1775. In Antonio Ferrer del Río, *Historia del reinado de Carlos III en España*, 3:134. Madrid: Matute y Compagni, 1856.

Antepara, J. M. *Miranda y la emancipación suramericana: Documentos, históricos y explicativos, que muestran los proyectos que están en curso y los esfuerzos hechos por el general Miranda durante los últimos veinticinco años para la consecución de este objetivo.* Edited by Carmen Bohórquez, Amelia Hernández, and Andrés Cardinale. Caracas: Biblioteca Ayacucho, 2006. First published 1810 in London.

Antolín Espino, María del Populo. "El virrey marqués de Cruillas." In *Los virreyes de la Nueva España en el reinado de Carlos III*, edited by José Antonio Calderón Quijano, 1:1-160. Sevilla: Consejo Superior de Investigaciones Científicas / Escuela de Estudios Hispano-Americanos, 1968.

Apear, Jennifer M. *Race, Sex, and Social Order in Early New Orleans.* Baltimore: Johns Hopkins University Press, 2009.

Araneder, Jeanne and Michèle Etchegoyhen. "Pierres de Soule," in *Harria eta Herria: pierre et pays*, 159-70. Bayonne, Bulletin du Musée Basque, 2003.

Archer, Christon I. *The Army in Bourbon Mexico, 1760-1810.* Albuquerque: University of New Mexico Press, 1977. Spanish ed., *El ejército en el México borbónico, 1760-1810.* México D.F.: Fondo de Cultura Económica, 1983.

Arciniegas, Germán. *Los Comuneros.* México D.F.: Guaranía, 1951. First published 1938.

Arena, Richard C. "Land Settlement Policies and Practices in Spanish Louisiana." In *The Spanish in the Mississippi Valley, 1762-1804*, edited by John Francis McDermott, 51-60. Urbana: University of Illinois Press, 1974.

Arístegui, Pedro de, *Misión en Managua.* Barcelona: Ediciones B, 1989.

Armillas Vicente, José Antonio. "Ayuda secreta y deuda oculta: España y la independencia de los Estados Unidos." In *Norteamérica a finales del siglo XVIII: España y los Estados Unidos*, edited by Eduardo Garrigues, Emma Sánchez Montañés, Sylvia L. Hilton, Almudena Hernández Ruigómez, and Isabel García-Montón, 171-96. Madrid: Fundación Consejo España-Estados Unidos and Editorial Marcial Pons, 2008.

———. "El criollismo luisianés bajo la administración española (una aproximación al tema)." In *Reformismo y sociedad en la América borbónica: In memoriam Ronald Escobedo*, edited by Pilar Latasa, 155-94. Pamplona: Ediciones Universidad de Navarra S.A., 2003.

———. "La educación femenina en la Nueva Orleans: El convento de ursulinas en el siglo XVIII." In *XIII Coloquio de Historia Canario-Americana, VIII Congreso Internacional de Historia de América (Anuario de Estudios Americanos) (1998)*, edited by Francisco Morales Padrón, 1273-82. Las Palmas de Gran Canaria: Cabildo Insular de Gran Canaria, 2000.

———. "El imperio ultramarino español." In *La España moderna*, edited by Enrique Martínez Ruíz, Enrique Giménez, José Antonio Armillas Vicente, and Consuelo Maqueda, 533-58. Madrid: Istmo, 1992.

———. "El nacimiento de una gran nación: Contribución española a la independencia de los Estados Unidos de América del Norte." *Cuadernos de Investigación del Colegio Universitario de Logroño* 3 (1977): 91-98.

———. "Nueva Orleans: El proyecto frustrado de una sociedad distinta (1763-1803)." In *Estrategias de poder en América Latina*, edited by Pilar García Jordán, 97-118. Barcelona: Universitat de Barcelona, 2000.

———. "Nuevas consideraciones sobre la deuda de guerra de los Estados Unidos con España." In *Actas del Congreso de Historia de los Estados Unidos, La Rábida, 5 a 9 de julio de 1976*, 51-63. Madrid: Ministerio de Educación y Ciencia, 1978.

———. "Organización eclesiástica de la Luisiana española: El vicariato." In *Homenaje a Alberto de la Hera*, edited by Soberanes Fernández, José Luis, and Rosa María Martínez de Codes, 21-55. México D.F.: Universidad Nacional Autónoma de México, 2008.

Armistead, Samuel G. "Coplas tradicionales de los isleños de Luisiana." In *Homenaje a José Pérez Vidal*, edited by Carmen Díaz Alayón, 175-83. La Laguna: Litografía A. Romero, 1993.

———. "Tres dialectos españoles de Luisiana." *LEA: Lingüística Española Actual* 13, no. 2 (1991): 279-96.

Arnaiz Amigo, Aurora. "Estudio preliminar a las Enfermedades políticas de la Nueva España de Hipólito Villaroel." In Hipólito Villaroel, *Enfermedades políticas de la Nueva España que padece la capital de esta Nueva España en casi todos los cuerpos de que se compone y remedios que se le deben aplicar para su curación si se quiere que sea útil al Rey y al público* [1785], edited by Genaro Estrada and Aurora Arnaiz Amigo, xvi-lxv México D.F.: Porrúa, 1979.

Aron, Stephen. *American Confluence: The Missionary Frontier from Borderland to Border State*. Bloomington: Indiana University Press, 2006.

Arredondo López, María Adelina. "Andanzas de un pueblo en pos de su escuela (Chihuahua, 1779-1820)." *Historia Mexicana* 49, no. 4 (2000): 549-92.

Arrom, Silvia Marina. *Containing the Poor: The Mexico City Poor House, 1774-1871*. Durham: Duke University Press, 2000.

———. "Vagos y mendigos en la legislación mexicana, 1745-1845." In Beatriz Bernal, coordinator, *IV Congreso de Historia del Derecho Mexicano*, 1:71-87. Barcelona: Montesinos, 1988.

Arsenault, Bona. *Histoire des Acadiens*. Québec: Fides, 2004.

Artacho y Pérez-Blázquez, Fernando de. "Cofradías, congregaciones y hermandades nobiliarias." *Anales de la Real Academia Matritense de Heráldica y Genealogía* 2 (1992-93): 89-112.

L'art de la guerre changes par l'usage de machines aerostatiques. Paris, 1784.

"El arte de la escritura." *El Correo UNESCO: Una ventana abierta al mundo*, year 17 (March 1964).

"*Artículos de Capitulación convenidos y acordados entre el Señor D. Bernardo de Gálvez, Caballero Pensionado de la Real y distinguida Orden de Carlos Tercero, Mariscal de Campo de los Reales Ejércitos de S.M. Católica, Inspector, Superintendente y Gobernador General de la Provincia de la Luisiana, y Comandante General de la*

Expedición; y los Excelentísimos Señores D. Pedro Chester, Escudero, Capitán General, Gobernador Comandante en Jefe, Canciller y Vice-Almirante por S.M. Británica de la Provincia de West-Florida, y Comandante General de las Tropas de S.M. Británica en dicha Provincia." In Bernardo de Gálvez, *Diario de las operaciones contra la plaza de Panzacola 1781*. Madrid: [1781?], 35-45. English translation in Scots Magazine 43, 1781.

Artículos de la Capitulación propuestos por D. Elías Durnford, Esquaire, Teniente de Gobernador de la Provincia de la Florida del Oeste, Capitán de Ingenieros y Comandante de las Tropas de S.M. Británica en el Fuerte Charlota de la Mobila, acordados por el Sr. D. Bernrrardo de Gálvez, Caballero pensionado de la Real y distinguida orden de carlos III, Brigadier de los Ejércitos de S.M., Inspector, Intendente y Gobernador General de la Provincia de la Luisiana y General de la expedición, Campo de la Mobila, March 13, 1780. In *Mercurio Histórico y Político*, July 1780, 315-22.

Artola, Miguel. "América en el pensamiento español del siglo XVIII." *Revista de Indias* 29 (1969): 51-77.

Atienza y Navajas, Julio de. *Nobiliario español: Diccionario heráldico de apellidos españoles y de títulos nobiliarios*. Madrid: Aguilar, 1948.

Atkin, Edmon. *The Appalachian Indian Frontier: The Edmon Atkin Report and Plan of 1755*. Lincoln: University of South Carolina Press, 1967.

Atkinson, James R. *Splendid Land, Splendid People: The Chicasaw Indians to Removal*. Tuscaloosa: University of Alabama Press, 2004.

Aulard, A. "La dette Américaine envers la France." *Revue de Paris* 10 (May 1925): 319-38.

Avilés Fernández, Miguel. *Carlos III y fin del antiguo régimen*. Madrid: EDAF, 1982.

Avilés Flores, Pablo. "La imagen de la independencia de México en Francia: Viajes, intereses científicos y económicos." In *El ejército y la armada en el noroeste de América: Nootka y su tiempo*, edited by Leandro Martínez Peñas and Manuela Fernández Rodríguez, 275-316. Madrid: Universidad rey Juan Carlos, 2011.

Axelrod, Alan. *The Real History of the American Revolution: A New Look at the Past*. New York: Sterling, 2007.

Axtell, James. "The Ethnohistory of Early America: A Review Essay." *William and Mary Quarterly* 35, no. 1 (January 1978): 110-44.

Ayala, Manuel Josef de. *Diccionario de gobierno y legislación de Indias*. Edited by Milagros del Vas Mingo. 13 vols. Madrid: Agencia española de Cooperación Internacional, 1988-96.

B*** D*** [sic]. *Voyage à la Louisiane, et sur le continent de l'Amérique septentrionale, fait dans les années 1794 à 1798*. Paris: Dentu, 1802.

Babcock, Matthew. *Apache Adaptation to Hispanic Rule*. Cambridge: Cambridge University Press, 2016.

Báez Macías, Eduardo. "La Academia de San Carlos en la Nueva España como instrumento de cambio." In *Las academias de arte, VII Coloquio Internacional en Guanajuato*, 38-55. México D.F.: Universidad Nacional Autónoma de México, 1985.

Bails, Benito. *Arismética [sic] para negociantes*. Madrid: Viuda de Ibarra, 1790.

Bails, Benito, and Jerónimo de Capmany. *Tratados de Mathematica que, para las escuelas establecidas en los Regimientos de Infantería, por particular encargo de su inspector general el Excmo. Señor conde de O-Reilly [sic]*. Madrid: Joachin Ibarra, 1772.

Baker, Maury, and Margaret B. Haas, eds. "Bernardo de Gálvez's Combat Diary for the Battle of Pensacola, 1781." *Florida Historical Quarterly* 56, no. 2 (1977): 176-99.

Bancroft, Hubert Howe. *History of Arizona and New Mexico, 1550-1888*. In *Collected Works*, vol. 17. San Francisco: History Company, 1889.

———. *History of Mexico, 1600–1803*. In *The Works of Hubert Howe Bancroft*, vol. 11. San Francisco: Bancroft and Co., 1883.

Banks, Joseph. "Sur un Moyen de Donner la Direction aux Machines Aérostatiques: Par M. Le Comte de Galvez." *Philosophical Transactions of the Royal Society of London* 74 (1784): 469–70.

Barcia, Ángel María de. *Catálogo de los Retratos de personajes españoles que se conservan en la sección de estampas y de bellas artes de la Biblioteca Nacional*. Madrid: Viuda é hijos de M. Tello impresor de cámara de S.M., 1901.

Barea, Juan Bautista. *Oración fúnebre del Excelentísimo Señor don Bernardo de Gálvez, conde de Gálvez*. Havana: Imprenta de la Curia Episcopal, 1787. Biblioteca Nacional, Madrid, VE/1233/15.

Barr, Julianna. *Peace Came in the Form of a Woman: Indians and Spaniards in the Texas Borderlands*. Chapel Hill: University of North Carolina Press, 2007.

Bartra, Roger. "Doce historias de melancolía en la Nueva España." *FRENIA* 4, no. 1 (2004): 31–52.

Bartroli, Tomás. "Presencia hispánica en la costa noroeste de América (siglo XVIII)." In *Actas del III Congreso de la Asociación Internacional de Hispanistas (1968)*, edited by Carlos H. Magis, 105–15. México D.F.: El Colegio de México, 1970.

Basso, Keith H. "Western Apache." In *Handbook of North American Indians*, edited by William C. Sturtevant, vol. 10, *Southwest*, edited by Alfonso Ortiz, 462–88. Washington, D.C.: Smithsonian Institution, 1983.

Batista González, Juan. "Significación político-estratégica de la ruta juniperiana." *Revista de Historia Militar* 59 (1985): 73–106.

Baudier, Roger. *The Catholic Church in Louisiana*. New Orleans: A. W. Hyatt Stationery, 1939.

Becker, Jerónimo. *España e Inglaterra, sus relaciones políticas desde las paces de Utrecht*. Madrid: Ambrosio Pérez y cía., 1906.

Beer, William. "The Surrender of Fort Charlotte, Mobile, 1780." *American Historical Review* 1, no. 4 (July 1896): 696–99.

Beerman, Eric. "An Aztec Emperor's Descendant, General Jeronimo Giron y Moctezuma: Spanish Commander at the Battle of Mobile, 1780." *Genealogist* 5, no. 2 (Fall 1984): 172–87.

———. "La bella criolla Felicitas de Saint Maxent, viuda de Bernardo de Gálvez, en España." In *Norteamérica a finales del siglo XVIII: España y los Estados Unidos*, edited by Eduardo Garrigues, Emma Sánchez Montañés, Sylvia L. Hilton, Almudena Hernández Ruigómez, and Isabel García-Montón, 281–96. Madrid: Fundación Consejo España–Estados Unidos and Editorial Marcial Pons.

———. "Bernardo de Gálvez and the 1779 Battle of Baton Rouge." *SAR Magazine* (Louisville, Sons of the American Revolution) 75, no. 1 (Summer 1980): 32–33.

———. "Bernardo de Gálvez y la ayuda a la independencia de los Estados Unidos." *Péndulo: Revista del Colegio Oficial de Ingenieros Técnicos Industriales de Málaga* (March 2007): 112–23.

———. "El conde de Aranda en la tertulia madrileña (1788–90) de la viuda de Bernardo de Gálvez." In *El Conde de Aranda y su tiempo*, edited by José A. Ferrer Benimeli, Esteban Sarasa, and Eliseo Serrano, 349–62. Zaragoza: Institución Fernando el Católico-Excma. Diputación de Zaragoza, 2000.

———. "El diario de Bernardo de Gálvez en la batalla de Mobila (1780)." *Cuadernos de Investigación Histórica* 13 (1990): 125–44.

———. *España y la independencia de Estados Unidos*. Madrid: MAPFRE, 1992.

———. "The French Ancestors of Felicite de St. Maxent." *New Orleans Genesis* 17, no. 68 (September 1968): 403-7. Also published in *Revue de Louisiana* 6, no. 1 (Summer 1977): 69-75.

———. "Governor Bernardo de Galvez's New Orleans Belle: Felicitas de St. Maxent." *Revista Española de Estudios Norteamericanos* 7 (1994): 39-44.

———. "The Last Battle of the American Revolution: Yorktown. No, the Bahamas! (The Spanish-American Expedition to Nassau in 1782)." *The Americas: A Quarterly Review of Inter-American Cultural History* 45 (July 1988): 79-95.

———. "¿Quién era el General Urrutia que Goya retrató?" *Revista Complutense de Historia de América* 19 (1993): 195-208.

———. "Yo solo not solo: Juan Antonio de Riaño." *Florida Historical Quarterly* 58, no. 2 (October 1979): 174-84.

———. *Yo Solo: The Battle Journal of Bernardo de Gálvez during the American Revolution, Introduction*. New Orleans: Polyanthos Press, 1978.

———, ed. "Last Will and Testament of Bernardo de Gálvez." *Louisiana Genealogical Register* 27, no. 2 (June 1980): 102-14; no. 3 (September 1980): 201-15; no. 4 (December 1980): 301-14.

Beerman, Eric, and Gilbert C. Din, trans. "Victory on the Mississippi, 1779." In *The Louisiana Purchase Bicentennial Series in Louisiana History, Vol. 2: The Spanish Presence in Louisiana, 1763-1803*, edited by Gilbert C. Din, 192-202. Lafayette: Center for Louisiana Studies, University of Southwestern Louisiana, 1996.

Beevor, Antony. *D-Day: The Battle for Normandy*. London: Viking, 2009.

Belden, Bauman L. *Indian Peace Medals Issued in the United States, 1789-1889*. New Milford, Conn.: N. Flayderman, 1966.

Béligand, Nadine. "La muerte en la ciudad de México en el siglo XVIII." *Historia Mexicana* 57, no. 1 (2007): 5-52.

Bemis, Samuel Flagg. *The Diplomacy of the American Revolution*. Bloomington: Indiana University Press, 1967. First published 1935.

———. *Pinckney's Treaty: A Study of America's Advantage from Europe's Distress, 1783-1800*. New Haven: Yale University Press, 1960. First published 1926.

Beristain, José Mariano. *Biblioteca Hispano americana septentrional o catálogo y noticias de los literatos, que o nacidos, o educados, o florecientes en la América septentrional española, han dado a luz algún escrito, o lo han dejado preparado para la prensa*. México D.F.: Alejandro Valdés, 1819. Quoted in Genaro Estrada, *Obras completas*, 2:256. México D.F.: Siglo XXI, 1988.

Berlin, Ira. *Many Thousands Gone: The First Two Centuries of Slavery in North America*. Cambridge, Mass.: Harvard University Press, 1998.

Bermúdez Plata, Cristóbal. "Historia de las banderas inglesas depositadas en 1786 en la Capilla de Nuestra Señora de los Reyes de la Catedral Hispalense." *Archivo Hispalense: Revista histórica, literaria y artística* 12, no. 39-41 (1950): 205-8.

Bernabéu Albert, Salvador. "La venganza de Sancho Panza: Cartas y sátiras de Juan Manuel de Viniegra, secretario de don José de Gálvez, 1765-1770." *Jahrbuch für Geschichte Lateinamerikas / Anuario de Historia de América Latina* 47 (2010): 37-58.

———, ed. *El Septentrión novohispano: Ecohistoria, sociedades e imágenes de frontera*. Madrid: Consejo Superior de Investigaciones Científicas, 2000.

Berry, Jane M. "The Indian Policy of Spain in the Southwest, 1783-1795." *Mississippi Valley Historical Review* 3, no. 4 (March 1917): 462-77.

Bethell, Leslie, ed. *Historia de América latina: vol. 5 la independencia*. Barcelona: Crítica, 1991. First published 1985 by Cambridge University Press.

Betts, C. Willys. *American Colonial History Illustrated by Contemporary Medals*. New York: Scott Stamp and Coin Co., 1894.

Bispham, Clarence Wyatt. "Contest for Ecclesiastical Supremacy in the Valley of the Mississippi, 1763–1803." *Louisiana Historical Quarterly* 1 (1917): 155–89.

Black, Jeremy. *European Warfare in a Global Context, 1600–1815*. New York: Routledge, 2007.

———. *Warfare in the Eighteenth Century*. London: Cassell, 1999.

Blackhawk, Ned. *Violence over the Land: Indians and Empires in the Early American West*. Cambridge, Mass.: Harvard University Press, 2006.

Blanch, Luis. *De la ciencia militar considerada en sus relaciones con las demás ciencias y el estado social: Nueve discursos*. Madrid: García Padrós, 1851.

Blanco Nuñez, José María. *La construcción naval en Ferrol, 1726–2011*. Madrid: Navantia, 2011.

Blume, Helmut. "El cultivo de la caña de azúcar en Andalucía, comparado con el cultivo de la caña en Luisiana." *Estudios geográficos* 19, no. 70 (1958): 87–120.

Blumenthal, Walter Hart, ed. *Eccentric Typography*. Worcester, Mass.: Achille J. St. Onge, 1963.

Blyth, Lance R. *Chiricahua and Janos: Communities of Violence in the Southwestern Borderlands, 1680–1880*. Lincoln: University of Nebraska Press, 2012.

Boeta, José Rodulfo. *Bernardo de Gálvez*. Madrid: Publicaciones Españolas, 1977.

Bohórquez Morán, Carmen L. *Francisco de Miranda: Precursor de Las Independencias de la América Latina*. Caracas: Gobierno Bolivariano de Venezuela, Ministerio de la Cultura, Fundación Editorial El Perro y la Rana, 2006.

Boissier de Sauvages de Lacroix, François. *Nosologie méthodique*. Lyon, 1772.

Boletín de la Sociedad Económica de Amigos del País de Málaga 9, September 30, 1861.

Bolton, Herbert Eugene. *Athanase de Mézières and the Louisiana-Texas Frontier, 1768–1780*. Cleveland: Arthur H. Clark, 1914.

———. "The Epic of Greater America." *American Historical Review* 38 (April 1933): 448–74.

———. *The Spanish Borderlands: A Chronicle of Old Florida and the Southwest*. New Haven: Yale University Press, 1921.

Bonilla, Antonio. *Breve compendio de los sucesos ocurridos en la Provincia de Texas desde su conquista ó reducción hasta la fecha, México, 10 de noviembre de 1772*. In Elizabeth Howard West, ed. and trans., "Bonilla's Brief Compendium of the History of Texas (1772)." *Texas Historical Association Quarterly* 8 (1904): 3–78.

Borah, Woodrow Wilson. "Alguna luz sobre el autor de las Enfermedades Políticas." *Estudios de Historia Novohispana* 8, no. 8 (1985): 51–79.

———. *Justice by Insurance: The General Indian Court of Colonial Mexico and the Legal Aides of the Half-Real*. Berkeley: University of California Press, 1983.

Borges, Pedro. "Primero hombres, luego cristianos: La Transculturación." In *Historia de la Iglesia en Hispanoamérica y Filipinas*, edited by Pedro Borges, 1:521–34. Madrid: Biblioteca de Autores Cristianos, 1992.

Borreguero Beltrán, Cristina. "Extranjeros al servicio del Ejército español en el siglo XVIII." In *Coloquio Internacional Carlos III y su Siglo: Actas, Poder y sociedad en la época de Carlos III*, 2:75–93. Madrid: Universidad Complutense / Departamento de Historia Moderna, 1990.

Böttcher, Nikolaus. "Juan de Miralles: Un comerciante cubano en la guerra de independencia norteamericana." *Anuario de Estudios Americanos* 57, no. 1 (2000): 171–94.

Boulle, Pierre Henri. "The French Colonies and the Reform of Their Administration during and Following the Seven Years' War." PhD diss., University of California, Berkeley, 1968.

Bourgoing, Jean-François, Baron de. *Modern State of Spain: Exhibiting a Complete View of Its Topography, Government, Laws, Religion, Finances, Naval and Military Establishments.* London: J. Stockdale, 1808.

Boussuge, Hains. Article without title in *Louisiana Creole; Gazette des salons, des arts et des modes.* Quoted in Virginia R. Domínguez, *White by Definition: Social Classification in Creole Louisiana*, 121. Newark: Rutgers State University, 1986.

Boyd, Mark F., and José Navarro Latorre. "Spanish Interest in British Florida, and the Progress of the American Revoluton." *Florida Historical Quarterly* 32 (1953): 92–130.

Brading, D. A. "Government and Elite in Late Colonial Mexico." *Hispanic American Historical Review* 53, no. 3 (1973): 389–414.

Brasseaux, Carl A. "The Moral Climate of French Colonial Louisiana, 1699–1763." *Louisiana History: The Journal of the Louisiana Historical Association* 27, no. 1 (Winter 1986): 27–41.

Braudel, Fernand. *La méditerranée et le monde méditerranéen à l'époque de Philippe II.* 2nd ed. Paris: Armand Colin, 1966.

———. *El mediterráneo y el mundo mediterráneo en la época de Felipe II.* 4th reimp. México D.F.: Fondo de Cultura Económica, 1997.

Bravo, Fernando Rodrigo. "Las élites militares en Venezuela (1760–1810)." *Estudios de Historia Social y Económica de América* 12 (1995): 505–86.

Bravo Ugarte, José. *Historia sucinta de Michoacán.* Morelia: Morevallado, 1995.

Breña, Roberto. "The Emancipation Process in New Spain and the Cádiz Constitution: New Historiographical Paths Regarding the Revoluciones Hispánicas." In *The Rise of Constitutional Government in the Iberian Atlantic World: The Impact of the Cádiz Constitution of 1812*, edited by Scott Eastman and Natalia Sobrevilla Perea, 42–62. Tuscaloosa: University of Alabama Press, 2015.

———. *El primer liberalismo español y los procesos de emancipación de América 1808–1824: Una revisión historiográfica del liberalismo hispánico.* México D.F.: Colegio de México, 2006.

———. *El imperio de las circunstancias: Las independencias hispanoamericanas y la revolución liberal española.* México: El Colegio de México/Marcial Pons, 2013.

Brewer, John. *The Sinews of Power: War, Money and the English State, 1688–1783.* Cambridge, Mass.: Harvard University Press, 1988.

Bright, Charles, and Michael Geyer. "Where in the World Is America? The History of the United States in the Global Age." In *Rethinking American History in a Global Age*, edited by Thomas Bender, 63–99. Berkeley: University of California Press, 2002.

Brinckerhoff, Sidney B., and Odie B. Faulk, ed. and trans. *Lancers for the King: A Study of the Frontier Military System of Northern New Spain, with a Translation of the Royal Regulations of 1772.* Phoenix: Arizona Historical Foundation, 1965.

Brooks, James F. *Captives and Cousins: Slavery, Kinship, and Community in the Southwest Borderlands.* Chapel Hill: University of North Carolina Press, 2002.

Brown, Thomas. *La Academia de San Carlos de la Nueva España.* México, D.F.: Secretaría de Educación Pública, 1976.

Bueno Carrera, José María. *Tropas virreinales.* Málaga: J. M. Bueno, 1983.

Burrus, Ernest J. "Pueblo Warriors Spanish Conquest." *Manuscripta* 11, no. 1 (1967): 58.

Bushnell, Amy. "Spain's Conquest by Contract: Pacification and Mission System in Eastern North America." In *The World Turned Upside-Down: The State of Eighteenth-*

Century American Studies at the Beginning of the Twenty-First Century, edited by Michael V. Kennedy and William G. Shade, 289-320. Bethlehem, Penn.: Lehigh University Press, 2001.

Bustelo García del Real, Francisco. "La transformación de vecinos en habitants: El problema del coeficiente." *Estudios Geográficos* 23, no. 130 (1973): 154-64.

Cabrera Leiva, Guillermo. "Bernardo de Gálvez (1746-1786)." *Diario Las Americas*, August 24, 1996.

Cabrera Ortíz, José Luis. "Cabrera, una familia de Macharaviaya y Vélez-Málaga en los siglos XVIII y XIX." *Isla de Arriarán: Revista Cultural y Científica* 9 (1997): 31-41.

Cabrero, Leoncio. "Francisco Sabatini y la fortificación de la Luisiana." *Revista Trabajos y Conferencias* 2, no. 3 (1958): 142-48.

Cadalso, José. *Cartas marruecas del coronel D. Joseph Cadahalso*. Madrid: Imprenta de Sancha, 1793.

Cadenas y Vicent, Vicente de. *Extracto de los expedientes de la Orden de Carlos III, 1771-1847*. 8 vols. Madrid: Consejo Superior de Investigaciones Científicas, 1979-86.

Calderón Cuadrado, Reyes. "Alianzas comerciales hispano-norteamericanas en la financiación del proceso de independencia de los Estados Unidos de América: La Casa Gardoqui e hijos." In *Norteamérica a finales del siglo XVIII: España y los Estados Unidos*, edited by Eduardo Garrigues, Emma Sánchez Montañés, Sylvia L. Hilton, Almudena Hernández Ruigómez, and Isabel García-Montón, 197-218. Madrid: Fundación Consejo España-Estados Unidos and Editorial Marcial Pons, 2008.

Calderón Quijano, José Antonio. "El banco de San Carlos y las comunidades de indios de Nueva España." *Anuario de Estudios Americanos* 19 (1962): 1-144.

———. "El fuerte de San Fernando de Omoa: Su historia e importancia que tuvo en la defensa del golfo de Honduras. Primera Parte." *Revista de Indias* 3/3 (1942): 515-48.

———. "El fuerte de San Fernando de Omoa: Su historia e importancia que tuvo en la defensa del golfo de Honduras. Continuación." *Revista de Indias* 4 (1943): 127-63.

———. "El ingeniero Simón Desnaux y su proyecto de Academias Militares en América." *Revista de Indias* 6 (1945): 635-50.

———. "Recensión de la *Política Marroquí de Carlos III* de Vicente Rodríguez Casado." *Revista de Estudios Políticos*, no. 27-28 (1946): 411-20.

———, ed. *Los virreyes de la Nueva España en el reinado de Carlos III*. 2 vols. Sevilla: Consejo Superior de Investigaciones Científicas—Escuela de Estudios Hispano-Americanos, 1968.

———, ed. *Los virreyes de la Nueva España en el reinado de Carlos IV*. Sevilla: Consejo Superior de Investigaciones Científicas—Escuela de Estudios Hispano-Americanos, 1972.

Calleja Leal, Guillermo, and Hugo O'Donnell y Duque de Estrada. *1762. La Habana inglesa. La toma de La Habana por los ingleses*. Madrid: AECI-Ediciones de Cultura Hispánica, 1999.

Calles Montaño, David Jacobo. "Territorio, cristiandad y rebelión en las misiones Jesuitas entre los Seris, 1679-1767." In *Misiones del noroeste de México, origen y destino*, edited by José Rómulo Félix Gastélum and Raquel Padilla Ramos, 135-51. México D.F.: Consejo Nacional para la Cultura y las Artes, Mexico, 2006.

Calloway, Colin G. *The American Revolution in Indian Country: Crisis and Diversity in Native American Communities*. New York: Cambridge University Press, 1995.

———. *First Peoples: A Documentary Survey of American Indian History*. 5th ed. Boston: Bedford and St. Martin's, 2016.

———. *New Worlds for All: Indians, Europeans, and the Remaking of Early America.* Baltimore: Johns Hopkins Unversity Press, 1997.
———. *One Vast Winter Count: The Native American West before Lewis and Clark.* Lincoln: University of Nebraska Press, 2003.
———. *The Scratch of a Pen: 1763 and the Transformation of North America.* Oxford: Oxford University Press, 2008.
Campillo y Cossío, José del [attrib]. *Nuevo sistema de govierno económico para la América.* Madrid: Imprenta de Benito Cano, 1789.
Campos, Rubén M. *Chapultepec, su leyenda y su historia.* México D.F.: Talleres gráficos de la Nación, 1922.
Canales Guerrero, Pedro. "Propuesta metodológica y estudio de caso ¿Crisis alimentarias o crisis epidémicas? Tendencia demográfica y mortalidad diferencial, Zinacantepec, 1613-1816." In *Problemas demográficos vistos desde la historia: Análisis de fuentes, comportamiento y distribución de la población en México, siglos XVI-XIX,* edited by América Molina del Villar and David Navarrete Gómez, 67-107. México D.F.: El Colegio de Michoacán / CIESAS, 2006,
Canga Argüelles, José. *Diccionario de Hacienda para el uso de los encargados de la suprema drección [sic] de ella.* Londres: Imprenta Española de M. Calero, 1827.
Cañizares-Esguerra, Jorge. *How to Write the History of the New World: Histories, Epistemologies and Identities in the Eighteenth-Century Atlantic World.* Stanford: Stanford University Press, 2001.
Cannon, Richard. *Historical Record of the Sixteenth, or the Bedfordshire Regiment of Foot; Containing an Account of the Formation of the Regiment in 1688, and of Its Subsequent Services to 1848.* London: Parker, Furnivall and Parker, 1848.
Cano Sordo, Víctor. *De la Luisiana a la Nueva España: La Historia de Juan Bernardo Domínguez y Gálvez (1783-1847).* México D.F.: Impresora Múltiple, 1999.
Cantillo, Alejandro del. *Tratados, convenios y declaraciones de paz y de comercio que han hecho con las potencias extranjeras los monarcas españoles de la casa de Borbón desde el año de 1700 hasta el día.* Madrid: Alegría y Charlain, 1843.
Carbajal López, David. "Los años del hambre en Bolaños (1785-1786): Conflictos mineros, escasez de maíz y sobremortalidad." *Relaciones: Estudios de historia y sociedad* 31, no. 121 (2010): 57-81.
Carbonero y Sol, León. *Índice de los libros prohibidos por el Santo oficio de la Inquisición Española desde su primer decreto hasta el éltimo, que espidió [sic: expidió] en 29 mayo 1819, y por los rdos. Obispos españoles desde esta fecha hasta fin de diciembre de 1872.* Madrid: Antonio Pérez Dubrull, 1873.
Cárdenas Gutiérrez, Salvador. "Las insignias del rey: Disciplina y ritual público en la ciudad de México (siglos XVI-XVIII)." *Jahrbuch für Geschichte Lateinamerikas / Anuario de Historia de América Latina* 39 (2002): 193-216.
Cárdenas Piera, Emilio de. *Propuestas, solicitudes y decretos de la Real y muy distinguida Orden de Carlos III.* Madrid: Hidalguía, 1966.
Carlisle, Jeffrey D. "Spanish Relations with the Apache Nations East of the Rio Grande." PhD diss., University of North Texas, 2001.
Carlos III. *Instrucción reservada que la Junta de estado, creada formalmente por mi decreto de este día, 8 de julio de 1787, deberá observar en todos los puntos y ramos encargados a su conocimiento y examen.* Edited by Andrés Muriel. Paris: Girard hermanos, sucesores de Teófilo Barrois y de Baudry, 1838.
Carlyle, Thomas. *History of Friedrich II of Prussia, called Frederick the Great.* Boston: Dana Estes and Charles E. Lauriat, 1884. First published 1858-65.

Carr, Henry. *Old Mother Mexico*. New York: Houghton Mifflin, 1931.
Carramolino, Juan Martín. *Historia de Ávila, su provincia y obispado*. Madrid: Librería Española, 1873.
Carrasco, Ricardo. *Francisco de Miranda, precursor de la independencia hispanoamericana, 1750-1792: Teniente coronel de España, coronel de Rusia, mariscal de campo de Francia y generalísimo de Venezuela*. Caracas: Bell, 1951.
Carreño, Alberto María. *La diplomacia extraordinaria entre México y Estados Unidos: 1789-1947*. México D.F.: Jus, 1961.
Carrillo, Joaquín. *Llanto de México en la muerte del Excmo. Sr. D. Matías de Gálvez, virrey*... México: Felipe de Zúñiga y Ontiveros, 1785. In Francisco de Solano, *Las voces de la ciudad: México a través de sus impresos, 1539-1821*, 206. Madrid: Consejo Superior de Investigaciones Científicas, 1994.
Carrillo y Gariel, Abelardo. *Datos sobre la Academia de San Carlos de Nueva España*. México D.F.: s.n., 1939.
Casas, Bartolomé de las. *An Account of the First Voyages and Discoveries Made by the Spaniards in America. Containing the Most Exact Relation Hitherto Publish'd of Their Unparallel'd Cruelties on the Indians, in the Destruction of Above Forty Millions of People. With the Propositions Offer'd to the King of Spain to Prevent the Further Ruin of the West-Indies*. London: J. Darby for D. Brown, J. Harris, and Andr. Bell, 1699. Library of Congress, Washington, D.C., F1411.C426 and F1411.C426.
———. *Apologética histórica*. Edited by Juan Pérez de Tudela Bueso. Madrid: Biblioteca de Autores Españoles-Atlas, 1958.
Cases, Victor. "El Censor: La prensa crítica en la Ilustración española." Murcia: Biblioteca Virtual de Pensamiento Político Hispánico Saavedra Fajardo, 2006.
Cashin, Edward J. *William Bartram and the American Revolution on the Southern Frontier*. Columbia: University of South Carolina Press, 2000.
Castañeda, José. *Informe jurídico dirigido al Rey por la muy noble y muy leal ciudad de México, cabeza de la Nueva España, a favor de los españoles nacidos en la América para que se les prefiera en los empleos eclesiásticos, políticos y militares*. Madrid: Pantaleón Aznar, 1786.
Castañeda Delgado, Paulino. *Don Vasco de Quiroga y su "Información en Derecho."* Madrid: José Porrúa Turanzas, 1974.
Castañeda Iturbide, Jaime. *Gobernantes de la Nueva España*. México D.F.: Departamento del Distrito Federal, 1986.
Castillo Meléndez, Francisco. "La aventura americana de unos labradores granadinos (1777-1787)." In *El Reino de Granada y el Nuevo Mundo, V Congreso internacional de Historia de América, mayo de 1992*, 109-33. Granada: Diputación Provincial de Granada, 1994.
Castro, José Agustín de. *Sentimientos de la América justamente dolorida en la temprana, inesperada muerte del Excmo. Sr. Conde de Gálvez, su virrey, gobernador y capitán general*. México: Felipe de Zúñiga y Ontiveros, 1786.
Castro Olivas, Jorge Luis. "Sociedades secretas y masonería en el proceso de emancipación peruano: La Logia Lautaro en el Perú." PhD diss., Universidad Nacional Mayor de San Carlos, 2009.
Castro Osores [*sic*: Ozores], Manuel. *Tiernos suspiros con que se procura explicar el verdadero y debido sentimiento de México en la dolorosa muerte de Excmo. Sr. Conde de Gálvez, su virrey*. México, 1786.
Catlin, George. *Last Rambles amongst the Indians of the Rocky Mountains and the Andes*. London: Sampson Low, Son and Marston, 1868.

Caughey, John Walton. "Bernardo de Gálvez and the English Smugglers on the Mississippi, 1777." *Hispanic American Historical Review* 12, no. 1 (February 1932): 46-58.

———. *Bernardo de Gálvez in Louisiana, 1776-1783*. Los Angeles: Pelican, Gretna, 1998. First published 1934, University of California Press.

———. *McGillivray of the Creeks*. Norman: University of Oklahoma Press, 1938.

———. "The Natchez Rebellion of 1781 and Its Aftermath." *Louisiana Historical Quarterly* 16 (January 1933): 57-83.

———. "The Panis Mission to Pensacola, 1778." *Hispanic American Historical Review* 10, no. 4 (November 1930): 480-89.

———. "Willing's Expedition Down the Mississippi, 1778." *Louisiana Historical Quarterly* 15 (January 1932): 5-36.

———, ed. *East Florida, 1783-1785: A File of Documents Assembled, and Many of Them Translated by Joseph Byrne Lockey*. Berkley: University of California Press, 1949.

Caulfield, Ruby van Allen. *French Literature of Louisiana*. New Orleans: Pelican, s.a.

Cavallo, Tiberius. *The History and Practice of Aerostation*. London: C. Dilly, 1785.

Cavo, Andrés, and Carlos María de Bustamante. *Los tres siglos de México durante el gobierno español, hasta la entrada del ejército trigarante*. México D.F.: Luis Abadiano y Valdés, 1836.

Cayton, Andrew, and Fredrika Tuete, eds. *Contact Points: American Frontiers from the Mohawk Valley to the Mississippi, 1750-1830*. Chapel Hill: University of North Carolina Press, 1998.

Ceano González, Diego. "Los Gálvez de Macharaviaya." *El Avisador Malagueño, Revista Cultural Malagueña* 4 (April 2006): 3-5.

Cebrián González, María del Carmen. "El obispado de Nueva Orleans." *Hispania Sacra* 40, no. 82 (1988): 777-89.

Certeau, Michel de. *L'invention du quotidien. 1. Arts de faire*. Paris: Gallimard, 1990. First published 1980.

Cervantes, Miguel de. *Don Quijote de la Mancha*. Barcelona: Instituto Cervantes-Crítica, 1998.

Céspedes del Castillo, Guillermo. *América Hispánica (1492-1898)*. Vol. 6 of *Historia de España*, edited by Manuel Tuñón de Lara. Barcelona: Lábor, 1985.

———. *Textos y documentos de la América Hispánica (1492-1898)*. Vol. 13 of *Historia de España*, edited by Manuel Tuñón de Lara. Barcelona: Lábor, 1985.

———. "La visita como institución indiana." *Anuario de Estudios Americanos* 3 (1946): 984-1025.

Chace, Jesse G. "Defining Asymmetric Warfare: A Losing Proposition." *Joint Force Quarterly* 61 (second quarter 2011): 123-28.

Chadwick, Ensor. *The Relations of the United States and Spain*. New York: Charles Scribner's Sons, 1909.

Chandler, Richard E. "Ulloa's Account of the 1768 Revolt." *Louisiana History: The Journal of the Louisiana Historical Association* 27, no. 4 (Autumn 1986): 407-37.

Chantreau, Pierre Nicolás. *Arte de hablar bien francés, ó gramática completa, dividida en tres partes*. Madrid: Antonio de Sancha, 1781.

Chaplin, Joyce E. "Expansion and Exceptionalism in Early American History." *Journal of American History* 89, no. 4 (2003): 1431-55.

Charlot, Jean. *Mexican Art and the Academy of San Carlos, 1785-1915*. Austin: University of Texas Press, 1962.

Chartrand, René. *American Loyalist Troops 1775-84*. Illustrated by Gerry Embleton and Samuel Embleton. London: Osprey, 2008.

Chauca García, Jorge. "Entre Andalucía y América: El malagueño José de Gálvez y la proyección de su red clientelar en Indias." In *Las élites en la época moderna: La monarquía española*, edited by Enrique Soria Mesa, Juan Jesús Bravo Caro, and José Miguel Delgado Barrado, 2:121-32. Córdoba: Universidad de Córdoba, 2009.

Chávez, Thomas E. *Spain and the Independence of the United States: An Intrinsic Gift*. Albuquerque: University of New Mexico Press, 2002.

———. "Spanish Policy and Strategy." In *Strategy in the American War of Independence: A Global Approach*, edited by Donald Stoker, Kenneth J. Hagan, and Michael T. McMaster, 163-75. New York: Routledge, 2010.

Chiva Beltrán, Juan. "El ocaso de un ceremonial: Las últimas entradas virreinales de la Nueva España." In *Actas XIV Congreso Internacional de Asociación de Historiadores Latinoamericanistas Europeos*, 1-12. Castellón: Universidad Jaume I, 2005.

———. *El triunfo del virrey. Glorias novohispanas: Origen, apogeo y ocaso de la entrada virreinal*. Castellón: Universitat Jaume I, 2012.

Chroniques de la régence d'Alger, traduites d'un manuscrit arabe intitule "El-Zohrat-el-Nayerat." Translated by Alphonse Rousseau. Alger: Imprimerie du Gouvernement, 1841.

Chul, Park. "La república utópica en el Quijote." *Revista de Educación*, special issue (2004): 177-87.

Churchill, Winston S. *A History of the English-Speaking Peoples*. London: Cassell, 1959. First published 1956.

Ciano, Count Galeazzo. *Ciano's Diary, 1939-1943*. London: Malcolm and W. Heinemann, 1947.

Claret, Pompeyo. *José de Gálvez, marqués de la Sonora*. Barcelona: Casulleras, 1963.

Clark, Emily. *Masterless Mistresses: The New Orleans Ursulines and the Development of a New World Society, 1727-1834*. Chapel Hill: University of North Carolina Press, 2012.

———, ed. *Voices from an Early American Convent: Marie Madeleine Hachard and the New Orleans Ursulines, 1727-1760*. Baton Rouge: Louisiana State University Press, 2007.

Clausewitz, Carl von. *On War*. London: Penguin, 1982. First published 1832.

Clavero, Bartolomé. "Delito y Pecado: Noción y escala de transgresiones." In *Sexo Barroco y otras transgresiones premodernas*, edited by Francisco Tomás y Valiente, 57-89. Madrid: Alianza Universidad, 1990.

Clavijo García, Agustín. *La Semana Santa malagueña en su iconografía desaparecida*. Málaga: Arguval, 1987.

"*Code Noir*: Edit du Roi, touchant l'Etat & la discipline des esclaves négres de la Louisiane, donné à Versailles au mois de mars de 1724." In *Recueils de règlements, édits, déclarations et arrêts concernant le commerce, l'administration de la justice et la police des colonies françaises de l'Amérique*, 135-56. Paris: Libraires associez, 1744-45.

Coker, William S. "Pensacola, 1686-1821." In *Archaelogy of Colonial Pensacola*, edited by Judith Ann Bense, 5-60. Gainesville: University Press of Florida, 1999.

———. *The Siege of Pensacola 1781 in Maps, with Data on Troop Stregnth, Military Units, Ships, Casualties and Related Statistics*. Pensacola: Perdido Bay Press, 1981.

Coker, William S., and Hazel P. Coker. "The Siege of Mobile, 1780, in Maps." In *Alabama and the Borderlands: From Prehistory to Statehood*, edited by Reid Badger and Lawrence Clayton, 162-83. Tuscaloosa: University of Alabama Press, 1985.

Coker, William S., J. D. L. Holmes, S. Proctor, and J. L. Wright. "Research in the Spanish

Borderlands: Bibliography." *Latin American Research Review: The Latin American Studies Association* 7, no. 2 (1972): 55-94.

Coker, William S., and Robert R. Rea, eds. *Anglo-Spanish Confrontation on the Gulf Coast during the American Revolution: Gálvez Celebration, Commemorating the Siege of Pensacola*. Pensacola: Gulf Coast History and Humanities Conference, 1982.

Cole, Shawn. "Capitalism and Freedom: Manumissions and the Slave Market in Louisiana, 1725-1820." *Journal of Economic History* 65, no. 4 (December 2005): 1008-27.

Colección de documentos inéditos relativos al descubrimiento, conquista y organización de las antiguas posesiones de América y Oceanía. Madrid, 1864-84.

Colección general de las providencias hasta aquí tomadas sobre el estrañamiento y ocupación de temporalidades de los Regulares de la Compañía que existían en los dominios de S.M. de España, Indias, e Islas Filipinas á consequencia del Real Decreto de 27 de Febrero, y Pragmática-Sanción de 2 de Abril de 1767. Madrid: Imprenta Real de la Gazeta, 1767.

Coleman, Emma Lewis. *New England Captives Carried to Canada, between 1677 and 1760 during the French and Indian Wars*. Westminster: Heritage Books, 2008.

Coleman, James J. *Gilbert Antoine de St. Maxent: The Spanish-Frenchman of New Orleans*. New Orleans: Pelican, 1968.

Colley, Linda. *Britons: Forging the Nation, 1707-1837*. New Haven: Yale University Press, 1992.

Comellas, José Luis. *Historia de España Moderna y Contemporánea*. Madrid: Rialp, 1967.

Concepción, Fray Juan de la. *Historia general de Philipinas: Conquistas espirituales, y teporales de estos españoles dominios, establecimientos, progresos y decadencias*. Pueblo de Sampaloc: Convento de Nuestra Señora de Loreto, 1792.

Conde y Oquendo, Francisco Javier. *Oración fúnebre que en las exequias militares celebradas por la Plaza de México en su Santa Iglesia catedral metropolitana el 28 de noviembre de 1786* [sic]. México: Felipe de Zúñiga y Ontiveros, 1787. Biblioteca Nacional, Madrid, VE/1340/5.

Confession del Coronel de Dragones de Edimbourg Don Carlos Caro, comandante que fué en el Sitio de la Plaza de La Habana de las Tropas del Campo, empezada hoy 15 de Octubre de 1763. Madrid, 1763[?]. Biblioteca Nacional, Madrid, VE/1463/11.

Connell, Royal W., and William P. Mack. *Naval Ceremonies, Customs, and Traditions*. Annapolis: Naval Institute Press, 2004.

Conrotte, Manuel. *España y los países musulmanes durante el ministerio de Floridablanca*. Sevilla: Espuela de Plata, 2006. First published 1909.

———. *La intervención de España en la independencia de los Estados Unidos de la América del Norte*. Madrid: Victoriano Suárez, 1920.

Constituciones de la Real y Distinguida Orden Española de Carlos Tercero, instituida por el mismo augusto rey a 19 de septiembre de 1771, en celebridad del felicísimo nacimiento del infante. Madrid: Imprenta del colegio nacional de sordo-mudos, 1839.

Contreras, Juan Senén de. *Compendio de los veinte libros de reflexiones militares, que en diez tomos en quarto escribió el teniente general don Álvaro de Navia Osorio, vizconde del Puerto y marqués de Santa Cruz de Marcenado*. Madrid: Imprenta Real, 1787.

Contreras Cruz, Carlos, and Claudia Patricia Pardo Hernández. "La ciudad de Puebla de los Ángeles (México) y su población entre 1777 y 1830." In *Actas del XIV encuentro de Lationoamericanistas españoles: Congreso internacional, 200 años de Iberoamérica (1810-2010), Santiago de Compostela, 15-18 de septiembre de 2010*,

edited by Eduardo Rey Tristán and Patricia Calvo González, 556-68. Santiago de Compostela: Universidade de Santiago de Compostela, 2010.
Cooke, William. *The Air Balloon: Or a Treatise on the Aerostatic Globe, Lately Invented by the Celebrated Mons. Montgolfier, of Paris.* London, 1783.
Corbitt, D. C. "James Colbert and the Spanish Claims to the East Bank of the Mississippi." *Mississippi Valley Historical Review* 24 (March 1938): 457-72.
Cordero, Antonio. *Descripción de los apaches del coronel Antonio Cordero incluida en sus Notas sobre la nación apache compuestas en 1796.* In Daniel S. Matson and Albert H. Schroeder, "Cordero's Description of the Apache." *New Mexico Historical Review* 32, no. 4 (October 1957): 335-56.
Cordoncillo Samada, José María. *Historia de la Real Lotería en Nueva España (1770-1821).* Sevilla: Dirección General de Tributos Especiales del Ministerio de Hacienda—Escuela de Estudios Hispano-Americanos, 1962.
Cortés, José. *Views from the Apache frontier, report on the northern provinces of New Spain* [1799]. Edited by Elizabeth A. H. John. Norman: University of Oklahoma Press, 1989.
Cossío, José Lorenzo. *Datos históricos sobre las propiedades urbanas de la Instrucción Pública y de la Beneficencia Privada.* México D.F., 1926.
Coutts, Brian E. "Boom and Bust: The Rise and Fall of the Tobacco Industry in Spanish Louisiana, 1770-1790." In *The Louisiana Purchase Bicentennial Series in Louisiana History, Vol. 2: The Spanish Presence in Louisiana, 1763-1803,* edited by Gilbert C. Din, 229-45. Lafayette: Center for Louisiana Studies, University of Southwestern Louisiana, 1996.
———. "Martín Navarro: Treasurer, Contador, Intendant, 1766-1788: Politics and Trade in Spanish Louisiana." PhD diss., Louisiana State University, 1981.
Covarrubias, José de. *Memorias históricas de última guerra con la Gran Bretaña, desde 1774 hasta su conclusion: Estados Unidos de la América, año 1774 y 1775.* Madrid: Imprenta de Andrés Ramírez, 1783. Biblioteca Nacional, Madrid, 2/45493 and HA/15440-1.
———. Discurso sobre el estado actual de la abogacía en los tribunales de la nación. Madrid: Antonio Espinosa, 1789.
Covarrubias, Sebastián de. *Tesoro de la lengua castellana o española.* Madrid: Luis Sánchez, 1611.
Cox, Steve. "The Rare Spanish Carlos III, Al Mérito Medals, a Chronology 1764 to 1783." *MCA Advisory: The Newsletter of Medal Collectors of America* 13, no. 7 (July 2010): 4-12.
Crane, Verner W. "The Origin of the Name of the Creek Indians." *Mississippi Valley Historical Review* 5, no. 3 (1918): 339-42.
Cresswell, Donald H. *The American Revolution in Drawings and Prints: A Checklist of 1765-1790 Graphics in the Library of Congress.* Washington, D.C.: Library of Congress, 1975.
Creté, Liliane. *La vie quotidienne en Louisiane 1815-1830.* Paris: Hachette, 1978.
The Critical Review, or, Annals of Literature. Vol. 60. London: A. Hamilton, 1785.
Croix, Marquis de. *Correspondance du marquis de Croix, Capitaine Général del Armées de S.M. C., Vice-roi du Mexique.* Nantes: Emile Grimaud, 1891.
Crosby, Alfred W., Jr. *The Columbian Exchange: Biological and Cultural Consequences of 1492.* Westport, Conn.: Greenwood Press, 1972.
———. *Ecological Imperialism: The Biological Expansion of Europe, 900-1900.* New York: Cambridge University Press, 1986.

———. *Throwing Fire: Projectile Technology through History*. Cambridge: Cambridge University Press, 2002.
Cruz Barney, Óscar. "Las milicias en la Nueva España: La obra del segundo conde de Revillagigedo (1789-1794)." *Estudios de Historia Novohispana* 34 (January-June 2006): 73-116.
Cubberly, Fred. "Fort George (St. Michael) Pensacola." *Florida Historical Quarterly* 6 (April 1928): 229-30.
Cuenya, Miguel Ángel. *Puebla de los Ángeles en tiempos de una peste colonial: Una mirada en torno al matlazahuatl de 1737*. Puebla: Colegio de Michoacán, 2009.
Cueto, Leopoldo Augusto de. *Poetas líricos del siglo XVIII*. Madrid: Biblioteca de Autores Españoles-Rivadeneyra, 1869.
Culver, Lawrence. *The Frontier of Leisure: Southern California and the Shaping of Modern America*. New York: Oxford University Press, 2010.
Cummins, Light Townsend. "The Gálvez Family and Spanish Participation in the Independence of the United States of America." *Revista Complutense de Historia de América* 32 (2006): 179-96.
Curley, Michael J. *Church and State in the Spanish Floridas (1783-1822)*. Washington, D.C.: Catholic University of America Press, 1940.
Cusachs, Gaspar, ed. "Diary of the Operations of the Expedition against the Place of Pensacola Conducted by the Arms of His Catholic Majesty, under the Orders of the Field Marshall Don Bernardo de Gálvez." *Louisiana Historical Quarterly* 1, no. 1 (1917): 45-84.
Cutter, Donald C., ed. and trans. *The Defenses of Northern New Spain: Hugo O'Conor's Report to Teodoro de Croix, 22 de Julio de 1777*. Dallas: Southern Methodist University Press, 1994.
D. Peza, Juan de. *La beneficencia en México*. México: Francisco Díaz de León, 1881.
Dailey, R. C. "The Role of Alcohol among the North American Indian Tribes as Reported in *The Jesuit Relations*." *Anthropologica* 10, no. 1 (January 1968): 45-57.
Dalrymple, William. *Travels through Spain and Portugal in 1774, with a Short Account of the Spanish Expedition against Algiers in 1775*. London: J. Almon, 1777.
Danvila y Collado, Manuel. *Reinado de Carlos III*. In *Historia general de España*, edited by Antonio Cánovas del Castillo, vol. 14. Madrid: El Progreso Editorial, 1894.
Darby, William. *A Geographical Description of the State of Louisiana, the Southern Part of the State of Mississippi, and the Territory of Alabama*. New York: James Olmstead, 1817.
Dart, Henry P., ed. "West Florida—The Capture of Baton Rouge by Gálvez, September 21, 1779, from Reports of the English Officers." *Louisiana Historical Quarterly* 12 (1929): 255-65.
———, trans. "Oath of Allegiance to Spain, September 10th, 1769." *Louisiana Historical Quarterly* 4 (1921): 205-15.
Davies, Andrew. "The War Years." In *Theatre and War, 1933-1945: Performance in Extremis*, edited by Michael Balfour, 54-64. London: Berghahn Books, 2001.
Davis, Andrew McFarland. "The Employment of Indian Auxiliaries in the American War." *English Historical Review* 2 (1887): 709-28.
Davis, Britton. *The Truth about Geronimo*. New Haven: Yale University Press, 1929.
Davis, David Brion. *The Problem of Slavery in Western Culture*. New York: Cornell University Press, 1966.
Dawson, Warrington. "A New Record of the Sieges of Yorktown and Pensacola." *Légion d'Honneur Magazine* 4, no. 2 (October 1933): 81-85.

———. "Les 2112 Français morts aux États-Unis de 1777 à 1783 en combattant pour l'indépendance américaine." *Journal de la Société des Américanistes* 28, no. 1 (1936): 1–154.

Declaraciones recibidas en Cádiz, y Bilbao à los tres Capitanes de Navío Don Joseph Díaz de San Vicente, Don Pedro Bermúdez, y Don Francisco Garganta, al tenor de los Interrogatorios formados por la Junta; con los respectivos Papeles de su remission al Señor Presidente. Madrid, 1763[?], Biblioteca Nacional, Madrid, VE/1463/10.

Deeds, Susan M. "New Spain's Far North: A Changing Historiographical Frontier?" *Latin American Research Review* 25, no. 2 (1990): 226–35.

Deiler, J. Hanno. "The German Waldeck Regiment and the Sixtieth or 'Royal American Regiment on Foot' in the War of 1779 to 1781." *German American Annals* 7 (1909): 202–7.

Delandine, Antoine-François. *Manuscrits de la bibliothèque de Lyon*. Paris and Lyon: Renouard, Schoel et Lenormand, 1812.

Delavillebeuvre, Juan. "Fort Panmure, 1779, as Related by Juan Delavillebeuvre to Bernardo de Galvez." Translated by Anna Lewis. *Mississippi Valley Historical Review* 18, no. 4 (March 1932): 541–48.

Delay, Brian. *War of a Thousand Deserts: Indian Raids and the U.S.-Mexican War*. New Haven: Yale University Press, 2008.

Deloria, Philip J., and Neal Salisbury, eds. *A Companion to American Indian History*. Malden: Blackwell, 2002.

De Pauw, Cornélius. *Recherches philosophiques sur les Américains, ou Mémoires intéressants pour servir à l'histoire de l'espèce humaine*. Berlin: G. J. Decker, 1768–69.

Desdevises du Dezert, Georges. "L'Inquisition aux Indes Espagnoles à la fin du dix-huitième siècle." *Revue Hispanique* 30 (1914): 1–118.

Díaz, Lilia. "El Jardín Botánico de Nueva España y la obra de Sessé según documentos mexicanos." *Historia Mexicana* 1 (1977): 49–70.

Díaz de la Vega, Silvestre. *Discurso sobre el objeto de los dramas, sus diferentes clases. Causas que, por razón de una sana política, obligan a los príncipes a mantener en sus estados los espectáculos dramáticos; y las que han precisado al Superior Gobierno de esta capital México, a la reforma y arreglo de su teatro*. México, 1786, Archivo General de Indias, Correspondencia de Virreyes, vol. 150, ex. 803, sheets 83–107. In Francisco de Solano, *Las voces de la ciudad, México a través de sus impresos, 1539-1821*, 128. Madrid: Consejo Superior de Investigaciones Científicas, 1994.

Díaz Nogueras, Rafael F. "Bernardo de Gálvez . . . ese desconocido." *Revista General de Marina* 254 (June 2008): 755–58.

Diez Muñiz, Evangelino. "El matrimonio de militares en España, Legislación y problemática canónica en el siglo XVIII a la luz de documentos inéditos." *Revista de Historia Militar*, year 13, no. 27 (1969): 57–87.

Din, Gilbert C. "Bernardo de Gálvez: A Reexamination of His Governorship." In *The Louisiana Purchase Bicentennial Series in Louisiana History, Vol. 2: The Spanish Presence in Louisiana, 1763-1803*, edited by Gilbert C. Din, 77–93. Lafayette: Center for Louisiana Studies, University of Southwestern Louisiana, 1996.

———. *The Canary Islanders of Louisiana*. Baton Rouge: Louisiana State University Press, 1988.

———. "La defensa de la Luisiana española en sus primeros años." *Revista de Historia Militar* 45 (1978): 151–72.

———. "For Defense of Country and the Glory of Arms: Army Officers in Spanish

Louisiana, 1766-1803." *Louisiana History: The Journal of the Louisiana Historical Association* 43, no. 1 (Winter 2002): 5-40.

———. *Francisco Bouligny: A Bourbon Soldier in Spanish Louisiana*. Baton Rouge: Louisiana State University Press, 1993.

———. "Lieutenant Raimundo DuBreüil, Commandant of San Gabriel de Manchac and Bernardo de Gálvez's 1779 Campaign on the Mississippi River." *Military History of the West*, 29, no. 1 (Spring 1999): 1-30.

———. "Loyalist Resistance after Pensacola: The Case of James Colbert." In *Anglo-Spanish Confrontation on the Gulf Coast during the American Revolution: Gálvez Celebration, Commemorating the Siege of Pensacola*, edited by William S. Coker and Robert R. Rea, 158-76. Pensacola: Gulf Coast History and Humanities Conference, 1982.

———. "Pierre Wouves D'Arges in North America: Spanish Commissioner, Adventurer, or French Spy." *Louisiana Studies* 12, no. 1 (1973): 354-75.

———. "Protecting the 'Barrera': Spain's Defenses in Louisiana, 1763-1779." *Louisiana History: The Journal of the Louisiana Historical Association* 19, no. 2 (Spring 1978): 183-211.

———. *Spaniards, Planters, and Slaves: The Spanish Regulation of Slavery in Louisiana, 1763-1803*. College Station: Texas A&M University Press, 1999.

———. "Spanish Control over a Multiethnic Society, Louisiana, 1763-1803." In *Choice, Persuasion, and Coercion: Social Control on Spain's North American Frontiers*, edited by Jesús F. de la Teja and Ross Frank, 49-76. Albuquerque: University of New Mexico Press, 2005.

———, ed. *The Louisiana Purchase Bicentennial Series in Louisiana History, Vol. 2: The Spanish Presence in Louisiana, 1763-1803*. Lafayette: Center for Louisiana Studies, University of Southwestern Louisiana, 1996.

Din, Gilbert C., and John E. Harkins. *The New Orleans Cabildo: Colonial Louisiana's First City Government, 1769-1803*. Baton Rouge: Louisiana State University Press, 1996.

Dirección general de estadística. *1er Censo de población de la Nueva España, 1790, Censo de Revillagigedo, "un censo condenado."* México D.F.: Dirección general de estadística, 1977.

Documentos para la historia de México. Cuarta Serie, México: Imp. de Vicente García Torres, 1856.

Documentos que hicieron un país. Bogotá: Archivo General de la Nación—Presidencia de la República, 1997.

Domínguez, Francisco Atanasio. *The Missions of New Mexico, 1776: A Description, with other Contemporary Documents*. Edited and translated by Eleanor B. Adams and Angelico Chavez. Albuquerque: University of New Mexico Press, 1956.

Domínguez, Virginia R. *White by Definition: Social Classification in Creole Louisiana*. Newark: Rutgers State University Press, 1986.

Domínguez Bordona, Jesús. *Manuscritos de América*. Madrid: Talleres de Blas, 1935.

Domínguez Ortiz, Antonio. "Política nobiliaria de la Ilustración." In *Homenaje a Marcelo Vigil Pascual: La historia en el contexto de las ciencias humanas y sociales*, edited by María José Hidalgo de la Vega, 269-80. Salamanca: Universidad de Salamanca, 1989.

———. *Sociedad y Estado en el siglo XVIII español*. Barcelona: Ariel, 1984.

Domínguez Rascón, Alonso. "Estado, frontera y ciudadanía: El septentrión entre el antiguo régimen y la formación de la nación Mexicana." PhD diss., Leyden University, 2013.

Donahue-Wallace, Kelly. "El grabado en la Real Academia de San Carlos de Nueva España, 1783-1810." *Tiempos de América: Revista de historia, cultura y territorio* 11 (2004): 49-61.

Donézar, Javier. "De las naciones-patrias a la 'nación-patria.' Del Antiguo al Nuevo Régimen." In *La monarquía de las naciones: Patria, nación y naturaleza en la monarquía de España*, edited by Bernardo García García and José Antonio Álvarez-Ossorio Alvariño, 93-120. Madrid: Fundación Carlos de Amberes, 2004.

Dos expediciones españolas contra Argel, 1541 y 1775. Madrid: Estado Mayor Central del Ejército-Servicio Histórico Militar-Imprenta del Servicio Geográfico del Ejército, 1946.

Dougnac Rodríguez, Antonio. *Esquema del Derecho de Familia Indiano*. Santiago de Chile: Ediciones del Instituto de Historia del Derecho Indiano Juan de Solórzano y Pereyra, 2003.

Drayton, Richard. *Nature's Government: Science, Imperial Britain and the "Improvement" of the World*. New Haven: Yale University Press, 2000.

Dueñas, Alejo. "*Rasgo épico en obsequio del excelentísimo señor don Bernardo de Gálvez, por la conquista de Panzacola*." In Joseph Antonio Álvarez y Baena, *Hijos de Madrid, ilustres en santidad, dignidades, armas, ciencias y artes, diccionario histórico por el orden alfabético de sus nombres*, 3:323. Madrid: Benito Cano, 1790. Also in Leopoldo Augusto de Cueto, *Poetas líricos del siglo XVIII*. Madrid: Biblioteca de Autores Españoles-Rivadeneyra, 1869, clxvi.

Duffy, Christopher. *The Military Experience in the Age of Reason*. London: Routledge, 1987.

Dull, Jonathan R. *A Diplomatic History of the American Revolution*. New Haven: Yale University Press, 1985.

———. *The French Navy and American Independence: A Study of Arms and Diplomacy, 1774-1787*. Princeton: Princeton University Press, 1975.

Dunbar-Nelson, Alice Moore. "People of Color in Louisiana." *Journal of Negro History* 1, no. 4 (October 1916): 361-76; 2, no. 1 (January 1917): 51-78. In *Creole: The History and Legacy of Louisiana's Free People of Color*, edited by Sybil Kein, 3-41. Baton Rouge: Louisiana State University Press, 2000.

Durell, Edward Henry. *New Orleans as I Found It*. New York: Harper and Brothers, 1845.

DuVal, Kathleen. "The Education of Fernando de Leyba: Quapaws and Spaniards on the Border Empires." *Arkansas Historical Quarterly* 60, no. 1 (Spring 2001): 1-29.

———. *Independence Lost: Lives on the Edge of the American Revolution*. New York: Random House, 2015.

———. "Indian Intermarriage and Métissage in Colonial Louisiana." *William and Mary Quarterly* 65, no. 2 (2008): 267-304.

———. "Interconnectedness and Diversity in 'French Louisiana.'" In *Powhatan's Mantle: Indians in the Colonial Southeast*, edited by Gregory A. Waselkov, Peter H. Wood, and Thomas Hatley, 133-62. Lincoln: University of Nebraska Press, 2006. First published 1989.

———. *The Native Ground: Indians and Colonists in the Heart of the Continent*. Philadelphia: University of Pennsylvania Press, 2006.

DuVal, Kathleen, and Gonzalo M. Quintero Saravia. "Bernardo de Gálvez: Friend of the American Revolution, Friend of Empire." In *Proceedings of the 2015 Sons of the American Revolution Annual Conference: The Marquis de Lafayette and the European*

Friends of the American Revolution, Mount Vernon, Virginia, June 13-15, 2015. Charlottesville: University of Virginia Press, forthcoming.

Eastman, Scott. "The Sacred Mantle of the Constitution of 1812." In *The Rise of Constitutional Government in the Iberian Atlantic World: The Impact of the Cádiz Constitution of 1812*, edited by Scott Eastman and Natalia Sobrevilla Perea, 1-18. Tuscaloosa: University of Alabama Press, 2015.

Eastman, Scott, and Natalia Sobrevilla Perea, eds. *The Rise of Constitutional Government in the Iberian Atlantic World: The Impact of the Cádiz Constitution of 1812*. Tuscaloosa: University of Alabama Press, 2015.

Echeverri, Marcela. *Indian and Slave Royalists in the Age of Revolution: Reform, Revolution, and Royalism in the Northern Andes, 1780-1825*. Cambridge: Cambridge University Press, 2016.

Eelking, Max von. *The German Allied Troops in the North American War of Independence, 1776-1783*. Edited by J. G. Rosengarten. Albany: Munsell's Sons, 1893. Abbreviated trans. of *Die Deutschen Hulfstruppen in Nordamerikanischen Befreiungskriege, 1776 bis 1783*. Hannover: Helwing, 1863.

Ekkberg, Carl J. *Colonial St. Genevieve: An Adventure on the Mississippi Frontier*. Gerald, Mo.: Patrice Press, 1985.

Elizondo, Domingo. *Noticia de la expedición militar contra los rebeldes seris y pimas del Cerro Prieto, Sonora, 1767-1771*. Edited by José Luis Mirafuentes and Pilar Máynez. México: Universidad Nacional Autónoma de México, 1990.

Elliott, John H. "Britain and Spain in America: Colonists and Colonized." Stenton Lecture, Reading, University of Reading, 1994. In John H. Elliott, *Spain, Europe and the Wider World, 1500-1800*, 149-72. New Haven: Yale University Press, 2009.

———. *Empires of the Atlantic World: Britain and Spain in America, 1492-1830*. New Haven: Yale University Press, 2006.

———. "Paz y Guerra con Inglaterra, 1554-1655." *Reales Sitios: Revista del Patrimonio Nacional* 152 (2002): 2-17.

Elorza, Antonio. "Peñaflorida, el sueño de la razón: Dos siglos de la muerte de un personaje clave de la Ilustración española." *El País*, January 14, 1985.

———. *Socialismo utópico español*. Madrid: Alianza Editorial, 1970.

The English Review, or, An Abstract of English and Foreign Literature for the Year 1789. Vol. 14. London: J. Murray, 1789.

Entick, John. *The General History of the Late War: Containing Its Rise, Progress and Event, in Europe, Asia, Africa and America . . .* London: Edward Dilly, 1764.

Epalza, Mikel de. "Intereses árabes e intereses españoles en las paces hispano-musulmanas del XVIII." *Anales de Historia Contemporánea* l (1982): 7-17.

Escrito Clásico del reinado de d. Carlos III. Madrid: Hijos de Catalina Piñuela, 1829.

Escudero, José Antonio. *Los orígenes del Consejo de Ministros en España*. Madrid: Ed. Complutense, 2001.

———. *El supuesto memorial del conde de Aranda sobre la independencia de América*. México D.F.: Universidad Nacional Autónoma de México, 2014.

Escuela de Genealogía, Heráldica y Nobiliaria. *Apuntes de Nobiliaria y nociones de Genealogía y Heráldica: Curso de grado de la Escuela de Genealogía, Heráldica y Nobiliaria*. Madrid: Hidalguía, 1960.

Esparza, José Javier. "Bernardo de Gálvez: La fuerza de un hombre solo." *Época* 1354 (2011): 70-73.

Esparza Castillo, Antoni. "El retablo perpetuo: Transcendencia de los artistas levantinos españoles en la formación de la Academia de San Carlos de México o el predominio del barroco." PhD diss., Universidad Politécnica de Valencia–Facultad de Bellas Artes de San Carlos, 2002.

Espinosa Cortés, Luz María, Fabiola Rueda Arroniz, and Rosa María Andrade. *Cronología de hambrunas en México 40000 a.c.–1985 d.c., Serie Historia del hambre en México, anexo 2*. México D.F.: Instituto Nacional de Nutrición, 1987.

L'Esprit de l'encyclopédie ou choix des articles les plus agréables, les plus curieux et les plus piquans dans ce grand Dictionnaire. Paris: Fauvelle et Sagnier, 1798.

Estado Mayor del Ejército. *Heráldica e historiales del Ejército, vol. 1, Infantería*. Madrid: Servicio Histórico Militar, 1969.

Estado militar de España año de 1769. Madrid: Antonio Sanz, 1769.

Estado militar de España año de 1774. Madrid: Antonio Sanz, 1774.

Estado militar de España año de 1775. Madrid: Antonio Sanz, 1775.

Estado militar de España, año de 1776. Madrid: Imprenta Real de la Gazeta, 1776.

Estado militar de España año de 1782. Madrid: Imprenta Real, 1782.

Estado militar de España del año 1783. Madrid: Imprenta Real, 1783.

Estado militar de España para el año 1781. Madrid: Imprenta Real de la Gazeta, 1781.

Estado Militar de España, año de 1784. Madrid: Imprenta Real de la Gazeta, 1784.

Estado militar de España para el año de 1800. Madrid: Imprenta Real, 1800.

Estala, Pedro, ed. *El viajero universal o noticia del mundo antiguo y nuevo, obra recopilada de los mejores viajeros, traducida al castellano y corregido el original e ilustrado con notas por don Pedro Estala*. Madrid: Villalpando, 1800.

Estatutos de la Real Academia de San Carlos de la Nueva España. México: Felipe de Zúñiga y Ontiveros, 1785. In Francisco de Solano, *Las voces de la ciudad, México a través de sus impresos, 1539–1821*, 118. Madrid: Consejo Superior de Investigaciones Científicas, 1994.

Estrada, Genaro. *Algunos papeles para la historia de las bellas artes en México: Documentos de la Academia de Bellas Artes de San Fernando de Madrid relativos a la Academia de Bellas Artes de San Carlos de México durante el siglo XX*. La Habana: Publicaciones de la Revista Universidad de La Habana, 1938.

———. "Introducción a las Enfermedades políticas de la Nueva España de Hipólito Villaroel." In Hipólito Villaroel, *Enfermedades políticas de la Nueva España que padece la capital de esta Nueva España en casi todos los cuerpos de que se compone y remedios que se le deben aplicar para su curación si se quiere que sea útil al Rey y al público* [1785], edited by Genaro Estrada and Aurora Arnaiz Amigo, v–xiii. México D.F.: Porrúa, 1979.

———. "El México de Villarroel." *Letras de México*, vol. 1, no. 7, May 12, 1937. In Genaro Estrada, *Obras completas*, 2:50–58. México D.F.: Siglo XXI, 1988.

———. *Obras completas*. México D.F.: Siglo XXI, 1988.

État militaire de la France 1758 pour l'année 1758. Paris: Guillyn, Michel Lambert & Nicolas-Bonaventure Duchesne, 1758.

Euclides. *Los seis primeros libros, y el undécimo, y duodécimo de los Elementos de Euclides traducidos de nuevo sobre la versión latina de Federico Comandino, conforme á la edición de ella publicada por Roberto Simson ilustrados con notas críticas y geométricas del mismo autor*. Madrid: Joachin Ibarra, 1774.

Evans-Pritchard, E. E. *Anthropology and History: A Lecture Delivered in the University of Manchester with the Support of the Simon Fund for the Social Sciences*. Manchester: Manchester University Press, circa 1961.

Ewers, John C. *Plains Indian History and Culture: Essays on Continuity and Change*. Norman: University of Oklahoma Press, 1998.

———. "Symbols of Chiefly Authority in Spanish Louisiana." In *The Spanish in the Mississippi Valley, 1762-1804*, edited by John Francis McDermott, 272-86. Urbana: University of Illinois Press, 1974.

Ezquerra, Ramón. "Un patricio colonial: Gilberto de Saint Maxent, teniente gobernador de Luisiana." *Revista de Indias* 10 (1950): 97-170.

Fabel, Robin F. A. "Anglo-Spanish Commerce in New Orleans during the American Revolutionary Era." In *Anglo-Spanish Confrontation on the Gulf Coast during the American Revolution: Gálvez Celebration, Commemorating the Siege of Pensacola*, edited by William S. Coker and Robert R. Rea, 25-53. Pensacola: Gulf Coast History and Humanities Conference, 1982.

Faragher, John Marck. *A Great and Noble Scheme: The Tragic Story of the Expulsion of the French Acadians from Their American Homeland*. New York: W. W. Norton, 2005.

Farmar, Robert. "A Journal of the Siege of Pensacola, from the Time the Enemy's Fleet First Appeared to the 10th of May, the Day We Surrendered to the Arms of Spain." Edited by Buckingham Smith. *Historical Magazine* 4, no. 6 (June 1960): 166-72.

Faye, Stanley. "British and Spanish Fortifications of Pensacola." *Florida Historical Quarterly* 20 (1942): 277-92.

Félix Gastélum, José Rómulo, and Raquel Padilla Ramos, eds. *Misiones del noroeste de México, origen y destino*. México D.F.: Consejo Nacional para la Cultura y las Artes, Mexico, 2006.

Fenn, Elizabeth A. "Whither the Rest of the Continent?" *Journal of the Early Republic* 24, no. 2 (Summer 2004): 167-75.

Fenton, William N. *American Indian and White Relations to 1830: Needs and Opportunities for Study*. Williamsburg: Chapel Hill, 1957.

———. "Field Work, Museum Studies, and Ethnohistorical Research." *Ethnohistory* 13 (Winter 1966): 71-85.

Fernández, Miguel Ángel. *Chapultepec, historia y presencia*. México D.F.: Smurfit Cartón y Papel de México, 1988.

Fernández-Carrión, Miguel-Héctor. "La familia Gálvez y el poder ilustrado." In *Familias y poderes: Actas del VII Congreso Internacional de la ADEH, Granada, 1-3 abril 2004*, edited by Francisco A. Chacón Gómez-Monedero, Xavier Roigé i Ventura, and Esteban Rodríguez Ocaña, 125-36. Granada: 2006.

———. "Incidencia de la frontera entre las poblaciones autóctonas americanas: El caso de Argentina y Chile." *Nóesis: Revista de Ciencias Sociales y Humanidades* 15, no. 30 (2006): 95-125.

———. "Vida privada del Virrey de la Nueva España Bernardo de Gálvez: A partir del testimonio expresado en su testamento el 9 de noviembre de 1786." In *Ocio y vida cotidiana en el mundo hispánico en la edad moderna*, edited by Francisco Núñez Roldán, 461-74. Sevilla: Secretariado de publicaciones de la Universidad de Sevilla, 2007.

Fernández de Castro y Pedrera, Rafael. "La expedición contra Argel en 1775." *África, Revista de tropas coloniales*, s.l., s.n., s.a., 11-16.

Fernández del Castillo, Francisco. *La facultad de medicina según el archivo de la real y pontificia universidad de México*. México D.F.: Consejo de Humanidades, 1953.

Fernández de Navarrete, Martín. *Biblioteca Marítima Española: Obra Póstuma*. Madrid: Viuda de Calero, 1852.

———. *Diccionario marítimo español, que además de las definiciones de las voces con sus equivalencias en francés, inglés e italiano, contiene tres vocabularios de estos idiomas con las correspondientes castellanas*. Madrid: Imprenta Real, 1831.

Fernández de San Salvador, Agustín Pomposo. *La América llorado por la temprana muerte de su amado, su padre, su bien y sus delicias: El Excmo. Sr. D. Bernardo de Gálvez, Conde de Gálvez*. México: Felipe de Zúñiga y Ontiveros, 1787.

Fernández de Uribe, José Patricio. *Solemnes exéquias del Excmo. Señor D. Matías de Gálvez, García, Madrid y Cabrera, Teniente General de los Reales Exércitos, Virrey, Gobernador y Capitán General del Reyno de Nueva España*. México: Imprenta Mexicana de Don Felipe de Zúñiga y Ontiveros, 1785.

Fernández de Velasco, Manuel. "El militarismo en la vida del mexicano hasta 1855." *Estudios de historia moderna y contemporánea de México* 2 (1967): 98-113.

Fernández Duro, Cesáreo. *Armada española, desde la unión de los reinos de Castilla y Aragón*. Madrid: Museo Naval, 1972-73. First published 1895-1903.

Fernández Fraile, María Eugenia. *La enseñanza del francés en España (1767-1936): Estudio histórico: Objetivos, contenidos y procedimientos*. Granada: Método, 1999.

Fernández Hernández, Rafael, ed. *Algunas cartas familiares de José Viera y Clavijo (1770-1807)*. Santa Cruz de Tenerife: Rescate, 2006.

Fernández Sebastián, Javier, ed. *Diccionario político y social del mundo iberoamericano: La era de las revoluciones, 1750-1850. (Iberconceptos-I)*. Madrid: Fundación Carolina / Sociedad Estatal de Conmemoraciones Culturales / Centro de Estudios Políticos y Constitucionales, 2009.

Fernández y Fernández, E. "Juan de Miralles, pionero de la diplomacia española en los Estados Unidos." *Cuadernos de la Escuela Diplomática* 5 (December 1990): 69-88.

Fernán-Núñez, Count de. "Diario de la expedición contra Argel." In *Vida de Carlos III*, 2:119-220. Madrid: Fernando Fé, 1898. First published 1791.

———. *La expedición militar española contra Argel de 1775 (según el Diario de un testigo ocular)*. Edited by Juan Antonio López Delgado. Murcia: J. A. López, 2001.

———. *Vida de Carlos III*. Madrid: Fernando Fé, 1898. First published 1791.

Ferreiro, Larrie D. *Brothers at Arms: American Independnece and the Men of France and Spain Who Saved It*. New York: Alfred A. Knopf, 2016.

Ferrer Benimeli, José Antonio. *La masonería espãnola en el siglo XVIII*. Madrid: Siglo XXI, 1986. First published 1974.

———. "Masonería española: Mito o realidad." *Tiempo de Historia* 1, no. 2 (1975): 18-49.

Ferrer Benimeli, José Antonio, Esteban Sarasa, and Eliseo Serrano. "El conde de Aranda, primer secretario de Estado (28 febrero-15 noviembre 1792)." In Frutos, Eugenio, ed. *Suma de estudios en homenaje al Dr. Canellas*, 353-78. Zaragoza: Facultad de Letras, 1969.

———, eds. *El Conde de Aranda y su tiempo*. Zaragoza: Institución Fernando el Católico / Excma. Diputación de Zaragoza, 2000.

Ferrer del Río, Antonio. *Historia del reinado de Carlos III en España*. Madrid: Matute y Compagni, 1856.

———, ed. *Obras originales del conde de Floridablanca y escritos referentes a su persona*. Madrid: Rivadeneyra, 1867.

Field, Martha R., Joan B McLaughlin, and Jack McLaughlin, eds. *Louisiana Voyages: The Travel Writings of Catharine Cole*. Jackson: University Press of Mississippi, 2006.

Fisher, David Hackett. *Washington's Crossing*. New York: Oxford University Press, 2004.

Fisher, John R. "Imperial 'Free Trade' and the Hispanic Economy, 1778-1796." *Journal of Latin American Studies* 13, no. 1 (1981): 21-56.

———. *El Perú borbónico, 1750-1824*. Lima: Instituto de Estudios Peruanos, 2000.

———. "Redes de poder en el virreinato del Perú, 1776-1824: Los burócratas." *Revista de Indias* 66, no. 236 (2006): 149-64.

Fitzpatrick, John C. *The Writings of George Washington from the Original Manuscript Sources, 1745-1799*. Washington, D.C.: Government Printing Office, 1931-44.

Flandrin, Jean-Louis. *Families in Former Times: Kinship, Household, and Sexuality*. New York: CUP, 1979.

Fleming, Thomas. "Bernardo de Gálvez: The Forgotten Revolutionary Conquistador Who Saved Louisiana." *American Heritage* 33 (1982): 31-39.

Florescano, Enrique. *Fuentes para la historia de las crisis agrícolas de 1785-1786*. México D.F.: Archivo General de Indias, 1981.

Florescano, Enrique, and Isabel Gil Sánchez. "La época de las reformas borbónicas y el crecimiento económico 1750-1808." In *Historia General de México*, 2:183-301. México D.F.: El Colegio de México, 1981.

Flores Hernández, Benjamín. "Organización de corridas de toros en la Nueva España del siglo XVIII y primeros años del XIX." *Anuario de Estudios Americanos* 61, no. 2 (2004): 491-515.

Flores Moscoso, Ángeles. "Protocolo del cabildo secular mexicano en los actos públicos en el siglo XVIII." In *Andalucía y América. Los cabildos andaluces y americanos. Su historia y su organización actual: Actas de las X Jornadas de Andalucía y América (Universidad de Santa María de la Rábida, marzo 1991)*, edited by Bibiano Torres Ramírez, 457-85. Sevilla: Diputación de Huelva, 1992.

Floridablanca, Count de. "Memorial presentado al rey Carlos III, y repetido a Carlos IV." In *Obras originales del conde de Floridablanca y escritos referentes a su persona*, edited by Antonio Ferrer del Río, 307-50. Madrid: Rivadeneyra, 1867.

———. "Representación hecha al señor Rey d. Carlos IV el 10 de octubre de 1788." In *Escrito Clásico del reinado de d. Carlos III*, 46-47. Madrid: Hijos de Catalina Piñuela, 1829.

Foley, William E. "Slave Freedom Suits before *Dred Scott*: The Case of Marie Jean Scypion's Descendants." *Missouri Historical Review* 79, no. 1 (October 1984): 1-23.

Fontana, Josep. "En torno al comercio libre." In *"El comercio libre" entre España y América (1765-1824)*, edited by Josep Fontana and Antonio Miguel Bernal, 7-14. Madrid: Fundación Banco Exterior, 1987.

Forbes, Jack D. *Apache, Navaho, and Spaniard*. Norman: University of Oklahoma Press, 1961.

Ford, Richard. *A Handbook for Travellers in Spain*. 3rd ed. London: John Murray, 1855. First published 1845. Spanish trans., *Manual para viajeros por España y lectores en casa, vol. VI, Galicia y Asturias*. Madrid: Turner, 2008.

Ford, Worthington Chauncey, ed. *The Writings of George Washington*. New York: Putnam's Sons, 1889.

Fortier, Alcée. *A History of Louisiana*. 4 vols. Edited by Jo Ann Carrigan. Baton Rouge: Claitor's Book Store, 1966. First published 1904.

———. *A History of Louisiana*. Vol. 1, *Early Explorers and the Domination of the French, 1512-1768*. Paris: Goupil & Co., 1904.

Foucault, Michel. *Historia de la locura en la época clásica*. Bogotá: Fondo de Cultura Económica Colombia, 1998. First published 1964.

———. *Il faut défendre la société: Cours au Collège de France (1975-1976)*. Edited by M. Bertani and A. Fontana. Paris: Seuil, 1997.

Frank, Ross. *From Settler to Citizen: New Mexican Economic Development and the Creation of Vecino Society, 1750-1820*. Berkeley: University of California Press, 2000.

Franklin, Benjamin. *The Complete Works of Benjamin Franklin*. Edited by John Bigelow. New York, 1888.

———. *The Papers of Benjamin Franklin.* Sponsored by the American Philosophical Society and Yale University. Digital edition by the Packard Humanities Institute, http://franklinpapers.org (accesed March 12, 2017).

———. *Writings of Benjamin Franklin.* Edited by Jared Sparks. Boston: Hilliard, Gray, 1840.

Frederick II of Prussia. "Des marches d'armée, et de ce qu'il faut observer à cet égard." In *Oeuvres de Frédéric le Grand*, 31 vols., 29:107-32. Edited by J. D. E. (Johann David Erdmann) Preuss. Berlin: Imprimerie Royale, 1856.

Fredericksen, John C. *American Military Leaders: From Colonial Times to the Present.* Santa Barbara: ABC-CLIO, 1999.

Freeman, Douglas Southall. *George Washington: A Biography.* New York: Scribner, 1948.

Frontela Carreras, Guillermo. *Biografía nobiliaria de don Bernardo de Gálvez.* Algeciras-Cádiz: Frontela, 1992.

Fuente, Alejandro de la. "Slave Law and Claims-Making in Cuba: The Tannenbaum Debate Revisited." *Law and History Review* 22, no. 2 (Summer 2004): 339-69.

Fuente, Alejandro de la, and Ariela Gross. "Comparative Studies of Law, Slavery, and Race in the Americas." *Annual Review of Law and Social Science* 6 (2010): 469-85.

Fuente, Vicente de la. *Historia de las Universidades, colegios y demás establecimientos de enseñanza en España.* Madrid: Viuda de Fuentenebro, 1889.

Fuentes, Carlos. *El Alma de México, capítulo: Luces de la independencia.* TV series. México D.F.: Televisa, 2000.

Fulton, Norman. *Relaciones diplomáticas entre España y los Estados Unidos a finales del siglo XVIII: Relaciones económico-comerciales.* Madrid: Universidad Complutense, 1970.

Füssel, Marian. *Der Siebenjährige Krieg, Ein Weltkrieg im 18, Jahrhundert.* München: Beck, 2010.

Galán Domingo, Eduardo. "De las Reales Caballerizas a la Colección de Carruajes del Patrimonio Nacional." *ARBOR Ciencia, Pensamiento y Cultura* 169 (May 2001): 221-38.

Galbis Díez, María del Carmen. "Bernardo de Gálvez." In *Los virreyes de la Nueva España en el reinado de Carlos III*, edited by José Antonio Calderón Quijano, 2: 327-62. Sevilla: Consejo Superior de Investigaciones Científicas / Escuela de Estudios Hispano-Americanos, 1968.

———. "El virrey don Miguel José de Azanza." In *Los virreyes de la Nueva España en el reinado de Carlos IV*, edited by José Antonio Calderón Quijano, 2:3-66. Sevilla: Consejo Superior de Investigaciones Científicas / Escuela de Estudios Hispano-Americanos, 1972.

Galí i Boadella, Montserrat. *Historias del bello sexo: La introducción del romanticismo en México.* México D.F.: Universidad Nacional Autónoma de México, 2002.

Galindo y de Vera, León. *Historia, vicisitudes y política tradicional de España respecto de sus posesiones en las costas de África, desde la monarquía gótica y en los tiempos posteriores a la Restauración hasta el último siglo.* Madrid: Manuel Tello, 1884.

Gallay, Alan. *The Indian Slave Trade: The Rise of the English Empire in the American South, 1670-1717.* New Haven: Yale University Press, 2002.

Gallego Gredilla, Enrique. "La figura de Bernardo de Gálvez, durante la intervención española en la guerra de la independencia de los EE.UU. (I)." *Revista de Historia Militar* 84 (1998): 85-134.

———. "La figura de Bernardo de Gálvez, durante la intervención española en la guerra de la independencia de los EE.UU. (II)." *Revista de Historia Militar* 85 (1998): 59-110.

Gálvez, Bernardo de. "Apuntes que [Bernardo de Gálvez] doy a don Ramón Posada para que con arreglo a ellos extienda mi testamento, dados en Tacubaya el 9 de noviembre de 1786," completados por dos disposiciones adicionales del 11 de ese mismo mes (Last Will and Testament of Bernardo de Gálvez). Published several times. In Souviron, *Bernardo de Gálvez, virrey de Méjico (Un infante de la marina española)*; Beerman, "Last Will and Testament of Bernardo de Gálvez," nos. 2-4; Fernández-Carrión, "Vida privada del Virrey de la Nueva España Bernardo de Gálvez: A partir del testimonio expresado en su testamento el 9 de noviembre de 1786."

———. *Diario de las operaciones contra la plaza de Panzacola 1781.* Madrid: [1781?]. Also published in Madrid: José Porrúa Turanzas, 1959. English trans., Cusachs, "Diary of the Operations of the Expedition against the Place of Pensacola Conducted by the Arms of His Catholic Majesty, under the Orders of the Field Marshall Don Bernardo de Gálvez."

———. "Diario que yo, d. Bernardo de Gálvez, brigadier de los Reales Ejércitos, gobernador de la provincia de la Luisiana, y encargado por S.M. de la expedición contra Panzacola y Mobila, formé de los acontecimientos que ocurren en ella." In *Mercurio Histórico Político, que contiene el estado presente de la Europa, lo sucedido en todas las Cortes, los intereses de los Príncipes, y generalmente todo lo mas curioso*, 198-226. Madrid: June, 1780.

———. *Instrucción formada en virtud de real orden de S.M., que se dirige al señor comandante general de provincias internas don Jacobo Ugarte y Loyola para gobierno y puntual observancia de este superior gefe y de sus inmediatos subalternos (Instruction for Governing the Interior Provinces of New Spain)*. México, 1786. Published several times. In *Boletín del Archivo General de la Nación* 8, no. 4 (1937): 491-540; Worcester, *Instructions for Governing the Interior Provinces of New Spain, 1786*; Velázquez Chávez, *La frontera norte y la experiencia colonial*; Hilton, *Las raíces hispánicas del Oeste de Nortemérica: Textos históricos*.

———. *Noticia y reflexiones sobre la guerra que se tiene con los indios apaches en las provincias de Nueva España*, Madrid, sin fecha (probablemente, sobre 1771). In Blas de Osés, documentación varia, Manuscript, México, 1817, the Hill Museum and Manuscript Library, Steiner Collection, Bush Centre, St. John's University, Collegeville, Minn., Steiner 27, Blas de Osés, Manuscripts, no. 2, 35-66. Published in Teixidor, "Noticia y reflexiones sobre la guerra que se tiene con los apaches en la provincia de la Nueva España, por don Bernardo de Gálvez"; John, "A Cautionary Exercise in Apache Historiography—Notes and Reflections on the War with the Apache Indians in the Provinces of New Spain—by Bernardo de Galvez, ca. 1785-86"; and John, "Bernardo de Gálvez on the Apache Frontier."

Gálvez, José de. *"Discurso y reflexiones de un vasallo."* In Luis Navarro García, *La política americana de José de Gálvez según su "Discurso y reflexiones de un vasallo."* Málaga: Algazara, 1998.

———. "Discurso y reflexiones de un vasallo sobre la decadencia de nuestras Indias españolas (extractos)." *Araucaria: Revista Iberoamericana de Filosofía, Política y Humanidades* (online) 5, no. 9 (first semester 2003) (accessed September 25, 2016).

———. *Informe general que el Excmo. Sr. Marqués de Sonora siendo Visitador General de este reyno al Excmo. Sr. Virrey Frey D. Antonio Bucarely y Ursua, con fecha de*

31 de diciembre de 1771. Se arregló y enquadernó siendo Secretario del Virreynato el Coronel de Dragones Antonio Bonilla. México: Sección de Fomento del Ministerio de Gobernación-Imprenta de Santiago White, 1867. In Suárez Argüello, *Informe general que en virtud de real orden instruyó y entregó el excelentísimo señor Marqués de Sonora siendo visitador general de este reino, al Excelentísmo señor virrey don Antonio Bucarely y Ursúa con fecha 31 de diciembre de 1771*.

———. *Informe sobre las rebeliones populares de 1767 y otros documentos inéditos*. Edited by Felipe Castro Gutierrez. México D.F.: Universidad Nacional Autónoma de México, 1990.

———. *Sobre el Estado y Honor de Salillas . . . por Don Miguel Pérez de Pomar Lope Fernández de Heredia . . . con el Marqués de Ariño*. Madrid[?], 1758[?]. Biblioteca Nacional, Madrid, VC/1019/50.

Los Gálvez de Macharaviaya. Madrid: Diputación Provincial de Málaga / Consejo Superior de Investigaciones Científicas, 1972.

Gannon, Michael V. "Church Influence in Louisiana and Florida in the Eighteenth Century." In *Cardinales de Dos Independencias (Noreste de México—Sureste de los Estados Unidos)*, edited by Francisco de Solano and Beatriz Ruiz Caytán, 138-60. México D.F.: Fomento Cultural Banamex, 1978.

Garavaglia, Juan Carlos, and Juan Marchena. *América Latina de los orígenes a la Independencia*. Barcelona: Crítica, 2005.

García, Sebastián. "El Príncipe de Asturias, soldado de honor del regimiento Inmemorial del rey." *El País*, May 29, 1977.

García Acosta, Virginia, Juan Manuel Pérez Zevallos, and América Molina del Villar. *Desastres agrícolas en México: Catálogo histórico, vol. 1, Épocas prehispánica y colonial (958-1822)*. México D.F.: Fondo de Cultura Económica / Centro de Investigaciones y Estudios Superiores en Antropología Social, 2003.

García de la Leña, Cecilio. *Conversaciones históricas malagueñas, Descanso VI, Continuación de los Ilmos. Obispos de esta ciudad*. Málaga: Luis de Carreras, 1793.

García de Segovia, Joseph. *Los Pastores de Macharavialla [sic]: Égloga a la muerte del Excmo. Sr. D. Joseph de Gálvez, Marqués de la Sonora, etc.* Málaga: Herederos de Francisco Martínez de Aguilar, 1787.

García García, Bernardo, and José Antonio Álvarez-Ossorio Alvariño, eds. *La monarquía de las naciones: Patria, nación y naturaleza en la monarquía de España*. Madrid: Fundación Carlos de Amberes, 2004.

García Hernán, David. *La nobleza en la España moderna: La historia en sus textos*. Madrid: Istmo, 1992.

García Hernán, Enrique, and Óscar Recio Morales, eds. *Extranjeros en el Ejército: Militares irlandeses en la sociedad española, 1580-1818*. Madrid: Ministerio de Defensa, 2007.

García Jordán, Pilar, ed. *Estrategias de poder en América Latina / Estratègies de poder a Amèrica Llatina*. Barcelona: Universitat de Barcelona, 2000.

García Lasaosa, José. "La política exterior de Carlos III y Carlos IV." In *Historia general de España y América*, edited by Luis Suárez Fernández, vol. 10/2:299-331. Madrid: Rialp, 1990.

García Lorenzo, Luciano. *Autoras y Actrices en la historia del teatro español*. Murcia: Servicio de Publicaciones de la Universidad de Murcia, 2000.

García Melero, Luis Ángel, ed. *La independencia de los Estados Unidos de Norteamérica a través de la prensa española ("Gaceta de Madrid" y "Mercurio Histórico y Político"). Los precedentes (1763-1776)*. Madrid: Ministerio de Asuntos Exteriores, 1977.

García Panes, Diego. *Diario particular del camino que sigue un virrey de México desde su llegada a Veracruz hasta su entrada pública en la Capital* [circa 1793]. Edited by María Lourdes Díaz-Trechuelo López Spínola. Madrid: Centro de Estudios Históricos de Obras Públicas y Urbanismo, 1994.

Garrigues, Eduardo, Emma Sánchez Montañés, Sylvia L. Hilton, Almudena Hernández Ruigómez, and Isabel García-Montón, eds. *Norteamérica a finales del siglo XVIII: España y los Estados Unidos*. Madrid: Fundación Consejo España-Estados Unidos and Editorial Marcial Pons, 2008.

Gascoigne, John. "Joseph Banks and His Abiding Legacy." *London Papers in Australian Studies* 2 (2001): 1-12.

Gates, Eunice Joiner. "Don José Antonio de Areche: His Own Defense." *Hispanic American Historical Review* 8, no. 1 (February 1928): 14-42.

Gayarré, Charles. *Histoire de La Louisiane*. Nouvelle Orléans: Magne and Weisse, 1847.

———. *History of Louisiana*. Vol. 3, *The Spanish Domination*. New York: William J. Widdleton, 1866.

———. *The History of Louisiana*. Vol. 4, *The American Domination*. New York: William J. Widdleton, 1866.

Gayol, Víctor. *Laberintos de justicia: Las reglas del juego*. México D.F.: Colegio de Michoacán, 2007.

"George Bert, Obituary." *Economist*, December 1, 2005.

Gerbi, Antonello. *La disputa del nuevo mundo: Historia de una polémica, 1750-1900*. México D.F.: Fondo de Cultura Económica, 1960.

Gerhard, Peter. *La frontera norte de la Nueva España*. México D.F.: Universidad Nacional Autónoma de México, 1996.

Gibson, Campbell. "Table 2. Population of the 24 Urban Places: 1790." In *Population of the 100 Largest Cities and Other Urban Places in the United States: 1790 to 1990*, Population Division Working Paper No. 27. Washington, D.C.: U.S. Bureau of the Census, 1998.

Gibson, Charles. *Los aztecas bajo dominio español*. México D.F.: Siglo XXI, 1991.

———. "Conquest, Capitulation, and Indian Treaties." *American Historical Review* 83 (February 1978): 1-15.

Gil Novales, Alberto. "Política y sociedad." In *Centralismo, Ilustración y agonía del antiguo régimen (1715-1833)*, edited by Emiliano Fernández de Pinedo, Alberto Gil Novales, and Albert Dérozier, 175-320. Barcelona: Labor, 1987.

Giraud de Vilette, André. Letter to the editor. *Journal de Paris*, October 20, 1783.

Gitlin, Jay. "On the Boundaries of Empire: Connecting the West to Its Imperial Past." In *Under an Open Sky: Rethinking America's Western Past*, edited by William Cronon, George Miles, and Jay Gitlin, 71-89. New York: W. W. Norton, 1992.

Godoy, Manuel de. *Memorias de don Manuel Godoy príncipe de la Paz, o sea cuenta dada de su vida política: Para servir a la historia del reinado del señor don Carlos IV de Borbón*. Gerona: Vicente Oliva, 1839.

Gold, Robert L. "Governor Bernardo de Gálvez and Spanish Espionage in Pensacola, 1777." In *The Spanish in the Mississippi Valley, 1762-1804*, edited by John Francis McDermott, 87-99. Urbana: University of Illinois Press, 1974.

Goldoni, Carlo. *La posadera feliz o El enemigo de las mujeres: Comedia en tres actos, en verso, escrita en italiano por Carlos Goldoni, abogado veneciano; y traducida e impresa conforme se representa por la compañía del señor Francisco Ramos por José López de Sedano*. S.l., s.a. Biblioteca Nacional, Madrid, MSS/14976.

Gómez, José. *Diario curioso de México de d. José Gómez, cabo de alabarderos:*

Documentos para la historia de México. México: Antigua Imde la voz de la religión, 1854.

Gómez de Olea y Bustinza, Javier. *La Nobleza Titulada en la América Española: Discurso de ingreso en la Real Academia Matritense de heráldica y genealogía*. Madrid: Real Academia Matritense de heráldica y genealogía, 2005.

Gomez de Ortega, Casimiro. *Continuación de la flora española, o Historia de las plantas de España que escribía don Joseph Quer*. Vol. 5. Madrid: Joachin Ibarra, 1784.

Gómez de Silva, Guido. *Diccionario breve de mexicanismos*. México D.F.: Academia Mexicana / Fondo de Cultura Económica, 2001.

Gómez Montoya, Mónica Liliana. "José Joaquín Granados y Gálvez: La reconciliación de la sociedad novohispana." PhD diss., Universidad Nacional Autónoma de Méjico, 2007.

Gómez Ruiz, M., and V. Alonso Juanola. *El ejército de los borbones, vol.3, Tropas de ultramar, siglo XVIII*. Madrid: Servicio Histórico Militar, 1992.

———. *El ejército de los Borbones, vol.4, Reinado de Carlos IV (1788-1808)*. Madrid: Ministerio de Defensa, 1995.

Gone with the Wind. Directed by Victor Fleming. Hollywood, CA: Metro Goldwyn Mayer, 1939.

González-Aller Hierro, José Ignacio. "Relación de buques de la Armada Española en los siglos XVIII, XIX y XX." In *El buque en la Armada Española*, edited by Enrique Manera Regueyra, 454-97. Madrid: Sílex, 1999.

González Batista, Batista. *La estrategia española en América durante el siglo de las luces*. Madrid: MAPFRE, 1992.

González Bueno, Antonio. "Plantas y luces: La Botánica de la Ilustración en la América hispana." In *La formación de la cultura virreinal, vol. 3, Siglo XVIII*, 107-28. Madrid and Frankfurt: Iberoamericana and Vervuert Verlagsgesellschaft, 2000.

González Bueno, Antonio, and Raul Rodríguez Nozal. "Conocimiento científico y poder en la España ilustrada: hacia la supremacía comercial a través de la botánica medicinal." *Antilia: Revista española de historia de las ciencias de la naturaleza y de la tecnología*, 1 (1995): 1-22.

González Cruz, David. "Celebraciones de victoria militares de la monarquía hispánica en sus dominios de Europa y América (siglos XVII y XVIII)." In *Ocio y vida cotidiana en el mundo hispánico en la edad moderna*, edited by Francisco Núñez Roldán, 231-44. Sevilla: Secretariado de publicaciones de la Universidad de Sevilla, 2007.

———. "Represión y trato a los indígenas enemigos en la América Hispana durante los enfrentamientos armados del siglo XVIII." In *Orbis incognitus: Avisos y legajos del Nuevo Mundo: Homenaje al profesor Luis Navarro García*, edited by Fernando Navarro Antolín, 2:221-34. Huelva: Universidad de Huelva, 2007.

González de la Vega, José Sixto. *México llorosa y México risueña, tristeza y alegría, pésames y parabienes por la sentida muerte del Excmo. Sr. D. Bernardo de Gálvez, conde de Gálvez, y por el feliz nacimiento de la señora doña Guadalupe Felícitas de Gálvez*. México: Rangel, 1787. Biblioteca Nacional, Madrid, VE/1239/3.

González Díaz, Falia, and Pilar Lázaro de la Escosura. *The Threads of Memory: Catalogue of the Exposition / El hilo de la memoria: Catálogo de la exposición*, s.l., s.a., 2011.

González Enciso, Agustín. "En torno al contrabando de tabaco en el siglo XVIII." In *Estudios de historia moderna y contemporánea: homenaje a Federico Suarez Verdeguer*, edited by Valentín Vázquez de Prada, 199-210. Madrid: Rialp, 1991.

González Enciso, Agustín, and Rafael Torres Sánchez. *Tabaco y economía en el siglo XVIII*. Pamplona: Ediciones Universidad de Navarra S.A., 1999.

González López-Briones, Carmen. "Reacciones diferentes ante una política similar: Los indios Osages y los Quapaws ante la política comercial franco-española en la Luisiana durante el siglo XVIII." *Anales del Museo de América* 3 (1995): 119-30.

González Obregón, Luis. "El funeral de los virreyes." In *México Viejo: Noticias históricas, tradiciones, leyendas y costumbres del período de 1521 a 1821*, 121-30. 2nd ed. México D.F.: Escuela correccional de artes y oficios, 1891.

González-Polo, Ignacio. "La ciudad de México a fines del siglo XVIII; disquisiciones sobre un manuscrito anónimo." *Historia Mexicana* 26, no. (1976): 29-47.

González-Ripoll Navarro, María Dolores. "Idea y representación del Caribe en la cartografía del siglo XVIII." *Contrastes, Revista de Historia* 12 (2001-2003): 81-92.

González Troyano, Alberto. "Algunos libros de toros en la época de la Ilustración." In *Estudios de Tauromaquia*, edited by Rafael Cabrera Bonet, 187-90. Madrid: Fundación Universitaria San Pablo CEU, 2006.

Gortari Rabiela, Hira de. "La ciudad de México de finales del siglo XVIII: Un diagnóstico desde la 'ciencia de la policía.'" *Historia Contemporánea* 24 (2002): 115-35.

Granados y Gálvez, José Joaquín. *El Andaluz Perseo: Elogios poéticos que a los insignes hechos del Excmo. Sr. Don Bernardo de Gálvez, escribía el P. Fray Joaquín Granados y Gálvez, franciscano observante, a un amigo suyo*. México: Felipe de Zúñiga y Ontiveros, 1785.

Gray, Edward G., and Jane Kamensky, eds. *The Oxford Handbook of the American Revolution*. Oxford: Oxford University Press, 2013.

Green, Michael. "The Creek Confederacy in the American Revolution: Cautious Participants." In *Anglo-Spanish Confrontation on the Gulf Coast during the American Revolution: Gálvez Celebration, Commemorating the Siege of Pensacola*, edited by William S. Coker and Robert R. Rea, 54-75. Pensacola: Gulf Coast History and Humanities Conference, 1982.

Greene, Jack P., ed. *Negotiated Authorities: Essays in Colonial Political and Constitutional History*. Charlottesville: University Press of Virginia, 1994.

———. "Negotiated Authorities: The Problem of Governance in the Extended Polities of the Early Modern Atlantic World." In *Negotiated Authorities: Essays in Colonial Political and Constitutional History*, edited by Jack P. Greene, 1-24. Charlottesville: University Press of Virginia, 1994.

Greenleaf, Richard E. "The Inquisition in Spanish Louisiana, 1762-1800." 1st ver. *New Mexico Historical Review* 50, no. 1 (1975): 45-72.

———. "The Inquisition in Spanish Louisiana, 1762-1800." 2nd ver. In *The Louisiana Purchase Bicentennial Series in Louisiana History, Vol. 2: The Spanish Presence in Louisiana, 1763-1803*, edited by Gilbert C. Din, 543-58. Lafayette: Center for Louisiana Studies, Univ. of Southwestern Louisiana, 1996.

———. "The Nueva Vizcaya Frontier, 1787-1789." *Journal of the West* 8, no. 1 (January 1969): 56-66.

Griffen, William B. *Apaches at War and Peace: The Janos Presidio, 1750-1858*. Albuquerque: University of New Mexico, 1988.

Griffiths, Naomi Elizabeth Saundaus. *L'Acadie de 1686 à 1784: Contexte d'une histoire*. Moncton: Ed. de L'Acadie, 1997.

Grossman, James, ed. *The Frontier in American Culture*. Berkeley: University of California Press, 1994.

Grundset, Eric G., ed. *Forgotten Patriots: African American and American Indian Patriots of the Revolutionary War; A Guide to Service, Sources, and Studies*. Washington, D.C.: National Society Daughters of the American Revolution, 2001.

Grupo de Estudios del Tabaco (GRETA). "El consumo del Tabaco en España en el siglo XVIII." *Cuadernos de Investigación Histórica* 19 (2002): 313-45.

Guardia Herrero, Carmen de la. "Hacia la creación de la República Federal: España y los Estados Unidos, 1783-1789." *Revista Complutense de Historia de América* 27 (2001): 35-67.

Guerra, François-Xavier. *Modernidad e independencias: Ensayos sobre las revoluciones hispánicas.* México D.F.: MAPFRE / Fondo de Cultura Económica, 1992.

Guibert, Jacques-Antoine-Hippolyte, Count de. *Essai général de tactique, précédé d'un Discours sur l'état actuel de la politique et de la science militaire en Europe, avec le plan d'un ouvrage intitulé: La France politique et militaire.* Londres: Libraires associés, 1772.

Guillén Robles, F. *Historia de Málaga y su provincial.* Málaga: Imp. Rubio y Cano, 1874.

Gutiérrez, Ramón. *Fortificaciones en Iberoamérica.* Madrid: Fundación Iberdrola, 2005.

———. *When Jesus Came the Corn Mothers Went Away: Marriage, Sexuality and Power in New Mexico, 1500-1846.* Palo Alto: Stanford University Press, 1991.

Gutiérrez, Ramón, and Richard J. Orsi, eds. *Contested Eden: California before the Gold Rush.* Berkeley: University of California Press, 1998.

Gutiérrez Escudero, Antonio, and María Luisa Laviana Cuetos, eds. *Estudios sobre América: Siglos XVI-XX.* X Congreso de la Asociación Española de Americanistas, Sevilla 2002. Sevilla: Asociación Española de Americanistas, 2005.

Guzmán Wolffer, Ricardo. "Entrevista con Rafael Barajas 'el Fisgón': El humor está en quien lo ve." *La Jornada Semanal* 516 (January 2005).

Hackel, Steven W. *Children of Coyote, Missionaries of St. Francis: Indian-Spanish Relations in Colonial California, 1769-1850.* Chapel Hill: University of North Carolina Press, 2005.

———, ed. *Alta California: Peoples in Motion, Identities in Formation, 1769-1850.* Berkeley: University of California Press, 2010.

Hadden, Sally. "The Fragmented Laws of Slavery in the Colonial and Revolutionary Eras." In *The Cambridge History of Law in America*, vol. 1, *Early America (1580-1815)*, edited by Michael Grossberg and Christopher Tomlins, 253-87, 646-57. Cambridge: Cambridge University Press, 2008.

Haley, James L. *Apaches: A History and Culture Portrait.* Norman: University of Oklahoma Press, 1997.

Hall, Gwendolyn Midlo. *Africans in Colonial Louisiana: The Development of Afro-Creole Culture in the Eighteenth Century.* Baton Rouge: Louisiana State University Press, 1992.

———. Review of *Building the Devil's Empire: French Colonial New Orleans*, by Shannon Lee Dawdy. *H-France Review* 10, no. 215 (December 2010): 922-27.

Hämäläinen, Pekka. *The Comanche Empire.* New Haven: Yale University Press, 2008.

———. "The Rise and Fall of Plains Indian Horse Cultures." *Journal of American History* 90, no. 3 (December 2003): 833-62.

———. "The Western Comanche Trade Center: Rethinking the Plains Indian Trade System." *Western Historical Quarterly* 29, no. 4 (Winter 1998): 485-513.

Hamer, Philip M. "John Stuart's Indian Policy during the Early Months of the American Revolution." *Mississippi Valley Historical Review* 17, no. 3 (December 1930): 351-66.

Hamilton, Earl J. *El florecimiento del capitalismo y otros ensayos de historia económica.* Madrid: Revista de Occidente, 1948.

Hamilton, Peter. *Colonial Mobile: An Historical Study, Largely from Original Sources, of the Alabama-Tombigbee Basin from the Discovery of Mobile Bay in 1519 until the Demolition of Fort Charlotte in 1821.* New York: Houghton Mifflin, 1897.

Hammond, George. "The Zuñiga Journal, Tucson to Santa Fé: The Opening of a Spanish Trade Route, 1778-1795." *New Mexico Historical Review* 6, no. 1 (January 1931): 40-65.

Hamnett, Brian R. "Absolutismo ilustrado y crisis multidimensional en el período colonial tardío, 17860-1808." In *Interpretación del siglo XVIII mexicano: El impacto de las reformas borbónicas*, edited by Josefina Zoraida Vázquez, 67-108. México D.F.: Nueva Imagen, 1992.

———. "Problemas interpretativos de la Independencia Mexicana." In *Visiones y revisiones de la independencia americana, México, Centroamérica y Haití*, edited by Izaskun Álvarez Cuartero and Julio Sánchez Gómez, 77-92. Salamanca: Aquilafuente / Universidad de Salamanca, 2005.

Hanger, Kimberly S. "Almost All Have Callings: Free Blacks at Work in Spanish New Orleans." In *The Louisiana Purchase Bicentennial Series in Louisiana History, Vol. 2: The Spanish Presence in Louisiana, 1763-1803*, edited by Gilbert C. Din, 414-32. Lafayette: Center for Louisiana Studies, University of Southwestern Louisiana, 1996.

———. "Avenues to Freedom Open to New Orleans' Black Population, 1769-1779." *Louisiana History: The Journal of the Louisiana Historical Association* 31, no. 3 (Summer 1990): 237-64.

———. "A Privilege and Honor to Serve: The Free Black Militia of Spanish New Orleans." In *The Louisiana Purchase Bicentennial Series in Louisiana History, Vol. 2: The Spanish Presence in Louisiana, 1763-1803*, edited by Gilbert C. Din, 391-413. Lafayette: Center for Louisiana Studies, University of Southwestern Louisiana, 1996.

Hanke, Lewis. "Conquest and the Cross." *American Heritage* 14, no. 2 (February 1963): 4-19, 107-11.

———. *La humanidad es una: Estudio acerca de la querella que sobre la capacidad intelectual y religiosa de los indígenas americanos sostuvieron en 1550 Bartolomé de las Casas y Juan Ginés de Sepúlveda.* Méjico D.F.: Fondo de Cultura Económica, 1974. English ed., *All Mankind Is One: A Study of the Disputation between Bartolomé de Las Casas and Juan Ginés de Sepúlveda in 1550 on the Intellectual and Religious Capacity of the American Indians.* DeKalb: Northern Illinois University Press, 1974.

Hart, William B. "The Unsettled Periphery: The Backcountry on the Eve of the American Revolution." In *The Oxford Handbook of the American Revolution*, edited by Edward G. Gray and Jane Kamensky, 30-46. Oxford: Oxford University Press, 2013.

Haydon, Frederick Stansbury. *Military Ballooning during the Early Civil War.* Baltimore: Johns Hopkins University Press, 2000. First published 1941.

Haynes, Robert V. *The Natchez District and the American Revolution.* Jackson: University Press of Mississippi, 1976.

Henderson, Ernest Flagg. *Blücher and the Uprising of Prussia against Napoleon, 1806-1815.* New York: G. P. Putnam's Sons, 1911.

Hernández Franco, Juan. *La gestión política y el pensamiento reformista del Conde de Floridablanca.* Murcia: Universidad de Murcia, 1984.

———. "El gobierno español ante la independencia de los Estados Unidos: Gestión de Floridablanca (1777-1783)." *Anales de Historia Contemporánea, Murcia* 8 (1992): 163-86.

Hernández González, Manuel. "Francisco de Miranda y Canarias." In *Miranda, Bolívar y Bello: Tres tiempos del pensar latinoamericano. Memoria de las VI jornadas de Historia y Religión. En homenaje a los doscientos años de la Expedición Libertadora de Francisco de Miranda*, 153-82. Caracas: Universidad Católica Andrés Bello, 2007.

———. *Francisco de Miranda y su ruptura con España*. Caracas: Academia Nacional de Historia, 2006.
Hernández Luna, Juan. *José Antonio Alzate*. México D.F.: Secretaría de Educación Pública, 1945.
Hernández Sánchez-Barba, Mario. "El americanismo del conde de Floridablanca." *Anales de Historia Contemporánea* 8 (1991): 45-57.
———. "Bernardo de Gálvez, militar y político en la Florida occidental. (Un bicentenario y una reparación histórica)." *Arbor* 109, no. 425 (1981): 41-56.
———. "El bicentenario de 1776: América y la estrategia de seguridad atlántica y el Reformismo español." *Revista de la Universidad Complutense* 26, no. 107 (1977): 9-48.
———. *La última expansión española en América*. Madrid: Instituto de Estudios Políticos, 1957.
Hernández Silva, Héctor Cuauhtémoc. *La expedición del visitador José de Gálvez al septentrión novohispano (1768-1770), o, la locura de la modernidad*. Sonora: UniSon, 2000.
Hernández Sorelo, Anel. "Hipólito de Villarroel y las enfermedades políticas de la Nueva España." *Boletín Cultural: Órgano Informativo y Cultural de la Escuela Nacional de Antropología e Historia* 18 (2003): 13-24.
Herzog, Tamar. "Los americanos frente a la Monarquía: El criollismo y la naturaleza española." In *La monarquía de las naciones: Patria, nación y naturaleza en la monarquía de España*, edited by Bernardo García García and José Antonio Álvarez-Ossorio Alvariño, 77-92. Madrid: Fundación Carlos de Amberes, 2004.
———. "Colonial Law and 'Native Customs': Indigenous Land Rights in Colonial Spanish America." *The Americas: A Quarterly Review of Inter-American Cultural History* 69, no. 3 (2013): 303-21.
———. *Frontiers of Possession. Spain and Portugal in Europe and the Americas*. Cambridge and London: Harvard University Press, 2015.
Hevia Bolaños, Juan de. *Laberinto de comercio terrestre y naval, donde breve y compendiosamente se trata de la mercancía y contratación de tierra y mar, útil y provechoso para Mercaderes, Negociadores, Navegantes y sus Consulados, Ministros de los Iuizios, profesores de Derecho y otras personas*. Madrid: Luis Sánchez, 1619.
Hidalgo, Dionisio. *Boletín bibliográfico español*. Madrid: Imprenta de las Escuelas Pías, 1864.
Higonnet, Patrice Louis-René. "The Origins of the Seven Years' War." *Journal of Modern History* 40, no. 1 (March 1968): 57-90.
Hilton, Sylvia L. "España y Norteamérica, 1763-1821." In *Legado: España y los Estados Unidos en la era de la Independencia, 1763-1848*, edited by Mercedes Águeda, 31-43. Madrid: Sociedad Estatal para la Acción Cultural Exterior, 2007.
———. "El Mississippi y la Luisiana colonial en la historiografía española, 1940-1989." *Revista de Indias* 50 (1990): 195-212.
———. "Las relaciones anglo-españolas en Norteamérica durante el reinado de Carlos III: Revisión historiográfica." In *Actas del Coloquio Internacional Carlos III y su siglo*, 839-82. Madrid: Universidad Complutense—Departamento de Historia Moderna, 1990.
———. "Spanish Colonies in North America: Recent Historical Scholarship from Spain." *American Studies International* 32, no. 1 (1994): 70-95.
———, ed. *Las raíces hispánicas del Oeste de Nortemérica: Textos históricos*. Madrid:

Fundación Histórica Tavera / Digilibris, CD-ROM, Clásicos Tavera, no. 21, ser. 2, 1999.

Hinderaker, Eric, and Rebecca Horn. "Territorial Crossings: Histories and Historiographies of the Early Americas." *William and Mary Quarterly* 67, no. 3 (July 2010): 395-432.

Historical Manuscripts Commission. *Report on American Manuscripts in the Royal Institution of Great Britain*. Dublin: John Falconer, 1904-6.

The History of Don Francisco de Miranda's Attempt to Effect a Revolution in South America, in a Series of Letters, by a Gentleman who was an Officer Under that General, to his Friend in the United States. Boston: Oliver and Munroe, 1809.

Hodge, Frederick Webb. "Early Western History." *Land of Sunshine* 12 (December 1900): 39-52.

———, ed. *Handbook of American Indians, North of Mexico*. Vol. 1, A-G. Washington, D.C.: Smithsonian Institution, 1912.

Hoffman, Paul E. *Luisiana*. Madrid: MAPFRE, 1992.

Holland Braund, Kathryn E. "The Anglo-Spanish Contest for the Gulf Coast as Viewed from the Townsquare [sic]." In *Anglo-Spanish Confrontation on the Gulf Coast during the American Revolution: Gálvez Celebration, Commemorating the Siege of Pensacola*, edited by William S. Coker and Robert R. Rea, 90-105. Pensacola: Gulf Coast History and Humanities Conference, 1982.

———. "The Creek Indians, Blacks, and Slavery." *Journal of Southern History* 57 (November 1991): 601-36.

———. *Deerskins and Duffels: The Creek Indian Trade with Anglo-America, 1685-1815*. Lincoln: University of Nebraska Press, 1993.

Holmes, Jack D. L. "Bernardo de Gálvez: Spain's 'Man of the Hour' during the American Revolution." In *Cardinales de Dos Independencias. (Noreste de México—Sureste de los Estados Unidos)*, edited by Francisco de Solano and Beatriz Ruiz Caytán, 161-74. México D.F.: Fomento Cultural Banamex, 1978.

———. *Honor and Fidelity: The Louisiana Infantry Regiment and the Louisiana Militia Companies, 1766-1821*. Birmingham: n.p., 1965.

———. *The 1779 "Marcha de Gálvez": Louisiana's Giant Step Forward in the American Revolution*. Baton Rouge: Baton Rouge Bicentennial Corporation, 1976.

———. "Some Economic Problems of Spanish Governors of Louisiana." *Hispanic American Historical Review* 42, no. 4 (November 1962): 521-43.

———, ed. *José de Evia y sus reconocimientos del Golfo de México, 1783-1796: Diarios, cartas, explicaciones, descripciones, planos y mapas*. Madrid: J. Porrúa Turanzas, 1968.

Holmes, Richard. *Redcoat: The British Soldier in the Age of Horse and Musket*. New York: Norton, 2001.

Hook, Jason. *The Apaches*. Oxford: Osprey, 1987.

Houck, Louis. *A History of Missouri from the Earliest Explorations and Settlements until the Admission to the State into the Union*. Chicago: Donnelley and Sons, 1908.

———. *The Spanish Regime in Missouri*. Chicago: Donnelley and Sons, 1909.

Houdaille, Jacques. "Frenchmen and Francophiles in New Spain." *The Americas: A Quarterly Review of Inter-American Cultural History* 13, no. 1 (July 1956): 1-29.

House of Lords Sessional Papers, Session 1794. Edited by F. W. Torrington. Dobbs Ferry, N.Y.: Oceana Publications, 1975.

Hu-Dehart, Evelyn. *Missionaries, Miners and Indians: Spanish Contact with the Yaqui*

Nation of Northwestern New Spain, 1533-1820. Tucson: University of Arizona Press, 1981.

Huerta Martínez, Ángel. "Preocupación de la familia Gálvez por la enseñanza primaria." In *El Reino de Granada y el Nuevo Mundo: V Congreso internacional de Historia de América, mayo de 1992,* 2:197-210. Granada: Diputación Provincial de Granada, 1994.

Hughes, Daniel. *Moltke on the Art of War: Selected Writings.* London: Random House, 2009.

Humboldt, Alexander von. *Essai politique sur le royaume de la Nouvelle-Espagne.* Paris: Schoell, 1811. Spanish trans., *Ensayo Político sobre el Reino de la Nueva España.* México D.F.: Porrúa, 2004. English trans., *Political Essay on the Kingdom of New Spain.* Translated by John Black. New York: I. Riley, 1811.

Index librorum prohibitorum et expurgandorum novissimus. Madrid, 1747.

Ingersoll, Thomas N. "Free Blacks in a Slave Society: New Orleans, 1718-1812." *William and Mary Quarterly,* 3rd ser., 48, no. 2 (April 1991): 173-200.

Ingrao, Charles. "'Barbarous Strangers': Hessian State and Society during the American Revolution." *American Historical Review* 87, no. 4 (October 1982): 954-76.

Inventario general de manuscritos de la Biblioteca Nacional. Madrid: Dirección General de Archivos y Bibliotecas (vols. 1-13) / Biblioteca Nacional (vols. 14-15), 1953-95.

Jacoby, Karl. *Shadows at Dawn: A Borderlands Massacre and the Violence of History.* New York: Penguin Press, 2008.

Jackson, George B. "John Stuart: Superintendent of Indian Affairs for the Southern District." *Tennessee Historical Magazine* 3, no. 3 (September 1917): 165-91.

James, James Alton. "Oliver Pollock and the Free Navigation of the Mississippi River." *Mississippi Valley Historical Review* 19, no. 3 (December 1932): 331-47.

———. *Oliver Pollock: The Life and Times of an Unknown Patriot.* New York: Appleton-Century, 1937.

———. "Spanish Influence in the West during the American Revolution." *Mississippi Valley Historical Review* 4, no. 2 (September 1917): 193-208.

Jane, Cecil. *Liberty and Despotism in Spanish America.* Oxford: Clarendon Press, 1929.

Jansen, A. "El Virrey Charles de Croix y la expulsión de los jesuitas de Méjico en 1767." *Hispania* 36 (1976): 321-54.

Jasanoff, Maya. *Liberty's Exiles: American Loyalists in the Revolutionary World.* New York: Alfred A. Knopf, 2012.

Jay, John. *The Correspondence and Public Papers of John Jay.* Edited by Henry P. Johnston. New York: G. P. Putnam's Sons, 1890-93.

Jay, John, and Sarah Livingston Jay. *Selected Letters of John Jay and Sarah Livingston Jay.* Edited by Landa M. Freeman, Louise V. North, and Janet M. Wedge. Jefferson, N.C.: McFarland, 2010.

Jiménez Meneses, Orián. *El frenesí del vulgo: Fiestas, juegos y bailes en la sociedad colonial.* Medellín: Universidad de Antioquia, 2007.

Jiménez Núñez, Alfredo. *El gran norte de México una frontera imperial en la Nueva España (1540-1820): Una frontera imperial en la Nueva España (1540-1820).* Madrid: Tebar, 2006.

Jiménez Quintero, José Antonio. "El Panteón de los Gálvez de Macharaviaya." *Jábega* (1974): 45-48.

John, Elizabeth A. H. "Bernardo de Gálvez on the Apache Frontier." *Journal of Arizona History* 29 (1988): 427-30.

———. "A Cautionary Exercise in Apache Historiography—Notes and Reflections on the War with the Apache Indians in the Provinces of New Spain—by Bernardo de Galvez, ca. 1785-86." *Journal of Arizona History* 25 (1984): 301-15.

———. *Storms Brewed in Other Men's Worlds: The Confrontation of Indians, Spanish, and French in the Southwest, 1540-1795*. 2nd ed. Norman: University of Oklahoma Press, 1996.

Johnson, Sandra. "Born to Destiny: Bernardo de Gálvez." In *Siege! Spain and Britain: Battle of Pensacola, March 9-May 8, 1781*, edited by Virginia Parks, 23-32. Pensacola: Pensacola Historical Society, 1981.

Jomini, Baron de. *Précis de l'art de la guerre, ou Nouveau tableau analytique des principales combinaisons de la stratégie, de la grande tactique et de la politique militaire*. Paris: Anselin, 1813.

Jones, John Paul. *John Paul Jones' Memoir of the American Revolution, Presented to King Louis XVI of France*. Edited by John R. Sellers. Honolulu: University Press of the Pacific, 2001.

Jones, Joseph R. "María Rosa de Gálvez: Notes for a Biography." *Dieciocho: Hispanic enlightenment* 18, no. 2 (1995): 173-87.

———. "María Rosa de Gálvez, Rousseau, Iriarte y el melólogo en la España del siglo XVIII." *Dieciocho: Hispanic enlightenment* 19, no. 2 (1996): 165-80.

Jones, Oakah L. *Nueva Vizcaya: Heartland of the Spanish Frontier*. Albuquerque: University of New Mexico Press, 1988.

Journals of the Continental Congress, 1774-89. Edited by Worthington C. Ford et al. 34 vols. Washington, D.C.: 1904-37.

Jovellanos, Gaspar Melchor de. "Memoria para el arreglo de la policía de los espectáculos y diversiones públicas, y sobre su origen en España, 29 diciembre 1790." In *Obras completes*, 2:241-97. Barcelona: La Anticuaria, 1865.

Jover Zamora, José María. *España en la política internacional: Siglos XVIII-XX*. Madrid: Marcial Pons, 1999.

Kalendario manual y guía de forasteros de Madrid para el año de 1784. Madrid: Imprenta Real, 1784.

Kalendario manual y guía de forasteros de Madrid para el año de 1785. Madrid: Imprenta Real, 1785.

Kalendario manual y guía de forasteros de Madrid para el año de 1786. Madrid: Imprenta Real, 1786.

Kalendario manual y guía de forasteros en Madrid para el año de 1774. Madrid: Imprenta Real, 1774.

Kalendario manual y guía de forasteros en Madrid para el año de 1775. Madrid: Imprenta Real, 1775.

Kalendario manual y guía de forasteros en Madrid para el año de 1793. Madrid: Imprenta Real, 1793.

Kamen, Henry. *The War of Succession in Spain, 1700-1715*. London: Weidenfeld and Nicolson, 1969.

Kavanagh, Thomas W. *The Comanches: A History, 1706-1875*. Lincoln: University of Nebraska Press, 1996.

Keegan, John. *Intelligence in War*. New York: Alfred A. Knopf, 2003.

———. *The Mask of Command*: London: Pimlico, 1998. Spanish trans., *La máscara del mando*. Madrid: Ministerio de Defensa, 1991.

Kein, Sybil. "Louisiana Creole Food Culture: Afro-Caribbean Links." In *Creole: The History and Legacy of Louisiana's Free People of Color*, edited by Sybil Kein, 244-51. Baton Rouge: Louisiana State University Press, 2000.

Keith, Robert G. "Encomienda, Hacienda, and Corregimiento in Spanish America: A Structural Analysis." *Hispanic American Historical Review* 51 (1971): 431-46.

Kelsay, Isabel Thompson. *Joseph Brant, 1743-1807: Man of Two Worlds*. Syracuse: Syracuse University Press, 1984.

Kinnaird, Lawrence. "American Penetration into Spanish Louisiana." In *New Spain and the Anglo-American West (Historical Contributions Presented to H. E. Bolton)*, 1:211-37. Los Angeles: 1932.

———. "Spanish Treaties with Indian Tribes." *Western Historical Quaterly* 10, no. 1 (1979): 39-48.

———. *Spain in the Mississippi Valley, 1765-1794*. Part 1, *The Revolutionary Period, 1765-1781*. Washington, D.C.: Government Printing Office, 1949.

Knaut, Andrew L. *The Pueblo Revolt of 1680: Conquest and Resistance in Seventeenth-Century New Mexico*. Norman: University of Oklahoma Press, 1997.

Krebs, Daniel. "The Making of Prisoners of War: Rituals of Surrender in the American War of Independence, 1776-1783." *Militaergeschichtliche Zeitschrift* 64, no. 1 (2005): 1-30.

Kroener, Bernhard H. "L'État moderne et la société militaire au XVIIIe siècle." In *Guerre et concurrence entre les états européens du XIVé au XVIIIe siècle*, edited by P. Contamine, 237-68. Paris: Presses universitaires de France, 1998.

Kuethe, Allan J. "The Development of the Cuban Military as a Sociopolitical Elite, 1763-83." *Hispanic American Historical Review* 61, no. 4 (November 1981): 695-704.

———. "Las milicias disciplinadas de América." 1st ver. In *Temas de historia militar: 2º Congreso de Historia Militar, Zaragoza, 1988*. Madrid: Servicio de Publicaciones del Estado Mayor del Ejército, 1988: 311-39.

———. "Las milicias disciplinadas de América." 2nd ver. In *Soldados del rey: El ejército borbónico en América colonial en vísperas de la independencia*, edited by Allan J. Kuethe and Juan Marchena Fernández, 101-26. Castelló de la Plana: Universitat Jaume I, 2005.

Kuethe, Allan J., and Kenneth J. Andrien. *The Spanish Atlantic World in the Eighteenth Century: War and the Bourbon Reforms, 1713-1796*. New York: Cambridge University Press, 2014.

Kuethe, Allan J., and Juan Marchena Fernández, eds. *Soldados del rey: El ejército borbónico en América colonial en vísperas de la independencia*. Castelló de la Plana: Universitat Jaume I, 2005.

Lachance, Paul F. "The Politics of Fear: French Louisianians and Slave Trade, 1786-1809." *Plantation Society in the Americas* 1 (June 1979): 162-97.

Lacou-Gayet, G. *La marine militaire de la France sous le régne de Louis XVI*. Paris: Honoré Champion, 1905.

Lacunza, José María. *Discursos Históricos: Leídos en la Academia del Colegio de S. Juan de Letran*. México D.F., 1845.

Ladrón de Guevara, Baltasar [attrib.]. *Discurso sobre la policía de México; reflexiones y apuntes sobre varios objetos que interesan la salud pública y la policía particular de esta ciudad de México), si se adoptasen las providencias o remedios correspondientes*. In *Antología de textos sobre la ciudad de México en el periodo de la Ilustración (1788-1792)*, edited by Sonia Lombardo de Ruiz, 17-152. México D.F.: Departamento de Investigaciones Históricas, INAH, Colección científica no. 113, 1982.

Lafarelle, Lorenzo G. *Bernardo de Gálvez: Hero of the American Revolution*. Austin: Eakin Press, 1992.

Lafora, Nicolás de. "Viaje a los presidios internos de la América Septentrional (1766-

1768).″ In *Bibliotheca Indiana: Viajes y viajeros: Viajes por Norteamérica*. Madrid: Aguilar 1958.

Lafuente, Antonio. "Las expediciones científicas del setecientos y la nueva relación del científico con el Estado." *Revista de Indias* 47, no. 180 (1987): 373-78.

Lamar, Howard R., and Sam Truett. "The Greater Southwest and California from the Beginning of European Settlement to the 1880s." In *The Cambridge History of the Native Peoples of the Americas*, vol. 1, *North America*, edited by Bruce G. Trigger and Wilcomb E. Washburn, 57-116. New York: Cambridge University Press, 1996.

Larios Martín, Jesús. "Ciencias complementarias de la nobiliaria." In *Apuntes de Nobiliaria y nociones de Genealogía y Heráldica: Curso de grado de la Escuela de Genealogía, Heráldica y Nobiliaria*. Madrid: Hidalguía, 1960.

Larrañaga, Bruno Francisco. *La América socorrida en el gobierno del Excmo. Señor don Bernardo de Gálvez, conde de Gálvez, virrey. Égloga*. México: Felipe de Zúñiga y Ontiveros, 1786. Biblioteca Nacional, Madrid, VE/1234/14 and VE/1236/20.

Laserna Gaitan, Antonio Ignacio. *El Fondo Saavedra*. Granada: Universidad de Granada, 1995.

Latasa, Pilar, ed. *Reformismo y sociedad en la América borbónica: In memoriam Ronald Escobedo*. Pamplona: Ediciones Universidad de Navarra S.A., 2004.

Latham, J. D., and W. F. Paterson. *Saracen Archery*. London: Holland Press, 1970.

Lauber, Almon Wheeler. *Indian Slavery in Colonial Times within the Present Limits of the United States*. New York: Columbia University, 1913.

Lavedan, Antonio. *Tratado de los usos, abusos, propiedades y virtudes del tabaco, café, té y chocolate. Extractado de los mejores autores que han tratado de esta materia, a fin de que su uso no perjudique a la salud, antes bien pueda servir de alivio y curación de muchos males*. Madrid: Imprenta Real, 1796.

La Vere, David. *The Texas Indians*. College Station: Texas A&M University Press, 2004.

Lázaro Ávila, Carlos. "Los tratados de paz con los indígenas fronterizos de América: Revolución histórica y estado de la cuestión." *Estudios de Historia Social y Económica de América* 13 (1996): 15-24.

Lawrence of Arabia. Directed by David Lean. Hollywood, CA: Columbia Pictures, 1962.

Leblanc, Robert A. "The Acadian Migrations." *Cahiers de géographie du Québec* 11, no. 24 (1967): 523-41.

Leclerc, Charles. *Bibliotheca Americana: Histoire, Géographie, Voyages, Archéologie et Linguistique des Deux Amériques et des Iles Philippines*. Paris: Maisonneuve et Cie, 1878.

Lediard, Thomas. *The life of John, Duke of Marlborough: Prince of the Roman empire*. London: J. Wilcox, 1743.

Lee, Dayna Bowker. "Indian Slavery in Lower Louisiana during the Colonial Period, 1699-1803." MA diss., Northwestern State University, 1989.

Legado: España y los Estados Unidos en la era de la Independencia, 1763-1848. Madrid: Sociedad Estatal para la Acción Cultural Exterior, 2007.

Lemmon, Alfred E. "Spanish Louisiana: In the Service of God and His Most Catholic Majesty." In *The Louisiana Purchase Bicentennial Series in Louisiana History, Vol. 2: The Spanish Presence in Louisiana, 1763-1803*, edited by Gilbert C. Din, 517-29. Lafayette: Center for Louisiana Studies, University of Southwestern Louisiana, 1996.

Lemon, James T. "Colonial America in the Eighteenth Century." In *North America: The Historical Geography of a Changing Continent*, edited by Robert Mitchell and Paul Groves, 121-46. Lanham: Rowman and Littlefield, 2001. First published 1987.

Leonard, Irving A. "The 1790 Theater Season of the Mexico City Coliseo." *Hispanic Review* 19, no. 2 (April 1951): 104-20.
León-Ignacio, Jacinto. *Bernardo de Gálvez ¡Seguid la bandera!* Madrid[?]: Cliper, s.a.
León Meza C., René de. "Ideas y lecturas de un minero ilustrado del siglo XVIII." *Boletín del Archivo General de la Nación* 6, no. 19 (2008): 121-45.
León-Portilla, Miguel, ed. *Crónicas indígenas: Visión de los vencidos*. Madrid: Historia 16, 1985.
———. *El reverso de la conquista: Relaciones aztecas, mayas e incas*. México D.F.: Joaquín Mortíz, 1964.
León Tello, Pilar, Concepción Menéndez, and Carmen Herrero. *Documentos relativos a la independencia de Norteamérica existentes en archivos españoles, vol. 3/1, Archivo Histórico Nacional. Correspondencia diplomática (años 1801-1820)*. Madrid: Ministerio de Asuntos Exteriores, 1976.
———. *Documentos relativos a la independencia de Norteamérica existentes en archivos españoles, vol. 3/2., Archivo Histórico Nacional. Correspondencia diplomática (años 1801-1820)*. Madrid: Ministerio de Asuntos Exteriores, 1976.
León Tello, Pilar, Concepción Menéndez, and Carmen Torroja. *Documentos relativos a la independencia de Norteamérica existentes en archivos españoles, vol.4, Archivo Histórico Nacional. Expedientes (años 1801-1820)*. Madrid: Ministerio de Asuntos Exteriores, 1980.
———. *Documentos relativos a la independencia de Norteamérica existentes en archivos españoles, vol.8, Archivo Histórico Nacional. Correspondencia diplomática (años 1821-1833)*. Madrid: Ministerio de Asuntos Exteriores, 1982.
———. *Documentos relativos a la independencia de Norteamérica existentes en archivos españoles, vol.10, Archivo Histórico Nacional. Expedientes (años 1821-1850)*. Madrid: Ministerio de Asuntos Exteriores, 1984.
Lepore, Amedeo. *Mercado y empresa en Europa: La empresa de González de la Sierra en el comercio gaditano entre los siglos XVIII y XIX*. Cádiz: Universidad de Cádiz, 2010.
Leroy-Beaulieu, Paul. *De la colonisation chez les peuples modernes*. Paris: Guillaumin et Cie., 1882. First published 1861.
Lesen y Moreno, José. *Historia de la Sociedad Económica de Amigos del País de Madrid*. Madrid: Imprenta del Colegio de sordo-mudos y ciegos, 1863.
Levaggi, Abelardo. "Aplicación de la política española de tratados a los indios de la Nueva España y sus confines: El caso de la Luisiana y las Floridas (1781-1790)." *Revista de investigaciones jurídicas* 20 (1996): 225-41.
———. *Diplomacia hispano-indígena en las fronteras de América: Historia de los tratados entre la Monarquía española y las comunidades aborígenes*. Madrid: Centro de estudios Políticos y Constitucionales, 2002.
———. "República de indios y república de españoles en los reinos de Indias." *Revista de Estudios Histórico-Jurídicos* 23 (2001): 419-28.
———. "Los tratados entre la Corona y los indios, y el plan de conquista pacífica." *Revista Complutense de Historia de América* 19 (1993): 81-91.
Lewis, James A. "Las Damas de La Habana, el Precursor, and Francisco de Saavedra: A Note on Spanish Participation in the Battle of Yorktown." *The Americas: A Quarterly Review of Inter-American Cultural History* 37 (July 1980): 83-98.
———. *The Final Campaign of the American Revolution: The Rise and Fall of the Spanish Bahamas*. Columbia: University of South Carolina Press, 1991.
Lieux, D. B. "Malaria in Florida." *Florida Entomologist* 34, no. 4 (December 1951): 131-35.

Lightfoot, Kent G. *Indians, Missionaries, and Merchants: The Legacy of Colonial Encounters on the California Frontier.* Berkeley: University of California Press, 2005.

Limerick, Patricia N. *The Legacy of Conquest: The Unbroken Past of the American West.* New York: W. W. Norton, 1987.

Linneo, Carl. *Genera morborum.* Upsala, 1763.

Lipski, John M. "El dialecto español de Río Sabinas: Vestigios del español mexicano en Luisiana y Texas." *Nueva Revista de Filología Hispánica* 35, no. 1 (1987): 111–28.

———. "Reducción de 's' y 'n' en el español isleño de Luisiana: Vestigios del español canario en Norteamérica." *Revista de filología de la Universidad de La Laguna* 4 (1985): 125–34.

Lira Montt, Luis. "La prueba de hidalgía en el derecho indiano." *Revista Chilena de Historia del Derecho* 7 (1978): 131–52.

Lizararrás, José. *Lamentos americanos por la muerte del Excmo. Sr. D. Bernardo de Gálvez, conde de Gálvez.* México, 1785. Biblioteca Nacional, Madrid, VE/1236/19.

Llanto con que responde México a la pregunta de un curioso sobre la muerte del virrey conde de Gálvez. México: Felipe de Zúñiga y Ontiveros, 1786.

Lockhart, James. "Encomienda and Hacienda: The Evolution of the Great State in the Spanish Indies." *Hispanic American Historical Review* 49 (1969): 411–29.

———. Review of *Gobierno del Peru (1567),* by Juan de Matienzo, edition by Guillermo Lohmann Villena. *Hispanic American Historical Review* 49, no. 1 (February 1969): 137–38.

Lombardo de Ruiz, Sonia, ed. *Antología de textos sobre la ciudad de México en el periodo de la Ilustración (1788–1792).* México D.F.: Departamento de Investigaciones Históricas, INAH, Colección científica no. 113, 1982.

Longchamps, Pierre Charpentier de. *Historia de la última guerra entre la Inglaterra, los Estados Unidos de América, la Francia, España y Holanda: Desde el año de 1775, en que se principió hasta el de 1783, en que se concluyó, con un plan exacto, y circunstanciado de todos los navíos, y buques de guerra de las potencias beligerantes, que fueron apresados, quemados, echados a pique, o destruidos.* Alcalá: Imprenta de la Universidad, 1793. First published 1785.

Longford, Elizabeth. *Wellington: The Years of the Sword.* New York: Harper and Row, 1966.

Lopez, T. "Indian Peace Medals." *Numismatist,* April 2007, 36–47.

López Alanís, Gilberto. "Mecanismos de violencia militar fronteriza en las Provincias Internas a finales del siglo XVIII." In *Memoria del XI Simposio de Historia y Antropología 1987,* 107–18. Hermosillo: Universidad de Sonora, 1987.

López Cantos, Ángel. *Don Francisco de Saavedra, segundo intendente de Caracas.* Sevilla: Consejo Superior de Investigaciones Científicas / Escuela de Estudios Hispano-Americanos, 1973.

López-Cordón Cortezo, María Victoria. "Secretarios y secretarías en la edad moderna: De las manos del príncipe a relojeros de la monarquía." *Studia historica: Historia moderna* 15 (1996): 107–31.

López Delgado, Juan Antonio. "Estado de la cuestión." In *La expedición militar española contra Argel de 1775 (según el Diario de un testigo ocular),* by Count de Carlos Gutiérrez de los Ríos Fernán-Núñez. Edited by Juan Antonio López Delgado, 14–21. Murcia: J.A. López, 2001.

López Estrada, Francisco. *Tomás Moro y España.* Madrid: Universidad Complutense, 1980.

López Piñero, José María. "La obra botánica de Cavanilles." In *Antonio José Cavanilles*

(1745-1804): Segundo centenario de la muerte de un gran botánico, 11–168. Valencia: Real Sociedad Económica de Amigos del País, 2004.

López Sarrelangue, Delfina. "Población indígena de la Nueva España en el siglo XVIII." *Historia mexicana* 12, no. 4 (1963): 516–30.

———. "La policía de la ciudad de México en 1788." *Revista de Indias* 32, no. 127-30 (1972): 227–40.

Losa Contreras, Carmen. "La formación de la milicia urbana en la Nueva España." *Anuario de la Facultad de Derecho* 24 (2006): 177–214.

Lourido Díaz, Ramón. *Marruecos y el mundo exterior en la segunda mitad del siglo XVIII: Relaciones político-comerciales del sultán Sīdī Muhammad B. Allāh (1757-1790) con el exterior*. Madrid: AECI, 1989.

Lowental, Mark M. *Intelligence: From Secrets to Policy*. Washington, D.C.: CQ Press, 2000.

Lucas, Ventura. *Desahogo fiel, festiva, y autorizada solemnidad, con que la muy noble, valerosísima, y fidelísima villa de Molina de Aragón (a imitación de los demás pueblos de España) reconoce, y proclama a nuestro cathólico monarca don Carlos III por Rey de España, y Señor de aquella*. Madrid: Imprenta del Diario, 1759.

Lucena Salmoral, Manuel. *Los Códigos negros de la América española*. Alcalá de Henares: UNESCO-Universidad de Alcalá, 1996.

———. "El derecho de coartación del esclavo en la América española." *Revista de Indias* 59, no. 216 (1999): 357–74.

———. *Regulación de la esclavitud negra en las colonias de América Española (1503-1886): Documentos para su estudio*. Alcalá: Universidad de Alcalá de Henares / Universidad de Murcia, 2005.

Luque Alcaide, Elisa. "Debate sobre el indio en el IV Concilio Provincial Mexicano (1771). Francisco Antonio de Lorenzana, peninsular, vs Cayetano Antonio de Torres, criollo." In *Estudios sobre América: Siglos XVI-XX*, edited by Antonio Gutiérrez Escudero and María Luisa Laviana Cuetos, 1353–72. X Congreso de la Asociación Española de Americanistas, Sevilla 2002. Sevilla: Asociación Española de Americanistas, 2005.

Luque Talaván, Miguel. *Un universo de opiniones: La literatura jurídica indiana*. Madrid: Consejo Superior de Investigaciones Científicas, 2003.

Lurie, Nancy Oestreich. "The World's Oldest On-Going Protest Demonstration: North American Indian Drinking Patterns." *Pacific Historical Review* 40, no. 3 (August 1971): 311–32.

Lussan, A. *La famille creole, drame en cinq actes et en prose*. Nouevelle Orleans: Fremaux, 1837.

Lynch, John. *La España del siglo XVIII*. 4th ed. Barcelona: Crítica, 2009.

———. "Los factores estructurales de la crisis: La crisis del orden colonial." In *Historia general de América Latina*, edited by Germán Carrera Damas and John V. Lombardi, 5:31–54. S.l.: UNESCO-Trotta, 1992.

———. *Historia de España, vol.5, Edad Moderna: Crisis y recuperación, 1598-1808*. Barcelona: Crítica, 2005.

———. "El reformismo borbónico e Hispanoamérica." In *El Reformismo borbónico: Una visión interdisciplinar*, edited by Agustín Guimerá, 37–60. Madrid: Alianza Universidad, 1996.

———. *Las revoluciones hispanoamericanas, 1808-1826*. Barcelona: Ariel, 2008.

———. *Bourbon Spain, 1700-1808*. Oxford, UK; Cambridge, Mass.: B. Blackwell, 1989.

M. ——. *Mémoires sur la Louisiane et la Nouvelle-Orléans, Accompagnés d'une dissertation sur les avantages que le commerce de l'Empire doit tirer de la stipulation faite par l'article VII du Traité de cession, du 30 avril 1803*. Paris: Ballard, 1804.

MacAndrew, Craig, and Robert B. Edgerton. *Drunken Comportment: A Social Explanation*. Chicago: Hawthorne, 1969.

MacUrdy, Raymond R. "Los 'isleños' de la Luisiana: Supervivencia de la lengua y folklore canarios." *Anuario de Estudios Atlánticos* 21 (1975): 471–594.

Madariaga, Salvador de. *El auge y el ocaso del imperio español en América*. Madrid: SARPE, 1985.

Maddison, Angus. "Historical Statistics for the World Economy: 1–2003 AD." At http://www.ggdc.net/maddison/oriindex.htm (accessed January 2, 2017).

Maduell, Charles R., Jr., ed. *The Census Tables for the French Colony of Louisiana from 1699 through 1732*. Baltimore: Genealogical Publishing Co., 1972.

Maeder, Ernesto J. A. "Libros, bibliotecas, control de lecturas e imprentas rioplatenses en los siglos XVI al XVIII." *Teología* 77 (2001): 5–24.

Magro y Zurita, Santiago, and Eusebio Ventura Beleña. *Elucidationes ad quatuor libros Institutionum Imperatoris Justiniani*. México: Felipe Zúñiga Ontiveros, 1787.

Malagón Barceló, Javier. *Código Negro Carolino (1784): Código de legislación para el gobierno moral, político y económico de los negros de la isla Española*. Santo Domingo: Ed. Taller, 1974.

Maldonado López, Celia. "Temblores de tierra y otras calamidades registrados en la capital de la Nueva España en los siglos XVII y XVIII." In *Historias para temblar: 19 de septiembre de 1985*, edited by Carlos San Juan, 11–26. México D.F.: Instituto Nacional de Antropología e Historia, 1986.

Maldonado Polo, José Luis. "La expedición botánica a Nueva España, 1786-1803: El Jardín Botánico y la Cátedra de Botánica." *Historia Mexicana* 50, no. 1 (2000): 5–56.

Malvido, Elsa. "Factores de despoblación y reposición de la población de Cholula (1641-1810)." *Historia Mexicana* 23, no. 89 (1973): 52–110.

Mañana gaditana, fiesta del estreno de el nuevo Noviciado del convento de N. R. P. San Francisco costeado por la singular beneficiencia [sic] de Cádiz y especialmente por Don Antonio de Gálvez. Cádiz: Juan Ximenez Carreño, 1783.

Mancall, Peter C. *Deadly Medicine: Indians and Alcohol in Early America*. Ithaca: Cornell University Press, 1995.

Mancall, Peter C., and James H. Merrell. *American Encounters: Natives and Newcomers from European Contact to Indian Removal*. 2nd ed. New York: Routledge, 2007.

Manera Regueyra, Enrique, ed. *El buque en la Armada Española*. Madrid: Sílex, 1999.

Manjarrez Cuellar, María Graciela. "Aproximación a la representación del espacio: Tres textos de viajeros españoles por la Nueva México." Master's diss. Universidad Iberoamericana, 2006.

Mañón, Manuel. *Historia del Teatro Principal de México*. México D.F.: Cultura, 1932.

Mansilla Legoburo, María E., and María C. Vidal Casero. "Casimiro Gómez Ortega, Director del Jardín botánico de Madrid." In *Actas II Congreso de la Sociedad Española de Historia de las Ciencias: Jaca, 27 de Septiembre-1 de Octubre 1982, vol. 3, Temas libres: comunicaciones*, edited by Mariano Hormigón Blánquez, 197–202. Madrid: Sociedad Española de Historia de las Ciencias y de las Técnicas, 1984.

Manuel, Dale. *Pensacola Bay: A Military History*. Charleston: Arcadia, 2004.

Mapelli, Enrique. "La liberación de un penado en la Semana Santa de Málaga." *Isla de Arriarán: Revista cultural y científica* 9 (1997): 159–69.

Mapp, Paul W. *The Elusive West and the Contest for Empire, 1713-1763*. Chapel Hill: University of North Carolina Press, 2011.

———. "French Geographic Conceptions of the Unexplored American West and the Louisiana Cession of 1762." In *French Colonial Louisiana and the Atlantic World*, edited by Bradley G. Bond, 134-74. Baton Rouge: Louisiana State University Press, 2005.

———. "Interpretive Implications of a Continental Approach." Paper presented at the 2009 William and Mary Quarterly / EMSI workshop, Williamsburg, Virginia.

Marañón Moya, Gregorio. "Bernardo de Gálvez, de capitán de granaderos a virrey." In *Huellas de España en América II*, edited by Jaime Delgado, 2:83-98. Cádiz: Aula Militar de Cultura, 1984.

Marchena Fernández, Juan. "El ejército de América y la descomposición colonial: La otra mirada en un conflicto de lealtades." *MILITARIA: Revista de Cultura Militar* 4 (1992): 63-91.

———. *Ejércitos y milicias en el mundo colonial americano*. Madrid: MAPFRE, 1992.

———. "La expresión de la guerra: El poder colonial. El ejército y la crisis colonial." In *Historia de América Andina*, edited by Germán Carrera Damas, 4:79-128. Quito: Universidad Andina Simón Bolívar, 2003.

———. *La institución militar en Cartagena de Indias en el siglo XVIII*. Sevilla: Escuela de Estudios Hispano-Americanos, 1982.

———. *Oficiales y soldados en el ejército de América*. Sevilla: Consejo Superior de Investigaciones Científicas / Escuela de Estudios Hispano-Americanos, 1983.

Marchena Fernández, Juan, Gumersindo Caballero Gómez, and Torres Diego Arriaza. *El ejército de América antes de la Independencia. Ejército regular y milicias americanas, 1750-1815. Hojas de servicio, uniformes y estudio*. CD-ROM. Madrid: Fundación MAPFRE-Tavera, 2005.

Marfil García, Mariano. *Relaciones entre España y la Gran Bretaña desde las paces de Utrecht hasta nuestros días*. Madrid: Hijos de R. Álvarez, 1907.

Marichal, Carlos, and Matilde Souto Mantecón. "Silver and Situados: New Spain and the Financing of the Spanish Empire in the Caribbean in the Eighteenth Century." *Hispanic American Historical Review* 74, no. 4 (1994): 587-613.

Mariluz Urquijo, José María. "Gestiones en torno de la formación de un código de Hacienda en España (1780-1790)." *Revista de Historia del Derecho* 12 (1984): 229-51.

Marín Leoz, Juana. "El gobierno interino de la Audiencia y la jurisdicción militar en el México borbónico (1776-1806)." In *Estudios sobre América: Siglos XVI-XX*, edited by Antonio Gutiérrez Escudero and María Luisa Laviana Cuetos, 1105-22. X Congreso de la Asociación Española de Americanistas, Sevilla 2002. Sevilla: Asociación Española de Americanistas, 2005.

Marston, Daniel S. *The French-Indian War, 1754-1760*. Oxford: Osprey, 2003.

Martin, François-Xavier. *The History of Louisiana, from the Earliest Period*. New Orleans: Penniman, 1829.

Martín, Norman F. *Instrucciones del virrey marqués de Croix*. México D.F.: Jus, 1960.

Martínez, María Elena. *Genealogical Fictions: Limpieza de Sangre, Religion, and Gender in Colonial Mexico*. Stanford: Stanford University Press, 2008.

Martínez Carreras, José U. "El africanismo español." In *La política exterior de España (1800-2003)*, 2nd ed., edited by Juan Carlos Pereira, 357-70. Barcelona: Ariel, 2009.

Martínez Gálvez, Inmaculada, and Valentín H. Medina Rodríguez. "La aportación de las familias malagueñas al poblamiento de la Luisiana, 1777-1779." In *El Reino de*

Granada y el Nuevo Mundo, V Congreso internacional de Historia de América, mayo de 1992, 1:97-108. Granada: Diputación Provincial de Granada, 1994.

Martínez Laínez, Fernando, and Carlos Canales Torres. *Banderas lejanas: La exploración, conquista y defensa por España del territorio de los actuales estados Unidos*. Madrid: EDAF, 2009.

Martínez Moreno, Carlos Francisco. "El establecimiento de las masonerías en México en el siglo XIX." PhD diss., Universidad Nacional Autónoma de México, 2011.

Martínez Paricio, Jesús Ignacio. "La Real Escuela Militar de Ávila de los Caballeros, ¿una experiencia imposible?" In *La enseñanza militar en España: Un análisis sociológico*, 51-64. Madrid: Consejo Superior de Investigaciones Científicas, 1986.

Martínez Peñas, Leandro. *El confesor del rey en el antiguo régimen*. Madrid: Ed. Complutense, 2007.

Martínez Peñas, Leandro, and Manuela Fernández Rodríguez, eds. *El ejército y la armada en el noroeste de América: Nootka y su tiempo*. Madrid: Universidad rey Juan Carlos, 2011.

Martínez y Gálvez, Inmaculada. "La mujer y la vida familiar en Nueva Orleans (1763-1803)." In *XIII Coloquio de Historia Canario-Americana, VIII Congreso Internacional de Historia de América (Anuario de Estudios Americanos) (1998)*, edited by Francisco Morales Padrón, 1380-94. Las Palmas de Gran Canaria: Cabildo Insular de Gran Canaria, 2000.

Martín Gaite, Carmen. *Usos amorosos en el dieciocho en España*. Madrid: Siglo XXI, 1972. English trans., *Love Customs in Eighteenth-Century Spain*. Berkeley: University of California Press, 1991.

Martín Galán, Manuel. "Nuevos datos sobre un viejo problema: El coeficiente de conversión de vecinos en habitantes." *Revista Internacional de Sociología* 43 (October-December 1985): 593-633.

Martín Merás, María Luisa. *Cartografía marítima Hispana: La imagen de América*. Madrid: Lundwerg, 1993.

———. "La toma de Pensacola a través de los mapas." In *Bernardo de Gálvez y su tiempo*, edited by Manuel Olmedo Checa, 38-53. Málaga: Colegio Oficial de Ingenieros Técnicos Industriales de Málaga, 2007.

Martirologio Romano, publicado por orden del Papa Gregorio XIII, y reconocido con la autoridad de Urbano VIII, de Inocencio XI, de Clemente X, y últimamente corregido y aumentado por el Sumo Pontífice Benedicto XIV, traducido al castellano por D. Agustín Álvarez Pato y Castrillón. Madrid: Imprenta Real, 1791.

Mathews, James A. "Journal of the Siege and Surrender of Pensacola." In *Mississippi, as a Province, Territory and State with Biographical Notices of Eminent Citizens*, edited by J. F. H. Claiborne, 126. Jackson: Power and Barksdale, 1880.

Matienzo, Juan de. *Gobierno del Perú*. Edited by Guillermo Lohmann Villena, Lima: Institut Français d'Etudes Andines, 1967. First published 1567.

Matilla Tascón, Antonio. *Catálogo de documentos notariales de nobles*. Madrid: Hidalguía, 1987.

Matos Fragoso, Juan de. *Comedia famosa Lorenzo me llamo y carbonero de Toledo*. Madrid: Biblioteca de Autores Españoles-Rivadeneyra, s.a. First published 1754.

Matson, Daniel S., and Albert H. Schroeder, eds. "Cordero's Description of the Apache." *New Mexico Historical Review* 32, no. 4 (October 1957): 335-56.

Maty, Henry. *A New Review with Literary Curiosities, and Literary Intelligence for the Year 1785*. London: J. Davis, 1785.

Matzke McCadden, Helen. "Juan de Miralles and the American Revolution." *The Americas: A Quarterly Review of Inter-American Cultural History* 29, no. 3 (1973): 359-75.
Maura, Duke de Gabriel Maura Gamazo. *Carlos II y su corte*. Madrid: F. Beltrán, 1911.
Mauss, Marcel. *The Gift: Forms and Functions of Exchange in Archaic Societies*. New York: Norton, 1967. First published 1923.
May, Robin. *The British Army in North America, 1775-83*. Illustrated by Gerry Embleton. London: Osprey, 1997.
McAlister, Lyle N. *El fuero militar en la Nueva España (1764-1800)*. México D.F.: Universidad Nacional Autónoma de México, 1982.
―――. "The Reorganization of the Army of New Spain, 1763-1766." *Hispanic American Historical Review* 33, no. 1 (1953): 1-32.
McCarty, Kieran R. "La educación de un virrey: Bernardo de Gálvez en la frontera Apache, 1769-1771." In *Memoria del XII Simposio de Historia y Antropología*, 2:96-102. México D.F.: Universidad de Sonora, 1988.
McConnell, Michael N. *Army and Empire: British Soldiers on the American Frontier, 1758-1775*. Omaha: University of Nebraska Press, 2004.
McCutcheon, Roger P. "Libraries in New Orleans, 1771-1833." *Louisiana Historical Quarterly* 20 (1937): 152-58.
McDermott, John Francis. "The Myth of the Imbecile Governor." In *The Spanish in the Mississippi Valley, 1762-1804*, edited by John Francis McDermott, 339-48. Urbana: University of Illinois Press, 1974.
―――, ed. *The Spanish in the Mississippi Valley, 1762-1804*. Urbana: University of Illinois Press, 1974.
McFarlane, Anthony. *Colombia before Independence: Economy, Society, and Politics under Bourbon Rule*. Cambridge: Cambridge University Press, 2002.
―――. "Los ejércitos coloniales y la crisis del imperio español, 1808-1810." *Historia Mexicana* 57, no. 1 (2008): 229-85.
McKusker, John J. *Money and Exchange in Europe and America, 1600-1775: A Handbook*. Chapel Hill: University of North Carolina Press, 1978.
McMichael, F. Andrew. *Atlantic Loyalties: Americans in Spanish West Florida, 1785-1810*. Athens: University of Georgia Press, 2008.
McMillin, James A. *The Final Victims: Foreign Slave Trade to North America, 1783-1810*. Columbia: University of South Carolina Press, 2004.
Medick, Hans, and David Warren. Introduction to *Interest and Emotion: Essays on the Study of Family and Kinship*, edited by Hans Medick and David Warren, 1-27. New York: Cambridge University Press, 1984.
Medina, José Toribio. *La imprenta en México (1539-1821)*. Santiago de Chile: Casa del autor, 1909.
―――. *Medallas coloniales Hispano-Americanas*. Santiago de Chile: Casa del autor, 1900.
―――. *Medallas europeas relativas a América*. Buenos Aires: Casa Jacobo Peuser, 1924.
Medina Bustos, José Marcos. "El Gobierno indígena en los Pueblos de Misión de la Provincia de Sonora en la etapa posterior a la expulsión de los Jesuitas." In *Misiones del noroeste de México, origen y destino*, edited by José Rómulo Félix Gastélum and Raquel Padilla Ramos, 66-84. México D.F.: Consejo Nacional para la Cultura y las Artes, Mexico, 2006.
Medina Encina, Purificación, and Rosario Parra Cala. *Documentos relativos a la independencia de Norteamérica existentes en archivos españoles, vol. 1/1., Archivo*

General de Indias, Sección de Gobierno (años 1752-1822). Madrid: Ministerio de Asuntos Exteriores, 1977.

———. *Documentos relativos a la independencia de Norteamérica existentes en archivos españoles, vol. 1/2., Archivo General de Indias, Sección de Gobierno (años 1752-1822)*. Madrid: Ministerio de Asuntos Exteriores, 1977.

Medina Encina, Purificación, Reyes Siles Saturnino, and Rosario Parra Cala. *Documentos relativos a la independencia de Norteamérica existentes en archivos españoles, vol.7, Archivo General de Indias, Sección Cuba: Correspondencia y documentación oficial de varias autoridades de Luisiana y de las dos Floridas (años 1778-1817)*. Madrid: Ministerio de Asuntos Exteriores, 1981.

Medina Rojas, F. de Borja. *José de Ezpeleta, Gobernador de La Mobila, 1780-1781*. Sevilla: Escuela de Estudios Hispano-Americanos / Consejo Superior de Investigaciones Científicas and Excma. Diputación Foral de Navarra, 1980.

———. "La reforma del ejército en Nueva España, 1785 (actuaciones y proyectos del inspector José de Ezpeleta)." *Anuario de estudios americanos* 41 (1984): 315-95.

Medina Rubio, Arístides. *La Iglesia y la producción agrícola en Puebla, 1540-1795*. México D.F.: Colegio de México, 1983.

Mejías, Inma. "Madera de Galvezton para el bergantín Galvezton." *El Mundo*, June 21, 2010.

Memorial instructivo y curioso de la corte de Madrid. Vol. 12, September 1787. Madrid: Imprenta Real, 1787.

Memorial literario, instructivo y curioso de la corte de Madrid. Vol. 4, January 1785. Madrid: Imprenta Real, 1785.

Memorias de la Real Academia de la Historia. Madrid: Imprenta de doña Sancha, 1796.

Mena, Chaz (author, dir., and actor). *Yo Solo, Bernardo de Galvez on the Stage of the American Revolution*. Play. http://www.youtube.com/watch?v=AoLcU-Nr_lU (accessed July 21, 2016).

Méndez Beltrán, Luz María. "Trabajo indígena en la frontera araucana de Chile." *Jahrbuch für Geschichte von Staat Wirtschaft und Gesellschaft Lateinamerikas* 24 (1987): 1987.

Menéndez Peláez, Jesús, ed. *José Moñino y Redondo, conde de Floridablanca (1728-1808): Estudios en el bicentenario de su muerte*. Gijón: Fundación Foro Jovellanos del Principado de Asturias, 2009.

Merino, José Patricio. *Las cuentas de la Administración central española, 1750-1820*. Madrid: Instituto de Estudios Fiscales, 1987.

Merino Navarro, José. *La Armada española en el siglo XVIII*. Madrid: Fundación Universitaria Española, 1981.

Merrill, Ellen C. *Germans of Louisiana*. Gretna: Pelican, 2005.

Merritt, Jane T. "Native Peoples in the Revolutionary War." In *The Oxford Handbook of the American Revolution*, edited by Edward G. Gray and Jane Kamensky, 234-49. Oxford: Oxford University Press, 2013.

México en el siglo XVIII. México D.F.: Secretaría de Relaciones Exteriores / Embajada de México en Madrid, 1983.

Meyers, Rose. *A History of Baton Rouge, 1699-1812*. Baton Rouge: Louisiana State University Press, 1976.

Middlekauff, Robert. *The Glorious Cause: The American Revolution, 1763-1789*. New York: Oxford University Press, 1982.

Mill, John Stuart. *Considerations on Representative Government*. Rockville: Serenity, 2008. First published 1861.

Millar Corbacho, René. "La Inquisición de Lima y la circulación de libros prohibidos (1700-1820)." *Revista de Indias* 66 (1984): 415-44.

Miller, Hunter. *Treaties and Other International Acts of the United States of America*. Washington, D.C.: Government Printing Office, 1931.

Miller, Wilbert James. *The Spanish Commandant of Baton Rouge, 1779-1795*. Baton Rouge: Louisiana State University Press, 1965.

Mills, Elizabeth Shown. "Quintanilla's Crusade, 1775-1783: 'Moral Reform' and Its Consequences on the Natchitoches Frontier." *Louisiana History: The Journal of the Louisiana Historical Association* 42 (Summer 2001): 277-302.

Mínguez, Víctor. "Héroes clásicos y reyes héroes en el Antiguo Régimen." In *La construcción del héroe en España y México (1789-1847)*, edited by Germán Carreras Damas, 51-70. Valencia: Publicaciones de la Universidad de Valencia, 2003.

Mirafuentes Galván, José Luis. *Movimientos de resistencia y rebeliones indígenas en el norte de México (1680-1821), Guía documental*. 2nd. ed. México D.F.: Universidad Nacional Autónoma de México, 1989.

Miranda, Francisco de. *Colombeia*. Caracas: Ediciones de la Presidencia de la República, 1988.

———. *Diario de lo ocurrido en la escuadra, y tropas, que al mando del Jefe de Escuadra Don Josef Solano; y del Mariscal de Campo Don Juan Manuel de Cagigal, salieron de La Habana el 9 de Abril de 1781, para socorrer al ejército español, que atacaba la plaza de Panzacola . . . Sitio de dicha plaza . . . Su rendición &a*. Caracas: Archivo Francisco de Miranda, Viajes, vol. 3, sheets 80-98. English trans., Worcester, "Miranda's Diary of the Siege of Pensacola, 1781."

———. *Diario de viajes y escritos políticos*. Madrid: Editora Nacional, 1977.

———. *Documentos fundamentales*. Edited by Elías Pino Iturrieta, Josefina Rodríguez de Alonso, and Manuel Pérez Vila. Caracas: Biblioteca Ayacucho, 1992.

Miranda, José. *Humboldt y México*. México D.F.: Universidad Nacional Autónoma de México, 1962.

Mitchell, Margaret. *Gone with the Wind*. New York: Macmillan, 1936.

Molina Bautista, José Manuel de. *Historia de Alhaurín de la Torre en la Edad Moderna, 1489-1812*. Alhaurín de la Torre: Excmo. Ayuntamiento de Alhaurín de la Torre, 2005.

Molina del Villar, América. "Comportamiento y distribución de la población en Santa María de Guadalupe, Atlacomulco, 1679-1860." In *Problemas demográficos vistos desde la historia: Análisis de fuentes, comportamiento y distribución de la población en México, siglos XVI-XIX*, edited by América Molina del Villar and David Navarrete Gómez, 117-56. México D.F.: El Colegio de Michoacán / CIESAS, 2006.

Molina Martínez, Miguel. "Conflictos en la Audiencia de Quito a finales del siglo XVIII." *Anuario de Estudios Americanos* 1, no. 65 (2008): 153-73.

———. "El 'Fondo Saavedra' del Archivo de los jesuitas en Granada." *Archivo Hispalense* 207-8 (1985): 373-80.

———. "El gobierno de Antonio de Ulloa en Huancavélica y Luisiana." In *Actas del II centenario de don Antonio de Ulloa*, edited by Manuel Losada and Consuelo Varela, 169-84. Sevilla: Escuela de Estudios Hispano-Americanos / Consejo Superior de Investigaciones Científicas / Archivo General de Indias, 1995.

———. "Ilustración y reforma, la biblioteca de Francisco de Saavedra: Segundo intendente de Caracas." *Estudios de Historia Social y Económica de América* 7 (1991): 1-21.

———. "La participación canaria en la formación y reclutamiento batallón de Luisiana." In *IV coloquio de Historia Canario-Americano (1980)*, edited by Francisco

Morales Padrón, 2:135-224. Las Palmas de Gran Canaria: Cabildo de Las Palmas de Gran Canaria, 1981.
Moncada Maya, José Omar. *El ingeniero Miguel Constanzó: Un militar ilustrado en la Nueva España del siglo XVIII*. México D.F.: Universidad Nacional Autónoma de México, 1994.
Monte, Nicolás del. *Rendido y fiel obsequio en festiva demostración de los felices días del Excmo. Señor d. Bernardo de Gálvez, Conde de Gálvez*. México: Joseph de Jáuregui, 1786.
Montesquieu. *De l'esprit des lois*. Paris: Laroussse, 1969.
Moore, John Preston. "Antonio de Ulloa: A Profile of the First Spanish Governor of Louisiana." *Louisiana History: The Journal of the Louisiana Historical Association* 8 (Summer 1967): 189-217.
———. *Revolt in Louisiana: The Spanish Occupation, 1766-1770*. Baton Rouge: Louisiana State University Press, 1976.
Moorhead, Max L. *The Apache Frontier: Jacobo Ugarte and Spanish-Indian Relations in Northern New Spain, 1769-1791*. Norman: University of Oklahoma Press, 1968.
———. *The Presidio: Bastion of the Spanish Borderlands*. Norman: University of Oklahoma Press, 1991.
———. "The Spanish Deportation of Hostile Apaches: The Policy and the Practice." *Arizona and the West* 17, no. 3 (Fall 1975): 205-20.
Morales Folguera, José Miguel. *Arquitectura y urbanismo hispanoamericano en Luisiana y Florida occidental*. Málaga: Secretariado de Publicaciones de la Universidad de Málaga, 1987.
———. "Fundación de ciudades en Luisiana y Florida con canarios en el siglo XVIII." In *IX coloquio de Historia Canario-Americano (1990)*, edited by Francisco Morales Padrón, 2:1533-46. Las Palmas de Gran Canaria: Cabildo de Las Palmas de Gran Canaria, 1993.
———. "Urbanismo hispanoamericano en el sudeste de los Estados Unidos (Luisiana y Florida): La obra del malagueño Bernardo de Gálvez y Gallardo (1746-1786)." 1st ver. In *Andalucía y América en el s. XVIII: Actas de las IV Jornadas de Andalucía y América*, 2:119-40. Sevilla: Consejo Superior de Investigaciones Científicas / Escuela de Estudios Hispano-Americanos, 1984-85.
———. "Urbanismo hispanoamericano en el sudeste de los Estados Unidos (Luisiana y Florida): La obra del malagueño Bernardo de Gálvez y Gallardo (1746-1786)." 2nd ver. *Castillos de España* 93 (June 1987): 41-45.
Morales Folguera, José Miguel, María Isabel Pérez de Colosía Rodríguez, Marion Reder Gadow, and Siro Villas Tinoco. *Los Gálvez de Macharaviaya*. Málaga: Junta de Andalucía, Consejería de Cultura y Medio Ambiente-Asesoría Quinto Centenario, 1991.
Morales Lezcano, Víctor. "Diplomacia y política financiera de España durante la sublevación de las colonias inglesas en América: 1775-1783." *Anuario de Estudios Americanos* 26 (1969): 507-64.
Morales Moya, Antonio. "La ideología de la ilustración española." *Revista de Estudios Políticos* (nueva época), 59 (January-March 1988): 69-105.
———. "Milicia y nobleza en el siglo XVIII (Apuntes para una sociología de las armas y de la nobleza en España." *Cuadernos de Historia Moderna* 9 (1988): 122-37.
———. "Movilidad social en la España del siglo XVIII: Aspectos sociológicos y jurídicos de la consesión de títulos nobiliarios." *Revista Internacional de Sociología* 50 (1984): 463-90.

Morales Padrón, Francisco. "Las Canarias y la política emigratoria a Indias." In *I coloquio de Historia Canario-Americano (1976)*, edited by Francisco Morales Padrón, 211–91. Las Palmas de Gran Canaria: Cabildo de Las Palmas de Gran Canaria, 1977.

———. *Teoría y leyes de la conquista*. Madrid: Ediciones de Cultura Hispánica del Centro Iberoamericano de Cooperación, 1979.

———, ed. *Los Decenios (Autobiografía de un sevillano de la Ilustración)*. Sevilla: Servicio de Publicaciones del Excmo. Ayuntamiento de Sevilla, 1995.

———, ed. *Diario de don Francisco de Saavedra*. Sevilla: Universidad de Sevilla / Consejo Superior de Investigaciones Científicas, 2004.

———, ed. *IX coloquio de Historia Canario-Americano (1990)*. Las Palmas de Gran Canaria: Cabildo de Las Palmas de Gran Canaria, 1993.

Morales Rodríguez, Julio. "Para contener al pueblo: El Hospicio de Pobres de la ciudad de México, 1774–1871 por Silvia Arrom." *Historia Mexicana* 60, no. 3 (2011): 1815–19.

Morel, Robert. *Effusions du cœur, ou entretiens spirituels et affectifs d'une âme avec Dieu, sur chaque verset des psaumes et des cantiques de l'Eglise*. Paris: Vincent, 1756. First published 1716.

Moreno Cabrera, María de la Luz. "La arqueología de Chapultepec en el Plano del Real Sitio de 1792." *Boletín de Monumentos Históricos*, 3rd period, no. 7 (2006): 21–37.

Moreno Cebada, Emilio. *Las herejías, los cismas y los errores de todos los siglos o sea la historia general de los extravíos de la razón humana con respecto al cristianismo escrita con presencia de las obras de los Santos Padres, de los más notables publicistas católicos y del diccionario de las herejías del abate Pluquet*. Barcelona: Moreno y Roig, 1880.

Moreno de los Arcos, Roberto. *La primera cátedra de botánica en México, 1788*. México D.F.: Sociedad Mexicana de Historia de la Ciencia y de la Tecnología, 1988.

Moreno de Vargas, Bernabé. *Discursos de la nobleza de España*. Madrid: María de Quiñones, 1636.

Moreri, Louis. *Le grand dictionnaire historique ou Le mélange curieux de l'histoire sacrée et profane*. CD-ROM. Genève: Slatkine Reprints, 1995. First published 1759.

Moreto, Agustín. *Comedia famosa: El desdén con el desdén*. S.l., s.a.

Morfí, Juan Agustín de. "Account of the Disorders in New Mexico, 1778." In Simmons, *Coronado's Land: Essays on Daily Life in Colonial New Mexico*, 156–57. Albuquerque: University of New Mexico Press, 1991.

Moriones, Ildefonso. "Historia del proceso de beatificación y canonización del Venerable Juan de Palafox y Mendoza." In *Palafox: Iglesia, Cultura y Estado en el siglo XVII*, edited by Ricardo Fernández Gracia, 515–58. Pamplona: Ediciones Universidad de Navarra S.A., 2001.

Morlas, Katy Frances. "La Madame et la Mademoiselle: Creole Women in Louisiana, 1718–1865." Master's diss., Louisiana State University, 2003.

Morris, Richard B. *The Peacemakers: The Great Powers and American Independence*. Boston: Northeastern University Press, 1983. First published 1965.

Morris, Robert. *The Papers of Robert Morris*. Edited by John Catanzariti. Pittsburgh: University of Pittsburgh Press, 1988.

Mouillard, Lucien. *Armée française: Les régiments sous Louis XV. Constitution de tous les corps de troupe à la solde de France pendant les guerres de succession, de l'Empire et de sept ans*. Paris: Dumaine, 1882.

Munguía Cárdenas, Francisco. *Panorama histórico de Sayula, capital de la antigua provincia de Ávalos*. Guadalajara: Departamento de Bellas Artes del Gobierno de Jalisco, 1976.

Muñoz, Juan Bautista. *Historia del Nuevo Mundo*. Madrid: Viuda de Ibarra, 1791.
Muñoz Rebolledo, María Dolores, and Juan Luis Isaza L. [*sic*]. "Naturaleza, jardín y ciudad en el Nuevo Mundo." *Theoria* 10, no. 1 (2001): 9–25.
Murphy, W. S. "The Irish Brigade of Spain at the Capture of Pensacola, 1781." *Florida Historical Quarterly* 38, no. 3 (1960): 216–25.
Narrett, David. *Adventurism and Empire: The Struggle for Mastery in the Louisiana-Florida Borderlands, 1762–1803*. Chapel Hill: University of North Carolina Press, 2015.
Nasatir, Abraham P. *Borderland in Retreat: From Spanish Louisiana to the Far Southwest*. Alburquerque: University of New Mexico Press, 1976.
———. *Before Lewis and Clark: Documents Illustrating the History of the Missouri, 1785–1804*. St. Louis: St. Louis Historical Documents Foundation, 1952.
Nash, Gary B. *Red, White, and Black: The Peoples of Early America*. Englewood Cliffs, N.J.: Prentice-Hall, 1974.
Navajas Josa, Belén. "El padre Kino y la Pimería: aculturación y expansión en la frontera norte de Nueva España." PhD diss., Universidad Complutense de Madrid, 2008.
Navarrete, Félix. *La masonería en la Historia y en las leyes de Méjico*. México: Jus, 1962.
Navarro Azcue, Concepción. "Las Reales Sociedades Económicas en América." *Torre de los Lujanes* 67 (2010): 39–61.
Navarro García, Luis. "La crisis del reformismo borbónico bajo Carlos IV." *Temas Americanistas* 13 (1997): 1–22.
———. *Hispanoamérica en el siglo XVIII*. 2nd ed. Sevilla: Universidad de Sevilla, 1991.
———. "El ilustrado y el bárbaro: La guerra Apache vista por Bernardo de Gálvez." *Temas americanistas* 6 (1986): 10–15.
———. *José de Gálvez y la comandancia general de las Provincias Internas del norte de Nueva España*. Sevilla: Consejo Superior de Investigaciones Científicas / Escuela de Estudios Hispano-Americanos, 1964.
———. "Nobleza criolla y milicia en México, 1776." *Temas Americanistas* 15 (2002): 56–74.
———. "El norte de Nueva España como problema político en el siglo XVIII." *Estudios Americanos (Revista de la Escuela de Estudios Hispanoamericanos)* 20, no. 103 (1960): 15–31.
———. *La política americana de José de Gálvez según su "Discurso y reflexiones de un vasallo."* Málaga: Algazara, 1998.
———. "El virrey marqués de Croix." In *Los virreyes de la Nueva España en el reinado de Carlos III*, edited by José Antonio Calderón Quijano, 161–384. Sevilla: Consejo Superior de Investigaciones Científicas / Escuela de Estudios Hispano-Americanos, 1968.
Navarro Loidi, Juan. "Las matemáticas en la Escuela Militar de Ávila (1774)." *Gaceta de la Real Sociedad Matemática Española* 14, no. 2 (2011): 309–32.
Nehru, Jawaharlal. *The Discovery of India*. New York: John Day, 1946.
Neumann-Holzschuh, Ingrid. "Español vestigial y francés marginal en Luisiana: Erosión lingüística en isleño/bruli y en cadjin." *Boletín de lingüística* 15 (2000): 36–64.
Nieto y Cortadellas, Rafael. *Dignidades nobiliarias en Cuba*. Madrid: Ediciones Cultura Hispánica, 1954.Noizet de Saint-Paul, Gaspard. *Traité complet de fortification*. Paris: Barrois l'aîné, 1792. Spanish translation, *Elementos de fortificación escritos en francés por Noizet Saint-Paul, coronel de ingenieros y traducidos al castellano para el uso de los caballeros cadetes del regimiento real de zapadores-minadores-pontoneros*. Madrid: Imprenta Real, 1818.

Notas genealógicas que para tomar el Hábito de Santiago, presentaron Don Mariano, Don Francisco y Don Rafael Pardo de Figueroa, naturales de Medina Sidonia. Medina Sidonia: Tipografía particular del Doctor Thebussem, 1889.

Noticiosa, verica, triunfante, y victoriosa relación que declara, y dà noticia del feliz vencimiento, y victorioso aplauso que han tenido las católicas armas de nuestro Augusto Monarca el Señor D. Carlos Tercero . . . en la restauración de la Plaza de Panzacola, la Florida, y otras diferentes que va restaurando la Corona de España à el Rey Británico, todo conseguido à la solicitud, y cuidado de los Excmos. Sres D. Josef Solano, General de Mar, y D. Bernardo de Galvez, General de Tierra, sucedido el día 8. de Mayo de 1781. con todo lo demás que verá el curioso . . . Sevilla: J. Padrino, 1781.

Nouvelle manière de fortifier les Places; tirée des méthodes du chevalier de Ville, du comte de Pagan, et de monsieur de Vauban. Paris: Estienne Michallet, 1689.

Nouveau recueil des troupes légères de France levees depuis la pésente guerre avec la date de leur creation, leur uniforme et leurs armes. Desiné d'après nature sous la direction des officiers, présenté á Monseig le Dauphin par son très-humble et trés obeisant serviteur F. Chereau. Paris: 1747. Bibliothèque nationale de France, département Estampes et photographie, RESERVE FOL-QB-201 (99).

Nunemaker, J. Horace, ed. "Documents: The Bouligny Affair in Louisiana." *Hispanic American Historical Review* 25, no. 3 (August 1945): 339–63.

Núñez Cabeza de Vaca, Alvar. *La relacion y comentarios del gouernador Alvar Núñez Cabeça [sic] de Vaca, de lo acaescido en las dos jornadas que hizo a las Indias*. Valladolid, 1555.

Núñez Roldán, Francisco, ed. *Ocio y vida cotidiana en el mundo hispánico en la edad moderna*. Sevilla: Secretariado de publicaciones de la Universidad de Sevilla, 2007.

Nussbaum, Arthur, and Luis García Arias. *Historia del Derecho Internacional*. Madrid: Revista de Derecho Privado, 1949.

Nute, Grace Lee. "Indian Medals and Certificates." *Minnesota History Magazine* 25, no. 3 (1944): 265–70.

Oberg, Michael Leroy. *Native America: A History*. Malden, Mass.: Wiley-Blackwell, 2010.

O'Brien, Greg. "The Choctaw Defense of Pensacola in the American Revolution." In *Pre-removal Choctaw History: Exploring New Paths*, edited by Greg O'Brien, 123–47. Norman: University of Oklahoma Press, 2008.

Ocampo Alfaro, Aurora María, ed. *Diccionario de escritores mexicanos, siglo XX, desde las generaciones del Ateneo y novelistas de la revolución hasta nuestros días, vol.9 (U-Z)*. México D.F.: Universidad Nacional Autónoma de México, 2007.

O'Conor, Hugo de. *The Defenses of Northern New Spain: Hugo O'Conor's Report to Teodoro de Croix, 22 de Julio de 1777*. Edited by Donald C. Cutter. Dallas: Southern Methodist University Press, 1994.

———. *Informe de Hugo de O'Conor sobre el estado de las Provincias Internas del norte (1771-1776)*. Edited by Francisco R. Almada and Enrique González Flores. México: Cultura, 1952.

O'Donnell, James H., III. "Hamstrung by Penury: Alexander Cameron's Failure at Pensacola." In *Anglo-Spanish Confrontation on the Gulf Coast during the American Revolution: Gálvez Celebration, Commemorating the Siege of Pensacola*, edited by William S. Coker and Robert R. Rea, 76–89. Pensacola: Gulf Coast History and Humanities Conference, 1982.

———. *Southern Indians in the American Revolution*. Knoxville: University of Tenessee Press, 1972.

Odriozola y Añativia, José. *Compendio de artillería o instrucción sobre armas y municiones de guerra*. Madrid: Fuentenebro, 1827.
Olavarría y Ferrari, Enrique del. *Reseña histórica del teatro en México*. México D.F.: La Europea, 1895.
Olmeda y León, José. *Noticia del establecimiento y poblacion de las colonias inglesas en la América Septentrional* . . . Madrid: Antonio Fernandez, 1778.
Olmedo Checa, Manuel. *Bernardo de Gálvez: In Memoriam*. Málaga: Real Academia de Bellas Artes de San Telmo, 2009.
———. "Bernardo de Gálvez, la recuperación de una egregia figura." *Anuario real academia de bellas artes de san Telmo* 10, no. 2 (2010): 244–49.
———. "El último homenaje de Estados Unidos a España y a Bernardo de Gálvez." *Péndulo*: *Revista del Colegio Oficial de Ingenieros Técnicos Industriales de Málaga* (March 2007): 134–35.
———, ed. *Bernardo de Gálvez y su tiempo*. Malaga: Colegio Oficial de Ingenieros Técnicos Industriales de Málaga, 2007.
Olmedo Checa, Manuel, and Francisco Cabrera Palacios. "Bernardo de Gálvez." *Péndulo*: *Revista del Colegio Oficial de Ingenieros Técnicos Industriales de Málaga* (March 2007): 54–111.
O'Neill, Charles Edwards. "The Louisiana Manifesto of 1768." *Political Science Reviewer* 19 (1990): 247–89.
Opler, Morris E. "The Apachean Culture Pattern and Its Origins." In *Handbook of North American Indians*, edited by William C. Sturtevant, vol. 10, *Southwest*, edited by Alfonso Ortiz, 368–92. Washington, D.C.: Smithsonian Institution, 1983.
———. *An Apache Life-Way: The Economic, Social, and Religious Institutions of the Chiricahua Indians*. New York: Cooper Square Publishers, 1965. First published 1941.
———. "Chiricagua Apache." In *Handbook of North American Indians*, edited by William C. Sturtevant, vol. 10, *Southwest*, edited by Alfonso Ortiz, 401–18. Washington, D.C.: Smithsonian Institution, 1983.
———. "Mescalero Apache." In *Handbook of North American Indians*, edited by William C. Sturtevant, vol. 10, *Southwest*, edited by Alfonso Ortiz, 419–39. Washington, D.C.: Smithsonian Institution, 1983.
Oración fúnebre dedicada a la memoria del Excmo. Sr. D. Mathias de Gálvez, teniente general de los ejércitos, virrey de Nueva España, etcétera, por d. José Goicoechea, en las honras que se le hicieron en la ciudad de Guatemala en 5 de febrero de 1785. Guatemala: Antonio Cubillos, 1785.
Ordenanza de la división de la nobilísima ciudad de México en cuarteles, creación de los alcaldes de ellos, y reglas de su gobierno: Dada y mandada observar por el Excelentísimo señor don Martín de Mayorga, virrey, gobernador, y capitán general de esta Nueva España. México: Felipe de Zuñiga y Ontiveros, 1782.
Ordenanzas de S.M. para el régimen, disciplina, subordinación y servicio de sus Exércitos. Madrid: Antonio Marín, 1768.
Ordenanzas de su Magestad [sic] para el Govierno [sic] Militar, Político, y Económico de su Armada Naval, Parte Primera. Madrid: Juan de Zúñiga, 1748.
Ordonnance . . . au sujet du régiment Royal-Cantabre . . . Acte royal de 1 août 1749. Paris: Impr. royale, 1749.
Ordonnance . . . portant augmentation dans le régiment des Cantabre, avec le titre de Royal Cantabre . . . , Acte royal de 1 juillet 1747. Paris: Impr. royale, 1747.
Ordonnance . . . portant création d'un régiment d'infanterie de troupes légères, sous le

nom de Cantabre volontaires . . . , Acte royal du 15 décembre 1745. Paris: Impr. royale, 1745.

Ordonnance . . . portant rétablissement du régiment Royal-Cantabre . . . , Acte royal de 8 juillet 1757. Paris: Impr. royale, 1757.

Ordonnance . . . portant une nouvelle réforme dans le régiment Royal-Cantabre . . . , Acte royal du 1 décembre 1748. Paris: Impr. royale, 1748.

Ordonnance . . . pour réformer une partie des compagnies à cheval du régiment Royal-Cantabre . . . , Acte royal de 8 septembre 1748. Paris: Impr. royale, 1748.

Ortega, Martha. "Ross: La colonización rusa frente a la española." In *El Septentrión novohispano: Ecohistoria, sociedades e imágenes de frontera*, edited by Salvador Bernabeu Albert, 123-38. Madrid: Consejo Superior de Investigaciones Científicas, 2000.

Ortega Noriega, Sergio, ed. *Historia general de Sonora, vol.2. De la conquista al Estado libre y soberano de Sonora*. Hermosillo: Gobierno del Estado de Sonora, 1996.

Ortega Pereyra, Ovidio. *El Real Arsenal de La Habana: La construcción naval en La Habana bajo la dominación colonial española*. La Habana: Letras Cubanas, 1998.

Ortelli, Sara. "De vándalos, godos y apaches: La frontera y el enemigo en el norte novohispano colonial." *Nostromo: Revista Crítica Latinoamericana* 3 (2010): 21-28.

———. "Enemigos internos y súbditos desleales: La infidencia en Nueva Vizcaya en tiempos de los Borbones." *Anuario de Estudios Americanos* 61, no. 2 (2004): 467-89.

———. "Las reformas borbónicas vistas desde la frontera: La élite neovizcaína frente a la injerencia estatal en la segunda mitad del siglo XVIII." *Boletín del Instituto de Historia Argentina y Americana Dr. Emilio Ravignani* 28 (July-December 2005): 7-37.

———. *Trama de una guerra conveniente: Nueva Vizcaya y la sombra de los apaches (1748-1790)*. México D.F.: Colegio de México, 2007.

Ortiz, Eduardo. *Bernardo de Galvez: Hero of the American Revolution*. New York: Scholastic, 2003.

Ortíz de Urbina Montoya, Carlos. "Un gabinete numismático de la Ilustración española: La Real Sociedad Bascongada de los Amigos del País y Diego Lorenzo del Prestamero." *Cuadernos Dieciochistas* 5 (2004): 203-50.

Orwell, George. *The English People*, "Part I: England at First Glance." In George Orwell, *The Collected Essays, Journalism, and Letters of George Orwell*, edited by Sonia Orwell and Ian Angus, vol. 3, 1-37. New York: Harcourt Brace Jovanovich, 1968. First published 1947.

Osborn, George C. "Major-General John Campbell in British West Florida." *Florida Historical Quarterly* 27, no. 4 (April 1949): 318-40.

———. "Relations with the Indians in West Florida, 1770-1781." *Florida Historical Quarterly* 31, no. 4 (April 1953): 240-72.

O'Shaughnessy, Andrew Jackson. *An Empire Divided: The American Revolution and the British Caribbean*. Philadelphia: University of Pennsylvania Press, 2000.

Osorio, Alfred J. *El Regimiento de la Luisiana: A description of the Colonial Spanish Regiment, 1777-1781, with their Manual of Arms of 1768*. Smashwords e-Book Edition, 2011.

Ossa Santa Cruz, Juan Luis. "La criollización de un ejército periférico, Chile, 1768-1810." *Historia* 2, no. 43 (2010): 413-48.

Ostendorf, Berndt. "Creole Cultures and the Process of Creolization." In *Louisiana Culture from the Colonial Era to Katrina*, edited by John Lowe, 103-35. Baton Rouge: Louisiana State University Press, 2008.

Ots y Capdequí, José María. *El Estado español en las Indias*. México D.F.: Fondo de Cultura Económica, 1975. First published 1941.

———. *Instituciones*. Barcelona: Salvat, 1959.

Ouweneel, Arij. "Eighteenth-Century Mexican Peonage and the Problem of Credits to Hacienda Labourers." *Rural History* 8, no. 1 (1997): 21-54.

Owsley, Frank L., Jr. "Review of *The Log of H.M.S. Mentor, 1780-1781: A New Account of the British Navy at Pensacola*, by James A. Servies." *Florida Historical Quarterly* 62, no. 1 (1983): 82-84.

Pacheco Martínez, Dionisio. *Las lágrimas de la aurora en dos distintos efectos: Discursos metafóricos, políticos e históricos que en la muerte del Excmo. Señor d. Bernardo de Gálvez, conde de Gálvez, virrey de esta Nueva España*. México: Felipe de Zúñiga y Ontiveros, 1787.

Padgett, James A., ed. "Bernardo de Gálvez's Siege of Pensacola in 1781 (as Related in Robert Farmar's Journal)." *Louisiana Historical Quarterly* 26 (1943): 311-29.

Paine, Thomas. "The American Crisis, Number I." First published in the *Pennsylvania Journal*, December 19, 1776. In *Complete Writings of Thomas Paine*, edited by Philip S. Foner, 1:49-57. New York: Citadel Press, 1945.

Pajol, Charles Pierre Victor, Comte de. *Les guerres sous Louis XV*. Paris: Firmin-Didot et Cie., 1881.

Palau y Dulcet, Antonio. *Manual del librero hispano-americano: Inventario bibliográfico de la producción científica y literaria de España y de la América Latina desde la invención de la imprenta hasta nuestros días: Con el valor comercial de todos los artículos descritos*. Barcelona: Librería Anticuaria, 1923-27.

Palma, Ricardo. "Cortar el revesino: Crónica de la época del vigésimo segundo virrey del Perú." In *Tradiciones peruanas, segunda serie*, 238-45. Las Palmas de Gran Canaria: Red ediciones, 2011.

Palmer, Jessica Dawn. *The Apache Peoples: A History of All Bands and Tribes through the 1800s*. Jefferson, N.C.: McFarland, 2013.

Papers of the Continental Congress, 1774-1789. 5 vols. Washington, D.C.: National Archives and Records Service, General Services Administration, 1959-78.

Paquette, Gabriel B. "The Dissolution of the Spanish Atlantic Monarchy." *Historical Journal* 52, no. 1 (2009): 175-212.

———. *Enlightenment, Governance, and Reform in Spain and Its Empire, 1759-1808*. New York: Palgrave Macmillan, 2008.

———. "The Image of Imperial Spain in British Political Thought, 1750-1800." *Bulletin of Spanish Studies* 81, no. 2 (2004): 187-214.

Pardo-Tomás, José. "El Protomédico Francisco Hernández en Nueva España (1570-1577)." *Eidon* 15 (2004): 45-49.

Park, Joseph F. "Spanish Indian Policy in Northern Mexico, 1765-1810." *Arizona and the West* 4, no. 4 (Winter 1962): 325-44.

Parks, Virginia, ed. *Siege! Spain and Britain: Battle of Pensacola, March 9-May 8, 1781*. Pensacola: Pensacola Historical Society, 1981.

The Parliamentary Register; or History of the Proceedings and Debates of the House of Commons; Containing an Account of the Most Interesting Speeches and Motions; accurate Copies of the Most Remarkable Letters and Papers; of the Most Material Evidence, Petitions, &, Laid Before and Offered to the House, During the First Session of the Fifteenth Parliament of Great Britain. London: J. Debrett, 1782.

Paul, Anita R. "Michael Nolden Henderson: The Story of the First African-American in Georgia Inducted into the National Society of the Sons of the American Revolution

(SAR)." *Our Heritage Magazine*, http://ourheritagemagazine.com (accessed March 22, 2016).

Peabody, Sue. "Slavery, Freedom, and the Law in the Atlantic World, 1420-1807." In *The Cambridge World History of Slavery*, vol. 3, *AD 1420–AD 1804*, edited by David Eltis and Stanley L. Engerman, 594-630. Cambridge: Cambridge University Press, 2011.

Pearl, Mary Segura, ed. and trans. "The Capture of the Bluff of Baton Rouge." *Louisiana History: The Journal of the Louisiana Historical Association* 17, no. 2 (1976): 203-7.

Peña, Margarita. "El teatro novohispano en el siglo XVIII." *Bulletin of the Comediantes* 1, no. 58 (2006): 155-72.

Peña, Pepe. *Dos siglos de risa mexicana*. México D.F.: Secretaría de Educación Pública, 1950.

Pérez de Colosía Rodríguez, María Isabel. "Historiografía sobre política americanista y políticos andaluces: La familia Gálvez Siglo XVIII." *Revista de Indias* 50 (1990): 289-304.

———. "Rasgos biográficos de una familia ilustrada." In *Los Gálvez de Macharaviaya*, edited by José Miguel Morales Folguera, María Isabel Pérez de Colosía Rodríguez, Marion Reder Gadow, and Siro Villas Tinoco, 20-134. Málaga: Junta de Andalucía, Consejería de Cultura y Medio Ambiente-Asesoría Quinto Centenario, 1991.

Pérez Frías, Pedro Luis. "Unidades extranjeras en el Ejército borbónico español del siglo XVIII." In *Los extranjeros en la Edad Moderna: Actas del I coloquio internacional celebrado en Málaga del 28 al 30 de Noviembre de 2002*, edited by M. B. Villar García and P. Pezzi Cristóbal, 2:631-43. Málaga: 2003.

Pérez Herrero, Pedro. "El crecimiento económico novohispano durante el siglo XVIII: Una revisión." *Revista de Historia Económica* 8, no. 1 (1989): 69-110.

Pérez-Mallaína Bueno, Pablo Emilio. "Generales y almirantes de la Carrera de Indias: Una investigación pendiente." *Chronica nova: Revista de historia moderna de la Universidad de Granada* 33 (2007): 285-332.

Pérez Marchand, Monelisa. *Dos etapas ideológicas del siglo XVIII en México: A través de los papeles de la Inquisición*. México D.F.: Colegio de México, 1949.

Pérez Rosales, Laura. *Familia, poder, riqueza y subversión: Los Fagoaga novohispanos 1730-1830*. México D.F.: Universidad Iberoamericana / Real Sociedad Bascongada de los Amigos del País, 2003.

Pérez Vejo, Tomás, and Marta Yolanda Quezada. *De novohispanos a mexicanos: Retratos e identidad colectiva en una sociedad en transición*. México D.F.: Instituto Nacional de Antropología e Historia, 2009.

Pérez Verdía, Luis. *Historia particular del estado de Jalisco, desde los primeros tiempos de que hay noticia, hasta nuestros días*. Guadalajara: Escuela de Artes y oficios, 1910-11.

Perkins, Bradford. "Bemis Regit! A Diplomatic History of the American Revolution (Review)." *Reviews in American History* 14, no. 2 (1986): 195-99.

Peset, José Luis. "José Antonio Alzate." In *Ciencia y Libertad: El papel del científico en la independencia Americana*, 23-139. Madrid: Consejo Superior de Investigaciones Científicas, 1987.

Pezuela, Jacobo de la. *Diccionario geográfico, estadístico, histórico de la Isla de Cuba*. Madrid: Mellado, 1863.

———. *Ensayo histórico de la isla de Cuba*. Nueva York: Imprenta española de R. Rafael, 1842.

———. *Historia de la Isla de Cuba*. Madrid: Carlos Bailly-Bailliere, 1878.

Phone, Wilhelmina, Maureen Olson, and Matilda Martínez. *Dictionary of Jicarilla*

Apache. Abáachi Mizaa Iłkee' Siijai. Alburquerque: University of New Mexico Press, 2007.

Picazo Muntaner, Antoni. "El impacto de las guerras nativas en el norte de Nueva España." *Illes i imperis: Estudios de historia de las sociedades en el mundo colonial y post-colonial* 12 (2009): 7-18.

Pickering, R. B., ed. *Peace Medals: Negotiating Power in Early America*. Norman: Gilcrease Museum / University of Oklahoma Press, 2012.

A Pictorial History of the Marines in the Revolution. Washington, D.C.: History and Museums Division, Headquarters U.S. Marine Corps, 1975.

Pike, Zebulon Montgomery. *An account of expeditions to the sources of the Mississippi and through the western parts of Louisiana to the sources of the Arkansaw, Kans [sic], La Platte, and Pierre Jaun Rivers: Performed by order of the government of the United States during the years 1805, 1806, and 1807 and a tour through the interior parts of New Spain when conducted through these provinces by order of the captain-general in the year 1807*. Philadelphia: C. & A. Conrad & Co., 1810.

Pineda, Juan de. *Diálogos familiares de la agricultura cristiana*. Salamanca: Pedro de Adurça y Diego Lopez, 1589.

Piñera Ramírez, David, ed. *Visión histórica de la frontera norte de México, vol.2, De los aborígenes al septentrión novohispano*. Mexicali: Universidad Autónoma de Baja California, 1987.

Pitot, James. *Observations on the Colony of Louisiana from 1796 to 1802*. Baton Rouge: Robert D. Bush, 1979.

Plater, Felix. *Praxeos medica*. Basilea, 1609.

Poe, Edgar Allan. "The Fall of the House of Usher." In *Tales*, 64-82. New York: Wiley and Putnam, 1845.

Pontalba, José Javier Delfau de. *Memoir on Louisiana* [1801]. In Alcée Fortier, *A History of Louisiana*, edited by Jo Ann Carrigan, 2:189-215. Baton Rouge: Claitor's Book Store, 1966. First published 1904.

Porras Muñoz, Guillermo. "Acta de matrimonio de Bernardo de Gálvez y Felicitas Saint Maxent." *Boletín del Archivo General de la Nación* 16, no. 2 (1945): 277-81.

———. "Bernardo de Gálvez." In *Miscelánea Americanista: Homenaje a D. Antonio Ballesteros Beretta*, 3:575-619. Madrid: Consejo Superior de Investigaciones Científicas / Instituto Gonzalo Fernández de Oviedo, 1952.

———. "El fracaso de Guarico." *Anuario de Estudios Americanos* 26 (1969): 569-609.

———. *La frontera con los indios de Nueva Vizcaya*. México: Nueva Imagen, 1980.

———. "Hace doscientos años: 'México llorosa.'" *Estudios de Historia Novohispana* 10 (January 1991): 309-24.

Porro, Jesús María. "La defensa y consolidación de las fronteras en el Septentrión novohispano: Geografía y desarrollos cartográficos (1759-1788)." *Anuario de Estudios Americanos* 68, no. 1 (2011): 19-50.

Portell Vila, Herminio. *Juan de Miralles, un habanero amigo de Jorge Washington*. La Habana: Sociedad Colombista Panamericana, 1947.

———. *Los "otros extranjeros" en la Revolución Norteamericana*. Miami: Ediciones Universal, 1978.

Porter, Rebecca I. "Physical Injuries; Psycological Treatment." In *The Oxford Handbook of Military Psychology*, edited by Janice H. Laurence and Michael D. Matthews, 29-36. New York: Oxford University Press, 2012.

Porter, Roy. *Flesh in the Age of Reason*. New York: W. W. Norton, 2003.

Powell, Donald M. "Addition of Rare Southwestern Historical Items to the University of Library." *Kiva* 19, no. 2/4 (1954): 26-28.
Powell, Lawrence N. *The Accidental City: Improvising New Orleans*. Cambridge, Mass.: Harvard University Press, 2012.
Powell, Philip Wayne. "The Chichimecas: Scourge of the Silver Frontier in Sixteenth-Century Mexico." *Hispanic American Historical Review* 25, no. 3 (1945): 315-38.
———. *Tree of Hate: Propaganda and Prejudices Affecting United States Relations with the Hispanic World*. New York: Basic Books, 1971. Spanish ed., *Árbol de odio: La Leyenda Negra y sus consecuencias en las relaciones entre EEUU y el mundo hispánico*. Madrid: José Porrúa Torranzas, 1972.
Poydras, Julien. *Le dieu et les nayades du fleuve St. Louis: A Don. Bernard de Galvez colonel des armées de Sa Majesté Catholique, gouverneur & intandant [sic] général de la province de la Louisianne. Sur sa convalescence, Poeme*. Nouvelle-Orléans: Antoine Boudoisquié, 1777.
———. *Épître á Don. Bernard de Galvez colonel des armées de Sa Majesté Catholique, gouverneur & intandant [sic] général de la province de la Louisianne 1777*. Nouvelle-Orléans: Antoine Boudousquié, 1777.
———. *La Prise du morne du Bâton Rouge par Monseigneur de Galvez, Chevalier pensionné de l'Ordre Royal distingué de Charles Trois, Brigadier des Armées de Sa Majesté, Intendant, Inspecteur et Gouverneur Général de la Province de la Louisiane*. Nouvelle-Orléans: Antoine Boudousquié, 1779.
Práctica de las enfermedades asténicas o de debilidad, fundada en la experiencia y en la doctrina Browniana. Edited by Vicente Mitjavila. Barcelona: Francisco Ifern y Oriol, circa 1800.
Pradells Nadal, Jesús. *Diplomacia y comercio: La expansión consular española en el siglo XVIII*. Alicante: Instituto de Cultura Juan Gil-Albert, 1992.
Pratt, Comfort. "El español del noroeste de Luisiana: Orígenes y pervivencia." *Interlingüística* 3, no. 13 (2002): 283-304.
Precursores ideológicos de la guerra de independencia, 1789-1794. México: Publicaciones del Archivo General de la Nación, 1929.
Price, Catherine. "The Comanche Threat to Texas and New Mexico in the Eighteenth Century and the Development of Spanish Indian Policy." *Journal of the West* 24, no. 2 (1985): 34-45.
Priestley, Herbert Ingram. *Jose Galvez: Visitor-General of New Spain, 1765-1771*. New York: Kraus Reprint, Millwood, 1974. First published 1916.
"El Príncipe de Asturias, soldado de honor." *ABC* (Madrid), May 29, 1977.
Pritchard, Diane Spencer. "Joint Tenants of the Frontier: Russian-Hispanic Relationships in Alta California." In *Russian America: The Forgotten Frontier*, edited by Barbara Sweetland Smith and Redmond J. Barnett, 81-93. Tacoma: Washington State Historical Society, 1990.
Pritzker, Barry M. *A Native American Encyclopedia: History, Culture, and People*. Oxford, UK: Oxford University Press, 2000.
Processo formado de orden del Rey N. Señor por la Junta de Generales que S.M. se ha dignado nombrar à este fin, sobre la conducta, que tuvieron en la defensa, capitulación, pérdida y rendición de la Plaza de La Habana, y Escuadra, que se hallaba en su Puerto. Madrid: Juan de San Martín, 1763. Biblioteca Nacional, Madrid, 2/17624 V.1 and 2/17625 V.2.
Proctor, Samuel, ed. *Eighteenth-Century Florida: The Impact of the American Revolution*. Gainesville: University Presses of Florida, 1978.

Prucha, F. P. *Indian Peace Medals in American History.* Lincoln: University of Nebraska Press, 1971.
Puig-Samper, Miguel Ángel. "Humboldt, un prusiano en la corte del rey Carlos IV." *Revista de Indias* 59, no. 216 (1999): 329-55.
Quarleri, Lía. "Gobierno y liderazgo jesuítico-guaraní en tiempos de guerra (1752-1756)." *Revista de Indias* 68, no. 243 (2008): 89-114.
Quatrefages, René. "La participación militar de Francia en la toma de Pensacola." *Revista de Historia Militar* 21, no. 42 (1977): 7-30.
Quesada, Alejandro M. de. *A History of Florida Forts: Florida's Lonely Outposts.* Charleston: History Press, 2006.
———. *Spanish Colonial Fortifications in North America, 1565-1822.* Illustrated by Stephen Walsh. Oxford: Osprey, 2010.
Quevedo y Villegas, Francisco de. *Las zahúrdas de Plutón.* Madrid: Espasa Calpe, 1924.
¿Quién manda en este mundo? Wall poster, México[?], 1784[?]. In Víctor Cano Sordo, *De la Luisiana a la Nueva España: La Historia de Juan Bernardo Domínguez y Gálvez (1783-1847)*, 9. México D.F.: Impresora Múltiple, 1999.
Quintero Saravia, Gonzalo M. *Don Blas de Lezo: Defensor de Cartagena de Indias.* Bogotá: Planeta, 2002.
Quirós y Campo-Sagrado, Manuel de. *Condigno llanto de las musas en la muerte del Excmo. Sr. Conde de Gálvez, virrey.* México: Gerardo Flores, 1786.
Radding Murrieta, Cynthia. *Wandering Peoples: Colonialism, Ethnic Spaces, and Ecological Frontiers in Northwestern Mexico, 1700-1850.* Durham: Duke University Press, 1997.
Rakove, Jack. "An Agenda for Early American History." *Historically Speaking* 6 (March-April 2005): 30-31.
Ramírez Meza, Benito. "La comandancia general de las Provincias Internas." *Clío* 2 (January-March, 1991): 41-46.
Ramos, Antonio. *Descripción genealógica de la casa de Aguayo, y líneas que se derivan de ella desde que se conquistó Andalucía . . . hasta el presente, de la que es cabeza . . . D. Gonzalo de Aguayo y Manrique . . . conde de Villaverde la Alta.* Málaga: El impresor de la Dignidad Episcopal, 1781.
Ramos Pérez, Demetrio. *Historia de América.* Vol. 9 of *Historia general de España y América*, edited by Luis Súarez Fernández. Madrid: Rialp, 1990.
Ramos Vázquez, Isabel. "Policía de vagos para las ciudades españolas del siglo XVIII." *Revista de Estudios Histórico-Jurídicos* 31 (2009): 217-58.
———. "La represión de los delitos atroces en el Derecho Castellano de la Edad Moderna." *Revista de Estudios histórico-jurídicos* (online) 26 (2004): 255-99.
Rangel, Nicolás. *Historia del toreo en México: Época colonial (1529-1821).* México D.F.: León Sánchez, 1924.
Raynal, Guillaume-Thomas. *Histoire philosophique et politique des établissemens & du commerce des européens dans les deux Indes.* Amsterdam, 1770.
Razón de entrar en Portugal las tropas españolas como amigas, y sinrazón de recibirlas como enemigas: Manifiesto reducido a las memorias presentadas de parte a parte. Lima: Librería de la calle de Palacio, 1763. First published 1762.
Rea, Robert R. "Florida and the Royal Navy's Floridas." *Florida Historical Quarterly* 60, no. 2 (1981): 186-203.
———. *Major Robert Farmar.* Tuscaloosa: University of Alabama Press, 1990.
Real Academia Española. *Diccionario de la lengua castellana.* 9th ed. Madrid: Francisco María Fernández, 1843.

———. *Diccionario de la lengua castellana compuesto por la Real Academia Española, reducido a un tomo para su más fácil uso.* Madrid: Joachín Ibarra, 1780.

———. *Diccionario de la lengua castellana compuesto por la Real Academia Española, reducido a un tomo para su más fácil uso. Segunda edición, el la qual [sic] se han colocado en los lugares correspondientes todas las voces del Suplemento, que se puso al fin de la edición del año 1780, y se ha añadido otro nuevo suplemento de artículos correspondientes a las letras A, B y C.* Madrid: Joachín Ibarra, 1783.

———. *Diccionario de la lengua castellana, en que se explica el verdadero sentido de las voces, su naturaleza y calidad, con las phrases o modos de hablar, los proverbios o refranes, y otras cosas convenientes al uso de la lengua . . .* Madrid: Imprenta de la Real Academia Española por la viuda de Francisco del Hierro, 1732.

———. *Diccionario de la lengua castellana, en que se explica el verdadero sentido de las voces, su naturaleza y calidad, con las phrases o modos de hablar, los proverbios o refranes, y otras cosas convenientes al uso de la lengua . . .* Madrid: Imprenta de la Real Academia Española, 1734.

———. *Diccionario de la lengua castellana, en que se explica el verdadero sentido de las voces, su naturaleza, y calidad, con las phrases [sic], o modos de hablar, los proverbios, o refranes, y otras cosas convenientes al uso de la lengua . . .* Madrid: Real Academia Española, 1739.

Diccionario de la lengua castellana compuesto por la Real Academia Española reducido a un tomo para su más fácil uso. 7th ed. Madrid: La viuda de don Joaquín Ibarra, 1803.

———. *Diccionario de la lengua española.* 22nd ed., Madrid: Espasa, 2001.

Real Academia Nacional de Medicina. *Catálogo de los Fondos Manuscritos del S. XVIII de la Real Academia Nacional de Medicina.* Madrid: Real Academia Nacional de Medicina, 1996.

Real Cédula y Reglamento para las Escuelas, Premios y Socorros establecidos en la villa de Macharaviaya. Madrid: Imp. Pedro Martín, 1783.

Real Ruiz, José Joaquín, and Antonia M. Heredia Herrera. "Martín de Mayorga." In *Los virreyes de la Nueva España en el reinado de Carlos III*, edited by José Antonio Calderón Quijano, 9–224. Sevilla: Consejo Superior de Investigaciones Científicas / Escuela de Estudios Hispano-Americanos, 1968.

Recaño, Joaquín, and Angels Torrens. "Algunos apuntes sobre los determinantes sociodemográficos en la mortalidad infantil en Cataluña (s. XVIII–XX)." *Papers de Demografia* 238 (2004): 1–26.

Recio Morales, Óscar. *La presencia irlandesa en los ejércitos de la monarquía hispánica, 1580–1818. / The Irish Military Presence in the Spanish Armies, 1580–1818.* CD-ROM. Madrid: Ministerio de Defensa, 2007.

———. "When Merit Alone Is Not Enough: Money as a 'Parallel Route' for Irish Military Advancement in Spain." *Irish Migration Studies in Latin America* 5, no. 2 (July 2007): 121–24.

Recopilación de las Leyes de estos Reynos [sic], hecha por mandado de la Majestad Católica del Rey don Philippe Segundo nuestro Señor. Alcalá de Henares: Juan Iñiguez, 1581.

Recopilación de Leyes de los Reinos de las Indias. 3rd ed. Madrid: Antonio Pérez de Soto, 1774.

Recopilación de Leyes de los Reynos [sic] de las Indias: Mandadas imprimir, y publicar por la magestad católica del rey Don Carlos II, nuestro señor. Madrid: Julián de Paredes, 1681. Facs. ed. Madrid: Ediciones de Cultura Hispánica, 1973.

Recueils de règlements, édits, déclarations et arrêts concernant le commerce, l'administration de la justice et la police des colonies françaises de l'Amérique. Paris: Libraires associez, 1744-45.

Reder Gadow, Marion, and Pedro Luis Pérez-Frías. "La regulación social de la muerte en el ejército español en la crisis del antiguo régimen." *Baetica, Estudios de Arte, Geografía e Historia* 33 (2011): 373-97.

Reeve, John. "British Naval Strategy: War on a Global Scale." In *Strategy in the American War of Independence: A Global Approach,* edited by Donald Stoker, Kenneth J. Hagan, and Michael T. McMaster, 73-99. New York: Routledge, 2010.

Reflexions sur le Feu de Joye, fait à la Haye le 17 Novembre 1649, pour le marriage du Roy d'Espagne. Amsterdam, 1649.

Reglamento e Instrucción para los Presidios que se han de formar en la Línea de frontera de la Nueva España, Resuelto por el Rey Nuestro Señor en Cédula de 10 de September de 1772. Madrid, 1772, Archivo General de Indias, Guadalajara, 522. In Sidney B. Brinckerhoff and Odie B. Faulk, ed. and trans., *Lancers for the King: A Study of the Frontier Military System of Northern New Spain, with a Translation of the Royal Regulations of 1772,* 11-67. Phoenix: Arizona Historical Foundation, 1965.

Reglamento para las milicias de infantería y caballería de la isla de Cuba: Aprobado por S.M. y mandado que se observen inviolablemente todos sus Artículos, por Real Cédula expedida en El Pardo á 19 de Enero de 1769 y que debe observarse en todo lo adaptable á las Tropas de Milicias del Reyno del Perú en conseqüencia [sic] de la Real Orden; va al fin añadida una Real declaración sobre puntos esenciales de este Reglamento. Lima: Imprenta de la Real Casa de los Niños Expósitos, 1793. Biblioteca de Palacio Real, I/I/439.

Reglamento para todos los presidios de las Provincias internas de esta Governación, con el número de Oficiales, y Soldados, que los ha de guarecer: Sueldos, Que unos, y otros avrán de gozar: Ordenanzas para el mejor Govierno, y Disciplina Militar de Governadores, Oficiales, y Soldados; Prevenciones para los que en ellas comprehenden: Precios de los Víveres y Vestuarios, con que a los Soldados se les asiste, y se les avrá de continuar. Hecho por el Excmo. Señor Marqués de Casa-Fuerte, Vi-Rey, Governador, y Capitán General de estos Reynos. México, 1729. In Vito Alessio Robles, ed. "Diario y derrotero de lo caminado, visto y observado en la visita que hizo a los presidios de la Nueva España Septentrional el Brigadier don Pedro de Rivera." *Archivo Histórico Militar Mexicano* 2 (1946): 199-234.

Reglas de gobierno de la sociedad de suscriptores del teatro de la ciudad de México, reino de la Nueva Espuña. México, circa 1786.

Reher, David S. "¿Malthus de nuevo? Población y economía en México durante el siglo XVIII." *Historia Mexicana* 41, no. 4 (1992): 615-64.

Reher, David Sven, and Fernando González-Quiñones. "Do Parents Really Matter? Child Health and Development in Spain during the Demographic Transition." *Population Studies* 57, no. 1 (2003): 63-75.

Reig Satorres, José. "Visita General a la Presidencia y Audiencia de Quito, realizada por el licenciado José García de León y Pizarro (1778-1784)." In *XI Congreso Internacional de Historia del Derecho Indiano: Actas y estudios,* 3:121-46. Buenos Aires: Instituto de Investigaciones de Historia del Derecho, 1997.

El Reino de Granada y el Nuevo Mundo, V Congreso internacional de Historia de América, mayo de 1992. Granada: Diputación Provincial de Granada, 1994.

Relación puntual de lo acaecido con motivo de la Expedición dispuesta contra Argel en el año de 1775. S.l., s.n., 1775[?]. Biblioteca Nacional, Madrid, VC/84/23.

Reparaz, Carmen de. *Yo Solo: Bernardo de Galvez y la toma de Panzacola en 1781: Una contribución española a la independencia de los Estados Unidos*. Madrid: Ediciones del Serbal-ICI, 1986.

Represa Fernández, María Francisca, Carlos Álvarez Gracía, Miguel Represa Fernández, and Amando Represa Rodríguez. *Documentos relativos a la independencia de Norteamérica existentes en archivos españoles, vol. 5/ 1 & 2, Archivo General de Simancas. Secretaría de Estado: Inglaterra (años 1750-1820)*. Madrid: Ministerio de Asuntos Exteriores, 1976.

Represa Fernández, María Francisca, María del Camino Represa Fernández, and Amando Represa Rodríguez. *Documentos relativos a la independencia de Norteamérica existentes en archivos españoles, vol.6, Archivo General de Simancas. Secretaría de Estado: Francia (años 1774-1786)*. Madrid: Ministerio de Asuntos Exteriores, 1981.

El retrato novohispano en el siglo XVIII, exposición presentada en Museo Poblano de Arte Virreinal, octubre 1999-febrero 2000. Puebla: Museo Poblano de Arte Virreinal, 1999.

Reygadas, Fermín de. *Liras que la Excma. Señora dña. Felicitas Maxan [sic] expresa su sentimiento en la muerte del Excmo. Sr. Vi-rey [sic] conde de Gálvez*. México, Jáuregui, 1787.

Ribes, Vicent. "Nuevos datos biográficos sobre Juan de Miralles." *Revista de historia moderna: Anales de la Universidad de Alicante* 16 (1997): 363-74.

Ribes-Iborra, Vicente. "La era Miralles: El momento de los agentes secretos." In *Norteamérica a finales del siglo XVIII: España y los Estados Unidos*, edited by Eduardo Garrigues, Emma Sánchez Montañés, Sylvia L. Hilton, Almudena Hernández Ruigómez, and Isabel García-Montón, 143-69. Madrid: Fundación Consejo España-Estados Unidos and Editorial Marcial Pons.

Rich, Obadiah. *Bibliotheca Americana Nova: A Catalogue of Books in Various Languages, relating to America Printed since the year 1700, including Voyages to the Pacific and Round [sic] the World and Collections of Voyages and Travels Compiled principally from the works themselves*. New York: Burt Franklin, 1846.

Rindfleisch, Bryan. "Rebels and Indians: The Participation of and Relationship between Native Americans and the American Patriots during the Revolutionary War, 1775-1783." BA diss., University of Wisconsin-Madison, 2007.

Río, Ignacio del. "Autoritarismo y locura en el noroeste novohispano: Implicaciones políticas del enloquecimiento del visitador general José de Gálvez." *Estudios de Historia Novohispana* 22 (2000): 111-38.

———. "El noroeste novohispano y la nueva política imperial española." In *Historia general de Sonora, vol. 2. De la conquista al Estado libre y soberano de Sonora*, edited by Sergio Ortega Noriega, 193-222. Hermosillo: Gobierno del Estado de Sonora, 1996.

Risco, Antonio. *La Real Academia de Santa Bárbara de Madrid (1730-1808): Naissance et formation d'une élite dans l'Espagne du XVIIIe siècle*. Toulouse: Université Le Mirail, 1979.

Riva Palacios, Vicente. *México a través de los siglos*. Barcelona: Espasa, s.a.

Rivas, Christine. "The Spanish Colonial Military: Santo Domingo 1701-1779." *The Americas: A Quarterly Review of Inter-American Cultural History* 60, no. 2 (2003): 249-72.

Rivera Cambas, Manuel. *Los gobernantes de México: Galería de biografías y retratos de los virreyes, emperadores, presidentes y otros gobernantes que ha tenido México, desde don Hernando Cortes hasta el c. Benito Juárez*. México D.F.: J. M. Aguilar Ortiz, 1872.

———. *Historia antigua y moderna de Jalapa y de las revoluciones del Estado de Veracruz*. México D.F.: Cumplido, 1871.
———. *México pintoresco, artístico y monumental*. México D.F.: Nacional, 1883.
Robène, Luc. *L'homme à la conquête de l'air: Des aristocrates éclairés aux sportifs bourgeois*. Paris: L'Harmattan, 1998.
Robertson, William. *The History of America*. London: W. Strahan, 1777.
Robertson, William Spence. *La vida de Miranda*. 2nd ed. Caracas: Publicaciones de Banco Industrial de Venezuela, 1982.
Rodas de Coss, Francisco. "José de Gálvez Gallardo, 1720-1787." In *México en el siglo XVIII*, vii-lxxvii. México D.F.: Secretaría de Relaciones Exteriores / Embajada de México en Madrid, 1983.
Rodger, Nicholas. *Command of the Ocean: A Naval History of Britain, 1649-1815*. New York: Norton, 2005.
Rodilla, María José. "Diálogo satírico de don Quijote y Sancho Panza sobre los males de la Nueva España (siglo XVIII)." *Anales Cervantinos* 43 (2011): 271-98.
Rodríguez, Antonio. "El origen de los indultos de Semana Santa." *El Tiempo*, March 26, 2013.
Rodríguez, J. E. *The Independence of Spanish America*. Cambridge: Cambridge University Press, 1998.
Rodríguez, Mario. *La revolución americana de 1776 y el mundo hispánico: Ensayos y documentos*. Madrid: Tecnos, 1976.
Rodríguez Álvarez, María de los Ángeles. *Usos y Costumbres Funerarias en la Nueva España*. México D.F.: Colegio de Michoacán / Colegio Mexiquense, 2001.
Rodríguez Baena, María Luisa. "El virrey Manuel Antonio Flórez." In *Los virreyes de la Nueva España en el reinado de Carlos IV*, edited by José Antonio Calderón Quijano, 1:3-86. Sevilla: Consejo Superior de Investigaciones Científicas / Escuela de Estudios Hispano-Americanos, 1972.
Rodríguez Campomanes, Pedro, Count de Campomanes. *Noticia geográfica del reyno y caminos de Portugal*. Madrid: Joachin Ibarra, 1762.
Rodríguez Casado, Vicente. "Política exterior de Carlos III en torno al problema indiano." *Revista de Indias* 5 (1944): 227-66.
———. *Política interior de Carlos III*. Valladolid: Consejo Superior de Investigaciones Científicas, 1950.
———. *Política marroquí de Carlos III*. Madrid: Consejo Superior de Investigaciones Científicas / Instituto Jerónimo de Zurita, 1946.
———. *Primeros años de la dominación española en la Luisiana*. Madrid: Consejo Superior de Investigaciones Científicas / Instituto González Fernández de Oviedo, 1942.
Rodríguez del Valle, Mariana, and Ángeles Conejo Díez de la Cortina. "Matías de Gálvez (1783-1784)." In *Los virreyes de la Nueva España en el reinado de Carlos III*, edited by José Antonio Calderón Quijano, 225-326. Sevilla: Consejo Superior de Investigaciones Científicas / Escuela de Estudios Hispano-Americanos, 1968.
Rodríguez García, Vicente. *El fiscal de Real Hacienda en Nueva España: Don Ramón de Posada y Soto, 1781-1793*. Oviedo: Universidad de Oviedo, 1992.
Rodríguez Moya, Inmaculada. *La mirada del virrey: iconografía del poder en la Nueva España*. Castelló de la Plana: Pubicacions de la Universitat Jaume I, 2003.
———. *El retrato en México, 1781-1867: Héroes, ciudadanos y emperadores para una nueva nación*. Sevilla: Consejo Superior de Investigaciones Científicas / Escuela de Estudios Hispano-Americanos / Universidad de Sevilla, 2006.

Rodríguez-Sala, María Luisa. *Los cirujanos del ejército de la Nueva España (1713–1820): ¿Miembros de un estamento profesional o una comunidad científica*. México D.F.: Universidad Nacional Autónoma de México, 2005.

Rojas, Rafael. *La nueva sociabilidad política: Facciones parlamentarias, grupos de opinión y logias masónicas en los orígenes del Estado mexicano, 1821–1829*. Documento de trabajo no. 76. México D.F.: Centro de Docencia e investigación económicas, 1997.

Rojas y Rocha, Francisco de. *Poema épico: La rendición de Panzacola y conquista de la Florida occidental por el Excmo. Sr. Conde de Gálvez*. México: Felipe de Zúñiga y Ontiveros, 1785.

Romero Flores, Jesús. *Chapultepec en la historia de México*. México D.F.: Secretaría de Educación Pública, 1947.

———. *Historia de Michoacán*. México D.F.: Gobierno de Michoacán / Imprenta Claridad, 1946.

———. *Michoacán histórico y legendario*. México D.F.: SEP, 1985.

Romero García, Rafael Eugenio. "Medidas antiguas españolas: Breve compendio de las medidas antiguas utilizadas en las diferentes regiones y provincias españolas." *Técnica Industrial* 254 (September 2004): 64–67.

Rosenzweig, Fernando, Rosaura Hernández, María Teresa Jarquín, and Manuel Miño Grijalva, eds. *Breve historia del Estado de México*. México D.F.: Colegio Mexiquense / Gobierno del Estado de México, 1987.

Roulet, Florencia. "Con la pluma y la palabra: El lado oscuro de las negociaciones de paz entre españoles e indígenas." *Revista de Indias* 64, no. 231 (2004): 313–48.

Rousseau, François. *Règne de Charles III d'Espagne (1759–1788)*. Paris: Plon, 1907.

Rubio Argüelles, Ángeles. *Un ministro de Carlos III: D. José de Gálvez y Gallardo, marqués de la Sonora, ministro General de Indias, visitador de Nueva España*. Málaga: Tall. Gráf. de la Excma. Diputación Provincial, 1949.

Rubio Mañé, J. Ignacio. "Itinerario del teniente coronel don Hugo O'Conor de la ciudad de México a la villa de Chihuahua." *Boletín del Archivo General de la Nación* 30 (July–September 1959): 393–407.

———. *El virreinato*. Vol. 1, *Orígenes y jurisdicciones, y dinámica social de los virreyes*. México D.F.: Fondo de Cultura Económica, 1992. First published 1955.

Rubió y Bellvé, Mariano. *Diccionario de ciencias militares*. Barcelona: Administración de la Revista Científico Militar y Biblioteca Militar, 1901.

Ruigómez de Hernández, María Pilar. *El gobierno español del despotismo ilustrado ante la independencia de los Estados Unidos de América: Una nueva estructura de la política internacional (1773–1783)*. Madrid: Ministerio de Asuntos Exteriores, 1978.

Ruíz Gomar, Rogelio. "Grabado y numismática hasta la consumación de la independencia." In *El Arte del siglo XIX, El arte mexicano*, vol. 9. México D.F.: Salvat Mexicana, 1982.

Rumazo González, Alfonso. *Francisco de Miranda: Protolíder de la independencia americana (biografía)*. Caracas: CONATEL, 2006.

Rumeu de Armas, Antonio. *Piraterías y ataques navales contra las Islas Canarias*. Madrid: Consejo Superior de Investigaciones Científicas / Instituto Jerónimo Zurita, 1947–50.

Rush, N. Orwin. *Spain's Final Triumph over Great Britain in the Gulf of Mexico: The Battle of Pensacola, March 9 to May 8, 1781*. Tallahassee: Florida State University, 1966.

Saavedra, Francisco de. *Los Decenios (Autobiografía de un sevillano de la Ilustración)*.

Edited by Francisco Morales Padrón. Sevilla: Servicio de Publicaciones del Excmo. Ayuntamiento de Sevilla, 1995.

———. *Diario de don Francisco de Saavedra*. Edited by Francisco Morales Padrón. Sevilla: Universidad de Sevilla / Consejo Superior de Investigaciones Científicas, 2004.

Sabin, Joseph. *Bibliotheca Americana: A Dictionary of Books Relating to America, from its Discovery to the Present Time. Begun by Joseph Sabin, Continued by Wilberforce Eames and Completed by R. W. G. Vail for the Bibliographical Society of America*. 29 vols. New York: Joseph Sabin and Sons, 1868-1936.

Sacristán, María Cristina. "Filantropismo, improductividad y delincuencia en algunos textos novohispanos sobre pobres, vagos y mendigos (1782-1794)." *Relaciones: Estudios de Historia y Sociedad* 9, no. 36 (1988): 21-32.

Salmon, Roberto Mario. *Indian Revolts in Northern New Spain: A Synthesis of Resistance (1680-1786)*. Lanham, Md.: University Press of America, 1991.

Salvucci, Linda K. "Costumbres viejas, 'hombres nuevos': José de Gálvez y la burocracia fiscal novohispana (1754-1800)." *Historia Mexicana* 33, no. 2 (1983): 224-64.

Samper, José Antonio, and Clara Eugenia Hernández. "La Luisiana." In *Enciclopedia del español en los Estados Unidos: Anuario del Instituto Cervantes 2008*, edited by Humberto López Morales, 75-79. Madrid: Instituto Cervantes-Santillana, 2009.

Sanadon, Barthélémy Jean-Baptiste. *Ensayo sobre la nobleza de los bascongados, para que sirva de introduccion á la historia general de aquellos pueblos compuesto en francès de las memorias de un militar bascongado por un amigo de esta nación*. Tolosa: Francisco de la Lama, 1786.

———. *Essai sur la noblesse des Basques, pour servir d'introduction à l'histoire générale de ces peuples, rédigé sur les Mémoires d'un militaire basque, par un ami de la nation*. Pau: impr. de J.-P. Vignancour, 1785.

Sánchez, Santos. *Colección de pragmáticas, cédulas, provisiones, autos acordados y otras providencias generales expedidas por el Consejo Real en el reinado del señor don Carlos III, cuya observancia corresponde a los tribunales y jueces ordinarios del reino, y a todos los vasallos en general*. 3rd ed. Madrid: Viuda e hijo de Marín, 1803.

Sánchez-Albornoz, Nicolás. "La población de la América colonial española." In *Historia de América Latina*, edited by Leslie Bethell, 4:3-21. Barcelona: Crítica, 1990.

Sánchez Álvarez-Insúa, Alberto. "Toros y sociedad en el siglo XVIII: Génesis y Desarrollo de un espectáculo convertido en seña de identidad nacional." *ARBOR Ciencia, Pensamiento y Cultura* 172 (November-December 2006): 893-908.

Sánchez-Bella, Ismael. "Las reformas en Indias del Secretario de Estado José de Gálvez (1776-1787)." In *Derecho y administración pública en las Indias hispánicas: Actas del XII congreso internacional de Historia del derecho indiano (Toledo, 19 a 21 de octubre de 1998)*, edited by Feliciano Barrios Pintado, 2:1517-54. Cuenca: Universidad de Castilla / La Mancha, 2002.

Sánchez Casado, Galo. *Los altos grados de la masonería*. Madrid: Akal, 2009.

Sánchez de Rivera y Alfaro, María de los Ángeles. "La Real y distinguida Orden de Carlos III." *Hidalguía* 66 (1964): 609-20.

Sánchez Doncel, Gregorio. *Presencia de España en Orán (1509-1792)*. Toledo: Estudio Teológico de San Ildefonso, 1991.

Sánchez-Fabrés Mirat, Elena. *Situación histórica de las Floridas en la segunda mitad del siglo XVIII (1783-1819): Los problemas de una región de frontera*. Madrid: Ministerio de Asuntos Exteriores, 1977.

San Miguel Pérez, Enrique. "La crisis de la estrategia política española en

Norteamérica: De Bernardo de Gálvez a Luis de Onís." In *El ejército y la armada en el noroeste de América: Nootka y su tiempo*, edited by Leandro Martínez Peñas and Manuela Fernández Rodríguez, 29-58. Madrid: Universidad rey Juan Carlos, 2011.

Santa Cruz y Espejo, Javier Eugenio. *Escritos del doctor Francisco Javier Eugenio Santa Cruz y Espejo*. Edited by Federico González Súarez. Quito: Imprenta Municipal, 1912.

Santa María y Sevilla, Manuel. *Suspiros que en la muerte del virrey de México, conde de Gálvez, exsaló [sic] el cadete del Regimiento de Dragones de España, Don Manuel de Santa Maria y Sevilla, en verso castellano*. México: Rangel, 1786.

Santana Perez, Juan Manuel, and José Antonio Sánchez Suárez. *Emigración por reclutamiento: Canarios en Luisiana*. Las Palmas de Gran Canaria: Universidad de Las Palmas de Gran Canaria, 1992.

Santana Perez, Juan Manuel, José Antonio Sánchez Suárez, and María Eugenia Monzón Perdomo. "Desertores en Canarias durante el siglo XVIII." In *VI Encuentro de la ilustración al romanticismo, Juego, Fiesta y Transgresión, 1750-1850*, edited by Alberto Romero Ferrer, 575-83. Cádiz: Servicio de Publicaciones de la Universidad de Cádiz, 1995.

Santayana Bustillo, Lorenzo. *Gobierno político de los pueblos de España y el corregidor, alcalde y juez en ellos*. Edited by Francisco Tomás y Valiente. Madrid: Instituto de Estudios de Administración Local, 1979. First published 1769.

Santiago, Mark. *The Red Captain: The Life of Hugo O'Conor, Commandant Inspector of the Interior Provinces of New Spain*. Tucson: Arizona Historical Society, 1994.

Santos Arrebola, María Soledad. "De la hidalguía a la nobleza: La familia Gálvez." In *Familia, parentesco y linaje*, edited by James Casey and Juan Hernández Franco, 335-41. Murcia: Universidad de Murcia, 1997.

———. *La proyección de un ministro ilustrado en Málaga: José de Gálvez*. Málaga: Publicaciones de la Universidad de Málaga, 1999.

Sanz, Raymundo, ed. and trans. *Diccionario militar: O recolección alfabética de todos los términos propios del Arte de la Guerra*. Madrid: Gerónimo Ortega, 1794.

Sarriá Muñoz, Andrés. "Las escuelas de primaria de Macharaviaya (1776-1791): Una obra ilustrada de los Gálvez." *Jábega* 70, no. 4 (1990): 39-45.

Satisfacción de Don Alexandro Arroyo de Rozas Coronel del Regimiento fixo de La Habana, al cargo . . . de la . . . Junta de Guerra formada de Orden de S.M. para conocer de la Defensa, Rendición y Pérdida de aquella Plaza. Madrid, 1764[?]. Biblioteca Nacional, Madrid, VE/1233/20(3).

Satisfacción de Don Juan Antonio de la Colina, Capitan de Navio de la Real Armada, al cargo, y escrito del Señor Fiscal de la excelentísima Junta de Guerra, formada de Orden de S.M. para conocer de la defensa, rendición, y pérdida de La Habana. Madrid, 1764[?]. Biblioteca Nacional, Madrid, VE/1233/20(2).

Satisfacción del Coronel D. Balthasar Ricaud de Tirgale, ingeniero que fue en gefe de la plaza de Habana, à los cargos que le hace, y de que le acusa el señor fiscal de la Junta creada por su Magestad para la instrucción del processo sobre rendición de aquella plaza y sus resultas. Madrid, 1763[?]. Biblioteca Nacional, Madrid, VE/1233/20(4).

Satisfaccion del Mariscal de Campo D. Juan de Prado, Governador que ha sido de la Plaza de la Habana, y Capitan General de la Isla de Cuba, a los cargos que se le han formado en la causa pendiente en la Junta de Generales nombrados por S.M. sobre la conducta, que tuvieron en la Defensa, Capitulacion, Rendicion, y Pérdida de la misma Plaza. Madrid, 1764[?]. Biblioteca Nacional, Madrid, R/36168.

Saunt, Claudio. "Go West: Mapping Early American Historiography." *William and Mary Quarterly*, 3rd ser., 65, no. 4 (2008): 745-78.

Saxon, Lyle. *Gumbo Ya-Ya: Folk Tales of Louisiana*. Gretna: Pelican, 2006. First published 1945.
Schama, Simon. *Landscape and Memory*. New York: Knopf, 1995.
Schmidt, Elisabeth Whitman. "Blacks and Indians of New Hampshire and Vermont in the American Revolution." In *Forgotten Patriots: African American and American Indian Patriots of the Revolutionary War; A Guide to Service, Sources, and Studies*, edited by Eric G. Grundset, Washington, D.C.: National Society Daughters of the American Revolution, 2001, 39–76.
Schroeder, Albert H. "Shifting for Survival in the Spanish Southwest." *New Mexico Historical Review* 43, no. 4 (October 1968): 291–310.
Scott, H. M. *British Foreign Policy in the Age of the American Revolution*. Oxford: Oxford University Press, 1990.
Scramuzza, V. M. "Galveztown: A Spanish Settlement in Colonial Lousiana." Master's diss., Louisiana State University, 1924.
Seebold, Herman de Bachelle. *Old Louisiana Plantation Homes and Family Trees*. New Orleans: Pelican Press, 1941.
Segovia Salas, Rodolfo. *Las fortificaciones de Cartagena de Indias: Estrategia e historia*. Bogotá: Tercer Mundo Editores, 1992.
Semprún Bullón, José. "El esfuerzo bélico realista en América durante la Guerra de la Independencia." *Revista de Historia Militar* 51, special issue (2007): 39–64.
Sepúlveda, Juan Ginés de. *Historia del Nuevo Mundo*. Edited by Antonio Ramírez de Verger. Madrid: Alianza Editorial, 1987. First published 1550.
Sermón de honras funerales, que celebraron a la memoria del Excmo. Sr. D. Matías de Gálvez, en la iglesia del convento de Santo Domingo en la Imperial Ciudad de Covan a expensas de d. Francisco Xavier de Aguirre, Alcalde mayor de dicha provincia, el trece de diciembre de 1785, predicado por el prior del mismo convento. Sevilla: Oficina de d. Josef de San Román y Codina, 1785.
Serrano y Sanz, Manuel, ed. *Documentos históricos de la Florida y la Luisiana: Siglos XVI al XVIII*. Madrid: Librería General de Victoriano Suárez, 1913.
Servicio Geográfico del Ejército. *Cartografía de Ultramar, carpeta II: Estados Unidos y Canada*. Madrid: Servicio Geográfico e Histórico del Ejército, 1953.
———. *Cartoteca histórica: Índice de mapas y planos históricos de América*. Madrid: Servicio Geográfico del Ejército, 1974.
Servies, James A. *The Siege of Pensacola, 1781: A Bibliography*. Pensacola: John C. Pace Library, 1981.
———, ed. *The Log of H.M.S. Mentor, 1780–1781: A New Account of the British Navy at Pensacola*. Pensacola: University Presses of Florida, 1982.
Shafer, Robert Jones. *The Economic Societies in the Spanish World, 1763–1821*. Syracuse: Syracuse University Press, 1958.
Shakespeare, William. *Coriolanus*. London: Penguin Classics, 2005. First published 1605–8.
Sheehan, Bernard W. "Indian-White Relations in Early America: A Review Essay." *William and Mary Quarterly*, 3rd ser., 26, no. 2 (1969): 267–86.
Shepherd, William R. "The Cession of Louisiana to Spain." *Political Science Quarterly* 19 (1904): 439–58.
Siebert, Wilbur H. "The Loyalists in West Florida and the Natchez District." *Mississippi Valley Historical Review* 2, no. 4 (March 1916): 465–83.
———. "The Loyalists of Pennsylvania." *Ohio State University Bulletin* 24, no. 23 supplement (1920).

Siete Iglesias, Marqués de. "¿Qué es nobleza de sangre?" In Escuela de Genealogía, Heráldica y Nobiliaria, *Apuntes de Nobiliaria y nociones de Genealogía y Heráldica: Curso de grado de la Escuela de Genealogía, Heráldica y Nobiliaria*, 105-18. Madrid: Hidalguía, 1960.

Las Siete Partidas del Rey Don Alfonso el sabio. Edited by Real Academia de la Historia. Madrid: Imprenta Real, 1807.

Siles Saturnino, Reyes, and Rosario Parra Cala, eds. *Documentos relativos a la independencia de Norteamérica existentes en archivos españoles, vol.2, Archivo General de Indias, Sección Cuba: Correspondencia y documentación oficial de los gobernadores de Luisiana (años 1777-1803)*. Madrid: Ministerio de Asuntos Exteriores, 1980.

Siles Saturnino, Reyes, Purificación Medina Encina, and Rosario Parra Cala, eds. *Documentos relativos a la independencia de Norteamérica existentes en archivos españoles, vol.9, Archivo General de Indias, Sección Cuba: Correspondencia y documentación oficial de autoridades de Luisiana y de Florida Occidental (años 1764-1819)*. Madrid: Ministerio de Asuntos Exteriores, 1986.

Silvestre Martínez, Manuel. *Adicción a la libreraía de jueces, utilísma y universal . . .* Madrid: Imprenta Real, 1791.

Simmons, Marc. *Spanish Pathways: Readings in the History of Hispanic New Mexico*. Albuquerque: University of New Mexico Press, 2001.

———, ed. *Coronado's Land: Essays on Daily Life in Colonial New Mexico*. Albuquerque: University of New Mexico Press, 1991.

Simpson, Thomas. *Elements of plane geometry: to which are added, an essay on the maxima and minima of geometrical quantities, and a brief treatise of regular solids; also the mensuration of both superficies and solids, together with the construction of a large variety of geometrical problems*. London: J. Nourse, 1747.

Sio, Arnold A. "Reviewed Interpretations of Slavery: The Slave Status in the Americas." *Comparative Studies in Society and History* 7, no. 3 (1965): 289-308.

Skelton, Ike. "America's Frontier Wars: Lessons for Asymmetric Conflicts." *Military Review* 81, no. 5 (September-October 2001): 22-27.

Smith, Barbara Sweetland, and Redmond J. Barnett, eds. *Russian America: The Forgotten Frontier*. Tacoma: Washington State Historical Society, 1990.

Smith, Paul H., et al., eds. *Letters of Delegates to Congress, 1774-1789*. Washington, D.C.: Library of Congress, 1976-2000.

Soberanes Fernández, José Luis, and Rosa María Martínez de Codes, eds. *Homenaje a Alberto de la Hera*. México D.F.: Universidad Nacional Autónoma de México, 2008.

Solano, Francisco de. *Cedulario de tierras: Compilación, legislación agraria colonial (1497-1820)*. 2nd ed. México D.F.: Instituto de Investigaciones Jurídicas / Universidad Nacional Autónoma de México, 1991.

———. "Reformismo y Cultura Intelectual: La biblioteca privada de José de Gálvez, Ministro de Indias." *Quinto Centenario* 2 (1981): 1-100.

———. "Los resultados científicos de la real expedición hispanofrancesa al virreinato de Perú, 1749-1823." *Historia Mexicana* 184, vol. 46, no. 4 (1997): 723-43.

———. *Las voces de la ciudad, México a través de sus impresos, 1539-1821*. Madrid: Consejo Superior de Investigaciones Científicas, 1994.

Solano, Francisco de, and Beatriz Ruiz Caytán, eds. *Cardinales de Dos Independencias. (Noreste de México—Sureste de los Estados Unidos)*. México D.F.: Fomento Cultural Banamex, 1978.

Solano Acosta, Fernando. "La emigración acadiana a la Luisiana española (1783-1785)." *Jerónimo Zurita Cuadernos de Historia* 2 (1954): 85-125.

Solbes Ferri, Sergio. "Los comerciantes extranjeros y el negocio del tabaco en la España del siglo XVIII." In *Los extranjeros en la España moderna: Actas del I Coloquio Internacional, celebrado en Málaga del 28 al 30 de noviembre de 2002*, edited by María Begoña Villar García and Pilar Pezzi Cristóbal, 1:643-55. Madrid: Ministerio de Ciencia y Tecnología, 2003.

Solórzano Pereira, Juan de. *De Indiarum Iure, sive de Iusta Indiarum Occidentalium Gubernatione*. Lugduni: Sumptibus Laurentii Anisson, 1672.

———. *Política indiana*. Edited by Miguel Ángel Ochoa Brun. Madrid: Biblioteca de Autores Españoles-Atlas, 1972. First published 1629.

Somolinos, Germán. *Vida y obra de Francisco Hernández*. Vol. 1 of *Obras completas de Francisco Hernández*. Edited by Germán Somolinos. México D.F.: Universidad Nacional Autónoma de México, 1960.

Soniat du Fossat, Guy. *Synopsis of History of Louisiana: From the Founding of the Colony to the End of the Year 1791*. New Orleans: Louisiana Historical Society, 1906.

Sorando Muzás, Luís. *Banderas, estandartes y trofeos del Museo del Ejército, 1700-1843: Catálogo razonado*. Madrid: Ministerio de Defensa, 2001.

Soria Mesa, Enrique. *La Nobleza en la España Moderna: Cambio y Continuidad*. Madrid: Marcial Pons, 2007.

Sotto, Serafín María de, Count de Clonard. *Historia Orgánica de las Armas de Infantería y Caballería Españolas desde la creación del ejército permanente hasta el día*. Vol. 7. Madrid: Boletín de Jurisprudencia, 1856.

———. *Historia Orgánica de las Armas de Infantería y Caballería Españolas desde la creación del ejército permanente hasta el día*. Vol. 8. Madrid: Boletín de Jurisprudencia, 1856.

———. *Historia Orgánica de las Armas de Infantería y Caballería Españolas desde la creación del ejército permanente hasta el día*. Vol. 9. Madrid: Boletín de Jurisprudencia, 1856.

———. *Historia Orgánica de las Armas de Infantería y Caballería Españolas desde la creación del ejército permanente hasta el día*. Vol. 10. Madrid: Boletín de Jurisprudencia, 1856.

———. *Historia Orgánica de las Armas de Infantería y Caballería Españolas desde la creación del ejército permanente hasta el día*. Vol. 11. Madrid: Boletín de Jurisprudencia, 1857.

———. *Historia Orgánica de las Armas de Infantería y Caballería Españolas desde la creación del ejército permanente hasta el día*. Vol. 13. Madrid: Boletín de Jurisprudencia, 1856.

———. *Memoria histórica de las academias y escuelas militares de España, con la creación y estado presente del Colegio General establecido en la ciudad de Toledo*. Madrid: Imp. de D. José M. Gómez Colon y Compañía, 1847.

Southey, Captain Thomas. *Chronological History of the West Indies*. London: Longman, Rees, Orme, Brown and Green, 1827.

Souviron, Sebastián. *Bernardo de Gálvez, virrey de Méjico (Un infante de la marina española)*. Málaga: Excma. Diputación Provincial, 1946.

Sparks, Jared, ed. *The Writings of George Washington: Being His Correspondence, Addresses Messages, and Other Papers, Official and Private*. New York: Harper and Brothers, 1847.

Spear, Jennifer M. *Race, Sex, and Social Order in Early New Orleans*. Baltimore: Johns Hopkins University Press, 2009.

Spicer, Edward H. *Cycles of Conquest: The Impact of Spain, Mexico, and the United States on the Indians of the Southwest, 1533-1960*. Tucson: University of Arizona Press, 1962.

Spring, Ted. *Las compañías de Infantaria [sic] de las Americas / The Spanish Colonial Era Infantry, 1739-1781*. St. Louis: Track of the Wolf, 1990.

Stahl, A. M., ed. *The Medal in America*. New York: American Numismatic Society, 1999.

Starkey, Armstrong. *European and Native American Warfare, 1675-1815*. Norman: University of Oklahoma Press, 1998.

Starr, Joseph Barton. "'Left as a Gewgaw': The Impact of the American Revolution on British West Florida." In *Eighteenth-Century Florida: The Impact of the American Revolution*, edited by Samuel Proctor, 14-27. Gainesville: University Presses of Florida, 1978.

———. *Tories, Dons, and Rebels: The American Revolution in British West Florida*. Gainesville: University Presses of Florida, 1976.

St. Clair Segurado, Eva María. *Expulsión y exilio de la provincia jesuita mexicana, 1767-1820*. Alicante: Publicaciones de la Universidad de Alicante, 2005.

———. "La participación del ejército en la expulsión de la provincia jesuita mexicana." In *Milicia y sociedad ilustrada en España y América (1750-1800): Actas XI jornadas nacionales de historia militar, Sevilla, 11-15 de noviembre de 2002*, 509-26. Madrid: Deimos, 2003.

Steck, Francis Borgia. *A Tentative Guide to Historical Materials on the Spanish Borderlands*. New York: B. Franklin, 1971. First published 1943.

Stein, Stanley J., and Barbara H. Stein. *El apogeo del imperio: España y Nueva España en la era de Carlos III, 1759-1789*. Barcelona: Crítica, 2005.

Sternberg, Mary Ann. "In Search of Galveztown: An Archeological Dig Uncovers Fragments of Life at a Spanish Outpost in 18th Century Louisiana." *Louisiana Cultural Vistas* (Spring 2009): 54-61.

Sturtevant, William C. "Anthropology, History, and Ethnohistory." *Ethnohistory* 13, no. 1/2 (1966): 1-51.

———, ed. *Handbook of North American Indians*. 17 vols. Washington, D.C.: Smithsonian Institution, 1978-2008.

Suárez, Santiago Gerardo. *Las milicias: Instituciones militares hispanoamericanas*. Caracas: Academia Nacional de la Historia, 1984.

Suárez Argüello, Clara Elena. "De caminos, convoyes y peajes: Los caminos de México a Veracruz, 1759-1835." *Relaciones: Estudios de historia y sociedad* 22, no. 85 (2001): 223-45.

———, ed. *Informe general que en virtud de real orden instruyó y entregó el excelentísimo señor Marqués de Sonora siendo visitador general de este reino, al Excelentísmo señor virrey don Antonio Bucarely y Ursúa con fecha 31 de diciembre de 1771*. México D.F.: CIESAS, 2002.

Suárez Fernández, Luís. *Historia general de España y América*. Madrid: Rialp, 1992.

Sucre, Luis Alberto. *Gobernadores y Capitanes General de Venezuela*. Caracas: Lit. y Tidel Comercio, 1928.

Suetonio, Cayo. *Las vidas de los doze cesares*. Tarragona: Phelipe Roberto, 1596.

Susane, Louis. *Histoire de l'acienne infanterie française*. Paris: Librairie Militaire, Maritime et Plytechnique de J. Corréard, 1851.

Swanton, John R. *Indian Tribes of the Lower Mississippi Valley and Adjacent Coast of the Gulf of Mexico*. Washington, D.C.: Smithsonian Institution, 1911.

Tallant, Robert. *The Romantic New Orleanians*. New York: E. P. Dutton, 1950.
Tanck de Estrada, Dorothy. *Pueblos de indios y educación en el México colonial, 1750-1821*. México D.F.: El Colegio de México, 1999.
Tannenbaum, Frank. *Slave and Citizen: The Negro in the Americas*. New York: Beacon Press, 1947.
Taylor, Alan. *American Colonies: The Settling of North America*. New York: Viking-Penguin, 2001.
———. *American Revolutions: A Continental History, 1750-1804*. New York: Norton, 2016.
———. *The Divided Ground: Indians, Settlers, and the Northern Borderland of the American Revolution*. New York: Knopf, 2006.
Taylor, J. G. *Louisiana: A Bicentennial History*. New York: Norton, 1976.
Taylor Hansen, Lawrence Douglas. "La riqueza escondida en el desierto: La búsqueda de metales preciosos en el noroeste de Sonora durante los siglos XVIII y XIX." *Religión y Sociedad* 20 (2008): 165-90.
Tayman Barry D., Tony Lopez, and Skyler Liechty. "Tomás Prieto's al Mérito Spanish Indian Peace Medals." In *Peace Medals: Negotiating Power in Early America*, edited by R. B. Pickering, 19-31. Norman: Gilcrease Museum / University of Oklahoma Press, 2012.
Tedde de Lorca, Pedro. "La Real Hacienda de Carlos III y la guerra de independencia de los Estados Unidos." In *Norteamérica a finales del siglo XVIII: España y los Estados Unidos*, edited by Eduardo Garrigues, Emma Sánchez Montañés, Sylvia L. Hilton, Almudena Hernández Ruigómez, and Isabel García-Montón, 219-36. Madrid: Fundación Consejo España-Estados Unidos and Editorial Marcial Pons.
Teijeiro de la Rosa, Juan Miguel. "La financiación de la guerra en el siglo XVIII." *Revista de Historia Militar*, special issue, 51 (2007): 97-118.
Teixeira, Pedro. *Descripción de España y de las costas y puertos de sus reynos*. Madrid, 1634. Hofbibliothek Wien, Codex Miniatus, 46. Spanish ed., *El Atlas del Rey Planeta*. "La descripción de España y de las costas y puertos de sus reinos," de Pedro Texeira (1634), edited by Felipe Pereda and Fernando Marías. Madrid: Editorial Nerea, 2002.
Teixidor, Felipe, ed. "Noticia y reflexiones sobre la guerra que se tiene con los apaches en la provincia de la Nueva España, por don Bernardo de Gálvez." *Anales del Museo Nacional de México* 3 (1925): 537-55.
Teja, Jesús F. de la, and Ross Frank, eds. *Choice, Persuasion, and Coercion: Social Control on Spain's North American Frontiers*. Albuquerque: University of New Mexico Press, 2005.
Tepaske, John J. "Economic Problems of Florida Governors, 1700-1763." *Florida Historical Quarterly* 37, no. 1 (1958): 42-58.
Terrón Ponce, José Luis. "La casaca y la toga: Luces y sombras en la reforma militar durante el último tercio del siglo XVIII." *De la paz de París a Trafalgar (1763-1805): Las bases de la potencia hispana, IX jornadas de historia militar*, Monografías del Centro Superior de Estudios de la Defensa Nacional, no. 70 (April 2004): 27-50.
———. *Ejército y política en la España de Carlos III*. Madrid: Ministerio de Defensa, 1997.
Terry y Rivas, Antonio. *Diccionario marítimo inglés-español y vocabulario marítimo español-inglés . . .* Madrid: Ministerio de marina, 1896.
Tesoros de los Palacios Reales de España: Una historia compartida, Galería de Palacio Nacional, Exposición temporal, 16 diciembre 2011 a 31 mayo 2012. México D.F.:

Consejo Nacional para la Cultura y las Artes / Instituto Nacional de Antropología e Historia, 2011.

Thackeray, William Makepeace. *The Luck of Barry Lyndon: A Romance of the Last Century*. New York: Appleton, 1853. First published 1844.

Thomas, Alfred B. "An Eighteenth-Century Comanche Document." *American Anthropologist* 3, no. 2 (1929): 289–98.

———. "The Gálvez Campaigns, 1779–1780." In *Siege! Spain and Britain: Battle of Pensacola, March 9–May 8, 1781*, edited by Virginia Parks, 39–44. Pensacola: Pensacola Historical Society, 1981.

Thwaites, Reuben G., ed. "Papers from de Canadian Archives." *Collections of the State Historical Society of Wisconsin* 12 (1888): 97–211.

Tinker, Edward Larocque. *Les écrits de langue française en Louisiane au XIXe siècle: Essais biographiques et biobliographiques*. Paris: Champion, 1932.

———. *Louisiana's Earliest Poet: Julien Poydras and the Paeans to Galvez*. New York: New York Public Library, 1929.

Torales Pacheco, María Cristina. "Los jesuitas y la independencia de México: Algunas aproximaciones." *Destiempos* 3, no. 14 (2008): 397–412.

Tornero Tinajero, Pablo. "Emigración canaria a América: La expedición cívico-militar a Luisiana de 1777–1779." In *I coloquio de Historia Canario-Americano (1976)*, edited by Francisco Morales Padrón, 343–54. Las Palmas de Gran Canaria: Cabildo de Las Palmas de Gran Canaria, 1977.

———. *Relaciones de Dependencia entre Florida y los Estados Unidos (1783–1820)*. Madrid: Ministerio de Asuntos Exteriores, 1979.

Torre Revello, José. *Don Juan de San Martín: Noticia biográfica con apéndice documental*. Buenos Aires: Instituto Nacional Sanmartiniano, 1927.

Torres, José Alejandro. *Al buen entendedo . . . breve antología del refrán*. México D.F.: Quarzo, 2004.

Torres, José María de la. *Lo que fuimos y lo que somos o La Habana antigua y moderna*. La Habana: Librería Cervantes, 1857.

Torres Pérez, José María. "Pliego suelto fechado en 1781." *Revista General de Información y Documentación* 18 (2008): 147–59.

Torres Ramírez, Bibiano. *Alejandro O'Reilly en las Indias*. Sevilla: Escuela de Estudios Hispano-Americanos / Consejo Superior de Investigaciones Científicas, 1969.

Torres Sánchez, Rafael. "Crecimiento y expansión económica en el siglo XVIII." In *Historia económica de España*, edited by Agustín González Enciso and Juan Manuel Matés Blanco, 135–58. Barcelona: Ariel, 2006.

Torre Villar, Ernesto de la, and Ramiro Navarro de Anda, eds. *Instrucciones y memorias de los virreyes novohispanos*. México D.F.: Porrúa, 1991.

Traer, James. *Marriage and the Family in Eighteenth-Century France*. Ithaca: Cornell University Press, 1980.

Tratado de la defensa de las plazas que escrivio [sic] Mr. de Vauban . . . para la instrucción del . . . Duque de Borgoña; traducido de francés en español por Don Ignacio Sala . . . ; y augmentado con algunas reflexiones, y addiciones . . . . Cádiz: Pedro Gómez de Requena, 1743.

Trentian, Jacques de. "*French Regiments and American Independence*." At http://www.xenophongroup.com/mcjoynt/regts.htm. Accessed September 27, 2017.

Trigger, Bruce G., and William R. Swagerty. "Entertaining Strangers: North America in the Sixteenth Century." In *The Cambridge History of the Native Peoples of the Americas*, vol. 1, *North America*, edited by Bruce G. Trigger and Wilcomb E. Washburn, 325–98. New York: Cambridge University Press, 1996.

Trigger, Bruce G., and Wilcomb E. Washburn, eds. *The Cambridge History of the Native Peoples of the Americas*, vol. 1, *North America*. New York: Cambridge University Press, 1996.

Troxler, Caroline Watterson. "Loyalist Refugees and the British Evacuation of East Florida, 1783–1785." *Florida Historical Quarterly* 60 (July 1981): 1–28.

Trumbach, Randolph. *The Rise of the Egalitarian Family: Aristocratic Kinship and Domestic Relations in Eighteenth-Century England*. New York: Academic Press, 1978.

Tsouras, Peter G. *Warrior's Words: A Quotation Book: From Sesostris III to Schwarzkopf, 1871 BC to AD 1991*. London: Arms and Armour Press, 1992.

Tucker, Robert W., and David C. Hendrickson. *The Fall of the British Empire: Origins of the War of American Independence*. Baltimore: Johns Hopkins University Press, 1982.

Turner, Frederick Jackson. *The Frontier in American History*. New York: Henry Holt, 1920.

Ubiella, Vicente José. *Demostración que en la muy sentida y lamentable muerte del Excmo. Sr. conde de Gálvez, virrey . . . hizo den Vicente José Ubiella, escribano de cámara de la Real Audiencia*. México: Rangel, 1787.

Usner, Daniel H. "American Indians in Colonial New Orleáns." 2nd ver. In *The Louisiana Purchase Bicentennial Series in Louisiana History, Vol. 2: The Spanish Presence in Louisiana, 1763–1803*, edited by Gilbert C. Din, 296–306. Lafayette: Center for Louisiana Studies, University of Southwestern Louisiana, 1996.

———. "American Indians in Colonial New Orleans." In *Powhatan's Mantle: Indians in the Colonial Southeast*, edited by Gregory A. Waselkov, Peter H. Wood, and Thomas Hatley, 163–88. Lincoln: University of Nebraska Press, 2006. First published 1989.

———. *Indians Settlers and Slaves in a Frontier Exchange Economy through the Lower Mississippi Valley before 1783*. Chapel Hill: University of North Carolina Press, 1992.

———. "Rescuing Early America from Nationalist Narratives: An Intra-imperial Approach to Colonial Canada and Louisiana." *Historical Reflections* 4, no. 3 (2014): 1–19.

Vaca de Osma, José Antonio. *Carlos III*. Madrid: Rialp, 2005.

Vachon, André. "L'eau de vie dans la societe indienne." *Report of the Annual Meeting of the Canadian Historical Association* 39, no. 1 (1960): 22–32.

Valdelvira González, Gregorio. *Los militares ilustrados del siglo XVIII: Su contribución a las ciencias humanas y sociales*. Madrid: Ministerio de Defensa, 1996.

Valdés, Antonio J. *Historia de la Isla de Cuba y en especial de La Habana*. La Habana: Oficina de la Cena, 1813.

Valdés, Manuel Antonio. *Apuntes de algunas de las gloriosas acciones del Excmo. Señor don Bernardo de Gálvez, conde de Gálvez, virrey . . . hacíalos en un romance histórico, Don Manuel Antonio Valdés, autor de la Gazeta Mexicana*. México: Felipe de Zúñiga y Ontiveros, 1787.

———. *Gazetas de México, compendio de noticias de Nueva España, desde principios del año de 1784 dedicadas al Excmo. Señor D. Matías de Gálvez, Virrey, Gobernador y Capitán general de la misma*. Mexico: Felipe de Zúñiga y Ontiveros, circa 1785.

Valery S., Rafael. *Miranda en Pensacola*. Caracas[?]: Los Teques, 1991.

Valle-Arizpe, Artemio. *Virreyes y virreinas de la Nueva España*. Madrid: Espasa Calpe, 1933.

Varela Marcos, Jesús. "Los prolegómenos de la visita de José de Gálvez a la Nueva

España (1766): Don Francisco de Armona y la instrucción secreta del Marqués de Esquilache." *Revista de Indias* 46, no. 178 (1986): 453–70.

Varela Tortajada, Javier. "Nación, patria y patriotismo en los orígenes del nacionalismo español." *Studia historica: Historia contemporánea* 12 (1994): 31–43.

Vargas, José Mariano de. *Carta de pésame por el fallecimiento del Excmo. Sr. D. Bernardo de Gálvez, conde de Gálvez, virrey... dirigida a todos los súbditos del reino por el licenciado d. José Mariano de Vargas, agente fiscal de la Real Audiencia*. México: Felipe de Zúñiga y Ontiveros, 1787.

Vargas Lugo, Elisa. "Imágenes de la inmaculada concepción en la Nueva España." *Anuario de Historia de la Iglesia* 13 (2004): 67–78.

Vargas Machuca, Bernardo de. *Milicia y descripción de las Indias escrita por el capitán D. Bernardo de Vargas Machuca, caballero castellano, natural de la villa de Simancas, reimpresa fielmente, según la primera edición hecha en Madrid en 1599*. Madrid: Librería de Victoriano Suarez, 1892. First published 1599. English trans., *The Indian Militia and Description of the Indies*. Durham: Duke University Press, 2008.

Varona, Cándido. *Apuntes para un libro de historia y arte militar, entresacados de las mejores obras que tratan del mismo asunto*. Madrid: R. Vicente, 1870.

Varona, Frank de. *Bernardo de Gálvez*. Milwaukee: Raintree, 1990.

Vauban, Sébastien Le Prestre de. *De l'Attaque et de la défense des places, par M. de Vauban*. La Haye, 1732.

———. *Le triomphe de la méthode ou le Traité de l'attaque des places de monsieur de Vauban, ingénieur du roi*. Edited by Nicolas Faucherre and Philippe Prost. Paris: Découvertes-Gallimard, 1992.

Vázquez, Josefina Zoraida. "Los apaches y su leyenda." *Historia Mexicana* 24, no. 2 (1974): 161–76.

Vázquez de Acuña, Isidoro. "El capitán general don Matías de Gálvez." *Revista de Historia Militar* 21 (1966): 55–74.

———. "El Conde de Gálvez." *Revista de Historia Militar* 9 (1961): 51–89.

———. *Historial de la Casa de Gálvez y sus alianzas: Hechos ilustres de sus hijos en España, Italia, México, Guatemala, Perú, Chile y otros países del Viejo y Nuevo Mundo*. Madrid: M. Artes Gráficas Villena, 1974.

———. "El Ministro de Indias don José de Gálvez, Marqués de Sonora." *Revista de Indias* 19, nos. 77–78 (1959): 449–73.

Vázquez de Prada, Valentín ed. *Estudios de historia moderna y contemporánea: Homenaje a Federico Suárez Verdeguer*. Madrid: Rialp, 1991.

Vega González, Jesusa. *Ciencia, arte e ilusión en la España ilustrada*. Madrid: Consejo Superior de Investigaciones Científicas, 2010.

Vega Juanino, Josefa. *La institución militar en Michoacán en el último cuarto del siglo XVIII*. México D.F.: Colegio de Michoacán, 1986.

Vegas, Antonio. *Diccionario geográfico universal que comprehende la descripción de las cuatro partes del mundo; y de las Naciones, Imperios, Repúblicas y otros Estados, provincias, territorios, ciudades, villas y lugares memorables, lagos, ríos, desiertos, montañas, volcanes, mares, puertos, golfos, islas, penínsulas, istmos, bancos, cabos, etc... que se encuentra en el globo terráqueo*. Madrid: Francisco Martínez Dávila, 1815.

Velázquez Chávez, María del Carmen. "Los Apaches y su leyenda." *Historia Mexicana* 24, no. 2 (1974): 161–76.

———. *El estado de guerra en Nueva España, 1760–1808*. México D.F.: El Colegio de México, 1950.

———. *Tres estudios sobre las Provincias Internas de la Nueva España*. México D.F.: Colegio de México, 1979.

———, ed. *La frontera norte y la experiencia colonial*. México D.F.: Secretaría de Relaciones Exteriores, 1982.

Vélez de Escalante, Silvestre. *The Dominguez-Escalante Journal: Their Expedition through Colorado, Utah, Arizona, and New Mexico in 1776*. Edited by Ted J. Warner. Provo: Brigham Young University Press, 1976.

Ventura Beleña, Eusebio. *Recopilación Sumaria de todos los autos acordados de la Real Audiencia y Sala del Crimen de esta Nueva España y providencias de su Superior Gobierno: De varias Reales Cédulas y Órdenes que, después de publicada la Recopilación de Indias, han podido recogerse, así de las dirigidas a la misma Audiencia ó Gobierno, como de algunas otras que por sus notables decisiones convendrá no ignorar*. México: Felipe de Zúñiga y Ontiveros, 1787.

Vicens Vives, Jaume. *Historia de España y América*. Vol. 4, *Burguesía, industrialización, obrerismo*. Barcelona: Vicens Vives, 1961.

Vicente y Monzón, Ramón, *Relación de la obra del Acueducto de Málaga*. Madrid: Impr. de Andrés de Sotos, 1786.

Victoria, Pablo. *España contrataca: De cómo Bernardo Gálvez, solo, derrota a los ingleses y precipita la independencia de los Estados Unidos*. Barcelona: Áltera, 2007.

Vigil, Ralph H., Frances W. Kaye, and John R. Wunder, eds. *Spain and the Plains: Myths and Realities of Spanish Exploration and Settlement on the Great Plains*. Niwot: University Press of Colorado, 1994.

Vigness, David M. "Don Hugo O'Conor and New Spain's Northwestern Frontier, 1764-1776." *Journal of the West* 6 (January 1967): 27-40.

———. "Nuevo Santander in 1795: A Provisional Inspection by Félix Calleja." *Southwestern Historical Quarterly* 75, no. 4 (April 1972): 461-506.

Villacañas Berlanga, José Luis ed. *El siglo de Floridablanca (1728-1808): La España de las reformas*. Murcia: Universidad de Murcia, 2009.

Villalba Pérez, Enrique. "La Orden de Carlos III: ¿nobleza reformada?" In *Coloquio Internacional Carlos III y su Siglo: Actas, Poder y sociedad en la época de Carlos III*, 2:671-81. Madrid: Universidad Complutense, 1990.

Villalpando, José Manuel. *El Virrey*. México D.F.: Planeta Mexicana, 2002.

Villarejo, Esteban, and Manuel P. Villatoro. "Gálvez: El marino español que se aventuró 'solo' contra las defensas inglesas de Florida." *ABC* (Madrid), November 30, 2012.

Villaroel, Hipólito. *Enfermedades políticas que padece la capital de esta Nueva España en casi todos los cuerpos de que se compone y remedios que se le deben aplicar para su curación si se quiere que sea útil al Rey y al público* [1785]. Edited by Genaro Estrada and Aurora Arnaiz Amigo. México D.F.: Porrúa, 1979.

———. *México por dentro y fuera bajo el gobierno de los virreyes, o sea, Enfermedades políticas que padece la capital de la Nueva España en casi todos los cuerpos de que se compone, y remedios que se deben aplicar para su curación*. Edited by Carlos María de Bustamante. México D.F.: Alejandro Valdés, 1831.

Villegas de Echeverría, José. *Coloquio tierno y lastimosos ayes de la América en la muerte del Excmo. Sr. Conde de Gálvez, virrey*. México: Felipe de Zúñiga y Ontiveros, 1786.

———. *Felicidad de México en su mayor congoja por el dichoso natalicio de la señorita, hija segunda de los señores condes de Gálvez*. México: José de Jáuregui, 1787.

Villena, Elvira. "The First Spanish Military Decorations: Tomás Francisco Prieto's Al Mérito Medals." *The Medal* 36 (Spring 2000): 25-32.

Villiers du Terrage, Marc de. *Les dernières années de la Louisiane Française*. Paris: Guilmoto, 1905.

Vindel, Pedro. *Catálogo de la Librería de P. Vindel calle del Prado no. 9*. Madrid: P. Vindel, 1896.

Vinson, Ben, III. *Bearing Arms for His Majesty: The Free-Colored Militia in Colonial Mexico*. Stanford: Stanford University Press, 2001.

Viqueira Albán, Juan Pedro. *¿Relajados y reprimidos? Diversiones públicas y vida social en la ciudad de México durante el Siglo de las Luces*. México D.F.: Fondo de Cultura Económica, 2005.

Voltes Bou, Pedro. *Carlos III y su tiempo*. Barcelona: Juventud, 1988.

———. "La tentativa de mediación de España en la guerra de independencia de los Estados Unidos." *Revista de Indias* 27 (1967): 313-34.

Vos, Jan de. *Vivir en frontera: La experiencia de los indios de Chiapas*. México D.F.: CIESAS-INI, 1994.

Waddington, Richard. *La Guerre des Sept Ans, Histoire diplomatique et militaire*. Paris: Firmin-Didot, 1899-1914.

Walker, Deward E. "Ethnology and History." *Idaho Yesterdays* 4, no. 1 (1970): 24-29.

Wallace, Nesbit Willoughby. *A Regimental Chronicle and List of Officers of the 60th, or the King's, Royal Rifle Corps, Formerly the 62nd Royal American Regiment of Foot*. London: Harrison, 1879.

Ward, Christopher. *The War of the Revolution*. New York: Skyhorse, 2011. First published 1952.

Ward, Robert J. "Los Estados Unidos y sus intereses en las colonias españolas: La Nueva España." *Estudios de Historia Moderna y Contemporánea de México* 4 (1972): 63-93.

Warhus, Mark. *Another America: Native Maps and the History of Our Land*. New York: St. Martin's Press, 1997.

Wartelet, Jorge d'. *Diccionario militar, contiene las voces técnicas, términos, locuciones y modismos antiguos y modernos de los ejércitos de mar y tierra*. Madrid: Luis Palacios, 1863.

Washburn, Wilcomb E. "Indians and the American Revolution." AmericanRevolution.org, http://www.americanrevolution.org (accessed April 21, 2016).

Wasserman, Fabio. "El concepto de nación y las transformaciones del orden político en Iberoamérica, 1750-1850." In *Diccionario político y social del mundo iberoamericano: La era de las revoluciones, 1750-1850. (Iberconceptos-I)*, edited by Javier Fernández Sebastián, 1:851-69. Madrid: Fundación Carolina / Sociedad Estatal de Conmemoraciones Culturales / Centro de Estudios Políticos y Constitucionales, 2009.

Waters, Frank. *Book of the Hopi*. New York: Viking Press, 1963.

Watson, Alan. *Slave Law in the Americas*. Athens: University of Georgia Press, 1989.

Watson, Thomas D. "A Scheme Gone Awry: Bernardo de Gálvez, Gilberto Antonio de Maxent, and the Southern Indian Trade." In *The Louisiana Purchase Bicentennial Series in Louisiana History, Vol. 2: The Spanish Presence in Louisiana, 1763-1803*, edited by Gilbert C. Din, 307-16. Lafayette: Center for Louisiana Studies, University of Southwestern Louisiana, 1996.

Way, Segyi, "Asymmetric Warfare." *Army Guide*. http://www.army-guide.com (accessed March 21, 2015).

Wayland, Virginia, Harold Wayland, and Alan Ferg. *Playing Cards of the Apaches: A Study in Cultural Adaptation*. Tucson: Screenfold Press, 2006.

Weber, David J. *Bárbaros, Spaniards and Their Savages in the Age of Enlightenment.* New Haven: Yale University Press, 2005.

———. *The Spanish Frontier in North America.* New Haven: Yale University Press, 1992. Spanish trans., *La frontera española en América del Norte.* México D.F.: Fondo de Cultura Económica, 2000.

———. "The Spanish Legacy in North America and the Historical Imagination." *Western Historical Quarterly* 23, no. 1 (February 1992): 5-24.

Webre, Stephen. "The Problem of Indian Slavery in Spanish Louisiana, 1769-1803." *Louisiana History: The Journal of the Louisiana Historical Association* 25 (Spring 1984): 117-35. Also in *The Louisiana Purchase Bicentennial Series in Louisiana History, Vol. 2: The Spanish Presence in Louisiana, 1763-1803,* edited by Gilbert C. Din, 352-65. Lafayette: Center for Louisiana Studies, University of Southwestern Louisiana, 1996.

Weddle, Robert S. *Changing Tides: Twilight and Dawn in the Spanish Sea, 1763-1803.* College Station: Texas A&M University Press, 1995.

———. "Galvez Crossings on the Pecos River." *Handbook of Texas Online,* www.tshaonline.org.

Weeks, Charles A. *Paths to a Middle Ground: The Diplomacy of Natchez, Boukfouka, Nogales, and San Fernando de las Barrancas, 1791-1795.* Tuscaloosa: University of Alabama Press, 2005.

Weir, David Stanley. "Ruin of Ruins: (Re)building Myth and Memory in Menard, Texas." Master's diss., Texas Tech University, 2004.

Wescott, Allan, ed. *Mahan on Naval Warfare: Selections from the Writings of Rear Admiral Alfred Thayer Mahan.* Boston: Little, Brown, 1941.

West, Elizabeth Howard. "The Indian Policy of Galvez." *Proceedings of the Mississippi Valley Historical Association* 8 (1914-15): 95-101.

———, ed. and trans. "Bonilla's Brief Compendium of the History of Texas (1772)." *Texas Historical Association Quarterly* 8 (1904): 3-78.

Wharton, Francis, ed. *Revolutionary Diplomatic Correspondence of the United States.* 6 vols. Washington, D.C.: Government Printing Office, 1889.

Whitaker, Arthur Preston. "Antonio de Ulloa." *Hispanic American Historical Review* 15, no. 2 (May 1935): 155-94.

———. "The Commerce of Louisiana and the Floridas at the End of the Eighteenth Century." In *The Louisiana Purchase Bicentennial Series in Louisiana History, Vol. 2: The Spanish Presence in Louisiana, 1763-1803,* edited by Gilbert C. Din, 219-28. Lafayette: Center for Louisiana Studies, University of Southwestern Louisiana, 1996.

———. *Documents Relating to the Commercial Policy of Spain in the Floridas, with Incidental Reference to Louisiana.* Deland: Florida State Historical Society, 1931.

White, Richard. *"It's Your Misfortune and None of My Own": A New History of the American West.* Norman: University of Oklahoma Press, 1991.

———. *The Middle Ground: Indians, Empires, and Republics in the Great Lakes Region, 1650-1815.* New York: Cambridge University Press, 1991.

———. *The Roots of Dependency: Subsistance, Environment, and Social Change among the Choctaws, Pawnees, and Navajos.* Lincoln: University of Nebraska Press, 1983.

White, Sophie. "Geographies of Slave Consumption: French Colonial Louisiana and a World of Goods." *Winterthur Portfolio* 45, no. 2/3 (2011): 229-48.

———. "'To Ensure That He Not Give Himself Over to the Indians': Cleanliness, Frenchification, and Whiteness." *Journal of Early American History* 2, no. 2 (2012): 111-49.

———. "'Wearing Three or Four Handkerchiefs around His Collar, and Elsewhere about Him': Slaves' Constructions of Masculinity and Ethnicity in French Colonial New Orleans." *Gender and History* 15, no. 3 (2003): 528-49.
———. *Wild Frenchmen and Frenchified Indians: Material Culture and Race in Colonial Louisiana*. Philadelphia: University of Pennsylvania Press, 2012.
Wilcox, William Bradford. *Portrait of a General: Sir Henry Clinton in the War of Independence*. New York: Knopf, 1964.
Williams, Harold D. "Bernardo de Gálvez and the Western Patriots." *Revista de Historia de América* 65-66 (1968): 53-70.
Williams, Jack S., and Robert L. Hoover. *Arms of the Apacheria: A Comparison of Apachean and Spanish Fighting Techniques in the Later Eighteenth Century*. Greeley: Museum of Anthropology, University of Northern Colorado, 1983.
Willie, Leroy Ellis. *Spanish and Natives of Louisiana Who Served under General Don Bernardo de Galvez in His Campaigns against the British*. Baton Rouge: God Country Heritage, 1996.
Wilson, James Grant, and John Fiske, eds. *Appleton's Cyclopaedia of American Biography*. New York: Appleton, 1888.
Wissler, Clark. "The Diffusion of Horse Culture among the North American Indians." *Proceedings of the National Academy of Sciences of the United States of America* 1 (April 1915): 254-56.
Wood, Peter H. "The Changing Population of the Colonial South: An Overview by Race and Region, 1685-1790." In *Powhatan's Mantle: Indians in the Colonial Southeast*, edited by Gregory A. Waselkov, Peter H. Wood, and Thomas Hatley, 57-132. Lincoln: University of Nebraska Press, 2006. First published 1989.
Woodward, Ralph Lee Jr., ed. and trans. *Tribute to Don Bernardo de Gálvez: Royal Patents and an Epic Ballad Honoring the Spanish Governor of Louisiana*. Baton Rouge / New Orleans: The Historic New Orleans Collection, 1979.
Worcester, Donald E. *The Apaches: Eagles of the Southwest*. Norman: University of Oklahoma Press, 1992.
———. "The Apaches in the History of the Southwest." *New Mexico Historical Review* 50, no. 1 (1975): 25-44.
———. "Early Spanish Accounts of the Apache Indians." *American Anthropologist*, n.s., no. 2, part. 1 (April-June 1941): 308-12.
———, ed. *Instruction for Governing the Interior Provinces of New Spain, 1786*. Berkeley: Quivira Society, 1951.
———, ed. "Miranda's Diary of the Siege of Pensacola, 1781." *Florida Historical Quarterly* 29, no. 3 (January 1951): 163-96.
World War II Veterans' Survey. Carlisle, Pa.: U.S. Army Military History Institute, U.S. Army War College.
Worsley, Richard. *Museum Worsleyanum; or a Collection of Antique Basso-Relievos, Bustos, Statues, and Gems*. London, 1794-1803.
Wright, J. Leitch. "British East Florida: Loyalist Bastion." In *Eighteenth-Century Florida: The Impact of the American Revolution*, edited by Samuel Proctor, 1-13. Gainesville: University Presses of Florida, 1978.
———. *Florida in the American Revolution*. Gainesville: University Presses of Florida, 1975.
———. "Lord Dunmore's Loyalist Asylum in the Floridas." *Florida Quarterly* 49 (1971): 370-99.
Yajima, Noboyuki, Naoki Izutsu, Takeshi Imamura, and Toyoo Abe. *Scientific*

Ballooning, Technology and Applications of Exploration Balloons in the Stratosphere and the Atmospheres of Other Planets. New York: Springer, 2009.

Yela Utrilla, Juan F. *España ante la independencia de los Estados Unidos*. Lérida: Academia Mariana, 1925.

Young, Perry. *Don Matías de Gálvez in Guatemala and His Son, the Count Bernardo*. S.l.: United Fruit Company, 1936.

Young, Peter. *Blücher´s Army, 1813-1815*. Illustrated by Michael Roffe. Oxford: Osprey, 1973.

Zabala, Silvio. *Ideario de Vasco de Quiroga*. México D.F.: Colegio de México, 1941.

Zahino Peñafort, Luisa. "La cuestión indígena en el IV Concilio Provincial Mexicano." *Relaciones: Estudios de Historia y Sociedad* 12, no. 45 (1991): 5-31.

———. *Iglesia y sociedad en México, 1765-1800: Tradición, reforma y reacciones*. México D.F.: Universidad Nacional Autónoma de México, 1996.

Zapatero, Juan Manuel. "Del castillo de San Fernando de Omoa." *Revista de Indias* 13 (1953): 277-306.

Zazo y Ortega, Ramón. *Blasón y genealogía de la casa de los Gálvez de Macharaviaya*. Málaga: Diputación Provincial de Málaga, 1972. First published 1771.

Zepeda Cortés, María Bárbara. "El *socio incómodo* del ministro: La carrera burocrática del comerciante Pedro Antonio de Cossío en Nueva España durante la era Gálvez (1765-1787)." In *De la Colonia al Estado Moderno: Ruptura, cambios y continuidades*, edited by José Alfredo Uribe Salas and Abel Padilla Jacobo, 427-42. Morelia, Michoacán: Universidad Michoacana de San Nicolás de Hidalgo, 2009.

Zinn, Howard. *A People's History of the United States: 1492-Present*. New York: Longman, 1980.

Zuno, José Guadalupe. *Historia de la Caricatura en México*. México D.F.: Universidad de Guadalajara, 1961.

Index

✳ ✳ ✳

Page numbers in *italics* refer to figures, tables, maps, or graphs.

Abarca, Silvestre, 20
Acadians, 17, 118, 123, 126
Acculturation, 309, 313. *See also* Assimilation
Acosta Rodríguez, Antonio, 110, 121
Acton, John, 71, 72
Acuña, Juan de, 38
Adams, John, 172–73
Aerostatic machines, 5, 274–77, *275, 276–77*, 474n172. *See also* Hot-air balloons
Africanism, Spanish, 69
African policy of Spain, 68–70
Agenois Regiment of France, d', 218, 454n220
Agriculture in Louisiana, 115, 126–27
Aguayo, house of, 274, 474n170
Aguilar Piñal, Francisco, 273
Aguirre, Manuel de, 65, 66
Alabardiers Corps, 288, 291, 292
Alamán, Lucas, 341
Albi, Julio, 18
Alcohol, 101, 102, 142, 312, 313, 320. *See also* Liquor
Aldea de la Mobila, 188–90. *See also* Mobile Village
Alderete, Miguel de, 203–4
Algiers, military expedition against: background of, 68–70, 408n62; disembarkation and attacks, 71–74, *74*, 409n83; preparations and deployment for, 70–71; reembarkation and conclusions of, 73–78
Allegiance to Spain, 98, 105, 111, 117, 180
Allen, William, 206
Al mérito medals, 103–4, *105*, 158, 418n184
Alsuvide, Jayme, 33–34
Álvarez, Francisco, 273
Álvarez, Julián, 151

Alzate, José Antonio de, 300, 319, 331
Ambulodi y Arriola, Teresa, 134
Amebiasis, 337
"American Crisis, The" (Paine), 80
American Revolution, *271*; background of, 80–82; contribution of Indians to, 181–83, 184–85; as a global war, 4–5; Seven Years' War and, 17. *See also* Spain and the American Revolution
American soldiers, 327–28
America's Dragoons, 218, 453n214
Amores Carredano, Juan Bosco, 278
Anderson, Fred, 17
Andrade, Rosa María, 302
Andreu Ocariz, Juan José, 90
Antigua, 257
Anza, Juan Bautista de, 310
Anzara, Félix de, 312
"Apache problem," 36–37, 397n117
Apachería, 35–36
Apaches, 34–36, 396n94, 396n99; Bernardo on, 58–61, 107–8; combat tactics of, 58–59; *Instrucción formada en virtud de Real Orden de S.M.* and, 309–12, 313–14, 316–18; realism and perception and, 39–42, *40*
Apaches, campaigns against: assessments of, 55–61; background of, 26–29, 36–42; in Nueva Vizcaya, 44–45, 50–53; objectives of, 29–32; Spanish policy and, 42–44
Aragon Regiment, Spanish, 90, 218, 451n214
Aranda, Count of: Algiers military campaign and, 69, 70; Felicitas de Gálvez and, 348; Seven Years' War and, 15; as Spanish ambassador to France, 82, 129, 140–41; Treaty of Paris and, 259–60, 261–62, 263–65

[585]

Aranda Plan, 262
Archer, Christon I., 325, 327
Arena, Richard C., 122
Arévalo, Antonio de, 20
Argelejos, Count of, 62
Arístegui, Pedro de, 130
Aristizábal, Gabriel de, 177, 178
Armillas Vicente, José Antonio, 129, 134
Armona, Francisco de, 10, 21-22, 32
Army in America, Spanish, 18-20; Americanization of, 326-28, 342, 490-91n316.
    See also specific military campaigns of
Arredondo, Nicolás, 279
Arredondo López, Maria Adelina, 318
Arriaga, Julián de, 51, 76
Arrows, 59, 101, 313-14
Art de la guerre changée par l'usage de machines aéristatiques, L', 274-75
Arte de hablar bien francés (Chantreau), 66
Articles of capitulation: of siege of Mobile, 171, 174; of siege of Pensacola, 2, 192, 224, 230-35, 238-39, 246, 263
Artillery units in Louisiana, 93
Art of Writing exhibition, 345
Assimilation: of Indians, 307, 310, 313, 318, 485n185; policies of Spain, 7, 42, 55
Asturias, Prince of, 296, 480n114
Atakapa Indians, 94, 105, 126
Audiencias in New Spain: Bernardo and, 22, 296-97, 335, 337, 338; *gañanes* and, 305; Guatemala and, 13, 42, 250; royal houses renovations and, 322, 323
Auler, Miguel, 62
Aunoy, Nicolás Favre D', 94
Avilés Flores, Pablo, 286
Azanza, Miguel José de, 46-48, 50

Babcock, Matthew, 318
Bahamas, 4, 252-55, 260, 377-78, 423n293
Bails, Benito, 65
Balearic Islands, 239, 459n312
Bambiteli, Francisco, 322-23
Banks, Joseph, 275, 276, 277
Barataria, 125
"Barbaric Indians" term, 307, 392n36, 485n185
Barbilampiños, 5, 66-67
Barbuda, 257
Barcelona, Cirilo de, 128, 133, 270

Bartolache, José Ignacio, 331
Baton Rouge, 123, 149, 150-53
Bautista Degruis, Juan, 126
Bayagoulas, 126
Baynton, Benjamin, 189
Bay of Bengal, 5
Beauvau-Craon, Charles Juste de, 15
Becerril, Diego de, 32, 44
Beerman, Eric, 346, 347
Béla, Chevalier de (Jeanne-Philippe de Béla), 15, 390n27
Belling, Wilhelm Sebastian von, 13
Berrotarán, José de, 38-39
Betancourt y Molina, Agustín de, 276
Biloxi Indians, 105
Black, John, 340, 495n1
Blackhawk, Ned, 314
Blacks, 94, 112-13, 114-15, 218
Blacks, Battalion of Havana Free, 218, 453n214
Blumenthal, Walter Hart, 345
Bolton, Herbert Eugene, 100
Bonet, Juan Bautista, 152, 174, 175-76, 177-79, 196, 240-41
Books, forbidden, 285, 286-87
Borders and Treaty of Paris, 262-63, 266-67
Botany, 331-32
Bouligny, Francisco de, 119-20, 122, 123-25, 131, 167-68
Bourbon reforms, 250, 260-61, 470n108
Boussuge, Hains, 132
Bows and arrows, 59, 101, 313-14
Boyd, Mark F., 183
Brant, Joseph, 182
Brasseaux, Carl A., 128
Braudel, Fernand, 69
Britain: Cartegena and, 19; debt of, 259, 469n98; Florida and, 387n2; Indians and, 99-100, 181-82, 183-84, 185, 227, 417-18n149; trade and, 97-98. *See also* Spain and war with Britain
Britania and Her Daughter—A Song, 162
British Lion Engaging Four Powers, The, 254
Brooks, James F., 310
Bucareli y Ursúa, Antonio María de, 42, 53, 54, 55, 56-57, 284, 342, 345
Buena y Alcalde, Mariano Antonio de, 46
Bullfighting, 51, 288, 290-92, 323, 478n69.
    See also Corridas

Burdon, George, 153
Burke, Edmund, 233
Bustamante, Carlos María Cavo, 291, 298, 341
Bustillo, Fernando, 29

Cabarrús, Francisco, 347–48
Cabildo of New Orleans, 110, 115–17
Cagigal, Juan Manuel de: Armesto and, 86; Jamaica and, 249–50, 251; New Providence and, 253, 255; Pensacola siege and, 192, 195, 214, 224, 228, 241
Calderón Cuadrado, Reyes, 141
Caledonian Mercury, 173
California, 26, 314
Calles Montaño, David Jacobo, 28
Calloway, Colin G., 100, 181, 182, 185
Calvo, José, 197–99, 200, 202–4, 228
Cambresis Regiment, French, 218, 454n220
Cameron, Alexander, 184, 186
Campbell, James, 246
Campbell, John (British General): on Bernardo, 211–12; dislike of West Florida of, 210–11; Indians and, 184, 185–86; Mobile and, 168, 170, 171; Natchez and, 84, 245, 246; New Orleans and, 146, 149, 152; Pensacola presiege and, 179, 191, 197, 202–3, 207, 209–11, 212, 216; Pensacola siege and, 219, 223, 225, 234, 235
Campbell, John (merchant smuggler), 98
Campillo y Cossío, José, 312
Canary Islands: Bernardo and, 13; immigration from, 91, 120–21, 123, 125, 146
Capace, Raimundo Minutolo, 347
Capmany, Jerónimo de, 65
Capuchin Friars, Order of the, 128
Carillo, Francisco, 335
Carlisle, Jeffrey D., 43
Carlos III (king of Spain), 64, 81; about, 18, 342, 390n41; Africa policy of, 68–69; Bernardo and, 152, 175, 242, 283; Britain and, 137, 138; on commemorative medals, 329; Jesuit expulsion and, 24; Louisiana and, 117; religion and, 283; Seven Years' War and, 14
Carlos IV (king of Spain), 138
Carlos V (king of Spain), 21, 68
Caron de Beaumarchais, Pierre-Augustin, 82

Carr, Henry, 302
Carriages, 295, 300, 479n103
Cartagena de Indias, 13, 19, 20
Carvajal, José de, 38
Casas, Bartolomé de las, 106
Castañeda, José de, 327
Castaño de Sosa, Gaspar, 36
Casualties: of Algiers expedition, 73, 75; of Apache campaigns, 52–53; of attack along the Mississippi, 150, 151; in Mobile, 189, 442n63; of Pensacola siege, 202, 222, 225–27, 226, 455n239
Catalonia Volunteers Light Infantry Regiment, Spanish, 218, 451n214
Catholicism: indigenous peoples and, 39, 42; in Louisiana, 111, 128–30; slavery and, 113, 117; Spanish reformation and, 283
Caughey, John Walton: on attacks along the Mississippi, 149, 154; on Jamaica, 269; on Louisiana, 85, 88; on Mobile campaign, 163, 169, 171; on Natchez revolt, 245, 247; on Pensacola siege, 175, 184, 201; on trade, 95, 97, 98
Cavallo, Tiberius, 275
Cavalry: Algiers campaign and, 69, 72, 73; Apache campaigns and, 31; in Louisiana, 93, 94–95, 415n97; New Spain military reform and, 315, 316, 325, 326, 328; Royal Cantabre Regiment and, 15; Royal Military Academy and, 65–66
Cavalry Company of Saint Louis, 94
Caymán (Spanish ship), 229
Cazenonpoint, 103–4
Ceballos, Pedro de, 70
Censor, 239
Censuses: of Louisiana, 93, 106, 110, *111*, 125; of Mexico City, 318–19. *See also* Population counts
Cerro Prieto, 28, 29, 30
Cervantes, Miguel de, 125
Céspedes del Castillo, Guillermo, 18
Cevallos, Pedro de, 20
Chadwick, Ensor, 260
Chalmers, Hamilton, 244, 461n343
Chalmers, James, 206
Chantreau, Pierre Nicolás, 66
Chapultepec, Royal Palace at, 321, 322–24, 324, 343–45, *344*
Chapultepec Hill, 322, 343

INDEX [587

Charleston, 118, 230
Charrúa Indians, 313
Cherokee Indians, 181, 182–83
Chester, Peter, 85, 206, 207, *208*, 210, 234, 235
Chichimeca revolt, 36–37
Chickasaw Indians, 180–81, 184
Chihuahua, 35, 44–45, 50–53, 54–55, 56
Choctaw Indians, 105–6, 180–81, 184, 185–88
Chouteau, Jean Pierre, 107
Chroniques de la régence d'Alger, 74
Churchill, Winston, 389n21, 396n98
Church of San Fernando, 337, 338, 339
Cimarrones, 116–17
Cis, Guillermo de, 46
Clinton, Henry, 207
Coartación, 114–15
Coats of arms: of Count of Gálvez, 202, *243*, 338; of Louisiana Fixed Infantry Regiment, *92*; of Spanish Louisiana, *109*
Cock, William, 253
Cocks, Charles, 233, 457n273
Code noir, 113–14, 116
Coffee shops, 286
Colbert, James, 247, 248
Colley, Linda, 261
Colonization, 26, 43, 117–21, 312, 319
Comanche Indians, 36, 43, 54, 58, 310
Comandancia general de las provincias internas, 39
Combat tactics, 58–59, 61, 154, 316–17
Commemorative medals, 329, *330*, 345
Committee of Commerce of Continental Congress, 138–39, 140
Committee on Indian Affairs of Continental Congress, 184
Communications interception, 83–84
Company of Louisiana, 93, 415nn97–98
Conquest by contract, 104
Conrotte, Manuel, 260
Continental Congress: American Revolution and, 80; Bernardo and, 2, 140, 159; Committee of Commerce of, 138–39, 140; Indians and, 184–85; Mississippi River navigation and, 265; Spain and, 138, 142, 160–61, 172–73
Contraband trade, 6, 95–98, 112, 127, 131, 234
Cordero, Antonio, 40
Córdoba, Fernando de, 335

Córdoba, Luis de, 240–41
Coronado, Francisco de, 36
Corridas, 51, 288, 290–92, 323, 478n69. *See also* Bullfighting
Corruption in presidios, 38
Cortés, Hernán, 37
Cortés, José, 41
Cossío, José, 33
Cossío, Pedro Antonio de, 29, 48
Council of the Indies, 22, 131, 306, 323
Count de Gálvez title, 242, *243*, 297, 347
Counterintelligence, 83, 84
Countess de Galvez (merchant ship), 447n219
Courrier d'Avignon, 173, 234, 236–38
Court of Mining of Mexico, 329
Creagh, Francisco and Tomás, 279
Creek Indians, 180–81, 183–84, 233, 440n12
Creoles: Bernardo and, 6, 60; as a free population, 112; in military, 91–93, 94–95; women, 132–33, *135*
Creole womanhood, myth of, 132
Creolization, 134–36
Crespo, Francisco Antonio, 325, 326, 328
Crimes, second-class, 47
Critical Review, or, Annals of Literature, 277
Croix, Marquis de (Carlos Francisco de Croix), 284; Bernardo and, 32, 34, 44, 56; as viceroy of New Spain, 23, 24–26, 51, 52, 56
Croix, Teodoro de, 23, 24, 57, *282*, 399n134
Cruillas, Marquis de (Joaquin de Montserrat), 22, 23, 325, 327
Cruzat, Francisco, 105, 117, 247
Cruz Barney, Óscar, 328
Cuauhtlatoatzin, Juan Diego, 283
Cuba, 108, 119; Aranda plan and, 262; Bernardo as governor of, 5, 278–80, 476n203; siege of Mobile and, 174; siege of Pensacola and, 175–76, 214, 241; slavery in, 114; Treaty of Paris and, 262. *See also* Havana, Cuba
Cucaña, 290, 292, 478n69
Cuddalore, battle of, 5
Cuéllar, Lope de, 32–33, 44–45, 46, 57
Cuerpos fijos, 18, 19

Dagobert, Friar, 128
Dalrymple, William, 66–67

Dancing, 289, 294
Darby, William, 132
Dauphin Island, 188
Deans, Robert, 209, 246
Death, commonality of, 11
Debt certificates, 143–44
Delavillebeuvre, Juan, 117, 152
Delaware Indians, 119
De l'esprit des lois (Montesqueiu), 312
Demographic imperialism, 318
Derby Mercury, 235
Desdén con desdén se paga (Moreto), 288
Diario curioso de México de d. José Gómez, cabo de alabarderos, 288
Díaz de la Vega, Silvestre, 289
Dickson, Alexander, 84, 212, 245
Dieu et les nayades du fleuve St. Louis, Le (Poydras), 134
Din, Gilbert C., 88, 112, 116, 123
Discipline of slaves, 116
Discurso sobre el estado actual de la abogacia en los tribunales de la nacion (Covarrubias), 273
Discurso sobre la policía de Mexico (Guevara), 319
Diseases, 19, 302
Divide and conquer policy, 310
Don Quixote (Cervantes), 125
Dragging Canoe, 183
Dragones de la cuera, 316
Dragoons, 93, 315
Dress in Louisiana, *135*, 136
Dunbar-Nelson, Alice Moore, 136
Durnford, Elias, 166–69, 170–71
Dutch Republic, 4–5
DuVal, Kathleen, 107

Eccentric Typography (Blumenthal), 345
Echeveste, José de, 55
Economic Societies of Friends of the Country, 64–65, 121, 273
Economic Society of Basque Country, 65
Eduardo, Miguel, 85–86
Effusions du coeur, ou entretiens spirituels et affectifs d'une âme avec Dieu (Morel), 287
Ejército de dotación, 18, 19
Ejército de refuerzo, 18, 19
Eleta, Joaquín de, 69
Elizondo, Domingo, 30, 31

Elliott, John H., 100, 319
Elogios poéticos que a los insignes hechos del Excmo. Sr. Don Bernardo de Gálvez (Granados), 298
Elorza, Antonio, 63
Empires of the Atlantic World (Elliott), 319
Encomienda system, 304, 484n172
Enconomienda of Bolaños of the Order of Calatrava, 272, 336, 472n151
Encyclopedia, 286
Encyclopédia, ou dictionnaire raisonné des sciences, des arts et des métiers (Diderot and D'Alembert), 286
Enfermedades politicas que padece la capital de esta Nueva España (Villaroel), 319
Engineers, military, 19–20
English Review, or, An Abstract of English and Foreign Literature for the Year 1789, 277
Enlightenment: arts, sciences, and leisure time and, 290, 292, 312, 319, 329, 331; Bernardo and, 5, 6, 286, 289, 318; childhood and family and, 324; education and, 64, 65; French influence on, 285, 347; Indians and, *40*, 41, 43, 312; war and, 235
Epidemics, 123, 302–3
Épître á Don Bernard de Galvez (Poydras), 134
Escudero, José Antonio, 261
Eslava, Sebastián de, 19
España Regiment, 151–52, 161, 172
Espinosa Cortés, Luz María, 302
Esquilache, Marquis de, 21–22
Essai général de tactique (Count de Guibert), 65
Estachería, Francisco, 78
Estrehan y Saint-Maxent, Adelaide d', 131, 257, 272, 335, 336, 347, 348
Eulogies, 342–43
Evia, José de, 123, 270
Exclusion, policy of, 100
Ezpeleta, José de, 67, *187*; as governor of Cuba, 280; as governor of Mobile, 185–88, 189–90; Pensacola and, 179, 192, 194, 197, 212, 222, 228; as provincial governor of Louisiana and Florida, 270; reform of New Spain army and, 325–26, 328; siege of Mobile and, 175–77, 179, 180
Ezquerra, Ramón, 131

INDEX [589

Fabianism, 138
Fabris, Felipe, 287
Fainí, José de, 44-45, 51, 52
Fair American (American corsair ship), 225, 229-30
Faloris, Felipe, 287
Famille creole, La (Lussan), 132
Family Compacts, 137
Famine, 298-304, 321-22, 480n122
Farmar, Robert Adolphus, 191, 219
Faveau, Antonio, 46, 48, 50, 402n198
Favrot, Pedro José, 153
Felipe II (king of Spain), 43, 313
Felipe IV (king of Spain), 106
Ferguson, John, 139
Fernández, Francisco, 331
Fernández Armesto, Bertolomé, 86-87
Fernán-Núñez, Count of, 69, 71
Ferrer del Río, Antonio, 69
Figueroa, Benito Pardo de, 347, 348
Figuerola, Pablo, 222
Fisher, David Hackett, 80
Fixed Infantry Battalion of Louisiana, 89, 90, 431n64
Fixed Infantry Regiment of Louisiana, 78, 79, 90-95, 92, 112, 121, 158-59
Flags: British, *158*; regimental, 92
Flanders Valon Infantry Regiment, 218, 452n214
Flax, 120, 126
Flon Tejada, Manuel, 286, 338
Flores, Juan Antonio, 303-4
Florescano, Enrique, 285
Flores Maldonado, Manuel Antonio, 317
Florida: Britain and, 387n2; Loyalist refugees and, 118, 119; Spanish population of, 119, 423n293; Spanish subsidies for, 108; Treaty of Paris and, 87, 260, 262-63. *See also* Pensacola; Pensacola and the war with Britain
Floridablanca, Count of (José Moñino y Redondo), 137, 138, 259-60, 336
Fort Bute, 149-50
Fort Carlota, 175
Fort Charlotte, 166-71, 179, 436n154
Fort Condé, 166
Fort George, 207-9, 218-19, 224-25, 449n167, 456n251, 460n332
Fortifications and Spanish reform, 19-20

Fort Manchac, 149-50
Fort Panmure, 151, 152-53, 246
Fossat, Guy Soniat du, 132, 426n393
France: American Revolution and, 4-5, 138, 141, 429n35; Battle of the Saints and, 255-56; debt of, 259; Indian policy of, 99-100, 417-18n149; Louisiana and, 87; Seven Year's War and, 17; Spain's war against Britain and, 145-46, 218, 248-49, 251-52, 256-57, 454n220; trade and, 96, 98
Franciscans, 28
Franklin, Benjamin, 82, *254*, 265, 269
Frederick II (king of Prussia), 5
Free blacks, 94, 112-13, 114-15
Freedom suits, 107, 115, 422n257
Freemasonry, 285, 287, 342
French Revolution, 347
Fuente, Vicente de la, 67
Fuentes, Concepción Valenzuela, 125, 134

Gachupines, 112, 327
Galbis Díez, María del Carmen, 304, 323
Galveston, Texas, 2, 123
Gálvez, Antonio de, 272, 346
Gálvez, Bernardo de: Algiers expedition and, 68, 71, 73; Apache campaigns and, 30-32, 35, 44, 45, 50-53, 54-56, 57-61; arrival in New Spain of, 32, 394-95n73; becoming a Creole, 134-36; birth and childhood of, 9-10, 11-13; "black legend" of, 287, 340-45, 346; books of, 286-87; burial of, 337-38; care of subordinates by, 155-56, 157-58, 171-72, 241, 295, 437n183; as colonel and acting governor in Louisiana (*See* Louisiana, Bernardo de Gálvez as colonel and acting governor in); dossiers processed by, 332-33, *333*; estate of, 336; fall of the Gálvez clan after death of, 346-48; in the French army, 13-14, 15, 17; funeral of, 337-38; funeral incident of, 294-95; genealogy interest of, 274; as governor of Cuba, 5, 278-80, 476n203; in Havana, 190, 193-96; hobbies and interests of, 5, 274-48, 295; honors and official recognitions of, 2, 229, 242, 272; illness and death of, 333-39, 342-43; José de Gálvez's mental illness and, 46, 48-49, 50, 401n174; journal of, 192-93, 212, 444n90; last will and testament of, 335-

590]   INDEX

36, 337, 492n356; marriage of, 133–34; military capabilities and mindset of, 155, 295–96; music, love for, 76, 295; overview of, 2, 4, 5–8; and partying, 294; personal life in Louisiana of, 130, 131, 133–34; popularity of, 147–48, 229, 278, 296–98, 303–4, 342–43; poisoning, legend of, 336–37, 493n364; portraits of, *3*, *247*, *258*, 345; promotions of, 33–34, 78, 79, 159, 240–41, 277–78; Royal Military Academy and, 63, 78; schedule of, 288; secret plan of to siege Pensacola, 194–96; in Seville Infantry Regiment, 62–63, 76, 78; support for American rebels by, 139–40, 141–42; theater attendance by, 288–89, 290; U.S. honorary citizenship of, 2

Gálvez, Bernardo de, as viceroy of New Spain, 281–339; *Afrancesamiento* of, 285–88; army reform and, 324–28, 341, *379–80*; becoming and arrival of, 279–80, 281–84; bullfighting and, 290–92; everyday business of, 332–33, *333*, *381*; funeral incident of, 294–95; governing of Mexico City by, 318–24; Indian labor and *solicitadores* policy and, 304–7; *Instrucción formada envirtud de Real Orden de S.M.* of (*See Instrucción formada envirtud de Real Orden de S.M.*); military mindset of, 295–96; overview of, 6–7; partying of, 294; popularity of, 296–98; prisoners' pardon of, 292–93; promotion of arts and sciences by, 288–89, 329–32; style of governance of, 284–85; theater and, 288–89; walking of, 292; year of the hunger and, 298–304, 480n122

Gálvez, Feliciana Saint-Maxent de, 131–32, 133–34, *297*, 335, 336, 338–39, 347–48, 477n28

Gálvez, José de, 1, 5, 9–10, *10*, 11, *64*; as an *Afrancesado*, 285; Apache campaigns and, 26–27, 28–29, 45, 55–56; appointment as minister of Indies of, 76, 399n134; attacks along the Mississippi and, 121, 144, 159–60; Bernardo and, 13–14, 156, 159; California and, 26; *comandancia general* and, 39; death of, 346; fall of the House of Gálvez and, 346; French alliance and, 254; intelligence and, 82, 84, 86; as Marquis of Sonora, 274; marriage of, 134; mental illness of, 31–32, 46–50, 401n174; Mobile and, 174–75; Pensacola and, 240–41, 460n330; poisoning, legend of, 346; return to Spain of, 55; as visitor general of New Spain, 21, 22–26

Gálvez, María Rosa de, 346, 348

Gálvez, Matías de, 9, 13, 272, 329; illness and death of, 279, 300, 342; as viceroy of New Spain, *12*, 242, 250, 284, 305, 320, 322, 325, 460n336, 476n6

Gálvez, Miguel de, 63, *64*, 273, 346; Bernardo and, 71, 335; military career of, 296

Gálvez clan, 9, 242, 345–48, 388n1. *See also specific members of*

Galvezton (Spanish ship), 153, 165, 199–200, *199*, 202, *243*, 446n119

Galveztown, 94, 122–23, *124*

Gálvez y Saint-Maxent, Guadalupe Felícitas de, 339, 343, 347

Gálvez y Saint-Maxent, Matilde Felicitas, 134, 272, 297, 336, 346–47

Gálvez y Saint-Maxent, Miguel de: as an adult, 297, 346–47; as a child, 133, 257–58, 259, 272, 294, 296, 336, 346

García, Francisco, 33–34

Gardens, 292, 322, 331–32, 344, *344*

Gardoqui, Diego María de, 140, 263, 265, 272

Gardoqui & Sons, 140, 141

Gayarré, Charles, 95, 150

Gazeta de Madrid: Algiers expedition and, 75–76; Bernardo and, 78, 192; Morocco and, 69; war against Britain and, 154, 161, 172, 234, 238–40

Gazeta de México: Bernardo and, 281, 288, 293, 294, 333, 334, 337; Royal Academy of San Carlos and, 329; year of hunger and, 299, 300, 480n122

Gazette de Leyde, 236

General Arnold (British corsair ship), 225

General visits, 21–22

Gentleman's Monthly Intelligencer, 235

George III (king of Britain), 145

Ger, Miguel, 66

Germain, George, Lord, 146, 233–34, 457n274

German Coast, 117, 130, 149

German-speakers as immigrants, 117–18

Gibraltar, 4, 5, 137, 144, 259–60, *268*

Gibson, Charles, 104

Gifts for Indians, 100, 101-4, 105, 108, 185-86, 311
Gil, Francisco, 29
Gil, Jeronimo Antonio, *10*, 224, 329, *330*
Gilabert, Francisco, 198, 200
Gillon, Alexander, 253
Gillray, James, *268*, 469n86
Girón y Moctezuma, Gerónimo, 166, 172, 177, 223, 228, 257
Gitanear, 186, 442n53
Gitlin, Jay, 111
Goicoechea, Miguel de, 177
Goldoni, Carlo, 288
Golillas, 26-27
Gómez, José, 288, 290, 292, 294, 333, 334
Gómez de Argüello, Juan Antonio, 46, 47, 48, 50
Gómez de Ortega, Casimiro, 276, 331
González, Manuel, 171-72
González Bueno, Antonio, 331
González de Castejón, Pedro, 70, 76, 203
González Enciso, Agustin, 127
González Troyano, Alberto, 290
Gordon, Hugh Mackey, 219
Gortari Rabiela, Hira de, 319
Governor of Louisiana, Bernardo de Gálvez as. See Louisiana, Bernardo de Gálvez as colonel and acting governor in
Grade and rank, military, 33. See also Rank, military
Granados y Gálvez, José Joaquín, 298
Grand dictionnaire historique ou Le mélange curieux de l'histoire sacrée et profane, Le (Moreri), 287
Grand Pré, Carlos de, 117, 153
Grasse, Count de, 249, 251, 255, 468n86
Grayden, Alexander, 98
Grimaldi, Marquis of, *10*, 69, 70, 75, 76
Grimaldo, Magdalena de, 9
Grimarest, Enrique, 177-78, 179, 185
Guadalajara Regiment, 90, 218, 452n214
Guadalupe, 283
Guaraní Indians, 313
Guardia Herrero, Carmen de la, 263
Guardias Españolas, 72
Guatemala, 4, 13, 42, 250
Guaymas, 30
Güemes Pacheco y Padilla, Juan Vicente, 317

Guevara, Baltasar Ladrón de, 319
Guibert, Count de, 65
Gypsies, 186, 442n53

Haciendas, 304-5
Haldiman, Frederick, 146
Haley, James L., 311
Half-Moon Fort, 1-2, 207, 209, 213, 218-23, 224, 226, 244
Hall, Gwendolyn Midlo, 115
Hamilton, Earl J., 143
Hanger, Kimberly S., 94, 112
Hanxleden, Colonel von, 188-89
Harkins, John E., 116
Harvesters of Malaga before King Carlos III, The (Inza), *64*
Havana, Cuba, *191*; as an intelligence center, 84; Bernardo in, 190, 193-96, 270-72, 277-80; conquest of Pensacola and, 201, 203-4, 214, 229, 240; population of, 319; Seven Years' War and, 17, 18, 19, 20. See *also* Cuba
Havana Fixed Infantry Regiment, 218, 452n214
Havana Fusiliers Company, 218, 453n214
Hawkins, Joseph, 447n119
Haynes, Robert V., 152-53
Hemp, 120, 126
Henderson, Michael Nolden, 422n257
Hernández Sánchez-Barba, Mario, 30, 31-32, 41, 394n68
Hernández Silva, Héctor Cuauhtémoc, 32
Herrero, Luciano, 82
Herzog, Tamar, 114
Hessians, 206
Hevia Bolaños, Juan de, 114
Hibernia Regiment, 54, 218, 242, 452n214
Hilton, Sylvia L., 137, 263
Hispanicization, 134-36
History and Practice of Aerostation (Cavallo), 275
History Detectives, 422n257
Holker (American corsair ship), 225, 229-30
Holmes, Jack D., 94-95
Holmes, Robert, 85
Honore d'Estrehen, Jean Baptiste, 131
Horn, Albrecht von, 222
Horses: in carriage teams, 295, 300; Indians and, 40, 50, 52, 312-13

Hoskins, James, 447n119
"Hospitality policy," 118-19, 139, 145
Hot-air balloons, 5, 274-77, 275, 276, 277, 474n172. *See also* Aerostatic machines
Houdaille, Jacques, 285, 287
Hound (British ship), 188, 189, 209, 442n64
House of Commons, British, 233
Houston, William C., 173
Huet, Luis, 163, 193, *220-21*
Humboldt, Alexander von, 132, 298-99, 302, 323, 340-41, 343, 348
Hunger, 51, 295, 298-304, 480n122. *See also* Year of the hunger
Huntington, Samuel, 230
Hurricanes, 147, 190, 195

"I alone" phrase, 201-2
"I alone" speech, 200-201
Ibn Abdallah, Sidi Muhámmad, 68
Idle, the, 321-22
Immigration to Louisiana, 117-21, 127
Indagación y reflexiones sobre la Geografía (Aguirre), 65
Index Expurgatorius, 287
Indian Militia and Description of the Indies (Vargas Machuca), 102
Indian peace medals, 103-4, 105, 417n171, 417n175, 418n184
Indian policy in Louisiana, 99-108; background and overview of, 6-7, 99-101, 416-17n149; guns, ammunition, alcohol, and gifts and, 101-3; Indian agreements and, 104-5, 418n186; Indian peace medals and, 103-4, 417n171, 417n175, 418n184; Indian relationship with Bernardo and, 105 6; repercussions in other regions of, 107-8; slavery prohibition and, 106-7
Indians: colonization and, 26; as *gañanes*, 304-7; neutrality of, 180, 184-85; population of, 304, 484n169; relationships among, 42; Seven Years' War and, 17; slavery and, 36, 106-7, 304, 305, 397n112; trade and, 272; treaties with, 104-5, 418n186; war against Britain and, 180-83, 227. *See also* Indian policy in Louisiana; *Instrucción formada en virtud de real orden de S.M.; specific Indian groups

Indians, supplying with guns and ammunition, 101-2, 313-14
Indigo, 126
Infant mortality, 11
Informe jurídico dirigido al Rey por la muy noble y muy leal ciudad de México (Castañeda), 327
Ingersoll, Thomas N., 114
Inglaterra, Guillermo [William] de (prince of Wales), 269-70
Inquisition, the, 129
Instrucción formada en virtud de real orden de S.M., 7, 307-17; Interior Provinces restructure and military reform of, 314-17; policy of, 307-14; results and assessments of, 317-18
Instrucción reservada, 117
Intelligence, 83-87
Inza, Joaquín, *64*
Irregular warfare, 100, 154, 188
Isabel I (queen of Spain, "The Catholic"), 106
Isaza, Juan Luis, 292

Jamaica: spies and, 82, 86-87; war with Britain and, 214, 248-52, 255-57, 269-71, 376
Jamud, Nodbas, 84
Jansenism, 286-87
Jasanoff, Maya, 119
Jay, John, 161, 173, 263, *264*, 265
Jay, Sarah Livingston, *264*
Jefferson, Thomas, 318
Jennings, Edmund, 232
Jerónimo, Friar, 345
Jesuits. *See* New Spain: expulsion of Jesuits from
Jesús, Pablo de, 345
Johnson, Guy, 182
Johnson, William, 182
Join or Die (Franklin), *254*
Joli, Antonio, *11*
Jomini, Baron of, 83
Jones, James, 98
Journal de Paris, 274
Journal Encyclopedique ou Universal, 276
Journal Historique et Littéraire, 173
"Journal of the Siege of Pensacola" (Farmar), 191

Journal Politique, ou Gazette des Gazettes, 173
Jovellanos, Gaspar Melchor de, 289, 348
Joven Feliciana, La (American merchant ship), 447n119
Juicio de residencia, 300, 336
Junta de conferencias, 300
Junta de Medios, 142–43

Keegan, John, 83, 295
Kein, Sybil, 136
Key, Philip B., 189
King's Immemorial Regiment, 71, 190, 296, 480n114
King's Regiment, 218, 453n214
Kino, Eusebio Francisco, 28
Kirkland, Samuel, 182
Knights of the order, 79
Knights of the Order of Malta, 71
Kuethe, Allan J., 19

Lacunza, José María, 341
Lafora, Nicolás de, 40, 396n99
Landowner tensions with royal officials, 302, 482n149
Land tenure and registration, 122
Las Felicianas, 126
Latorre, José Navarro, 183
Lavedan, Antonio, 126–27
Lee, Arthur, 82
Lee, Charles, 82
Leeds Intelligencer, 235
León Meza, René de, 286
León Portilla, Miguel, 396n98
Lèse majesté crimes, 47
Letters from an English Traveler in Spain in 1778, 235–36
Levaggi, Abelardo, 99, 104
Leyes Nuevas, 304
Leyva, Fernando de, 103–4, 154
Lezo, Blas de, 13, 19
Lichtenstein Johnston, Elizabeth, 119
Light infantrymen, about, 71
Lincoln, Benjamin, 230
Lincoln, Thomas "Tad," 296
Liquor, 101, 102, 142, 312, 313, 320. *See also* Alcohol
Llano de Alguazas, Marquis de los, 273
Lloyd, Thomas, 97–98

Loende, Guillermo, 244, 461n343
London Gazette, 151, 234
London Magazine, 235
Longoria, Colonel, 202
Lopez Carrizosa, Felipe, 228
López Delgado, Juan Antonio, 69
Lorenzana, Francisco Antonio, 50
Losa Contreras, Carmen, 328
Louisiana: authority transfer to Spain of, 20, 39, 391n56; Bernardo as acting governor of (*See* Louisiana, Bernardo de Gálvez as colonel and acting governor in); Indian policy in (*See* Indian policy in Louisiana); planters in, 6, 107, 114, 115–16, 127; postwar, 270–71; religious policy of, 111, 127–30; settlement of, 122–26. *See also* New Orleans
Louisiana, Bernardo de Gálvez as colonel and acting governor in: agriculture and, 126–27; contraband trade and, 95–98; Fixed Infantry Regiment of Louisiana and, 90–95, 415n96; free population and, 111–13; immigration and colonization and, 117–21; intelligence and, 83–86, 87; military and government distinction and, 108–10; military reorganization and, 87–89; overview and appointment of, 6, 79; population and demographics and, 110–11, *111*; religion and, 127–30; settlement and, 122–26; slavery and, 113–17
Louisiana Creole, 132
Louisiana Fixed Infantry Regiment: Bernardo's appointment in, 79, 99; Catalonia Volunteers Light Infantry Regiment and, 451n214; flag of, 92; Miró's appointment in, 158–59; recruitment for, 90–93, 431n64; war against Britain and, 157, 158–59
Loyalists: loss of Pensacola and, 230, 232–33, 242–44, 248; militias of, 206, 207, 222, 225, 230; in Natchez, 248; as refugees, 118–19, 423n293
Loyalty: importance of to Bernardo de Gálvez, 202, 314, 317; of Indians, 100, 103–4, 105–6, 181, 185; of local populations, 6, 87–88, 112, 114, 115, 413n63
Lucena Salmoral, Manuel, 113
Lussan, A., 132
Lynch, John, 27, 69, 75

Macharaviaya, Spain, 9, 120, *158*
Madrid, María Josefa de, 11
Madrid, Spain, *11*, 319; Bernardo in, 272-78; Saint-Maxent de Gálvez family in, 347-48
Madrid (Joli), 11
Maduell, Charles R., Jr., 106-7
Mahón, 239, 459n312
Malaga, immigration from, 6, 120, 121, 123-25, 126
Malaria, 31, 149, 213, 334
Maldonado Polo, José Luis, 332
Mallorca Regiment, 218, 452n214
Malnutrition, 302
Mangino, Fernando José, 338-39
Manila, Philippines, 17, 18, 19
Marching pace of soldiers, 149, 431n71
Maritime security, 69-70
Marriage law, 133, 427n403
Martínez, María Elena, 79
Martinez Carreras, José U., 68
Martínez Paracio, Jesús Ignacio, 63
Maryland Loyalists, 206, 207, 222, 225, 230. *See also* Pennsylvania and Maryland Provincial Militia, British
Mathews, James A., 191, 217
Mathews, Thomas, 14
Mathieu, Agnes, 115
Matienzo, Juan de, 106
Mauss, Marcel, 102
Maximus, Quintus Fabius, 138
Maxwell, John, 253
Mayorga, Martín de, 284, 319, 476n6
Mayronne, Francisco, 447n119
Mbororé, battle of, 313
McCarty, Kieran R., 61
McDonald, John, 222
McFarlane, Anthony, 93
McGillivray, Alexander, 183
McKean, Thomas, 265
Medals: *al mérito*, 103-4, 105, 158, 418n184; commemorative, 329, *330*, 345; Indian peace, 103-4, 105, 417n171, 417n175, 418n184
Mediation between Britain and North American colonies, Spanish, 138
Medina Bustos, José Marcos, 28
Medina Rojas, F. de Borja, 194, 455n230
Melancholy, term of, 31
Melilla, 68, 69

Mémoire sur la Louisiane, 95
Memoirs of Francisco de Quevedo, 235-36
Memorias históricas de la última guerra con la Gran Bretaña (Covarrubias), 273
Mendinueta y Múzquiz, Pedro, 337
Mengs, Anton Rafael, *81*
Mentor (British ship), 188, 189, 209, 246, 449n169, 462n16
Mercurio Histórico Político, 165, 238-39, 241
Mercury mining, 23
Merit as criterion for advancement, 5, 60, 66, 125, 274, 315-16
Mexico City, *282*, 318-19; Bernardo in (*See* Gálvez, Bernardo de, as viceroy of New Spain); José de Gálvez in, 22-23, 26
Meyers, Rose, 153
Mézières, Athanase de, 100, 182-83
Miguel, Eduardo de, 82
Military rank versus grade, 33
Military Reflections (Marcenado), 155
Military regulations, Spanish, 90, 93, 201, 431n71
Militias, 18-19; attacks along the Mississippi and, 150, 157, 158; Cuban, 279; Indian, 313; in Louisiana, 93-94, 108, 148; reform in New Spain and, 325-26, 328; siege of Pensacola and, 189, 206, 218
Mill, John Stuart, 154
Mills, Elizabeth Shown, 128
Mindanaoans, 106
Mínguez, Victor, 281
Minorca, 4, 5, 144, 239, 259-60, 459n312
Miralles, Juan de, 160-61
Miranda, Francisco de: on Bernardo, 13; Jamaica and, 249-50, 251; New Providence and, 253; siege of Pensacola and, 191-93, 197, 198-99, 202, 203-4, 219, *222*, 223-24
Miranda, José, 285
Miró, Esteban, 158-59, 163-64, 175, 176-77, 194, 229, 248, 263
Misión en Managua (Arístegui), 130
Missions as a colonizing institution, 26, 43
Mississippi River, navigation of, 263-69, 471n132
Mobile, campaigns at, 161-77; British attack and, 188-90, 209; impact of Spanish victory of, 171-75; lack of Spanish aid from Cuba and, 175-77; press coverage of, 165,

172, 173–74, 235, 236; Spanish landing and siege of, 166–71, *167*, 436n160; Spanish plans and preparations for, 144, 161–64, *352–54*; Spanish traveling to, 164–66
Mobile, Indian attacks on, 185–88
Mobile Village, 188–90
Moltke, Helmut von, 71, 214
Moñino y Redondo, José, 137
Monserrat, D. Fernando, 22
Monteil, Chevalier de: Jamaica campaigns and, 248–49, 251; Pensacola siege and, 191, 196, 213–14, 218, 219, 228, 236, 450–51n202
Montepío militar, 335
Montesquieu, 312
Montgolfier brothers, 274, 474n172
Moorhead, Max L., 41
Morales Padrón, Francisco, 120
Moratín, Leandro Fernández de, 348
More, Thomas, 125
Morel, Robert, 286–87
Morenos, 94, 112–13, 114–15, 218
Moreri, Louis, 287
Moreto, Agustín, 288
Morocco, 68, 69
Morris, Robert, 139
Morris (American ship), 153, *199*
Mortality, 11
Mount Vernon, 389n21
Mozos viejos, 5, 67
Mulattoes, 94, 112–13, 115, 149, 157
Muñoz Rebolledo, María Dolores, 292
Murray, John, 248
Mutual Aid Society of Wine, Liquor, Raisins, Figs, Almonds and Oil Harvesters of Malaga, *64*
"Mystery of Avila," 5, 66–67

Narrett, David, 98, 140, 232
Natchez, 151, 152–53, 160; revolt in, 245–48
Natchitoches, 128
Navajo Indians, 34, 310
Navarra Regiment, 65, 66, 67, 163, *187*, 218, 452–53n214
Navarro, Diego José: Pensacola siege and, 194, 196, 227–28, 229, 240–41; on Spain's neutrality in American Revolution, 145; undermining Bernardo by, 159, 161, 163, 175

Navarro, Martín, 95, 109, 127, 154, 156
Navarro García, Luis, *37*, 41, 45
Navas, Francisco de, 177
Navia, Victorio de, 74, 190, 196, 240, 451–53n214
Navy, British Royal, 14, 209, 242, 256
Navy, Spanish Royal: hemp and, 120; Mobile attack and, 174, 176; New Providence and, 254–55; reform and, 18, 19–20; siege of Pensacola and, 177, 195, 199–204, *205*, 216, 228
Navy, U.S., 141
Nepotism, 32, 120, 159
Neptune (American ship), 236
Neutrality: Indian, 180, 184–85; Spanish, 119, 139, 145
New Bahama Channel, 144
New Hampshire Gazette State Journal, and General Advertiser, 233
New Orleans: hurricane in, 147; revolt of 1768 in, 130–31; as a spy hub, 84; war against Britain and, 146–48, *148*, 155. *See also* Louisiana
New Orleans Artillery Militia Company, 94, 415n108
New Orleans Colored Militias, 94, 218, 415n109, 453n214
New Orleans Infantry Militia Battalion, 94, 415n106
New Orleans Militia Company of Distinguished Carabineros, 94–95, 415n112, 415n114
New Orleans's Dragoons, 93, 415nn97–98
New Providence, 4, 252–55, 260, *377–78*
New Review with Literary Curiosities, and Literary Intelligence, 276
New Spain: Americanization of army of, 326–28, 342, 490–91n316; civilian versus military authority in, 27–28; conspiracy theory regarding independence of, 340–45, 346; defenses of northern frontier of, 37–39, *37*, 398n123; expulsion of Jesuits from, 24–26, *25*, 28, 392n24; interior provinces of, 101, 108, 307–8, 314–18; troops of the army of, 325–28
New Spain Crown Regiment, 32, 33, 34, 251, 294, 296, 326, 395n73
Nezahualcóyotl, 322

Nieto, Vicente, 328
Nobility of blood, 79-80
Nobility of privilege, 79
"Noble savage" myth, 40, *40*, 318
Norfolk Chronicle, 235
Noria system, 18
Northampton Mercury, 235
Noticia breve de la expedición Militar de Sonora y Cinaloa, 56
Noticia del establecimiento y poblacion de las colonias inglesas en la América Septentrional (Álvarez), 273
Noticia y reflexiones sobre la guerra que se tiene con los indios apaches (Gálvez), 7, 57-61, 405-6n246
Nueva Gálvez, 126
Nueva Granada, 39, 250, 399n132
Nueva Iberia, 120, 123-25
Nueva Vizcaya, 32, 34, 36, 41, 44-45, 50-52, 54-57
Núñez Cabeza de Vaca, Alvar, 36, 397n107

O'Brien, Greg, 184
O'Conor, Hugo, 53-55, 56-57, 396n99, 403n217
O'Donnell, James H., III, 182
Ohio Valley Indians, 119
Old boys, 5, 67
Old Mother Mexico (Carr), 302
Olmeda y León, José, 273
Olmedo Checa, Manuel, 337
Oñate, Juan de, 36
O'Neill, Arturo, 104, 242, 244
Order of the Capuchin Friars, 128
Ordinances of Felipe II, 43, 313
O'Reilly, Alejandro, 53, 77; Algiers expedition and, 70, 71-76; Apache campaigns and, 56-57; Bernardo and, 78; Chalmers and Loende and, 244; as Louisiana's governor, 88-89, 90, 93, 94, 100, 103, 107, 113, 130-31; Royal Military Academy and, 63, 65, 66, 67-68; Seville Infantry Regiment and, 62
Orozco, Rafael, 280
Ortelli, Sara, 41, 309
Ortiz Cortés, Fernando, 321
Orwell, George, 132
Osborn, George C., 185
O'Shaughnessy, Andrew Jackson, 255

Ostendorf, Berndt, 132
Oubel, Luis Fernando de, 41-42

Pace of soldier marching, 149, 431n71
Paine, Thomas, 80
Palafoz y Mendoza, Juan, 282-83
Palma, Ricardo, 175-76
Paniagua, Diego, 79, 278
Panis, Jacinto, 85, 163
Pardos, 94, 112-13, 115, 149, 157
Pareja-Obregón, José Joaquín Domínguez, 274
Particular visits, 21
Partos ocultos, 321-22
Pasmo, 213
Patriotic Society of Cuba, 279
Paul III (pope), 106
Payne, John Willet, 153
Peace and Commercial Treaty between Morocco and Spain, 68
Pedagogic utopia, 63
Pedrosa, Miguel de, 62
Peñafort, Luisa Zahino, 24
Peñalver y Cárdenas, Luis Ignacio, 129
Pennsylvania and Maryland Provincial Militia, British, 189, 206, 207, 222, 225, 230
Pennsylvania Journal, 80, 233
Pennsylvania Journal and Weekly Advertiser, 160
Pennsylvania Loyalists, 206, 207. *See also* Pennsylvania and Maryland Provincial Militia, British
Pensacola, *193*, 210, 449
Pensacola and the war with Britain, 144, 205; after siege of, 242-44; British forces and defenses at, 206-9, *368*; consequences of siege of, 240-42; contemporaneous accounts of, 190-93; crossing the bar to, 197-204; first attempt to siege, 163-64, 175-79, 190, *355-63*; Indians and, 184; preparations for second attempt to siege, 193-96, 213, *364-67*; reaction in America to Spanish victory at, 229-33; reaction in Europe to Spanish victory at, 233-40; reinforcements for second siege attempt of, 212-17, *369-73*; Santa Rosa island taking and, 196-97; siege of, 1-2, 217-24, 220-21, *224*, *374-75*; start of

the siege of, 209-12, 448n152; victory at, 224-29, 239, 456n251
Pérez, Enrique San Miguel, 262-63
Pérez Marchand, Monelisa, 286
Pérez Rosales, Laura, 301
Pesquisa, 21
Philosophical Transactions of the Royal Society of London, 275, 277
Pickles, William, 153
Piernas, Pedro, 148
Pijao Indians, 106
Pima Indians, 26, 28, 44, 52, 61
Pineda, Juan de, 46
Pío (Spanish ship), 229
Pirates and privateers, 18, 69-70
Pitic, 30
Pitot, James, 129-30
Platilla, Mateo, 115
Pliego de mortaja, 337
Poema épico: La rendición de Panzacola y conquista de la Florida occidental por el Excmo. Sr. Conde de Gálvez (Rojas), 298
Poitou Regiment, French, 218, 454n220
Policing, 317, 319
Policy of exclusion, 100
"Political Considerations on the Present State of the Province of Louisiana" (Navarro), 95
Political Essay on the Kingdom of New Spain (Humboldt), 340-41, 495n1
Pollock, Oliver, 97, 139, 140, 142, 149, 152, 265
Ponce, Nicolás, 329
Pondicherry, siege of, 5
Pontalba, José Javier Delfau de, 130
Poor, the, 6, 300-301, 321-22
Population counts: of Europe, 319; of Indians, 36, 106, 304; of Louisiana, 106, 110, 111, 115, 117-21; of New Spain, 282, 304, 319, 484n169; of North America, 319. *See also* Censuses
Portrait of a Golilla (Santa Cruz y Espejo), 27, 392-93n41
Portrait of Carlos III (Mengs), 81
Port Royal (British ship), 209
Portugal, 14, 15-17
Posadera feliz o el enemigo de las mujeres, La (Goldoni), 288
Potts, Richard, 232
Powell, Philip Wayne, 37

Poydras, Julien, 134, 156-57
Presidiales, 59-61, 308
Presidios, 26, 28, 37-38, 43, 53, 315, 398n123
Prince of Wales Redoubt, 207, 209, 218, 222, 224
Prince's Regiment, 218, 453n214
Príncipe de Asturias (Spanish ship), 178
Príncipe Fort, 251
Príncipe Negro (American ship), 236
Prise du morne du Bâton Rouge par Monseigneur de Galvez, La (Poydras), 156-57
Prisoners of war, 150, 151-52, 160, 171, 224-25, 350-51
Prisoners' pardon, 292-93, 341
Project for the Arrangement of the Army of New Spain (Crespo), 325, 328
Promotion of Algiers list, 76-78
Propaganda, 75, 84, 161
Public grain storehouses, 302
"Public happiness," 6
Public opinion, 76, 239
Public street lighting, 320
Puebla, 282-83, 300
Pueblo revolt, 37
Puente, Eligio de la, 86
Puerto Rico, 250, 262
Pulque, 102, 313, 320
Pulquerías, 320
Punta Cortada, 105

Queen's Redoubt, 1-2, 207, 209, 213, 218-23, 224, 226, 244
Querétaro Provincial Cavalry Regiment, 328
Quintanilla, Luis de, 128
Quiroga, Vasco de, 106

Racial differences, 260
Rada, Josef, 189
Raffelin, Antonio, 82
Ramos, Antonio, 274
Ramos Pérez, Demetrio, 304-5
Ramos Vázquez, Isabel, 321
Rangel, José, 314
Rank, military, 33, 200, 446n118. *See also* Grade and rank, military
Reading Mercury, 235
Reales Ordenanzas, 90, 431n71
Recio Morales, Óscar, 55
Recopilación de Leyes de Indias, 21

Recopilación de Leyes de los Reynos de las Indias, 133
Recruitment, military, 91, 93-94, 121, 326-28
Red Cliffs, 197, 202, 209, 225, 244, 460n339
Redoubts: of British Royal Navy, 203, *204*, 209, 225; Prince of Wales, 207, 209, 218, 222, 224; Queen's, 1-2, 207, 209, 213, 218-23, *224*, 226, 244
Reforms: Bourbon, 250, 260-61, 470n108; Economic Societies and, 64-65; Imperial, 18-20; of Louisiana's military, 87-90; in New Spain, 314-17, 324-28, 341, *379-80*
Refugees of the American Revolution, 118-19, 122, 423n293
Reglamento para la dirección del Coliseo de Mexico, 289
Reglamento para las milicias de infantería y caballería de la isla de Cuba, 279
Rendón, Francisco, 225, 230
Revillagigedo, Count of, 39, 286, 287, 317, 319, 323
Revolt of 1768, New Orleans, 130-31
Riaño, Juan Antonio de, 200, 286, 335, 477n30
Ricaurd, Francisco, 70
Ricla, Count of, 63, 66
Rillieux, Vicente, 153
Rindfleisch, Bryan, 182
Rio de la Plata, 20, 39, 399n132
Rivera Cambas, Manuel, 286
Robertson, Little Page, 84
Rodney, George, 255-56, 467-68n86
Rodríguez Álvarez, María de los Ángeles, 321-22
Rodríguez Moya, Inmaculada, 345
Rodríguez-Sala, María Luisa, 325, 328
Romero Flores, Jesús, 303
Romet y Richelin, Lucía, 9
Rosario (Spanish ship), 165
Ross, Robert, 98
Royal Academy of San Carlos of New Spain, 329, *330*, 345
Royal Alabardiers, 288
Royal American Gazette, 232-33
Royal American Regiment of Foot, 206
Royal audiencia, 296-98
Royal Cantabre Regiment, 14-17, *16*, 390n32, 390n35

Royal Economic Societies of Friends of the Country, 64-65, 121, 273
Royal Foundling House, 322
Royal Hospice House, 301, 320-22
Royal Military Academy of Avila, 5, 63-68, 70, 78
Royal Navy, British, 14, 209, 242, 256
Royal Navy, Spanish. *See* Navy, Spanish Royal
Royal Navy's Redoubt, 203, *204*, 209, 225
Royal Order of Carlos III, *12*, 79-80, *81*
Royal Palace at Chapultepec, 321, 322-24, *324*, 343-45, *344*
Royal pardons, 30-31, 293
Royal Treasury of Spain: American Revolution and, 141-42; funding of the war with Britain and, 143-44; Indians and, 27, 29, 37-38, 308; Louisiana and, 95, 96, 108, 109, 127, 129, 242; New Spain sources of income for, 290, 320, 323
Rubio Mañé, José Ignacio, 284
Rueda Arroniz, Fabiola, 302
Ruiz de Alarcón, Lorenzo Montalvo, 134
Runaway slaves, 116-17
Rush, N. Orwin, 210
Russians in America, 37, 398n120

S. Laurent, Raim de, 276
Saavedra, Francisco de, *215*, 287; Algiers expedition and, 68; Bernardo and, 1, 76, 269, 270-71, 295, 334; Jamaica and, 248-49, 251, 256; New Providence and, 252; Pensacola and, 1, 192, 194, 196, 201, 203, 213-17, 219, 228-29, 455n230; Royal Military Academy and, 65, 66, 67
Sabatini, Francisco de, 90, 348
St. Augustine, 108, 119, 270
St. Clair Seguarado, Eva María, 24
Saint-Maxent, Felicitas, 131-32, 133-34, *297*, 335, 336, 338-39, 347-48, 477n28
Saint-Maxent, Gilberto Antonio, 125, 130-31, 150, 272
Saint-Maxent, María Isabel, 131
Saint-Maxent, Mariana de, 477n30
Saint-Maxent, Marie-Anne, 130
Saint-Maxent, Maximiliano, 157
Saint-Maxent, Victoire, 477n30
Saints, Battle of the, 255-56
Salaries, 38, 305

INDEX [599

Sanadon, Barthélémy Jean-Baptiste, 390n27
San Agustín de las Cuevas, 294
San Bernardo, 126
Sánchez Pareja, Eusebio, 337
San Fernando de Omoa, 250
San Ildefonso Treaty, 144
San Josef (Spanish ship), 120
San José y San Joaquín (Spanish ship), 225, 230
San Juan, Nicolás de, 78
San Juan Bayou fort, 89
San Luis de Ilinueses, 94, 154
San Martín, Juan de, 278
San Ramón (Spanish ship), 177, 197–98, 202, 203
Santa Cruz de Marcenado, Marquis de, 154–55
Santa Cruz y Espejo, Francisco Javier de, 27, 392–93n41
Santa Fe agreement, 310
Santa María de Gálvez Bay, 242
Santa Rosa Island, 196–97, 209, 213
Santelises Pablo, Juan Eugenio, 286
Santiago, Felipe, 305
Santísima Trinidad, Joaquín, 47
Santo Domingo, 108, 114
Santo Domingo (Spanish ship), 270
Saugrain, Monsieur, 285–86
Schmidt, Elisabeth Whitman, 182
Science, 5, 331–32
Science Academy of Lyon, 275
Scipioville settlement, 109
Scypion, Marguerite, 107
Secret Committee of U.S. Congress, 140
Security: for Bernardo as viceroy of New Spain, 292; foreign policy and, 138; maritime, 69–70
Sedella, Antonio, 129
Seri, 26, 28, 29, 30–31, 37, 44
Sessé, Martín, 331
Settlers, 38, 41–43
Seven Years' War, 4, 13, 14–20, 100, 389n19
Seville Brigade, 71
Seville Infantry Regiment, 62–63, 71, 74, 76
Sgraffito, 345
Shawnee Indians, 119, 181
Sheehan, Bernard W., 182

Ship construction, 20
Shopkeepers Infantry Regiment, 328
Sicre y Béjar, Jorge, 66
Simplified signature system, 335
Sinaloa, 26, 28, 29
Sint Eustatius, 4
Sint Maarten, 4
Sioux Indians, 36, 43
Situados for Spanish territories, 108–9
Sixteenth Infantry Regiment, British, 206, 207
Sixtieth Infantry Regiment, British, 188, 189, 206
Slavery: Indians and, 36, 106–7, 304, 305, 397n112; in Louisiana, 113–17, 422n257; punishment and, 116; tobacco and, 127
Slave trade, 106, 115, 447n119
Smuggling, 95–98, 127, 142, 249, 251
Solalinde, Juan de, 33, 34
Solano, José (navy captain), 201
Solano Acosta, Fernando, 110, 118
Solano y Bote, José (admiral): Jamaica and, 250; as naval commander in Cuba, 241, 250, 254; Pensacola and, 190, 192, 195, 213, 216, 217, 218, 227–28, 236
Soldiers, 59–60, 149, 327–28, 431n71
Solicitadores, 306–7
Solórzano Pereira, Juan de, 21, 99
Sonora, 26, 28, 29–30, 35, 44–45, 56, 314
Sonora, Countess of, 348
Soria Regiment, 218, 453n214
Sosier, Francisco, 126
Spain: African policy of, 68–70; assimilation policies of, 7, 42, 55; empire of, 2–4; foreign policy of, 137–39, 428n1; France and, 137, 145–46, 218, 248–49, 251–52, 256–57; imperial reforms of, 18–20, 390n43; Indian policy and, 185–86; oaths of allegiance to, 98, 105, 111, 117, 180; obsession with keeping papers of, 49; post–American Revolution interest in North America of, 273; Seven Years' War and, 14, 17–19, 87–88; social mobility in, 5; system of defense for America of, 18–20, 390n43; U.S. Continental Congress and, 138, 142, 160–61, 172–73. *See also* Royal Treasury of Spain
Spain and war with Britain: attacks on British settlements along the Missis-

sippi of, 148–53, 154; Bernardo's preparations and strategy for, 146–48, *148*; British attack on San Luis de Illinueses and, 154; campaign against Mobile and (*See* Mobile, campaigns at); cost, funding, and debt of, 142–44, *143*, 249, 251, 259, 430n43, 469n98; entering, 137–38, 144–46; future problems caused by peace treaty of, 260–62; Indians and, 180–81, 185–88; Jamaica and, 214, 248–52, 255–57, 269–71, *376*; military operations on the Mississippi and, 153, *351–52*; Mississippi River navigation and, 263–69; Natchez revolt and, 245–48; New Providence and, 252–55, *377–78*; peace treaty of, 259–60, 262–63, *266–67*, 269; Pensacola and (*See* Pensacola and the war with Britain); results of initial campaigns of, 154–61

Spain and the American Revolution: economic impact and, 272; foreign policy and, 138–39; overview of, 2–5, 82–83; support for American rebels and, 139–42, 155, 262, 429n30, 429n32, 429n34, 430n43; Treaty of Paris and, 260–63

Spain Regiment, 218, 451–52n214

Spanish army, promotion system of, 33, 60; regulations of, 33, 37–39, 44, 90, 93, 201, 431n71

Spanish military officers, appeal of being, 91–93

Spanish territories, subsidies for, 108–9

Spear, Jennifer M., 114, 117

Speculation, 248, 302–3

Spying, 83, 84–87, 141–42, 146, 163

Starkey, Armstrong, 59, 182

Starr, Joseph Barton, 183, 210, 244, 247–48

Steuernagel, Carl Philipp, 191, 216, 443n76

Storehouses, public grain, 302

Street lighting, 320

Stuart, Charles, 181

Stuart, John, 182, 183–84, 206

Suárez Argüello, Clara Elena, 56

Sublimis Deus, 106

Superiority, European, 327

Surrender rituals, 171

"Sur un Moyen de Donner la Direction aux Machines Aérostatiques" (Banks), 275–76, *277*

Swift, Joseph, 225

Tannenbaum, Frank, 113

Tapados y preparados, 291

Taxes: famine and, 300, 481n135; Mississippi River navigation and, 268, 471n132; pulque and, 320; slavery and, 115, 116; trade and, 96

Tepeyac, 283

Texas, 2, 35, 43, 107, 123

Thackeray, William Makepeace, 14

Thayendanegea, 182

Tierra de Bueyes, 126

Times, The (Gillray), *268*

Tinker, Edward Larocque, 134

Tlaxcala, 282–83, 482n149

Tobacco, 22, 23, 109, 126–27

Tocas, 133, 427n403

Toluca, road to, 321, 322

Tomaso, Juan, 195

Tonantzin, 283

Toreras (women bullfighters), 290–91

Torre Campo, Marquis de, 33–34

Torres Ramírez, Bibiano, 89

Trade: as a civilizing tool, 312; contraband, 6, 95–98, 112, 127, 131, 234; foreign policy and, 137; with Indians, 272, 312–14; regulation, 95–98; slave, 106, 115, 447n119; Spain with U.S., 141; of tobacco, 22, 23, 127

Tratados de Mathematica (Bails and Capmany), 65

Treasures of the Royal Palaces of Spain exhibit, 345

Treasury Council of Spain, 142–43

Treaties with Indians, 104–5, 418n186

Treaty of Aranjuez, 144

Treaty of Friendship, Limits, and Navigation between Spain and the United States, 268–69

Treaty of Paris (1763), 17–18, 37, 87, 137, 144

Treaty of Paris (1783), 263–65, *266–67*, 269

Treaty of Utrecht, 118, 137

Troncoso, Bernardo, 280

Tufiño, Juan, 250

Tupí Indians, 313

Ugalde, Juan, 315

Ugarte y Loyola, Jacobo de, 307, 308, 314–15, 316, 317

Ulloa, Antonio de, 88, 95, 113, 130

Ulloa, Pascual de, 62
Uniforms: children wearing, 296; of Louisiana military groups, 415nn96–98, 415n106, 415nn108–9, 415n114; of Royal Cantabre Regiment, 390n35
United Corps of Pennsylvania and Maryland Loyalists, 206
United States: Seven Year's War and, 17; Spain's war against Britain and, 145, 160–61, 172–73, 230–33, 253–54; Spanish foreign policy and, 138–39. *See also* American Revolution
Unzaga, Luis de, 80, 83, 90, 95, 129, 131, 280, 411n5
Unzuaga, Isabel Saint-Maxent de, 347
Urbina, Luis de, 71
Urriza, Juan Ignacio de, 251, 253
Urrutia, José Ramón de, 66
Ursuline convent, 129, 336
U.S. Congress. *See* Continental Congress

Valcárcel, Domingo de, 28
Valdelomar, Luis de, 272
Valdelvira González, Gregorio, 65
Valenzuela, 125, 131
Valera, Juan Antonio, 48
Vales reales, 143–44
Valière, José, 157
Varela, Manuel, 29
Vargas Lugo, Elisa, 283
Vargas Machuca, Bernardo de, 102
Vauban, Sébastien Le Prestre de, 166, 219, 454n223
Vázquez, Bartolomé, *258*
Vega Juanino, Josefa, 328
Velázquez, Juan, 45
Velázquez Chávez, María Luisa Rodríguez-Sala, 325
Vélez's Rock, 68, 69
Ventura Beleña, Eusebio, 31, 49
Veracruz, Mexico, 22–23, 24, 48, 281
Vernon, Edward, 389n21
Vicens Vives, Juame, 272
Viceroyalties, new, 39
Viera y Clavijo, José, 238, 276
Vildósola, Gabriel Antonio de, 31, 46
Vilette, André Giraud de, 274
Villacañas Berlanga, José Luis, 137

Villalba, Juan de, 19, 23, 27, 54, 325, 327
Villareal, José Luciano de, 257, 334
Villaroel, Hipólito, 319, 320
Villena, Marquis of, 71
Viniegra, Juan Manuel de, 31, 46, 47, 48–50, 394n68, 401n174, 402n201
Viqueira Albán, Juan Pedro, 289, 290, 291
Viscount of Gálvez-town, 242
Volante (Spanish ship), 89, 165, 201
Volantes companies, 315
Volontaires Cantabres, 15. *See also* Royal Cantabre Regiment

Waldeck Regiment, British, 153, 188, 191, 203, 206, 207, 222, 225, 443n76
War as a business, 235
Warfare, asymmetric, 100, 154, 188
War of Jenkins' Ear, 14, 389n21
"War with the whole world and peace with England" axiom, 137, 428n1
Washington, George, 80–82, 160, 161, 184–85, 230–32, *231*, 389n21
Washington, Lawrence, 389n21
Weapons, 59, 320. *See also* Indians, supplying with guns and ammunition
Weber, David J., 41, 104
Webre, Stephen, 107
Wervik, Duke of, 241
West Florida. *See* Florida; Pensacola; Pensacola and the war with Britain
West Florida (British ship), 153, *199*
White, Sophie, 136
Who's Afraid (British ship, former American ship *Mentor*), 209
Widow of Excribano's Bookshop, 240
Wild Geese, 54–55, 77
Willing, James, 84, 139–40
Wisherd, Edwin L., *135*
Worsley, Richard, 276
Wright, J. Leitch, 242

Year of the hunger, 298–304, 321–22, 333, 342, 480n122
Yo solo phrase, 201–2, 243, 344, *344*
Yuta Indians, 310

Zayas y Ramos, Ana de, 11
Zinn, Howard, 396n98

www.ingramcontent.com/pod-product-compliance
Lightning Source LLC
Chambersburg PA
CBHW031659230426
43668CB00006B/51